THE
SINGING GAME

BY

IONA AND PETER OPIE

Oxford   New York
OXFORD UNIVERSITY PRESS
1988

Oxford University Press, Walton Street, Oxford ox2 6DP

Oxford New York Toronto
Delhi Bombay Calcutta Madras Karachi
Petaling Jaya Singapore Hong Kong Tokyo
Nairobi Dar es Salaam Cape Town
Melbourne Auckland

and associated companies in
Beirut Berlin Ibadan Nicosia

Oxford is a trade mark of Oxford University Press

First published 1985 by Oxford University Press
First issued as an Oxford University Press paperback 1988

356654/

British Library Cataloguing in Publication Data

Opie, Iona
The singing game.
1. Singing games—Great Britain—History
I. Title II. Opie, Peter
398'.8'0941 GV1215
ISBN 0-19-284019-3

Library of Congress Cataloging in Publication Data
Opie, Iona Archibald.
The singing game / by Iona and Peter Opie.
p. cm.
Reprint. Originally published: Oxford; New York:
Oxford University Press, 1985.
Bibliography: p. Includes indexes.
1. Singing games—Great Britain. I. Opie, Peter. II. Title.
[GV1215.065 1988]
796.1'3—dc19 87-22918
ISBN 0-19-284019-3

Printed in Great Britain by
The Guernsey Press Co. Ltd.,
Guernsey, Channel Islands.

Preface

In this work we present the singing games and clapping games that used to be played, or are still played, by children in Great Britain, and set forth as much of their histories as could be discovered. What we have tried to show is that these games, now enjoyed by children, are the final flowering of a tradition known since antiquity.

The present-day material has chiefly been drawn from the nationwide surveys undertaken for *The Lore and Language of Schoolchildren* in the 1950s, and for *Children's Games in Street and Playground* in the 1960s. Since then contributions from a further 112 schools have been received, many new correspondents have sent us news of children's games, and further tape-recordings have been made by ourselves and our helpers.

Singing games were already thought of as being suitable for children in the eighteenth century when they appeared in such juvenile compilations as *Tommy Thumb's Pretty Song Book*, 1744, and *Gammer Gurton's Garland*, 1784. But it was not until William Carleton published *Traits and Stories of the Irish Peasantry* in 1830, and Robert Chambers completed his collection of *Popular Rhymes of Scotland* in 1842, 'to supply a presumed desideratum in popular antiquities', that the games could be seen in a social context.

Charlotte Burne included sections of choral and dramatic games in *Shropshire Folk-Lore*, 1883, though stating 'It is of course impossible to give all variants of the ditties', and her introductory remarks extended to no more than a firm conviction that the games were 'relics of the old May-games' and 'survivals from very old and rudimentary dramas, invented and first performed by grown-up players'. Alice Bertha Gomme's substantial two-volume *Traditional Games*, 1894–8, has long been the standard work on the subject, and, since her real enthusiasm was for the singing games, has provided the main corpus of orally collected texts and tunes. Having obtained the greatest possible number of singing game texts, she then analysed and interpreted them according to the tenets of the anthropological school of folklore, of which her husband George Laurence Gomme was a leading exponent. Thus game-songs mentioning water are linked with well-worship, choosing-and-pulling games with tribal marriage-by-capture, and the game of 'In and Out the Windows', in which a circle of players stand still while a single player threads in and out between them, with the ceremonial perambulation of a village. Alexander Haggerty Krappe, who objected, in *The Science of Folklore*, to Alice Gomme's derivation of singing games 'in sudden leaps' from primitive customs, nevertheless acknowledged her undeniable achievement, that she had 'generously placed at our disposal the very materials on which we base our criticism of her theories'.

The folklorist William Wells Newell, compiler of *The Games of American Children*, 1883, was more erudite and more detached than Alice Gomme. He brought to the study of children's games his knowledge of history and languages, his poetic talent, and his European affinities. When he was headmaster of a school in New York he learned the singing games of that city from the children on the sidewalks; and his enthusiasm was such that, as with Alice Gomme, his friends sent him games from every part of the country.

Knowledge of children's games is easier to obtain in the present day than it was in Gomme's or Newell's time. Children no longer feel inhibited from talking about their games to any grown-up who has the sense to be interested. There is no longer the awe felt in the days when the games-collector, having made contact through the local vicar, was introduced to children sitting in sedate rows in the village school under the surveillance of the headmistress. (Nowadays, in our grateful experience, a head teacher to whom one has only just introduced oneself is likely to say 'They'll be going out to play in ten minutes—help yourself'.) The local vicar himself, or the lady of 'the big house', fared no better when collecting games. J. S. Udal, writing in the 1880s, said sadly in *Dorsetshire Folk-Lore*, 'the children nowadays seem to me to be more shy and more reluctant to afford information on the subject than they were in former days, and oft-times when one comes suddenly upon a party of them playing at their games in a country lane or corner of a field (especially if you happen to belong to the class known as "gentry") they will either break off their game altogether, or, if they continue it, they do so in a subdued and half-hearted kind of way that shows to you more eloquently than words that your room would be far preferable to your company'.

It has been easier, too, to note the tunes accurately. Michael Hurd has been able to reproduce the tunes of the contemporary games from our tapes, and from Father Damian Webb's, exactly as the children sang them: and from this point of view they must be regarded as the wild flowers of music rather than its cultivated species, for children can preserve the tunes no more accurately than they can the words.[1] The tunes keep, for the most part, within a fairly restricted compass. The children seem inclined to

---

[1] Father Damian Webb's superb recordings have been published as *Children's Singing Games*, record and cassette, 1983, by Saydisc Records, The Barton, Inglestone Common, Badminton, Glos.

choose a rather lower pitch than might be expected—sometimes a little too low for comfort. Possibly the lower pitch is due to the fact that they are also doing something and therefore do not want to be bothered with 'singing' as such—the tunes being a kind of heightened speech. This is also borne out by the way the tunes often revolve round a very few notes: the alternation between notes a third apart is very frequent. Almost all employ major, diatonic keys. Most of them are in a lilting 6/8 or 12/8 rhythm, as might be expected from the flowing nature of the games. It is also an easier, lazier rhythm to sing in. Many of the tunes are recognizably part of the common stock; and echoes of old and well-known airs can be heard in them: 'Sherrifmuir', 'The Keel Row', 'So Early in the Morning', 'I Had a Little Nut Tree', 'Blaydon Races' (related to the game 'The Best Bed's a Feather Bed'), and, frequently, 'Bobby Shaftoe'.[2] In all instances we have given the tune as it fits the first verse; and subsequent verses may require some rhythmic adjustment. We have given more than one tune in the few cases in which there are several well-established tunes for the same game, but we have not given all variants.

As for the games themselves, we have, in the apparatus which follows each main article, aimed to provide an outline history in terms of printed sources and oral collectings, rather than to give every available reference. If no source is given for a game it should be taken that it was sent by a correspondent.

A printed page cannot convey the exuberance of children singing these games on their own. We have tried to give the book life by assembling as much evidence as we could of a still rich tradition, and by using the children's own words to describe it. Nevertheless we are aware that, had it not been time to draw a line beneath our researches, we could have gone out into the cities and countryside of Great Britain again and come home with ten times as many recordings as we possessed already, with possibly some 'extinct' games among them, and certainly some new ones. The tradition is truly a living one, and while some parts of it are declining others are burgeoning. The songs and actions may change, but the important thing is that childhood continues to sing in the freedom of its own tatterdemalion world.

I. O. & P. O.

West Liss in Hampshire
1970–1984

[2] We have seldom attempted to relate one tune to another. The question of whether a tune is 'the same as' another is endlessly debatable and endlessly debated, and is, in the last analysis, a question of definition and degree. All we can offer music-genealogists is a reference to Bayard's 'Prolegomena to a Study of the Principal Melodic Families of Folk Song' in *The Critics and the Ballad*, M. Leach and Tristam P. Coffin (Carbondale, Illinois), 1961, and the wide-eyed astonishment of a Liss schoolchild: 'It doesn't really matter, does it?'

Acknowledgements

THIS is our third disquisition into the teeming traditions of school-children. The mass of material gathered in the 1950s showed us that one volume, *The Lore and Language of Schoolchildren*, would not suffice, and that the games would have to be left for another volume. A second amassment in the 1960s showed that the games were so many and various that three more volumes would be needed to contain them. The first of these, describing the active and competitive games in which 'only the players themselves are needed', was *Children's Games in Street and Playground*, 1969; the present book of singing and clapping games is the second; the third, of games needing equipment, remains to be written. We would therefore like to renew our thanks to the schools, and the many corre-spondents, who contributed to this not-yet-fully-worked mine of informa-tion, and who are listed in the first two volumes. In addition we are grateful to the schools who have, since 1969, sent material or allowed us to visit them and record the children:

Alton, Hants, Anstey County Junior School (head: Mr P. Cockerham) and Alton County Junior School (head: Mr D. S. Hall); Ashbourne, Derbyshire, St Oswald's Infant School (head: Mrs J. A. Dawson); Aylesbury, Bucks., Meadowcroft Middle School (head: Mr G. L. Coath); Basingstoke, Hants, Cranbourne Bilateral School (teacher responsible: Mr R. Hare); Bedford, Livingstone First School (head: Mrs B. Lawry); Birmingham 23, The Abbey Junior and Infant School (head: Mr Philip Hindle); Bramley, Surrey, Bramley C. of E. Primary School (teacher responsible: Miss Joan Ford); Driffield, E. Yorks., Driffield Junior School (head: Mr O. H. Curtis); Fringford, Oxon., Fringford C. of E. Primary School (heads: Mr and Mrs J. Woodworth); Garforth, W. Yorks., St Benedict's RC Primary School (head: Mr P. Jordan) and Garforth Parochial C. of E. Controlled Junior School (head: Mr J. H. Hall); Goring-by-Sea, Sussex, West Park Junior School (teacher responsible: Mrs A. Edgeler); Huddersfield, St Patrick's RC Primary School (head: Mr B. Hepworth); Ilkley, Yorks., All Saints First School (head: Mr A. C. Heslop); Kirkby Malham, Yorks., Kirkby Malham United School (head: Mr N. Longbottom); Lilliput, Dorset, Lilliput C. of E. First School (head: Miss B. Graves); Lymington, Hants, Lymington County Junior School (head: Mr D. S. Caistor); Macclesfield, Cheshire, Hurdsfield County Infants School (head: Miss S. J. Stothert); Manchester, Wythenshawe,

Rackhouse Junior School (head: Mr M. W. Milner); Nottingham, Whitemoor Junior School (head: Mr D. F. Sayers); Oxford, St Ebbe's C. of E. First School (head: Miss R. E. Marshall) and St Barnabas First School (head: Mr P. H. Penfold); Redditch, Worcs., Crabbs Cross County Primary School (head: Mr E. J. Jackson); Rocester, Staffs., The Dove First School (head: Mr E. Wood); Salford, Lancs., St Clement's Primary School (head: Mr N. Akister), North Grecian Street Junior School (head: Miss D. F. Pearson), St Clement's C. of E. Junior School (head: Mr R. R. Graham); Selborne, Hants, Selborne C. of E. Primary School (head: Miss J. M. Butler); South Baddesley, near Lymington, South Baddesley C. of E. Primary School (head: Miss J. Stott).

We owe a particular debt of gratitude to: Mr E. H. G. Chitham, who organized a large survey of games 1969–71, chiefly conducted by his students at Dudley College of Education when out on teaching practice; Mr Graham Stephen, whose enthusiasm called forth contributions from schools in every part of Scotland; Mr N. G. N. Kelsey, head master of Michael Faraday Junior School, London SE17, who sent us items from his own collection of games; Mrs Kathleen Hunt, who made recordings for us in Cambo, Northumberland, and Fringford, Oxon.; Mrs Pat Palmer, who allowed us to use her Birmingham recordings; Peter Charlton of 'Play-school', for recordings from Hoxton and North London, and for other help; Martin Freeth of the BBC, for a recording from Chiswick, London W4; Mr R. A. Smith, head master of Blue Bell Junior School, Nottingham, and Mrs Mary E. Milson, head mistress of Wereham County Primary School, Norfolk, for sending us their schools' own 'books' of games; Mandy Davies and Form 3R, of Prenton High School, Birkenhead, for recollections of their younger days; Mrs Jean Shuttleworth, for lending photostats of Crofton's diaries; Mrs Anne Salmon, for recording the Glasgow version of 'Best Bed's a Feather Bed'; and, always, to our neighbour, Mr D. J. Mason, head master of Liss County Junior School, who has accepted us as part of the ecology of his playground during the past fourteen years.

Friends have kept us in touch with children's play in other countries, and we would especially like to thank: Miss Ruth Brinton, for a copy of her thesis 'Le Folklore de Bon Encontre' and useful correspondence; Mrs Mary Chatterjee, Ramapura, India; Miss Bertha Longin and Professor Roger Pinon, both of Belgium; Berit Østberg (author of *På livets landvei*, 1976) not only for Norwegian games and translations, but for her field recordings in Leeds, London and Dublin. For translations, we are indebted to: Professor Christabel Braunrot (Pierre de Lancre, in 'Witch Dances'); Mrs Joyce Houwaard-Wood (medieval and modern Dutch);

Robert Knowles of the Oxford University Press (the Portuguese 'Condessa' in 'Three Brethren out of Spain'); Michael Mann (French); Kerstin Osborne (Swedish versions of 'London Bridge'); Dr Veronica Salusbury (the medieval French dancing song 'A l'entrada del tems clar').

Other constant friends to our work have been: Dr Dorothy Howard and the late Ian Turner, whose collections of American and Australian lore, respectively, have given this work an extra dimension; Miss Carrol Jenkins; Mr Rowland Kellett; Mr Julian Pilling (especially for the Nelson version of 'Jenny Jones'); Mrs Wendy Rix; and our *buona fata* Mrs Diana Mann.

Father Damian Webb, OSB, has most generously allowed us to use his magnificent collection of tapes and photographs. The games were recorded when he was a curate at Workington and could make day trips to Scotland; as curate at Leyland, Lancs.; as parish priest at Garforth near Leeds; and on holidays in Portugal, Italy, and Ireland. (Copies of the tapes are with Peter Kennedy, Folk Institute and Resources Centre.) And in this volume, as in *Children's Games in Street and Playground*, Father Damian's photographs show the vitality of the games when in their natural environment.

We should like to say a particular thank you to Michael Hurd, who notated the tunes from our and Father Damian's tapes, both for his interest in the singing games and his patience with their vagaries.

Finally, we once again thank Miss F. Doreen Gullen, for she, like Mr Greatheart in *The Pilgrim's Progress*, has always held us on our way.

The authors and publishers are grateful for permission to include the following copyright material:

Norman Gimbel and Larry Coleman: 'Tennessee Wig-Walk'. Copyright 1953 Village Music Co. (USA). Reproduced by permission of EMI Music Publishing Ltd., 138–140 Charing Cross Road, London WC2H 0LD.

Jimmy Kennedy: 'The Cokey Cokey'. Copyright © 1942 by Kennedy Music Co. Ltd., London W1. Used by permission of Campbell Connelly & Co., Ltd. All Rights Reserved.

Bob Merrill: 5 lines from 'She Wears Red Feathers'. Copyright © 1952 Joy Music Inc., USA. Reproduced by permission of Intersong Music Ltd., and International Music Publications.

Willa Muir: 8 bars of tune to 'Father, Mother, may I go?' from *Living With Ballads*. Reproduced by permission of the Author's Literary Estate and The Hogarth Press.

John J. Stamford: 4 lines from 'Macnamara's Band'. Copyright J. H. Larway 1914. Reproduced by permission of Music Sales Limited.

Contents

Illustrations

Clapping (Ch. XX), Bamber Bridge, Lancs., 1984.   448
  Father Damian Webb.

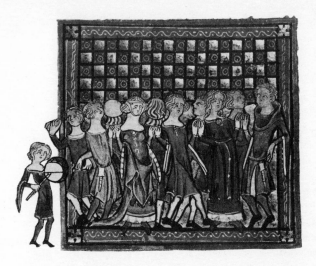

Men and Women carolling, *Roman de la Rose*, first half of fourteenth century.
The British Library MS Royal 20 A xvii f. 9.

Abbreviations

Böhme	F. M. Böhme, *Deutsches Kinderlied und Kinderspiel*, 1897; continuous pagination, but first book, *Kinderlied*, and second book, *Kinderspiel*, have independent numbering.
Crofton MS	Revd Addison Crofton, 'Children's Rhymes', 2 MS vols.; a fair copy, written out for his friend E. W. B. Nicholson, Keeper of Printed Books at the Bodleian, 1901. (Bodleian Library MS Eng. misc. e 39–40.) Crofton was incumbent at Reddish, Lancs, 1877 onwards.
English County Songs	*English County Songs*, words and music collected and edited by Lucy E. Broadwood and J. A. Fuller Maitland, 1893.
Fowke, 1969	Edith Fowke, *Sally Go Round the Sun*, 1969 (games collected in Toronto unless otherwise stated).
Fuld	James J. Fuld, *The Book of World-Famous Music*, revised edition 1971.
Games of American Children	*Games and Songs of American Children*, W. W. Newell, 1883; augmented 1903.
Games of Argyleshire	*Games and Diversions of Argyleshire*, R. C. Maclagan, 1901.
Gilchrist MSS	singing games, with tunes, collected by Anne Geddes Gilchrist; the MSS are in the library of the English Folk Dance and Song Society.
Golspie	*Golspie: contributions to its folklore*, E. W. B. Nicholson, 1897. Nicholson was Keeper of Printed Books at the Bodleian Library, and the schoolchildren's papers, the basis of his book, are stored there.
Gomme papers	letters sent to Alice Gomme after the publication of *Traditional Games*.
Howard MSS	games collected by Dr Dorothy Howard in USA, 1931 onwards. Also Australia.
JAFL	*Journal of American Folklore*.
Journal of EFDSS	*Journal of the English Folk Dance and Song Society*.
London Street Games	*London Street Games*, Norman Douglas, 1916.

Macmillan Collection	collection of 243 children's letters written in 1922 to A. S. Macmillan, Juvenile Editor of the West Country paper *Pulman's Weekly News*.
Mass Observation	Mass-Observation Ltd. Contributions to their August directive, 1949.
North Carolina Folklore	*The Frank C. Brown Collection of North Carolina Folklore*, vol. i, 1952.
ODNR	*The Oxford Dictionary of Nursery Rhymes*, Iona and Peter Opie, 1951.
Pandrich thesis	J. A. Pandrich, 'Child Lore . . . with particular reference to the North-East of England', 1967.
Popular Rhymes of Scotland	*Popular Rhymes of Scotland*, Robert Chambers, 1826, 1842, 1847, 1869. Robert and his brother William founded the firm of W. & R. Chambers, Edinburgh, publishers of Chambers's Journal and Chambers's Encyclopaedia.
Shropshire Folk-Lore	*Shropshire Folk-Lore: a sheaf of gleanings*, edited by Charlotte Sophia Burne from the collections of Georgina F. Jackson, 1883.
Street and Playground	*Children's Games in Street and Playground*, Iona and Peter Opie, 1969.
Sutton-Smith	Brian Sutton-Smith, *The Games of New Zealand Children*, 1959.
Those Dusty Bluebells	*Those Dusty Bluebells: children's rhymes from the Cumnock area*, published by Cumnock Academy, 1965.
Traditional Games	*The Traditional Games of England, Scotland, and Ireland*, Alice Bertha Gomme, 2 vols., 1894–8. This appeared as Part I of Sir Laurence Gomme's projected *Dictionary of British Folk-Lore* and was the only part to be completed.
Turner	Ian Turner, *Cinderella Dressed in Yella* (Melbourne, Australia), 1969.
Turner MS	Australian rhymes collected by Ian Turner in the 1950s and 1960s.

I

The Singing Game

ON a hot summer's day in July 1974, in Coram Fields in Bloomsbury, a small cockney sang with energy and conviction a game-song she had just learnt from her cousin:

> There's a lady on the mountain,
> Who she is I do not know,
> All she wants is gold and silver,
> All she wants is a nice young man.
>
> Open the gates and let me through!
> Now I can show you black and blue,
> So open the gates and let me through!
>
> Kneel down, lord,
> Kiss the ground, lord,
> Stand up, lord.
>
> Open the gates and let me through,
> Now I can show you black and blue;
> Here's my black and here's my blue,
> So open the gates and let me through!

The song seemed as mysterious as a fairy tale, and the singer possessed of ancient authority, as indeed she was.

After Thomas Hardy had heard his friend Canon Pentin repeating children's game-songs in the winter's dusk at Dorchester Museum, the words stayed with him, he said, all the next day, 'upstairs, downstairs, across the meads and in the garden'. The older singing games have the sound of poetry, even though sometimes nonsensical in meaning: 'Early and fairly the moon shines above, A' the lads in our town are dying for love', 'Our spurs are bright and richly wrought, In this town they were not bought, In this town they'll not be sold, Neither for silver nor for gold', 'The wind, the wind, the wind blows high, The rain comes scattering down the sky, She is handsome, she is pretty, She is the girl of the royal city'. William Barnes, who kept a scrapbook of folk poetry, cherished the game of 'Green Gravel', and admired the version of 'A Duke a-Riding' in which the suitors are 'all too black and brawny, They sit in the sun uncloudy, With golden chains around their necks, They are all too black and brawny'. Robert Graves has been entranced by the words of 'King William' and the 'Merry-ma-tansie'.

Singing games and their tunes are part of the well of tradition from which writers and composers draw. 'Here We Go Round the Mulberry Bush' has a significant place in Chesterton's *Manalive* and Eliot's 'The Wasteland'. The tune of 'Nuts in May' was not written for the celebrated song of 'Nancy Dawson' in 1760; it already existed as a dance tune in 1740, and was then probably taken from a singing game. Henri Hemy borrowed the tune of the game 'Queen Mary' for his famous hymn 'Hail, Queen of Heaven, the Ocean Star'. Humperdinck gave Gretel a folk game to sing in 'Hansel und Gretel', 1893—'Mit den Füszen tapp, tapp, tapp, Mit den Händen klapp, klapp, klapp'—a game which is related to the 'Wee Melodie Man' (p. 406). And singing games have been put to less exalted uses: they have been adopted by the Boy Scouts for singing round camp fires, and recalled with relief by song writers writing new songs under pressure.

The playing of singing games was, by at least the beginning of the nineteenth century, considered too unsophisticated a pastime to be fit for any but children, and the games are now under the haphazard guardian-ship of girls of about seven to nine years old. Songs eroded by generations of adult use are sung by children who are still not in command of everyday English, who have undeveloped memories, and who think the game itself more important than the words and tune which accompany it. On the other hand, they ardently defend what they believe to be the 'right' version of a song, especially if they themselves have introduced it to their mob. A young virago in Poole, who had brought a new game back from Pimlico, rounded on a friend who was unwise enough to retail the game to us. 'You don't know how it goes, Jennifer, so shut up!' 'They don't know it down here,' she complained. 'I've told *'er* once, and *'er* once, and I've told Michelle. But they don't really *know* it.' Likewise, they will defend their version against adult criticism. If the words are questioned they retort 'It's *like* that. That's what it *says*', as if the game were a living entity, which perhaps, by virtue of tradition, it is. They become irritable if a game is held up by adults asking irrelevant questions. They know the game itself is all that matters: 'We can't explain', they protest, 'We'll show you.' They would be uninterested to hear that they are perpetuating an amusement as old as the earliest written records or the beginnings of sculptural art.

RING DANCING IN THE ANCIENT WORLD

In Heraklion Museum four small naked men of baked clay, about 3,500 years old, with features pinched as a child might pinch them in plasticine, dance round a threshing floor in the way men still dance in Crete today. Almost as ancient a group from Palaikastro, in the same museum, depicts women dancing round a female lyre-player. In a later pottery group in Nicosia Museum, of 700–500 BC, six men dance with joined hands round a smaller man who looks as if he is nibbling the end of a French loaf, but must be playing a wind instrument; and in New York's Metropolitan Museum of Art are many more terracotta ring-dancers from Cyprus, pressed from moulds of a late Hellenistic style.

There is no doubt the ancient world was much given to dancing, in line as well as ring form. One has only to think of the scene Homer described, one of those adorning Achilles' shield (*Iliad*, *c*.800 BC):

... a dancing floor like the one that Daedalus designed in the spacious town of Cnossus for Ariadne of the lovely locks. Youths and marriageable maidens were dancing on it with their hands on one another's wrists, the girls in fine linen with lovely garlands on their heads, and the men in closely woven tunics showing the faint gleam of oil, and with daggers of gold hanging from their silver belts. Here they ran lightly round, circling as smoothly on their accomplished feet as the wheel of a potter when he sits and works it with his hands to see if it will spin; and there they ran in lines to meet each other.

Or witness the ring dance of the gods in Olympus in one of the Homeric hymns:

> ... Harmonia now and Hebe take their places
> With heaven-born Aphrodite, all in a ring
> Joined hand to wrist, and merrily round they swing.[1]

Songs often accompanied the dances. The Greeks, who played many games which are still part of the European tradition, may have played choral and choosing games as well. However, the only lines to survive which have the sound of a game-song are the question and response, from before 600 BC, 'Where are my roses, where are my violets, And where is my fine parsley? Here are your roses, here are your violets, And here is your fine parsley'.[2]

The first intimation of the courtship type of singing game, as later known in Europe, is found in the Bible, when the surviving men of the tribe of Benjamin were told to capture wives for themselves from among

[1] III, 182–206, trans. T. F. Higham.
[2] *Oxford Book of Greek Verse in Translation*, p. 196.

the girls dancing in the vineyards at the annual feast in Shiloh (Judges, 21: ninth century BC); and Rabbi Simeon ben Gamaliel, referring to c.AD100–200, vividly elucidates the nature of the vineyard dancing when he describes how, on the Day of Atonement, 'the daughters of Jerusalem went out in white dresses so that no one need be ashamed if she had none. And the daughters of Jerusalem went forth and danced in a circle in the vineyards. And what spake they? "Youth, lift up thine eyes and behold her whom thou wouldst choose" ' (*Mishnah*, Ta'an 4: 8). Thus the choosing of a sweetheart from a dancing ring is shown to have been a custom in the time of Christ and probably for centuries before.

Another ancient circular dance was that in which a leader stood in the centre of the ring and sang the verse, and the ring acted as chorus. This seems to be described in the 'Titanomachia', a poem of unknown authorship probably written before the mid-seventh century BC, in which Zeus,

> Himself, the sire of men, of gods the sire,
> The centre took, and led the dancing quire.[1]

In the apocryphal Acts of St John, of the mid-second century AD, Christ takes the central role while the apostles dance round him:

He bade us therefore make as it were a ring, holding one another's hands, and himself standing in the midst he said: Answer Amen unto me. He began, then, to sing an hymn and to say:
   Glory be to thee, Father.
And we, going about in a ring, answered him: Amen.
   Glory be to thee, Word: Glory be to thee, Grace. Amen.
   Glory be to thee, Spirit: Glory be to thee, Holy One:
   Glory be to thy Glory. Amen.

   Grace danceth. I would pipe; dance ye all. Amen.

   The number Twelve danceth on high. Amen.
   The Whole on high hath part in our dancing. Amen.
   Whoso danceth not, knowing not what cometh to pass. Amen.

   Now answer thou unto my dancing.
   Behold thyself in me who speak, and seeing what I do, keep silence about my mysteries.

I have leaped: but do thou understand the whole, and having understood it, say: Glory be to thee, Father. Amen.

   Thus, my beloved, having danced with us the Lord went forth.[2]

---

[1] *Oxford Book of Greek Verse in Translation*, p. 180.
[2] *The Apocryphal New Testament*, ed. M. R. James, 1955, 253 f.

THE MEDIEVAL CAROLE

It is not to be supposed that dancing ceased during the Dark Ages, but not until the monk Goscelin included the legend of the sacrilegious dancers of Kölbigk in his *Life of St Edith of Wilton*, *c.*1080, is there any further documentation. The story is best known from Robert Mannyng of Bourne's metrical version, 'Handlyng Synne', 1303, itself a retelling from William of Wadington's Norman-French *Manuel des Péchés*. Twelve revellers gather on Christmas Eve to dance in the churchyard of St Magnus at Kölbigk in Saxony, and bring the priest's daughter out to join their ring. The leader of the dance sings, 'as telleth the Latin tunge':

> Equitabat Bouo   per siluam frondosam
> Ducebat sibi   Mersuindem formosam:
> Quid stamus?   Cur non imus?

for which Robert Mannyng provides the translation:

> By þe leued [leaved] wode rode Beuolyne,
> wyþ hym he ledde feyre Merswyne;
> why stonde we? why go we noght?

When matins are over, the priest comes to the church porch to tell the dancers that Mass is about to begin, bidding them 'carolleth no more, for Cristes awe'. When they take no notice he condemns them to go on dancing for a year and a day. Too late, he sends his son to pull his daughter from the ring, and, in horrifying and absurd sequence, the girl's arm breaks off, does not bleed, will not be buried, and finally is exhibited in the church. When the year is up the dancers fall to the ground exhausted, and lie there for three days. The priest's daughter is found to be dead; soon afterwards the priest himself dies, and the carollers go their separate ways, still hopping about as if dancing.

The Kölbigk dancers' song helps to explain how such dances were performed. The dancers must have skipped round while singing the story of Bevoline riding through the woods with fair Merswine by his side, and marked time while singing 'Why stand we? Why go we not?' It is also significant that Robert Mannyng, in 1303, called the dance a 'carole', whilst Goscelin (*c.*1080) did not. 'Carole', a French word signifying a dance accompanied with song (cf. Italian *carola*), is not found in English until about 1300. Thereafter, until about 1550, 'carolling' appears as one of the chief recreations at feasts and merrymakings. Sir Gawain (in the fourteenth-century poem) takes part in 'kynde caroles of knyʒtez and ladyes' at Christmas. The jay-bird, in Sir Richard Holland's *Buke of the*

Howlat, *c*.1450, conjures up wonderful scenes for the birds at the banquet:

> . . . Thus jowkit with juperdys [juggled with hazard] the jangland Ja:
> Fair ladyis in ryngis,
> Knychtis in caralyngis,
> Boith dansis and syngis;
>   It semyt as sa.

Gavin Douglas, portraying a contemporary scene in the twelfth prologue to his translation of Virgil, 1513, described how the ladies

> . . . sang ring-sangs, dancis, ledis and roundis,
> With vocis schil, quhil all the dale resoundis;
> Quhareto they walk into thare karoling,
> For amourus layis dois all the rochis ring;
> Ane sang, 'The schip salis over the salt fame,
> Will bring thir merchandis and my lemane [lover] hame,
> Some other sings, 'I will be blyith and licht,
> My hert is lent apoun sae gudly wicht'.

And Sir Richard Maitland exhorted 'all boroughs towns' to make bonfires, act plays, and dance *caroles* through the streets, to celebrate the marriage of the fifteen-year-old Mary, Queen of Scots, to the sickly young dauphin Francis in April 1558 (*Maitland Quarto MS*, ed. W. A. Craigie, pp. 19–23).

The precise way in which the *carole* was danced has been the subject of much speculation and argument. R. L. Greene, *The Early English Carols*, 1977, summarizes the arguments for the two main contentions: that the dancers stood still while the song-leader led the singing of the stanza, or story-line, which was different each time, and circled round while singing the refrain, which was always the same; or that the dancers circled while the stanza was sung and stood still while singing the refrain (as, presumably, did the dancers of Kölbigk while singing 'Why stand we? Why go we not?'). The Kölbigk refrain would be the only real evidence that exists, were it not that the medieval *carole* has survived in the Faroes. Hjalmar Thuren explains, in *Folk Songs in the Faroes*, 1908, that in Germany in the early Middle Ages young girls danced lively ring dances ('Reigen') to lyrical songs, and the slow, more formal and courtly *carole*, danced 'with extreme gravity', spread through Europe during the period of the minnesingers in the twelfth to fourteenth centuries. While the Faroese dances are quicker or slower according to the nature of the song, the general mode of dancing is always the same. A chain of dancers gradually forms behind the leader, who is also the leader of the song, and when it is long enough it closes into a ring, which circles to the left. 'The dance steps are simple: the left foot takes a step to the left, the right foot is brought up to the left, the left foot takes another step to the left, the right closes to the left again; finally the right foot steps to the right, and the left foot is brought up to the right foot, and these steps are repeated.' 'Sometimes', Thuren adds, 'the Faroese dance on the same spot, when the stanza is being sung, although they move during the singing of the refrain, as before' (also see p. 248).

Claude Fauriel also contributes to our knowledge of how the *carole* was danced in his *Histoire de la Poésie Provençale*, 1846 (ii, p. 87). He remembered seeing peasants playing the game 'L'Avoine' ('Oats and Beans and Barley Grow', p. 178) and, not being aware of the *carole*, and possibly seeing it from a libertarian standpoint, thought that the slow tempo of the song, while the singers stood and imitated the farming actions through the year, represented 'the fatigue and sullen air of the poor labourer'; and that the refrain, sung to a lively air, was 'the dancers giving way to all their gaiety'. This marking time while singing the stanza and moving round while the refrain is sung, together with the slow and stately movement said to be characteristic of the *carole*, can be found in some of the earlier recordings of singing games. 'London Bridge' was danced in this fashion in Bristol *c.*1785. Robert Chambers saw girls dancing the 'Merry-ma-tansie' as a *carole* in Lanarkshire before 1842, with even a song-leader in the centre of the ring:

A number of girls join hands in a circle, round one of their number, who acts as a kind of mistress of the ceremonies. The circle moves slowly round the central lady, observing time with their feet, and singing to a pleasing air,

> Here we go the jingo-ring,
> The jingo-ring, the jingo-ring . . .

And in his 'Hinkumbooby' ('Okey Kokey'), also danced slowly and with a song-leader, the dancers move while singing the refrain and make the grotesque gestures called for while in their places:

The party form a circle, taking hold of each others' hands. One sings, and the rest join, to the tune of Lullibullero [*sic*]:

> Fal de ral la, fal de ral la;

while doing so, they move a little sideways, and back again, beating the time (which is slow) with their feet. As soon as the line is concluded, each claps his hand and wheels grotesquely round, singing at the same moment the second line of the verse:

> Hinkumbooby, round about.

J. S. Udal noted that children playing 'The Mulberry Bush' in Symonds-bury in the 1880s, who had learnt the game from other children, took hands and sang the refrain while slowly moving or dancing around,

Cretan ring dance of *c.*1350 BC, a
pottery group in Heraklion Museum.

Shepherds carolling,
with their dance-leader
standing outside the
ring; from a
mid-fifteenth century
book of hours.

Detail from Bruegel's
Kermesse d'Hoboken,
showing two of the chief
pleasures of a
sixteenth-century
fair—drinking, and the
playing of singing
games. This game could
well be 'The Farmer's in
His Den' (No. 38).

Top: The heavenly ring dance; detail from Fra Angelico's *Last Judgement*, early fifteenth century. A saint and angel hold up their hands to make an arch, through which the others will 'thread the needle' (see p. 33).

Bottom: A young man is invited into a courtship ring, where his sweetheart waits to crown him with a chaplet of flowers. *Roman de la Rose, c.*1490.

unloosing their hands and standing while they did the actions; and it is obvious that any action game would, for convenience sake, be danced with the players standing still to perform the actions. But carolling must not be thought of as being confined to circular dances. Other dances accompanied by song, some of which have been preserved by children to the present day, were probably embraced in the term. Chains of dancers can not only make closed or open circles, but can move across country with serpentine movement, pause and wind into a snail shape, and progress again by means of 'threading the needle', when the dancer at the end of the chain runs through an arch made by the two at the front, pulling the rest of the chain after her (see pp. 33–6).

COURTSHIP DANCES

The entertainments of the later Middle Ages were graceful and courtly, humorous and vulgar, according to their setting, but always radiated a love of life that defied pestilence, poverty, and war. The singing games can now be recognized as having a place beside the folk and mystery plays, the music and singing, that constituted the social pleasures of the time. A herald of arms, Jacques Bretel, describing actual events at the Tourney of Chauvency in 1285, gave a detailed account of the singing game, then called 'Le Chapelet', which was played to hearten the knights who had been wounded in the tournament. A lady, who is supposed to be in a wood, stands inside the ring playing with a chaplet of flowers. A 'minstrel of old' comes to her, and asks in song 'Why are you here alone, without a friend?', and then, 'Sweet lady, do you want a husband?' She replies she would rather keep her chaplet (that is, remain a virgin) than have a bad husband. The minstrel, acting as master of ceremonies, brings forward a knight from among the spectators, telling him to come and search for the lady. The knight pretends reluctance, but is led to where the lady waits impatiently; and she takes him by the hand, 'singing with great joy, "Thanks be to God, I have gained what I longed for".'[1]

Another game-song on the theme of a girl reluctant to give her chaplet of flowers to a young man is found in the Netherlands, in the Hulthem MS of c.1400:

> In a bower where I came
> Did I find fair flowerets stand;
> There I gathered for my love
> Of violets this garland.

[1] For the French text, see Joseph Bedier, *Revue des Deux Mondes*, V, xxxi, 1906, 'Les Plus Anciennes Danses Françaises'; and, for a translation of the whole piece, Peter Dronke, *The Medieval Lyric*, 1968, pp. 198–9.

Does it suit me well?
Do I wear it well?
How do you like it?

Young maiden, that garland
Doth suit you well.
Most over-chaste slender fair one
Give me that garland,
Then thou dost well.
Give me that garland!

The girl says that only her 'dearest love' will wear that garland, the young man says that in that case he will die on the sharp sword of love, and, as often happens in real life, the girl relents: 'Surely my sin would be most great, If thus I slew my lover dead, Stand up now, we shall depart, Blithely, with a gladsome heart'.[1]

The same scene of pastoral love was being enacted within a ring in the 1930s. Arnold Van Gennep said 'Le Bois charmant' was 'well-known throughout France' and selected a version from St Bueil:

Dans un petit bois charmant,	(In a delightful little wood,
Quand on y est, l'on est bien aise,	Where one is glad to be,
Dans un petit bois charmant,	In a delightful little wood,
Quand on y est, l'on est content.	Where one is happy to be.
La belle y va s'y promenant . . .	The beautiful girl goes strolling . . .
Son amant rentre en la suivant . . .	Her lover follows her there . . .
Ils s'asseyent bien gentiment . . .	And they sit down most prettily . . .
Ils font l'amour en souriant . . .	Smiling, they pay court to each other . . .
Ils s'embrassent bien tendrement . . .	They embrace most tenderly . . .
Ils se retirent lestement . . .	Then they withdraw without further ado . . .)

[1] *Het dietse lied in de middeleeuwen*, H. Godthelp and A. F. Mirande, 1940, p. 91: translation, Joyce Houwaard. Surrendering her chaplet or coronet of flowers has long been symbolic of a girl becoming a woman. Károly Viski, *Hungarian Peasant Customs*, 1932 (1937, pp. 112–13), says that it is usually the task of the best man to remove the bride's wreath at weddings, and shows that the custom goes back many centuries. 'In the 17th century, at Transylvanian aristocratic weddings, the wreath was cut off the bride's head as a memento that "she shall thus behave herself in holy wedlock, that if she besoils it a sword will fall onto her head" . . . The son of the Hungarian king Béla IV in 1264 also cut the wreath off the head of his bride, Kunigund, with a sword, according to a German chronicler—*juxta ritum suae gentis* (according to the custom of his own nation).' In Sweden a common wedding custom is 'dancing the coronet off the head of the bride'; the bride is blindfolded and, while the bridesmaids dance round her in a ring, she places the coronet on one of their heads—the belief being that that girl will be next to find a husband (E. E. Westermarck, *History of Human Marriage*, ii, 1921, pp. 588–9).

The structure of the dance would have been familiar to the knights and ladies of 1285: 'Two players enter the circle, perform the movements indicated, and then leave, each to a different side of the ring, to be followed by two other players'.[1]

The courtship round was part of the social machinery of the Middle Ages. A dance-leader conducted the proceedings, and, in the chief Maytime round, 'Le Rosier', which has analogues throughout Europe, he addressed the young dancers as 'rose' or 'rose tree'. In most printed versions only words and tune are given, but Ernest Gagnon, in *Chansons Populaires du Canada*, 1865, places the game in its social context. The round, which he speaks of as being a popular amusement of the past, was danced to this song:

Dans ma main droite je tiens rosier,	(In my right hand I hold a rose tree,
Dans ma main droite je tiens rosier,	In my right hand I hold a rose tree,
Qui fleurira, manon lon la,	Which will flower, manon lon la,
Qui fleurira au mois de mai.	Which will flower in the month of May.
Entrez en danse, joli rosier!	Come into the dance, pretty rose tree!
Entrez en danse, joli rosier!	Come into the dance, pretty rose tree!
Et embrassez (saluez) manon lon la!	And kiss (bow to) manon lon la!
Et embrassez (saluez) qui vous plaira.	And kiss (bow to) the one you like.)

He explained:

The young people all hold each other by the hand, making a circle, and begin to go round; the old parents are wallflowers and see to the proprieties. The oldest or the best singer then intones: 'Dans ma main droite je tiens rosier . . .' The other dancers sing with him *ad libitum*, but always letting the voice of the soloist dominate *obbligato*. At the second verse the singer brings into the round the young boy or girl whom he holds with his right hand, saying 'Entrez en danse, joli rosier . . .', then, if the dancers are all in the family, he adds 'Et embrassez manon lon la . . . qui vous plaira'; but if there are strangers in the dance one almost always says 'Et saluez . . . qui vous plaira'. Then the dancers stop, then, the embrace or bowing done, they begin to circle again. He who was in the centre of the chain passes to the left of the singer, who goes through the same ceremony with his new neighbour on the right, and so on till each boy and girl has declared his preference before the assembled company.

It seems likely that this was the way the game was danced in Europe and that the simple choose-and-change ring games played by children in the present day once had this more elegant and sophisticated structure.[2]

[1] *Le Folklore du Dauphiné, Isère*, ii, 1933, p. 666.

[2] 'Le Rosier' was part of the Maytime festivities in Provence, especially in Nice, until the outbreak of World War II (*Folklore de la Provence*, C. Seignolle, 1963, p. 187). The equivalent game in Holland is 'Alhier ne meiboom in mijn hand' (Here is a may tree in my hand), *Kinderspel in Zuid-Nederland*, A. de Cock and I. Teirlinck, ii, 3, p. 248; in French Flanders, 'Roza, willen wy

The office of dance-leader has a long history. In the *carole*, as has been shown, a principal singer led the company in both singing and dancing. In the wedding-houses or *Tanzhäuser* of medieval Jewish ghettos, dance-leaders organized and announced the dances throughout the evening and made sure the dancers behaved with decorum. (Beau Nash, Master of Ceremonies at Bath Assembly Rooms, later fulfilled the same function.) Alessandro Falassi has shown that the *caposala* of public dance halls in Tuscany occasionally resorts, in his capacity as match-maker, to the medieval ritual of bringing young people forward to dance with one another. In 'Ballo a i' canto' ('Dance to the Singing') he gives a man direct instructions to dance with a particular girl:

> This dance is no good
> If Beppino doesn't come over here.
> It would be much better
> If Beppino came over here.

Beppino then comes to the foot of the platform and the girl who is to partner him is invited to dance:

> And this dance is no good
> If Rosa doesn't come over here.

Often the dancers have confided their preferences to him beforehand, as must have happened in medieval days. Dances were being conducted in the same way, and with the same dance-song, in Tuscany in the sixteenth century, as Falassi points out. In the Riccardiano MS 2352 is a description of a dance at Rovezzano in 1552. The head of the dance sang 'Questo ballo non sta bene' ('This dance is no good'—a pronouncement reminiscent of the cushion dance, see pp. 190–7); and the dancers were told 'You (name), my companion, go near your desired one, and there remain'.[1]

Slowly, as the surviving singing games are sifted, a picture emerges of the European games as they were played by young adults long ago. In another of the courtship games, for instance, a girl was led outside the ring, was consulted about her choice of young man, and was brought back to declare her choice and to have it approved by the ring. Often in such a game the players curtsied at the end of the first verse, and it was the last

---

dansen?' (Rose, shall we dance?), *Chants Populaires des Flamands de France*, C. E. de Coussemaker, 1856, pp. 330–1; in Germany, 'Rosen, Rosen auf unser'm Hut' (Roses, roses on our hat), Böhme, p. 576; in Sweden, 'Är det någon kavaljer er behagar? Ja, ja min rosa . . .' (Is there some cavalier for her delight? Yes, yes my rose), *Svenska folklekar och danser*, C. Tillhagen and N. Dencker, ii, 1950, pp. 394–5. In the USA cf. Newell's game from Deerfield, Mass., *c.*1810, 'There's a rose in the garden for you, fair maid, There's a rose in the garden, pluck it if you can, Be sure you don't choose a false-hearted one' (p. 110).

[1] *Folklore by the Fireside, text and context of the Tuscan Veglia*, 1980, pp. 192–3.

to rise who was escorted out of the ring by the match-makers. This can still be seen in some present-day games: in 'Orange Balls' for instance (pp. 232–5). Often the chooser and her friends asked for gates to be opened, and this, as well as selection-by-falling, is found in a version of 'Merry-ma-tansie' from County Louth (*Traditional Games*, ii, pp. 84–5) where the girls sang 'Open the gates and let the bride through'. In its imagery, the great Italian ring game 'Madame Dorè' might be a medieval illumination brought to life. The match-maker chooses a girl from the ring, singing 'Most beautiful girl in the city, come outside' and, after agreeing on a suitable match with the mother, re-enters singing 'Open the gates for me, Madame Dorè' and asks that the carpets be put down for the wedding.[1] Byron, rambling through Albania in the autumn of 1809, was fascinated by the choral dances he heard and had the following song taken down 'by one who understands the dialect perfectly'. The first words were a refrain, 'merely a kind of chorus without meaning'. Thereafter the game unfolds a story of a gate opening to let in a lover:

I come, I run; open the door that I may enter. Open the door by halves, that I may take my turban. Caliriotes with the dark eyes, open the gate that I may enter. Lo, lo, I hear thee, my soul. An Arnaout girl, in costly garb, walks with graceful pride. Caliriot maid of the dark eyes, give me a kiss. If I have kissed thee what hast tho.. gained! My soul is consumed with fire. Dance lightly, more gently, and gently still. Make not so much dust to destroy your embroidered hose.[2]

Another pattern for a courtship game was one in which a girl, having been brought into the ring, had to perform certain dancing steps before kissing the one she loved best and returning to her place. It is this figure which seems to have been preserved in 'Wallflowers' (pp. 244–7) where the girl in the centre must once have had to match with actions the now corrupted words 'She can dance, and she can skip, And she can turn the candlestick'. The most typical of such dances in Italy is 'Maria Giulia', which must serve as an example for the whole genre:

Maria Giulia,	(Maria Julia,
Da dove sei venuta?	Where have you come from?
Alza gli occhi al cielo,	Raise your eyes to the sky,
Fa un salto, fanne un altro,	Make a leap, make another,
Levati il cappelletto,	Take off your cap [originally chaplet?]
Fa la riverenza,	Make a bow (or curtsy),
Fa la penitenza,	Do a penance,

[1] *Giochi descritti dai bambini*, M. M. Lumbroso, 1967, pp. 101–3, from Grignano Prato, near Florence.

[2] Byron's note to 'Childe Harold', canto xi, stanza lxxii.

Un di su,	Once look up,
Un di giù,	Once down,
Da un bacio a chi vuoi tu.	Give a kiss to whom you like.)

Rome, c.1892, Notes & Queries, *8th ser., i, p. 250*

This game was being played in sixteenth-century Italy and is recorded in the Florentine MS Riccardiano 2352:

Danza chi danza	(Dance who dances,
Che fai una bella danza.	Who dances a pretty dance.
E danza tu (*name*)	And you must dance (*name*)
Che l'hai la tua speranza.	So that you will have the one you hope for.
Per amor facci un salto,	For love make a leap,
Per gentilezza un altro,	For courtesy make another,
Con una riverenza	With a bow (or curtsy)
E una continenza,	And a moderation,
E torna alla tua stanza.	And return to your place)[1]

The 'riverenza' and 'continenza' were dance steps taught in Italy, France, and Spain in the fifteenth century, appearing for instance in Cornazano's *Libro dell'arte del danzare*, 1455, the 'continenza' being a swaying step. The game is still a favourite in modern Italy, but sometimes the central character is 'Maria Maddalena', who washes handkerchiefs, spreads them out, gives a jump and another jump, turns around, curtsys, does penance, and kisses the one she loves.

Other survivals of medieval dance-games are 'Thread the Needle' in its various forms and the bridge games, such as 'Oranges and Lemons' (see ch. II, 'Chains and Captives'); and it seems highly probable that the games in chapters III and XI, 'Match-Making' and 'Contests', which are played like the old German stepping dance in two lines, some of the 'Dramas' (ch. X), the 'Cushion Dances' (ch. VI) and the 'Witch Dances' (ch. IX), also date from the later Middle Ages.

May, and thereafter through the summer, was the season for dancing. It was not only a celebration of springtime and the return of fair weather, but fulfilled the function of pairing off the young and shaming the reluctant into what was considered a normal sexual rôle. Bachelors, spinsters, and homosexuals were not considered to take a responsible part in society, and a number of singing games express scorn for the unpaired: the cushion dance 'Silly Old Man', for instance, which begins 'Here's a silly old man that lies alone', the adult German version of 'The Farmer's in His Den', where the farmer is pushed and shoved till he chooses a wife, and a

[1] Printed in *Canzonette antiche*, E. Alvisi, 1884, p. 15.

German singing game, 'Die schwarze Köchin', in which the girl left alone at the end must hide her face in shame while the others taunt 'There stands the black cook!' and hiss at her (Böhme, no. 267).[1]

Fifteen seems to have been the optimum age for marriage. At fourteen a girl could sing 'How should you want me to marry, I am not yet fifteen' (though a nightingale answers 'Come, my beauty, I will find you a charming lover').[2] Another singing game exhorts:

La mère Bontemps	(Mother Fairweather
Disait aux jeunes fillettes:	Said to the young girls:
'Dansez, mes enfants,	'Dance, my children,
Tandis que vous êtes jeunettes.	While you are young.
La fleur de gaîté	The flower of gaiety
Passe avec l'été.	Passes with summer.
Au printemps, comme la rose,	Gather it in the spring, like the rose,
Cueillez-la dès qu'elle est éclose.	As soon as it is open.
Dansez à quinze ans;	Dance at fifteen;
Plus tard, il n'est plus temps.'	Later, is not the time.')[3]

At sixteen a girl might think she had lost her chance of marrying: 'J'ai seize ans, ma mère, J'ai seize ans passés. Vous ne songez guère a me marier' (I am sixteen, mother, I am sixteen already. You are not thinking much about getting me married).[4] These dance-songs, though not written down till the nineteenth century, agree with other evidence that the age of marriage was about fifteen in the late Middle Ages, leaving aside the very early contractual marriages of nobility and royalty, which were not consummated until the age of puberty. In the ballad of 'Earl Brand' (Child 7, A) the bride was 'na fifteen years o' age, Till she came to the Earl's bed side'. In fairy tales, girls are thought marriageable at fourteen or fifteen. And in hard legal terms, girls in the district of Arezzo in Tuscany in 1427–30 who expected to have tax deducted when the marriage contract was concluded had an average age of 15.4 years.[5] Literary evidence of a later date can be

---

[1] To understand the pressure upon young people to get married, one has to remember that, even as late as the seventeenth century, 'No single man would usually take charge of the land, any more than a single man would often be found at the head of a workshop in the city. The master of a family was expected to be a householder, whether he was a butcher, a baker, a candlestick maker or simply a husbandman, which was the universal name for one whose skill was in working the land. Marriage we must insist, and it is one of the rules which gave its character to the society of our ancestors, was the entry to full membership, in the enfolding countryside, as well as in the scattered urban centres' (Peter Laslett, *The World We Have Lost*, 2nd edn. 1971, p. 286 n.).

[2] 'J'ai cueilli la rose rose', in *Chants du Cambresis*, A. Durieux and A. Bruyelle, i, 1864, pp. 284–6.

[3] *Jeux des Jeunes Filles*, Mme de Chabreul, 1856, pp. 223–4.

[4] *Folklore du Dauphiné, Isère*, A. Van Gennep, ii, 1933, pp. 617–18.

[5] *The World We Have Lost*, P. Laslett, 1971, p. 286.

discounted; Shakespeare's fourteen-year-old Juliet, for instance, and the song in Beaumont and Fletcher's *Cupid's Revenge* (I, i), 1615, 'the God hath said, Fifteen shall make a mother of a maid'. But Geiler von Kaisersberg, preaching at the beginning of the sixteenth century, illumines the short and joyous years between childhood and womanhood when he chides: 'Do you still want to dance "Den faulen Brucken" ("The Rotten Bridge", cf. "London Bridge" pp. 61–7) as you did when you were twelve or fourteen years old? It becomes you ill: older people must not behave like young ones do.'[1]

ECCLESIASTICAL ATTITUDES

The Christian church seems to have been opposed to secular dancing throughout its history, and especially during the years of the Inquisition and the Protestant Reformation. For more than a thousand years the ecclesiastical councils sought to stamp out the sin of 'obscene' dancing without much success. It is impossible for us in the twentieth century to know in what spirit the common people danced, but it is likely that their dancing was often wild and bawdy. Certainly the dancing sometimes seems to have been carried to excess, when a kind of mania took hold of the dancers so that they could not stop. The malady known as St Vitus's dance broke out in the Rhine valley about the middle of the fourteenth century, when for months people danced travesties of the *carole* from town to town until they fell foaming at the mouth. Nearly two centuries earlier Giraldus, Archdeacon of Brecon, in Wales, had watched the parishioners of St Almedha dancing in the church and round the churchyard, 'falling on the ground as in a trance, then jumping up as in a frenzy, and representing with their hands and feet, before the people, whatever work they have unlawfully done on feast days; you may see one man put his hand to the plough, and another as it were goad on the oxen . . . one man imitating the profession of a shoemaker; another that of a tanner. Now you may see a girl with a distaff, drawing out the thread, and winding it again on the spindle; another walking, and arranging the threads for the web; another, as it were, throwing the shuttle and seeming to weave.'[2] It seems likely, however, that—far from expiating their sins—the villagers had carried to extremes the widespread European singing game in which different occupations are imitated (see 'When I Was a Lady', pp. 294–6), and that Giraldus, as a fisher of men, probably saw the game from as slanted a viewpoint as that from which the libertarian Claude Fauriol was to watch

[1] Böhme, p. 533.
[2] *The Itinerary of Archbishop Baldwin*, trans. Sir Richard Colt Hoare, 1806, I, pp. 35–6.

the peasants of Provence dancing 'L'Avoine' six hundred years later (see p. 7).

On other occasions dancers were seized by an enthusiasm which fell not far short of madness. A delirious dance across country took place in Switzerland in the mid-fourteenth century when the Count of Gruyère, returning to his castle, found a company of young men and maidens dancing a *carole* at its foot. The Count joined the *carole* and 'someone proposed that they should go, dancing all the while, as far as the village of Enny, without stopping, and from that place continue the carole to Chateau d'Oex in the district of Enhaut; and it was a marvellous thing to see the people of the villages they passed through joining this happy band'.[1] And on the castle meadow at Greyerz, also in Switzerland, one Sunday evening, seven people started a ring dance which only ceased on Tuesday morning in the great market place of Saanen, after seven hundred youths and maidens, men and wives, had joined on to the line, 'till the whole looked like a snail shell'.[2]

The dance songs were, it is true, not elevating, being entirely concerned with earthly love. A sermon of the early thirteenth century describes as 'worthless' the ring song it takes as a text:

> Atte wrastlinge my lemman [lover] i ches,
> and atte ston-kasting i him for-les.[3]

The Maytime ring songs are instinct with carnal joy, and lyrical with love's emblem, the rose: 'Qui mari 'rons-nous, Dans ce petit jardin d'amour' the dancers sang, and 'Me arrodillo a los pies di mi amante' ('I kneel at the feet of my beloved . . . Give me a kiss of your lovely mouth'), and 'Rosier chargé de roses, de roses et de fleurs, Mademoiselle, retournez-vous, Que derrière vous il y a un amoreux'. The kissing itself could scarcely have been disapproved, since it was the ordinary polite greeting of the time. More disreputable was the horseplay with which some of the games ended, as can be seen from the jostling at the end of 'The Big Ship', 'Winding Up the Clock', and the foreign versions of 'Wallflowers'; the thumping at the end of 'The Farmer's in His Den' (especially the German feast-day versions), the hitting with fists at the end of the eighteenth-century French 'L'Avoine' ('Oats and Beans'), and the disorderly chases at the end of 'Old Roger', 'Jenny Jones', 'Milking Pails', and 'La Porte du Gloria' (the French equivalent of 'Oranges and Lemons') where the pursuers are armed with knotted handkerchiefs. When such games were

[1] *La Danse Populaire dans le Pays de Vaud sous le Regime Bernois*, J. Burdet, 1958, p. 87.
[2] *Labyrinth-Studien*, Karoly Kerényi, Albae vigiliae, Neve folge, Heft 10, 1950, pp. 28–9.
[3] Trinity College, Cambridge, B. I. 45, f. 41ᵛ. Quoted *Early English Carols*, R. L. Greene, 1977, 1.

played by tipsy adults on feast days, they may well have given cause for alarm.

Another reason for ecclesiastical unease was the preference people had for dancing in churchyards (as did the dancers of Kölbigk, see p. 5). Étienne de Bourbon, who was appointed Inquisitor soon after 1235, denounced in his *Preachers' Manual* 'those most sacrilegious persons who tread down the bodies of holy Christian folk in the churchyards, where they dance on Saints' eves and kindle the living temples of God with the fire of lechery, flocking to the churches on Saints' days and eves and holding dances and hindering the service of God and his Saints'. But, later, Sir Thomas Overbury's franklin held a more kindly view: he did not think 'the bones of the dead anything bruised, or the worse for it, though the country lasses dance in the churchyard after evensong'.

However, the church commended *caroles* if they were danced to the glory of God. As early as the fourth century AD St Chrysostom of Constantinople congratulated his flock on performing ring dances 'in the spirit of St Paul' at Whitsun, rather than 'dancing the indecent dances of the drunken'. Perhaps even at that time religious ring dances were being composed as substitutes for secular ones, as they were in later centuries. Böhme (pp. 367–71) prints a considerable number of religious songs for ring dances in his *Altdeutsches Liederbuch*: one is based on the Lord's prayer; another has words from the Twenty-third Psalm; another is a '*Kranzsingen*' or 'singing of the garland'. Religious ring dances were also sung in England, as 'Hand by hand we shule us take' and 'A ferly thing it is to mene, That a maid a child have borne', with its refrain 'Ay, ay, this is the day, That we shal worship ever and ay'.[1] By the sixteenth century books of religious games were in print, of which the most important was *Een devoot ende profitelyck boecxken*, Antwerp, c.1539.[2] Here we read of Christ joining the heavenly maidens in a dance:

> Maria, the most beautiful maiden,
> There leadeth she the dance,
> And all the sweet little maidens,
> They wear a golden garland.

In Hermann's *Historien von der Sindfluth* (History of the Flood), 1563, appears 'A dialogue between two Christian maidens on the use and virtue of holy baptism. Set as an evening ring song', which has the refrain 'If no

---

[1] *Oxford Book of Medieval Verse*, nos. 79 and 211.

[2] '*A devout and profitable little book, containing many spiritual songs and leizen*. Printed in the triumphant commercial town of Antwerp, at the Lombardy fastness, opposite the Golden Cock. By me, Simon Cock.' The most important collection of spiritual songs, according to G. Kalff, *Het Lied in der middeleeuwen*, 1884; it is in the library at Haarlem.

one will sing, then I will, The King of all glory is wooing me'; and Böhme has matched this with its secular antecedent (from Peter Schöffer II, *Sammlung 65 Lieder*, *c*.1537): 'If no one will sing, then I will, There is a youth a-courting me'. It seems that the church has been converting secular songs to religious purposes throughout the Christian era (as the Salvation Army has done in our own day) and ring dances along with them. Thus are explained the religious singing games still played on the continent in the present century, such as the Flemish 'Myn moeder gaat naar Laken' ('My mother goes to Laken, Sacré, sacré, Maria; Then we fall on our knees . . . Then we kiss a statue . . . Then we dance in the ring')[1] and 'Balliam, balliamo O virgini', recorded in Sardinia by Father Damian Webb in 1962: 'Let us dance, dance O virgins, for whom the angels play music. Let (*name*) turn round that the angel may embrace her. Full of flowers, full of flowers, With the beautiful angel let us make love.'

Religious carolling was to be enjoyed on earth and also, as is shown in poetry and picture, to be enjoyed with the saints in heaven. A heavenly *carole*, depicted in 'The Last Judgement' by Fra Angelico (1387–1455) in the Convent of St Mark in Florence, shows the blessed being welcomed into heaven by the angels, given haloes, and led into the dance.[2] John Lydgate (1370?–1450), in his long poem 'A Kalendare', implores the saints that he may, when he passes hence, be brought into their dance; and to St Appollinare he says 'teche me ȝoure games', an interesting use of the word 'game' in the general context of the ring dance—did he mean what we now know as singing games? In her cell in the Buurkerk of Utrecht, in the second half of the fifteenth century, the anchoress St Bertha pours out her 'Song about Heaven' ('Een lied op de Hemel') and, saying goodbye to her earthly nature, joins Christ, personifying love, in an ecstatic circling dance:

> Love doth have a rose garland,
> The lilies perform a dance,
> They have been purified within;
> They step ahead, forward advance,
> At love's most high demand.
>
> Love's splendour is, as I shall tell,
> The lilies bend, they stand quite still,
> Love wishes to rise high:
> The lilies float in ecstasy,
> Who may praise love enow?

---

[1] *Vlaamsche Kinderspelen uit West Brussel*, Aimé de Cort, 1931, pp. 132–3.
[2] See p. 9.

> Love doth stand, love doth go,
> Love doth sing, love doth spring,
> Love rests in those he loveth,
> Love doth sleep, love doth wake,
> How can one comprehend it?[1]

In so doing, St Bertha describes one of the delights of her girlhood, before she became a hermit.

During the sixteenth century the rapturous pleasures of the medieval age were further frowned upon: no more might saints or mortals dance in rings, or lovers go a-maying. The Catholic church, as well as the Protestant, tried to put down the vice of carolling, as A. J. Mill shows in *Medieval Plays in Scotland*. The Catholic Archbishop of St Andrews, in his *Catechism*, 1552, sought to prevent unnecessary drinking, lecherous songs, whoredom, card-playing and dicing, 'and specially carreling and wanton singing in the kirk', on Sundays. In 1574 fourteen women of Aberdeen were charged with 'plaing, dansin and singin off fylthe carrolles on Yeull Day, at evin, and on Sunday, at even, thairafter'. Later, witches were accused of the same wanton behaviour; one Isobel Gowdie confessed at Auldearne, 1662, 'the Devil always takes the Maiden in his hand next him, when we dance Gillatrypes'.[2]

The Puritans were the most virulent in their condemnation of dancing, and since they took their beliefs with them to America, it is natural that scruples against dancing should have lingered on there. The consequence was the development of that purely American festivity, the play-party (the term itself is not found before 1904). Play-parties are simply evening gatherings for young folk, at which singing games are played. As they are games and not dances, and as there is no music other than the singing, the church was not likely to object. Even so, as B. A. Botkin says (*American Play-Party Song*, p. 21), 'On the one hand—and this was the more general attitude—it might tolerate and even encourage the play-party as the lesser of two evils; on the other hand, fanaticism might proceed to the point where the play-party was outlawed along with the dance'.[3]

---

[1] *Het dietse lied in de middeleeuwen*, H. Godthelp and A. F. Mirande, 1940, pp. 227–8; translation, Joyce Houwaard.

[2] *The Witch-Cult in Western Europe*, M. A. Murray, p. 133.

[3] It is interesting that the church in Italy, about 1300, was making the same distinction between dances and games. See V. de Bartholomaeis, *Origini della Poesia Drammatica Italiana*, 1924, p. 80; he refers to the *Pungilingua* of Domenico Cavalca (*c.*1270–1342) and the *Prediche* of Giordano da Rivalto, 29 August 1305.

THE ROMANTIC REVIVAL

The revival of singing games in the late nineteenth century was part of a general yearning for all things romantically old; part, indeed, of the movement that Dr J. A. H. Murray defined for his dictionary, under *aesthetic* (1883), as 'recent extravagances in sentimental archaism as the ideal of beauty'. The movement had been gathering force during the century. Antiquarianism manifested itself in Pugin and Barry's medieval palace of Westminster, begun in 1840; in Henry Shaw's books on medieval decoration, of the 1840s; in the paintings of the Pre-Raphaelite brotherhood; in the invention of 'folklore' in 1846, and the founding of that swap-shop for antiquaries, *Notes & Queries*, in 1849. William Morris aimed to bring the beauty of hand-made furniture back into English homes; Liberty's provided textiles in subtle colours, dyed with vegetable dyes; Jaeger promoted clothes woven from natural fibres. Singing games, which had sunk to the lower end of the social scale, were ready to be discovered by the cultured classes and re-fed to the poor.

At least by 1885 the philanthropic classes had become convinced that poor children needed to be taught how to play. Frances Lord, who translated Froebel's *Mutter- und Kose-Lieder*, said in her preface: 'Children who go to Board Schools have no idea of playing as children play who have a nursery and a kind nurse and merry, clever parents. The infant mistresses in a Board School are often distressed to find how long it takes to get the little ones into the spirit of a game, and to see what a listless, brutalized, neglected home-life it points to.' She suggested that 'girls who live in towns should try to arrange with the Board or National Schools in their neighbourhood to go and play games . . . If play were thus cultivated, clumsy games, like "Kissing in the Ring", would disappear; the masses of children would want to play better games.'

At about the same time the intelligentsia discovered the old singing games, as fairy tales had been discovered earlier in the century and folk songs towards its end. A girl from Madeley in Shropshire was nursemaid to Charlotte Burne's sister's children in Derbyshire, and was persuaded to teach her singing games to the Derbyshire village children for a parish festivity. Miss Burne described the success of the venture to Mrs (later Lady) Alice Gomme, who began teaching singing games to the local children in Barnes. When Alice Gomme was asked to contribute to a *conversazione* in the rooms of the Society of Antiquaries in Burlington House, as part of the International Folk-Lore Congress of 1891, she brought the children from Barnes to demonstrate 'Oranges and Lemons' and 'Poor Mary Sits a-Weeping', and 'had the success of the Congress'.

Encouraged, she went ahead with her collection of traditional games, and published the first of her two substantial volumes of *Traditional Games* in 1894. It was she who established the term 'singing game'. Evelyn Carrington had used it in the title of an article in the *Folk-Lore Record*, III, 1, in 1880; but Charlotte Burne wrote of 'choral' and 'dramatic' games in 1883, and Babcock of 'song-games' in 1887 (*Folk-Lore Journal*, v). When Alice Gomme's popular illustrated edition of *Children's Singing Games* was published, also in 1894, Cecil Sharp took up both the games and the term and it was 'children's singing games' that he later taught to his students at Chelsea polytechnic.[1]

The artistic and progressive world was entranced by the old singing games. Together with folk songs and morris dancing they were seen as a panacea for the stricken life of the city slums. No matter that Samuel Butler had said 'the want of fresh air does not seem much to affect the happiness of children in a London alley: the greater part of them sing and play as though they were on a moor in Scotland', and that the Revd Stewart Headlam, who believed in the dignity of childhood, commented in his School Board Notes for *The Church Reformer*, June 1894:

Benevolent West-end ladies who have not yet recognised that their main duty towards the poor is to see that all unauthorised people get off their backs, have once or twice lamented to me that 'poor' children do not know how to play. So being in a school in the poorest part of Hoxton talking to the girls about temperance, I asked them what games were then in season. I had a chorus of answers, and not being able altogether to understand the descriptions, they wisely suggested an object lesson in the playground after school, which resulted in my introduction to the following seven games, all of which are new to me . . .

A distinction should perhaps be drawn between those who observe, reflect, and understand, and those who, having looked on the surface, are immediately swept away on a wave of emotion. The majority of idealists in the late nineteenth century believed that the grime of the industrial revolution had blighted the souls of the workers, and they felt guilty. The joys of merrie England were to be brought back. The hobby horse was to prance through the streets once more, and children plait ribbons round maypoles (the fact that plaited maypoles were foreign was of little consequence). The enthusiasm reached its height during the first decade of this century, and *Punch* applauded (13 November 1907):

Among many movements that have for their excellent object a return to the land and the cultivation of old simplicities, none wears a more inviting mien than that

---

[1] In Germany the term had been familiar since the beginning of the century, and also the idea that the games belonged to children. The anonymous *Dichtungen aus der Kinderwelt*, Hamburg, 1815, contains songs, counting-out rhymes, and 'Singspiele für Kinder'.

which originated with the Espérance Club for Working Girls some two or three years ago, and has by this time attained to such a stature that a public Conference is to be held at the Goupil Gallery on November 14 to consider the steps by which it might be, if not exactly nationalised, at any rate organised to the full. We refer to the revival of Folksongs, Games, and Morris Dances, which, under the direction of Miss NEAL and Mr H. C. MACILWAINE, of the Espérance Club, and Mr Cecil SHARP, the musician, has led to several charming performances at the Queen's Hall, where such enthusiasm was kindled that, through the generosity of certain of the audience, in many villages of England at this moment teachers are at work instructing the children in the steps of those delightful measures to which our ancestors danced when England was merrie.

The Times devoted a fourth leader to 'The Value of Play' (15 February 1909):

Mrs HUMPHRY WARD has recently told us of the admirable efforts that are being made to teach the children of the London poor how to play. There are now twelve play centres in London open on five evenings a week. The system has been established for three years, and in that time the attendance of children has risen from 5,000 to 23,000 a week. This fact is enough to show that the system provides something which the children want, that they are ready enough to learn to play, if only some one will teach them . . . The younger children learn singing games; and these, it is interesting to hear, have a strong civilising effect on them . . .

The Board of Education was in the vanguard of the crusade. In its *Suggestions for the Consideration of Teachers and others concerned in the work of Public Elementary Schools*, 1905, it had drawn the attention of teachers to various classes of traditional song suitable for Infant Schools, though saying that their use was 'not obligatory'. As well as 'French Nursery Rhymes (translated)' and 'German Kindergarten Songs (translated)' they recommended 'Old English Singing Games'. The main drift of traditional singing games into the infant-teaching system took place at this time (though 'The Mulberry Bush' had been adapted for infant use in the 1840s) and they proved their worth by long outlasting the prosaic action songs which were also being taught.[1] Cecil Sharp held classes in singing games at the South-Western Polytechnic in Chelsea, after he parted company with Mary Neal and her Espérance Club in 1909. He had collected the games from children in Somerset and was now re-cycling them by means of his ardent young woman-students, who went out to

---

[1] 'Action songs' could mean traditional games like 'Oats and Beans and Barley Grow', but chiefly referred to invented games either reflecting everyday life, e.g. 'Little Bakers' in L. Jesse's *Games for Busy Babies*, 1905, or encouraging a sympathy with nature or the fairy world, e.g. 'Gathering Bluebells' and 'Water Fairies' in *The Daisies and the Breezes: Action Songs for Children*, L. O. Chant, 1903. Many were suffocatingly sentimental, with the word 'little' much used: small children imitated 'Dear little birdies' or stumped along singing 'See the little babies go, Marching in a merry row'.

teach them to other children in every corner of the country. Some of these games, such as 'In and Out the Windows', 'Jolly Miller', and 'Oats and Beans and Barley Grow', may already have been declining; others, such as 'Romans and English', 'Nuts in May', 'Jenny Jones', and 'Old Roger', were finally removed from oral tradition and domesticated in the classroom.

So great was the adult enjoyment of singing games that versifiers tried their hands at writing new ones. Mrs G. T. Kimmins, who ran the Guild of Play at the Bermondsey University Settlement, taught the children dances, games, and songs which were insecurely 'based upon genuine antiquarian facts',[1] and wrote, in the euphoric mood of the time:

The beauty and setting of the play means so much more than we think, and our play must be clothed in beautiful garments if it is to give its full message. There is no mistaking the return of the public thought of today to the delights of colour, song, and dance. Think of the many pageants of the past year, and of the fancy dresses and riotous fun set in historical setting, which would have been severely censured not so very many years ago. There has been, and is still going on, a distinct revival of old customs, dances, and recreations, and in no place has it been more keenly welcomed than in the long, grey, monotonous streets of South-east London.

Rose Fyleman wrote singing games; and Eleanor Farjeon wrote singing games (her *Singing Games for Children*, 1919, were used in the Morecambe Festivals). May Gillington, already in the action-song business, wrote *Twelve New Singing Games on Traditional Lines*, 1900, before making the collections of genuine games, illustrated with photographs of girls in pinafores and button boots, for which she is still remembered. None of these games took root in oral tradition; they were too self-conscious and insipid. May Gillington's 'One Fair Maid a-Dancing' was picked up in the streets of London by Norman Douglas (1916), and that was all. Educationists were not much more successful. 'Days of the Week' (p. 292), of unknown and apparently pedagogic origin, was never popular, and 'Three Jolly Fishermen' (p. 386) had only regional popularity. 'Punchinello' (p. 412) only achieved success through its licence to invent funny actions, and 'One Little Elephant' (p. 367) through its comical progression, borrowed from an old burlesque dance.

THE INHERITORS

Cecil Sharp and his followers were perhaps being optimistic if they thought to revive, for antiquarian and aesthetic reasons, games whose *raison d'être* had largely disappeared. The youths and maidens who played

---

[1] See *Guild of Play Book*, pt. 4, 1912, p. 5 onwards; ibid., pt. 2, 1909, introduction.

the games in previous centuries were on the verge of adulthood, and were getting to know each other within the security of a social framework. The girls who play the games in the present day enjoy them for reasons unconnected with the choosing of sweethearts. They enjoy (though they may not be able to say so) the gaiety, warmth, sociability, excitement; the chance to thump their friends on the back or tangle with them in helpless laughter; and the chance to star (most singing games provide two opportunities for the ego to shine: once when the soloist plays her part in the centre of the ring, and once when she chooses her successor). Girls, too, seem to like games that are rhythmic and repetitive, formal and enigmatic. They accept them uncritically, not worrying that the words make little sense; in fact the stranger the words are, the greater is the liberation into fantasy. Singing games are now played almost exclusively by seven to nine-year-olds, with older and younger girls joining in on occasion. Individual attitudes vary, however, and ten-year-olds who are happily playing singing games at one end of a playground may be despised by girls of the same age group at the other end, who say scornfully 'We never play them sort of games, they're boring', and go back to their netball.

Some games have always been played by girls on their own. A dancing song in the twelfth-century *Chansonnier de St Germain* describes the May queen dancing alone with her maidens:

A l'entrada del tems clar, eya,   (At the coming of Spring, eya,
per joja recommençar, eya,   So as to renew joy, eya,
e per jelos irritar, eya,   And to vex the jealous one, eya,
vol la regina mostrar   The queen wanted to show
qu'el' est si amoroza.   How amorous she is.
alavi' alavia, jelos,   Away, away, jealous one,
laissaz nos, laissaz nos ballar entre   Leave us, leave us to dance
   nos, entre nos.   among ourselves, among
                        ourselves.)[1]

In a song from the thirteenth-century manuscript *Carmina Burana* girls sing defiantly:

> Who are these circling here?
> Girls every single one:
> They want to spend all summer
> Dancing without a man.[2]

And one remembers the 1798 version of 'The Mulberry Bush':

---

[1] *Chrestomathie provençale*, C. Bartsch, 2nd edn. 1868, cols. 107–110. The game, E. K. Chambers says, *Mediaeval Stage*, I, p. 170, 'recalls the conventional freedom of women from restraints in May'.

[2] *The Mediaeval Lyric*, Peter Dronke, p. 189.

> The gooseberry grows on an angry Tree,
> About ye Maids and about ye Maids.
> Others are merry as well as we,
> Then about ye merry Maids all.

But already in 1842 Robert Chambers was witnessing courtship games being played by girls alone. He describes two, 'The Widow of Babylon' and 'The Merry-ma-tansie', in which girls imitate the progress of a wedding, choosing girl lovers from the circle and kissing them at the conclusion. J. M. McBain remembered, from about the same period in Arbroath, a group of girls dividing into sides to play 'Romans and English'. The Revd Addison Crofton, observing children in the 1870s and 1880s, seemed to take it for granted that the singing games belonged to girls alone. Flora Thompson recalled in *Lark Rise* how the girls would gather to play singing games on a green open space between the houses, in the 1880s: 'The boys of the hamlet did not join in them, for the amusement was too formal and restrained for their taste, and even some of the rougher girls when playing would spoil a game, for the movements were stately and all was done by rule.' And Alice Gomme, asking the readers of *Notes & Queries* to help her collect singing games in November 1891, said: 'These games are, I believe, now almost solely played by girls and very small boys', and in 1896, after the publication of her first volume, she said in a paper read to the South Place Institute that girls had almost the monopoly of the games, 'which do not meet with the approval of the other sex'.

Against this and other evidence that, through the nineteenth century, singing games were played exclusively by girls, with boys as jeering spectators, must be set observations that sometimes, in some places, boys did join in. Boys and girls were playing 'Oats and Beans and Barley Grow' together in a Lincolnshire Wold village in the mid-century (*Notes & Queries*, 7th ser., xii). J. S. Udal talks of his Dorsetshire choral games as being played by boys and girls together (*Folk-Lore*, vii, 1889). In *Living London*, 1903, Edwin Pugh says:

Boys will take part in 'Kiss-in-the-Ring' and the other innumerable love-making games . . . These little ones seem to play at love for practice; they blush and are tremulous and constrained; the boys cut awkward capers to show how terribly they are at ease.

Rowland Kellett, remembering Leeds in the 1920s, says 'The boys used to join in singing games. By and large boys and girls laiked with each other up to the age of eleven to thirteen.' And, as late as 1952, a teacher at Welshpool sent us a large number of singing games known to her pupils, saying 'At Primary School they often played them in the playground, but quite as frequently, if not more so, with brothers and sisters and neighbours at home. Six to twenty would take part, and boys join in with the girls.'

However, the participation of boys is the exception rather than the rule. When a craze for a game sweeps through a school boys can be found, somewhat shamefaced, in the huge singing circles of swaying lines. 'They are all playing "Nuts in May",' a Wilmslow headmaster wrote in 1960, 'Even the boys joined in, to the openly expressed disgust of the women members of the staff.' Small brothers, not yet conscious of their manhood, are included in games played in front gardens on summer evenings. Little boys of a retiring disposition take refuge in girls' games: 'Richard Broughton always plays with us,' said eight-year-old girls in Wells, 1964. 'He's rather shy. He gets scared if he has to play with the boys.' A boy playing 'The Big Ship Sails' with girls in Sheet playground, 1974, explained blandly: 'I've got two sisters, so I like to do girls' games. They're fun, aren't they, and I like them better than the hurting games.' In village schools the boys may join in the girls' games; but generally, however, boys consider singing games beneath their dignity, though they sometimes watch, fascinated, with assumed detachment. 'You don't catch *us* joining in,' they bluster. 'We're not going to make fools of ourselves—it's cissy.' Nevertheless when boys and girls can play unselfconsciously together, as West Indian children were doing in Bedford in 1975, the games have a special vitality and grace.

Certain general laws of folklore, and characteristics of children's lore in particular, which were demonstrated in *The Lore and Language of School-children* and *Children's Games in Street and Playground*, hold true for the singing games. Oral traditions are subject to continual change and, while some of the older singing games are in as lusty a condition as ever—'The Farmer's in His Den', 'King William', 'A Duke a-Riding', and 'Looby Loo' in Jimmy Kennedy's modern version 'The Hokey Kokey'—others, such as 'Three Brethren out of Spain' and 'Romans and English', have only been retained for the charm of their tunes or the excitement of the action, and exist as shrunken parodies of their former selves. Others again, perhaps too slow and dreary, are nearly extinct: 'Jenny Jones', 'Old Roger', 'Widow from Babylon'. Yet whenever a game seems finally to have disappeared it is found again, usually in the depths of a city. A version of 'Three Brethren out of Spain' was sent to *Notes & Queries* in 1852 which might be 'sufficiently interesting to rescue from oblivion', the writer said, 'as National Schools are fast sweeping away all charms, fairies, folk lore, and old village sports and pastimes'. Yet ten-year-olds were playing the same game enthusiastically, in its full dramatic form, in Salford in 1975.

Tattered lines from old game-songs combine to make patchwork songs of strange beauty. Actions change, and are transferred from one game to another. The stronger and simpler actions and tunes oust the weaker. The older games are found in the north of England and Scotland, and in the USA. Immigrant children play English singing games before they can speak English, reproducing the words as pure sound.[1]

Of the 133 games in this book (leaving aside the clapping chants) only 82 could be considered true singing games, in the sense that they fulfilled a social function in days gone by; and some of these are only hodge-podges of old games, which have achieved an identity of their own. The others are songs, or parts of songs, or misrememberings of songs, which have been commandeered to make singing games on the old pattern—for once a pattern exists, it will be copied. The casual use of half-forgotten songs is not new. Gomme's 'Ball of Primrose', played in 1869, may have been as ephemeral a game as Crofton's 'What Shall We Do With the Old Piano?', played in the 1880s, and as 'Lady of Spain I Adore You', played in the present day. The attractions of circling while singing are strong, and as the older games fade out others take their place. Whether the total amount of children's dance-and-song is less than it was, for instance, before the First World War, is difficult to say; certainly the general impression is that it is less—but grown-ups have been bewailing the disappearance of children's games ever since the advent of the railways. Television is blamed, and lack of quiet playing space, the dangers of traffic and predatory men, and the abolition of segregated playgrounds. Children, we must believe, will continue to enjoy themselves in their own ways, and it will be interesting to see, in another thirty years, if the singing game tradition is still alive.

Singing games are played in school playgrounds, in front gardens and cul-de-sacs, in the back lanes (where they still exist) of northern cities, and on the grass islands of housing estates during long summer evenings. Girls learn the games from each other at school, from their neighbours who go to other schools, informally at Brownie meetings and at other social clubs, from the 'dinner ladies' during the school dinner hour, occasionally from books or television, and, frequently, from their cousins. They learn games on holiday ('There was this girl in the swimming pool at Plymouth, she taught it me'; 'Last year at Gretna Green I learned a game from the people in the next caravan—they came from Glasgow'). And Army children bring

---

[1] Leah Yoffie remembered, as a newly-arrived immigrant in St Louis, c.1895, 'We children were learning English in the public schools, but the language in our homes was still Yiddish. It is the more surprising, therefore, that we assimilated so quickly and played so avidly the old traditional games of Great Britain.'

to British schools games which they have learnt in the playgrounds of Army schools abroad.

Whether a child straightaway passes on the games she knows depends on her personality. A natural impresario of any age starts organizing the other children as soon as she sets foot inside a new school. Others may wait for reinforcements. The nine-year-old who introduced 'I know a girl who lived in Majorca' to Four Marks primary school had played it at her old school in Alton two years before. 'But I didn't tell 'em it till not long ago,' she said, 'I was too scared. It was when my friend arrived from Alton, we taught 'em it together.' Years ago the teachers were more likely to be maternal thirteen-year-olds in the all-age village schools which did not long survive the Second World War; or were the nursemaids, scarcely more than children themselves, who had the care of small children even in quite humble households. But children learn as much by watching and listening as by being taught. The following are typical comments:

You just pick it up off the other children. You just watch and then try to join in the best you can, and after a bit you get used to it. In the yard, you know, we just run up and they separate hands. They don't really bother. You just join in. Usually in the street you have to ask them, but in the yard you can just join in all together.

9-year-old, Salford, 1970

Somebody's at home, they hear something on the streets, they bring it into the school, tell their friends, then all the friends pass it round the school. That's how we do it.

I live in a big round sort of thing. We've got a big island in front of us, we play games on that. We got houses all around, and we go on the island and we all make up songs, all the children. There are ten in our gang. We call it a gang cos it's outdoors.

We've got sixty in our road. Sixty people, and they usually come out, you know—like on a Saturday and Sunday, when they have free time, and sometimes we go into the park.

9 and 10-year-olds, Birmingham, 1977

Children, as the old proverb says, 'pick up words as pigeons pease, And utter them again as God shall please'. They are conservationists by accident, keeping what adults have discarded because, to them, it is new. Since the games are their own they can play them with affectionate disrespect. They can play *with* the games, as well as playing them, guying the actions and making witty alterations in the words. Being inexperienced, they cannot—even if they wanted to—discriminate between the old-and-picturesque and the new and (some adults would say) shoddy or sophisticated: the 'Lady on the Mountain' and 'Shirley Temple' are equally romantic in their eyes. Yet in the circling of these unselfconscious, casual creatures, we can sometimes glimpse the young people of the Middle Ages 'all arrayit in a ring', dancing in the springtime long ago.

II

Chains and Captives

THESE games once moved like living embroidery across the continent of Europe; the chains of dancers were the bright-coloured threads, the captives trapped by falling arms were the sombre emblems of mortality.

'Threading the needle' must be the happiest and most ingenious way ever invented of possessing a town or encircling a village. In the Middle Ages it was thought an entertainment worthy of Heaven, for in Fra Angelico's 'Last Judgement', c.1420, in the Museum of St Mark in Florence, angels and saints can be seen dancing an open round dance together, the pair at one end making an arch with their arms for the other end of the line to file through. And earlier, Ambrogio Lorenzetti (*fl.* 1319–48) painted a fresco for the town hall of Siena, an allegory of Good and Bad Government, which shows nine ladies dancing 'Thread the Needle' (see p. 34). Small untarnished phrases can be found entangled in the words of other games in Latin America, which are evidence of lost European imagery: 'Thread of gold, thread of silver, little thread of St Gabriel', 'Threads, golden threads, My foot is breaking', 'Come let us play at the thread of gold, and at the thread of silver'. Some of the verses that survive in Europe have been reduced to practicalities ('It is so dark we cannot see, To thread the tailor's needle') or to inappropriate nonsense ('Tiggotty tiggotty gutter, Call the hogs to supper'); but others, especially on the Continent, retain a weird fairy-tale quality. And nearly always the arched arms of the dancers are transformed by the song into not a humble needle, but the gates of a city, or a bridge.

Probably it has occurred to few British children to wonder why, after they have had their heads chopped off in the game of 'Oranges and Lemons', they should apparently be offered a choice of fruit drinks; or to German children to ask why, after having chosen an apple or a pear, they should find themselves turned into angels or devils and taking part in a struggle resembling Armageddon. A game carries its own authority; and in the games where the last child in the line is caught between the two making the gate or bridge, the prisoner cannot avoid death and the hereafter. In the German versions assembled by Böhme there are enough details left to convince one that, as Mannhardt suggested, this game was once an enactment of the end of the world—a drama which had been Christianized but was founded on Germanic mythology. The bridge was the golden bridge linking earth and hell. Over the bridge drove Death in his coach, taking with him the soul he had come to fetch; and on the bridge sat its guardian, the virgin Modgud, judging the souls who passed over. The tug of war may have represented Ragnarok, the last battle of all, fought between the heroes of Valhalla and the inhabitants of the underworld, when the bridge was shattered by the enemy hosts. Christianity saw the struggle in terms of angels and devils fighting over individual souls in front of the gates of Paradise.

I

Thread the Needle

Thread the needle, thread the needle,
Eye, eye, eye;
Thread the needle, thread the needle,
Eye, eye, eye.

The game of 'Thread the Needle', the joy and exercise of generations of our forebears, could no longer be played in its street form even before the appearance of the motorcar, the game being perilous if played where there was the possibility of any kind of fast-moving traffic, such as a coach; and the more gentle dance-like form seems by the middle of the nineteenth century to have been largely displaced by related competitive games. Even so, traces of the old game are still to be found in children's play; and its successor 'The Big Ship Sails' (p. 50) is to be numbered amongst the best-loved of contemporary amusements. In its vigorous form the players, the more the better, held hands in a line. The two players at one end of the line made an arch by each raising the hand with which they were linked, and, without anyone letting go of his neighbour, the player at the other end of the line ran through the arch and kept running until everyone in the line had been drawn through after him and the two players who made the arch were forced to twist round and follow. The two players in the lead now made an arch themselves, and the player in the rear, who formerly made part of the arch, doubled up to the front, bringing after him the rest of the line, which had momentarily been checked; and everyone passed under the new arch which in turn was pulled along at the end of the line until the new leaders who had first formed an arch decided to make another one,

THREAD THE NEEDLE

Facing, top: Ambrogio Lorenzetti's fresco in Siena town hall, showing ladies dancing 'Thread the Needle' in the early fourteenth century.

Facing, bottom: Rubens's *Peasant's Dance*, in an Italian setting, *c*.1630. This is the 'Grandy Needles' variety of the game (No. 2) with the couples holding handkerchiefs between them to form the arch. The musician, as was customary, is perched in a tree. A man dancer hastens to mend the break in the chain; but the dance progression itself seems to have been subordinated to artistic requirements.

Above: The only surviving, and very popular, thread-the-needle game. 'The Big Ship Sails', at Micklefield, Yorkshire, 1978.

and the tail once again raced forward to lead the way under it. This process continued for as long as strength remained or space permitted; for much ground could be covered as the line moved ever forward. In fact, played like this, the game was scarcely more than a boisterous form of progression; and the ideal setting was an empty street or series of streets, a requirement not easy to obtain other than on a holiday, and then perhaps only in the evening.

Thus at Bradford-on-Avon, in the first half of the nineteenth century, it was customary on the evening of Shrove Tuesday, which was a partial holiday, for the boys and girls of the town to 'run through the streets in long strings playing "Thread the Needle", and whooping and hollering their best as they ran, and so collecting all they could together by seven or eight o'clock, when they would adjourn to the churchyard'. Here they joined hands in one long line until the church was encircled, and then walked round three times to 'clip the church'. Likewise at Trowbridge in Wiltshire on the evening of Shrove Tuesday, as also at Longbridge Deverell on Shrove Tuesday, and on no other day in the year, playing 'Thread the Needle' was traditional, the vocal accompaniment always being the seasonal verse:

> Shrove Tuesday, Shrove Tuesday, when Jack went to plough,
> His mother made pancakes she didn't know how;
> She tipped them, she tossed them, she made them so black,
> She put so much pepper she poisoned poor Jack.

It was also a part of the proceedings, according to a correspondent, of 'an ancient and almost forgotten custom at Marlborough called Jacky John's Fair, in the course of which children used to dance in and out of the pent house pillars in the High Street singing:

> The tailor's blind, and he can't see,
> So we must thread the needle.'

At Ellesmere in Shropshire the game preceded the clipping of the church, as at Bradford-on-Avon, only here it was called 'Crewduck', the boys in the line having to duck under the arms of the leading pair as they progressed along the street, and their shouts and hurrahs as they did so collected other boys from all parts of the town. First they made for the 'Green Mount', the site of the old castle; and from there went to the church hoping to form a complete circle round it. Then, not content with clipping the church they proceeded to the market-hall, and 'clipped' that building too in like manner. Even young men and women, it was said, did not disdain to take part, though the custom seems to have died out sometime between 1815 and 1820, as it did also at South Petherton in Somerset, where the procedure was similar.

At Evesham in Worcestershire Easter Monday was the one day in the year for 'Thread the Needle', which took place at sunset and was played throughout the town, led, apparently, by the older folk, followed by the younger men and women, with the children bringing up the rear; and the children's repeated call (in the 1840s) was for fresh arches to be made:

> Open the gates as high as the sky,
> And let Victoria's troops pass by.

A further place where the sport was traditional on Easter Monday was Minchinhampton in Gloucestershire. Here, until about 1875, people of all ages used to foregather in Manor Park, where various games were played always ending with 'Crooked Mustard', a serpentine game (depicted by Bruegel in 1560) in which a long string of players swerved their way around trees and persons seated on the ground. They then made for the park gates and 'Thread the Needle' was played through the streets in the growing darkness.

At Tenby in Pembrokeshire, however, the day for 'Thread the Needle' was May Day. In preparation for this day maypoles decorated with flowers, coloured papers, and bunches of variegated ribbon would be raised in different parts of the town. On the day itself each group of young men and women danced first round their own maypole, and then set off 'threading the needle', sometimes fifty to a hundred dancers in the line, working their way from one pole to another, till they had traversed the town; and if, incidentally, they met another party coming in the opposite direction they made a 'lady's chain', which was probably a 'hey', the members of each line weaving their way through the other line, taking alternately the right hand and the left hand of those they met, and passing by as appropriate on the near or off side.

May Day was also the special day in the east of Britain. At Saffron Walden in Essex 'Thread the Needle' was, as elsewhere, played in the evening, although under the curious name of 'Tig-in-the-Gutter' or 'Pig-in-the-Gutter', names which were glossed, though not exactly explained, at Linton in Cambridgeshire, where a string of children, with the bigger boys at each end, used to pass down the whole length of the village street 'threading the needle' and singing as they did so:

> Tiggotty tiggotty gutter,
> Call the hogs to supper;
> That's fat, that's lean,
> That's to go for the butcher e'en.

This ritual participation in 'Thread the Needle' was not confined, it is evident, to any one part of Britain (London's Threadneedle Street probably acquired its name from being a traditional site for the game), nor to any particular season of the year. Away in Cornwall, in the towns and villages around Mounts Bay, the most spectacular celebration of the year used to be that which greeted Midsummer. On the vigil of St John every man, woman, and child crowded into the streets. Blazing torches were carried, enormous bonfires were lit, tar barrels were hoisted aloft, and fireworks were set off. Then, when everything might have been expected to be over there was a happening that seems to have been almost more remarkable than the fire festival itself. According to an observer in Penzance in 1801:

No sooner are torches burnt out, than the inhabitants of the quay-quarter (a great multitude) male and female, young, middle-aged, and old, virtuous and vicious, sober and drunk, take hands, and forming a long string, run violently through every street, lane, and alley, crying, 'An eye! an eye! an eye!' At last they stop suddenly; and an eye to this enormous needle being opened by the last two in the string (whose clasped hands are elevated and arched) the thread of populace run under and through; and continue to repeat the same, till weariness dissolves their union, and sends them home to bed; which is never till near the hour of midnight.

Small wonder that Philip Stubbes (1583) should be concerned that such an activity might lead to scandal:

I thinke that all good minstrelles, sober and chast musitions (speking of suche drunken sockets and bawdye parasits as range the Cuntreyes, ryming and singing of vncleane, corrupt, and filthie songs . . .) may daunce the wilde Moris thorow a needles eye. For how should thei bere chaste minds, seeing that their exercyse is the pathway to all vncleanes.

In fact allusions to 'Thread the Needle', most of them joyous, abound in literature. In Middleton and Rowley's *The Spanish Gipsie*, performed 1623, the gipsy's song begins:

> Trip it Gipsies, trip it fine,
> Shew tricks and lofty Capers;
> At threading Needles we repine,
> And leaping over Rapiers.

In *Poor Robin's Almanack*, 1738, the summer quarter is said to follow spring 'as close as Girls do one another, when playing at Thread-my-Needle'. In *A Little Pretty Pocket Book*, first printed 1744, 'Thread the Needle' is described as 'a very pleasing Sight' when 'Hand in Hand the Boys unite', and it is thus depicted (see p. 330).

David Copperfield, however, struggling to learn his tables of weights and measures, used to find they went in at one ear and out the other, like 'threading my grandmother's needle'. Festus Derriman in *The Trumpet-Major* taunted his comrades that if the French landed they would never again enjoy 'Thread-the-Needle' at Greenhill Fair. And William Barnes was clearly referring to the gentle, but nonetheless lively form of the game when he recalled in his idyll 'The Welshnut Tree':

> There we do play 'thread the woman's needle',
> An' slap the maïdens a dartèn drough.

This form of the game, it will be appreciated, was far from being a ritual rush through the streets. A correspondent in Hone's *Every-Day Book*, who spent Whit Monday at Greenwich in 1826, thought 'one of the prettiest sights' amongst the holiday-makers was a game of 'Thread My Needle' played 'by about a dozen lasses, with a grace and glee that reminded me of Angelica's nymphs', and, in tune with the romanticism of his time, he 'indulged a hope that the hilarity of rural pastimes might yet be preserved'. In such a game, later to be witnessed by young Boz at the same place, the emphasis will, in the manner of a medieval *carole*, have been on the quality of the performance rather than its velocity ('the pace is a kind of dance, and is accompanied by a sort of song', noted one observer), the words being such as were sung in Sussex:

> Open the gates as wide as wide,
> And let King George go through with his bride.
> It is so dark we cannot see
> To threaddle the tailor's needle.

Little ground will have been traversed, for the leader of the line will have come round in a circle and made his new arch next to or close to the old one. Alternatively, in Penzance at the beginning of the century, the arch or 'eye' could be provided not by the first two players in the line but by the last two, the players in the lead thus being required to double back. In *School Boys' Diversions*, 1820, as also in Holloway's *Provincialisms*, 1839, the players are said to commence the game by forming up in a ring. While in Dublin, today, according to Eilís Brady, when the children are getting themselves into a knot, in the manner of 'The Big Ship Sails', they chant: 'Sew, sew, sew, thread a needle' which may be compared with 'Dan, Dan, thread the needle' at Four Marks today (see under 'The Big Ship Sails').

The game seems always to have been played differently in the United States, and to have resembled 'Through the Needle-ee' as played in Scotland (p. 42). But in France 'L'Aiguille' appears to be an ancient game, and to have been played exactly as in England, the children singing as they passed under the arch:

Enfilons, l'aiguille, l'aiguille;
Enfilons, l'aiguille de bois. -

Britain: *Sports and Pastimes of the People of England*, Joseph Strutt, 1801, p. 285 | *A Nosegay for the Trouble of Culling*, 1813, p. 25 | *History of Cornwall*, Richard Polwhele, i, 1803, p. 50 n. | *History of Evesham*, George May, 1845, p. 319 | *Dolly Pentreath*, John Trenhaile, 1854 (1869, p. 6), possibly based on Polwhele, 1803 | *Tales and Traditions of Tenby*, G. P. W. Scott, 1858, pp. 21–3 | *Girl's Own Book*, re-edited Madame de Chatelain, 1858, p. 108 | *Notes & Queries*, 3rd ser., xii, 1867, p. 530; 5th ser., xi, 1879, p. 226; 6th ser., viii, 1883, p. 387; and cxc, 1946, p. 151 | *Shropshire Folk-Lore*, C. S. Burne, 1883, pp. 321–3 | *Traditional Games*, ii, 1898, p. 231, South Petherton account | *Folk-Lore*, xxiii, 1912, pp. 196–203 | Correspondents 1952 and 1953, including Knighton, *c.*1925, 'Come thread the long needle, Come thread the eye'.
　　Ireland: *All In! All In!* Eilís Brady, 1975, pp. 162–3.
　　France: Termonde, *c.*1815, 'Willen wy, willen wy 't Haesken jagen deure de Hey?' (Shall we, shall we, chase the little hare through the heather?) (*Chants populaires des Flamands de France*, E. de Coussemaker, p. 327) | *Jeux de Societé*, Madame Celnart, 1846, p. 37, 'L'Aiguille enfilée' | *Revue des Traditions Populaires*, xiii, 1898, p. 10 | Bordeaux, 1958, 'Enfilons les aiguilles de bois, Les aiguilles ne sont pas à moi; Elles sont au petit Chinois' | *Les Comptines*, Jean Baucomont et al, 1961, pp. 311–12, 'Enfilons les aiguilles de bois' reported to be still known in France, Switzerland, and Canada.
　　Belgium: Bailleul, *c.*1855, 'Ma seurtje, gae ye meê' (E. de Coussemaker, op. cit., pp. 326–7).

2

Grandy Needles

Grandy needles, thread my needles, set! set! set!
Through the long valley we go, we go,
To see the blue bells of Je-ho, Je-ho.
Open the gates as wide as wide
And let King George come through with his bride.

'Grandy Needles' (i.e. Grandmother's Needles) was another and even more eye-catching way of progressing along a street on a high day or holiday. Those taking part used to line up behind each other in pairs, each player holding up his partner's hand to make an arch. The last pair then dashed through the avenue of arches and made a new arch at the front, with the next pair following close behind, so that progression could be quite rapid; and if, as reported, those making the arches sometimes—at the words 'set! set! set!'—thumped those who were running through, this simply made their passage brisker.

In the Midlands the sport was known as 'Duck under Water' or 'Duck-under-the-Water-Kit' (Gainsborough, *c.*1820), 'Dig under the Water Hole' (High Peak of Derbyshire), 'Long Duck' (Sheffield), or 'High Gates' (Boston, Lincolnshire, *c.*1920); there was little vocal accompaniment, and each pair of players customarily held a handkerchief between them to make their arch wider. Thus Thomas Miller, who was born in Gainsborough, 1807, recalled:

Two of us held up a handkerchief at arms'-length, one taking hold of each end, and keeping it nearly tight; under this the next couple passed, and, halting two or three yards from us, they also held up their handkerchief, as we did ours; a third, a fourth, and a fifth couple went under in the same way—sometimes as many as fifty of us; and a pretty sight it was to see that long arcade of handkerchiefs, of all colours, arching across a country road, and held by as merry a group as ever sent their deep laughter through the green lanes.

'Few', he added, 'unless they had seen us, would believe how soon we managed to run over a mile of ground.'

Another poet who found the sport to his taste was John Clare (born 1793), who refers to it at least four times. In his account of May Day celebrations at Helpstone, his native village in Northamptonshire, he describes how, after the girls had carried round their May garland to be admired by the cottagers:

> Then at *duck under water* adown the long road,
> They run with their dresses all flying abroad;
> And ribbons all colours how sweet they appear!
> May seems to begin the new life of the year.

In his autobiography he confesses he 'never had much relish for the pastimes of youth' – but 'Duck under Water' was something different; and he was able to take part in it on the First of May even, apparently, when still a little fellow: 'We were too young to be claimants in the upgrown sports but we joined our little interferences with them and ran under the extended handkerchiefs with the rest unmolested.'

Amongst the 'recreations and sports . . . used by our Country Boys and Girls' listed by Randle Holme of Chester in 1688 is 'Duck under water', which may be presumed to be this entertainment (*Academy of Armory*, III, xvi, 91); and in Germany, as also in Switzerland, the game seems to have been widespread under the name 'Macht auf das Thor', the runners demanding that the gate be opened on the premise, apparently, that they were bringing the devil in a wagon, who was carrying out his business of fetching sinners.

Descriptions of the game: *Country Year Book*, Thomas Miller, 1847, pp. 44–5 | *Northamptonshire Glossary*, A. E. Baker, i, 1854, p. 204 | *Notes & Queries*, 3rd ser., xii, 1867, p. 329; and 9th ser., xii, 1903, p. 474 | *Sheffield Glossary*, S. O. Addy, 1888, p. 138 | *Traditional Games*, i, 1894, pp. 112–13 | *English Dialect Dictionary*, ii, 1900, *Duck* sb³ 1 (3) | *Folk-Lore*, xxiii, 1912, p. 200 | Correspondents, 1951, and 1952, recollection of Kendal, *c.*1870, as text.

The formation is the same as the Northumbrian Ribbon or Handkerchief Dance, described by H. M. Neville, *A Corner in the North*, 1909, and as the 'Arch Dance' in Curt Sachs's *World History of the Dance*, p. 162.

Germany: *Hessische Kinderliedchen*, G. Eskuche and Johann Lewalter, 1891, no. 204, 'Macht auf das Thor! macht auf das Thor, wir kommen mit unsern Wagen! Wer sitzt darin? Wer sitzt darin? Ein Mann mit rothen Haaren. Was will er denn? Was will er denn? Er will die Tochter holen. Was hat sie denn? Was hat sie denn? Sie hat ja was gestohlen. Was ist es denn? Was ist es denn? Es ist ein Korb mit Kohlen' (Open the gate, open the gate, We are coming with our coach! Who sits inside? Who sits inside? A man with red hair. What does he want? What does he want? He has come for the daughter. What has she done? What has she done? She has stolen something. What is it then? What is it then? It is a basket of coals). The song is also used for the German equivalent of 'Oranges and Lemons' (see p. 60) | *Deutsches Kinderspiel*, Johann Lewalter, 1911, pp. 340–1, 12 further references.

Netherlands: the couples going under sing a song of gentle farmyard lunacy, 'Geeft de duiven, Da ze snuiven, Geeft de vogelen Kempzaad!' (Give the doves So that they take snuff, Give the doves hemp seed!) (*Kinderspel & Kinderlust in Zuid-Nederland*, I, i, 1902, pp. 247–50).

3

Through the Needle-ee

Brother Jack, if ye were mine,
I would give you claret wine;
Claret wine's gude and fine—
Through the needle-ee, boys.

As early as 1801 the name 'Thread the Needle', which ordinarily had been the name of the non-stop arch game already described (pp. 33–40), was being given to an amusement in which the last player passing through the arch was captured and questioned ('Now, what do you like best, plum-pudding or plum-pie? Plum-pudding. Oh, he is on my side!'); and in Scotland, where the game—however played—was generally known as 'Through the Needle-ee' or 'Through the Needle-ee, Boys', the capturing of the last player was common throughout the nineteenth century, the game being played to determine who should take which side in a round of 'Scots and English' or 'Tug o' War'. However the songs in these Scots games were notably conciliatory, containing such lines as 'If ye were mine, I would give you claret wine' (Edinburgh, 1821), or 'If you want a bonnie lassie, Just take me' (Fraserburgh, 1898); and there may be a connection here with the more romantic needle-threading of the United States.

Scores of Americans, in regions where the play-party tradition was strong, have taken part in the 'Needle's Eye', when the arch was formed with a boy on one side and a girl on the other, and verses were sung such as,

The needle's eye that doth supply
The thread that runs so true;
Many a beau have I let go
For the sake of kissing you.

Or,

> The needle's eye that doth espy
>   The thread that's running through;
> Many a lass have I let pass
>   Because I wanted you.
> Not one's so neat, or dressed so sweet,
>   We do intend
>   Before we end
> To have this couple meet.

In this game the player who was trapped while filing through the arch effected his release by kissing whichever side of the arch was appropriate. Alternatively the players passed under the arch in couples, and the pair who were caught were under the obligation, which they had ensured by their pairing should be no hardship, of kissing each other. Newell said the game was played like this, with the couples kissing, in the 1830s, and the game has certainly been much played like this since then.

Britain: *Youthful Sports*, 1801, p. 6 | *Blackwood's Edinburgh Magazine*, August 1821, p. 36, as text | *Scottish Dictionary, Supplement*, John Jamieson, ii, 1825, pp. 563–4 | *Popular Rhymes of Scotland*, Robert Chambers, 1842, p. 63 | Baverstock, Wiltshire, *c*.1850, undescribed but verse went 'Thread the needle, thread the needle, who am I? One, two, three, if you want a pretty girl, come and fetch me' (*Folk-Lore*, xxiii, p. 203) | Forfar, *c*.1890 (*Lang Strang*, Jean C. Rodger, 1948, p. 28) | *Traditional Games*, ii, 1898, pp. 289–90, Fraserburgh, 'Clink, clink, through the needle ee, boys, One, two, three, If you want a bonnie lassie, Just tak me', also Galloway and Northumberland | Selkirk, 1960, 'Through the needle eye boy, eye boy, eye boy, Through the needle eye boy, one, two, three' (*Scottish National Dictionary*, s.v. needle).
    USA: *Games of American Children*, 1883, pp. 91–2, and 1903, pp. 241–2, similar to quotes | Bowling Green, Virginia, pre-1887, coloured informant, 'Here we go two by two. Do you want to get married? Yes, I do. Marry by love, and let it be true, Salute your bride, and pass on through. The needle works finely, The thread runs through. I courted a many pretty girls Before I court you. Hug so neat, Kiss so sweet, Take all that to make it look neat' (*Folk-Lore*, v, p. 137) | Rains County, Texas, *c*.1908, 'Needle and I' as side-picking game (*Dorothy's World*, Dorothy Howard, pp. 223–4) | North Carolina, 1920s, four versions and many references *North Carolina Folklore*, pp. 108–9) | *American Play-Party Song*, B. A. Botkin, 1937, p. 29 n., 62 Oklahoma variants of 'Needle's Eye' said to have been collected | *Play Party Songs in Western Maryland*, Florence Warnick, 1942, p. 10 | *Singing Games of the Illinois Ozarks*, D. S. McIntosh, 1974, pp. 94–5, version collected 1948; and further references.
    Canada: *Toronto Globe*, 20 November 1909, 'Bread and wine is too fine, Through the needle-eye, boys' (*JAFL*, xxxi, p. 58).

4

How Many Miles to Babylon?

> How many miles to Babylon?
> Three score and ten.
> Can I get there by candlelight?
> Yes, and back again.
> Open your gates as wide as the sky
> And let the king and his men pass by.

'How Many Miles to Babylon?' is one of the games which displaced 'Thread the Needle' in the nineteenth century, or which, to be precise, was grafted on to it, to its detriment. In *The Boy's Own Book*, 1828, it is still called 'Thread the Needle' and, indeed, is little more than a slowing-down of the basic game. A number of boys joined hands in a line, and the game commenced with the player at one end calling out: 'How many miles to Babylon?'

The player at the other end responded: 'Three score and ten.'

The first asked: 'Can I get there by candlelight?'

The other replied: 'Yes, and back again.'

Whereat the first demanded: 'Then open the gates without more ado, And let the king and his men pass through.'

In obedience to this mandate, the player who stands at the opposite end of the line and the one next him, lift their joined hands as high as possible; the other outside player then approaches, runs under the hands thus elevated, and the whole line follows him, if possible, without disuniting. This is threading the needle. The same dialogue is repeated, the respondent now becoming the inquirer, and running between the two players at the other end, with the whole line after him. The first then has his turn again.

This procedure must have been tedious, and the game was often enlivened—usually by having the last in the line captured by the gatekeepers, and asked to take a side as in 'Oranges and Lemons' (p. 54). However William Barnes who, like many another poet, was attracted by the words, reported that in Dorset the children stood opposite each other in pairs, with one pair, who acted king and queen, singing: 'How many miles to Gandigo?'

The rest replied: 'Eighty-eight, almost or quite.'

King and queen: 'Can we get there by candlelight?'

Chorus: 'Yes, if your legs are long and light.'

King and queen: 'Open the gates as high as the sky, And let the king and his queen go by.'

The players then formed a line of arches for the king and queen to run through, as in 'Grandy Needles', and the next pair took their place.

In Scotland the dialogue used to end: 'Open the gates and let us through'; and the gatekeeper replied: 'Not without a beck an' a boo.' Those seeking to pass through were obliged to make a curtsy and a bow, and to acquiesce:

> Here's a beck an' here's a boo,
> Open your gates an' let us through.

This method of signalling submission was in fact well recognized in Scotland. In *Rob Roy* (1818) Mr Jarvie remarks how he and Mattie, to avoid being pelted with snowballs in Glasgow, 'are fain to make a baik and a bow, or rin the risk o' our harns (brains) being knocked out'. In England such language has always, of course, been incomprehensible. In Coram Fields in 1974 we heard a small cockney singing:

> Here's my black and here's my blue,
> So open the gates and let me through.

In North America the 'Oranges and Lemons' type of game was played with the single couplet:

> Open the gates sky high,
> And let King William's troops pass by!

Or,

> Hoist the gate as high as the sky,
> And let King George's host pass by!

The lines 'How many miles to Babylon?' (or to Bethlehem, or to Boston, or 'How far is it to Molly Bright?') were, and are, still known, but generally in association with a catching game in which two groups of children run to change places while one in the middle hopes to intercept them (*Street and Playground*, pp. 124–6). And this catching may, in fact, have been the original sequel to the dialogue. In a Latin sermon of the thirteenth century, the preacher compared the behaviour of those Christians who at one moment make haste to Heaven and at another relapse with the play of boys, and instances this very game: 'Quot leucas habeo ad Beverleyham?' The other says 'Eight'. The first asks if he can get there in daylight: 'Possum venire per lucem?' The other assures him he can, 'Ita potes', and begins running quickly, gets to where he wants, and then dances back to his original place, jeering at the other's slowness: 'Ha ha petipas (small pace) 3uot ich am Per ich was.'

Further, as if to forestall any doubters in years to come that this play-chant was being passed on from child to child through the centuries, Gerard Langbaine (1609–58), who attended the free school at Blencow in Cumberland, commented on this passage: 'As I remember, when I was a young boy at schole I have seene this play, and then the Questions and responses were these.

Q.   Pe, pe, postola. How many miles to Beverlay?
R.   Eight, eight, and other eight.
Q.   Think you I shall gett thither to-night?
R.   Yes if your horse be good and swift (or light).

'The rest,' Langbaine commented, 'I have forgott.'

Happily children are alive today who can, if required, supply his deficiency.

Britain: Balliol MS 230, f. 153v, late thirteenth century (*MSS of Balliol*, R. A. B. Mynors, p. 242) | Blencow, Cumberland, *c.*1620 (Bodleian SC 8617, Wood donat 4, p. 384, see Mynors, ibid.) | Scotland, 1796, 'How many miles to Babylon?' (*Notes & Queries*, 4th ser., vii, p. 141) | Looe, Cornwall, *c.*1820, ending 'Open your gates as high as the sky, And let King George and me pass by' (ibid., p. 271) | *Boy's Own Book*, 2nd edn., 1828, pp. 35–6, description as quote, much copied in subsequent books for boys | *Popular Rhymes of Scotland*, Robert Chambers, 1847, p. 261 | *Popular Rhymes*, J. O. Halliwell, 1849, p. 118, 'How many miles to Barley-bridge?' | *Letters of Bishop Shirley*, 1849, p. 415, 'How many miles to Hebron?' | Reddish, Cheshire, 1879, 'How many miles to Bethlehem . . . Not without a bend and a bow . . . And let the King and all go by. All a bye, all a bye, Oh! oh! oh!' (Crofton MS, i, 42) | Arbroath, J. M. McBain, 1887, pp. 343–4 | *Folk-Lore*, vii, 1889, pp. 230–1 | *Traditional Games*, i, 1894, pp. 231–5 | *Joyous Book of Singing Games*, John Hornby, 1913, pp. 96–7, 'How many miles to Banbury?' | Berry Hill, Gloucestershire, 1961, an introduction to the game 'The Big Ship Sails': 'Show me black and show me blue And I will open the gate and let you through'. The full dialogue continues to be well known, but not usually in association with a game. See *ODNR*, pp. 63–4.

USA: *Girl's Own Book*, L. M. Child, 1831, 'King William's Troops' (1832, p. 39) | *American Girl's Book*, Eliza Leslie, 1831, 'The King and his Train' (1835, pp. 23–4) | *Our Young Folks*, vi, 1870, p. 168, recollection, presumably of this game, *c.*1835 | *Games of American Children*, 1883, p. 212, 'Open the Gates'; and pp. 153–4, 'How many miles to Barbary-cross?' and 'Marlow, marlow, marlow bright, How many miles to Babylon?' in association with the catching game. | *Games for the Playground*, J. H. Bancroft, 1909, pp. 108–9 | North Carolina, 1920s, 11 versions of catching game (*North Carolina Folklore*, pp. 74–8) | *JAFL*, lx, 1947, p. 32 | *Singing Games of the Illinois Ozarks*, D. S. McIntosh, 1974, p. 85.

Cf. France: *Jeux de l'Enfance*, E. Rolland, 1883, p. 141, 'La Porte Saint-Nicolas'.

5

Winding Up the Clock

Winding up the clock, winding up the clock,
Tick tock, tick tock, winding up the clock.

'Winding Up the Clock' is the only game in this section in which there is not an arch. The players join hands in a line with, very often, the tallest amongst them at one end, and everyone begins singing. The tall player stands still, while the boy or girl at the other end leads the line round the stationary figure, and continues going round until everyone is wrapped about the player in the middle and unable to move further forward. At this point the singing stops, and the game itself may stop; but, in the nineteenth century, the players jogged up and down chanting 'A bundle of rags, a bundle of rags', or 'Tags and jags, and a bundle of rags', and continued to do so until somebody fell over. Alternatively the players shouted 'Row-chow-tobacco', and did not disperse until they had given each other what was termed, doubtless euphemistically, 'the fraternal hug' (Roxburgh-shire, 1825); or the girl in the middle attempted to burrow her way out, and hoped to pull the rest of the chain after her (Aberdeen, c.1880); or the players tried to tread on each other's toes (Sheffield, 1894); or they shouted 'The clock is run down', and turned about, and unwound as fast as they could (Taunton, c.1910).

However in the earliest American account of the game, in *The Little Girl's Own Book*, 1831, the proceedings, under the name 'Twine the Garland, Girls!', were more decorous:

A line of young ladies take hold of each other's hands: one stands perfectly still, while the others dance round her, winding and stopping—winding and stop-ping—until they are all formed into a knot. Then they gradually untwist in the same manner. As they form the knot they sing, 'Twine the garland, girls!' and when they unwind, they sing, 'Untwine the garland, girls!'

That this was the original way the game was played (as it continues to be when supervised) is quite possible. Certainly it was played like this in France, where the children likened themselves to a ball of yarn, 'Mon peloton'; as also in Germany, where one of its names was 'Garnwinden'. But the game has also long been played on the Continent with children trying, as in England, to knock each other over; or with the central player trying to worm his way out, as in Aberdeen.

In Antwerp the game was called 'Horloge wind op', and in the south Netherlands, commonly, 'Horloge opwinden'. In Rotterdam, c.1910, however, the children likened themselves to a tree which became thicker as they wound themselves round the tallest player, or, on occasion, they wound themselves round an actual tree, singing: 'De boom wordt hoe langer hoe dikker'. And as they unwound themselves they declared the tree was becoming thinner: 'De boom wordt hoe langer hoe dunner'. This, too, has parallels in England. S. O. Addy told Alice Gomme that in Sheffield young men and women playing this game would say, as if the middle player was an alder tree, 'The old eller tree grows thicker and thicker'. Other informants told her that in Nottinghamshire, and at Anderby in Lincolnshire, the children sang:

> The old oak tree grows thicker and thicker every Monday morning.

While in Lincoln, and further parts of the county, where the game was known as 'The Old Oak Tree', the words were:

> Round and round the old oak tree:
> I love the girls and the girls love me.

Further, when the children were coiled up against the 'tree', they started dancing up and down crying 'A bottle of rags, a bottle of rags'; and Lady Gomme did not fail to remark the coincidence that the hanging of rags on special trees is a venerable custom, and that these games might therefore be connected with an ancient form of tree-worship. However the Spanish 'Baile de Cintas' or 'Baile del Cordón' might be noticed; and a less contiguous encirclement of trees is referred to, of course, under 'Here We Go Round the Mulberry Bush'.

The European dance-figure 'L'Escargot', as also the semi-ritual 'Snail Creep', at one time an entertainment in mid-Cornwall (*Western Antiquary*, April 1881, p. 10), has been compared with this game, but possesses only a spiral relationship, since in 'L'Escargot' the leader of the file himself leads the way gradually inwards until he reaches the centre—then leading the way out again—whereas in 'Winding up the Clock' the leader is always on the outside.

The movement is, in fact, one of the figures of the old Scandinavian weaving dance 'Veva vadmaal' (Weave Homespun). The dancers dance the setting up of the warp, the winding, the shuttles, the weaving, the rolling up of the cloth, the pounding, and the proving, and they sing all the time:

> So we weave homespun,
> So we beat together,
> Weave homespun,
> Beat together,
> Let the shuttles go.

When they imitate rolling up the cloth each takes her neighbour's hand in a long line. They swing inwards around one who stands still at the end. When they are all 'rolled' tight together, the one who is innermost must get out and pull the row after her till the whole web has unrolled.

But a movement as simple and satisfying as this is likely to have been invented independently, anywhere in the world. Malinowski, in *The Sexual*

Life of Savages, 1929, describes how boys and girls play a game exactly like 'Winding up the Clock'.

The players stand in a long chain holding hands, and then walk, reciting a chant, round the person who stands at one end. This end remains immovable and the person at the other end leads the chain round in gradually narrowing circles until the whole group is pressed together into a tight knot. The fun of the game consists in squeezing the knot very tightly. It is then unrolled gradually by reversing the motion faster and faster, till at the end the others run round and round the fixed end until the chain breaks.

He then makes a remark which is true of Europeans and Trobriand Islanders alike; in this game 'close proximity lends itself to the preliminaries of love making'. Stewart Brand (author of the American *Whole Earth Catalog*) invited idealists to bring their 'own new games' to his New Games Tournaments, 1973 onwards. One of the games was Spirals: 'get the group to give itself a big hug'. When the spiral is wound up, 'Now feel the group energy. You're all one body'. Which seems the culmination of the 'fraternal hug' known in Roxburghshire in 1825.

Britain: Teviotdale, 1825, 'Row-Chow-Tobacco' and 'Tuilyie-wap'; west of Scotland, *c.*1860, 'Rowity-Chowity-Bacco' (Jamieson's *Scottish Dictionary, Supplement*, ii, pp. 316 and 603; new edition, iv, p. 67) | Shrewsbury, 1850, 'Wind-up Jack', and Ellesmere, 1883, 'Roll up the tobacco-box' (*Shropshire Folk-Lore*, p. 521) | *Every Boy's Book*, *c.*1860, p. 20, 'My Grandmother's Clock' | Minchinhampton, Gloucestershire, *c.*1875, 'Bundle of Matches' (probably this game: *Folk-Lore*, xxiii, p. 201) | Aberdeen, *c.*1880, 'Maypole' | West Cornwall, 1886, 'Roll Tobacco' (*Folk-Lore*, iv, p. 235) | Weston Rhyn, Shropshire, 1892, 'Lap Lap Tobacco' (*Bye-Gones*, 2nd ser., ii, p. 234) | Warwickshire, 1892, 'Thread the Needle', starting with arch, and chanting 'Thread the needle thro' the skin Sometimes out, and sometimes in'. Otherwise as above | Sheffield, 1894, 'Eller Tree' (*Traditional Games*, i, pp. 119–20) | Lincolnshire and Nottinghamshire, 1898, 'The Old Oak Tree'; Essex, 'Wind up the Bush Faggot'; Wolstanton, 'Wind up the Watch' (ibid., ii, pp. 384–6) | Taunton, *c.*1910, 'Winding up the Clock' | Staffordshire, 1924, 'Jack o' the Clock' | Alton, 1953 | Wells, Somerset, 1964, as text.

USA: *Little Girl's Own Book*, L. M. Child, 1831 (1832, p. 48) | Cincinnati, 1908, 'Twist, tobacco, tight, tight, tight,' and child's comment, 'Chu the tobact ti ti ti. I like it because you fall down and all on top of you' (*JAFL*, xl, pp. 28 and 66) | *American Nonsinging Games*, Paul G. Brewster, 1953, pp. 174–5, 'Twist Tobacco, Twist' and 'Neighbor, Lend Me Your Hatchet', the latter played as in Warwickshire, 1892.

France: *Revue des Traditions Populaires*, xiii, 1898, p. 10.

Germany: *Deutsches Kinderspiel*, F. M. Böhme, 1897, pp. 554–5 | *Zeitschrift für Volkskunde*, lx, 1899, p. 104, 'die Tonne binden' in Schlesien.

Netherlands: *Kinderspel in Zuid-Nederland*, A. de Cock and I. Teirlinck, I, i, 1902, pp. 264–8 | Correspondent, 1972.

6

The Big Ship Sails

Ashbourne, Derbyshire, 1977

The big ship sails on the alley alley oh,
  The alley alley oh, the alley alley oh;
The big ship sails on the alley alley oh,
  On the last day of September.

We all dip our heads in the deep blue sea,
  The deep blue sea, the deep blue sea;
We all dip our heads in the deep blue sea,
  On the last day of September.

The captain said, 'This will never never do,
  Never never do, never never do';
The captain said, 'This will never never do,
  On the last day of September'.

'The Big Ship Sails' is now the most played of arch games; a development
of 'Thread the Needle' that little girls find almost mesmeric in the
neatness with which it works out. Eight or nine players, sometimes more,
hold hands in a line; and the girl at one end, who may be at the end because
she is the tallest, clamps her free hand against a wall. Everyone begins
singing, and the girl at the other end of the line leads the way through the
arch made by the tall girl and the wall. As the last player passes through,
the girl at the wall finds her arm being pulled under her so that her body is
twisted round to face the other way, and her arms are crossed. The leader
of the line then circles round and passes through the arch (or 'alley' as
some call it) between the player at the wall and her neighbour; and this

second player, likewise, is forced to turn round and stay in position with her arms crossed, almost as if she was a stem stitch. The line then goes through the space between the second girl from the wall and the third, everyone continuing to sing the first verse over and over again until the last player has her arms crossed and is facing in the new direction. The two ends of the line then join up to make a circle, the second verse is sung, and heads are lowered to emphasize the words. The players then let go hands, and wag forefingers at each other while singing the third verse, 'This will never never do'. Or, as in Birmingham, they dance round singing:

> Sally had a bike and the wheels went round,
>   The wheels went round, the wheels went round;
> Sally had a bike and the wheels went round,
>   On the last day of September.

Or, as at Swanage, they sink to the ground singing:

> The big ship sank to the bottom of the sea,
>   The bottom of the sea, the bottom of the sea;
> The big ship sank to the bottom of the sea,
>   On the last day of December.

And only adults, recalling the game from their childhood, are concerned whether the big ship sailed on the last day of September or of December, or on the fourteenth of November, or 'on Christmas Day in the morning'. Indeed no one knows the correct words, or whether there ever were any correct words, or what they are about. The explanation most often heard is that the song celebrates the opening in 1894 of the Manchester Ship Canal ('an alley-like channel'); but this seems to be precluded by a recollection of the game in New Zealand in 1870. The suggestion that the nautical order 'Lee-oh' is intended (the order to swing the bow to leeward when a ship is about to set sail into the wind) seems almost as improbable, although the cry 'a lee, a lee-oh' or 'ee-lee-ay-lee-oh' is to be found in songs of the sea. And the possibility that the words developed from the line 'Through and through shall you go' (recorded 1849 in the related arch game 'How Many Miles to Barley-bridge?') is no more than a possibility, although it is recurrent; for instance 'Through and through the shally go' (Durham, 1898), and

> Through and through, Sally go,
> Them that comes last shall be catched.

(Scarborough, c.1900)

On the other hand in Hampshire in 1909 'The Big Ship' was recorded as sailing 'thro' the Holly, Holly O!'; Norman Douglas in London found children singing, similarly, 'holly holly ho'; and Scots versions have always been recognizable with their 'eely ally oh'.

After the *Lusitania* went down, 7 May 1915, the children added verses that were still being sung a decade later:

> The big ship's name was the Lusitania,
>   Lusitania, Lusitania,
> The big ship's name was the Lusitania,
>   On the fourteenth of November.
>
> The Germans sank the Lusitania,
>   Lusitania, Lusitania,
> The Germans sank the Lusitania,
>   On the fourteenth of November.
>
> My father was the captain of the Lusitania,
>   Lusitania, Lusitania,
> My father was the captain of the Lusitania,
>   On the fourteenth of November.

In the Manchester district between the wars the game ended with the players jumping up and down as they sang:

> My mother's back door goes
> Flipperty, flopperty, bang!

In a number of places, both before and since the last war, the game ended with the circle whirling round as fast as possible to the words:

> Dash, dash, dash, my blue sash,
> Sailing on the water like a cup and saucer,
> Dash, dash, dash.

At South Molton, in 1954, the circle was found to be chanting 'A bunch o' rags, a bunch o' rags' at the end of the game, as children did in the nineteenth century at the end of 'Winding up the Clock' (p. 46).

And at Four Marks in Hampshire the children still play 'Dan, Dan, Thread the Needle', which to an outsider is scarcely to be distinguished from 'The Big Ship Sails' (which they also play)—the children merely repeating 'Dan, Dan, thread the needle' as they do their human stitching. But in doing so they are the unwitting caretakers of words that brought pleasure to their great-great-grandparents in Hampshire when playing 'Thread the Needle'.

'The Big Ship Sails' was unknown to Alice Gomme in 1898, and unknown to our correspondents before about 1900; yet the form of the game is not new. The actions are almost exactly those of the country dance 'Wind up the Ball Yarn', otherwise known as 'Killiecrankie' or 'The

Grapevine Twist' or 'Winding up the Maple Leaf', which Cecil Sharp found being danced in the Southern Appalachian Mountains in 1917, although the hillbilly dancers, instead of keeping their hands at waist level as the children do when they twist round, crossed their right hand over their left shoulder. A similar threading and twisting-round takes place in the 'Durham Reel', as also apparently in 'Winding the Bobbin', a figure in the Hebridean Weaving Lilt. And the game is well known in parts of the Continent. In Holland it is usually played under the name 'K zou zo graag een ketting breien' (I should so like to knit a chain), and in Italy under such names as 'La Fornaia' (The Baker's Wife) and 'Mamma, cotto pane?' (Mama, is the bread baked?), the players first engaging in a dialogue as in Britain in the old game of 'How many miles to Babylon?' Thus, in a performance witnessed in Capri in 1976, the children joined hands in a half circle, and the following exchanges took place between the children at each end of the line:

Il fornaio ha fatto il pane?	*Has the baker baked the bread?*
Si.	*Yes.*
Come l'ha fatto?	*How has he made it?*
Bruciato.	*Burnt.*
E chi è stato?	*And who is standing here?*
Anna.	*Anna.*

Anna, who supposedly had burnt the bread, was the player next to the respondent; and the player at the other end of the line led the way through the arch between them, effectively tying her up:

Povera *Anna* è in mezzo le catene,	*Poor* Anna *is in chains,*
Passano le pene,	*They suffer pain*
Prima di morir, prima di morir.	*Before dying, before dying.*

Up to a generation ago, this game was known as 'Tira la tela' (Pull the Cloth), or 'Stienne mia cortina' (Stretch my Curtain); and 'Stienne mia cortina' was one of the thousand games played by the story-tellers in Basile's *Pentamerone*, 1634, Day Two.

The tune of 'The Big Ship Sails' has become well known through the film 'A Taste of Honey' (1961), and the Frankie Vaughan recording 'The Alley Alley Oh' (1964).

Britain: Midgley near Halifax, and Quantock Hills, *c.*1900 | *Old Hampshire Singing Games*, A. E. Gillington, 1909, p. 24 | Chesterton near Newcastle-under-Lyme, Clifton, Durkar near Wakefield, Gainsborough (last line 'Ee-oh, my big toe'), *c.*1910 | Edinburgh, *c.*1912 | *Joyous Book of Singing Games*, John Hornby, 1913, p. 58, 'Illy Ally O' | *London Street Games*, 1916, p. 66 | Common thereafter. Versions from 89 places since 1950.

New Zealand: Nelson, *c.*1870, 'The Eely Ily Oh' (Sutton-Smith, p. 24) | 'The Alley Alley Ooh' included in Education Department's Infant Syllabus in 1920s.

South Africa: Pietermaritzberg, 1975.

Netherlands: *Kinderspel in Zuid-Nederland*, A. de Cock and I. Teirlinck, I, i, 1902, pp. 254–63. Children sing 'Karikolle! karikolle! karamelle bollen!' as they thread their way through arches, leaving each child with his arm over his shoulder. They then dance round singing 'Slinge slinge slange! Boter in de panne, Kees in de pot! Is Marjanneke nog nie zot?' (Slinge slinge slange, Butter in the pan, Kees in the pot, Is Marjanneke not a clot?) | *De Verborgen Schat in het Kinderspel*, Mellie Uyldert, 1962, 'Ik zou zo graag een ketting breien' | Olst, Overijssel, *c.*1970, 'K zou zo graag een ketting breien, Dat gaat naar de stad van Leiden. Ha, ha, Victoria' (I would so much like to knit a chain, That goes to the town of Leiden) | Ecken Wiel, Zelderland, 1972.

Italy: *Giuochi fanciulleschi Siciliani*, G. Pitrè, 1883, pp. 241–5, 'A Tila, tila, tila' | *Giochi*, M. M. Lumbroso, 1967, pp. 110–14, versions from both the north and the south, and two from Sardinia | Capri, 1976.

Columbia: Cali, 1951, 'El Traidor'. Version similar to Capri—the traitor is the one who burnt the bread (*Rique Ran*, M. L. Goodwin and E. L. Powell, pp. 30–1).

7

Oranges and Lemons

Stepney, London E1, 1976

Oranges and lemons, say the bells of Saint Clemens;
I owe you five farvins, say the bells of Saint Martins;
When will you pay me? say the bells of Old Bailey;

> When I grow rich, say the bells of Shoreditch;
> When will that be? say the bells of Stepney;
> I do not know, say the great bells of Bow.
> Here comes a candle to light you to bed,
> Here comes a chopper to chop off your head:
> Chip, chop, the last man's *head*.

Thus nine-year-olds in Stepney: 'You 'ave to pick Oranges or Lemons, see. Two people 'ave to pick what they are, Oranges or Lemons, and the person who's 'ad their 'ead chopped off 'as to say Oranges or Lemons, and they go on their side, and then in the end there's a tug of war and see who wins.' Despite being an adult-sponsored party game children still sometimes play 'Oranges and Lemons' when outside, taking pleasure perhaps in the number of killings it promotes. In fact the game itself may be truncated to speed the slaughter. The two children who make the arch may chant merely a couple of lines before bringing their arms down around the player who is passing through:

> Oranges and lemons, say the bells of St Clement's,
> I owe you five farthings to-chop-off-your-*head*.

In the playground the words are shouted rather than sung. A cheer goes up when a girl is caught, and a further cheer when she chooses Orange or Lemon. (She scarcely bothers to whisper her choice, yet those who follow still seem to choose at random.) When asked what they like about the game they say, surprisingly, 'It's got singing in it', and they enjoy 'the heaving bit'. As soon as everyone's head has been cut off, and the players are aligned on one side or the other of the arch, they shout 'Tug of war, tug of war', and although in one game witnessed (Oxford), the Lemons far outnumbered the Oranges, a gratifyingly fierce contest took place to shouts of 'Heave! Heave!' before the Lemons pulled the Oranges to their side. 'That chopping bit,' confided a seven-year-old after the contest, 'It's not really true because we only come down over their heads. They should be laying down, so we could go "Whack!" '

The date when 'Oranges and Lemons' became the game it is today, played like 'London Bridge Is Falling Down', is anyone's guess. Texts of the song recorded in the eighteenth century (the earliest in 1744) confirm that the verses already belonged to children, but provide no evidence that there were accompanying actions. 'Oranges and Lemons' was, however, listed as a game for 'both boys and girls' by Edward Moor in 1823. 'I believe,' he said, 'It is nearly the same as plum pudding and roast beef'; and 'Plum Pudding and Roast Beef' he gave as 'nearly the same I think, as

"English and French".' That 'Oranges and Lemons' was then some such game as is played today seems apparent from the fact that 'Pudden or beef?' has long been the challenge among children when a random decision has to be made about which side a person should take in a game; and 'French and English' (though rarely 'English and French') was the common name at that time for tug of war. Nevertheless, in the earliest known description of the game, in Eliza Leslie's *American Girl's Book*, 1834, although the game begins with the two players making an arch for the others to pass under, no head-chopping or tug of war takes place, the players merely wrapping themselves round the two in the middle when they have taken sides, almost as if playing 'Winding Up the Clock'; and when, says the editor, they come to 'great bell of Bow' the two in the centre had to 'give a sudden push and extricate themselves by throwing down all the rest'. This way of playing the game was copied by Mrs Valentine in *The Home Book of Pleasure and Instruction*, 1867, although further on, under 'Indoor Games', she described 'Oranges and Lemons' almost exactly as played today, even to the brevity of the song:

> Oranges and lemons, say the bells of St Clement's,
> Here comes a candle to light you to bed,
> And here comes a hatchet to chop off your head.

That the game was not as well known at the beginning of the century as at the end, when it was very popular, seems to be confirmed by the fact that J. O. Halliwell (born 1820), who gave a literary text in his *Nursery Rhymes of England*, 1842, did not add the head-chopping until the third edition, 1844, and did not describe the game until he prepared the fifth edition in 1853. A reference to the game as a party game, with two sides pulling against each other, appears in *Peter Parley's Annual*, 1855, p. 78.

Since the bells of St Clement's, and the oranges and lemons, feature in only two of the four known texts of the eighteenth century, and then not prominently, and since the head-chopping figures not at all, stories about the ancient significance of the game have a counterfeit look to them; for instance that it commemorates the exposure of criminals on their way to execution accompanied by the tolling of the death bell and the carrying of torches ('Here comes a candle to light you to bed'). In the eighteenth and nineteenth centuries, and doubtless earlier, sayings purporting to give voice to particular sets of bells were not uncommon in all parts of the country, the content of the verses being dictated, however, more by the need for rhyme than for reason, as for example in Shropshire:

> Roast beef and be merry,
> say the bells of Shrewsbury.

Itchy and scabby,
　　say the bells of the Abbey.

Three naked lads,
　　say the bells of St Chads.

The one feature, perhaps, that differentiates the bells of the City from those in country places is that, due to the proximity of the churches, they could be presumed to address each other. The well-known tune was first given by E. F. Rimbault in 1846 (that supplied by Arnold in 1796 is unrelated), yet even Rimbault's 'Merry Bells of London Town' do not include those of St Clement's; and the present mechanical peal of St Clement Danes in the Strand (installed 1958), however familiar-sounding and agreeable to the ear, may be taken to be an example of practice echoing a tradition rather than tradition echoing a practice. The custom of presenting an orange or a lemon to each child attending an annual service in March was started by a publicity-conscious vicar in 1920.

Even so, the form of the game may be old, possibly very old, and only its conjunction with the singing of 'Oranges and Lemons' be fortuitous. Although no versions of the game have been found on the Continent associated with the chimes of bells, in the way that international equivalents abound to 'London Bridge Is Falling Down' (p. 61), the French game 'La Porte du Gloria', depicted in *Les Trente-six figures*, 1547, is a game of much the same type. Rolland, in *Rimes et Jeux de l'Enfance*, 1883, described how it was played in the department of Loiret. The two girls making the arch represented one the sun, and the other the moon. The players filed under the arch singing:

> Passez trois fois, la dernière, la dernière, la dernière,
> Passez trois fois, la dernière, la dernière restera.

The two girls made a prisoner of the last in the line; and a dialogue followed in which the captive's mother attempted to purchase her release, but failed to offer enough to save her from being hanged. The girl was then asked to choose sun or moon, as were those caught after her, and when all had been caught and had taken sides, it was revealed that the sun represented paradise and the moon hell (or the other way round, as determined secretly beforehand), and those who found themselves in paradise rushed after the damned, hitting them with knotted handker-chiefs. This distinction between two sides of sun and moon has also been found amongst children in Alexander County, North Carolina, an area possessing traditions dating back to the early settlers. In the game 'Sun

ORANGES AND LEMONS

Top: In Philippe Pigouchet's *Heures a lusaige de Paris*, 1497.
Bottom: In Workington, Cumberland, 1965.

and Moon' the players sang, as in other such amusements in England:

> Raise the gates as high as the sky,
> And let all the King's horses come marching by.

Each child captured was asked to choose between sun and moon, and the game ended with a tug of war. That this method of taking sides dates back to Elizabethan times seems evident from an entry in John Higins's *Nomenclator*, 1585, where the game *Dielcystinda* of ancient Greece is likened to a sport familiar to the editor, who defined it as 'a kinde of play wherein two companies of boyes holding hands all in a rowe, doe pull with hard holde one another, till one side be overcome: it is called sunne and moone'.

Texts: *Tommy Thumb's Pretty Song Book*, ii, 1744, pp. 50–1, begins 'Two Sticks and Apple, Ring ye Bells at Whitechapple', followed by bells of Aldgate, St Catherine's, St Clement's, Old Bailey, Fleetditch, Stepney, and Paul's | *Top Book of All for Little Masters and Misses*, *c.*1760, pp. 9–10, similar to 1744 but 'You owe me ten shillings, Say the Bells of St Hellens', instead of 'oranges and lemons', 'Shoreditch' instead of 'Fleetditch', 'great bell at Bow', instead of Paul's | *Tommy Thumb's Pretty Song Book* (Worcester, Massachusetts), 1788, pp. 26–7, similar to 1744 | *Juvenile Amusement, No. 17*, Samuel Arnold, *c.*1797, 'Lend me five shillings says the bells of Saint Helens', followed by bells of Old Bailey, Shoreditch, Stepney, and Bow | *Songs for the Nursery*, 1805, pp. 64–5, similar to *c.*1797, followed by the bells of Whitechapel, St Martin's, St Clement's, St Ann's, St Giles', St Peter's, and St John's | *Gammer Gurton's Garland*, 1810, pp. 28–9, begins 'Gay go up and gay go down, To ring the bells of London Town', continues with the bells of St Marg'rets, St Giles', St Martin's, St Clement's, St Peter's, Whitechapel, Aldgate, St Helen's, Old Bailey, Shoreditch, Stepney, and Bow | *Nursery Rhymes*, E. F. Rimbault, 1846, pp. 22–4, as 1810 but omitting St Clement's and adding St John's and St Ann's, with tune.

Recordings as a game: *Suffolk Words*, Edward Moor, 1823, p. 260 | *American Girl's Book*, Eliza Leslie, 1831, 'Bells of London' (*Girl's Book of Diversions*, 1835, pp. 43–4) | *Nursery Rhymes of England*, J. O. Halliwell, 1854, pp. 156–7 | *Peter Parley's Annual*, 1855, p. 78 | *Home Book of Pleasure and Instruction*, Mrs R. Valentine, 1867, p. 9, 'The Chimes', and p. 40 'Oranges and Lemons' | *Cassell's Book of In-door Amusements*, 1881, p. 36, captives asked to choose English or French | Hersham, Surrey, 1882, 'And the last one that comes shall be chop, chop' (*Folk-Lore Record*, v, p. 86) | Derbyshire, 1883 (*Folk-Lore*, i, p. 386) | *Merrie Games in Rhyme*, E. M. Plunket, 1886, pp. 44–5 | Dorset, 1889, 'a very favourite game'; Symondsbury version, 'Oranges and Lemons, Say the bells of St Clemen's; I owe you five farthin's, Say the bells of St Martin's; When shall I pay you? Monday, Tuesday, Wednesday, Thursday, Friday, Saturday, or Sunday?'; Broadwinsor version 'many years ago', 'I owe you five farthings. When will you pay me, today or tomorrow? Here comes a candle to light you to bed; Here comes a chopper to chop off your head' (*Folk-Lore*, vii, pp. 216–17) | *Traditional Games*, ii, 1898, pp. 25–35, 11 additional versions; also variants, pp. 232–3, and 456, 'Apples and oranges, two for a penny', 'Pancakes and flitters is the wax of cantailers', and 'Three Days' Holidays' | *London Street Games*, 1916, p. 99, 'Oranges and Lemons . . . Everybody knows that!'

Versions from 28 places in Britain since 1950.

Australia: Powelltown, Victoria, *c.*1935, 'Oranges and lemons, the bells of St Clement's, Let's cut the next man's head, head, head off'.

Tasmania: New Norfolk, *c.*1910, 'Oranges and lemons, the bells of St Clement's, I owe you three farthings; When will you pay me, tomorrow or the next day? Chip chop the last man's head off'.

New Zealand: Avonside, Christchurch, 1876, '. . . And when will you pay me Tomorrow or the next day?' 'Oranges and lemons' said to have become subsequently the most popular singing game in the country (Sutton-Smith, p. 21).

Canada: Willowdale, 1963 (Fowke, 1969, p. 31).

USA: *American Girl's Book*, 1831, see above. Not much played in twentieth century.

Netherlands: Hoogwoud, north Holland, 1972, 'Groene zwanen, witte zwanen, wie gaat er mee naar Engeland varen? Engeland is gesloten, de sleutel is gebroken, en is er dan geen smid in 't land, die de sleutel maken kan? Laat doren, laat doren, van achteren en van vo-ren!' (Green swans, white swans, who sails with me to England? England is closed, the key is broken. Then is there no smith in the land who can mend the key? Let us through, let us through, From behind and from front). The captured child chooses between golden apples and silver pears. In Germany this is a game of fighting to get out of a ring.

India: Ramapura, Uttar Pradesh, 1975, 'they file under the arch singing "The dacoit (bandit) is coming, Will steal, take your food, catch you". The one caught has to choose between two names, and at the end there is a tug of war.'

Germany: Bremer, 1836, *Kinder- und Ammenreime in plattdeutscher Mundart*, H. Smidt (quoted by Böhme, p. 522, from the 1859 edn.), 'Dat Osterdoor dat is tobraken, Morgen wollen wi't wedder maken; Mit 'n Speigel, mit 'n Dreier—Krunp unner dör, is wöhl' (The Easter door is broken, We will rebuild it tomorrow, With some spittle, with a coin, Creep under the door, it is lucky). The captured child is asked 'What will you have, Heaven or Hell?' and the game ends with a tug of war. A Westphalian version, 1859, has a tug of war between Sun and Moon | Krombach, 1952, 'Machen auf das Tor! Es kommt ein Goldener Wagen. Wer sitzt darin? Ein Mann mit grossem Kragen. Was will er denn? Er will die *Laura* holen. Was hat sie denn? Die *Laura* hat gestohlen. Wo denn? Wo denn? In dem Lande Polen. Was denn? Was denn? Ein Sack von Kohlen'. (Open the gate! Here comes a golden coach. Who sits inside? A man with a big cape. What does he want? He has come for *Laura*. What's wrong with her? *Laura* has stolen. Where? In Poland. What, then? A sack of coals. The tug of war is between Angels and Devils.

Portugal: Lisbon, 1960, 'Que linda falua'.

Italy: *Giuochi Popolari Veneziani*, G. Bernoni, 1874, pp. 46–8, 'Le porte xè serate, Col girum, girum, gela; Le porte xè serate, Col girum, girum, già' (The gates are shut, With girum, girum, gela; The gates are shut, With girum, girum, gia). The children in the line say 'We will smash them down . . .' at which the arch surrenders, singing 'The gates are open'. The last child through is asked 'Do you want some wine?' and then 'Do you want some water?' If 'wine', she goes behind Hell; if 'water', behind Heaven. At the end the two lines wander about making suitable hellish or heavenly noises | Sicily, 1974, 'Le porte son' aperte', with children, having chosen between a fork and a spoon, finding themselves in Heaven or Hell. The game ends with the heavenly children shouting 'Inferno, inferno' at the others.

Spain: *Cancionero Infantil Español*, S. Córdova y Oña, 1947, p. 24, 'A la vibora del amor, por aquí pasaré yo. Por aquí yo pasaré y una niña dejaré; y esa niña cuál será, la de alante o la de atrás; la de alante corre mucho, la de atrás se quedará. Pásame, si; pásame ya; por la puerta de Alcalá (To the viper of love, through here will I pass. Through here will I pass, and a girl I will leave behind; And that girl will be either the first or the last; The one in front runs very fast, so it will be the last. Pass along, pass along, through the gate of Alcalá). Girls making the arch have names of flowers or colours.

8

London Bridge

Liss, 1978

London Bridge is falling down,
  Falling down, falling down,
London Bridge is falling down,
  My fair lady.

Build it up with sticks and stones,
  Sticks and stones, sticks and stones,
Build it up with sticks and stones,
  My fair lady.

Sticks and stones will wear away,
  Wear away, wear away,
Sticks and stones will wear away,
  My fair lady.

Build it up with iron and steel,
  Iron and steel, iron and steel,
Build it up with iron and steel,
  My fair lady.

Iron and steel will rust away,
  Rust away, rust away,
Iron and steel will rust away,
  My fair lady.

Build it up with bricks and clay,
  Bricks and clay, bricks and clay,
Build it up with bricks and clay,
  My fair lady.

Bricks and clay will wash away,
  Wash away, wash away,
Bricks and clay will wash away,
  My fair lady.

Build it up with silver and gold,
  Silver and gold, silver and gold,
Build it up with silver and gold,
  My fair lady.

Silver and gold is stole away,
  Stole away, stole away,
Silver and gold is stole away,
  My fair lady.

'You make a bridge with two people, and all the other people line up, and you sing "London Bridge is falling down" and they all go round under the bridge,' the nine-year-olds explained. 'And when you get to "My fair lady" you catch somebody. And then when you're singing "Sticks and stones will wear away" you swing them about backwards and forwards and round and round—any way you like—as if you'd got them in a sieve. And then you take them away and they whisper what they'll have, *sticks* or *stones*, and they go to whichever side of the bridge they've chosen. Then you sing "London Bridge" again; but first you have to whisper what the next verse is going to be, and which person is going to be which thing. The bridge never is mended, but it doesn't matter. You have a tug of war at the end.'

Here, in the present day, young singers give new life to an old song. Admittedly, in the early part of the game, the song we heard in Liss playground in 1978 would have been familiar to nine-year-olds in the eighteenth century; but a forceful song-leader (one of the players forming the arch takes the lead) can obtain acceptance of some curious fancies. The game continued with 'Build it up with paper and card . . . Paper and card will float away', 'Build it up with bread and butter . . . Bread and butter's eaten away', 'Build it up with pencils and pens . . . Pencils and pens will snap away', and the rest of the children, especially the younger ones, were enchanted with this minor act of folk creation.

It is difficult to know how long children have been making up verses for the game (in fact almost everything about it is a mystery). For a hundred and fifty years it has been agreed that 'London Bridge Is Falling Down' is one of the most renowned songs in the English language, 'a song of which there is, perhaps, not a single dweller in the Bills of Mortality, who has not heard somewhat', as Richard Thomson remarked in 1827; 'yet it is a song,'

Thomson continued, 'of which not one person can tell you more concern-
ing it, than that they have heard it sung "many years ago", as the gossiping
phrase is'. In 1888 Babcock, writing in Washington, declared that it had
'held its own in the favor of children and the memory of adults for many
generations'. And Newell, in New York, said no game was more popular,
adding that it could be seen any summer evening in the poorer quarters of
the cities.

Yet there is no certainty that the song has always been part of a game; or
if the game was originally played with a line of children passing under an
arch. At Clun in the 1880s the children moved round in a ring as they sang
'London bridge is broken down, Gay ladies, gay!' And in *The Chronicles of
London Bridge*, 1827, Richard Thomson's fictitious narrator Mr Barbican,
having sung 'London Bridge is broken down, Dance o'er my Lady Lea',
added 'I learn from a manuscript communication, from a Mr J. Evans of
Bristol, which has been most kindly placed in my hands, that "about forty
years ago, one moonlight night, in a street in Bristol, his attention was
attracted by a dance and chorus of boys and girls, to which the words of this
ballad gave measure. The breaking down of the Bridge was announced as
the dancers moved round in a circle, hand in hand; and the question, 'How
shall we build it up again?' was chaunted by the leader, whilst the rest stood
still"'.' About 1790, then, 'London Bridge' was being danced in exactly the
manner of a medieval *carole*. It may well have been danced the same way in
the seventeenth century, when, in the 'witty comoedy' *The London Chaunticleres*, 1659 (sc. viii), the dairywoman Curds said she had danced 'the
building of London-Bridge' in her youth, at the Whitsun ales. It would be
good to know what words, if any, were used on such occasions, for an old
lady born in the reign of Charles II, who recollected the song from her
childhood (reported in *The Gentleman's Magazine*, 1823), called it merely
'a ballad'. Her version began:

> London Bridge is broken down,
> *Dance over the Lady Lea:*
> London Bridge is broken down,
> *With a gay lady.*

And by 1725, when Henry Carey quoted them in the satirical *Namby
Pamby*, the lines were already looked upon as being nursery property:

> *Namby Pamby* is no Clown,
> London Bridge is broken down:
> Now he courts the gay Ladee
> Dancing o'er The Lady-Lee.

The song's first appearance in print was in a children's book, *Tommy*

Thumb's Pretty Song Book, c.1744, where the words agreed closely with those remembered from the late seventeenth century: 'London Bridge Is Broken down, Dance over my Lady Lee. London Bridge Is Broken down, With a gay Lady. How shall we build it up again ... Build it up with Gravel, and Stone ... Gravel and Stone will wash away ... Build it up with Iron, and Steel ... Iron and Steel Will bend, and Bow ... Build it up with Silver, and Gold ... Silver, and Gold Will be stolen away ... Then we'l set A man to Watch.'

Thus it is well established that a song of 'London Bridge', with chorus 'Dance over my Lady Lee', was sung in the seventeenth century and used for a ring dance at least by the 1820s. It tells of a bridge that has fallen down, and the plans, practical or impractical, for building it up again (the dialogue could serve as a text for Eric Berne's psychology-game 'Why Don't You—Yes But'). The song ends with a watchman being set to guard the bridge, and this is apparently not only because it is to be made of silver and gold. Bridge building is a hazardous undertaking, and it has long been thought sensible to propitiate the river with a sacrifice, a human life if possible. (The Pope has played a kindlier role as Pontiff, a title which means not only 'master bridge-builder' but also 'the one who makes the propitiatory offering'.) The Romans used to throw an old man into the Tiber once a year from the Pons Sublicius (later, osier figures were thrown instead). A foundation sacrifice of human bones and the bones of cattle and sheep was found beneath an arch of Old Blackfriars Bridge, built 1760–8; and as recently as 1939 an engineer constructing a bridge in Assam was brought a live month-old baby to build into the foundations ('My Indian workmen were most enthusiastic'). Songs reflecting this belief are known throughout Europe and the East, one of the most famous being that sung about the Bridge of Arta, in which the bridge would not stand until the master-mason built his wife into the masonry. (Also see *ODNR*, under 'London Bridge'.)

'London Bridge is broken down' was listed with other singing games in *Blackwood's Magazine*, 1821, as a rhyme 'sung in concert' to the tune of 'Nancy Dawson' (i.e. 'Nuts in May'), and it is interesting that the solo part in *The Chronicles of London Bridge* is sung to the same tune. A fanciful version of the song ('London Bridge is falling down, Dan's sister and Lady Ann') was remembered from childhood in the vicinity of Glasgow c.1855, but no actions were given (*Rymour Club*, i, 1906). Newell (*Games of American Children*, 1883, pp. 208–9) provided the first record of what might be called the arch-game wording, from Boston, and Savannah, Georgia:

London Bridge is falling down,
Falling down, falling down,
London Bridge is falling down,
My fair lady.

Both have 'robber' verses attached (see the game 'Watch and Chain', p. 68).

The game was still taking shape (if it has ever acquired a permanent shape) in the 1890s. Alice Gomme gave either versions of the old song, or contemporary versions which included the 'robber' verses from 'Watch and Chain', or, in the addenda, some inexplicit and ragged versions from Scotland (which are, however, the first traces of the distinct Scottish variety, 'Broken Bridges Falling Down'). She considered the game to be 'more or less in a state of decadence', and said 'it is now generally played like "Oranges and Lemons", only there is no "tug-of-war" at the end'. So 'London Bridge' seems never to have had a heyday as an arch game, and to have acquired its limited popularity only through the addition of the 'Watch and Chain' verses, with their licence for manhandling a prisoner.

Perfunctory game-versions have been noted in the north country and Scotland from the 1920s to the 1970s, usually consisting, in the north, of 'London Bridge is falling down . . . My fair lady' and an invitation to have an apple or a pear (Leeds, 1920s; Bacup, 1960); or, in Scotland, of 'Broken Bridges falling down, falling down, falling down, Broken Bridges falling down, My fair lady. Breakfast, dinner, tea, supper, Nip her, grip her, take her away. A golden shoe or a silver shoe?' (Forfar, 1951; Kingarth, Isle of Bute, 1960, '. . . Nupper, grupper. Apple or an orange?') And thereafter, as we have seen, revivals have sprung up in some places where children have discovered that the game lends itself to jubilant inventiveness.

The arch game of 'London Bridge' might be supposed to be a late development from the song, were it not that similar bridge games abound throughout Europe and have been played for centuries. In the Germanic tradition, especially, the game has sinister undertones. The bridge has been broken, and 'the last will be caught, with spears and with stakes', or, in Württemberg c.1862, a King and an Emperor make the arch and whoever has the most players behind him beheads the other, while the children crowd round cheering 'Bloody man! bloody man!' The following from a children's book published in Hamburg in 1815 is typical of many of the versions gathered together by Böhme (p. 526):

Wir wollen gern auf die Merseburger Brücke!	(We want to go over the Merseburger Bridge!
Sie ist zerbrochen.	It is all broken.
Wer hat sie denn zerbrochen?	Who has broken it?
Der Goldschmied mit seiner Tochter.	The goldsmith with his daughter.
Wir wollen sie wieder machen.	We will build it up again.
Mit was und welcherlei Sachen?	With what, with what?
Mit Steinen, mit Beinen,	With stones, with bones,
Mit Gold und Silber und Edelgesteinen.	With gold and silver and precious stones.
Zieht immer hin, zieht immer hin,	Keep moving through, keep moving through,
Der Letzte muss bezahlen.	The last must pay.)

The words are as rich and strange as a medieval tapestry. In many places the bridge is golden, and the tug of war between angels and devils. The reward for rebuilding the bridge may be 'the hindmost horse, with saddle and pistol'. And this diversity already existed in Germany in the sixteenth century, for Johann Fischart (1546–90) knew the game by three different names: 'Der faule Brucken' (The rotten bridge), 'Ritter durch Gitter' (Knight through the lattice-work), and 'Auf der Brucken suppern in glorie' (On the bridge we feast in glory). It seems that the bridge in question was neither in London, Dresden, nor Magdeburgh, but was what Carlyle called 'that stupendous Arch from Hell-gate to the Earth'.

The tune for the game is different from that for the song 'London Bridge is broken down, Dance over the Lady Lea', which appears in Arnold's *Juvenile Amusements*, c.1797, no. 47, and in E. F. Rimbault's *Nursery Rhymes*, 1846, where the first phrase, only, is the same. Fuld does not find the game-tune, as now known, earlier than 1879, when it was printed with the words in A. H. Rosewig, *Illustrated National Songs and Games* (Philadelphia) by W. F. Shaw. The tune for the dance 'London Bridge' in *The Dancing-Master*, 1718, bears no relationship to that for either the song or the game.

Britain: *Traditional Games*, i, pp. 333–50; ii, pp. 441–2.

Germany: Böhme, pp. 522–35 | *Das Berliner Kinderspiel der Gegenwart*, Reinhard Peesch, 1957, pp. 17–18, 'Ziege durch, ziege durch, durch die goldne Bröke, sie ist ent-zwei, sie ist ent-zwei, wir wolln sie wieder flöken, mit was denn, mit was denn, mit ei-ner-lei, mit stei-ner-lei. Der erste kommt, der zweite kommt, der dritte muss gefangen sein' (Pass through, pass through, through the golden bridge, it is in two . . . we will mend it again. What with then? with just the same, with stones. The first comes, the second comes, the third must be caught). The children making the arch are Angel and Devil; the captives choose between Apple and Pear.

Netherlands: *Kinderspel in Zuid-Nederland*, A. de Cock and I. Teirlinck, I, i, 1902, p. 236, 'Is de steenen brug gemaakt?' 'Neen! we zullen ze maken, Met steenen en met staken; Al die er laatst aankomt, Zal zijn leven laten!' (Has the stone bridge been built? No! we shall build it, With stones and with stakes; The one who comes last shall lose his life!).

Denmark: *Bórneses Musik, Sange etc*, 1879, 'Bro bro Brille, Klokken ringer elleve . . .'

Norway: *Norske Barnerim og Leikar*, B. Støylen, 1899, 'Bru, bru breie, Brui ligge bratt yver heii, Med stolpar og naglar og alle gode greior, I fjor for me herifraa, I aar gjer me like so. Lat upp, lat upp, Den høgaste topp! Lat oss gaa igjenom lund, Lat oss fara gjenom sund. Far, far fredeleg, Freden skal du nyta, Den litle fuglen som etter kjem, Han skal upp i gryta' (Bridge, bridge broad, The bridge lies over the plain, With pillars and nails and all. Last year we left from here, This year we do the same. Open, open the highest top! Let us go through the greenwood. Let us sail through the strait. Sail, sail peacefully, You shall enjoy peace. The little bird which comes after, He shall end in the pot). Players choose between Sun and Moon | Trondheim, 1976, *På livets landevei*, Berit Østberg, pp. 124–5, 'Bro bro brille, klokken slager elve. Keiseren stå på det høyeste slott, så hvit som sne, så sort som gull. Fari, fari krigsmann, døden skal du lide. Den som kommer aller sist, skal i den sorte gryte' (Bridge, bridge broad, the clock strikes eleven. The Emperor stands in his high castle, As white as snow, As black as gold. Go, go soldier, You shall suffer death. The one who comes last shall be thrown in the pot).

Sweden: *Svenska fornsånger*, A. I. Arwidsson, iii, 1842, pp. 250–3, 'Bro bro, breda, Brona ligger nere; Hvad fattas brona? Stockar och stenar. Ingen slipper nu här fram, Förr'n han sagt sin kärestas namn, Hvad heter han (hon)? (NN) hafver (honom) henne fäst Med tolf guldringar och appelgrå häst; Han rider åstad, Han vill henne ha; Ty han vill henne försörja bra. Till hösten de skära, Till vatten de bär'n; De bär'n för fast, De plocka nu ax, (NN) ska' göra godt barnsöl i år; Hon pår välle det! (NN) tar sin knyppeldyna, Hon sätter sig i fönstret; Mer ser hon på fästemannen, Än uppå mönstret. Hå, hå! du (NN) lilla, Hå, hå, du (NN) lilla, Du äst min, Jag är din, I alla vara lefnadsdagar!' (Bridge bridge broad, The bridge falls down. What does it need? Sticks and stones. Nobody is let through until he says his sweetheart's name. What is she called? (Name) has plighted her troth With twelve gold rings and dapple grey horse; He rides off, He will have her, For he will support her well. In the autumn they cut, Water they carry, they carry it well. They thresh the corn, (Name) will make a good lying-in this year, She may well do so! (Name) takes her lace-pillow, She sits in the window; She looks more at her betrothed than upon the pattern. Ha, ha, you little (Name), Ha, ha, you little (Name), You are mine, I am yours, All our living days) | *Visor, ramsor och andra folkrim*, F. Ström, 1941, pp. 143–9, 17 variants from oral tradition. Children choose between Sun and Moon, or Gold and Silver | *Svenska folklekar och danser*, C. Tillhagen and N. Dencker, ii, 1950, pp. 320–1, 'Bro bro breda'.

Spain: *Baile de la Maya* (Dance of the May Queen), Miguel Sanchez, 1615, '*Ora, lirón, lirón*, Whence are you come? *Ora, lirón, lirón*, From San Pedro el Altare . . . What did Don Roldane tell you? . . . That you shouldn't pass . . . The bridges are broken . . . I'll have them fixed . . . We have no money . . . I'll give you some . . . What is money made of? . . . Of eggshells . . . How will we count it? . . . On tables and blackboards . . . What will you give us in payment? . . . A love that is true' (translation from *Lirica Infantil Mexicana*, No. 162, XX, 1973, p. 104) | *Cancionero Infantil Español*, S. Córdova y Oña, 1947, p. 23, '*Al álimon, al álimon*, el puente se ha caído. *Al álimon, al álimon*, mandadle componer . . . no tenemos dinero . . . nosotras lo tenemos . . . pasen los caballeros . . . nosotras pasaremos . . . de qué es ese dinero . . . de cáscaras de huevo . . . el puente se arregló . . . el juego se acabó' (*Al alimon, al alimon*, The bridge has fallen . . . command that it be mended . . . We have not got the money . . . we have some . . . let the gentlemen pass . . . we will pass . . . what is money made of? . . . of eggshells . . . the bridge is mended . . . the game is finished). The choice is between Rose and Jasmine, and there is a tug of war at the end. The game is played in all Spanish-speaking countries.

Japan: *Folk Songs of Japanese Children*, D. P. Berger, 1969, pp. 59–63; the equivalent game is called 'Toryanse' and the players filing under the arch are trying to gain admittance to the Tenjin shrine.

An article by H. F. Feilberg, 'Bro-brille-legen', in *Nyare bidrag til kannedom om svenska landsmal och svenskt folklif*, 1905, brings together all the European bridge games.

9

Watch and Chain

Tune: 'London Bridge Is Falling Down'

Who has stole my watch and chain,
　　Watch and chain, watch and chain;
Who has stole my watch and chain,
　　My fair lady?

Off to prison you must go,
　　You must go, you must go;
Off to prison you must go,
　　My fair lady.

The popularity of this game, which is played like 'Oranges and Lemons' but with one significant difference, seems to be on the increase. 'There's two children holding hands and about five to ten other children keeping going under the two children's hands, and there's a song to it "Who has stole my watch and chain?". When you've stopped the song, you catches the person who's going through, and you swing them between your arms and sing "Off to prison you must go". They've got to pick "watch" or "chain". Say they picked "watch", and it was Linda; they got to go behind Linda. And in the end, when all the people have gone to prison, you have a tug of war.' The significant difference between 'Watch and Chain' and 'Oranges and Lemons' is the swinging or shaking back and forth of each new captive, or—as a Camberwell girl put it—'the torture'. In some places a third verse is sung:

> Stamp on her toes and let her go,
> 　　Let her go, let her go,
> Stamp on her toes and let her go,
> 　　My fair lady.

Naturally this injunction is acted upon. It is not the players' business to inquire into the original wording, which almost certainly was 'Stamp your foot and let her go', or 'Stamp your foot and away we go'.

　　The question whether 'Watch and Chain' is an offshoot of 'London Bridge Is Falling Down', or is the remnant of a game with a separate history that now often gets attached to 'London Bridge', is difficult to answer. The earliest notice of it as a separate game is in 1892 when Belloc's friend Rachel Busk reported that in the village of Shipley, near

Horsham in Sussex, children formed themselves into two lines and, alternating with two or three children who called themselves robbers and swaggered between the lines, sang as follows:

> Hark! at the robbers going through;
>> Through, through, through; through, through, through;
> Hark! at the robbers going through,
>> My fair lady.

Robbers: What have the robbers done to you;
>> You, you, you; you, you, you?
> What have the robbers done to you,
>> My fair lady?

Lines: Stole my gold watch and chain;
>> Chain, chain, chain; chain, chain, chain;
> Stole my gold watch and chain,
>> My fair lady.

Robbers: How many pounds will set us free;
>> Free, free, free; free, free, free?
> How many pounds will set us free,
>> My fair lady?

Lines: A hundred pounds will set you free;
>> Free, free, free; free, free, free;
> A hundred pounds will set you free,
>> My fair lady.

Robbers: We have not a hundred pounds;
>> Pounds, pounds, pounds; pounds, pounds, pounds;
> We have not a hundred pounds,
>> My fair lady.

Lines: Then to prison you must go;
>> Go, go, go; go, go, go;
> Then to prison you must go,
>> My fair lady.

Robbers: To prison we will not go;
>> Go, go, go; go, go, go;
> To prison we will not go,
>> My fair lady.

After uttering their defiance the robbers rushed away with the rest of the children after them, and whoever was caught was put in an imaginary prison. Under the name 'Robbers', 'See the Robbers', 'Hear the Robbers', or 'Hark the Robbers', the game was well known at the end of the nineteenth century. Alice Gomme knew of it being played in six places in England and one in northern Ireland; and Anne Gilchrist found it in Southport and Sunderland Point. There was little agreement between one place and another on how the game should be played, but everywhere the song was much the same. The only out-of-the-way text was that published by Kidson in 1907, which he had obtained some years earlier from children in Liverpool. Here the players sang, first 'Shootman, Shootman, the very very last man', and then 'What has my poor prisoner done?'. The prisoners replied 'Robbed a church and killed a man', and the rest responded 'Tread upon his toes, and let him go, My fair lady'.

However these verses, or ones very like them, were being sung in the 1880s at Clun in Shropshire, as the second part of a ring game, 'Gay Ladies', in which two players outside the ring started by singing 'Over London Bridge we go', and when London Bridge had broken down and been built up, first with lime and sand, and then with penny loaves that were stolen away, one of the players outside the ring went inside and sang:

> O, what has my poor prisoner done,
> O, what has my poor prisoner done,
> O, what has my poor prisoner done,
>   Gay ladies, gay?

And the game continued:

> Robbed a house and killed a man,
> Robbed a house and killed a man,
> Robbed a house and killed a man,
>   Gay ladies, gay.

> What will you have to set her free,
> What will you have to set her free,
> What will you have to set her free,
>   Gay ladies, gay?

> Fourteen pounds and a wedding gown,
> Fourteen pounds and a wedding gown,
> Fourteen pounds and a wedding gown,
>   Gay ladies, gay.

> Stamp your foot and let her go,
> Stamp your foot and let her go,
> Stamp your foot and let her go,
>   Gay ladies, gay.

Of the six non-literary versions of 'London Bridge' that Alice Gomme obtained in England in the 1880s and 1890s all but one ended with the sequence of verses 'What has this poor prisoner done?' Yet no such verses about robbers, ransoms, going to prison, or getting married to escape going to prison, have been found in the first half of the nineteenth century. However, in the game 'La Porte du Gloria' played in France (see under 'Oranges and Lemons') the prisoner's mother attempts to secure her daughter's release, although at a bargain price:

> Ah! rendez-moi ma fille,
> Les zig, les zag, les marionnettes;
> Ah! rendez-moi ma fille,
> A moins de six cent francs.

And when this fails the prisoner, as in England, undergoes an ordeal. The two girls making the arch hang her by passing their arms under her armpits and raising her until she is suspended in the air.

In Britain, to this day, when children are on their own playing 'London Bridge Is Falling Down', they are likely to repeat one or more of the prisoner verses, probably because of the licence they give to shake or otherwise discomfort the player who has been seized. Indeed a verse may be supplied for the purpose. Thus in Salford:

> Shake her up in a carrier bag,
> Carrier bag, carrier bag;
> Shake her up in a carrier bag,
> My fair lady.

And at Haggate, near Burnley:

> Chop her up for fi-er-wood,
> Fi-er-wood, fi-er-wood;
> Chop her up for fi-er-wood,
> My fair lady.

The game of 'Watch and Chain' seems to have acquired its current abridged form in the 1940s.

Britain: Shipley, Sussex, 1892 (*Notes & Queries*, 8th ser., i, pp. 210–1) | *Traditional Games*, i, 1894, pp. 192–9, seven versions including one from Belfast | Southport, 1898 and 1900. Children choosing sides were asked whether they would rather have 'a golden piano with God on it, or a golden church with a piano in it with angels on it?' (Piagetists may like to note that most children inclined to the piano with angels on it). Also Sunderland Point (Gilchrist MSS 231 Aiii) | Hartlebury, Worcestershire, 1899 (*Folk-Lore*, xxxv, p. 266) | *Eighty Singing Games*, Frank Kidson, 1907, p. 58 | *Children's Singing Games*, Cecil Sharp, iv, 1912, p. 14 | *Street Games of North Shields Children*, M. and R. King, 1930, p. 19 | Swansea, c.1939 | *Children's Games Throughout the Year*, Leslie Daiken, 1949, pp. 99–100, 'More widely in circulation than London Bridge' | 13 places since 1950.

Australia: *The Bulletin* (Sydney), 26 February 1898 (Turner, pp. 121–2).

New Zealand: Collingwood, Nelson, 1895, 'Here's a prisoner we have got'; and Onehunga, Auckland, 1905, 'What have the robbers done to you?' Prisoners tortured by ear-twisting: 'Pull her ears and let her go, My fair lady' (Sutton-Smith, pp. 21–2). See also version linked to 'London Bridge'.

USA: *North Carolina Folklore*, p. 140, one recording, *c.*1927.

Canada: Guelph, Ontario, *c.*1900, 'Here are the robbers coming through' (Fowke, 1969, p. 31).

Versions linked to 'London Bridge':

Britain: *Shropshire Folk-Lore*, 1883, pp. 518–19 | *Merrie Games in Rhyme*, E. M. Plunket, 1886, pp. 22–3 | *Traditional Games*, i, 1894, pp. 335–40; ii, p. 441 | Highfields, Sussex, 1898, 'Where are these fine folks a-going? Over London Bridge they go' etc (Gilchrist MSS 231 Aiii f. 13) | Belford, Northumberland, *c.*1900 (*County Folk-Lore*, iv, pp. 113–14) | *100 Singing Games*, 1916, p. 6 | Somerset, 1922 (Macmillan Collection) | Versions from 9 places since 1960.

New Zealand: Tahataki, Otago, 1875, 'London Bridge is broken down, Who's going to mend it?' followed by 'Off to prison you must go' and 'Pull her ears and let her go' (Sutton-Smith, p. 22).

USA.: Boston, Massachusetts, apparently a number of years prior to 1883, 'London Bridge is falling down, My fair lady!' followed by 'You've stole my watch and kept my keys', 'Off to prison you must go', and 'Take the key and lock her up'. Also similar from Savannah, Georgia (*Games of American Children*, pp. 208–10) | St Louis, 1895–1900, 'London Bridge is falling down, So merrily', 'Here's a prisoner we have caught', 'He stole my watch and stole my chain', and 'Off to prison he must go' (*JAFL*, lx, pp. 24–5) | Cincinnati, 1908, 'London Bridge is falling down, Hi-diddlum dey', 'Here's a prisoner we have caught', and 'Take a key and wind her up' (ibid., xl, p. 38).

III

Match-Making

THESE games belong to a group of European entertainments which make fun of the old system of match-making, and are in fact known as 'Brautwerbung' in Germany. In some, the suitors demand from a mother one of her large family of daughters, the suitors standing in one line, with the mother and her daughters in a line opposite—a variation, as in 'Three Sailors', being that only one daughter is courted. In others, notably 'A Duke a-Riding', the girls themselves receive the man who comes to woo, when an agreeably insulting dialogue ensues. In 'Green Grass' the formula is different again, the suitors proceeding without hindrance or badinage, and their proposals being marked by an unusual note of chivalry.

The mother acts as match-maker in the majority of these games. She makes difficulties, prevaricates, and finally strikes a bargain. She may be open to the highest bidder, as in the Dutch game 'Killemandee' when, in one version, she relinquishes her daughter only when the girl is promised a dress of blue satin; and in another, when she will allow her daughter to go on condition that she cleans not the house, but the family diamonds. Madame Dorè, in the much-loved Italian game 'O quante belle figlie!', perhaps not unnaturally refuses the hand of her daughter to a serpent, or a rose, but is satisfied when Prince Blue is suggested by the match-maker. More comprehensible, to the modern way of thinking, is the mother who, in the French 'Chevalier du Guet', allows the Chevalier to choose a wife from among her daughters when it is at last understood that 'gold and jewels' are not the approved present, he must give his heart instead. Only one game exists in Britain, apparently, in which the mother is anxious to get rid of her girls—'The Widow from Babylon'; although to judge from the many Continental games on the theme ('Rich and Poor' being the best known), there may have been others now forgotten. Indeed, in these islands, numerous features of this great dance-game cycle have been lost, including the match-maker himself. The duke a-riding to get married must once have had to negotiate with a counterpart to the German 'Man from Nineveh'; but even as it survives today the game is robust enough to recall a Europe echoing to the sound of feet plunging forward and back, and to cheerful shouts of 'Ransom, tansom, terrimus hey!' and 'Heiza fipilatus!'

10

The Lusty Wooer

Nursery Rhymes, *E. F. Rimbault, 1846*

Here comes a lusty wooer,
    My a dildin, my a daldin;
Here comes a lusty wooer,
    Lily bright and shine-a.

Pray, who do you woo,
    My a dildin, my a daldin?
Pray, who do you woo,
    Lily bright and shine-a?

For your fairest daughter,
    My a dildin, my a daldin;
For your fairest daughter,
    Lily bright and shine-a.

Then there she is for you,
    My a dildin, my a daldin;
Then there she is for you,
    Lily bright and shine-a.

'I am a lusty Wooer' appears as the name of a children's game in *The Craftsman*, 4 February 1737/8; and confirmation that the song was well known at this time is supplied by Henry Carey, in whose burlesque *Tragedy of Chrononhotonthologos*, 1734, sc. vii, occurs a medley of popular refrains beginning:

See Venus doth attend thee,
  My dilding, my dolding.
Love's goddess will befriend thee,
  Lily bright and shiny.

The full text appeared ten years later in the first collection of children's traditional verse, *Tommy Thumb's Pretty Song Book*, 1744. It was thereafter included in Ritson's *Gammer Gurton's Garland*, 1784; and, in more recent times, has often been anthologized, notably in *Come Hither*, although de la Mare's renovated text is not, it must be said, one that would survive oral transmission. In the nineteenth century the game was displaced by its more amusing relative 'A Duke a-Riding' (p. 76); although it is named by Sutton-Smith, in *Games of New Zealand Children*, as being played at Avondale, Christchurch, in 1875; and direct descendants still existed in Britain at the end of the century, as is apparent from two games given by Alice Gomme, 'Jolly Hooper' and 'Jolly Rover'. In 'Here comes a jolly hooper', at Sheffield, the hooper said he came for 'one of your daughters', was asked which one, and on naming her, was told:

Then take her and welcome,
On this bright shining night.

And in 'Here comes one jolly rover', from Derbyshire, the rover, after saying he roved for his pleasure, was asked what was his pleasure, and replied:

My pleasure's for to marry you,
Lily white and shining.

In an eighteenth-century MS addition to our copy of Ray's *English Words*, 1737, the term *dilding* is equated with '*A dilling*; a Darling, or best-beloved Child'.

II

A Duke a-Riding

Manchester, 1975

Preston, Lancs, 1961

Here comes a duke a-riding,
   Riding, riding,
Here comes a duke a-riding,
   Rancey, tancey, teena.

What are you riding here for,
   Here for, here for?
What are you riding here for?
   Rancey, tancey, teena.

We're riding here to marry,
   Marry, marry,
We're riding here to marry,
   Rancey, tancey, teena.

Marry one of us, sir,
   Us, sir, us, sir;
Marry one of us, sir,
   Rancey, tancey, teena.

You're too black and dirty,
　　Dirty, dirty;
You're too black and dirty,
　　Rancey, tancey, teena.

Not as black as you, sir,
　　You, sir, you, sir;
Not as black as you, sir,
　　Rancey, tancey, teena.

Will you marry me?
No.

You're too fat and greasy,
　　Greasy, greasy;
You're too fat and greasy,
　　Rancey, tancey, teena.

Not as fat as you, sir,
　　You, sir, you, sir:
Not as fat as you, sir,
　　Rancey, tancey, teena.

Will you marry me?
Yes.

A classic singing game in that it is of old stock, has international analogues, enacts an outmoded practice, possesses little appeal to adults, was immensely popular with children in the nineteenth century, and is played with equal gusto by the young today. Further the words, and even the manner of playing the game, continue to vary from place to place up and down the country. Essentially there are two sides, though they are not in direct opposition, and one side may consist of a single player and the other side of everyone else. The two sides face each other with enough room between them to advance and retire as they sing the alternate verses. Sometimes the girl the duke has chosen gives herself up willingly, sometimes—indeed usually—she refuses him, is subjected to further abuse, and then submits. Sometimes she has to be pulled over, sometimes she is pushed from behind. Occasionally her side tries to save her.

　　The earliest the game is known to have been played, 'acted with much energy, and gestures and tones of servility, scorn, etc.', is in Lancashire, 1820–30, the song beginning:

> Here comes three dukes a-riding,
>   With a rancy tancy terry boy's horn!
> Here comes three dukes a-riding,
>   With a rancy tancy tee!

These words were given by Charlotte Burne in *Shropshire Folk-Lore*, 1883, as a footnote to her Salopian version, which went as follows, the burden being understood after each response:

First party:	Here comes three dukes a-riding, a-riding,
	With a ransome dansome day!
Second party:	Pray what is your intent, sirs, intent, sirs?
	With a ransome dansome day!
1st:	My intent is to marry, to marry!
2nd:	Will you marry one of my daughters, my daughters?
1st:	You are as stiff as pokers, as pokers!
2nd:	We can bend like you, sir, like you, sir!
1st:	You're all too black and too blowsy, too blowsy,
	For a dilly-dally officer!
2nd:	Good enough for *you*, sir! for *you*, sir!
1st:	If I must have any, I will have this,
	So come along, my pretty miss!

Apparently the early Lancashire version was similar, but Miss Burne noted that the reply 'You're all too black and too blowsy' had an additional line, 'With your golden chains about your necks'; and it is apparent that some of the verses were spoken rather than sung. In a version 'There's a young man that wants a sweetheart', known to the Dorset poet William Barnes in 1874, the young man's reservations about the 'fine daughters' he had been offered were distinctly off-beat:

> They are all too black and brawny,
> They sit in the sun uncloudy,
> With golden chains around their necks,
> They are too black and brawny.

To which the girls replied:

> Quite good enough for you, sir,
> For you, sir, for you, sir;
> Quite good enough for you, sir,
> For the ransome tansome tidi-de-o.

The boys then relented, speaking as though they were one:

> I'll walk in the kitchen and walk in the hall,
> I'll take the fairest among you all,
> The fairest of all that I can see,
> Is pretty *Miss Watts*, come out to me.
> Will you come out?

Top: 'A Duke a-Riding' in the days when it was felt that 'the children of the well-to-do . . . might find pleasure for themselves and give pleasure to their elders' by learning and playing such games. *Merrie Games in Rhyme*, E. M. Plunket, 1886.

Bottom: 'A Duke a-Riding' at Leyland, Lancs, 1968.

Such verses have been found elsewhere. 'You're all too black and too browsy, You sit in the sun so drowsy' comes in a Yorkshire version probably of the 1870s; and the line 'I'll walk in the kitchen and walk in the hall' (an echo of ballad and folk song: 'There's blood in the kitchen, and blood in the hall') was common at this time. Indeed such verses were still known in the West Country fifty years later. In a number of places in East Devon and West Dorset three players joined hands and advanced towards the others singing:

> Here come three dukes a-riding,
> A-riding, a-riding,
> Here come three dukes a-riding,
> With a ransom, dansom, diddle-hi-ho.

The others replied:

> And what is your good will, sirs?
> Will, sirs? Will, sirs?
> And what is your good will, sirs?
> With a ransom, dansom, diddle-hi-ho.

Dukes: Our will is to get married,
> Married, married;
> Our will is to get married,
> With a ransom, dansom, diddle-hi-ho.

The others: Will any of my fine daughters do,
> Daughters do, daughters do?
> Will any of my fine daughters do?
> With a ransom, dansom, diddle-hi-ho.

Dukes: They are too black and brownie,
> They sit in the sun so clownie,
> They have no chains around their necks,
> They are too black and brownie.

The others: They are good enough for you, sirs,
> You sirs, you sirs;
> They are good enough for you, sirs,
> With a ransom, dansom, diddle-hi-ho.

Dukes: We'll hunt the kitchen, we'll hunt the hall,
> And find the fairest of them all.
> The fairest one that we can see,
> Is *Polly Smith*, will you come with me?

Polly Smith answered 'No!' The three dukes joined hands in a small circle, and (unwittingly borrowing from the cushion dance) skipped round singing:

> The naughty girls they won't come out,
> They won't come out, they won't come out;
> The naughty girls they won't come out,
> To join us in our dancing.

The three dukes again approached Polly, and invited her, as before, to join them. This time the answer was 'Yes'. Polly joined hands with them, and they danced in a ring singing:

> Now we've got a bonny lass,
> A bonny lass, a bonny lass,
> Now we've got a bonny lass,
> To join us in our dancing.

The game then recommenced; and was played over and over again until all the bonny lasses had been chosen.

Although dukes continue to go a-riding to this day in some places (they usually set out one at a time, not in threes), other personages have been taking their places in the twentieth century, often to the accompaniment of curious staccato fanfares. The following are examples:

*c.*1900, Inverary, 'Here's the King arriving, Oh! Ay! Oh!'

*c.*1905, Forfar, 'O, where do you come from, My ring-a-ding, my darling?'

*c.*1910, Devonport, 'Here comes a little nigger boy, A-rin-ting, my darling'

1911, Edinburgh, 'Here's the King's arrival, E-I-O' (*Rymour Club*, i, pp. 154–5)

1911, Sunderland Point, Lancaster, 'There come three knights a-courting' (Gilchrist MSS 231 B iv)

*c.*1920, Liverpool, 'There came a duke a-riding, I-O-U'

*c.*1930, Kirkby Stephen, Westmorland, 'There came three gipsies riding'

1952, Shrewsbury, 'There came a duke a-riding, Alaba talaba tishoo'

1952, Lincoln, 'Here comes a prince a-riding, Hey! Hi! Ho!'

1957, Penrith, 'There came a gipsy riding, Y-O-U'

1960, Accrington, 'Three gipsies came a-riding, Ee-by-gum'; Banbury, 'There came a king a-riding, Y-O-U'; Berry Hill, Gloucestershire, 'Three young men came a-riding, E-I-O'; Bristol, 'A gipsy came a-riding, Tom, Tom, Terrier'; Cranford, Middlesex, 'I'm the Duke of Gloucester, Y-O-U'; Knighton, 'There came two gipsies striding, Y-O-U'; Market Rasen, 'A soldier came a-riding one fair summer's day'

1961, Workington, 'There came a gipsy riding, Y-O-U'

1962, Newcastle upon Tyne, 'Here came three gipsies riding, With a ramsey tamsey tay'

1966, Birmingham, 'A gipsy came a-riding, Alaba tambarina'

1969, Basingstoke, 'A prince came a-riding, Y-O-U'

1969, Thornbury, Gloucestershire, 'Gipsy come a-riding, Tom Tom Terio'

1973, Leeds, 'A gipsy came a-riding, Y-O-U'; St John's Wood, London, 'A
  Prince came a-riding, Ipsy opsy over'
1975, Ayr, 'There came a duke a-riding, Upon a Sunday morning'; Salford,
  'Came a duke a-riding, I tie tiddley-i'
1976, Dublin, 'Here's gipsy riding, Y-O-U'
1978, Huddersfield, 'There came a duce a-riding, Y-O-U'

The emphasis tends now to be on the suitor's choice rather than on the
suitor, a change that gives opportunity for further badinage. The performance of a group of Waunarlwydd seven-year-olds seen in 1960 may be
considered typical, with the exception (there is always an exception if the
performance is genuine) that due to the waywardness of oral transmission,
and children's desire to do precisely as tradition instructs, a delightful
irrelevancy had been added. Their song's refrain was 'Alla balla kiss-me-
toe' (compare in the nineteenth century, 'Ransom, tansam, tisum ma tea'
and 'Nancy pancy disimi oh!') and each time after one or other party had
skipped forward, prettily holding hands and singing their verse, they
retired and, lifting a foot with one hand, unconcernedly kissed the toe of
their shoe. Then they waited expectantly for the other side to perform.
The girls had split into two equal parties and faced each other about ten
feet apart:

> *Dukes*:   Here comes a Duke a-riding,
>   A-riding, a-riding;
>   Here comes a Duke a-riding,
>   Alla balla kiss-me-toe.
>
> *Maidens*:   What are you riding here for,
>   Here for, here for;
>   What are you riding here for?
>   Alla balla kiss-me-toe.
>
> *Dukes*:   We're riding here to marry,
>   Marry, marry;
>   We're riding here to marry,
>   Alla balla kiss-me-toe.
>
> *Maidens*:   Who do you want to marry,
>   To marry, to marry;
>   Who do you want to marry?
>   Alla balla kiss-me-toe.
>
> *Dukes*:   We want to marry Bacon Face,
>   Bacon Face, Bacon Face;
>   We want to marry Bacon Face,
>   Alla balla kiss-me-toe.

Maidens: Who the 'eck is Bacon Face,
              Bacon Face, Bacon Face;
              Who the 'eck is Bacon Face?
              Alla balla kiss-me-toe.

Dukes, giving the name of one of the maids:

              Her Christian name is *Vivian*,
              Vivian, Vivian;
              Her Christian name is *Vivian*,
              Alla balla kiss-me-toe.

The dukes then swaggered forward again, and demanded with strident little voices, 'Will you come?' The maid, equally boldly, said 'No', whereon the singing and dancing recommenced:

Dukes: You-er legs are bandy,
              Bandy, bandy;
              You-er legs are bandy,
              Alla balla kiss-me-toe.

Maidens: Just the same as yours are,
              Yours are, yours are;
              Just the same as yours are,
              Alla balla kiss-me-toe.

The dukes demanded again, 'Will you come?' This time the maid said 'Yes'. The dukes asked, 'Who will you pull?' The maid chose the duke she thought the weakest. The two advanced to the centre, took each other's right hand, and pulled. The duke was much the stronger, and pulled the maid to his side. Thereafter she played on the dukes' side, and the singing and dramatics began again from the beginning, only this time the dukes said they wanted not 'Bacon Face' but 'Fish Fingers'. When asked 'Who the 'eck is Fish Fingers?' the dukes said her Christian name was Wendy, and when Wendy refused to come to them they said her legs were dirty (turning their backs to her, and kicking their legs out backwards); when she refused a second time they said her legs were pokers (and demonstrated their stiffness). She then agreed to come, the pulling was arranged, the duke she chose was stronger than her, and she too joined the dukes.

Alice Gomme, commenting on the nineteenth-century recordings of this game, made the good point, which can be repeated today, that there is no individual courtship, that 'love' is not mentioned, and that the proceedings are wholly practical. 'The marriage formula does not appear, nor is there any sign that a "ceremony" or "sanction" to conclude the marriage

was necessary, nor does kissing occur in the game.' She herself believed
the game to be a survival of exogamous marriage, the banter between the
parties being to enhance the value of the protagonists, to display their wit,
and to give each individual a chance 'to have as good a look round as
possible' before accepting the offer.

In the nineteenth century gifts or bribes to aid the transaction seem to
have been as uncommon as they are today, although Lady Gomme printed
one version, from Earls Heaton, a suburb of Dewsbury, to which attached
the courting song, 'I will buy a silk and satin dress, to trail a yard as we go to
church' (cf. p. 140); and this form of the game was still being played at
Wythenshawe, Manchester, in 1975. The game started in an ordinary
enough manner with one girl, the duke, out in front facing the rest. She
skipped forward and back twice as she sang each of her verses, and the rest
did likewise when they sang the alternate verses:

> There came a duke a-riding, a-riding, a-riding,
> There came a duke a-riding,
> I tie tiddley-i.

> What are you riding here for, here for, here for,
> What are you riding here for?
> I tie tiddley-i.

> I'm riding here to marry, marry, marry,
> I'm riding here to marry?
> I tie tiddley-i.

> Who are you going to marry, marry, marry,
> Who are you going to marry?
> I tie tiddley-i.

> I'm going to marry white socks, white socks, white socks,
> I'm going to marry white socks,
> I tie tiddley-i.

> Who the 'eck is white socks, white socks, white socks,
> Who the 'eck is white socks?
> I tie tiddley-i.

> Her first name is Andrea, Andrea, Andrea,
> Her first name is Andrea,
> I tie tiddley-i.

> Who the 'eck is Andrea, Andrea, Andrea,
> Who the 'eck is Andrea?
> I tie tiddley-i.

> Her second name is Jackson, Jackson, Jackson,
> Her second name is Jackson,
> I tie tiddley-i.
>
> Who the 'eck is Jackson, Jackson, Jackson,
> Who the 'eck is Jackson?
> I tie tiddley-i.

At this point, remarkably, the duke went up to Andrea Jackson, led her by the hand to a corner, and sang to her:

> If I give you ten white horses,
>> Ten white horses, ten white horses,
> If I give you ten white horses,
>> Will you marry me?

The girl replied 'No', and the duke continued:

> If I give you a diamond ring,
>> A diamond ring, a diamond ring,
> If I give you a diamond ring,
>> Will you marry me?

Andrea again replied 'No'—we were told she could have said 'Yes' if she had wanted—and the duke went on:

> If I give you baby Jesus,
>> Baby Jesus, baby Jesus,
> If I give you baby Jesus,
>> Will you marry me?
>
> If I give you the key to Heaven,
>> The key to Heaven, the key to Heaven,
> If I give you the key to Heaven,
>> Will you marry me?

To this she agreed; and the two of them danced round together, with everybody singing:

> Now we've got the princess,
>> The princess, the princess,
> Now we've got the princess,
>> I tie tiddley-i.

The game then began again; but this time the duke's wish was for a child, and thereafter a nurse for the child, and then a dog. The game, they assured us, could 'last for hours and hours'.

This dancing round, sometimes twizzling round, confirms that the game has descended from the old German stepping dance (see 'Romans

and English'). In some places, particularly in the north, the performance
may end with the curious words:

> Round and round the banisters, the banisters, the banisters,
> Round and round the banisters, Y-O-U.

In Preston they chant 'Now we've got a merry ring'. In Birmingham the
gipsies make a circle round the girl they have pulled to their side, and sing
'Now we've got our fairy, our fairy, our fairy'. In Middleton Cheney they
chant 'Now we've got the silly old maid'. In the nineteenth century a
variant, sometimes beginning 'Forty dukes (or ducks) a-riding' and having
the refrain 'My dilsey dolsey officer' (cf. 'My a dildin, my a daldin', in 'The
Lusty Wooer', p. 74), or having the 'dilsey dolsey officer' in the principal
role, was played in a ring, and at the end they 'opened the gate' (as in
'Merry-ma-tansie', p. 150) to let the dolsey officer and his bride out of the
ring. But in the latest development we have noticed, at Poole, Dorset, in
1975, a gipsy comes 'arrivin', and when asked what 'he' has come 'arri for',
he says 'for a furry coat', and thereafter 'for some gold', and then 'for a
mirror, Tittley tattley teaser'; and each time the gipsy grabs someone from
the other side and takes them back to his own. In Poole, it seems, goods are
more in demand than brides.

In Italy the game 'È' rivato l'ambasciatore' is remarkably similar, and
widely played. The children form up in two lines facing each other, they
sing as they advance and retire, as do their counterparts in Britain, and
their verses are in the same form, a single action line being followed by a
nonsense refrain and then repeated. The proceedings open with the
announcement of the ambassador's arrival:

> È' rivato l'ambasciatore,
>   Olì olì olela;
> È' rivato l'ambasciatore,
>   Olì olì olà.

The other side, using the same metrical form, ask what he wants. He says
he wants one of their daughters. They ask what he wants her for. He says
he wants to give her away in marriage. They ask to whom he wants to give
her. He replies 'To a knight of the king's'. They ask what gift he will give
her. He replies 'A basket of flowers'. They tell him the gift is too small. He
offers a palace of gold. The offer is accepted:

> Questo fa per me,
>   Olì olì olela,
> Questo fa per me,
>   Olì olì olà.

The game, versions of which are known in other Romance languages, was even more like the English game when played in Venice a hundred years ago. The ambassador, after being asked what he wanted, and saying he wanted one of the daughters, was asked which one he wanted. He replied the most beautiful one, was asked to name her, did so, and was then asked who the bridegroom would be, and replied a chimney-sweep. He was immediately told this would not do: 'Questo non va bene, Ola, ola, ola'. Whereupon he said he would give her the King of France; and he, of course, was accepted: 'Questo sì va bene, Ola, ola, ola'.

In Swedish-speaking Finland, where a similar drama is popular (Otto Andersson gives nine versions), the game is known as 'Simon i Sälle', as it also is in its country of origin, Sweden. 'Simon i Sälle' is apparently a corruption of 'syv Mands Ædelig', the seven noble men of a parallel game that has been known in Denmark at least since the beginning of the nineteenth century. Simon i Sälle arrives in the company of 'honest gentlemen—southernmen all', represented by one of the lines of players, who dance forward as they sing.

> Här kommer Simon i Sälle!
> Här komma redeliga herrar!
> Här komma Södermänner alla!

The women reply, in the same way, asking what they want. Simon says he wants to propose a marriage. The women ask what he offers, and he offers at first comical characters such as a clown, chimney-sweep, and bootblack, whom the women refuse. Only when a man of higher degree is suggested is the offer accepted, the women singing 'Ja! får Simon i Sälle', and so on.

In Germany, where this type of game has been much played, children taking part in 'Herr von Nineve' or 'Brautwerbung' (match-making) formed up in two rows facing each other, and advanced and retired, singing as they did so, in the manner customary elsewhere. At Dresden, in 1872, when the 'youngest daughter' was given away, the match-maker had to pull her across to his side as the Duke pulled the chosen girl in Glamorgan in 1960. The man from Nineveh had been asked what he would do with the youngest daughter, and said he would get her a man. When asked what sort of a man, he replied he would be the miller's fool:

> Das wird der Müllers August sein,
> Kaiser fipilatus.

Surprisingly, the daughter's side agreed:

> So nehmt sie hin die jüngste Tochter,
> Kaiser fipilatus.

But in earlier versions, for instance in Prussia in 1867, the proposition was not accepted until the Crown Prince, or the Czar of Russia, or the Roman Emperor was offered. In yet other versions, however, acceptance was procured by the threat of smashing a window, or of setting fire to the home. While in further versions the visitor, who is variously designated, demands first of all to see the father, who must read a letter that has been brought and then hand over the daughter, and very often she is not to be some man's bride, but 'Heaven's bride'. Sometimes, indeed, the body-snatchers are not men but women, as at Cassel about 1860, where came three ladies riding:

> Es kommen drei Damen geritten,
>   Heisa Fipilatus!
> Von Adel und von Sitten,
>   Heisa Fipilatus!

The noble ladies say that they want 'the first daughter'. They are asked what they want the first daughter for, and say they want to put her in a convent. 'What will she do in the convent?' ask the girl's family. 'She will learn embroidery and knitting', say the ladies. 'She has been taught that well by us', respond the family. 'Then we'll teach her washing and ironing', say the ladies, and demand she be brought to them, whereon the daughter sings an affecting farewell:

> Adieu, adieu, beloved mother,
> Now I must leave you,
> I am going into a convent
> And must do much work there;
> I shall be beaten with a rod
> Till my fingers bleed.
> Adieu, adieu, adieu!

This game, or something very like it, has a long history in Germany. In a book of merriments, *Alle Arten von Schertz- und Pfänder-spielen*, printed about 1750, a sport is described in which a row of men stand opposite a row of women, each of them paired off 'in the manner customary in English dances'. The men are monks, the women nuns, and at one end stands an extra man, who is not paired off, denominated 'the wise man'. The women begin, all singing together, 'Here come the bold nuns':

> Hier kommen die kecken Nonnen daher,
> Sera, Sera, sancti nostri Domine!

Then the monks opposite come forward, asking what the nuns want:

> Was ist der Nonnen ihr Begehr,
> Sera, Sera, sancti nostri Domine!

The nuns say they want the wise man who can show them the seal:

> Wir fragen nach dem weisen Mann,
> Der uns das Petschaft zeigen kann,
> Sera, Sera, sancti nostri Domine!

The monks reply the wise man is not there, he is in his writing-closet:

> Der weise Mann der ist nicht hier,
> Er ist in seinem Schreib-Loschier,
> Sera, Sera, sancti nostri Domine!

The nuns say they want the wise man to read a letter for them:

> Wir fragen nach dem weisen Mann,
> Der uns den Brief recht lesen kann,
> Sera, Sera, sancti nostri Domine!

The wise man then sings that in the letter it is written each man shall love his little nun:

> In diesem Briefe steht geschrieben:
> Ein Jeder soll sein Nönnjen lieben,
> Sera, Sera, sancti nostri Domine!

On this each monk kisses the nun standing opposite him, and processes with her to the wise man, singing a wedding song:

> Wir wünschen der Braut ein neues Jahr,
> Was wir wünschen, das werde wahr,
> Sera, Sera, sancti nostri Domine!

This simple amusement seems to have been old (the Hamburg poet Conrad von Hövel listed 'Hi kommen wir käkken Nonnen her, herr Domine' amongst social games in 1663), and to have been the diversion not only of common folk but of royalty. Princess Elisabeth Charlotte of the Palatinate (born 1652), who became the Duchess of Orleans, was one who took part in the game when she was young, and remembered it throughout her lifetime. In a letter to her half-sister, 7 July 1718, she wrote:

This morning I had become attached to the lie so that I could really have wished from my heart that it was true, namely that the princess of Wales had seen the king [George I of England]. I felt like singing, as at the end of the game:

> Here we come fools and nuns,
>   Her Domine, her Domine!
> And what is not, still may be,
>   Cede, cede, sancte, quit, nostre Domine!

It is a foolish game. I don't know whether it is still played in Germany.

It is difficult to imagine all these years afterwards in what spirit such games of monks and nuns were danced, for there were many of them. Were they making fun of the religious (in the way Boccaccio made fun of them); or were the games played on the Feast of Fools, on or near 1 January, when the priests outdid the common people in rioting and revelry, and laity and priesthood mockingly exchanged clothes and rôles; or were the games danced by monks and nuns in an ordinary sociable fashion, as Louis Cognet says they were at the beginning of the seventeenth century at Maubuisson Abbey (*La Mère Angélique*, 1951, p. 28)? He quotes from the Prioress's sister and biographer:

When the weather was fine, after vespers had been finished with, the Prioress used to take the community for a walk a good way from the Abbey, beside the ponds by the Paris road, when often the monks of Saint-Martin de Pontoise, who live near by, would come and dance with these nuns, and this as naturally as one would do something nobody would dream of criticizing.

A ritual curiously similar to 'A Duke a-Riding' was performed at the *rèiteach*, the formalized 'arranging' or 'clearing the way' for a marriage in the Western Isles of Scotland. The School of Scottish Studies recorded descriptions of the occasion from some of the older people (*Tocher*, 30, 1979). In Harris, for instance, the bridegroom and a supporter went to the bride's house, where the neighbours had gathered, about a week before the wedding. Two or three boys were selected

to go amongst the girls, grabbing one here and one here and dragging her along to the top of the table . . . And we [girls] used to hide, from shyness, in case we were taken up to the groom. And they would appear in the doorway with this one and that one, asking, 'Is this her?' 'Oh no. No. That one's too difficult to winter.' And one was so ugly, one so fat, one was too thin, and everything was wrong—each one had a fault. But at last, now, the right one was got hold of, and she would be taken up to the top of the table and seated next to the man. And the man who was asking for the young woman would say, 'Oh, here she is, here she is. We'll accept that one.' That's how they were. 'That one will do.'

Presumably this identity parade was helpful in ensuring that the bridegroom was going to marry the right girl (it has echoes of the theme of the true and false bride in many old fairy stories); and one wonders whether, some centuries ago, this grabbing of young girls and dragging them to the bridegroom was not cast in the more gracious form of a game like 'A Duke a-Riding'.

Britain: Lancashire, 1820–30 (*Shropshire Folk-Lore*, p. 517 n.) | Isle of Man, *c.*1840, 'Here come three dukes a-riding, With a ransome, tansom, tissimy tee' (*Traditional Games*, ii, p. 246) | Dorset, 1874 (*Folk-Lore Journal*, vii, pp. 223–4) | Bocking, Essex, 1880 (*Folk-Lore Record*, iii, pp. 170–1) | Lanarkshire?, 1881, 'There came three dukes a-riding, With a tinsy, tinsy, tee' (*Folk-

Lore Record, iv, p. 174) | Chirbury, 1883 (*Shropshire Folk-Lore*, p. 517) | *Merrie Games in Rhyme*, E. M. Plunket, 1886, pp. 38–9 | *The Besom Maker*, Heywood Sumner, 1888, pp. 20–1 | Madeley, Shropshire, 1891, 'Here come three dukes a-riding, With a rancy, tancy, tay!' | Numerous recordings hereafter, e.g. *Traditional Games*, ii, 1898, pp. 233–55 and 414–15 | *Eighty Singing Games*, Frank Kidson and Alfred Moffat, 1907, p. 25 | *Old Surrey Singing Games*, A. E. Gillington, 1909, p. 4 | *Joyous Book of Singing Games*, John Hornby, 1913, p. 38 | *London Street Games*, 1916, p. 75 | Text and tune based on a version from Ipswich, 1953.

New Zealand: 'Played in all the provinces' in period 1870–1920 (Sutton-Smith, pp. 25–6). Some versions, such as 'Saucy Duke' and 'Saucy Jack', were probably more like 'Three Brethren out of Spain'.

Australia: Sydney, *The Bulletin*, 26 February 1898, 'Here come two Dukes a-riding, A-ree, a-row, a-riding' (Turner, pp. 55–6).

USA: Concord, Massachusetts, 1883, 'Here comes a duke a-roving, With the ransy, tansy, tea!' A well-mannered version: 'Pretty fair maid, will you come out, To join us in our dancing?' 'No.' 'Naughty girl she won't come out, To join us in our dancing.' 'Yes.' 'Now we've got the flowers of May, To join us in our dancing.' The more usual form said to be common in the Middle States. But in New York, 1883, 'Forty ducks are riding, My dilsey dulsey officer' (*Games of American Children*, pp. 47–9) | Washington DC, 1886, 'Here comes one duke a-riding, Sir Ransom Tansom tiddy bo-teek' (*Lippincott's Magazine*, xxxvii, p. 245) | Virginia, 1888, 'Here comes a dude a-riding by, So ransom, tansom, titty bo tee' (*Counting-Out Rhymes*, H. C. Bolton, p. 118) | St Louis, 1895–1900, 'Here come three dukes a-riding, With a ransum, tansum, cinnamon tea'; also 1944 'known today on nearly every playground and schoolyard' (*JAFL*, lx, pp. 3–7) | Cincinnati, 1908, 'There came a Jew (duck, duke) ariding, He, hi, ho!' (ibid., vol. xl, pp. 8–9) | *Negro Folk Rhymes*, T. W. Talley, 1922, pp. 85–6, 'Here comes a young man a courtin'! It's Tidlum Tidlum Day' | North Carolina, 1920s, eight versions (*North Carolina Folklore*, pp. 89–93) | *American Play-Party Song*, B. A. Botkin, 1937, pp. 328–30 | Washington County, Maryland, 1950, 'Here come three dukes a riding, With a ransom, tansom tee yi o. What are you coming here for? Our good will is to marry. Marry one of us, sirs. You're all too black and dirty. We're good enough for you, sir. You're all as stiff as pokers. We can bend as well as you, sir. Through the kitchen and through the hall, We choose the fairest of you all. The fairest one that we can see Is ——, come walk with me.' Also St Mary's County, 1950, version in which girls say they will lock all the doors and otherwise obstruct the dukes. Dukes then say 'I'll give to you a package of pins To pin your veil when you get married', etc., ending 'I'll give to you the keys of heaven To count the angels seven by seven' (Howard MSS) | Illinois, 1959, 'Here comes Dr Robey. What have you come for? I've come to get me a kewpie doll, kewpie doll, kewpie doll.'

Canada: Toronto, 1888, 'Here comes our king arriving To my Nancy Tancy Tisabyo; To my Nancy Tancy Tee' (*JAFL*, viii, p. 253) | Ontario, 1909, 'Here come three kings a-riding, My tipsy topsy officer', and two other versions (ibid., xxxi, pp. 52–3) | Harriston, Ontario, *c*.1920, 'Here come three kings a-riding, With a rancy, tancy, titty-i-o' (Fowke, 1969, p. 36).

Barbados: 1930, 'Seven Jews arrivin', Around the Darmee Sea' (*JAFL*, xliii, p. 327).

Denmark: *Danmarks Sanglege*, S. Tvermose Thyregod, 1931, pp. 1–7, 'Her kommer Offer, her kommer Ædelig, Her kommer syv Mands Ædelig, Og her kommer Kongens Bønder alle' (Here come the willing, here come the noble, Here come seven noble men, And here come the king's freemen all). The action has elements of 'Three Brethren out of Spain' (p. 92 | Copenhagen, 1973, 'Der kom en mand fra det Rode Hav, Ej-sikke-lej-sikke-ladetus. Og hva vil han fra det Rode Hav? Ej-sikke-lej-sikke-ladetus' etc. (There came a man from the Red Ocean. And what does he want, from the Red Ocean? I want to woo the king's daughter. And what will be her name? Her name will be ——. Then be pleased to take her.) The tune is similar to that usual for 'Here Comes a Duke a-Riding', as is also the manner of playing. A second game, 'Der kom en pige gående, gående, gående' (There came a girl a-walking, a-walking, a-walking) also bears comparison: the girl is offered employment at the home of a witch, refuses with the excuse that 'She looks so grim and ugly, ugly, ugly', and is told 'She is just as nice as you are, you are, you are'. Also played in Norway, 'Det kom en pike vandrende, vandrende, vandrende'.

Sweden: Uppsala, 1973, 'Vi komma ifrån Riara, Aske daske då'. (*Riara*, presumably from the Danish *Røde Hav*, Red Ocean, is here meaningless.)

Germany: *Alle Arten von Schertz- und Pfänder-spielen*, Bruder Lustigen, p. 12 (Böhme, pp. 519–

20) | *Das deutsche Kinderbuch*, Karl Simrock, 1848, p. 163, 'Hier kommen die Herren aus Nonnefei, Heiza fi Pilatus!' | *Preussische Volksreime*, Friedrich Frischbier, 1867, p. 700, as quote | *Deutsches Kinderspiel*, F. M. Böhme, 1897, pp. 508–21, 16 versions of 'Herr von Nineve'. He says the game resembles the old German stepping dance of the Middle Ages: movement forward and backward in lines, three steps sideways, and at the end a ring dance or leaping dance.

Italy: *Giuochi Popolari Veneziani*, D. G. Bernoni, 1874, pp. 43–6 | Anghiari in Tuscany, 1961 | Mantua in Lombardy, Terni in Umbria, and Sassari in Sardinia, 1967 (*Giochi*, M. M. Lumbroso, pp. 91–4, 365–6).

Chile: Santiago, 1951, 'Buenos días, su señoría, Man-dan-di-run-di-run-dan'. The suitor is asked what he wants, says he wants one of the daughters, is asked what her name will be, says she will be called 'wash-the-dishes', this does not please her. Finally suitor says she will be called 'little angel'. Mother and daughters are pleased with this name (*Rique Ran*, M. L. Goodwin and E. L. Powell, pp. 6–7).

Brazil: *Varios Juegos Infantiles del Siglo XVI*, F. R. Marín, 1932, p. 63, 'Bom dia, meu senhorio, Manda o tiro-tiro-lá'. Similar to Chile. Mother asks suitor 'What is your work?' Suitor says he is a shoemaker and is told his job is not good enough.

12

Three Brethren out of Spain

Milford Haven, Pembs., c.1910

We are three brethren out of Spain,
Come to court your daughter Jane.

My daughter Jane she is too young,
And has not learned her mother tongue.

Be she young, or be she old,
For her beauty she must be sold.
So fare you well, my lady gay,
We'll call again another day.

Turn back, turn back, thou scornful knight,
And rub thy spurs till they be bright.

Of my spurs take you no thought,
For in this town they were not bought.
So fare you well, my lady gay,
We'll call again another day.

Turn back, turn back, thou scornful knight,
And take the fairest in your sight.

> The fairest maid that I can see,
> Is pretty *Nancy*, come to me.
>
> Here comes your daughter safe and sound,
> Every pocket with a thousand pound,
> Every finger with a gay gold ring;
> Please to take your daughter in.

This game has brought glamour to school yards and back streets for two hundred years. The lines were collected, as above, by the antiquary Joseph Ritson, who printed them in *Gammer Gurton's Garland: or, The Nursery Parnassus*, 1784; and it can be assumed that at that time they were well known to the young. Most of the other rhymes in the collection were familiar ones (Ritson had asked his schoolboy nephew to write down any he knew); and the first eight lines had already appeared, as follows, in *Mother Goose's Melody*, 1780, a collection of oral verse which had possibly been assembled by Goldsmith around 1765:

> We're three brethren out of Spain
> Come to court your daughter Jane:
> My daughter Jane she is too young,
> She has no skill in a flattering tongue.
> Be she young, or be she old,
> Its for her gold she must be sold;
> So fare you well my lady gay,
> We must return another day.

It will be noticed that the wording here differs slightly from Ritson's, that both versions seem to have been set down exactly as received from oral tradition, and that neither is wholly intelligible. It is to be imagined the responses scarcely made more sense to children playing the game in the eighteenth century than they do to the young today. This, of course, adds to their wonder. The game was, and is, played like 'A Duke a-Riding' (p. 76) with which it is sometimes confused, especially when it begins 'Here comes a duke out of Spain'. It varies in that the suitors (or emissaries) are after a particular girl who is named; and that the girl is in the charge of a mother or guardian; and that the older woman, whose initial doubtfulness about the match may well be feigned, is probably bribed. In 'A Duke a-Riding' on the other hand the girls are on their own, have a girlish eagerness for a lover, and say in effect 'Take one of us—which would you like?' Yet the principal difference between the two games lies in their verse patterns. In 'A Duke a-Riding' the verses ordinarily consist of a single line and nonsense refrain, which is then repeated. In the present game the dialogue is in the form of a poetic drama; and this difference is noticeable in the parallel games in other countries; the Scots variant hereafter (p. 103), which probably had an art origin, being an exception.

Despite the quaintness of the language (compare the seventeenth-century ballad *The Maidens Delight: Or A dainty New Dialogue*), the verses retained their shape and content in the nineteenth century to a remarkable degree. In 1820 at a dame school in the City of Gloucester the little players stood in a line with one child out in front who advanced towards them saying:

> Here comes a noble knight of Spain,
> Courting to your daughter Jane.

One of the girls, acting the mother, replied:

> My daughter Jane is much too young
> To hear your false and flattering tongue.

To this the juvenile knight replied:

> Be she young, or be she old,
> For a price she must be sold.

The mother, alerted, it seems, to the chance of material gain, called after him:

> Turn back, turn back, thou scornful knight,
> And rub thy spurs, they are not bright.

To which the knight, jealous of the badge of his knighthood, responded:

> My spurs are bright and richly wrought,
> For a price they were not bought,
> Nor for a price shall they be sold,
> Neither for silver nor for gold.
> And so goodbye, my lady gay,
> For I must ride another way.

The criticism of the knight's spurs is clearly of significance. In one mid-century recording he defends them as being 'as bright as snow, and fit for any king to show'. In another, he says they are bright and were 'laid in stable all last night'. In a third, from Eccleshall in Staffordshire (1849), he declares them to be 'of a costliest wrought':

> My spurs they are of a costliest wrought,
> And in this town they were not bought;
> Nor in this town they won't be sold,
> Neither for silver nor for gold.

> So, fare you well, my lady gay,
> For I must turn another way.

And in yet another version, also mid-nineteenth century, but from Cornwall, the point is also made that the spurs were not obtained locally.

This Cornish text is also significant on other counts. It begins 'Here comes three dukes a-riding', showing the early influence of the sister game. It interposes a name-calling line 'Come back! Come back! you Spanish Jack', or, as the informant also recollected, 'Come back! Come back! you coxcomb'; and it retains the curious quatrain, reported by Ritson, in which the daughter is returned, seemingly with a reward for her services. The three dukes stood in front of the other players, who were in a long line with hands linked, the mother in the middle and the taller girls next to her. The players advanced and retreated as they sang, and one of the dukes, acting as spokesman, began:

> Here comes three dukes a-riding, a-riding,
> Here comes three dukes a-riding, to court your daughter Jane.

Mother: My daughter Jane is yet too young
        To bear your silly, flattering tongue.

Duke: Be she young or be she old,
        She for her beauty must and shall be sold.
        So fare thee well, my lady gay,
        We'll take our horse and ride away,
        And call again another day.

Mother: Come back, come back! you Spanish knight,
        And clean your spurs, they are not bright.

Duke: My spurs are bright as rickety-rock [and richly wrought?],
        And in this town they were not bought,
        And in this town they shan't be sold,
        Neither for silver, copper, nor gold.
        So fare thee well, my lady gay,
        We'll take our horse and ride away,
        And call again another day.

Then came the name-calling—paralleled in some folk plays:

Mother: Come back! come back! you Spanish Jack (*or* coxcomb).

Duke: Spanish Jack is not my name,
        I'll stamp my foot and say the same.[1]

---

[1] Compare William Walker's edition of *The Peace Egg*, originally printed before 1850:

> *St George*: Why, Jack, did ever I do thee any harm?
> *Fool*:   Thou proud saucy coxcombe, begone!
> *St George*: A coxcombe, I defy the name!
>   With a sword thou ought to be stabbed for the same.

[*cont. on p. 96*]

Whereat the mother recanted:

> Come back! come back! you Spanish knight,
> And choose the fairest in your sight.

The dukes retired, consulted together, and selected a daughter, singing:

> This is the fairest I can see,
> So pray young damsel walk with me.

Then, when all the daughters had been taken away one by one they were returned to their mother in the order they had been taken, the dukes chanting a verse that had been recorded in 1784:

> We've brought your daughter, safe and sound,
> And in her pocket a thousand pound,
> And on her finger a gay gold ring,
> We hope you won't refuse to take her in.

The circumstances leading to this request are not divulged. Whether the riches the girl brought with her confirmed that the match had been successful (as the children undoubtedly feel), or that it had failed (as a cynic might suppose), we are left to guess. We do not know whether the ring was on her wedding finger or no; nor the cause of the dukes' concern that the mother might not take her back. Were the dukes relieved, as seems to be the case, when they heard the mother's reply?

> I'll take her in with all my heart,
> For she and me were loath to part.

At Bocking in Essex, 1881, the 'gentleman' from Spain returned the girl with the words:

And *Notes & Queries*, 20 October 1860, p. 318:

> *He*:   Why, Madam, why? did I ever do you any harm?
> *She*:   Yes, yes, you saucy coxcombe, get you gone.
> *He*:   Coxcombe! Madam, I defy that very name;
>   Step to me equally as the same.

The banter turns up again in the game 'Two Old Jews' played by children at Belford about 1900 (*County Folk-Lore: Northumberland*, p. 115):

> *Mother*:   My daughter Jane she cannot come,
>   She cannot bear your flattering tongue.
>   Go away, Corkscrew!
>
> *Jew*:   My name is not Corkscrew!
>   I'll stamp my foot, and away I'll go!
>
> *Mother*:   Come back, come back, your coat is green,
>   Your feathers are the fairest seen!

And the man from Spain was still being called a corkscrew (or coxswain or cock sparrow) instead of a coxcomb in Somerset in 1922, in County Durham about 1945, and in Edinburgh in 1951.

> I've brought your daughter home safe and sound,
> With money in her pocket here, a thousand pound:
> Take your saucy girl back again.

While in London, at the end of the century, the daughter, who had left home with a thousand pounds in her pocket, was returned with neither cash nor character:

> Here's your daughter not safe or sound,
> And in her pocket no thousand pound,
> And on her finger no gay gold ring;
> Open the door and take her in.

Fortunately the young, who are able to sing complacently that 'the fate of beauty's to be sold', are untroubled by the ethics of the situation; and ordinarily, indeed, the drama ends happily. At Eccleshall in 1849, the suitor, a duke from Spain, was invited to go

> Through the kitchen, and through the hall,
> And take the fairest of them all.

He then apparently did so, replying:

> The fairest is, as I can see,
> Pretty Jane, come here to me.

And the game ended with the verse:

> Now I've got my pretty fair maid,
> Now I've got my pretty fair maid
> To dance along with me—
> To dance along with me!

The ease with which 'Three Brethren out of Spain' and 'A Duke a-Riding' can amalgamate will be appreciated; and around the turn of the century, when the suitor was often a Jew, the game very nearly lost its separate identity. Thus at Westcliff-on-Sea, about 1900, one child stood in front of the other players and sang:

> I am a Jew, just come from Spain,
> I come to see your daughter Jane,
> Your daughter Jane she is so young
> I cannot hear her rattling tongue.

The child in front offered her hand to one of the players in the row whose response was to shake her head. At this the suitor danced round and round, singing—as if taking part in a cushion dance (see p. 190):

> Naughty girl, she won't come out,
>   She won't come out, she won't come out;
> Naughty girl, she won't come out,
>   To see the ladies dancing.

The child playing the Jew then held out her hand a second time, was
accepted, and the two players joined hands and danced round together
singing:

> Pretty girl, she has come out,
>   She has come out, she has come out;
> Pretty girl, she has come out
>   To see the ladies dancing.

The game then began again, with the pair advancing while they sang 'We
are two Jews, just come from Spain'; another girl was invited to join them
from the line, and the game continued until all the girls had joined the
Jews. Alternatively the framework was retained but the dialogue became
clipped and practical, as at Axminster, in the early 1920s, where the Jew
came up announcing:

> Here comes a Jew, all dressed in blue,
> Come to court your daughter Sue.

Mother: My daughter Sue is much too young,
            To be compelled by such a one.

Jew: Let her be old, let her be young,
            'Tis her duty she should come.

Mother: Search the kitchen and the hall,
            Take the fairest of them all.

Jew: Fairest, fairest, I can see,
            Please, *Miss Mabel*, come to me.

By the 1950s the wording had been further eroded. In Aberdeen, in
1952, the children stood in a line with their backs to a wall with one player
facing them, who skipped forward and back again as she sang:

> There came a Jew, a Jew from Spain,
> To call upon my sister Jane,
> My sister Jane was far too young
> To marry a man of twenty-one.
> Fly away, flay away,
> Come back another day;
> Face to face, back to back,
> Choose the one that you love best.

She then picked someone out of the line of players standing against the wall. The person she chose said 'No'; and the Jew sang:

> Oh! the dirty rat she widdna come,
>   Widdna come, widdna come,
> Oh! the dirty rat she widdna come,
>   Ee-i-oh.

The Jew asked her again to come. This time the answer was 'Yes'; and the two players danced round together in a circle singing:

> Now we've got the fairy queen,
>   The fairy queen, the fairy queen;
> Now we've got the fairy queen,
>   Ee-i-oh.

In the third quarter of the twentieth century this soliciting by a 'king' of twenty-one (or 'a hundred-and-one'), the flying away, and the coming back face to face and back to back, was enacted throughout the land. Between 1951 and 1970 we had sightings in places as far apart as Bristol, Workington, Wolverhampton, Forfar, and Dublin, so that the old form seemed past recovery. Then in Salford, in 1975, we saw a ten-year-old wobbling backwards and forwards on her platform-soled shoes in front of a group of other ten-year-olds, singing as fluently as if it were the latest pop-song:

> There came a Jew, a Jew from Spain,
> To marry marry, me daughter Jane.
> Me daughter Jane is far too young
> To understand the Spanish tongue.
> Ku-well, ku-well, come back, come back,
> And choose the fairest you love the best.

Where, we asked them, had they learnt the game. 'Miss,' they said, 'we learned it at North Grecian Street, in the Infants.' 'Ah, you were taught it by a teacher.' 'No, Miss, we learned it off of the Juniors.'

That a game that has been sung through the years should also dance across frontiers is perhaps only to be expected. Yet it is undoubtedly a curiosity if, as appears, 'Three Brethren out of Spain' originated in the country its chief characters have always maintained they came from. Thus although it is recorded that in Württemberg, about 1850, a game of *Brautwerbung* or match-making was played in which a suitor came a-riding, asked the mother for her most charming daughter, was told she would not be allowed out of the house (her hair was not plaited, her skirt had not yet come back from the tailor), so that the gentleman bid her 'farewell', whereon the mother told him to stay (her daughter's hair was now plaited, the skirt had now arrived, and so on), reports of the game in Germany are few compared with those for 'Herr von Nineve'; and in France, likewise, the game of 'Bonjour madame La Marceline' or 'Bonjour, madame La Postologne', in which the visitor seeks a girl for a convent, has the request refused even in return for gold, and falls into a passion, seems to have had only local circulation. In Portugal, however, an entertainment has long been popular which will be instantly recognized, the following version being recorded by Father Damian Webb in Sta Leocádia, Minho, in 1960:

Condessa, linda Condessa,	(Countess, lovely Countess,
Condessa do Alagar,	Countess of the Alagar,
Venho-te pedi-las filhas	I come to ask for one of your daughters
Para comigo casar.	To marry me.
Minhas filhas não tas dou	I'm not giving you my daughters,
Nem por ouro nem por prata,	Not for gold, nor for silver,
Nem por fio d'algodão,	Nor for thread of cotton,
Nem por laço de lagarta.	Nor for lizard's blood.
Que as quero meter freira	For I want to put them as sisters
No convento de Jesus;	In the convent of Jesus;
Que là está o nome escrito—	For there is written the name—
Condessa Dona da Cruz.	Countess Lady of the Cross.
Que tão contente que eu vinha,	How happy I was as I was coming,
Tão triste me vou achar;	How sad I must be in the end.
Pedi filhas a condessa—	I asked the countess for her daughters—
Condessa não mas quis dar.	The countess didn't want to give me them.
Volt' atrás ó cavalheiro	Turn back, sir,
Que eu abri os meus portais:	Because I've opened my gates.
Escolhei as mais bonitas	Choose the most beautiful ones
Que neste rancho achais.	That you find in this company.
Não quero esta por ser cravo,	I don't want this one as she is a pink,
Nem quero esta por ser lagarta,	Nor do I want this one as she's a lizard,
Quero esta por carvalhinha,	I want this one: a *carvalhinha* (a flower),
Condessa que eu vi com dor.	Countess whom I have met with suffering.)

This game, 'A Condessa', which Portugal's poet-president, Theophilo Braga (born 1843), thought worthy of being considered an organic part of the Portuguese theatre, is renowned in Latin America where closely-related songs have been found in the Argentine, Bolivia, Brazil, Chile, Mexico, and Nicaragua. Yet it is in Spain where the most significant texts are to be found and the roots are most deeply embedded. In a Catalan version, 'La Conversa del Rey moro', the dialogue takes place between an ambassador and the king of the Moors. The ambassador arrives, and after making a low bow, and observing the formalities of the court, he informs the king:

> Of the daughters that you have
> I should like you to give me one.

The king replies:

> If I have any, or if I have none,
> I do not have them to give away;
> If I have any, or if I have none,
> I do not have them for you.
> The bread that I eat
> They shall eat also.

At this the ambassador begins to leave:

> I go away much discontented
> From the palace of the King.

But the king calls after him:

> Turn back, turn back, thou knight[1]
> I will give you the most lovely,
> The most lovely and the bravest,
> The bonniest rose upon the tree.

The ambassador returns, saying:

> This one I will take for bride,
> For bride and for wife.

The king bids him take good care of her, and the ambassador assures him:

> She will be cosseted,
> Seated in a chair of gold;
> She will sleep in the arms of the King.
> Adieu, pearl and carnation!

Happily, what might have been mere speculation, that such a game was played in Spain in the days of Don Quixote, can be shown to be virtual

---

[1] *Escudereta*. In other versions he is referred to as *escuders*, *caballero*, and *cavaleiro*.

certainty. In an anonymous comedy quoted by Marín, *Baile curioso de Pedro de Brea*, printed in Barcelona in 1616, several children's games are introduced, and the following lines are amongst them:

> —I am the Heron, the Heron am I,
> How well I am attended!

> —I bow to you, Heron.

> —I bow to you, Count.

> —If one of these maidens
> Who you have about you
> You like to give me for wife
> I will bless my good luck.

> —Be assured, Sir Count,
> That they are not for you;
> That to a higher rank
> Their haughty character aspires.
> I am the Heron, the Heron am I,
> How well I am attended!

> —I depart very angry
> To the palaces of the King;
> For the daughter of the Moorish king
> Is not given me for wife.

Further, in *Daca mi mujer*, an interlude by Lope de Vega (born 1562), another quotation is apparent, the game seeming to have been so well known it was felt a mere allusion would raise a smile:

> *Sacristán*: Suegro, a mi mujer.
> *Padre*:   ¿Suegro? Daca la mohosa.
> *Sacristán*: Pues me niegas la suegrez,
>   *enojado me voy, enojado*
>   *a los palacios del rey . . .*

(Because you deny her to me, *Angered I go, angered to the palaces of the king . . .*)

Britain: *Mother Goose's Melody: or, Sonnets for the Cradle*, 1780 (1791, p. 67), as quote | *Gammer Gurton's Garland*, 1784, as text | *Notes & Queries*, 1st ser., iv, 1852, pp. 241–2, 'Here comes a poor Duke out of Spain', believed to be 'common in many parts of England' | Gloucester and Kent, c.1820 (*Notes & Queries*, 5th ser., iv, pp. 51 and 157) | Cambridgeshire, and Eccleshall in Staffordshire, 1849 (*Popular Rhymes*, J. O. Halliwell, pp. 123–4) | Cornwall, c.1851 (*Folk-Lore*, v, pp. 46–7) | Kendal, Westmorland, c.1865 | Bocking, Essex, 1881, 'I am a gentleman come from Spain' (*Folk-Lore Record*, iii, p. 171) | *Cassell's Book of In-door Amusements*, 1881, pp. 42–3,

'I am a nobleman from Spain' | Market Drayton, and elsewhere in Shropshire, 1883, 'Here comes Three Knights all out of Spain' described as 'common' (*Shropshire Folk-Lore*, C. S. Burne, p. 516) | Eyemouth, Berwickshire, 1893, 'Here's one old Jew, just come from Spain' (*Antiquary*, xxx, pp. 15–16) | *Merrie Games in Rhyme*, E. M. Plunket, 1886, pp. 60–1, 'I am a knight all out of Spain' | *Traditional Games*, ii, 1898, pp. 257–79, 35 recordings, including 'We are three suitors come from Spain', from Dublin, and 'There were three lords they came from Spain', from Belfast; also the suitors' retort 'Eighteen pence would buy such a wench, As either you or your daughter Jane', from Middlesex | Frequently recorded hereafter. Versions from 9 places since 1960.

Australia: Toowoomba, Queensland, *c*.1900, 'We are three Jews from Spanish main'.

New Zealand: Auckland, *c*.1887, 'Here comes a Duke a-riding, a-riding', and similar (Sutton-Smith, pp. 25–6).

USA: New York, 'early part' of nineteenth century, 'Here come three lords out of Spain'; also New England, *c*.1840, Philadelphia, and Cincinnati, *c*.1880 (*Games of American Children*, pp. 39–42) | Avery County, North Carolina, *c*.1927, 'We are three fine kings of Spain', played by grown-ups at a molasses boiling (*North Carolina Folklore*, p. 93).

Spain: *Baile curioso de Pedro de Brea* in *Comedias de diferentes autores*, pt. v, 1616, 'Yo la Garza' | *Jochs de la Infancia*, F. Maspons y Labrós, 1874, pp. 47–9 | *Varios Juegos Infantiles del Siglo XVI*, F. R. Marín, 1932, pp. 55–63.

Portugal, and Portuguese language: *O Povo Portuguez*, Theophilo Braga, i, 1885, pp. 335–7, 'Aqui as vimos pedir Pera com ellas casar'. To which the Condessa replies 'Neither for gold, nor for silver, Nor for dragon's blood, Will I give my daughters Nor show where they are'. The seven boys respond 'Tão alegres que vinhemos!'—'With what joy we came! With what sorrow we go! That the daughters of the Condessa Are not to be taken as wives.' The Condessa summons them back, 'Volvei a mim cavalleiros', and with compliments on both sides each boy in turn chooses the daughter he likes best | *Revista de Dialectologia y Tradiciones Populares*, x, 1954, pp. 591–643, 60 versions of 'A Condessa' from Portugal, Spain, and South America, brought together by Theó Brandão.

Mexico: *Artes de Mexico*, no. 162, 1973, p. 28.

13

Three Brethren Come from Spain (Scots version)

We are three brethren come from Spain,
　　All in French garlands;
We are come to court your daughter Jean,
　　And adieu to you, my darlings.

Our daughter Jean she is too young,
　　All in French garlands;
She cannot bide your flattering tongue,
　　So adieu to you, my darlings.

Be she young, or be she old,
　　All in French garlands;
It's for a bride she must be sold,
　　So adieu to you, my darlings.

A bride, a bride she shall not be,
    All in French garlands,
Till she go through this world with me,
    So adieu to you, my darlings.

Come back, come back, you courteous knight,
    All in French garlands;
Clear up your spurs, and make them bright,
    And adieu to you, my darlings.

Smell my lilies, smell my roses,
    All in French garlands;
Which of my maidens do ye choose?
    And adieu to you, my darlings.

Are all your daughters safe and sound?
    All in French garlands;
Are all your daughters safe and sound?
    And adieu to you, my darlings.

In every pocket a thousand pound,
    All in French garlands;
On every finger a gay gold ring,
    And adieu to you, my darlings.

This text was reprinted, with minor alterations, by Robert Chambers in 1842. It had first appeared as a recollection, believed to be imperfect, in *Chambers's Edinburgh Journal*, 26 October 1833. Since Robert Chambers was himself the chief contributor to the *Journal*, as well as being the Joint-Editor, it is not unlikely the description of the game was his; particularly as, seven years earlier, he had listed 'We are three brethren come from Spain' amongst games 'upon which our information is already almost complete'. In this 'operatic game', stated the *Journal*, 'One range of girls take their station at a wall, while another, twining their arms together behind their backs, commence moving backwards and forwards to the measure of the music'. They sang the first verse 'to a very pretty air' while advancing, and when they had finished retreated at the same measured pace, while the 'wall-stationed party' sang the second verse. The 'moveable party' then advanced again singing the third verse; and the mother, who remained by the wall all the while, refused her consent. At this point the writer thought—incorrectly as it now seems—that a verse or verses had been forgotten, since 'the maternal party' immediately relented; and offered 'a choice of their daughters, in the following elegant terms':

> Smell my lilies, smell my roses,
>   All in French garlands;
> Which of my maidens do ye choose?
> And adieu to you, my darlings.

'The lover now becomes fastidious in proportion to the concessions of the opposite party, and affects to scruple about the bodily sanity of the young ladies.' However he seemed reassured by the answer he received, and the match-making proceeded.

This ballad-style version of 'Three Brethren out of Spain' (p. 92) appears to have had a fair circulation in Scotland in the nineteenth century. Four little girls were heard singing at least the first verse on the pier at Kirkwall, Orkney, sometime in the middle of the century:

We three— suit - ors— come from Spain,
My dear— dar - ling: All— [for] to court your
daught -er Jane, And a -dieu to you— my— dar - ling.

Ancient Orkney Melodies, *D. Balfour, 1885*[1]

It was picked up by a Scots contributor to *Notes & Queries* in 1864. It was found in Perth, though in poor health, by Walter Gregor at the end of the century. And, interestingly, the flower-smelling sequence was reported in Argyllshire at the beginning of the present century, although the words accompanied a guessing game played in the manner of 'Queenie' (*Street and Playground*, pp. 290–2). Three girls, representing the Spanish brothers, stood out in front while the rest faced them in a row, one being the mother and the others being daughters, one of whom tried not to show that she was holding a ball. The brothers advanced, singing:

[1] In the fifteenth-century Scots poem 'Cockelbie Sow' a dance is named called 'My deir derling', but it appears to have been a ring dance.

> Here's three brethren come from Spain,
> For to court your daughter Jane.

Mother: My daughter Jane is too young,
She cannot bear a flattering tongue.

Brothers: Come be she young, come be she old,
A bride, a bride she must be sold.

Mother: A bride, a bride she'll never be
Till she comes through this world with me.

The brothers made no reply. They began walking away, making believe they would leave without a daughter, knowing full well this was something no mother could endure—although only in the world of childhood could her invitation to prospective sons-in-law be thought conventional:

> Come taste of my lily and smell of my rose,
> And which of them all do you choose?

The brothers named the girl they thought was secreting the ball; and if they guessed correctly, she and her mother and one other girl took their place; but if they guessed incorrectly the mother showed her disdain:

> The ball is ours, it's none of yours,
> Go to the garden and pluck your flowers.
> We have pins to pin our clothes,
> You have nails to nail your nose.

The flower-smelling lines had earlier occurred in the old game of 'Lady Queen Anne', played in the same way, which Chambers had recorded in Scotland in 1847:

> Come smell my lily, come smell my rose,
> Which of my maidens do you choose?

And curiously, somewhat similar imagery occurs in parallel games on the Continent. In 'Golden Ear-rings', as recorded by Katherine Lee Bates, in *Spanish Highways and Byways*, 1900, the following dialogue takes place between a suitor and one of the daughters:

> 'Will you come with me, my Onion?'
> 'Fie! that's a kitchen smell.'

> 'Will you come with me, my Rosebud?'
> 'Ay, gardens please me well.'

In the Iberian game 'A Condessa', which has been traced back to the sixteenth century (see p. 100), the chosen daughter is often said to be a

rose amongst carnations. In a version collected at Sta Leocádia, Geraz-
do-Lima, in Portugal in 1960, the suitor sang:

> I don't want this one as she is a carnation,
> Nor do I want this one as she is dark,
> I want a rose, as this one is,
> The queen of the lily.

And in Italy, likewise, in the game 'Madame Dorè', as played in Florence
in the 1960s, there is a floral interlude when the match-maker says:

> I'll marry her to a rose, Madame Dorè,
>   I'll marry her to a rose.

'No, no,' responds the mother, 'we are not happy about that.'

Scotland: *Popular Rhymes of Scotland*, Robert Chambers, 1826, p. 299, listed; 1842, p.
66 | *Chambers's Edinburgh Journal*, ii, 1833, pp. 308–9 | Kirkwall, Orkney, *c.*1850 (*Ancient
Orkney Melodies*, David Balfour, 1885, pp. 71 and 86) | *Notes & Queries*, 3rd ser., v, 1864, p.
393 | Perth, 1898 (*Traditional Games*, ii, p. 270) | *Games of Argyleshire*, R. C. Maclagan, 1901,
pp. 90–1.

14

Six Virgins

> There comes six virgins on their knee.
>
> When do they come?
>
> They come by night as well as by day,
> To take thy daughter *Mabel* away.
>
> My daughter *Mabel* is yet too young,
> To stay away from her mam.
>
> Whether she's old or whether she's young,
> We'll take her as her am.
>
> Don't let her gallop or don't let her trot,
> Don't let her carry the mustard pot.
>
> She shall gallop and she shall trot,
> And she shall carry the mustard pot.

In the early 1920s A. S. Macmillan collected four versions of this game,
three being from East Devon (Alfington, Kilmington, and, as above, from

Yarcombe), and one from a place unknown. All were of a similar pattern with the virgins in a line on one side and the mother with her daughters lined up facing them, although at Alfington the game opened with only three virgins, and at Kilmington with but one:

> Here comes a virgin on bended knee,
> To ask for your daughter *Mary*.

However the number of virgins at the beginning is scarcely important, since, as in other games of this type, the predatory side usually increases as the game proceeds. The virgin, having advanced and announced herself, was asked where she came from. She replied:

> I came by night, I came by day,
> To take thy loving daughter *Mary* away.

She was rebuffed without courtesy: 'My daughter is far too good to mix with such as you.' At which the virgin began to walk away; but in three of the four versions the delegation was recalled with such words as: 'Come back, come back, and show me your dirty boots.' The virgin or virgins replied:

> Behold my boots both clean and bright,
> I bought them at the shop last night.

The mother then agreed to the daughter being taken, provided she was not allowed to gallop or trot, or to carry, or to be thrown into, the mustard pot, a memory, it seems, of the servant-hiring game 'Widow from Babylon' (p. 113) as played in Dorset in the 1880s, which in turn is reminiscent of the nursery dobbin who could amble and could trot, and could carry a mustard pot (*ODNR*, pp. 209–10).

Clearly the game is an offshoot of 'Three Brethren out of Spain'; and might have been thought to have been merely a local aberration, were it not that Alice Gomme reported the same game being played some thirty years earlier at Hurstmonceux, under the name 'Here Comes One Virgin'. There, too, the virgin arrived on one knee, was asked when she came, explained that she came by night and by day, and admitted she had come 'To steal poor *Edie* away'. Presumably it is a relic of a game that once existed in England, as commonly on the Continent, in which a daughter was sought not to become a bride but to enter a convent.

Hurstmonceux, Sussex, 1894 (*Traditional Games*, i, p. 203) | East Devon, *c.*1922, four places.

15

Three Sailors

last two verses:

adapted from Traditional Games, *ii*

Here come three sailors, three by three,
To court your daughter, fair lady,
And down by the door we bend our knee,
Can we have lodgings here?

Sleep, my daughter, do not wake,
For here are sailors we can't take;
By the door they bend their knee,
They cannot have lodgings here.

Here come three soldiers, three by three,
To court your daughter, fair lady,
And down by the door we bend our knee,
Can we have lodgings here?

Sleep, my daughter, do not wake,
For here are soldiers we can't take;
By the door they bend their knee,
They cannot have lodgings here.

> Here come three princes, three by three,
> To court your daughter, fair lady,
> And down by the door we bend our knee,
> Can we have lodgings here?
>
> Wake, my daughter, do not sleep,
> For here are princes we can take;
> By the door they bend their knee,
> They can have lodgings here.
>
> Here's my daughter, safe and sound,
> And in her pocket one thousand pounds,
> And on her finger a golden ring,
> She is fit to marry a king.
>
> Here's your daughter, not safe nor sound,
> And in her pocket no thousand pounds,
> And on her finger no golden ring,
> She is not fit to marry a king.

These verses were sung in South Wales in the 1880s in yet another game in which a line of suitors approach, are rejected, go away, try again, and are eventually accepted. Elsewhere in Britain the would-be lodgers have declared themselves to be 'sweeps', 'bakers', 'butchers', 'farmers', and 'kings'; but the verses themselves were sung with little variation in the nineteenth century wherever the game was played—an indication, perhaps, that it had been adopted in the playground only recently. In addition the last two verses seem to be borrowings from elsewhere (see 'Widow from Babylon' and 'Three Brethren out of Spain'); although it must be remarked they were also a regular feature of the game in America. In Charleston, West Virginia, for instance, in the 1880s, the daughter was handed over with the words:

> Here is my daughter safe and sound,
> And in her pocket five hundred pound,
> And on her finger a plain gold ring,
> And she is fit to walk with the king.

She was taken away, and then returned with the words:

> Here is your daughter *not* safe and sound,
> And in her pocket *not* five hundred pound,
> And on her finger no plain gold ring,
> And she's not fit to walk with the king.

In America as in Britain, this verse was rationalized with the explanation

that the travellers were not princes or kings but robbers in disguise. The
players went through the motions of stripping the daughter of her purse,
ring, and finery, and pushing her back to her mother, who then usually
gave chase to the robbers, and the one she caught became the mother in
the next round. The basic theme of a guardian rejecting all suitors not
known to be of noble blood is commonplace on the Continent of Europe.
However in North Carolina, and some other states, a game called 'Hog
Drovers' or 'Swine Herders' was more tolerant in its attitude, and seems to
have been wonderfully popular at play-parties, and to have been still a part
of homestead jollifications in the 1920s. Generally a girl and a man—often
an oldish man—sat on chairs side by side or with the girl on the man's
knee, and another man and a girl walked round them singing:

> Hog-drivers, hog-drivers, hog-drivers we air [are].
> A-courtin' your darter so sweet and fair;
> And kin we git lodgin' here, O here—
> And kin we git lodgin' here?

The father replied:

> Now this is my darter that sets by my side (*or*, on my knee),
> And no hog-driver can get 'er fer a bride (*or*, from me);
> And you kain't git lodgin' here, O here—
> And you kain't git lodgin' here, O here.

The hog-drivers retorted:

> Yer darter is pretty, yer ugly yerself,
> So we'll travel on further and seek better wealth,
> And we don't want lodgin' here, O here—
> And we don't want lodgin' here.

In the meantime the girl had told her father who she would like as a
partner, and the father made known his name, singing:

Now this is my darter that sets by my side,
And Mr —— kin git 'er fer a bride,
And he kin git lodgin' here, O here—
And he kin git lodgin' here.

The girl then left her father, joined her chosen partner, and another girl
took her place. This continued until all the players were paired. Then the
last girl and the father stood up and joined hands to make an arch, singing:

Come under, come under, my honey, my love, my heart's above—
Come under, come under, below Galilee.

The other players passed under in pairs; but each time a pair attempted to
pass under a second time they were caught by the arch, with the words:

We've caught you as a prisoner, my honey, my love, my heart's above—
We've caught you as a prisoner, below Galilee.

They would then be instructed to kiss, and not be released until they had
done so:

Then hug 'er neat, and kiss 'er sweet,
    My honey, my love, my heart's above—
Then hug 'er nice, and kiss 'er twice,
    Below Galilee.

Whether the game 'Three Jolly Butchers', named by Edward Moor in
his *Suffolk Words* as being played in Suffolk in the eighteenth century, was
some such game as the 'Three Sailors' or the 'Hog Drovers' is now
impossible to say.

Britain: Juniper, Oxfordshire, 1880s, 'Here come three tinkers' (*Lark Rise*, F. Thompson, 1939,
pp. 160–1) | South Wales, *c*.1885, as text | *Merrie Games in Rhyme*, E. M. Plunket, 1886, pp.
28–9, 'Here come three tinkers'. Ends: 'A fig for your daughter, another for yourself, Three
farthings more would get a far better wife, We will not take a lodging here, Oh! here, We will not
take a lodging here' (probably from Ireland) | Golspie, 1892, 'Here's three sweeps' (*Golspie*, E.
W. B. Nicholson, pp. 169–70) | Berkshire, 1893 (*Antiquary*, xxvii, p. 194) | Aberdeen,
Norfolk, London, Surrey, Kent, and Isle of Man, 1898 (*Traditional Games*, ii, pp. 283–9) | *Old
Hampshire Singing Games*, A. E. Gillington, 1909, pp. 12–13 | Taunton, *c*.1910 | Somerset,
1912 (*Children's Singing Games*, Cecil Sharp, iii, pp. 6–7) | Glasgow, 1912, 'Here's three
beggars, three by three' (*Kerr's Guild of Play*, p. 39).
    Cf. County Leitrim, *c*.1875, prank-like game played at wakes, 'Here's a tailor so neat and so

fine, He's come to court a daughter of thine'. Father: 'I'll set my nine daughters down by my knee, And it's no tailor will get a wife from me' (*Folk-Lore*, v. p. 190) | *Irish Wake Amusements*, Seán Ó Súilleabháin, 1967, pp. 93–4, 'Nine Daughters'.

USA: Charleston, West Virginia, 1883 (*Games of American Children*, pp. 46–7) | Washington DC, 1888, 'Here come three sweeps' (*American Anthropologist*, i, pp. 259–60) | St Louis, 1895 (*JAFL*, lx, pp. 2–3) | Rutherford County, *c*.1927, 'Three Bakers'. After the bakers have become farmers, soldiers, sailors, and finally kings, and been accepted, the kings reply 'If she won't have us when we're pore, We'll leave your house and court no more' (*North Carolina Folklore*, pp. 99–100) | Hog-driver versions: Blue Ridge Mountains, N. Carolina, *c*.1850 (*JAFL*, xiii, p. 104) | Asheville, N. Carolina, 1903 (*Games of American Children*, pp. 232–4) | Ypsilanti, *c*.1915, 'Two Wagoners' (*JAFL*, xxiii, p. 131) | *North Carolina Folklore*, pp. 94–8, four texts from the 1920s | Oklahoma, *c*.1930, three texts, including the hog-drivers' retort 'Don't care for your daughter, much less for yourself, I'll bet you five dollars we better ourselves' (*American Play-Party Song*, B. A. Botkin, pp. 206–8).

16

Widow from Babylon

Kerr's Guild of Play, *Glasgow*, *1912*
(*accompanies a shorter text*)

Here's a poor widow from Babylon,
With six poor children all alone;
One can bake, and one can brew,
One can shape, and one can sew,
One can sit at the fire and spin,
One can bake a cake for the king.
Come choose you east, come choose you west,
Come choose the one that you love best.

'Here's a Poor Widow from Babylon' was moderately popular in England and Scotland from the 1840s to the 1920s, and is still so in Ireland. In Scotland, as described in 1842, the game was played by a ring of girls with

one player in the middle who was asked, in the above words, to choose the
one she loved best. She replied, with the felicity granted by tradition:

> I choose the fairest that I do see,
> *Jeanie Hamilton*, ye'll come to me.

The girl named entered the ring, and those who remained sang with one
voice:

> Now they're married, I wish them joy,
> Every year a girl or boy;
> Loving each other like sister and brother,
> I pray this couple may kiss together.

The two girls within the ring then kissed; the girl who was first in the
middle joined the circle, and she who had been chosen became the
chooser, the game continuing until everyone had had a turn.

This manner of playing the game was also described in England in
1849. But the girls' interpretation of their rôles may, under the influence
of 'Here's a poor widow, she's left alone' (see 'Silly Old Man', p. 202),
have been over-romantic. When Halliwell first met the game, under the
name 'The Lady of the Land', there was no kissing, no marrying, and no
loving 'like sister and brother'. In the text he printed in 1844 the mother
was not on the look-out for suitors for her daughters but for situations in
domestic service:

> Here comes a poor woman from baby-land,
> With three small children in her hand:
> One can brew, the other can bake,
> The other can make a pretty round cake.
> One can sit in the garden and spin,
> Another can make a fine bed for the king;
> Pray ma'am will you take one in?[1]

Subsequent descriptions have mostly told of the game being played in
the manner of the others in this section. The poor woman brought her
children forward to be inspected by a mistress, singing as she did so. One
of them was chosen, she parted with the child, and retired. In Dorset in the
1880s, and for years thereafter in the West Country, the mother brought
her children up to the mistress, saying or singing:

---

[1] Halliwell (1844) also gave a culinary couplet which he suggested belonged to the game:

> I can make diet bread, Thick and thin;
> I can make diet bread, Fit for the king.

But almost certainly he had obtained these lines independently. They appear in *Tom Tit's Song
Book*, *c.*1790.

> Here comes the lady of the land,
> With all her children in her hand,
> Please do you want a servant today?

The lady asked:

> What can she do?

The mother replied:

> She can brew, she can bake,
> She can make a wedding cake
> Fit for you or any lady in the land.

The lady would say:

> Leave her.

The mother would say—unexpectedly in the circumstances:

> I leave my daughter safe and sound,
> And in her pocket a thousand pound,
> And on her finger a gay gold ring,
> And I hope to find her so again.[1]

This procedure was repeated until all the children had been taken, the mistress sometimes assuring the mother:

> I'll take her in with all my heart,
> And if I do I'll dress her smart.

A few days or weeks were then supposed to elapse; and the mother returned to see how her children were faring. The lady, however, refused to let her see them. The mother called again; and the lady again made excuses why the children could not be seen. Then the children began to escape from the lady and return to their mother, who asked each of them in turn, 'What did she do to you, my dear?' One child would answer 'She cut off my nose and made a nose pie'. Another would say 'She took out my eyes and made a figged pudden, and woulden give me none'. Each child told of a terrible operation she had endured; and the game ended with the mother and children chasing the lady and putting her in prison. William Brighty Rands had good cause, it seems, for saying that the 'Poor Woman from Baby's Land' was a children's game 'I do not understand'.

---

[1] In Scotland, more realistically:

> And now, poor Mary, she is gone,
> Without a farthing in her hand,
> Without as much as a guinea gold ring,
> Goodbye, Mary, goodbye.

Some of our older informants have recalled the poignancy of the game. 'At this point a sensitive child was known to burst into tears.'

Britain: *Popular Rhymes of Scotland*, R. Chambers, 1842, p. 65, as text | *Nursery Rhymes of England*, J. O. Halliwell, 1844, p. 121 | *Popular Rhymes*, J. O. Halliwell, 1849, pp. 132–3 | Milngavie, Glasgow, *c.*1875, 'Here's an old widow from Sandy's land' (Crofton MS, ii, p. 36) | Dorset, 1889, 'Here comes the Lady of the Land' and 'There camed a lady of the land' (*Folk-Lore Journal*, vii, pp. 227–9) | Golspie, 1892 (*Golspie*, E. W. B. Nicholson, p. 158) | Berkshire, 1893, 'Here comes an old woman from Cumberland' (*Antiquary*, xxvii, p. 254) | *Traditional Games*, i, 1894, pp. 313–19, 'Here is a poor widow from Sandy Row' (Belfast), 'from Sandalam' (Forest of Dean), 'from Sandyland' (Ballynascaw, County Down), and others; also ii, 1898, pp. 438–9, 'There came a poor widow from Sunderland' (Fraserburgh), 'from Sankelone' (Cullen, Banffshire), 'We're three young mothers from Babylon' (Isle of Man) | *Games of Argyleshire*, 1901, pp. 63–5, 'Here's a poor widow from land and sand' | *Whittingham Vale, Northumberland*, D. D. Dixon, 1895, p. 270 | Banffshire, *c.*1910, 'I'm a poor woman from Switzerland' | Forfar, *c.*1910 | Glasgow, 1912 (*Kerr's Guild of Play*, p. 17) | Lanarkshire *c.*1915? (*Dae Ye Min' Langsyne?* A. S. Fraser, p. 124) | Devon and Somerset, 1922 (Macmillan Collection) | *Street Games of North Shields Children*, M. and R. King, 1926, p. 22 | Golspie, 1953 | Swansea, 1960, for skipping.

Ireland: Dublin, 1975, 'Here's the old woman from Sandy Land' (*All In! All In!*, Eilís Brady, pp. 105–6) | Dublin, 1976, 'still very popular'.

USA: Philadelphia, 1883, 'There comes a poor widow from Barbary-land' (*Games of American Children*, p. 56) | Washington, DC, 1886, 'Here comes an old woman from Barbary' (*Lippincott's Magazine*, xxxvii, p. 246) | Cincinnati, 1908, 'There came an old lady from Germany' or 'Barbary'. Version much influenced by 'A Duke a-Riding' (*JAFL*, xl, pp. 9–10).

Cf. 'Mother the Cake is Burning' in *Street and Playground*, pp. 317–29, especially pp. 324–5.

17

Green Grass

Forfar, c.1880

A dis, a dis, a green grass,
    A dis, a dis, a dis;
Come all ye pretty fair maids,
    And dance along with us.

For we are going a-roving,
    A-roving in this land;
We'll take this pretty fair maid,
    We'll take her by the hand.

Ye shall get a duke, my dear,
   And ye shall get a drake;
And ye shall get a young prince,
   A young prince for your sake.

And if this young prince chance to die,
   Ye shall get another;
The bells will ring, and the birds will sing,
   And we'll all clap hands together.

'Green Grass' was in vogue from the 1820s to the 1920s, during which time it seems to have been known in three or four forms according to where it was played. The above verses, recorded in Scotland in 1842, were general in the northern part of Britain from, it is believed, about 1825 to the end of the century, the game being a simple one with a number of girls standing in a row 'from which two retire, and again approach hand in hand' singing the first couple of verses, then selecting a girl from the group, taking her by the hand, and singing the next two verses. 'Then there is a chorus and clapping of hands' (Chambers). In the north midlands the verses differed in that the suitors offered bribes, which at first were resisted. They might begin 'Dossy, dossy green grass' and invite the others to dance; but often the opening was rationalized and the two suitors out in front were matter-of-fact in their approach:

Stepping up the green grass,
   Thus and thus and thus,
Will you let one of your fair maids
   Come and play with us?

We will give you pots and pans,
   We will give you brass,
We will give you anything
   For a pretty lass.

The rest refused the offer:

We won't take your pots and pans,
   We won't take your brass;
We won't take your anything
   For a pretty lass.

The pair retired, and advanced again, singing as before, but with an increased bid:

> Stepping up the green grass,
>   Thus and thus and thus;
> Will you let one of your fair maids
>   Come and play with us?
>
> We will give you gold and silver,
>   We will give you pearl,
> We will give you anything
>   For a pretty girl.

This time the row yielded. The two children took the first girl in the row, and danced round with her singing 'Come my dearest *Mary*', or whatever was her name:

> Come my dearest *Mary*,
>   Come and play with us;
> You shall have a young man,
>   Born for your sake.
> And the bells shall ring,
> And the cats shall sing,
> And we'll all clap hands together.

The performance continued until each girl had been led out in turn, the last part of the game being called 'the wedding' (Sheffield, 1888).

In the south of England, and also possibly in Ireland, the game was beholden to the cushion dance. The older children formed a line and sang as they advanced:

> Here we come up the green grass,
>   The green grass, the green grass;
> Here we come up the green grass
>   On a dusty, dusty day.
>
> Fair maid, pretty maid,
>   Give your hand to me,
> You shall see the prettiest sight
>   That ever you care to see.
>
> You shall see the cuckoo,
>   The blackbird and the wren,
> You shall see the pretty man
>   That wanted you to come.

'Will you come?' they asked. The youngest of the younger children answered 'No'; and, according to Emmeline Plunket (1835–1924), the elders danced off 'in high dudgeon', singing as they went:

> Naughty Miss, she won't come out,
>   She won't come out, she won't come out;
> Naughty Miss, she won't come out,
>   To help us with our dancing.

The elders advance again and sing the first verse. The youngest child now answers 'Yes', and the elders take her by the hand, and dance off singing:

> Now we have our bonny lass,
>   Our bonny lass, our bonny lass,
> Now we have our bonny lass,
>   To help us in our dancing.

In America the game, or rather the verses, seem to have been known only in a close-cropped state, the strange 'dis a dis' being literarily, if not literally, worn to dust, as in Philadelphia, about 1860:

> Tread, tread the green grass,
>   Dust, dust, dust;
> Come all ye pretty fair maids
>   And walk along with us.
>
> If you be a fair maid,
>   As I suppose you be,
> I'll take you by the lily-white hand
>   And lead you across the sea.

Collaterals of 'a dis, a dis' include 'a diss, a dass', 'a dish, a dish', 'dissy duss', 'dossy doss', 'dusty dust', 'dusty day', 'a dust, a dust', 'thus and thus', and 'the merry buss', a concordance of sounds that naturally promotes speculation. Newell thought 'a dis, a dis' might come from the Scots word *adist* meaning 'on this side', as opposed to *ayont*, 'on the far side', as in 'I wish you was neither adist her, nor ayont her', when a person is seen in the company of a woman of ill-repute. Again 'a dis, a dis' may be thought to invoke the name of Dis, from whom, according to the Gauls, the Druids were descended; and to non-sequitarians the fact that his name should be remembered in the Scottish lowlands where the people have been declared to be of Gallic extraction is considered significant. Again, it cannot be certain that green is here a colour, and not the old Scottish verb *grene* or *green*, 'to long for' (cf. *gern*, 'to yearn'), and that grass or griss does not come from *greis* or *gries*, meaning gravel, which is not so out-of-the-way as might appear when the widespread funereal witch-dance is remembered, 'Green gravel, green gravel, the grass is so green' (p. 239). And most strange is the account of saining or blessing of a corpse in the Scottish lowlands given by William Henderson in *Notes on the Folk Lore of the Northern Counties*, 1866, pp. 36–7, apparently on the strength of a manuscript of some fifty years earlier. When the body had been washed and laid out, a candle lit, a dish of salt placed on the breast of the corpse, and three empty dishes arranged near the fire or on a table, the attendants went out of the room and returned into it backwards. This rite was called 'Dishaloof'—which is also the name of a boys' game in which hands are piled on top of each other, the bottom-most being withdrawn and smacked on the top of the pile—and the proceedings continued with the customary sports and prognostications of a lyke-wake. But before the refreshments were brought in, according to Henderson, 'the company join hands and dance round the dishes, singing this burden, "A dis, a dis, a dis, a green griss, a dis, a dis, a dis".' Only then were bread, cheese and spirits placed on the table, and when the company had partaken of them they were at liberty to go home. Thus perhaps the game belongs more to a burial than a wedding. The reassuring last verse was not uncommon in the nineteenth century, as at Berrington in Shropshire, 1883:

> Suppose this young man was to die,
>   And leave the poor girl a widow;
> The bells would ring and we should sing,
>   And all clap hands together.

North Britain: *Popular Rhymes of Scotland*, 1842, p. 66 | Lanark, *c.*1855, and Biggar, *c.*1860? (*Traditional Games*, i, pp. 154–5) | *Notes & Queries*, 3rd ser., v, 1864, p. 393 | Morpeth, 1879, and recalled from Durham, *c.*1825 (*Folk-Lore of the Northern Counties*, W. Henderson, 2nd edn., 1879, p. 26) | Forfar, *c.*1880 | Peterhead and Perth, 1898 (*Traditional Games*, ii, pp. 426–7).

North Midlands: *Sheffield Glossary*, 1888, p. 239 | Frodingham, Lincolnshire; Nottinghamshire; and Congleton, Cheshire, 1894 (*Traditional Games*, i, pp. 157–8 and 161–2) | Cf. *Nursery Rhymes of England*, J. O. Halliwell, 1842, pp. 126–7 | *Shropshire Folk-Lore*, C. S. Burne, 1883, p. 511.

South: Middlesex, *c.*1850 (*English County Songs*, p. 107) | London and Liphook, 1894 (*Traditional Games*, i, pp. 159–61) | Somerset?, 1909, 'Walking up the hillside' (*Children's Singing Games*, Cecil Sharp, i, pp. 12–15) | Chard, and elsewhere in West Country, 1922 (Macmillan Collection) | Cf. *Merrie Games in Rhyme*, E. M. Plunket, 1886, pp. 26–7.

USA: Philadelphia, *c.*1860, and Maryland, 1903 (*Games of American Children*, pp. 50–1 and 226–7) | Florida, 1902, 'Walking on the green grass, Walking side by side; Walking with a pretty girl—She shall be my bride' (*JAFL*, xv, pp. 193–4) | Cincinnati, 1908 (ibid., xl, p. 29) | Callaway, Virginia, 1918, 'We go walking on the green grass, thus, thus, thus'. First verse as introduction to song 'Soldier Boy for Me' (*English Folk-Songs from the Southern Appalachians*, Cecil Sharp, ii, p. 382) | Rutherford County, *c.*1927, 'Walking up the green grass Raising heavy dust' (*North Carolina Folklore*, pp. 98–9) | Cleveland County, Oklahoma, *c.*1930 (*American Play-Party Song*, B. A. Botkin, pp. 344–5).

IV

Mating

THE nature of children being what it is, and the age of the games in this section being unknown, it is understandable that the words of the game-songs have become confused, and the actions of the games simplified. Verses from one mating game can appropriately be added to another mating game, and so much have they been interchanged that it is impossible to be certain to which song they originally belonged (and as this is not literary criticism but oral tradition it does not matter). The romantic purpose of the games has not been lost sight of: either they are cushion dances which retain only the kneeling and kissing, like 'King William' and 'Pretty Little Girl'; or, mostly, they are ring games in which one person, in the centre of the ring, makes her preference known by choosing someone from the ring, who will stand or dance round with her for a while before taking her place. In some versions the games have been varied with actions from other games. The secret agreeing by intermediaries on the sweet-heart's name (characteristic of the Wedding Rings); the alluring inside-out circle from 'Wallflowers'; and the new-fangled 'wheel of fortune' ending, when the one in the centre shirks her responsibility and leaves her choice to fate, have all been used to enliven these games, now that the choice itself has not the momentous consequences it had when the players were young people on the brink of marriage.

18

King William

Huddersfield, 1978

King William was King James's son,
All the royal races run;
Upon his breast he wore a star
Pointing to the Russian war.

Choose to the east, and choose to the west,
Choose the one that you love best;
If she's not here to take her part,
Choose another with all your heart.

Down on the carpet you shall kneel,
While the grass grows in yon field,
Salute your bride and kiss her sweet,
Rise again upon your feet.

Not least of the curiosities of this game, with its seeming memory of a
conflict for the British Succession, is that it is better known and earlier
recorded in the United States than in the United Kingdom. Traditionally
a boy or girl in the centre of the ring chooses a sweetheart from the other

players; and the pair carry out the actions prescribed during the singing of the last verse, a verse, incidentally, that recalls the cushion dance (p. 190); and, in fact, a description of the game played in Connecticut in 1865, during the course of an 'Evening Party', further links the game with the cushion. A young man stood with a broad-brimmed hat in his hand, and, as the singing proceeded, presented himself to one of the girls, placing the hat on her head:

> King William was King George's son,
> And from the royal blood he sprung;
> Upon his breast he wore a stowe,
> Which denotes the sign of woe,
> Say, young lady, will you 'list and go?
> Say, young lady, will you 'list and go?
> The broad-brimmed hat you must put on,
> And follow on to the fife and drum.

The pair then marched arm-in-arm until the girl, in her turn, put the hat on the head of another young man; and so the play continued until everyone had been crowned with the hat, and the whole company marched round the great central chimney of the house 'singing with a will the words over and over'.

The announcement that 'King William was King James's son' has been the customary opening to the song in both continents, yet children are not everywhere agreed, and perhaps not overmuch concerned, with the niceties of genealogy. King William has been sung of as being King David's son, King George's son, and King Simon's son. Alternatively King Henry has been credited with being King James's son; King Charles, with more accuracy, has been given as King James's son; and King Arthur as King William's son.

In Britain, during the past hundred years, the game has been played mostly in Yorkshire, especially, it appears, in the areas of Halifax, Huddersfield, and Pickering. In Yorkshire, too, it has been an encouragement to romantic association. S. O. Addy told Alice Gomme (1894) that in Sheffield young men and women used to form the ring which, like other Yorkshiremen since, they referred to as a kissing ring; and when a man had made known his fancy he walked arm-in-arm with her inside the circle. At Pickering the words, though similar, were distinct:

> King Henry was King James's son,
> And all the royal race is run;
> Upon his breast he wears a star
> Right away to the ocean far.

> Choose to the east, and choose to the west,
> And choose to the one that you love best;
> If they are not here to take their part,
> Choose another with all your heart.
>
> Down on the carpet you shall kneel,
> As sure as the grass grows in the field,
> Allelulia bright, and a kiss so sweet,
> Please to rise upon your feet.

An old lady in Pickering recollected (1967) that she first met her husband 'seriously' during a 'King Henry', and was probably not alone in her experience (cf. *Street and Playground*, pp. 201–2). Right up to the 1930s the chapels in the district celebrated their anniversaries with a public supper followed by the playing of 'King Henry' in an adjoining field, some older members of the congregation taking part as well as the younger ones, and the play continuing to a late hour. The couplet that was characteristic in Halifax and Huddersfield,

> Upon his breast he wore a star,
> Pointing to the Russian war,

was in the United States in the nineteenth century commonly

> Upon his breast he wore a star,
> And it was called the sign of war,

or 'Which was carried in time of war', a puzzlement to commentators as well as children, who have rendered it

> On his breast he wore a star,
> And that's the way to the pickle jar,[1]

or 'Upon his breast he wore a star, And in his hand a big guitar', or 'Upon his vest he wore a star, And in his mouth a large cigar'. However the third verse of the song 'Lewie Gordon', given by Hogg in his *Jacobite Relics*, second series 1821, and supposedly written about a younger son of the Duke of Gordon who declared for Prince Charles in the rising of 1745, invites comparison:

> The princely youth that I do mean
> Is fitted for to be a king;
> On his breast he wears a star,
> You'd take him for [the] god of war.

---

[1] Robert Graves said that in this version the king must certainly have been William IV, and the last line originally 'And that's the way that Billy's a tar'.

(The tune of 'Lewie Gordon', which Hogg says is the original or northern set of 'Tarry woo', is not similar to 'King William' as usually chanted.)

USA: Missouri, *c.*1860 | Ashford and Eastford, Connecticut, 1865 (*JAFL*, xiv, p. 299) | *Games of American Children*, 1883, pp. 73–5, 'exceedingly familiar, throughout the Middle and Southern States, as a kissing-round'; also 1903 edn., pp. 246–8 | Washington DC, 1886 (*Lippincott's Magazine*, xxxviii, pp. 323–4) | St Louis, 1895 (*JAFL*, lx, pp. 15–16. The song stated to be one of the most widely known to persons attending the 1916 meeting of the Missouri Folk-Lore Society. References given to further printed sources) | North Carolina, 1920s, nearly 50 texts collected, and further references to printed sources (*North Carolina Folklore*, pp. 113–17) | Oklahoma City, *c.*1930 (*American Play-Party Song*, B. A. Botkin, pp. 226–7, the game reputed to have been played in Kentucky when Daniel Boone, born 1734, was a boy) | Maryland, 1944 (Howard MSS).

Canada: Highgate, Kent County, Ontario, 1909, and Toronto, *c.*1910 (*JAFL*, xxxi, pp. 50 and 131) | St Elmo, Ontario, *c.*1915 (Fowke, 1969, p. 24).

Britain: Giggleswick, *c.*1875, played like Drop Handkerchief (Crofton MS, i, p. 100) | Pickering, *c.*1890, *c.*1910, and *c.*1932 | Hanging Heaton and Sheffield, 1894 (*Traditional Games*, i, p. 302) | Co. Durham, 1896, as adult kiss-in-the-ring game (*Longman's Magazine*, xxviii, p. 584, in story by Margaret Hunt) | Upper Calder Valley, *c.*1900, last verse, 'Oh, what a beautiful choice you've got, Don't you wish you was going to stop? Give her a kiss and send her away, And tell her to come another fine day' | Halifax district, *c.*1900 and *c.*1920 | Huddersfield district, *c.*1900, *c.*1939, *c.*1941, and *c.*1950 | Leigh, Lancashire, 1906 (Gilchrist MSS 231 B iv) | Forfar, *c.*1950 | Holmfirth, near Huddersfield, 1954 | Slaithwaite, near Huddersfield, *c.*1959 | Workington, 1960 and 1961.

19

Pretty Little Girl of Mine

Joyous Book of Singing Games, *John Hornby, 1913*

See this pretty little girl of mine,
She's brought me a bottle of wine;
A bottle of wine and a guinea too,
See what my little girl can do.

On the carpet she shall kneel,
While the grass grows in the field;
Stand upright upon your feet
And choose the one you love so sweet.

Now you're married we wish you joy,
First a girl and then a boy;
Seven years to come, seven years to pass,
Many a happy kiss at last.

The players form a circle and skip round, with one player in the middle who, during the second verse, kneels, stands upright again, and chooses the person she wishes to join her in the ring. During the last verse the two in the middle join hands (formerly they used to kiss) and swing round together. The game was at the peak of its popularity at the turn of the nineteenth century (Alice Gomme collected twenty-four recordings); but since 1950 it has been found only in Radnorshire. The opening verse, in which the second line can be less idyllic, 'She's cost me a bottle of wine', is the only one exclusive to the game. 'On the carpet she shall kneel', with its echo of the cushion dance, is also a constituent of 'King William' (p. 122); and 'Now you're married we wish you joy' is, of course, tagged on to many a love game (see esp. pp. 148–50).

Britain: Thornes near Wakefield, 1874, one verse only 'On the carpitt you shall kneel, While the grass grows in the field. Stand up, stand up, on your feet; Pick the one you love so sweet' (*Notes & Queries*, 5th ser., iii, p. 482) | Reddish, Lancashire, *c*.1880, 'See what a pretty little girl I am, It's brought me many a bottle of wine, Bottle of wine to make me shine, See what a pretty little girl I am. On the carpet you shall kneel, While the grass grows in the field; Stand up, stand up, on your feet, And choose the one you love so sweet,' with finale (to 'For He's a Jolly Good Fellow') 'My sister's gone to be married, Hip, hip, hooray!' (Crofton MS, i, p. 26) | Berrington, 1883, similar to 1874 (*Shropshire Folk-Lore*, p. 509) | Derbyshire, 1883, similar to *c*.1880 (*Folk-Lore*, i, p. 385) | Maxey, 1885, 'Oh! this pretty little girl of mine, Has cost me many a bottle of wine; A bottle of wine and a guinea or two, So see what my little girl can do' (*Northamptonshire Notes & Queries*, i, p. 214) | Symondsbury, Dorset, 1889, 'Boys and girls often play this together, and then the words are changed to suit the circumstances' (*Folk-Lore*, vii, pp. 207–8) | Tyneside, *c*.1895, 'See what a pretty little girl I've got, She gave me a penny and a bottle of pop' | *Traditional Games*, ii, 1898, pp. 67–77 | *Old Isle of Wight Singing Games*, A. E. Gillington, 1909, no. 2 | Chard, and elsewhere in Somerset, 1922 (Macmillan Collection) | Wootton Bassett, *c*.1950 | Dolyhir, Radnorshire, 1953, 'See this pretty little boy of mine, He cost me many a bottle of wine, A bottle of wine and a biscuit too, To see what my little boy can do' | Evancoyd, Radnorshire, 1960.
Australia: Toowoomba, Queensland, *c*.1900.

New Zealand: Has been known in all provinces, e.g. Tahataki, Otago, 1875, and Hawkes Bay, 1920 (Sutton-Smith, pp. 13–14).

Cf. USA: Cincinnati, 1908, 'See what a pretty little girl I am! Many bottles of wine she drank, Bottles of wine to make her shine, See what a pretty little girl I am!' (*JAFL*, xl, p. 23).

20

Down by the Riverside

Mosspark, Glasgow, 1961

Down by the riverside the green grass grows,
There stands *Tracy* hanging out her clothes;
She sang and she sang and she sang so sweet,
She sang for her true love across the street.

True love, true love, will you marry me,
Yes dear, yes dear, at half past three.
Ice cakes and cream cakes all for tea,
And I will marry you at half past three.

A ten-year-old at Knighton says:

This game is played with one person in the middle, and all the others standing in a ring holding hands. When the song starts they skip around in a ring. Then the person in the middle chooses a person from out of the ring. Then she says to her partner 'True love, true love, will you marry me?' True love says 'Yes dear, yes dear, at half past three'. Together they say 'Ice cakes and cream cakes all for tea . . .' Then those two people go out, and we start all over again.

On a practical point she adds, 'You choose the person in the middle by saying "Each, peach, pear, plum, out goes Tom Thumb, in comes another one, out goes you".'

   This gentle singing game has been found being played in the 1960s and
1970s in places as far apart as Street in Somerset and Whalsay on
Shetland. None of the texts appears to have regional significance, but in
the south-west of Scotland the opening is usually the old-fashioned
'Down in yonder meadow', as in the version collected in Glasgow by
Father Damian Webb in 1961, the tune being that given above:

> Down in yonder meadow where the green grass grows,
> Where *Mary Johnson* she bleaches all her clothes,
> And she sang, and she sang, and she sang so sweet,
> That she sang *Robert Richards* [shouted] across the street.
>
> And she huddled and she cuddled, and she sat him on her knee,
> Saying, 'My dear *Robert*, I hope you will agree,
> AGREE, AGREE, I HOPE YOU WILL AGREE [shouted],
> For tomorrow is my wedding day and I must go.'
>
> Mary made a dumpling, she made it awfu' nice,
> She cut it up in slices and gave us all a slice.
> Saying 'Taste it, taste it, don't say no,
> For tomorrow is my wedding day and I must go.'

   In 1975 children in Glasgow were singing almost the identical words;
and they are indeed the words of a 'bottling song' sung at the all-female
parties at workplaces in Glasgow when one of the party is leaving to get
married. The first two verses are also little different from how J. S. Kerr
set them down in Glasgow in his *Guild of Play*, 1912, while the last six lines
seem to have been sung around Glasgow since about 1855 (see 'Up the
Street', p. 145). Likewise the words of the game at Knighton are similar to
those noted by A. E. Gillington in *Old Hampshire Singing Games*, 1909,
sung with the children standing in a line facing the chosen one. The oldest
notice of the game yet found is, in fact, not much earlier (in *Northamptonshire Notes & Queries*, ii, 1888), although the distribution of Alice Gomme's
six recordings, the accretions to her texts from other games, and the fact
that the game was already played in America (*American Anthropologist*, i,
1888, p. 248; also *JAFL*, xl, Cincinnati, 1908, p. 27), make it probable it
was not new at the end of the nineteenth century.
   Alice Gomme's premier text, printed 1894, was from Cowes in the Isle
of Wight:

> Down in the valley where the green grass grows
> Stands E—— H——, she blows like a rose.
> She blows, she blows, she blows so sweet.
> In came F—— S—— and gave her a kiss.
> E—— made a pudding, she made it nice and sweet,

F—— took a knife and fork and cut a little piece.
Taste of it, taste of it, don't say nay,
For next Sunday morning is our wedding day.
First we'll buy a money box,
Then we'll buy a cradle;
Rock, rock the bottom out,
Then we'll buy another.
Bread and cheese all the week, cork [pork?] on Sunday,
Half a crown on Saturday night, and a jolly good dance on Monday.

This may be compared with the game, recollected by a correspondent, which children played 'on the short goose-cropped grass at the edge of Chobham Common' about 1905:

> Down in the valley where the violets grow,
> Look at [girl's name] how she blow.
> She blows like a rose, she blows so sweet,
> Come along [boy's name] and tell us your true love.
> First we'll buy a wedding ring,
> And then we'll buy a cradle;
> Rock, rock, the bottom come out,
> And then we'll buy another.
> Bread and cheese all the week,
> Sheep's head o' Sunday,
> Half a crown o' Saturday night
> And pay the rent o' Monday.
> [Girl] on a white horse, [boy] on a grey,
> Here we go, here we go, riding away.

Although the precise source of 'Down by the riverside', 'Down in the meadow', or 'Down in the valley where the violets grow', may never be known, the words probably stem from an Arcadian song such as 'The Wars are all O'er', which appears on a slip sheet in our possession printed in the 1770s:

> Down in the meadows the violets so blue,
> There I saw pretty Polly a milking her cow,
> The song that she sung made all the grove ring,
> My Billy is gone and left me to serve the King.

> I stept up to her and made her this reply,
> And said my dear Polly what makes you to cry,
> My Billy is gone from me whom I love so dear,
> The Americans will kill him so great is my fear.

I said my dear Polly can you fancy me,
I'll make you as happy as happy can be,
No, no, said the fair maid that never can be,
I ne'er shall be happy till my Billy I see.

A version of the game unlikely to accord with the original words is one that children have picked up in the Manchester–Birmingham area (recordings from Salford, Tipton, and Great Barr) which turns the wedding feast into a tea-party, and sounds as if it comes from *Tiny Tots Annual*:

Down by the river where the green grass grows,
There sits *Mary* washing her clothes.
She sings, she sings, she sings so sweet,
She calls for her playmate across the street.
Playmate, playmate, will you come to tea,
Come next Sunday at half past three.
Tea cakes, pancakes, lovely things to eat,
Won't we have a jolly time at half past three.

Nevertheless girls of nine and ten have been found chanting these words, choosing a partner, and playing the parts of host and guest, with perfect equanimity. The words are, however, a provocation to the lusty, and the boys are more likely to sing about the heroine taking off her clothes than washing them.

It is remarkable the singing game continues to be played when, from the early years of the century, the words have also been chanted in the skipping rope.

21

All the Boys in Our Town

Forfar, c.1905

All the boys in our town lead a happy life,
Excepting So-and-so, he wants a wife.
A wife he shall have, and a-courting he shall go,
Along with So-and-so, because he loves her so.
He huddles her, he cuddles her, he sits her on his knee,
He says, 'My dearest darling, will you marry me?
If I love you, and you love me,
We shall be as happy as birds upon a tree.'

These are the chief recurring lines of a singing game that had its vogue at
the turn of the century, and has been reported only once in the 1970s
(from Ayr). Alice Gomme published four versions, from widely separated
areas, in 1894–8; Flora Thompson knew the game in north Oxfordshire in
the 1880s (*Lark Rise*, 1939, p. 165); and two informants recollect it around
1910 (Romsey and Forfar). The game, played in the usual manner of a
courtship game, with one child naming another to come into the ring, was

innocuous in itself, perhaps too innocuous, but became over-grown with other verses, notably the bridal pudding-making chant, which is sometimes played as a game on its own and sometimes found as part of 'Down by the Riverside'; the lines about the domestic chattels or wedding gifts, usually a feature of 'Up the Street and Down the Street' (p. 145); and the roving doctor with his motley crew, who have now attached themselves (as members of the same profession) to the skipping game 'Mother, Mother, I Am Ill', and the clapping chant 'The Johnsons Had a Baby' (p. 472). 'Up the heathery mountains, down the rushy glen' appears as an introduction in some versions, lines which formed part of the song 'Charlie is my darling' (J. Hogg, *Jacobite Relics of Scotland*, ser. ii, 1821) and were later used by William Allingham. Thus the recital collected in Deptford for Lady Gomme, while of interest to folklorists for making comparison with, for instance, a skipping game played in Soho a few years later, must have been tiresome to urchins only wishing to know which girl Charley Allen would name:

> All the boys in our town leads a happy life,
> Excepting *Charley Allen*, and he wants a wife;
> And a-courting he shall go
> Along with [Charley's choice], because he loves her so.

> He kisses her, he cuddles her, he sets her on his knee,
> And says, My dearest darling, do you love me?
> I love you and you love me;
> We'll both be as happy as birds on the tree.

> Alice made a pudding, she made it nice and sweet,
> Up came *Charley*, cut a slice off—
> A slice, a slice, we don't say No;
> The next Monday morning the wedding goes.
> I've got knives and forks, I've got plates and dishes,
> I've got a nice young man, he breaks his heart with kisses.

> If poor Alice was to die,
> Wouldn't poor *Charley*, he *would* cry.
> He would follow to the grave
> With black buttons and black crape,
> And a guinea for the church,
> And the bell shall ring.

> Up came the doctor, up came the cat,
> Up came the devil with a white straw hat.
> Down went the doctor, down went the cat,
> Down went the devil with a white straw hat.

Such a prolongation seems to have added nothing to the action of the game, and like all organisms that become monstrous its extinction was predictable. However, unlike the dinosaur, the chant kept its head and came back to life with increased vigour as a skipping game.

Britain: *Popular Rhymes of Scotland*, R. Chambers, 1847 (1869, p. 137), 'Early and fairly the moon shines above, A' the lads in our town are dying for love, Especially [Jamie Anderson], for he's the youngest man, He courts [Helen Simpson] as fast as he can. He kisses her, he claps her, he ca's her his dear; And they're to be married before the next year' etc. | *Games of Argyleshire*, 1901, p. 256, 'All the girls in our town live a happy life, Except M.P., she wants a man, a man she shall have, A dicky, dicky dandy, a daughter of her own. Send her upstairs, put her to bed, Send for the doctor before she is dead. In comes the doctor, out goes the cat, In comes Jimmie with his chimney hat. . .' | *London Street Games*, 1916, p. 59, 'All the boys in our town, eating apple-pie, Excepting (Georgie Groves), he wants a wife—A wife he shall have, according he shall go Along with (Rosie Taylor), because he loves her so. He kisses her and cuddles her, and sits her on his knee, And says, my dear, do you love me? I love you, and you love me. Next Sunday morning, the wedding will be, Up goes the doctor, up goes the cat, Up goes a little boy in a white straw hat' | *St Anne's Soho Monthly*, June 1907, p. 156, for skipping, 'All the boys in our town lead a happy life, Excepting Freddy ——; he wants a wife. A wife he shall have, and a courting he shall go Along with Florrie ——, because he loves her so. He huddles her and cuddles her And sets her on his knee, Says, "Darling do you love me?" "I love you and you love me"; Next Sunday morning the wedding shall be. Up comes the doctor, up comes the nurse, Up comes the devil in a dirty white shirt. Down goes the doctor, up comes a cat, Up comes the devil in a dirty straw hat. *Salt, mustard, vinegar, pepper*.'

USA: Washington DC, 1886, 'I went to Mr Johnson's To buy a rocking-chair, And who should I see there But Willie and his dear! He kisses her, he hugs her, He calls her his dear, He makes her a present Of a handsome rocking-chair' (*Lippincott's Magazine*, xxxviii).

22

The Wind Blows High

> The wind, the wind, the wind blows high,
> The rain comes scattering down the sky.
> She is handsome, she is pretty,
> She is the girl of the golden city.
> She goes a-courting, one, two, three,
> Please and tell me who is she.
>
> *Terry Johnson* says he loves her,
> All the boys are fighting for her;
> Let the boys say what they will,
> *Terry Johnson* loves her still.
>
> He loves her, he kisses her, he sits her on his knee,
> He says, 'Dear darling, won't you marry me?'
> He says tomorrow, and she says today,
> So let's get a taxi and drive them away.

In Manchester the girls take the initiative in the courting, and then may be as inconstant as in real life.

One of the girls calls out 'I'll be in' and stands to one side. Somebody thinks of a boy to be the girl's sweetheart, and they all whisper the name round to each other so that it shall be a secret. Then they make a ring round the girl and begin singing:

> The wind, the wind, the wind blows high,
> The rain comes scattering down the sky.
> She is handsome, she is pretty,
> She is the girl of the London city.
> She goes a-courting, a-one, two, three,
> And *Paul Stewart* will you marry me?
> She loves him, she kisses him,
> She sits him on her knee,
> She says 'You lucky darling,
> Will you marry me?'
> If you love him, clap your hands,
> If you hate him, stamp your feet.

If the girl claps her hands, the others chant:

> North, south, east and west,
> You shall be my very best.
> Shall it be a boy or girl,
> North, south, east and west?

The girl in the middle shuts her eyes and spins round with her arm outstretched, like a wheel of fortune. The person at whom she is pointing when the verse finishes changes places with her. If she stamps her feet, on the other hand, she chases the person who thought of the boy's name, and if she catches them they go in the middle. She knows who thought of the boy's name because 'either they own up, or everybody else tells'. The borrowed lines are from 'All the Boys' and 'Orange Balls' (pp. 130 and 232).

At Nelson in Lancashire they sing:

> The wind, the wind, the wind blows high,
> The rain comes scattering down the sky.
> He is handsome, she is pretty,
> She is a girl of the London City,
> He comes a-courting of one, two, three,
> And may I tell you who it be?
>
> *Julian Pilling* says he loves her,
> All the boys are fighting for her.
> He takes her in the garden, he sits her on his knee,
> And says, Pretty girl, will you marry me?
>
> Pick up a pin and knock at the door,
> And say has Johnny been here before?
> She's in, she's in, she's never been out,
> She's in the parlour walking about.
> She comes down as white as snow,
> With a baby in her arms all dressed in silk.

At the end of the first verse (which is the only one sung to the formal tune) all go down on their haunches, the last down chooses a sweetheart from amongst the other players, and the two go in the middle, join hands and walk round until the end of the song, when they rejoin the ring, but facing outwards. The game is repeated until the whole ring is turned inside out. (Compare both words and actions with 'Wallflowers (II)', p. 143).

Scottish versions are recognizable by an extra two lines after the opening couplet, naming the principal girl:

> *Myra Fraser* says she'll die
> All for the love of a rovin' eye.

Alternatively for 'a rolling eye', 'a golden eye', or 'a tartan tie'. In Edinburgh the game is further extended with verses from 'Merry-ma-tansie'. The players hint at the sweetheart's name by giving his initials:

J is his first name, his first name, his first name,
J is his first name, around the merry ma tansie.

M is his second name, his second name, his second name,
M is his second name, around the merry ma tansie.

The full name being assembled, the principal player is instructed to hide her face, to show her face, and to choose a player to take her place.

'I used to like this game when I was younger,' commented an eleven-year-old in the Royal Mile. But it was not for its romance that she liked it. 'I liked it because when you go round fast it is very hard to hold hands and very often you fall, which if you don't hurt yourself is great fun.' The game seems to have been less exciting and less played in the nineteenth century (Alice Gomme collected only seven versions 1894–8). The player in the middle herself (or himself) chose the person to join her in the ring, and this person had to be one of the opposite sex, an unvarying rule that meant, as a little girl at Southport confided to an adult spectator in 1900, 'We can't play this game without *young boys*!'

Britain: Giggleswick, *c.*1875, 'The wind, the wind, the wind blows high, The rain comes falling from the sky; She is handsome, she is pretty, She is the girl of London city. She goes courting one, two, three; Can you tell me who is he? Johnny Bulcock says he loves her! All the boys are fighting for her; Let the boys say what they will, Johnny Bulcock's got her still! He knocks at the knocker, and he rings at the bell, Please, my dear, is your daughter in? She is neither ways in, she is neither ways out. She is in the back parlour walking about. Out she comes, as white as snow, With a rose in her breast as soft as silk. "Please my dear, will you have a drop of this?" "No my dear, I would rather have a kiss!" ' (Crofton MS, i, p. 88) | *Shropshire Folk-Lore*, 1883, p. 510, ending 'He takes her by the lily-white hand And leads her over the water, Gives her kisses, one, two, three, Mrs ——'s daughter!' | South Wales, *c.*1885, ending, 'I went to Mrs —— to buy a frying pan, There I saw her kissing her young man, She offs with her gloves and puts on a ring, Next Monday morning the wedding shall begin.' | Warwickshire, 1892 (*English Folk-Rhymes*, G. F. Northall, p. 379 | *Traditional Games*, ii, 1895, pp. 387–90, includes variants from north-east Scotland | Southport, 1898 and 1900; Highfields, Sussex, 1905 (Gilchrist MSS, notebooks 231 A iii, A ii, and B iv) | Shetland, *c.*1900, begins 'Rain, rain high, and wind doth blow' and ends 'Down she comes all dressed in silk With a rose in her bosom as white as milk. She pulls off her glove and shows him the ring. Tomorrow, tomorrow, the wedding will begin' | Argyllshire, 1901, the ring stands still and sings 'The wind and the rain, and the wind blows high, The rain comes dashing through the sky, Peggie Mactavish says she'll die, if she'll not get the boy with the laughing eye. She is handsome, she is pretty, She's the flower of the golden city, She has lovers, one, two, three, Pray can you tell me who they be?' Two in the centre 'retire and fix upon names of suppositious rival lovers and return singing 'Duncan Maclarty says he'll have her, Sandy Grant is fighting for her' and the whole company proclaim 'Let them say what they will, Duncan Maclarty will have her still' (*Folk-Lore*, xvi, p. 202) | 25 other versions 1900–50. Versions from 30 places since 1950, although now more often used as a skipping song. The opening bars became familiar to the whole nation in the 1970s as the signature tune of BBC Radio 4.
Australia: North Queensland, 1957 (Turner).
USA: Washington DC, 1886, 'The wind blows low, the wind blows high, The stars are dropping from the sky, And Jennie says she'll surely die If she don't get a lover with a dark-blue eye. He is happy, he is pretty, He is the boy of Washington City' (*Lippincott's Magazine*, xxxvii, p. 242) | Illinois, 1898, 'The wind blows high, the wind blows cool, Stars are gathering to and fro;

Miss —— says she'll die, Couldn't get a fellow with a dark blue eye. She is handsome, she is pretty, She is the belle of New York City; She has lovers one, two, three, Please come and tell me who they be. —— says he loves her; All the boys are fighting for her, Let them fight as long's they will, —— —— has her still' (*JAFL*, xxviii, p. 278) | Cincinnati, 1908, 'Rain, rain high, and the wind blows cold, And the stars are shining two and two, And Mrs *Emma* said she would die For the sake of a fellow with a rosy eye' (*JAFL*, xl, p. 19) | Holland, Michigan, 1914, 'The Ring Ring's eye, the Ring Ring's eye, The rain is falling from the sky. Some one says —— will die, If she doesn't get married in the Ring Ring's eye.'

23

Johnny the Sailor Boy

In 1891 Frank Kidson published a game-song 'heard and seen played by Liverpool children', which he believed to be old but hitherto unrecorded:

> Johnny Todd he took a notion
>   For to go across the sea,
> And he left his love behind him,
>   Weeping by the Liverpool sea.

The words were, he admitted, imperfectly remembered; and the succeeding verses are (to our ear at least) those of an improviser rather than a recorder:

> For a week she wept full sorely,
>   Tore her hair and wrung her hands,
> Till she met another sailor
>   Walking on the Liverpool sands.
>
> Why, fair maid, are you a-weeping,
>   For your Johnny gone to sea?
> If you'll wed with me tomorrow,
>   I will kind and constant be.
>
> I will buy you sheets and blankets,
>   I'll buy you a wedding ring,
> You shall have a gilded cradle
>   For to rock your baby in.
>
> Johnny Todd came back from sailing,
>   Sailing o'er the ocean wide;
> But he found his fair and false one,
>   Was another sailor's bride.

> All young men who go a-sailing,
> For to fight the foreign foe,
> Don't you leave your love like Johnny—
> Marry her before you go.

Frank Kidson was not to know that five years earlier an American anthropologist had come across children in Washington DC playing a ring game that, at the least, confirmed his claim that the song was not new:

> Charlie took a notion
> To go sail the sea,
> And left poor Minnie a widow
> Under the willow-tree.
> Minnie, Minnie, nurse your baby;
> Drink the wine that Charlie's sent you.

Nor was he to know that thereafter collectors of children's song would find little difficulty obtaining authentic copies of the verses. For instance, in 1892 E. W. B. Nicholson had heard little girls in Golspie singing,

John-ie John-son took a no-tion For to go and sail on sea:

There he left his own dear Maggie Weep-ing at a wil-low tree.

The tune, he said, was 'suspiciously like "The Grecian Bend", a comic song of about 1867', but more probably the song-writer had filched the traditional tune. Alice Gomme was sent versions from Fochabers, Laurieston, and Perth, which she published (1898) under the titles 'Dig for Silver' and 'Hear all! Let me at her'. A member of the Rymour Club found the game being played in the Gorgie district of Edinburgh:

> Johnnie Johnston's ta'en a notion,
> For to go and sail the sea;
> He has left his own true lover
> Weeping by the willow tree.

And James Kerr published a similar text in 1912, sung by children in Glasgow.

From these versions, and from the recollections of informants who grew up in the twentieth century, two strands of song can be distinguished. In one, the verses become entangled with 'The Keys of Heaven'. A would-be suitor or seducer chants:

> I will buy you beads and earrings,
> I will buy you diamond stones,
> I will buy you a horse to ride on,
> Bonny lassie, marry me.

To which the forlorn girl replies:

> What care I for beads and earrings,
> What care I for diamond stones,
> What care I for a horse to ride on,
> When my true love's far from me.

In the other (reflected in the Washington game) the sailor lover, who is also a father, reassures the girl:

> Weep no more my own dear *Jeanie*
> Take your baby on your knee;
> Weep no more for a gallant sailor
> I'll come back and marry thee.

The tune 'Johnnie Todd' was arranged by Bridget Fry and Fritz Spiegl, and became familiar to every home in Britain in the 1960s as the signature tune of the BBC television series *Z Cars* which is set in Liverpool. In fact Kidson's song 'Johnny Todd' has been taken up by Liverpool folk groups and has become a sort of scouseport anthem, in the belief that children customarily skip to it in the streets of Liverpool. Several attempts to collect it from children have, however, failed. But in Radcliffe, south of Bury, in 1952, children were to be heard singing while they skipped, as if in direct communication with the capital city of the United States:

> Johnnie the sailor boy took no notice,
> Sailed across the deep blue sea.
> There he met his dearest *Hazel*,
> Weeping by the willow tree.
> Weep no more my dearest *Hazel*,
> Sit your baby on your knee,
> I'll be back in ten more minutes
> Asking you to marry me.

A ten-year-old in the second half of the twentieth century could help repair the deficiencies of a folksong collector in Victorian days.

USA: Washington DC, 1886 (*Lippincott's Magazine*, xxxviii, pp. 321–2).

Britain: *Traditional Tunes*, Frank Kidson, 1891, pp. 103–4 | *Traditional Games*, ii, 1898, pp. 413–14, 428–9 | *Rymour Club*, i, 1911, p. 151 | *Kerr's Guild of Play*, 1912, p. 25 | Glasgow, *c.*1900; Clifton, *c.*1910; Morecambe, *c.*1920; children, Radcliffe, 1952.

24

I'll Give to You a Paper of Pins

adapted from Old Nursery Rhymes with Chimes, *1863*

I'll give to you a paper of pins
To prove to you my love begins,
If you will marry, you will marry,
You will marry me.

I won't accept the paper of pins
To prove to me your love begins,
And I'll not marry, I'll not marry,
I'll not marry you.

I'll give to you a dress of blue
To prove to you my love is true,
If you will marry, you will marry,
You will marry me.

I won't accept the dress of blue
To prove to me your love is true,
And I'll not marry, I'll not marry,
I'll not marry you.

I'll give to you a dress of red
Sewed all round with golden thread,
If you will marry, you will marry,
You will marry me.

I won't accept the dress of red
Sewed all round with golden thread,
And I'll not marry, I'll not marry,
I'll not marry you.

I'll give to you a dress of green
To prove you're like a fairy queen,
If you will marry, you will marry,
You will marry me.

I won't accept the dress of green
To prove I'm like a fairy queen,
And I'll not marry, I'll not marry,
I'll not marry you.

I'll give to you the key to my chest
Full of the very, very best,
If you will marry, you will marry,
You will marry me.

I won't accept the key to your chest
Full of the very, very best,
And I'll not marry, I'll not marry,
I'll not marry you.

I'll give to you the key to my heart
To prove we'll marry and never part,
If you will marry, if you will marry,
If you will marry me.

> I *will* accept the key to your heart,
> To prove we'll marry and never part,
> And I *will* marry, I *will* marry,
> I *will* marry you.

Whether these words have always been part of a dialogue game, as here, is not clear. Halliwell recorded a romantic rendering 'Madam, I am come to court you', in which the girl rejects her suitor on the grounds that he is not handsome enough, in the 1844 edition of his *Nursery Rhymes of England*, p. 153; and added, in 1846, a materialistic version, 'The Keys of Canterbury', in which personal appearance mattered not at all:

> Oh, sir, I will accept of the keys of your chest,
> To count your gold and silver when you are gone to rest,
> And I will walk abroad with thee,
> And I will talk with thee!

But Halliwell did not indicate how the words were sung. In *Old Nursery Rhymes with Chimes*, 1863, they were, again, simply a song, beginning:

> Madam, I present you these six rows of pins,
> The very first token my true love brings.
> Madam, will you walk with me, me, me,
> And, madam, will you walk with me?

and the lover spurns the lady when she accepts his offer of 'a little golden watch'. Robert Chambers, *Popular Rhymes of Scotland* (1869), gives similar verses, beginning:

> I'll gie you a pennyworth o' preens,
> That's aye the way that love begins;
> If ye'll walk with me, leddy, leddy,
> If ye'll walk with me, leddy,

as part of a nursery tale 'The Tempted Lady', in which the suitor, equally successful with his bribes, is revealed to be Auld Nick. And Newell in America in 1883 also gives the verses for straightforward singing. But folksong collectors at the end of the century found the verses being used, as might be expected, for acting games. Lucy Broadwood reported she had seen it 'prettily performed by a little Yorkshire village boy and girl, who sang words beginning "Madam, I present you with a paper of pins" to the nursery tune "What have you got for dinner, Mrs Bond?" ' Alice Gomme twice came across children in Marylebone repeating the words (rather vestigial versions) in ring games. And Yoffie knew them as a singing game in St Louis 1895–1900 (*JAFL*, lx, pp. 7–11). The age of the song is uncertain; but a paper of pins was at one time a recognized lover's gift. In 'A wooing Song of a Yeoman of Kents Sonne' in *Melismata*, 1611, the young man reminds his intended:

> One time I gaue thee a paper of pins
> anoder time a taudry lace:
> And if thou wilt not grant me loue
> in truth ich die beuore thy vace.

Britain: *Traditional Games*, ii, 1898, pp. 437–8, 'Keys of Heaven', and pp. 450–1, 'Paper of Pins' | Chardstock, 1922, starts 'Dear madam, I will give you a new lace cap' (Macmillan Collection) | Forfar, 1952, as text. See also Wythenshawe, 1975, under 'A Duke a-Riding'.

Ireland: Dublin, 1975, 'I'm a soldier brave and strong, After coming from the war, Will you marry, marry, marry, marry, Will you marry me?' The game is played by two rows who advance and retire, and the inducements are a golden ball, a golden spoon, a piece of cake to throw to the swans in the lake, the 'keys of the press, And all the money I possess', which offer, being accepted, is then withdrawn (*All In! All In!*, Eilís Brady, pp. 111–12).

USA: (game versions only) *Games of American Children*, 1883, pp. 51–5, three versions | Cincinnati, 1908 (*JAFL*, xl, p. 9) | American versions may stem from *Paper of Pins* by 'A Lady', music by E. Mack, copyrighted 31 December 1869 (noted by James Fuld, *World-Famous Music*, 1971, p. 294). Song begins 'I'll give to thee a paper of pins, if that's the way that love begins'.

Compare 'Lady on the Mountain' and 'Johnny the Sailor Boy'.

25
Wallflowers (II)

> Wallflowers, wallflowers, growing up so high,
> All young ladies they are sure to die;
> Excepting *Cathie Hunter*, she shall live.
> Turn your back against the wall
> And tell me who your sweetheart is.
>
> *Tom Drummond* is a nice young man,
> He came to the door with his hat in his hand;
> He took off his glove and he showed her the ring,
> Tomorrow, tomorrow, the wedding will begin.

Like 'Green Gravel' (p. 239) the game 'Wallflowers' is sometimes a sweetheart-revealing game and is played with a distinctive second verse also used in 'Uncle John (II)' (p. 161). A twelve-year-old girl in North Devon told us what happens.

We stand in a ring and pick out four girls. They stand out of the ring so they can't hear which of them we pick. When one is chosen all four come back to the ring. The children hold hands and go round clockwise saying the first half of the song and naming the girl. She leaves the ring and stands against the wall. She says who her sweetheart is and then, returning to the middle of the ring, the children all circle her saying the second half of the song.

Two further versions, separated by forty years and the width of the Atlantic, will confirm that this was no temporary alliance of verses:

> Water, water, wild flowers, growing up so high,
> One of you young ladies shall surely die;
> And that shall be *Miss Perkins*.
> She can dance and she can sing,
> And she can play the organ;
> Turn your face towards the wall,
> And tell me what your sweetheart's called.
>
> *Tommy Jones* is a nice young man
> He came to the door with his hat in his hand;
> Took off his glove to show his ring,
> Tomorrow, tomorrow, the wedding begins.
>
>

Girl, Bradford-on-Tone, Somerset, 1922

> Water, water, wild flowers, growing up so high,
> We are all young ladies, and we are sure to die,
> Excepting *Susie Allen*, she is the finest flower.
> Fie, fie, fie for shame;
> Turn about and tell your beau's name.
>
> *Mr Nobody* is a nice young man,
> He comes to the door with his hat in his hand.
> Down she comes all dressed in silk,
> A rose in her bosom, as white as milk.
> She takes off her gloves, she shows me her ring,
> Tomorrow, tomorrow, the wedding begins.
>
>

'Played in New York streets',
Games of American Children, *1883, p. 68*

Newell also says that in Concord, Massachusetts, before 1800, the following was sung as the second part of 'Little Sally Waters' and 'Uncle John (II)':

> He knocks at the door, and picks up a pin,
> He asks if Miss —— is in.
> She neither is in, she neither is out,
> She's in the garret a-walking about.
> Down she comes as white as milk,
> A rose in her bosom, as soft as silk.
> She takes off her gloves, and shows me a ring;
> Tomorrow, tomorrow, the wedding begins.

Some of these lines remain in the memories of older folk in Workington, of playing 'Walty, Walty, Wild Flowers'; and they were also part of 'Water, Water, Wild Flowers' at Ogbourne in Wiltshire, as recorded by Alice Gomme in *Traditional Games*, 1898, p. 339:

> I pick up a pin, I knock at the door,
> I ask for ——
> She's neither in, she's neither out,
> She's up in the garden skipping about.
> Down come ——, as white as snow,
> Soft in her bosom as soft as glow.
> She pulled off her glove, and showed us her ring,
> Tomorrow, tomorrow, the bells shall ring.

Britain: Hurstmonceux, Sussex, and Ogbourne, Wiltshire, 1898 (*Traditional Games*, ii, pp. 338–9) | Workington, pre-1920 | Chard, Axminster, and Bradford-on-Tone, 1922 (Macmillan Collection) | Bishop's Nympton, 1954.
   USA: New York, 1883 (*Games of American Children*, p. 68) | Philadelphia, 1899, and three places in Michigan, 1914 (*JAFL*, xii, p. 292, and xxxiii, pp. 132–3).

26

Up the Street and Down the Street

> Up the street and down the street,
> The windows made of glass.
> Isn't *Molly Watson* a nice young lass?
> Isn't *Terry Hunter* as nice as she?
> They shall be married if they can agree.

This simple ring game was still being played in the 1920s (A. S. Macmillan collected six versions in Somerset), but seems eventually to have been engulfed by 'All the Boys in Our Town', itself now obsolescent. The words undoubtedly go back to the eighteenth century and its life-span as an independent game may be traced in the following sightings:

> Up street and down street,
>   each window's made of glass;
> If you go to Tom Tickler's house,
>   you'll find a pretty lass:
> Hug her, and kiss her,
>   and take her on your knee,
> And whisper very close:
>   Darling girl, do you love me?

Gammer Gurton's Garland, *1810, p. 34.*
Not in earlier editions.

Up the street, and down the street,
With windows made of glass,
Call at *Mary Muskett's* door,
There's a pretty lass.

With rosy in her bosom,
With a dimple in her chin,
Come all you lads and lasses
Let this fair maid walk in.

*Song for 'lace telling', sung by children in
the lace schools, from the recollection of two
old lace-makers, reported by Elizabeth
Wilson,* Olney and the Lace-Makers,
1864, pp. 66–7

The following three versions, though separated by time and space, are
interestingly similar:

Up streets and down streets and windows made of glass,
Isn't *Janet Rankin* a nice young lass?
Isn't *Willie Walker* as nice as she?
When they are married I hope they will agree—
    Agree, agree, agree.
Clean sheets and blankets and pillow-slips an' a',
A little baby on her knee and that's the best of a'.

Calder Ironworks, near Glasgow, c.1855.
Rymour Club, *1911, p. 7*

Up the streets the windows made of glass,
Isn't *Essie Baisley* a nice young lass?
Isn't *Callum Nichol* as nice as she?
When they get married I hope they'll agree.
Essie made a pudding, nice and sweet,
Callum took the fork and tasted it.
Taste love, taste, and don't say no,
For tomorrow morning to church they shall go.
Clean sheets and blankets, pillow slips and a',
A little baby on her knee and that's the best of a'.
Some say gold, some say brass,
Some say come owre the hill and kiss your bonny lass.

*Loanhead, Argyll, from the singing of a
maid, 1900 (Gilchrist MSS 231 A iii,
p. 92)*

Up Hill Street and down Hill Street, windows made of glass,
I see *Molly Jones*, a nice young lass.
Molly made a pudding, she made it very nice;
She forgot to put the fork in, till her sweetheart came at night.

Oh, *Freddie*, will you take a piece, and don't say no,
For next Sunday morning the wedding will go.
He kissed her, he cuddled her, he took her on his knee,
And said, Oh my darling, what shall I give to thee?
A china cup and saucer, a guinea gold ring,
A plate to put your porridge on, and ding, dong, ding.

Chaffcombe, Somerset, 1922
(Macmillan Collection)

But the song has kept a place in the affections of children to the present day. After we had been watching a long programme of skipping in a Lymington playground, during a heatwave, a gallant ten-year-old exclaimed 'Oh, there's that other one, Oh *yes*.

The church is made of marble stone,
The window's made of glass,
She goes down yonder
To see her bonny lass.
Her name is ("you choose a girl's name")
Catch her if you can,
Before she marries ("and then you choose a boy")
Before he's a man.
She kissed him, she hugged him,
She sat upon his knee,
She said "Dear ——, won't you marry me?"
Salt, mustard, vinegar, pepper,
Yes, no, yes, no, yes . . .

You go on till you get puffed out, and if it's "yes" he's going to marry her.'

Gammer Gurton's Garland, 1810 | *Nursery Rhymes of England*, J. O. Halliwell, 1843, p. 51 | *Traditional Games*, ii, pp. 323–4.

V

Wedding Rings

IN the prototype wedding game one player, sometimes selected by lot through her slowness in sinking to the ground, was led from the circle, and confided to a close friend or friends, who acted as intermediaries, the name of the person he or she wished to marry. The choice was then approved or disapproved by the rest of the players; and, if approved, bride and groom were welcomed into the middle of the circle through 'open gates' or 'high arches'. A wedding ceremony was then enacted, or symbolized by a kiss, and the pair were enjoined to love one another and be fruitful. (See chapter I, pp. 10–17.)

It is tempting to see, in these games, survivals of actual wedding ceremonies from the days when the poor and illiterate married by pledging themselves, without religious rite. The phrase 'Lead her across the water' for instance (in 'Rosy Apple' and 'Uncle John') may well describe what happened in betrothals conducted across running water, such as that entered into by Burns and Highland Mary. But we prefer to think of them as part of the graceful and functional social life enjoyed in the late Middle Ages, when young people could declare preferences for each other within the formal framework of a game—a facility which continued to the early years of this century.

The dance-songs are simple and repetitive, in the manner of the traditional ballads, and the language is the standard phraseology of ballad literature. Maidens are 'soft as silk and white as milk', their hands are 'lily-white', and they carry roses in their bosoms. But time has so fretted at the words, it is impossible, sometimes, to tell in which game the lines originated. The end verse (a combination of benediction and admonition) is now only regularly sung as part of 'Sally Water' and 'Oats and Beans and Barley Grow', yet used, it seems, to be considered the proper conclusion to any wedding game. In 1842 Robert Chambers's Scottish version of the 'Widow from Babylon' had the finale:

> Now they're married I wish them joy,
> Every year a girl or a boy;
> Loving each other like sister and brother,
> I pray this young couple may kiss together.

And in George IV's time an Irish version of 'Silly Old Man' ended:

> Now, young couple, you're married together . . .
> You must obey your father and mother,
> And love one another like sister and brother—
> I pray young, people, you'll kiss together!

> W. Carleton, *Traits of the Irish Peasantry*

The curiously casual assumption in versions of 'Sally Water' (the text version, for instance, and that in *Shropshire Folk-Lore*, 1883) that the marriage will only last seven years, has perhaps derived from the folk belief that a marriage has ended when a couple have lived apart for seven years. Alice Gomme (*Traditional Games*, ii, pp. 177–8) reported that 'early in November in 1895, a man tried for bigamy gave as his defence that he thought his marriage was ended with his first wife, as he had been away seven years'. Lina Eckenstein (*Comparative Studies*, 1906, p. 70) took this further with remarks she had gleaned from country folk: 'Thus a woman whose husband had gone from her, after seven years felt justified in looking upon him as dead, and had the bell tolled for his funeral.'

Such wedding formulas were cautionary, rather than romantic. The young couple were to obey their parents, and to love each other only like sister and brother (a restraint more suited to a period of betrothal than to matrimony itself). The 'wood-chopping' verse always attached to 'Oats and Beans and Barley', on the other hand, deals with married life at its most practical; and in 1883 Newell commented that in New England, where 'splitting the wood' was a troublesome part of the farmer's daily work, the 'amatory chorus' was liable to be of greater length, though showing signs of artistic embellishment:

> And now you're married in Hymen's band,
> You must obey your wife's command;
> You must obey your constant good,
> And keep your wife in hickory wood—
> Split the wood and carry it in,
> Split the wood and carry it in,
> And then she'll let you kiss her again.

Seemingly a song-writer had been at work, as had Nicholls and Clendon in Britain, with their music-hall song 'Now You Are Married I Wish You Joy' (1884 or earlier). The performer's patter was expressed in the sentiment of the day:

And when it came to kiss in the ring, ah! I fancy I see myself now, with a lot of other kids hand in hand dancing round two little duffers, and shrieking out at the tops of our voices—

> Now you are married I wish you joy,
> First a girl, and then a boy,
> Seven years after son and daughter,
> Pray young couple, kiss together.

A few years later the two Harrys, Wincott and Leighton, were to rewrite the words more realistically for Dan Crawley:

> Now you're married I wish you joy!
> Two fat girls and a bouncing boy,
> Seven years after next November,
> You'll have something to remember . . .

But the children, unaffected by the flippancy of their elders, keep to the traditional words.

27

Merry-ma-tansie

Tune: 'Nuts in May'

Here we go round the jingo-ring,
  The jingo-ring, the jingo-ring,
Here we go round the jingo-ring,
  Around the merry-ma-tansie.

Twice about and then we fall,
  Then we fall, then we fall,
Twice about and then we fall,
  Around the merry-ma-tansie.

Choose your maidens, one or two,
  One or two, one or two,
Choose your maidens, one or two,
  Around the merry-ma-tansie.

Sweep the house till the bride comes in,
  The bride comes in, the bride comes in,
Sweep the house till the bride comes in,
  Around the merry-ma-tansie.

A guinea-gold ring to tell her name,
  To tell her name, to tell her name,
A guinea-gold ring to tell her name,
  Around the merry-ma-tansie.

Jeannie is her first name,
  Her first name, her first name,
Jeannie is her first name,
  Around the merry-ma-tansie.

Macdonald is her second name,
  Her second name, her second name,
Macdonald is her second name,
  Around the merry-ma-tansie.

A bottle of wine to tell his name,
  To tell his name, to tell his name,
A bottle of wine to tell his name,
  Around the merry-ma-tansie.

Robbie is his first name,
  His first name, his first name,
Robbie is his first name,
  Around the merry-ma-tansie.

Bruce is his second name,
  His second name, his second name,
Bruce is his second name,
  Around the merry-ma-tansie.

This leisurely ceremony, once the chief marriage game in Scotland, is now cut down to child-size. Today the game usually begins abruptly 'Here's the bride just new come home' or 'Choose your partners one and two', so that the divulging of the sweethearts' names may not be too long delayed; for children in junior schools gossip as much about who is 'going with' whom, as do their elders. Thus some graceful features of the game are disappearing which identified it as a medieval *carole*: the opening of gates or raising of arches for the returning bride (e.g. the verse 'High gates till the bride comes in' in Nairnshire, 1898); and the sweeping of the floor 'till the bride comes in', which is an echo, it seems, of the old custom in Scotland of 'Sweepin' the bride', a symbolic sweeping at weddings when the Bride's Reel was danced, the original purpose of which was apparently to sweep away evil spirits, and let bride and groom begin life together free from their influence. (One is reminded of Puck, 'sent with broom before, to sweep the dust behind the door' on a bridal night in Athens.)

The game used to begin with the children dancing round in a circle singing. At the end of the second verse they dropped to the ground, and the last down went into the middle. After the next verse, the player in the middle chose one or two others, went out of the ring with them, and confided the name of her sweetheart. In the meantime the rest sang 'Sweep the hoose (house) till the bride comes in'. They then went back to the middle of the ring; and in Aberdeenshire the circle thought it time the bride should cover her face:

> Time for the bride to be happin her face,
>   Happin her face, happin her face,
> Time for the bride to be happin her face,
>   Sing round about merry me tanzie.

Those in the middle responded:

> What will you give to tell her name,
>   Tell her name, tell her name,
> What will you give to tell her name?
>   Sing round about merry me tanzie.

The circle offered a 'guinea-gold ring'; and the game continued until the names of the sweetheart had been revealed, and the benediction given; although Chambers reported in 1842 that in Lanarkshire, if the girls did not approve the choice, they might reply:

> Apples are sour, and so is he,
>   So is he, so is he;
> Apples are sour, and so is he,
>   About the merry ma tanzie.

The earliest mention of the game is in *Blackwood's Magazine*, August 1821, p. 37, where children in Edinburgh are said to have been singing 'Here we go by gingo-ring' to the favourite tune of 'Nancy Dawson', a tune also associated with 'Nuts in May' and 'Here We Go Round the Mulberry Bush' (pp. 276, 286). In 1825 children in Tweeddale, and Fife, were described playing 'Merry-metanzie', but in a peculiar manner:

They form a ring, within which one goes round with a handkerchief, with which a stroke is given in succession to every one in the ring; the person who strikes, or the *taker*, still repeating the rhyme:

> Here I gae round the jingie ring,
>   The jingie ring, the jingie ring,
> Here I gae round the jingie ring,
>   And through my merry-metanzie.

Then the handkerchief is thrown at one in the ring, who is obliged to take it up and go through the same process.

No confirmation or explanation of this form of the game has been found, and it is probably an aberration.

The term 'jinga-ring' or 'jingo-ring' has long been proverbial in Scotland for a lively circle dance. William Miller, in the first half of the nineteenth century, spoke of the seasons as 'hand in hand they jink about, Like weans at jingo-ring'; and Robert Louis Stevenson, in the second half of the century, wanted an illustration of one of his poems to show children 'dancing in a jing-a-ring'. The uncertain origin of the term 'merry-ma-tansie', variously found as 'merry-ma-tansa', 'merry-ma-tandy', 'merry-me-tanzie', 'merry-my-tanzie', etc., provides a springboard for conjectural gymnasts. Some have suggested 'merry-ma-tansie' may be a transmutation of 'merry maids dancing', or of 'merry maids all' (as in the refrain of 'The Gooseberry Grows on an Angry Tree'), or of the German *Mit mir tanzen*, 'Dance with me', or even of *matanza*, the ceremonial pig-killing in Spain. In 1868 an observer in Glasgow was certain the words were 'And round about Mary matan'sy'; and remarked on the way children bent to the ground when they repeated them, in the way children did in Antwerp when playing a similar game, to the same tune, with the figure of the Madonna in the centre. The line might therefore, he suggested, mean 'Round about Mary our matins say', and certainly children at this time moved round slowly, rather than briskly, and curtsied to the ground rather than fell to the ground, the one who last regained her position being the one who was required to say her sweetheart's name. Possibly 'Ring a Ring o' Roses' (p. 220) was once merely the start of a game of the same kind, as indeed it was in Westmorland in 1903; while in Connecticut, about 1840, children used to sing:

> A ring, a ring, a ransy,
> Buttermilk and tansy,
> Flower here and flower there,
> And all—squat!

If children had one song about the tansy, why not others? (Indeed they also had 'And my delight's in tansies'.) In the north there is tansy pudding, tansy tea, tansy cake, and a 'tansy' can be a merry-making, although one assisted more by beer than tea and cake. In some versions of the game, however, there is no 'Merry-ma-tansie', the refrain being 'On a cold and frosty morning' or 'My fair lady'. And sometimes there is no jingo ring either. The texts of the game are in fact very various and probably corrupted; and the song may begin 'Three times round goes the gala, gala ship' (1893) or include 'A bowlful of nuts we sat down to crack' (R. Ingpen, 1903).

Scotland: *Scottish Dictionary, Supplement*, John Jamieson, ii, 1825, p. 116 | *Popular Rhymes of Scotland*, Robert Chambers, 1842, pp. 64–5, 'The Merry-ma-tanzie is one of the most universally prevalent of these pretty games' | Glasgow, 1868, 'a favourite game' (*Notes & Queries*, 4th ser., ii, p. 324) | *Merrie Games in Rhyme*, E. M. Plunket, 1886, pp. 50–1 | *Arbroath*, J. M. McBain, 1887, 'that merry rollicking game which has delighted our mothers and grandmothers time out of mind', p. 346 | *Weekly Scotsman*, 16 October 1893, starts 'Three times round goes the gala, gala ship' | *Traditional Games*, i, 1894, pp. 369–71, Biggar, Lanarkshire; ii, 1898, pp. 422–4, Laurieston and St Andrews, 'Galley, Galley Ship'; pp. 443–6, versions from north-east of Scotland | *Games of Argyleshire*, 1901, pp. 55–6 | *One Thousand Poems for Children*, Roger Ingpen, 1903, p. 90, 'A bowlful of nuts we sat down to crack Around about merry ma Tansy' | Forfar, *c.*1910 | *Kerr's Guild of Play*, 1912, p. 11 | Langholm, 1957 | Montrose, and Bellshill, Lanarkshire, 1975.

New Zealand: Moeraki, Otago, 1890s, and elsewhere, apparently played in a variety of ways (Sutton-Smith, p. 16).

Canada: London, Ontario, 1909, 'Hally-go-round my ging-a-ring' (*JAFL*, xxxi, p. 57).

Cf. USA: Washington DC, 1886, game begins 'Johnny is his first name, His first name, his first name, Johnny is his first name, Among the lily-white daisies.' After first and second names have been given of both boy and girl, song continues 'And now poor Johnny's dead and gone . . . And left poor Emma a widow. . . With twenty-four children round her feet' (*Lippincott's Magazine*, xxxvii, p. 241) | Cincinnati, 1908 (*JAFL*, xl, p. 20) | Maryland, 1948, ends 'Now poor —— is dead and gone. . . Where shall we bury him?. . . Bury him in the coo coo's nest, Among the little white daisies' (Howard MSS). Jean Ritchie's rendering, *Folkways Record* no. FC 754, 1957, is very similar.

Cf. also: Co. Louth, Ireland, 1898, 'Round about the punch bowl, one, two, three; Open the gates and let the bride through. Half a crown to know his name. . . On a cold and frosty morning,' etc. (*Traditional Games*, ii, pp. 84–5).

28

Gentle John

As I go round ring by ring,
A maiden goes a-maying,
Here's a flower, and there's a flower,
In my lady's garden.
If you set your foot awry,
Gentle John will make you cry;
If you set your foot amiss,
Gentle John will give you a kiss.

This lady is none of ours,
Has put herself in *Jamie's* power,
So clap all hands and ring all bells,
And make the wedding o'er.

Such lines were probably part of a ring game of the type in which the leader of the dance conducts a maiden round inside the ring, induces her to name

one from the ring for partner and proceeds, if the others approve the
match, to stage a mock wedding. The lines are adapted from two game-
songs set down by Halliwell in 1842, of which Alice Gomme could find no
further trace in 1894, but of which we have two further records. At Askam-
in-Furness about 1890, children held hands in a circle, picked one player
to go in the middle, and sang, to the tune of 'I Saw Three Ships Come
Sailing By':

> Here we go round some rings and jings,
> And ladies goes a walking.
> Here's a flower, and there's a flower,
> In Gentle Johnny's garden.
> If you set your foot awry,
> Gentle Johnny will make you cry;
> If you set your foot amiss,
> Gentle Johnny will give you a kiss.

The girl in the ring enacted the words, setting one foot awry, pretending to
cry, and at the end choosing one in the ring she would like to kiss. In
Somerset, in the early 1920s, children similarly formed a ring, selected
one player to go in the middle, and danced round her to the words:

> All round the mulberry bush,
>   Boys and girls together,
> Pick a flower and leave a flower,
>   Curtsy all together;
> If by chance your foot should slip,
>   Uncle Joe will give you a kiss;
> Oh, for shame! Oh, for shame!
>   Tell me who your sweetheart is.

The girl in the middle named her sweetheart, who joined her in the ring,
and the children continued their dance, singing:

> If Mister *Brian* was to die
> And leave his wife behind him,
> Oh, what should we do to save her!
> She's either in, she's either out,
> Or up in the garden dressing herself;
> Then it's off with the glove, and on with the ring,
> This is the way the wedding begins.

The game ended with the pair pretending to get married.

Is it possible that the Gentle John commemorated was Gentil Johne the
English fool who 'brocht japis' to the Scottish King in 1489 and was paid
£10 for his performance (*Mediaeval Plays in Scotland*, Anne Jean Mill,
1927, p. 314)?

Nursery Rhymes of England, J. O. Halliwell, 1842, pp. 123–4 and 125, one starting with the line 'Ring me, ring me, ring me rary', which is probably not integral. The whole verse was used to count-out a girl who must select a sweetheart; but she must not join in the general applause at her choice, or the selected one had to take the place in the middle. However, Halliwell admitted he was not sure of the procedure | Askam-in-Furness, Lancashire, *c.*1890 (Professor E. M. Wilson) | Somerset, *c.*1922 (Macmillan Collection).

Cf. 'Uncle John (II)', p. 161.

29

Glasgow Ships

Games of Argyleshire, *1901*

Glasgow ships come sailing in,
Come sailing in, come sailing in;
Glasgow ships come sailing in,
On a fine summer morning.

You dare not stamp your foot upon,
Your foot upon, your foot upon;
You dare not stamp your foot upon,
Or Gentle John will kiss you.

Three times kiss you,
Four times bless you,
Send a piece of bread and butter
Upon a silver saucer.

> Who shall we send it to,
> Send it to, send it to,
> Who shall we send it to?
> To Mrs Murray's daughter.
>
> She washes her face, she combs her hair,
> She leaves her lad at the foot of the stair;
> She wears a gold ring and a velvet string,
> And she turns her back behind her.

This game was played with everyone joining hands in a circle, singing the song (text from Argyllshire), and whoever was named to receive the gift turned her back to the centre, the verses being sung again and again until everyone had 'got themselves played' and was facing outwards. The game was known in Aberdeenshire, Berwickshire ('Let the Ships Come Sailin' In'), Morayshire, Perthshire, and elsewhere in Scotland, as well as Argyllshire, at the turn of the century; but the opening verse had probably emerged only recently, prompted by the tune 'I Saw Three Ships Come Sailing In'. When recorded in 1847 the song had no Glaswegian or nautical associations, although the sound of the words, it will be noticed, was similar:

> Here is a lass with a golden ring,
> Golden ring, golden ring;
> Here is a lass with a golden ring,
>   So early in the morning.
>
> Gentle Johnie kissed her,
> Three times blessed her,
> Sent her a slice o' bread and butter,
>   In a silver saucer.
>
> Who shall we send it to,
> Send it to, send it to;
> Who shall we send it to?
>   To Mrs *Ritchie's* daughter.

No mention was made of anyone turning her back; and the game was probably played like 'Uncle John (I)' hereafter, the maiden perhaps simply turning away her face in modesty when her lover was named. Clearly the song is related to both 'Uncle John' and 'Gentle John', but the records are insufficient to show the line of development. A memory of the game seems to have been preserved in the skipping verse current in Cumnock in 1961:

Glasgow waves go rolling over,
Rolling over, rolling over,
Glasgow waves go rolling over,
Early in the morning.

The tune is a version of 'Sheriffmuir', first printed by James Hogg in *Jacobite Relics*, 1819, pp. 149–50, with the comment 'but the air has long been popular'.

Scotland: *Popular Rhymes of Scotland*, Robert Chambers, 1847, p. 256 | Milngavie, Glasgow, *c.*1875, 'She dare not set her foot upon, for Gentle John 'll court her!', the child informant explained; ' "her foot upon" means "upon the ship" ' (Crofton MS, ii, p. 76) | *Antiquary*, xxx, 1894, p. 16, Eyemouth and Beauly Firth | *Traditional Games*, ii, 1898, pp. 424–5, five versions | *Games of Argyleshire*, 1901, pp. 81–3 | *Children's Rhymes*, Robert Ford, 1904, pp. 81–3 | *Eighty Singing Games*, Frank Kidson, 1907, pp. 16–17.

30

Uncle John (I)

Uncle John is very sick,
What shall we send him?
Three good wishes, three good kisses,
And a slice of ginger.

What shall we send it in?
In a piece of paper.
Paper is not fine enough;
In a golden saucer.

Who shall we send it by?
By the governor's daughter.
Take her by the lily-white hand,
And lead her over the water.

Newell reported (1883) that this was one of the most familiar of all children's rounds in America. The words were sung by a ring of dancers, who, when they came to 'governor's daughter', fell to the ground: 'The last down stands apart, selects her confidential friend, and imparts with great mystery the *initials* of some boy in whom she takes an interest. She then returns, and takes her place in the ring with face reversed, while the friend announces the initials, and the dancers sing a verse borrowed from 'Rosy Apple' (p. 164), using the letters given:

> *A. B.*, so they say,
> Goes a-courting night and day,
> Sword and pistol by his side,
> And —— —— to be his bride;
> Takes her by the lily-white hand,
> And leads her o'er the water—
> Here's·a kiss, and there's a kiss
> For Mr ——'s daughter.'

One of the girls who played this game—in Minnesota in the 1870s—was the future author Laura Ingalls Wilder. Another was to be the librarian Caroline M. Hewins, who knew the game at children's parties around Boston in the 1850s. But the game was familiar in Britain as well as America. In Shrewsbury, in the 1880s, the children went round singing:

> Uncle John is ill in bed,
> What shall I send him?
> Three good wishes and three good kisses,
> And a race of ginger.
>
> Who shall I send it by?
> By the carrier's daughter,
> Catch her by the lily-white hand
> And carry her over the water.

They then stooped down, the last to do so had to reveal her sweetheart's name, and they continued the game singing:

> *Sally* goes a-courting night and day,
> Histal, whistal, by her side,
> *Johnny Everall* by her side.

At Bridport, likewise, in the early 1920s, children formed a ring and danced round as they sang:

> Uncle John is very sick
> And what shall we send him?
> A piece of pudding as long as our arm,
> And send it in a basin.
> Who shall we send it by?
> By the governor's daughter.

At the words 'governor's daughter' they fell to the ground, and the last to get up again had to tell her sweetheart's name. The others then sang:

> All the boys in Bridport shall lead a happy life,
> Except *John Jones*, and he shall have a wife;
> A wife he shall have, and a-courting he shall go,

Along with *Mary Smith*, because he loves her so.
He kisses her, he cuddles her, he takes her on his knee,
He says, My dear old *Mary*, how happy we shall be.
Mary made a pudding, she made it very sweet,
In comes John, and cuts it very deep:
One on the right hand,
The other on the left.

Everyone then clapped hands, and the game began again. This linking of lines from 'All the Boys in Our Town' (p. 130) with a patient who might be cured with fondness and good feeding (as all patients should be) had already been traditional for two or three generations. In 1847 Chambers reported a 'courtship dance' in Scotland which, beginning with the universal tragedy of 'A' the lads in our town are dying for love', concluded with the names of the two performers chosen to be sweethearts:

> *Helen Simpson* lies sick,
> Guess ye what'll mend her?
> Twenty kisses in a clout,
> Which *Jamie Anderson* sends her.
> Half an ounce o' green tea,
> A pennyworth of pepper,
> Take ye that, my bonny dear,
> And I hope you'll soon be better.

Further, a piquant little dance verse, crooned to the tune 'Cawdor Fair', is still rightly remembered in the land of Burns, and may be presumed to be the game's ancestor:

> Cockie Bendie's lyin' sick,
> Guess you what will mend him,
> Twenty kisses in a cloot
> Lassie, will ye send them?

'Cockibendy' was almost certainly already venerable when 'A New Song called Cockibendy', embodying the well-known lines, was printed about 1820.

Britain: *Popular Rhymes of Scotland*, Robert Chambers, 1847, p. 273 | *Shropshire Folk-Lore*, 1883, p. 511 | Bridport, Somerset, 1922 (Macmillan Collection) | Kington St Michael, 1924 (*Wiltshire Magazine*, Dec. 1942, p. 44).
   USA: Minnesota, *c*.1875 (*On the Banks of Plum Creek*, L. I. Wilder, 1937, ch. xxi) | Hartford, Connecticut, 1883 (*Games of American Children*, p. 72) | Cincinnati, 1908 (*JAFL*, xl, pp. 13 and 70) | Wake County, 1920s? (*North Carolina Folklore*, pp. 132–3).

31

Uncle John (II)

Uncle John is very sick,
What shall I send him?
A piece of bread, a piece of cake,
A piece of apple dumpling.

Who shall I send it by?
By the governor's daughter.
Take her by the lily-white hand
And lead her across the water.

I knock at the door, I pick up a pin,
And ask Mrs *Buchan*, 'Is *Sheila* within?'
'She's neither within, she's neither without,
She's up in the garret walking about.'

Down she comes as white as milk,
A rose in her bosom as soft as silk;
She off with her glove, and shows me a ring,
Tomorrow, tomorrow, the wedding begins.

Enough evidence exists to suggest that the game 'Uncle John' flourished in two forms, and that lines such as these (the text is a slight reconstruction) were the usual ones in the eighteenth century. Newell says the third and fourth verses were known in Concord, Massachusetts, before 1800; and followed the playing of 'Little Sally Waters' or 'Uncle John'. In Maryland in the 1940s children were playing a game, 'Uncle Johnny's Sick in Bed', in which, during the second verse, a player in the centre of the ring had to choose another, who must name her boy-friend (in this case), so that his mother's name, and his own, could be given when they sang:

> I went to the door, I picked up a pin,
> I asked Mrs —— if —— was in.

The game also seems to have been known in Scotland—again, one player being chosen whose duty it was to pick another—and all the lines were repeated except, apparently, the couplet about going to the door and picking up the pin (i.e. tirling the pin or rattling the latch). However these lines, and the succeeding ones, turn up in England in a version of 'Sally Water', played by children at Hersham, Surrey, in 1882.

Although schoolchildren and scholars alike have hitherto chosen to think of the song as commemorating a happy romance, another interpretation is possible. In the old Scots ballad 'Clyde's Water' or 'The Drowned Lovers' (recorded 1802–3) the climax occurs when the hero, who has rashly made his way late at night through the flood to visit his sweetheart Margaret, arrives at her door in some distress:

> And when he come to his love's gates,
>   He tirled at the pin:
> Open your gates, Meggie,
>   Open your gates to me.

His cry, however, is heard not by the girl but by her ill-disposed mother, who pretends to be Margaret, and replies:

> I hae nae lovers thereout,
> I hae nae love within.

This response sends the young man to his doom. In the game-song the enigmatic line 'She's neither within, she's neither without', begins to make sense if spoken by a mother who is prevaricating; and the possibility cannot be discounted that when the daughter descends from the garret, with a rose in her bosom, and removes her glove announcing that the wedding is to be the next day, the ring she shows is one given her by another man.

Scotland: Nairn, and Laurieston, Kirkcudbright, 1898, 'Uncle Tom is very sick' (*Traditional Games*, ii, p. 322) | Cairnbulg, Aberdeenshire, *c.*1915, 'Uncle Tommie's very sick'.

USA: Concord, Massachusetts, pre-1800, 'He knocks at the door, and picks up a pin, And asks if Miss —— is in, She neither is in, she neither is out, She's in the garret a-walking about. Down she comes as white as milk, A rose in her bosom, as soft as silk. She takes off her gloves, and shows me a ring; Tomorrow, tomorrow, the wedding begins' (*Games of American Children*, p. 67) | Maryland, 1944 (Howard MSS).

Cf. *Lilliput Levee*, W. B. Rands, 1864, p. 111, 'But here comes Marjorie, white as milk, A rose in her bosom as soft as silk, On her finger a gay gold ring; The bridegroom holds up his head like a king!' | *Folk-Lore Record*, v, 1882, p. 88, 'Sally, Sally Water' | *Traditional Games*, i, 1894, p. 175, 'Green Gravel', and pp. 312–13 'Knocked at the Rapper'—'He knocked at the rapper, and he pulled at the string, Pray Mrs ——, is —— within? O no, she has gone into the town; Pray take the arm-chair and sit yourself down' | *St Anne's Soho Monthly Magazine*, July 1907, p. 180, skipping chant, 'All right *Florrie*, pretty little *Florrie*: All the boys are waiting for you; They go to the door and lift up the latch, And ask Mrs —— if *Florrie* is in. *Florrie*'s always in; *Florrie*'s always out; *Florrie*'s in the parlour walking about' | Cincinnati, 1907, 'I went up stairs to pick up a pin, I asked if Mrs Jenny is in, She neither was in, she neither was out' etc. (*JAFL*, xl, 1927, p. 12).

32

Oh Dear Doctor

Oh dear doctor, can you tell
What will make poor *Annie* well?
Annie's sick and going to die,
That will make poor *Frankie* cry.
Frankie's here and *Frankie's* there,
Frankie's on the water,
Frankie's got the prettiest girl
Of Mrs *Burton's* daughters.

A simple ring game in which the lovesick maiden in the centre is cured by a kiss from the boy called into the ring. About 1800 the first couplet was being addressed to the Doctor in the folk play: 'Doctor, doctor, can you tell What will make a sick man well?' (Hone, *Every-Day Book*, 1827, p. 75).

USA: *Games of American Children*, 1883, pp. 99–100 | Cincinnati, 1907, as end part of the game 'The Wind Blows High' (*JAFL*, xl, p. 19) | *Play-Party in Indiana*, L. J. Wolford, 1916, p. 97 | Forest City, *c.*1927 (*North Carolina Folklore*, p. 177) | New York, New Jersey, and East Texas, 1938 (Howard MSS) | Marissa, 1948, as second part of 'Uncle Johnny Sick in Bed' (*Singing Games of the Illinois Ozarks*, D. S. McIntosh, 1974, p. 67; tune given is an adaptation of 'Yankee Doodle').

Britain: Southport, *c.*1905.

Cf., for the motif, *Jeux de Société*, Madame Celnart, 1827, Le Médecin: 'Donne-moi ton bras que je te guérisse, Car tu m'as l'air malade!' 'Embrasse monsieur pour te guérir. C'est un fort bon remède.'

33

Rosy Apple

Dearham, Cumberland, 1962

Rosy apple, lemon and a pear,
A bunch of roses she shall wear,
A sword and pistol by her side,
She shall be a bride.
Take her by the lily-white hand,
Lead her across the water,
Blow her a kiss and say goodbye—
She's the captain's daughter.

One of the loveliest songs for 'playing ring' that ever haunted a city back street (Martin Shaw said he would have given all his musical compositions to have composed it); and the song is appreciated by the children too, who sing it when skipping as well as when circling. The game is played with one person in the middle of the ring choosing someone from the circle to be the bride, and then blowing kisses or symbolically saluting her before withdrawing to the perimeter; or with the player in the middle taking 'the lily-white hand' of the chosen one, and the pair weaving their way in and out of the arches which the circle make by holding up their arms (Liss); or the pair may themselves make a two-armed arch, and the ring run round under it until the arch descends on one of the runners who becomes the new chooser (Preston); or, again, the players may stand in a line with one

'Rosy Apple' (No. 33) near the gasworks at Leyland, Lancs., 1968; the local version is played with an arch.

girl out in front who dances backwards and forwards, takes hold of the right hand of the chosen one with her right hand, and swings her round leaving her to become the chooser, when the game starts again (Workington). The text has remained remarkably stable over the years. The line 'Lead her across the water' is sometimes rationalized to 'Lead her to the altar'; and 'Gold and silver by her side' becomes 'Golden pistol by her side' or 'Sword and pistol by her side'. But such divergencies, if divergencies they are, are themselves traditional. 'Lead her to the altar' was already an alternative version in 1882; the line 'Sword and pistol by his side' was current in Connecticut in 1883 (see under 'Uncle John' I); and the opening 'Rosy apple, mellow pear', instead of 'Rosy apple, lemon and pear', heard in Brighton in 1964, was the opening of the song when recorded in 1877:

> Rosy apple, mellow pear,
> Bunch of roses she shall wear;
> Gold and silver by her side;
> I know who shall be my bride.
>
> Take her by the lily-white hand,
> Lead her 'cross the water,
> Give her kisses, one, two, three,
> Mrs *Harrison's* daughter.

The song may well be of some antiquity, despite the lack of early recordings. It has the grace and simplicity of age, and 'take her by the lily-white hand' is a phrase from balladry (appearing for instance in 'Young Andrew', Child 48).

Britain: *Nursery Rhymes and Country Songs*, M. H. Mason, 1877, p. 21 | Hersham, Surrey, 1882 (*Folk-Lore Record*, v, p. 85) | Symondsbury, Dorset, 1889 (*Folk-Lore*, vii, p. 210) | Berkshire, 1893 (*Antiquary*, xxvii, p. 254) | Ipswich, 1893, 'Golden apple, lemon and a pear' (*County Folk-Lore: Suffolk*, E. C. Gurdon, p. 64) | Ropley, Hampshire, 1895 (*Notes & Queries*, 8th ser., vii, p. 383) | Guildford, 1897 or 1898 (*Song Time*, Percy Dearmer and Martin Shaw, p. 88) | *Traditional Games*, ii, 1898, pp. 117–21, 11 further versions, including five from Scotland | Frequently recorded in twentieth century. Versions from 12 places since 1960.

   Canada: Bruce School, 1962 (Fowke, 1969, p. 68) | *Victoria Daily Times Weekend Magazine*, 30 May 1970, p. 10, slick version for skipping, 'Red rose the apple, Five cent affair, A box of roses she shall wear' etc.

   Cf. USA: Hartford, Connecticut, 1883, '——— ———, so they say, Goes a-courting night and day, Sword and pistol by his side, And ——— ———, to be his bride,' etc. (*Games of American Children*, p. 72) | Jackson and St Johns, Michigan, c.1914, 'Johnny, Johnny, so they say, Goes a-courting night and day; Sword and pistol by his side, Takes ——— to be his bride,' etc. (*JAFL*, xxxiii, pp. 106–7) | North Carolina, c.1927, 'a kissing game', similar to Michigan (*North Carolina Folklore*, pp. 128–9).

   Cf. Scotland: Kirkcaldy, c.1910, ring game, 'Logan's waters they are deep, But I'm nae fear'd tae weet ma feet, Weet ma feet an' away I go To meet the bonnie lassie o' the Logans O!' (Chooses a girl.) 'Take her by the lily white hand, Lead her o'er the water: Give her kisses one, two, three, For she's a lady's daughter' (Girl is kissed, and stays in centre).

34
Sally Water

Southport, 1898, Gilchrist MSS 231 A iii

Sally, Sally Water, sprinkle in the pan,
Rise Sally, rise Sally, for a young man,
Choose to the east, and choose to the west,
Choose the very one that you love best.

Now they are married I hope they will be joy,
First a girl and then a boy,
Seven years after, seven years to go,
Now it is time for a kiss and I go.

These lines, sung by children in Welshpool in 1952, and Alton in 1954, during a simple ring game in which one girl crouched down while the others walked round until they came to the word *best*, and the girl in the middle chose someone to join her, are not materially different from those Charles Bennett knew in 1858 as the general introduction to 'Kiss in the Ring':

Sally, Sally Waters, sprinkle in the pan,
Hie, Sally! Hie, Sally, for a young man!
Choose for the best, choose for the worst,
Choose for the prettiest that you love best.

In Aberystwyth, 1953, in Amlwch on Anglesey, 1952, and in Liverpool, 1945 and 1968, the children sang:

> Little Alexandra sitting on the sand,
> Weeping and crying for her young man;
> Rise up, Sally, wipe your tears,
> Choose the very one you love so dear.

The player in the middle likewise chose someone to enter the ring, and danced round with her while the others continued:

> Now Sally's got married I hope she'll enjoy
> For ever and ever a girl and a boy;
> If one won't do, I hope she'll have two,
> So I pray you young people to kiss two by two.

Almost identical words were sung at Southport in 1898, and at Stockport about 1905, and fairly similar lines at Beddgelert, near Mount Snowdon, before 1898.

In Hackney, 1965, the verse the girls knew may well have been considered 'wrong' by the children of other boroughs:

> Little Sally Masters sitting in a saucer,
> Rise, Sally, rise, and dry your eyes;
> Sally, turn to the east, Sally, turn to the west,
> Sally turn to the very one you love the best.

Yet in County Kerry in 1938, and in New Jersey about the same year, in St Louis, 1944, in Michigan about 1914, in Cincinnati in 1908, and in Jamaica before 1906, children were all singing about a 'Little Sally Water' or 'Walker' or 'Sally Sally Saucer' who sat in a saucer; and, in the earliest account of the game being played—at Stixwould in Lincolnshire, about 1828—the child in the middle, 'Sally, Sally Salter', is said to have held in her hands something 'resembling a saucer', and to have given the saucer to the one whom she chose (cf. Uncle John's gold or silver saucer, p. 158).

The singularity of the words, the fidelity of the transmission during the period they have been recorded, and the wide distribution of the game in the English-speaking world, inevitably arouse curiosity about the game's origin and possible significance. Alice Gomme made an analysis of the forty-eight British texts known to her in 1898, and found twenty-three of them to contain the name *Sally Water* or *Waters*, seventeen the name *Sally Walker*, and two the name *Sally* only, leaving six with another name altogether. If it is allowed that Sally Walker derives from Sally Water, or that anyway Sally Walker and Sally Water are cognate, then 83 per cent of the versions may be agreed to contain a related name-sound, a high proportion when it is appreciated some of the verses were fragmentary or hybrids. Further, in two versions where the name was not Sally Water or Walker, the word *water* appeared later; in twenty-one versions there was mention of 'sprinkling the water'; and in some other versions there was 'sitting by the water', 'water your can', 'springin' in the pan', and 'tinkle in a can', which may be presumed to be derivative. The conjunction of an aquatic name with this sprinkling of water, and with a marriage game, easily leads to the presumption that the game contains reference to water-worship or, at the least, reference to the special place water has been accorded in wedding customs. Thus in ancient Rome the bride is said to have been sprinkled with water; in Albania the bride's mother sprinkles the bridegroom with water, or did so in the nineteenth century; in Turkey the bridegroom upset water on the stairs to the bride's apartment; and in Little Russia the parents of both bride and groom were the ones who were soused (H. N. Hutchinson's *Marriage Customs*).

In classical Greece bride and groom bathed in water drawn from a particular fountain; and in Mohammedan countries, especially Morocco (according to Westermarck), ritual importance is attached to the bathing of both the bride and groom before they meet; and nearer home Burns and Highland Mary were possessed of an ancient memory of what was fitting when they plighted their troth across a 'small purling brook' after ceremoniously laving their hands in the stream. So it will be no surprise to the student of students of folklore that the female divinity Sul, or Sula, who presided over the waters of Bath, where the Roman temple was dedicated to Sulis-Minerva, has been seriously considered to be Sally's ancestor (Lina Eckenstein); and few folklorists, if any, have yet been impolite enough to doubt Lady Gomme's deduction that the game of 'Sally Water' is 'a relic of the pre-Celtic people of these islands'.

However an examination of the texts that have been in circulation in North America, where until recently oral lore has been under less stress than in Britain, presents a different picture. In the twenty texts known to us, collected in Canada and the United States between 1883 and 1976, much crying and weeping takes place, but the only other sign of moisture, other than in Sally's surname, is a possible allusion in the line 'Rise up, Sally, and tinkle the pan' (Southern Appalachians, *c.*1927). Most versions are in the form that was recorded in 1883:

> Little Sally Waters, sitting in the sun,
> Crying and weeping for a young man.
> Rise, Sally, rise, dry your weeping eyes,
> Fly to the east, fly to the west,
> Fly to the one you love best.

It should also be noted that recent recordings of the text in the United Kingdom show that the name Sally Water or Walker is disappearing; and that the game is undergoing a metamorphosis, if indeed it can still be thought of as the same game. The usual text today is one that was formerly confined to the north of Britain. It is sung to the tune of 'Best Bed's a Feather Bed' (p. 210):

> I'm a little sandy girl sitting on a stone,
> Crying, weeping, all the day alone,
> Stand up, sandy girl, wipe your tears away,
> Choose the one that you love best, and run the other way.

Or, in the vicinity of Glasgow and Dundee:

> Two little sandy girls sittin' by the shore,
> Cryin' and weepin' till their eyes are sore;
> Stand up *Annie*, and wipe away your tears,
> Choose the one that you love best and that's—
> and that's—and that's *Lucy* dear.

The game is now a version of 'Bump-on-the-Back' (see *Street and Playground*, p. 203). The player who has been sitting or crouching in the middle of the circle while the verse was sung springs up, touches someone who is part of the circle, and immediately races round the outside of the ring hoping to complete the circuit before the other player can race round the circle in the other direction and regain her place. And no matter whether this late-twentieth century ascendancy is due to its publication in *Traditional Singing Games for Brownies*, 1936, the ease with which a fundamental change can take place, and the rashness of reading deep meaning into words that have been orally transmitted, without supporting historical evidence, will, it is hoped, have been well-enough exemplified.

Britain: Stixwould, Lincolnshire, *c*.1828 (*Traditional Games*, ii, p. 157) | *Popular Rhymes*, J. O. Halliwell, 1849, p. 133, 'Sally, Sally Waters, why are you so sad? You shall have a husband either good or bad: Then rise, Sally Waters, and sprinkle your pan, For you're just the young woman to get a nice man' | *Old Nurse's Book*, C. H. Bennett, 1858, p. 35 | Altrincham, Cheshire, *c*.1870 (Gilchrist MSS. 231 Aiii) | Thornes, near Wakefield, 1874 (*Notes & Queries*, 5th ser., iii, p. 481) | Castle Carey, *c*.1875, 'Sally, Sally, Washdish, Sprinkle in the pan; Rise Sally, rise, Sally, For a young man' | Chudleigh Knighton, Devon, 1878, also Morpeth, Northumberland, 1879, 'Sally Walker, Sally Walker, Come spring time and love, She's lamenting, she's lamenting, All for her young man' (W. Henderson, *Folk-Lore of the Northern Counties*, pp. 26–7) | Market Drayton, and elsewhere, 1883, 'This is the most popular game of all' (*Shropshire Folk-Lore*, p. 509), ending, 'Now you are married I wish you good joy, First a girl and then a boy; Seven years now, and seven years to come, Take her and kiss her, and send her off home' | *Notes & Queries*, 7th ser., x, 1890, pp. 449–50, many versions | *Traditional Games*, ii, 1898, pp. 149–79, 453–4 | Chaddesley Corbett, Worcestershire, 1899, 'Rise, Sally, rise, Sally, Catch me if you can' (*Folk-Lore*, xxxv, p. 267) | *Games of Argyleshire*, 1901, pp. 60–1, 'Little Alexander, sitting on the grass, Weeping and crying, a nice young lass. Rise up, Sandie, wipe away your tears, Choose the very one you love so dear.' Player in the centre chooses someone from the ring, takes her hands and the pair whirl round while the rest sing: 'Now Sandie's married, I hope you'll enjoy For ever and ever to be a good boy' | Lanarkshire, *c.*1902, 'Two little sandy girls sitting on a stone' | *London Street Games*, 1916, p. 90, 'Little Sally Sanders, sitting on the sand' | *Traditional Singing Games for Brownies*, R. Cowan Douglas and K. M. Briggs, 1936, reissued 1955, 'There's a little Sandy girl' to be played as 'Bump-on-the-Back' type race-game | 38 versions since 1950.

New Zealand: Game being played *c.*1863 (*Shropshire Folk-Lore*, p. 509 n.) | Christchurch, 1870, and subsequent reports from all provinces (Sutton-Smith, pp. 15–16).

West Indies: *Jamaican Song and Story*, Walter Jekyll, 1907, pp. 190–1, the game said to be so well known that the name 'Sally Water' is generic for ring games | *Song Games of Trinidad and Tobago*, J. D. Elder, 1961, p. 12, 'There was a little sandy girl'.

USA: *Games of American Children*, 1883, p. 70 | Washington DC, 1886 (*Lippincott's Magazine*, xxxviii, pp. 324–5) | St Louis, *c.*1895 and 1944 (*JAFL*, lx, pp. 14–15 and 39) | Cincinnati, 1908 (ibid., xl, pp. 12–13) | Michigan, *c.*1914 (ibid., xxxiii, pp. 122–3) | Southern Appalachians, *c.*1927, three versions (*North Carolina Folklore*, pp. 130–1) | East Orange, New Jersey, *c.*1938, and Maryland, 1947 (Howard MSS) | *One Potato, Two Potato*, Mary and Herbert Knapp, 1976, p. 150, 'Little Sally Waters, sittin' in a saucer' played by contemporary children.

Canada: Peterborough, 1880, and Toronto, 1895 (*JAFL*, viii, p. 254) | Ottawa, *c.*1900, and Ontario, *c.*1900 and 1909 (ibid., xxxi, pp. 159–60, 147, and 55) | Toronto, 1962 (Fowke, 1969, p. 26).

35

Isabella

adapted from Joyous Singing Games, *John Hornby, 1913*

Isabella, Isabella, Isabella, farewell,
Last night when we parted,
I left her broken-hearted,
And on the green mountain
There stands a young man.

Choose your lover, choose your lover,
Choose your lover, farewell.

Open the gates, love, open the gates, love,
Open the gates, love, farewell.

Go to church, love, go to church, love,
Go to church, love, farewell.

Kneel down, love, kneel down, love,
Kneel down, love, farewell.

Say your prayers, love, say your prayers, love,
Say your prayers, love, farewell.

Stand up, love, stand up, love,
Stand up, love, farewell.

Put the ring on, put the ring on,
Put the ring on, farewell.

Return love, return love,
Return love, farewell.

Give a kiss, love, give a kiss love,
Give a kiss, love, farewell.

'Isabella' was still being played in the West Country in the 1920s. One child stood in the middle of the ring while the others circled round her singing. When they sang 'Choose your lover', she chose someone from the ring (a boy, if a boy was playing), and went out of the ring with him through the 'open gates', the gap where he had been standing. The pair then did as instructed, kneeling down, praying, standing up, putting on the ring, returning to the middle of the ring, and kissing. Usually the game ended here. But in some districts a dialogue followed in which the young couple were asked what they would have for dinner, tea, and supper, and replied variously:

'Roast beef and plum pudding.'
'Roast beef and rotten onions.'
'Dry bread and black beetles.'
'Bread and butter and watercress.'
'Bread and cheese and strong beer.'

Although 'Isabella' was much played in the last quarter of the nineteenth century in the midlands and the south (Alice Gomme collected it from a London nursemaid in 1878), the game was already being assimilated by its more dominant cousin 'Lady on the Mountain' (p. 174). The only sound of 'Isabella' we ourselves have heard was in 1974 in Coram Fields, Bloomsbury, where a little eight-year-old sang a curious medley of verses including the lines:

> Here's my black and here's my blue,
> So open the gates and let me through.
> Kneel down, lord,
> Kiss the ground, lord,
> Stand up, lord.

The recurrent end-word 'farewell' appears in almost every recording of the game, and lends weight to the evidence of the first verse that the words stem from a sentimental ballad. The only significant variation found was current in the Calder Valley in the early years of this century:

> The green leaves are falling,
> Are falling, are falling,
> The green leaves are falling,
> Are falling for me.
>
> Last night when we parted
> She was nigh broken-hearted,
> Isabella, Isabella (or 'She's a bell-a, she's a bell-a'),
> Isabella for me.
>
> Then give me your hand, love,
> Your hand, love, your hand, love,
> Then give me your hand, love,
> And a sweet kiss for me.

Somewhat similar lines from North Derbyshire, beginning 'Last night when we parted' and ending 'Then give me your hand, love, Isabella for me', were known to Alice Gomme in 1894.

Britain: London, 1878 (*Traditional Games*, i, pp. 251–2) | West Grinstead, Sussex, 1892, 'Isabella, Isabella, Isabella, farewell; Last night I met you downhearted and sad, And down by the river I met your young man. Choose a lover, a lover, a lover, farewell' (*Notes & Queries*, 8th ser., i, p. 249) | Berkshire, 1893 (*Antiquary*, xxvii, p. 193) | *Traditional Games*, i, 1894, pp. 247–56, 11 further versions; ii, 1898, p. 431, three Scots versions, including 'Isabella, fare ye wella', from Fochabers | Stalbridge, Dorset, 1895 (*Somerset and Dorset Notes & Queries*, iv, p. 265) | Wrecclesham, Surrey, *c*.1895 | Halifax district, *c*.1900 and *c*.1915, as quote | New Pitsligo, *c*.1900 (*Buchan Observer*, 16 April 1929, p. 2) | *Old Hampshire Singing Games*, A. E. Gillington, 1909, pp. 2–3 | *Joyous Book of Singing Games*, John Hornby, 1913, pp. 54–5 | Somerset and Devon, 1922 (Macmillan Collection) | *Street Games of North Shields Children*, M. and R. King, 1926, pp. 14–15.
    Cf. USA: Maryland, *c*.1920 and *c*.1940, 'Molly, Molly May, as we go rolling, Down the banks so swiftly rolling, Choose your own, your own dear lover, And be sure you never choose another, Oh farewell! Here's my hand, my heart I give you; One sweet kiss, and then I leave you, Oh farewell!' (Boy stands in middle as children circle round, chooses lover, puts one hand on heart while giving her the other one, kisses her, and leaves her in the centre for the game to restart.)

36

Lady on the Mountain

Children's Singing Games, *iii, 1912*

Stands a lady on the mountain,
Who she is I do not know.
All she wants is gold and silver,
All she wants is a nice young man.
Madam will you walk,
Madam will you talk,
Madam will you marry me?

No!

Not if I buy you a nice armchair
To sit in the garden when you take the air?

No!

Not if I buy you a nice silver spoon
To feed your baby in the afternoon?

No!

Not if I buy you a nice straw hat
With three coloured ribbons hanging down the back?

Yes!

Go to church, luv,
Go to church, luv, farewell.
Go to church, luv,
Go to church, luv, farewell.

Back from church, luv,
Back from church, luv, farewell.
Back from church, luv,
Back from church, luv, farewell.

What's for breakfast, luv,
What's for breakfast, luv, farewell?
What's for breakfast, luv,
What's for breakfast, luv, farewell?

Bread and butter and watercress,
Bread and butter and watercress,
Bread and butter and watercress,
And you shall have some.

What's for dinner, luv,
What's for dinner, luv, farewell?
What's for dinner, luv,
What's for dinner, luv, farewell?

Bread and butter and beetles,
Bread and butter and beetles,
Bread and butter and beetles,
And you shall have some.

What's for supper, luv,
What's for supper, luv, farewell?
What's for supper, luv,
What's for supper, luv, farewell?

Bread and butter and rats,
Bread and butter and rats,
Bread and butter and rats,
And you shall have some.

At the beginning of the 1970s only a few lines of this game-song seem to have been remembered; but in 1975–6 versions such as the above were collected in quick succession from nine-year-olds in Salford, from an eight-year-old at Wool in Dorset, and from ten-year-olds in Oxford. In the Salford game one girl stood in the centre while the others processed round her singing the first verse. She then stood in front of one of the players in the ring asking her to marry her. When the player agreed, the others in the circle regrouped to make an avenue of arches, and sang 'Go to church, luv' while the bridal pair passed through. They then sang 'Back from church, luv', while the pair came back through the arches; the circle was formed again, husband and wife sat down in the middle, as if at home, and the husband learnt, apparently without dismay, the kind of house-keeper he had married. The words are virtually those of the game 'There Stands a Lady' published by Cecil Sharp in 1912 and most of the children had, in fact, learnt the song from a young man with a guitar on the TV schools programme 'Music Time'. A detailed study of the reasons for this particular revival being so successful would make interesting reading; though it should be remembered that the game had never completely died out. Certainly this extended version belongs to the period 1905–25 when Norman Douglas and A. S. Macmillan recorded it, as well as Sharp; but the first four lines have been continuously popular in the skipping rope, as well as forming the basis of a simple ring game, first noted by John Hornby for his *Joyous Book of Singing Games*, 1913, and wellish known in the 1950s and 1960s, in which the player in the middle called another player to take her place, as at Berry Hill in 1961:

> On the mountain stands a lady,
> Who she is I do not know,
> All she wants is gold and silver,
> All she wants is a nice young man.
> So come in my *Josie* dear,
> *Josie* dear, *Josie* dear,
> So come in my *Josie* dear,
> While I go out to play.

This game, often reported in the last years of the nineteenth century (Alice Gomme gave eight versions), seems to be related to a further ring game 'Yonder Stands a Lovely Lady' or 'There She Stands a Lovely Creature' of which a version, containing more than one familiar echo, was obtained by Newell in New York, in or before 1883:

> There she stands, a lovely creature,
>   Who she is, I do not know;
> I have caught her for her beauty,
>   Let her answer, yes or no.
>
> Madam, I have gold and silver,
>   Lady, I have houses and lands,
> Lady, I have ships on the ocean,
>   All I have is at thy command.
>
> What care I for your gold and silver,
>   What care I for your houses and lands,
> What care I for your ships on the ocean—
>   All I want is a nice young man.

The second and third verses come from the nursery song 'Madam, I Am Come to Court You', recorded by Halliwell in 1844, just as lines 5–7 of the text song are to be found in versions of 'The Keys of Heaven' or 'The Keys of Canterbury', first printed 1846; and the offers of 'a nice armchair' or, to be precise, 'a nice easy-chair, To sit in and comb your yellow hair', and 'a silver spoon, To feed your babe in the afternoon', come in another old song 'I'll Give to You a Paper of Pins' (p. 140), while the 'Go to church' passage appears to be a borrowing from the game 'Isabella' (p. 171). In addition the four lines beginning 'There she stands a lovely creature', or 'On yonder hill there stands a creature', will be recognized as the opening lines of the folk songs 'Ripest Apples', 'Twenty Eighteen', 'The Disdainful Lady', and 'My Man John', as also, of course, of the song Cecil Sharp purified, 'O No John', a masquerade folk song that, inevitably, has become the anthem, more or less, of the chumpians of Arcady.

Extended versions: Over Stowey, 1900; Bridgwater, 1906; Littleport, 1911 (Cecil Sharp MSS. 1416, 874 and 2639) | *Children's Singing Games*, Cecil Sharp, iii, 1912, Bridgwater version with phrases from Littleport, plus unwarranted prolongation of opening borrowed from Over Stowey | *London Street Games*, 1916, pp. 85–7, much as text but 'Not if I buy you a nice silk hat With seven yards of ribbon hanging down the back? . . . Not if I buy you the keys of Heaven To let yourself in at half-past seven?' | Somerset, 1922 (Macmillan Collection) | Leeds, 1973 | Oban, 1974 | Salford and Wool, 1975 | Oxford, January 1976.

The three-stanza versions apparently derived from folk song: *Games of American Children*, 1883, pp. 55–6, as quote | Washington DC, 1888 (*American Anthropologist*, i, p. 247) | Askam-in-Furness, *c.*1892, 'Over yonder stands a lady, Who she is I do not know; I would like her for my beauty If she'll answer yes or no.' 'Will you come?' 'No.' 'I've got gold and I've got silver, I've got copper, I've got brass; I've got all this world of pleasure If I had that bonny lass.' 'Will you come?' 'Yes.' Boy and girl then whirl round to jingle ending 'Tiddle-i-umpty-umpty-umpty, Now I've got this bonny lass' | Balham, 1912 | *American Play-Party Song*, B. A. Botkin, 1937, p. 357, 'Yonder comes a heavenly creature', from Medford, Grant County, Oklahoma | Cf. *Traditional Games*, i, pp. 323–4, 'Lady on Yonder Hill'.

Simple game: *Shropshire Folk-Lore*, 1883, pp. 509–10, version from Berrington | *County Folk-Lore:Suffolk*, E. C. Gurdon, 1893, p. 62 | *Traditional Games*, i, 1894, pp. 320–3, 'Lady on the Mountain' | Wrecclesham, Surrey, *c.*1895 | Portsmouth, *c.*1905 | *Old Hampshire Singing Games*, A. E. Gillington, 1909, pp. 8–9 | *Street Games of North Shields Children*, M. and R. King, 1926, p. 20 | Versions from 15 places 1950–74. The tune to which the words are now usually sung was noted by Anne Gilchrist at Highfields, Sussex, in 1905 (Gilchrist MSS 231 B iv).

37

Oats and Beans and Barley Grow

East Tisted, Hants, 1964

Oats and beans and barley grow,
Oats and beans and barley grow,
Do you or I or anyone know
How oats and beans and barley grow?

First the farmer sows his seed,
Then he stands and takes his ease,
Stamps his foot, and claps his hand,
And turns around to view the land.

Waiting for a partner,
Waiting for a partner,
Waiting for a partner,
So open the ring and let one in.

Now you're married you must obey,
You must be true to all you say;
You must be kind, you must be good,
And help your wife to chop the wood.
Chop it thin and carry it in,
And kiss your partner in the ring.

Children are in league with folklorists when they feel this game is ancient
and somehow magical. They skip round in a ring, holding hands and
singing, with one player, the farmer, in the middle. The farmer scatters
seed, takes his ease with hands on hips, stamps his foot and claps his hands
(some say to bring on rain), turns round to view the land, and chooses a
partner from the circle, who takes her place beside him while the rest sing
the last verse. The first player then joins the ring; the game begins again
with the 'wife' playing the part of the farmer; after a further dispersal of
seed subjection to a mate is enjoined; and the children every now and again
are half certain they are engaged in something life-giving and important.
The words of 'Oats and Beans and Barley Grow' were not recorded until

the 1880s, but the game was well known then, both in Britain and America, and memories of it apparently went back some years. Indeed the game was, it seems, a favourite on formal occasions, at children's parties and Sunday School treats. A Lincolnshire countrywoman has recalled that in rural districts it was a favourite even with adults. As late as the 1930s, she reports, 'more than one courtship started from a couple meeting in the ring on a summer's evening after the meeting which followed the Sunday anniversary service at various country chapels'. Another informant recollects that at the turn of the century the game was played at her 'Victorian Spartan' boarding-school at Bangor on the evenings of Saints' Days, which were whole holidays for all the girls. The words varied from those usually sung. The girls, aged ten to fifteen, formed a large circle, holding hands, with one in the middle who was addressed by the others:

> Where the wheat and barley grow,
>   You and I and somebody know,
> Where the wheat and barley grow,
>   We're waiting for a partner, waiting for a partner!
> Open the ring and choose your Queen
>   And kiss her when you got her in!

The girl in the centre would then take a player out of the circle, the pair of them would kneel, the circle would reassemble, and the singing continue:

> On the carpet you shall meet,
>   Where the grass grows in the wheat,
> Stand up now upon your feet
>   And kiss the one you love so sweet.

Understandably a newly-arrived English mistress was heard to murmur 'This all seems very pagan for a Saint's Day'. However in English-speaking countries, it will be noticed, the male players are clearly more concerned with the little goddesses in front of them than with the spirits of seedtime. In the earliest recollection of the game in England (Lincolnshire) no mystery was felt about the growth of the crops, which were referred to only in the refrain:

> A-waitin' fur a pardner,
> A-waitin' fur a pardner,
> You an' I, an' iv'ryone knows
> How whoats an' beans an' barley grows.

In fact collation of the texts leads to only one conclusion, that the verses emanate from two separate sources. A contributor to *Notes & Queries* in 1908, whose memory went back to a Derbyshire village in the middle years of the previous century, remembered the pleasure with which boys and girls played a game called 'Chop the Wood':

It was a ring game, and started with a girl or boy in the ring, the rest, boys and girls, with hands joined, dancing round singing:

> You're waitin' for a partner,
> Open th' ring an' take one in.

The boy or girl selected one from the ring by 'ticking' on the breast, and together, with hands joined, they stood in the middle, the rest of the players dancing round, singing:

> Now you're married, you must obey;
> You must be true to all you say;
> You must be kind, you must be good,
> An' help your wife to chop the wood!

Then, while the couple kissed, the rest, with hands free, imitated the motion of chopping, saying 'Chop! chop! chop!'

'Chop the Wood', or a game like it, would seem to have had an agricultural game superimposed on it. On the Continent the equivalents to 'Oats and Beans and Barley Grow' contain no reference to obtaining partners and the matrimonial duties which go with them. In France the opening of the well-known 'Ronde de l'Avoine', recorded as long ago as 1724, closely corresponds to the opening of the English game:

> Qui veut ouïr, qui veut sçavoir
> Comme on sème l'avoine?
> Mon pèr' la semoit ainsi,
> Puis se reposoit un p'tit,
> Tapoit des pieds, battoit des mains
> Et faisoit le tour du vilain.
> Avoine, avoine, avoine,
> Le beau temps te ramène.

The eighteenth-century players were instructed, while singing these lines, to imitate a man sowing, then to take a rest, to tap their feet on the ground, clap hands, and do a pirouette. Then, at the words 'Avoine, avoine, avoine', they were to join hands again and to continue dancing while they called for good weather. But this was not a ribald song like 'Der Bauer', popular in Germany, which ended with the farmer or his wife dissipating their earnings (see under 'The Peasant', p. 298). It was and is an accumulating song in which the enactment becomes increasingly intense as the game proceeds. After demonstrating how the seed was sown the singers asked, 'Who wants to hear, who wants to know, how they cut the oats?' Reaping was imitated, and thereafter binding the sheaves, stacking the sheaves, winnowing the oats, and finally threshing the oats, whereupon they ran after each other hitting each other on the back with their fists, much in the manner British children 'pat' the dog in the game 'The Farmer's in His Den' (p. 183), a game that might otherwise seem unrelated. And since 'L'Avoine' is known to have survived for two hundred and fifty years, and is played across Europe from Sweden to Sardinia, it may already have been known for two hundred and fifty years and more before 1724. When Rabelais (born c.1494) says Gargantua played 'a semer l'avoyne' (Book I ch. xxii), and even earlier when Froissart (born c.1337) recalled playing 'a l'avainne' in his childhood near Valenciennes ('L'Espinette amoureuse', l. 226), the game may have been little different; and onlookers were probably already saying the sport was a relic of ancient ritual. Certainly, if the words are to be taken at their face value 'Oats and Beans and Barley Grow' is a spring song. In the Middle Ages oats and beans and barley, along with peas, were the crops planted in early spring; wheat and rye being sown in the season between Michaelmas and Christmas; and, as if to confirm this, most American versions begin 'Oats, peas, beans, and barley grows'. But whether the game ever had more meaning than now appears—none of the records mention leaping, the usual feature of planting rituals—is simply conjecture. Both Lucy Broadwood and Anne Gilchrist equate the tune with the country dance 'Dr Faustus'.

Britain: Lincolnshire, c.1870 (*Notes & Queries*, 7th ser., xii, p. 493) | Much Wenlock, 1883 (*Shropshire Folk-Lore*, p. 508) | Raunds and Maxey, 1885 (*Northamptonshire Notes & Queries*, i, pp. 163–4) | Shipley, 1888 (*Yorkshire Folk-Lore Journal*, i, p. 3) | Lincolnshire, 1893 (*English County Songs*, p. 87) | Devonport, c.1893 | *Traditional Games*, ii, 1898, 15 further recordings. Very common thereafter up to present day, especially among younger children.

Cf. Lodsworth, Sussex, c.1870, song sung at harvest suppers, 'There sits the hand that ploughs up the land, Where the peas, beans, oats and the barley stand. Drink off your liquor, and then you will know Where the peas, beans, oats, and the barley grow!' (*Journal of EFDSS*, i, p. 67).

USA: New Hampshire, early part of nineteenth century, 'Thus my father sows his seed, Stands erect and takes his ease, Stamps his foot, and claps his hands, Whirls about, and thus he stands' (*Games of American Children*, 1883, pp. 80–4: 'Oats, Pease, Beans, and Barley Grows' is described as 'very familiar to all American children') | Washington DC, 1886, 'O sweet beans and barley grows' (*Lippincott's Magazine*, xxxvii, p. 247) | St Louis, 1895, 'Oats, peas, beans, and barley grows, As you and I and everyone knows' (*JAFL*, lx, 1947, p. 16, with numerous references attesting to the game's popularity) | Cincinnati, 1908, 'Rosy beans and morning glories' (*JAFL*, xl, p. 14), the game a generation earlier, apparently, being 'Where old sweet peas and barley grows' | *North Carolina Folklore*, 1952, pp. 87–8, versions from 1920s.

Canada (English-speaking): Kingston, Ontario, 1940s (Fowke, 1969, p. 14).

Belgian Flanders: *Vlaamsche Kinderspelen uit West-Brussel*, Aimé de Cort, 1929, pp. 109–10, 'Hoe zaait de boer zijn graan, Hoe zaait de boer zijn Koren graan, Van de ran plan plan, Van den boereman, Hoe zaait de boer zijn graan, Hoe zaait de boer zijn graan'. The leader shows how the farmer sows his grain, and, in response to further questions from the ring, shows how he gathers, binds, dries, malts, bakes, and eats his grain.

France: *Les rondes, chansons à danser*, Christophe Ballard, 1724, p. 99, as quote (E. Rolland, *Jeux de l'enfance*, 1883, pp. 99–101) | *Manuel Complet des jeux de société*, E. F. Celnart, 1827 (1846, pp.

10–11) | *Jeux et exercises des jeunes filles*, Mme de Chabreul, 1856, pp. 142–4 | *Chantons Gaiement*, E. Van de Velde, *c*.1938, no. 50.

Canada (French-speaking): Saint-Constant, nr. Montreal, *c*.1890, 'Avoine, avoine, avoine, Que le printemps ramène! Le laboureur fait comme ceci, Et puis se repose comme ceci, et comme cela'. Players stamped their feet, clapped their hands, and took a turn with their neighbour (*JAFL*, xxxiii, pp. 343–4).

Sweden: *Svenska Fornsånger*, A. I. Arwidsson, iii, 1842, pp. 326–9, 'Viljen J veta och viljen J förstå, Hur bönderna bruka sin hafra så? Jag hade en fader han såde sa här, Och sedan så stälde han sig så här. Han stampade med fot, han klappade med hand, Han gick omkring, så glader var han' (Do you want to see and do you want to know, How the farmers sow their oats? I had a father, he sowed like this, And after he'd done, he stood like this. He stamped with his foot, He clapped with his hand, He walked around, so glad was he). Followed by the 'summonsing', 'See what i have in my hand . . .' | *Svenska folklekar*, C. Tillhagen and N. Dencker, ii, 1950, pp. 358–9.

Denmark: *Børneses Musik*, S. and S. Hagen, 1879, p. 99, 'Og ville I nu vide, og ville I forstaa, hvorledes den Bondemand sin Havre monne saa?' etc (And will you now see, and will you know, How the farmer must sow his oats? He sowed, he sowed, And the green field it grew. He clapped his hands; He wriggled his hips; He stamped with his feet; he turned himself around) | *Danmarks Sanglege*, S. Tvermose Thyregod, 1931, pp. 256–8.

Italy: *Giuochi Popolari Veneziani*, G. Bernoni, 1874, pp. 37–9, 'La bela vilana, La va in campagna, La impianta la fava, L'impianta cussì. La l'impianta a poco a poco; 'N' altro poco riposa cussì' (The lovely peasant, She walks in the country, She plants the beans, She plants them like this. She plants them little by little, Then rests a little like this). When the beans have been threshed, dried, shelled, and eaten, the game ends with a good male peasant, who walks in the country, plants the beans, stamps his foot, claps his hands, and hits himself | *The Second Gilwell Camp Fire Book*, 1962, pp. 60–1, 'Quando si planta la bella polenta, la bella polenta, si planta così', and thereafter growing, flowering, cutting, gathering, grinding, and eating the maize pudding | Lotzorai, Sardinia, 1962, 'Ara la fava la bella villana, Quando l'ara l'ara così, E l'ara a poco a poco, E poi si mette le mani così' (The lovely peasant she ploughs the beans, When she ploughs, she ploughs like this, And she ploughs little by little, And then she puts her hands like this). The lovely peasant then gathers, shells, cooks, and eats the beans in the same manner.

38

The Farmer's in His Den

Langton Matravers, Dorset, 1975

Montrose, 1978

Deutsches Kinderspiel, F. M. Böhme, 1897

Games of American Children, W. W. Newell, 1883

The farmer's in his den,
The farmer's in his den,
E I, E I,
The farmer's in his den.

The farmer wants a wife,
The farmer wants a wife,
E I, E I,
The farmer wants a wife.

The wife wants a child,
The wife wants a child,
E I, E I,
The wife wants a child.

The child wants a nurse,
The child wants a nurse,
E I, E I,
The child wants a nurse.

The nurse wants a dog,
The nurse wants a dog,
E I, E I,
The nurse wants a dog.

The dog wants a bone,
The dog wants a bone,
E I, E I,
The dog wants a bone.

We all pat the bone,
We all pat the bone,
E I, E I,
We all pat the bone.

The best known of ring games, played endlessly by the younger children, apparently everywhere, even in the middle of London. In a courtyard off Trafalgar Square a boy and girl told us they often played it: 'Boys *and* girls. It's good. We often play it here. And there's a really big yard up there where you can't see.' A big space is preferred because 'the more players there are the better'. One player, the farmer, stands in the middle, and the rest form a large circle round him. The farmer picks a wife from the circle (sometimes, as in life, with his eyes shut). She joins him in the middle and chooses another player from the circle to be her child. The child has the privilege of choosing his nurse. The nurse selects a dog. The dog picks someone, preferably a boy, to be the bone. There are now six players in the middle of the circle. Occasionally those in the middle themselves form a ring, and move round in the opposite direction to the outer circle. However the attraction of the game is the 'patting' (in Scotland 'clapping') which occurs while the last verse is being sung. Everyone crowds round the bone and thumps him on the back or head. He is then reincarnated to become the farmer in the next round. Sometimes the 'patting' is prolonged with the unsought bonus: 'One for luck, two for luck, three for the old man's coconut' (Swanage), or 'One for luck, two for luck, hit him on the coconut' (Ipswich). In Scotland they chant, 'The bone won't break, the bone won't break', and try to prove the words untrue. In Poole, after they have patted the bone, they lift the child up, chanting:

The bone goes crack,
The bone goes crack,
E—I—E—I
The bone goes crack.

They hold the bone in the air and, explained an eight-year-old, 'All the people, they try to push and bang—they bang 'ard though'. Usually it is easy to see how such refinements have arisen. The bone, first reported by Cecil Sharp in 1912, is now itself sometimes allowed a choice: 'the bone wants a plate' (Salford), 'the bone wants a-picking' (Swansea), 'the bone wants a maggot' (Middleton). In Langton Matravers, Dorset, the dog wants a cat, the cat wants a mouse, the mouse wants cheese, and 'we all pat the cheese'. (In Somerset, c.1922, 'we all eat the cheese'.) In Welshpool the child wants a nurse, the nurse wants a doll, the doll won't stand, so 'we lift her up, we lift her up'. If the game was not usually learnt early in life ('You learn it when you're a baby,' giggled a nine-year-old), the improvements might be more radical. As it is, the game itself is young as far as Britain is concerned (Alice Gomme included it only in her addenda); and it retains, even in its variations, some of the minor characteristics of its Continental forebears. (The game seems to have arrived via America, whence it had been taken by West Germanic immigrants.) Indeed the 'den', which puzzles serious-minded children, who picture the farmer as a Daniel closeted with wild beasts, may be explained by the game 'Es fuhr ein Bauer ins Holz'. If in Germany the farmer went to a wood, in England may he not have entered a woodland pasture? (The Old English *denn*, surviving in place names such as Tenterden, refers to a clearing in the woods, just as *dell*, in American and Australian versions, signifies a hollow surrounded by trees.) If, in some versions of the game, the dog (or the bone) is 'left alone' at the end, so, in the game 'In Holland steht ein Haus', after the chosen players have been called into the middle of the ring they successively leave it (an excuse for kissing) until eventually the house is left alone, 'Das Haus, das steht allein'. Originally this 'very old social game', as Böhme calls it, seems to have been a roisterous amusement at the annual fair, a game for people to get to know each other, show their preferences, push and shove each other, kiss and become involved with each other. Only part of this has come through to the British game, that part in fact—the heavy-handed patting—which is not encouraged in nursery schools. The Scottish and American tune, which is reminiscent of 'A-Hunting We Will Go', seems to be descended from the student song 'Was kommt dort von der Höh?', through the student song 'In Leipzig war ein Mann', a verse of which was quoted familiarly in a Danish comedy *Jeppe paa Bierget*, by Ludwig Holberg, 1722. The English tune, after some vacillation, settled down into the form above, which was first noted by Anne Gilchrist in 1921 (Gilchrist MSS 231, B iv, p. 36). In English, the earliest recorded refrain is 'Heigh ho! for Rowley O!' In recent times it has been found as 'Heigh ho the cherry ho', 'Hey hi cherry-i', 'Hey ho me daddy oh' (Scotland), 'I tie tiddly-i', 'E–I–E–I', 'E O the alley oh', 'E–I–O my laddie-o', 'E–I–E–O', 'E–I–N–E–O', 'E–I–N–D–O', and 'B–I–N–G–O', as well as, chiefly in the midlands, the football cry 'Ee-aye-addy-o'. If the game was not known to be a late nineteenth-century importation the temptation might be strong to equate such meaninglessnesses with the medieval vowel refrains, 'With I and E, borne ar we' and 'With an O & an I my talle thou atende'.

USA: New York, 1883, 'The farmer in the dell, The farmer in the dell, Heigh ho! for Rowley O! The farmer in the dell'. The nurse takes the dog, the dog takes the cat, the cat takes the rat, the rat takes the cheese, 'The cheese stands alone' (*Games of American Children*, pp. 129–30) | Washington DC, 1888, 'The man in the cell, High O! Cherry O!' (*American Anthropologist*, i, pp. 254–5) | Virginia, 1888, 'The farmer's in his den, Hi-oh, my cherry, ho!' (*Counting-out Rhymes*, H. C. Bolton, p. 119) | St Louis, 1895, as New York but 'Heigh-ho the cherry, O'. Described as very popular, and found to be still so in 1944. 'It has now become a kindergarten and primary grade school song, and is consequently known everywhere in the United States' (*JAFL*, lx, pp. 23 and 40) | North Carolina, 1920s, the ending 'The dog takes a bone' is commonly reported. Refrains include 'Hi oh the dairy oh', 'High ho! Victoria!' and 'Hooray, Victorious'. 'We did not talk to any child, white or black, who was not familiar with it' (*North Carolina Folklore*, pp. 146–50). The game continues to be much played, the players being encouraged to clap their hands at the end, rather than clap the last player on the back.

Canada: Toronto, 1893, similar to New York, 1883, but 'The farmer in his den, Highery O Valerio!' and ending 'The cheese stands still' (*JAFL*, viii, pp. 254–5) | Often reported since, including 'Le père est dans le puits'; the father being followed into the well by the mother, son, daughter, dog, cat, rat, and mouse. When the mouse is seen they come out of the well. This is possibly a direct translation from the American, 'dell' having been misheard as 'well' and rendered *puits* (*JAFL*, liii, 1940, pp. 170–1).

Germany: *Deutsche Liedertafel*, C. G. Kenser, i, 1826, p. 171 (Böhme) | *Volksreime und Volkslieder in Anhalt-Dessau*, Eduard Fiedler, 1847, pp. 61–2,

> Es fuhr ein Bau'r ins Holz,
> Es fuhr ein Bau'r ins Holz,
> Es fuhr ein Bau'r ins Kirmessholz,
> Ki-ka Kirmessholz,
> Es fuhr ein Bau'r ins Holz.

Farmer chooses a wife, who chooses a child, who chooses a maid, who chooses a serving-man. Serving-man then leaves the maid, etc. Kissing and hitting noted in variants | *Kinderlieder und Kinderspiele aus dem Vogtland*, Hermann Dunger, 1874, p. 176, 'Es fuhr ein Bauer in's Holz, Si sa Kirmesholz (viva).' The farmer, sitting on stool, is given a shove, has coat pulled, has shoes cleaned (in fact trodden upon), and is kissed. He takes a wife, who sits on his lap and takes a child, who sits on her lap and chooses a maid, who sits on her lap and chooses a serving-man. The stool may then be pulled from beneath them, and/or they may kiss, or leave one by one | *Deutsches Kinderspiel*, F. M. Böhme, 1897, p. 673, game collected in Thüringen, Sachsen, and Brandenburg, similar to 1874, but kissing on leaving seems usual | *Deutsches Kinderlied und Kinderspiel*, Johann Lewalter, 1911, pp. 125–6, version from Kassel, 'In Holland steht ein Haus'. An old man lives in the house, takes wife, child, doll; doll then leaves child, etc., and the house stands alone. Also related games, pp. 78–9, 'Der Bauer fährt ins Holz' beginning with farmer polishing his shoes:

> Der Bauer wichst seine Schuh',
> Der Bauer wichst seine Kirmesschuh',
> Vivat Kirmesschuh',
> Der Bauer wichst seine Schuh',

and only then choosing his household; and pp. 115–16, 'Da oben auf dem Berg', on which stands an old house, with an old man, child, cow, and milk, from which is made cheese. The players called into the middle of the circle form a small circle which goes round inside the large circle │ *Allerleirauh Viele schöne Kinderreime*, Hans Enzensberger, 1961, pp. 250–1, 'Es fuhr ein Bauer ins Holz, heissa Viktoria'. The farmer takes a wife, child, aunt, maid, manservant, dog, and bone. The farmer then leaves his wife, and so on, until the bone stands alone:

> Da steht der Knochen alleine,
> da steht der Knochen alleine,
> heissa Viktoria,
> da steht der Knochen alleine.

Switzerland: Basle, 1898, 'Once a peasant drove into the forest, Hurrah Viktoria!' He took a wife, child, nurse, man servant, and dog, who took a sausage. The peasant then left his wife etc., until the sausage is left alone (*The Study of Man*, A. C. Haddon, p. 338).

Netherlands: *Nederlandsche Baker- en Kinderrijmen*, J. Van Vloten, Leiden, 1894, p. 104, 'In Holland staat een huis, ja huis, Falderie faldera, Falderopsasa'. A lord lives in the house and assembles a family of wife, child, manservant, and maid. The servants are chased away, the lord goes into a wood, the wife leaves home, the child is left alone. The ring ask 'Where is your father? What is he doing in the wood?' and then set the house on fire ('Nu steekt men 't huis in brand') │ Amsterdam, *c.*1936 and 1963, 'In Holland staat een huis, ja, ja, Van tsjingelingelingelinge hopsasa'. In the house lives a lord, who has a wife, who has a child, who has a dog. Also played by Afrikander children, Pretoria, 1975 │ In the south Netherlands, however, the game is usually played in a different way, with no choosing. The children circle, and sing a form of 'In Holland staat een huis' resembling the student song 'In Leipzig war ein Mann' (see p. 186), in which the man makes a purse to save his money in, so that he can buy a child to send to school to learn his ABC; or a woman sells beer to make money to buy a son who will go to school, learn his ABC, and 'quickly become accomplished' (see *Kinderspel in Zuid-Nederland*, A. de Cock and I. Teirlinck, II, iii, pp. 102–14).

Denmark: *Danmarks Sanglege*, S. Tvermose Thyregod, 1931, pp. 25–30, 'Den Arme Bonde'.

Sweden: *Svenska folklekar och danser*, C. Tillhagen and N. Dencker, ii, pp. 317–18, 'På stolen sitter Herr Bollerman'.

French Flanders: *Chants populaires des Flamands de France*, C. E. de Coussemaker, 1856, pp. 329–30, 'Sa, boer, Gaet naer den dans, Gaet al naer den kermisdans, Kermis, kermis, kermisdans, Gaet al naer den dans . . . zit op den stoel . . . kiest uw wuf . . . kust uw wuf . . . gaet uyt den dans' (The peasant goes into the dance, sits on a stool, chooses a wife, kisses her, and goes out of the dance).

France: 'Le meunier dans son pré'. The miller takes a wife, and the sequence is child, nurse, cat, mouse, cheese (R. Brinton, *Folklore Enfantin de Bon-Encontre*, unpublished dissertation, 1978) │ Lille, 1978, 'Le fermier dans son pré . . . Ohé ohé ohé . . . femme . . . enfant . . . nourrice . . . chat . . . souris . . . fromage . . . Le fromage est battu, Tout cru, Dans la rue, Chapeau pointu!'.

Britain: Auchencairn, Kirkcudbrightshire, 1898, 'For it's oh! my dearie, the farmer's in his den' (*The Study of Man*, A. C. Haddon, p. 337; *Traditional Games*, ii, p. 420) │ *Old Hampshire Singing Games*, A. E. Gillington, 1909, p. 19, 'Heigh ho, heigh ho' or 'Ee ei, cherry pie, The farmer's in his den', ending 'We all pat the dog!' Everyone begins to pat the dog, which must bark and howl till the game breaks up │ *Children's Singing Games*, Cecil Sharp, iii, 1912, pp. 14–15, two versions, one ending 'The bone stands alone', the other 'The farmer's all alone', having been forsaken successively by dog, nurse, child, and wife │ *Joyous Book of Singing Games*, John Hornby, 1913, p. 64, 'He-i-daddy-o!' Everyone 'chases the dog and pretends to beat it' │ *London Street Games*, 1916, p. 68 │ 'Listen with Mother', BBC radio programme, recording played intermittently, 1975.

Australia: Poweltown, Victoria, *c*.1935, 'Hi, ho the merrio, the farmer's in the dell', ending 'The mouse takes a cheese', 'The cheese stands alone' | Cairns, North Queensland, *c*.1953, 'Hi ho the merry oh, the farmer's in the dell', ending 'We all pick the bone'.

South Africa (English-speaking): Pretoria, 1972, starting 'The farmer wants a wife', continuing with child, dog, cat, mouse, and ending with the cheese being smacked.

VI

Cushion Dances

FOR three hundred years temporary possession of a cushion gave a man the right, on convivial occasions, to kiss the woman he most fancied. In the middle of the nineteenth century 'the Cushion' was one of the robust joys of May Day that John Clare commemorated in his exultation of Helpstone in Northamptonshire; and it was one of the most popular games at parties during the Christmas holidays in Derbyshire 'amongst the farmers' sons and daughters and the domestics, all of whom were on a pretty fair equality, very different', as a writer observed in *Notes & Queries*, 19 December 1885, 'from what prevails in farmhouses of today'. In 1845, or thereabouts, the cushion dance was performed with boisterous fun:

The company were seated round the room, a fiddler occupying a raised seat in a corner. When all were ready, two of the young men left the room, returning presently, one carrying a large square cushion, the other an ordinary drinking-horn, china bowl, or silver tankard, according to the possessions of the family. The one carrying the cushion locked the door, putting the key in his pocket. Both gentlemen then went to the fiddler's corner, and after the cushion-bearer had put a coin in the vessel carried by the other, the fiddler struck up a lively tune, to which the young men began to dance round the room, singing or reciting to the music:–

> 'Frinkum, frankum is a fine song,
> An' we will dance it all along;
> All along and round about,
> Till we find the pretty maid out.'

After making the circuit of the room, they halted on reaching the fiddler's corner, and the cushion-bearer, still to the music of the fiddle, sang or recited:–

> 'Our song it will no further go!'

The fiddler:–

> 'Pray, kind sir, why say you so?'

The cushion-bearer:–

> 'Because Jane Sandars won't come to.'

The fiddler:–

> 'She must come to, she shall come to,
> An' I'll make her whether she will or no!'

The cushion-bearer and vessel-holder then proceeded with the dance, going as before round the room, singing 'Frinkum, frankum,' &c, till the cushion-bearer came to the lady of his choice, before whom he paused, placed the cushion on the floor at her feet, and knelt upon it. The vessel-bearer then offered the cup to the lady, who put money in it and knelt on the cushion in front of the kneeling gentleman. The pair kissed, arose, and the gentleman, first giving the cushion to the lady with a bow, placed himself behind her, taking hold of some portion of her dress. The cup-bearer fell in also, and they danced on to the fiddler's corner, and the ceremony was again gone through as at first, with the substitution of the name of 'John' for 'Jane', thus:–

The lady:–

     'Our song it will no further go!'

The fiddler:–

     'Pray, kind miss, why say you so?'

The lady:–

     'Because John Sandars won't come to.'

The fiddler:–

     'He must come to, he shall come to,
     An' I'll make him whether he will or no!'

The dancing then proceeded, and the lady, on reaching her choice (a gentleman, of necessity), placed the cushion at his feet. He put money in the horn and knelt. They kissed and rose, he taking the cushion and his place in front of the lady, heading the next dance round, the lady taking him by the coat-tails, the first gentleman behind the lady, with the horn-bearer in the rear. In this way the dance went on till all present, alternately a lady and gentleman, had taken part in the ceremony. The dance concluded with a romp in file round the room to the quickening music of the fiddler, who at the close received the whole of the money collected by the horn-bearer.

This manner of performing the dance had, it seems, altered little since the seventeenth century. The significant details are confirmed in a description (here paragraphed to ease comparison) printed with tune in the 1686 edition of Playford's *Dancing Master*:

'JOAN SANDERSON, *or* The Cushion Dance, *A Round Dance*'.

This Strain twice.   This once.

Play this as oft as is required.

This Dance is began by a single Person, (either man or woman) who taking a Cushion in his hand dances about the room, and at the end of the Tune he stops, and sings,

     This Dance it will no farther go.

The Musician answers,

> *I pray you, good Sir, why say you so?*

Man.   *Because Joan Sanderson will not come to.*
Music. *She must come to, and she shall come to,*
       and she must come whether she will or no.

Then he lays down the Cushion before a woman, on which she kneels, and he kisses her, singing,

> *Welcom Joan Sanderson, welcom, welcom.*

Then she rises, takes up the Cushion, and both dance, singing,

> *Prinkum, Prankum, is a fine Dance,*
> *And shall we go dance it once again,*
> *once again, and once again,*
> *and shall we go dance it once again.*

Then making a stop, the Wo. sings, as before,

> *This Dance, &c.*
> Music.   *I pray you, Madam, &c.*
> Woman. *Because John Sanderson, &c.*
> Music.   *He must, &c.*

And so she lays down the Cushion before a man, who kneeling upon it, salutes her, she singing,

> *Welcom John Sanderson, &c.*

Then he taking up the Cushion, they take hands and dance round, singing as before: And thus they do till the whole Company are taken into the Ring.

At the end the editor added: '*Note*, That the woman is kiss'd by all the men in the Ring at her coming in and going out, and the like of the man by the women.'

That this frolic dated back to the sixteenth century, and was known at the court of Elizabeth I, is to be understood from Selden's contemporary censure of Charles I's predilections:

The court of England is much altered. At a solemn dancing, first you had the grave measures, then the corantoes, and the galliards, and all this is kept up with ceremony; at length they fall to Trench-more, and so to the cushion dance, and then all the company dance, lord and groom, lady and kitchen-maid, no distinction. So in our court in Queen Elizabeth's time, gravity and state was kept up; in King James's time things were pretty well; but in King Charles's time, there has been nothing but Trench-more and the cushion dance, *omnium gatherum, tolly polly, hoyte cum toyte.*

Although no mention of the dance has been found actually in the sixteenth century—since those who suppose Tudor accounts of gentlemen 'missing the cushion' to be references to the cushion dance are clearly in more than one sense, *missing the mark*—it is evident Thomas Heywood was familiar with it at the beginning of the seventeenth century. In *A Woman kilde with Kindnesse*, performed 1603, the 'Cushion Dance' is one of the nine dances named by a disputatious group of youths and 'countrey wenches', the others being 'The Beginning of the World', 'Rogero', 'Iohn, Come Kisse Mee Now', 'Tom Tyler', 'The Hunting of the Fox', 'The Hay', 'Put On Your Smocke a Monday', and 'Sellinger's Round'.

Customarily the dance, which John Taylor the 'water-poet' termed 'pretty provocatory', was the last of the evening's entertainment, a fact noted as early as 1659 in *The London Chaunticleres*: 'When we were a weary with dauncing hard, we alwaies went to the Cushion daunce'; and within living memory in Scotland a man was expected to 'see home' the girl he selected in the 'Kissing Dance'. Understandably, the sport was a favourite at the junketings following a wedding, when traditionally more than ordinary licence was permitted. In the description of a wedding entertainment in the *Witty Apopthegms* collected by Thomas Bayly, 1658, it is said that when at last 'the Masque was ended, and time had brought in the Supper, the Cushion led the dance out of the Parlour into the Hall'. In Tom D'Urfey's song 'The Winchester Wedding', 1684, little is left to the imagination about the guests' inclinations following the dance:

> Pert Stephen was kind to Betty,
>   And blithe as a Bird in the Spring;
> And Tommy was so to Katy,
>   And Wedded her with a Rush Ring:
> Sukey that Danc'd with the Cushion,
>   An Hour from the Room had been gone;
> And Barnaby knew by her Blushing,
>   That some other Dance had been done.

Small wonder that Robert Burton should instance the cushion dance in his *Anatomy of Melancholy* as an entertainment unlikely to support a wise man's dignity.

In *Astrea's Booke for Songs & Satyrs*, 1688 (MS, Firth c. 16), 'The Cushion Dance' is given 'to the tune of Joan Sand'. In *The Dancing Master* it is denominated 'Joan Sanderson, or The Cushion Dance, a Round Dance'; and the name 'Jane Sandars' survived, as we have seen, to the nineteenth century in Derbyshire; as also did 'Mrs Sargesson', in a children's ring game played at East Kirkby, Lincolnshire. In Alice Gomme's *Traditional Games*, 1894, p. 91, children are said to have formed a ring, with one in the middle who had a cushion, and to have danced round singing to the tune of the 'Mulberry Bush':

> We've got a new sister in our degree,
> And she's welcome into our companee, companee.

The player in the middle chose one of the children in the ring, and the others responded:

> Mrs Sargesson says she weänt come to,
> We'll make her whether she will or no,
>   Will or no, will or no,
> We'll maäke her whether she will or no.

The player in the middle then apparently dragged the chosen child to the centre of the ring, forced her on to the cushion, and kissed her, whereon it was the newcomer's turn to select a player from the ring.

Another name for the dance was 'Frinkum-frankum', or 'Prinkum-prankum' as in Randolph's *The Muses Looking-Glasse*, licensed 1630 ('No wanton jig, I hope: no dance is lawful But prinkum-prankum!'), and also in William Davenant's *The Play-house to be Let*, performed 1663 ('Call in the Fidlers . . . Yet let 'em play us but princum and prancum'). In Ireland where an extension of the cushion dance has long been in order at wakes, the sport was known as 'Frimsy Framsy', 'Frincy-francy', 'Fronsy-fronsy', 'Frumsy-framsy', 'Frumso Framso', and 'Fraunces' (*Irish Wake Amusements*, 1967, pp. 94–5). This continuation of the cushion dance was explained in the 1721 edition of *The Dancing Master*:

And if there is Company enough, make a little Ring in the middle, and within that Ring set a Chair, and lay the Cushion in it, and the first Man set in it. Then the Cushion is laid before the first Man, the Woman singing, *This Dance &c.* (as before) only instead of—*come too*, they sing—*go fro*; and instead of *Welcome* John Sanderson, &c. they sing *Farewell* John Sanderson, *Farewell, Farewell*; and so they go out one by one as they came in.

Yet another name for this extension was 'Chair' and a description of the game played in South Tyrone at the beginning of the nineteenth century appears in William Carleton's *Traits and Stories of the Irish Peasantry*, 1830 (vol. I, 1836 edn., pp. 251–2):

A chair or stool is placed in the middle of the flure, and the man who manages the play sits down upon it, and calls his sweetheart, or the prettiest girl in the house. She, accordingly, comes forward, and must kiss him. He then rises up, and she sits down. 'Come now,' he says, 'fair maid—Frimsy framsy, who's your fancy?' She then calls them she likes best, and when the young man she calls comes over and kisses her, he then takes her place, and calls another girl—and so on, smacking away for a couple of hours.

In Scotland, according to the Fletts, in their *Traditional Dancing in Scotland*, 1964, the dance went under an abundance of names. In the Borders and in Aberdeenshire it was known as 'Babbity Bowster'; in Fife and Lanarkshire it was 'Be Bo Babbity'; in the Highlands it was sometimes 'Ruidhleadh nam Pòg' (The Kissing Reel); and other of the names included 'Blue Bonnets', 'The Bonnet Dance', 'The Bonny Lad', 'Pease Straw', and 'The White Cockade'. Nor were the Scots stingy about its performance—anyway up to the First World War—but danced and knelt with a lengthening procession of dancers (though carrying a handkerchief to kneel on rather than a cushion),[1] and thereafter formed a circle with one in the middle who might choose whom he liked to kiss, then leaving his chosen one to make her own choice from those who remained, and so on; the whole performance requiring, when the company was large, above an hour of strenuous but enjoyable activity. In Orkney, forms of the dance were still bringing to a close the evening's *official* programme in 1925; while in the Hebrides some modified forms continued into the 1960s.

In Newfoundland Maud Karpeles found both parts of the dance being performed when she was there in 1929, a handkerchief being carried round, as in Scotland, which the man might place, for the sake of decorum, over the face of the woman he wished to kiss (*Journal of the English Folk Dance and Song Society*, vol. iii, pp. 133–4).

In Tristan da Cunha, the British island in the South Atlantic that lies more than a thousand miles from anywhere, the 'Pillow Dance' and the 'Chair Dance' are looked upon as separate entertainments. When the islanders were evacuated to Britain following the volcanic eruption in 1961, they demonstrated both dances, along with others which they had kept in memory from the early part of the nineteenth century; and in 1971, after they had returned to the island, a visitor found that the 'Pillow Dance' and 'Chair Dance' continued to be the source of 'knowing laughter' on dance nights at the Prince Philip Hall. The rule is maintained on Tristan that during the dance a man may choose any woman except his wife and a woman any man other than her husband (*Journal of the EFDSS*, ix, p. 164, and *Sunday Times*, 12 December 1971, p. 26).

With the story of the cushion dance in mind it is possible to detect vestiges surviving in children's play; and to make sense of phrases that would otherwise be meaningless. In the north country the source of one

---

[1] As in Bohemia where the dance is, or was, called 'Satecek' (The Little Cloth). More often on the Continent a cushion or stool seems to have been traditional, as in the country game in Germany, 'Amor ging und wollte sich erquicken', and the equally amorous amusement in Languedoc, 'Qui mettrons-nous sur l'escabeau?'.

verse is immediately apparent, however far removed from the chiding of Joan Sanderson:

> The dirty slut she won't come out,
>   She won't come out, she won't come out,
> The dirty slut she won't come out
>   To help us with the dancing.

So is the following when it is recollected that 'Pease Straw' was one of the names of the dance in Scotland:

> Pease straw is dirty,
>   And will dirty all my gown.
> But never mind my bonny lass,
>   Just lay the cushion down.

And in 'King William', as also in 'Pretty Little Girl of Mine' (pp. 122 and 125), the line 'On the carpet she shall kneel' will jog the memory of readers of Rumer Godden's *The Greengage Summer* (1958). When the men and women at the Brass Instrument Factory, in the Champagne country of the Aisne, attend their centenary dinner, they take part in the 'danse du tapis', the carpet dance. In this the bearer of a small square of carpet kneels upon it in front of whomever he chooses, and receives a kiss.

The significance becomes apparent, too, of the verse in 'Babity Bowster' (Bob at the Bolster) which girls sang in the streets of Glasgow in the 1860s:

> Wha ga'e you the keys to keep,
>   Babity Bowster, Babity Bowster,
> Wha ga'e you the keys to keep,
>   Babity Bowster, brawly?

And if the importance of the key is appreciated in the successful performance of the cushion dance (as emphasized by a contributor to Hone's *Every-Day Book*, 1827, cols. 161–2, who remarked that those young women who had an 'invincible aversion' to being saluted by the gentlemen would certainly make their escape were it not that the bearer of the cushion 'prevented their flight by locking the door, and putting the key in his pocket') the reason for the familiar name of the game or dance in New York, which puzzled Newell in 1883, will be apparent, it being 'Pillow' or 'Pillow and Keys'. Incidentally a contributor to *St Nicholas Magazine*, xxiv, p. 217, giving the name of the game as 'Pillow and Keys' when played in New York about 1850, recalled that he did not much care for the game when he was young until, that is, he 'became courageous enough to kneel before somebody besides his maiden aunts'.

In the cushion dance we may have the source of the game 'Scorn', an amusement, Newell remarked, 'of a not very agreeable nature, familiar at children's parties in New England', in which a girl was seated on a chair in the middle of the room, and one child after another was led up to her, from whom she turned away with an expression of contempt, 'until someone approached that pleased her, who, after a kiss, took her place'. Newell wondered whether this game might be the same as 'Derision', mentioned by Froissart (Froissart recorded he played 'aux risées' in his boyhood, *c.*1350), and certainly the playing of games such as 'Scorn' is international, since we ourselves have taken part in such a sport in Capri. Here the tarantella dancers regularly conclude their entertainment for visitors with a dance, similar to that described in Playford's *Dancing Master*, in which one spectator after another—man and woman alternately—is invited to join an ever-growing line of dancers. Thereafter a chair is placed in the middle of the room, and a girl from among the dancers sits on it, holding a mirror. A man comes up and looks over her shoulder. If the girl does not like the man she sees in the mirror, she wipes his image away with a cloth, and another man looks over her shoulder. But if she accepts the man, she dances round the floor with him, and the man takes her place on the chair, with the mirror and the cloth, and one woman and then another comes up behind him to see who he will select.

Vestiges of cushion dances are to be found in other countries. For instance in Austria the ring game 'Blauer, blauer Fingerhut' ends 'Maiden, you shall kneel down, Kneel down at my feet. Whoever you love the best, You shall kiss' (*Oberösterreichische Kinderspiele*, O. Kampmüller, 1965, pp. 78–9); and in the Italian game 'O Quante Belle Figlie' the girl who is choosing from the circle sings 'Put down the carpets for me, Madame Dorè, Put down the carpets for me' (*Giochi*, M. M. Lumbroso, 1967, pp. 101–3).

39

Jolly Sailors

Dearham, Cumberland, 1962

> There was a jolly sailor boy
>> Who lately came on shore.
> He spent his money with a right good will
>> And wished he had some more:
>>> As we go around and round,
>>> As we go around and round,
>>> For he who loves a jolly jolly lass
>>> Must kiss her, must kiss her,
>>> Must kiss her to the ground.

> There were two jolly sailor boys. . .

A circle is formed, the singing starts, and one player goes round inside and keeps going round until the children sing 'As we go around and round', when the sailor picks someone from the circle, and the two of them go round together; a third player is picked who joins on behind, and in turn chooses a fourth player, who joins on behind and chooses a fifth player from the circle 'until the ring is finished and everyone is joined on and they all go round singing'. This is the game as played in Dearham in 1962. It was played in much the same way in Somerset in the 1920s, the song starting:

> One jolly little sailor boy,
>> Just come from shore,
> He spent his money on a moonlight night,
>> As you have done before.

Or it began with two children in the middle:

> There came two jolly sailor boys,
>> Just lately come ashore,
> They spend their days in merry, merry ways,
>> As they have done before.

> And we will have a round and a round,
> [?And we will have a round,]
> And the lad that delights in a bonny, bonny lass,
> Let him spin her round and round.

Evidence abounds that in the nineteenth century the game was a cushion dance. Mary Jagger in her *History of Honley* (1914) says the merrymakers at a 'Laking' or 'Playing night' would sing 'Here comes three jolly, jolly sailor boys', and march around in couples on stone-flagged cottage floors. 'The lilting strain of the old ditty is trilled forth with a youthful vigour, the only requirement for enjoyment being a pillow or cushion to be "kissed on the floor".' The verse sung at Honley was probably akin to that at Goathland, where the Easter Monday folk play was followed by a cushion dance:

> For we are valiant sailor lads
> Who've lately come on shore,
> And he that delights in a bonny, bonny lass,
> May kiss her on the floor.

An eye-witness to a performance at the Lord Nelson Inn, Beckhole, about 1855, reported that 'the one who had the cushion dropped it before a girl and knelt on it, and usually the girls also knelt down on the cushion, and then they kissed'.

In *Rob Roy*, published 1817, Justice Inglewood pledges the health of the absent Diana Vernon with the lines:

> And let her health go round, around, around,
> And let her health go round;
> For though your stocking be of silk,
> Your knees near kiss the ground, aground, aground.

Scott believed this 'pithy verse' occurred in Shadwell's play *Bury Fair*, though it is not found in the edition of 1689, or any other that we have examined. But a song even more to the purpose was included in Mark Lonsdale's *The Savages*, performed at Sadler's Wells in 1792:

> We be three poor fishermen,
> Who daily troll the seas;
> We spend our lives in jeopardy,
> While others live at ease.
> The sky looks black around, around,
> The sky looks black around,
> And he that would be merry, boys,
> Come haul his boat aground.

This stanza, and indeed the singing game, may be compared with one of

Freemens Songs of 3. Voices.

TREBLE.

Ee be three poore Mariners, newly come from the seas,

Wee spend our liues in ieopardy, whiles others liue at ease : Shall we goe

daunce the round, the round, the round, and shall we goe daunce the round?:‖:

and he that is a bully boy, come pledge me on the ground. :‖:

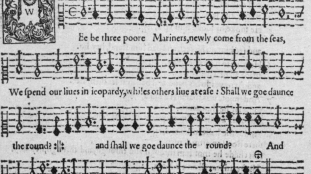

TENOR.

Ee be three poore Mariners, newly come from the seas,

We spend our liues in ieopardy, whiles others liue at ease : Shall we goe daunce

the round? :‖: and shall we goe daunce the round? And

he that is a bully boy, come pledge me on the ground. :‖:

The song 'Wee be three poore Mariners' from *Deuteromelia*, 1609. It has survived as the singing game 'Jolly Sailors' (No. 39).

the Freemen's Songs that Henry VIII is supposed to have delighted in, which was set down by Thomas Ravenscroft in his *Deuteromelia*, 1609:

> Wee be three poore Mariners,
>   newly come from the seas,
> Wee spend our liues in ieopardy,
>   whiles others liue at ease:
> Shall we goe daunce the round, the round, the round,
>   and shall we goe daunce the round?
> And he that is a bully boy,
>   come pledge me on the ground.

It is nicely apparent that the song collected in Shakespeare's day is more likely to be the ancestor of the children's game than is the eighteenth-century paraphrase; that the lines are but a slight sophistication of a traditional song; and that the words, even at this time, probably accompanied a cushion dance.

Britain: Goathland, Yorkshire North Riding, c.1855, as quote (*Yorkshire Dialect Society*, iv, pt. 27, p. 38) | Kendal, 1870s, 'Here comes one jolly sailor Lately come on shore, We'll spend our money like jolly, jolly sailors, Then we'll work for more'. Played at annual Sunday School Treat of the Plymouth Brethren | Raunds, 1886, 'Here comes four jolly sailor boys ... And he that choose his bonny, bonny lass Must kiss her on the floor' (*Northamptonshire Notes & Queries*, i, p. 232) | Shipley, Horsham, 1892, 'Here comes three jolly, jolly sailors' (*Notes & Queries*, 8th ser., i, p. 210) | *Traditional Games*, i, pp. 294–6; ii, p. 436, seven versions | Grayrigg, Kendal, 1903, Brighton, 1912, also South Elmsall and Sunderland Point (Gilchrist MSS, printed *Journal of EFDSS*, xix, pp. 224–5) | Enmore, Somerset, 1908, 'There came three jolly fishermen' (Sharp MSS no. 1750 and five other recordings) | Chaffcombe and elsewhere in Somerset, 1922, as quotes (Macmillan Collection) | Leek, Staffordshire, c.1925, 'There were two couples a-courting, A-courting on the shore' | *Baker's Dozen: Singing Games for Brownies*, Mary Chater, 1947, p. 20, 'There were two jolly sailor boys, Just home from Calais shore' | Glasgow, 1960 | Compare Ireland: Roscommon, 1960, 'We're three jolly bachelors, We come from jolly Dundee, We all own a silver house, And we're jolly bachelors three'.

USA: New York, 1883, 'Here comes a set of jolly sailor-boys' (*Games of American Children*, p. 124) | New York, 1884, 'Here comes a crowd of jolly sailor boys, That lately came on shore. They spend their time in drinking wine, As they have done before. So we go round and round, And round we go once more, And this is the girl—A very pretty girl—A kiss for kneeling down.' Played by children from slums on an Aid Society holiday at Long Island (*Street Arabs*, G. C. Needham, p. 265) | Washington DC, 1886, 'And kisses her on the ground' (*Lippincott's Magazine*, xxxvii, p. 243) | St Louis, 1895, Cincinnati, 1908, Missouri, 1914 (*JAFL*, lx, pp. 20–1; xl, pp. 24–5; xxvii, pp. 301–2) | *American Play-Party Song*, B. A. Botkin, 1937, pp. 221–2.

40

Silly Old Man

Tune: 'Nuts in May'

Silly old man, he walks alone,
He walks alone, he walks alone;
Silly old man, he walks alone,
He wants a wife and he can't get one.

All go round and choose your own,
Choose your own, choose your own;
All go round and choose your own,
Choose a good one, or else choose none.

Now young couple you're married together,
Your father and mother you must obey;
Love one another like sister and brother,
Now you're happy, come kiss one another.

The earliest description of this game, which is also the best, appears in Carleton's *Traits and Stories of the Irish Peasantry*, 1830, where the diversions congenial to wakes are related in the idiom of South Tyrone:

A ring of the boys and girls is made on the flure—boy and girl about—houlding one another by their hands; well and good—a young fellow gets into the middle of the ring, as 'the silly ould man'. There he stands looking at all the girls to choose a wife, and, in the manetime, the youngsters of the ring sing out—

> Here's a silly ould man that lies alone,
>   That lies all alone,
>   That lies all alone;
> Here's a silly ould man that lies all alone,
> He wants a wife, and he can get none.

When the boys and girls sing this, the silly ould man must choose a wife from some of the colleens belonging to the ring. Having made choice of her, she goes into the ring along with him, and they all sing out—

> Now, young couple, you're married together,
>   You're married together,
>   You're married together,
> You must obey your father and mother,
> And love one another like sister and brother—
> I pray, young people, you'll kiss together!

And you may be sure this part of the marriage is not missed, any way.

The words of the game seem to have been sung with some uniformity in the nineteenth century both in Ireland and the north-east of England; although sometimes the silly old man was identified as an old soldier 'come from the war', or as a lonely soldier who 'wants a wife and can't get none', or as one who, when he does find a partner, finds himself 'tied to a peg', having 'married a wife with a wooden leg'. Yet there were, and remain, several bleak characters who are clearly of the same family:

One poor widow left all alone,
With only one daughter to marry at home.
Come choose to the east, come choose to the west,
Come choose the young man that you love the best.

Now you're married we wish you good joy,
Every year a girl and a boy,
Love one another like sisters and brothers,
And kiss each other for joy.

Norfolk and Suffolk, 1890s

Here's a poor widow, she's left alone,
She has no one to marry upon.
Come choose to the east, come choose to the west,
Come choose the one that you love the best.

Now they're married we wish them joy,
Every year a girl and a boy,
Loving each other like sister and brother;
We pray the couple to kiss together.

Midlothian and Perthshire, c.1900. Still known 1950

Two old bachelors left alone,
Nothing to do but mind their own;
Choose to the east and choose to the west,
Choose the one you love the best.

Why don't you marry the girl,
Why don't you marry the girl?
You've got the ring and everything;
Why don't you marry the girl?

Swansea, 1952. Known since c.1910. Game starts with two players in the middle

Three old bachelors all in a row,
Nothing to do and nowhere to go,
Choose to the east and choose to the west,
Choose to the one that you love best.
Oh, Britannia, Britannia all the way,
Three times never, never, never shall be slay.
Why don't you marry a girl, you boy,
Why don't you marry a girl?
You bought the ring, you silly old thing,
Why don't you marry a girl? *Fire!*

Porthleven, Cornwall, 1961. Game starts with three in the middle, who choose members of the opposite sex

Also related, presumably, although the game is played differently, is 'I'm an Old Bachelor', as described by a West-Country girl in the 1920s, in which an equal number of boys and girls joined hands in a circle and danced round singing:

> I'm an old bachelor, isn't it sad,
> Lasses won't love me, it's too bad,
> Thousands of pretty girls daily I see,
> Yet not one of them will love me.

The circle then broke up, the children got together in couples, and they swung each other round while rejoicing, it seems, in the compensatory pleasures of the stomach:

> Peach or pear, cherry or plum . . .
> Yummy yum, yummy yum, yum-yum-yum.

The 'Poor Widow' was also known in the United States. In Philadelphia in the 1870s, or early 1880s, the children sang:

> Sister, O Phoebe, how happy we be,
> As we go under the juniper-tree!
> We'll put on our night-caps to keep our heads warm,
> And two or three kisses will do us no harm—
> Will do us no harm, Io!
>
> I am a poor widow, a-marching around,
> And all of my daughters are married but one;
> So rise up my daughter, and kiss whom you please,
> And kiss whom you please, Io!

In New York, again according to Newell (1883), one street child stood in the middle of the ring representing the widow, while the rest sang; and a daughter reclined as if asleep, her head resting on her hands, until told to 'rise up':

> Here stands a poor widow a-walking around,
>   Io! Io! Io!
> So put on the night-cap to keep her head warm,
>   To keep her head warm, Io!
> So rise up my daughter, and kiss whom you please,
>   And kiss whom you please, Io!

This game continued to be played in the twentieth century at play-parties, a chair sometimes being placed in the ring, a man choosing a girl, seating her in the chair, marching round and placing a hat on her head, and kissing her at the appropriate place in the song:

> Now take this hat on your head, keep your head warm,
> And take a sweet kiss, it will do you no harm,
> But a great deal of good, I know, I know.
> But a great deal of good, I know.

The man then left her, and the singing was renewed: 'Sister Phoebe, go choose her a man'. The girl chose a man from the ring, she led him to the chair, and the courtship was celebrated in song:

> Oh dear brother, how merry were we,
> The night we sat under the juniper tree.

These play-parties were attended, of course, by flirtatious teenagers rather than by children, and however correct the surroundings the lines of the songs were sometimes nicely sophisticated:

> Here is a young lady sits down to sleep,
> And wants a young gent to keep her awake . . .

Thus the game is, it seems, a direct descendant in performance as well as in spirit of the chair dance, or second part of the cushion dance, with its choosing and saluting of a person of the opposite sex; with the progressive role of chosen player becoming chooser; and with the vestige, even if only in song, of the badge of office in the hat or night-cap. In fact the head-covering as a badge of office survived elsewhere. In a Cornish version of 'I am a poor widow', printed by Alice Gomme in 1898, the child acting the daughter not only knelt in the ring but had a white handkerchief spread over her head, while the circle of children walked round chanting 'slowly and dismally':

> I put on a nightcap to keep her head warm,
> To keep her head warm, to keep her head warm, my own.

Ireland: County Tyrone, c.1800–15 (*Irish Peasantry*, William Carleton, i, 1830; i, 1836, pp. 262–3) | County Louth, 1894 | Dublin, 1898; Belfast, 1898, 'Here's a poor widow who lies alone' and 'I am an old Soldier' (*Traditional Games* under the names 'Here's a Soldier', 'Silly Old Man', 'Poor Widow', and 'Soldier') | *Children's Games*, Leslie Daiken, 1949, p. 80.

Britain: Belper, Derbyshire, 1842, 'The seely old man', and Lancashire, 1875 (*Notes & Queries*, 5th ser., iv, pp. 51 and 157) | Manchester, 1870s (Gilchrist MSS 231 A iii) | Glapthorn, 1884, 'Here stands a young man who wants a sweetheart' (*Northamptonshire Notes & Queries*, i, p. 214) | Norfolk and Suffolk, c.1890, 'One poor widow left all alone' (*English Folk-Rhymes*, G. F. Northall, p. 374, and *County Folk-Lore: Suffolk*, E. C. Gurdon, p. 67) | *Traditional Games*, 1894–8, versions from regions as far apart as Cornwall, Perthshire, and Isle of Man, see under names above, also 'Here stands a Young Man' and 'Widow' | The game was fairly common in early years of twentieth century | Since Second World War: Co. Durham, 1948, 'Three old fisher wives left alone'; Swansea, 1952; Porthleven, 1961.

USA: Connecticut, 1860s, 'I am a rich widow, I live all alone' (*JAFL*, xiv, pp. 298–9) | Boone County, Missouri, c.1880, called 'The Juniper Tree' (*JAFL*, xxiv, pp. 305–6) | *Games of American Children*, 1883, pp. 56–7; 1903, p. 256, 'I am a rich widow, I live all alone' | Lancaster, Massachusetts, 1897, 'formerly played' (*JAFL*, x, pp. 325–6) | Michigan, 1914 (ib. xxxiii, p. 107) | *American Play-Party Song*, B. A. Botkin, 1937, p. 162, many further references.

Newfoundland: St John's, 1929, adult kissing dance, 'There was an old woman lived in Athlone, She had one daughter to marry at home' (*Journal of EFDSS*, iii, pp. 133–4).

It is perhaps worth pointing out in relation to the American versions that in Norway there is a strong tradition that 'when the gipsies want to marry they run three times round a juniper bush' (Eilert Sund, *Fante-eller Landstrygerfolket*, 1852, p. 189).

41

Pray, Pretty Miss

Tune: 'Nuts in May'

Pray, pretty Miss, will you come out?
Will you come out? Will you come out?
Pray, pretty Miss, will you come out,
To help me in my dancing?

—No!

Then you are a naughty Miss,
A naughty Miss, a naughty Miss,
Then you are a naughty Miss,
Won't help me in my dancing.

Pray, pretty Miss, will you come out?
Will you come out? Will you come out?
Pray, pretty Miss, will you come out,
To help me in my dancing?

—Yes!

Now you are a good Miss,
A good Miss, a good Miss,
Now you are a good Miss,
To help me in my dancing.

The earliest description of this game is from Cornwall in the middle of the nineteenth century. 'The children (a boy and girl alternately) formed a ring. One stood in the middle holding a white handkerchief by two of its corners; if a boy he would single out one of the girls, dance backwards and forwards opposite to her' and sing the first verse. If the answer was 'No!' spoken 'with averted head over the left shoulder', she was told she was a naughty girl, and another player was chosen. 'Occasionally three or four in turn refused' before the request was granted, and that player was told she was good. 'The handkerchief was then carefully spread on the floor; the couple knelt on it and kissed', and the child first in the middle either remained there or joined the ring. The girl would then choose a boy: 'Pray, pretty Sir, will you come out?'—the last to go into the middle always having 'the privilege of selecting the next partner'. The game thus reproduced, it will be seen, the salient features of the cushion dance, although subsequently the children usually seem to have stood in a row, and to have been chosen by a player or players dancing forward to make the selection, there being no handkerchief and no kisses.

Britain: Cornwall, *c.*1850 (*Folk-Lore*, v, pp. 47–8) | Hurstmonceux, Sussex, *c.*1850, 'Oh, will you come dance with me?' (*Traditional Games*, ii, pp. 65–7) | Sheffield, 1882, 'Pray, pretty Miss, will you come out to help us with our dancing? Yes. Now we've got our jolly old lass to help us with our dancing' (*Folk-Lore Record*, v, pp. 87–8) | Fochabers, 1898, 'Priperty Miss, will you come out?' and Winterton, Lincs, 1898, 'Pretty Miss Pink, will you come out?' Players have colours | Workington, *c.*1925, 'Will you come out this moonlight night to help us with the dancing? The fairest one that I can see is *Sheila Cook*, will you come with me? No! The dirty slut she won't come out . . . to help us with the dancing.' Verses from the game, sung to the tune of 'Nuts in May', were sometimes found attached to 'Three Brethren out of Spain' (p. 92).

42
Bee Baw Babbity

Paisley, 1961

> Bee baw babbity,
> > Babbity, babbity,
> Bee baw babbity,
> > A lassie or a wee laddie.
>
> Kneel down, kiss the ground,
> > Kiss the ground, kiss the ground,
> Kneel down, kiss the ground,
> > Kiss a bonny wee lassie.
>
> I widna hae a lassie-o,
> > A lassie-o, a lassie-o,
> I widna hae a lassie-o,
> > I'd rather hae a wee laddie.

Choose, choose, wha ye'll tak',
  Wha ye'll tak', wha ye'll tak',
Choose, choose, wha ye'll tak',
  A lassie or a wee laddie.

Generally played at parties, but sometimes kept going in the playground despite the protest of one ten-year-old that she did not like the game 'because I do not like kissing boys'. The players join hands in a circle, with one in the middle, and go round singing. When they have sung 'Choose, choose, wha ye'll tak', the player in the middle, who sometimes holds a handkerchief, chooses someone, kisses them, and that person takes the handkerchief and goes in the middle.

The ten-year-old's protest at the choice of this game is justifiable. Originally it was for older folk. 'Bab at the Bowster' or 'Bab wi' the Bowster' (i.e. bolster) was customarily, like 'the Cushion' in England, the last dance at weddings and merry-makings. Jamieson, in his *Scottish Dictionary, Supplement*, 1825, considered it 'a very old Scottish dance, now almost out of use', although a Paisley contributor to *Notes & Queries*, 18 January 1851, looked upon it as all but commonplace:

The manner of dancing it is, the company having formed itself into a circle, one, either male or female, goes into the centre, carrying a pillow, and dances round the circle with a sort of shuffling quick step, while the others sing:

Wha learn'd you to dance,
  You to dance, you to dance,
Wha learn'd you to dance,
  Bab in the Bowster brawly?

To which the dancer replies:

Mother learn'd me to dance,
  Me to dance, me to dance,
Mother learn'd me to dance,
  Bab in the Bowster brawly.

He or she then lays down the pillow before one of the opposite sex, when they both kneel on it and kiss; the person to whom the pillow has been presented going over the above again, &c., till the company tires.

The writer added that in Paisley it was a favourite dance, 'particularly among young people, and at children's parties in particular it is never omitted'. Robert Chambers, in 1862, gave a longer version 'sung by girls playing on the streets in Glasgow':

Wha learned you to dance,
   Babity Bowster, Babity Bowster,
Wha learned you to dance,
   Babity Bowster, brawly?

My minny learned me to dance,
   Babity Bowster, Babity Bowster,
My minny learned me to dance,
   Babity Bowster, brawly.

Wha ga'e you the keys to keep,
   Babity Bowster, Babity Bowster,
Wha ga'e you the keys to keep,
   Babity Bowster, brawly?

My minny ga'e me the keys to keep,
   Babity Bowster, Babity Bowster,
My minny ga'e me the keys to keep,
   Babity Bowster, brawly.

Clearly 'Babity Bowster, brawly' is related to 'Bumpkin Brawly'—'An old dance, the dance which always ends balls, the same with the "Cushion" almost', that Mactaggart knew at the beginning of the nineteenth century in Kirkcudbrightshire:

Wha learn'd you to dance,
You to dance, you to dance,
Wha learn'd you to dance—
A country bumpkin brawly?
My mither learn'd me when I was young,
When I was young, when I was young,
My mither learn'd me when I was young,
The country bumpkin brawly.

Brawly may here mean 'finely'; or may echo the term 'Brawl', the English rendering of *Branle*, the French round dance, performed with the dancers singing, which seems to have arrived in Britain early in the sixteenth century, and to be referred to in *The Complaynt of Scotland*, 1549, where the shepherds 'dansand base dansis, pauans, galʒardis, turdions, braulis and branglis, buffons, vitht mony vthir lycht dancis'. 'Bee Baw Babbity' appears to be a simplified version of the tune 'Country Bumkin' in John Walsh's *Caledonian Collection of Country Dances*, 1733, though 'Country Bumkin' has a more instrumental feel about it. 'Round Robin', in Playford's *Dancing Master*, 1686, has a slight resemblance to 'Bee Baw Babbity' in the second bar, but otherwise would seem to bear no relationship. As for the lute piece 'Who Learned Yow to Dance and a

Towdle' in the Skene MS of the reign of James VI (i.e. James I of England), the relationship appears to be confined to the first three notes. Possibly the commentators who have supposed a closer relationship have been unduly influenced by the coincidence in the words.

Scotland: *Gallovidian Encyclopedia*, John Mactaggart, 1824, p. 101, as quote │ Glasgow and Paisley, 1851 (*Notes & Queries*, 1st ser., iii, pp. 45 and 282) │ Glasgow, 1862 (*Songs of Scotland Prior to Burns*, Robert Chambers, p. 244) │ Biggar, 1894 (*Traditional Games*, i, pp. 9–11) │ Loanhead, 1900, 'Be bo babbity, bowster barley' (Gilchrist MSS. 231 Aiii, p. 89) │ *Games of Argyleshire*, R. C. Maclagan, 1901, pp. 57–8, 'Be Bo Babbity, Babbity, Babbity Bouster Boully . . . Kneel down and kiss the ground, kiss a bonnie lassie . . . Take any one you choose, sir, the fairest in the ring' │ North-east Scotland, pre-1906, 'Cocky Breeky Brawly' (*Rymour Club*, i, p. 52) │ *Minstrelsy of Childhood*, Frank Kidson and Alfred Moffat, 1911, p. 42 │ *Kerr's Guild of Play*, 1912, p. 4 │ *Joyous Book of Singing Games*, John Hornby, 1913, p. 8 │ Common between the wars. Since 1950: Glasgow, 1952, 1958 (the best known singing game) and 1961 │ Kingarth, 1960 │ Cumnock, Paisley, and Stirling, 1961 │ Avoch, Ross-shire, 1975.

　In Roxburghshire 'Bab-at-the-bowster' was a name for the boys' game 'Hi Jimmy Knacker'.

43

Best Bed's a Feather Bed

Glasgow, 1978

The best bed's a feather bed,
　The best bed of all;
The best bed in our house
　Is clean pease straw.
Pease straw is dirty,
　And will dirty all my gown;
But never mind, my bonny lass,
　Just lay the cushion down.

A game which has always belonged to the north-east, and which continues to be suggestive of blowzy eighteenth-century merrymaking, although its sentiment is usually lost on today's players. Like 'Bee Baw Babbity' it is generally played at children's parties. The players form a large circle, often squatting on the floor, and during the singing one player or sometimes two, a girl and a boy, skip around inside the circle, each carrying a cushion. At the end of the song the carriers 'lay the cushion down' in front of whomever they please. Chooser and chosen one kneel on the cushion, the chosen one receives a kiss, and in recompense is free to skip around while the song is sung again, and to become the chooser at the end of the song. The game was clearly popular at the close of the nineteenth century, although Alice Gomme's collectors did not report it. The tune, which is just about the same as that used for the bawdy 'Ball of Kirriemuir', written in the 1880s, is also that of the Scottish version of 'Sally Water', 'I'm a little sandy girl' (p. 170).

Britain: *Northumberland Words*, R. O. Heslop, i, 1892, p. 211 | Tyneside, 1895, 'The pigsty is dirty, and will dirty all your gown'. Subsequent recollections are in *English Dance and Song*, 1967, pp. 45–6, 89–90 | Morpeth, *c.*1914 | Forfar, *c.*1925 | Glasgow, *c.*1945 and 1978, 'The pease straw was dirty, Lying on the ground, But never mind my bonny wee lassie, Lay the cushion down, Lay it down, lay it down, Lay it down at someone's feet, feet, feet, feet' | Birmingham, 1966, sung by girls while skipping or just for fun (Roy Palmer, *Songs of the Midlands*, p. 2) | *Folk Songs from the North*, G. and M. Polwarth, 1970, p. 21 | Cambo, near Morpeth, 1978.

VII

'Longways for as many as will'

THESE four frivolities illustrate the off-hand manner in which children treat tradition. Each appears to be a country dance 'longways for as many as will', such as was popular from the mid-seventeenth century onwards, but cannot be said to have descended from any of the dances in John Playford's *Dancing Master*, 1651, and its successors. Each has a rollicking tune none the worse for having been borrowed from an older song or infiltrated by a rival tune. Each has words blithely irrelevant to childhood experience; and each is played with equal gusto inside the school 'with the teacher playing the piano', or outside 'on our own by ourselves'.

44

A-Hunting We Will Go

Aylesbury, 1978

> A-hunting we will go,
> A-hunting we will go,
> We'll catch a fox and put him in a box,
> And never let him go.

You all stand in two lines, and you have a partner, and the top pair hold hands and go up and down the middle while all the other people clap, and then the two people at the top go down outside the sides and make an archway at the bottom and the other people follow them and come up through (*girl, 11, Aylesbury, 1978*).

This is the way the game was played at Ellesmere before 1883 ('the two lines march to the other end and meet again, as in the country-dance Sir Roger de Coverley') and in the West Country in 1922 ('The girls stand in one row and the boys in the other. The boy and girl at the top of the rows join hands and dance together down the space between the rows and back again, whilst all the players sing: "A-hunting we will go . . . We'll catch a fox and put him in a box And never let him go. We'll ask John Brown to tea, We'll ask John Brown to tea, If he can't come we'll ask his son, And all his family" '). But it has also been played in a ring, with the hunter in the middle trying to grab a fox when the singing stopped.

Two tunes have been used, and both are given in *Traditional Games* (i, p. 243). The first is the same as that used for 'The Grand Old Duke of York' (p. 214). The second, as above, most often used in the present day, is similar to the tune printed with Henry Fielding's song 'The Dusky Night Rides Down the Sky—chorus, A hunting we will go' in the musical broadside versions (e.g. *Vocal Music, or The Songster's Companion*), though in his ballad opera *Don Quixote in England* it was sung to a tune from the previous century, 'A Begging We Will Go' (see Chappell, vol. ii, pp. 650–2). The first two phrases of this second tune reflect the eighteenth-century German 'Bei Hall ist eine Mühl' which, probably because it sounds like a hunting horn, accompanied various comic songs about hunting a mole or a fish and making it into a purse (in Holland and Flanders) as well as the old German student song making fun of a 'fox' or freshman (see 'The Farmer's in His Den', p. 186).

Britain: Ellesmere, 1883, 'A-hunting we will go . . . We'll catch a little fish And put him in a dish, And never let him go!' (*Shropshire Folk-Lore*, p. 514) | Derbyshire, 1883, 'fox . . . box' (*Folk-Lore*, i, p. 386) | *Children's Singing Games*, Cecil Sharp, ii, 1909, p. 14, top pair cross hands and dance round to the left in column of two to the bottom of the dance. Tune is 'The Grand Old Duke of York' | West Country, 1922 (Macmillan Collection) | Since 1950s, 18 places as text, occasionally with 'A-fishing we will go' as second verse ('But it's stupid really,' said a Louth, Lincs, 9-year-old, 1961, 'because you don't hunt fish like you do a fox').

USA: Michigan, 1914, 'Oh, have you seen the Sha? . . . He lights his pipe on a starlight night, Oh, have you seen the Sha? For a-hunting we will go, etc.' (*JAFL*, xxxiii, p. 102) | Missouri, 1950 (*JAFL*, lxiii, p. 431).

It would be nice to think this was the dance decided upon by the yokels in Thomas Heywood's *A Woman Kilde with Kindnesse*, 1607, I, ii. Jenkin says that now the gentlefolk 'are busie in the parlor . . . weele have a crash heere in the yard'. Various dances are suggested and rejected until Jenkin says firmly 'No weele have the hunting of the Fox'.

45

The Grand Old Duke of York

Cambo, Northumberland, 1978

Oh, the grand old Duke of York,
He had ten thousand men,
He marched them up to the top of the hill,
And he marched them down again.
And when they were up they were up,
And when they were down they were down,
And when they were only half way up
They were neither up nor down.

Played with the same down-the-middle-and-back, cast-and-all-follow, first-couple-make-arch-at-the-bottom-and-all-through progression as 'A-Hunting We Will Go'. How long this lampoon on Frederick Duke of York has been used for a dancing game is not known. Anne Gilchrist learned, from a 'temporary' called Lily Petch, that it was played as a marching game at holiday time by large numbers of young men and girls in South Elmsall, *c.*1900. They 'would march in a long procession of couples up some hill and down again, singing the words. Lily . . . told me it was great fun, and that whenever a couple tripped and fell as not infrequently happened if the hill was steep, they lost their place in the ranks and had to fall in again at the tail of the procession' (notebook 231 Aii, p. 20).

Frank Kidson included an eccentric version in *Eighty Singing Games*, 1907, to which the children must parade like soldiers:

> Oh! the famous Duke of York,
>   He marched his men to war;
> But none of them got to the battlefield
>   Because it was too far . . .

But it was not until Cecil Sharp suggested that the song might be added to, or substituted for, 'O! A-Hunting We Will Go', that it appeared as the song-accompaniment to the country-dance (*Children's Singing Games*, ii, 1909).

Britain: *100 Singing Games*, F. Kidson, 1916, p. 15, as country-dance │ West Country, 1922, as text, 'and in some places they add "Rule Britannia" ' (Macmillan Collection) │ Since 1950, recordings from 14 places in England, Scotland, and Wales. Often the mention of 'boys and girls' indicates that it is a party game. Words are fairly consistent, though the commander-in-chief can be 'The merry Duke of York' (Berry Hill, Glos., 1961) or 'The good old Duke of Kent' (Swansea, 1952); and he may have only 'a thousand men' (Swansea, 1961) or 'so many men' (Kingarth, Isle of Bute, 1960). For the history of the rhyme see *ODNR*, pp. 442 and 176. The tune is old French, a version of 'Le petit tambour'.

46

O Belinda

Glasgow, 1960

Right hand up, O Belinda,
Right hand up, O Belinda,
Right hand up, O Belinda,
Won't you be my darling?

Left hand up, O Belinda, etc.

Both hands up, O Belinda, etc.

Back to back, O Belinda, etc.

A dance found only in Glasgow, 1960, with the off-hand instructions 'All the girls and boys begin in a ring and one girl goes out and starts to go round'. Richard Chase published a longways country-dance version from North Carolina in *Old Songs and Singing Games*, 1938, pp. 43–4. The first boy and last girl meet for the various movements as in 'Sir Roger de Coverley'; then the top couple cast off to the left and return up the middle to their places before moving down the bottom of the dance under a tunnel of raised hands. The words are 'Bow, bow, O Belinda . . . Won't you be my darling? Right hand 'round . . . Left hand 'round . . . Both hands 'round . . . Shake that big foot, shy all around her . . . Roll under, O Belinda'. Chase had known the dance in New York City, and said it was played as 'O Betty Liner' in Tennessee; and it appears in Botkin's *American Play-Party Song*, p. 299, as 'Lead 'er up an' down, Rosa Becky Diner' (danced like the better-known 'Boston', in which the line of girls marches round the line of boys and *vice versa*, and sharing the same tune). This vagrant play-party game was also found as a game for two small children in Pietermaritzburg, 1975 ('Baa baa, O Belinda').

47

Pop Goes the Weasel

Gloucester, 1935

Half a pound of tuppenny rice,
Half a pound of treacle,
That's the way the money goes,
Pop goes the weasel!

How to play. You make several circles of three or four. Each circle has a weasel in the middle, and there is an extra weasel outside. You dance round singing the song and when it comes to 'Pop' the weasels must run to the middle of a different ring and the odd weasel must try to get inside one before it is filled. It is a bit like Musical Chairs (*girl, 11, Stirling, 1961*).

In other places the third line is 'Mix it up and make it nice'; and sometimes another verse is added:

> Every night when I get home
> The monkey's on the table,
> Take a stick and knock it off,
> Pop goes the weasel!

The earliest appearance of this 'Pop Goes the Weasel' game is in *The Book of Cub Games*, V. C. Barclay, 1919; but the formula was used for a number of organized games at that period, when squirrels and cuckoos also tried to get into unoccupied rings. The game always seems to be played to the rice-and-treacle verse even when, as reported to Alice Gomme from Earls Heaton, Yorkshire, it was played by two rows of children moving backwards and forwards and whirling with partners at the end (*Traditional Games*, ii, 1898, pp. 63–4).

The Earls Heaton version was, perhaps, a misremembrance of the 'celebrated comic dance' which took England by storm in 1853. A music sheet in the British Library (h. 970/18, acquired 14 March 1853) describes the dance 'Pop Goes the Weasel' as 'An Old English Dance, as performed at Her Majesty's & The Nobilities Balls, with the Original Music' and gives the movements 'as taught by Madame Soutten at her Academy No. 27 Queen Ann Street':

The Ladies and Gentlemen form themselves into lines, as in the Country dance.

The couple at the top begin the figure by running forward within the line (four bars) and back again (four bars) and then without the line, and back again (in the same interval).

After this, they form a circle of three with one of the couple next to them on the line, and turn once round to the right, and once to the left; then making the one they have selected pass quickly under their arms to his place (while singing 'Pop goes the Weasel') they return direct to the other line, and repeat the same figure with the partner of the last chosen.

The same couple then runs forward and backward inside and outside the line, repeating the figure with the next couple on the right and left. After they have passed three or four couples, the Lady and Gentleman at the top begin and continue the same figure, which is performed by all in their turn.

The tune was close to that known today, and the only words were 'Pop goes the weasel', sung when a dancer was popped back into his place under the arms of the leading couple. But soon everyone was fitting words to the catchy, ubiquitous tune. Charles Sloman, for instance, celebrated its arrival with a comic song 'sung with unbounded success by Mr Charles Rice', which began:

> Something new starts every day,
>   Pop goes &c.
> Fashion ever changes sway,
>   Pop goes &c.
> As one comes in another goes out,
>   Pop goes &c.
> The newest one there is no doubt is
>   Pop goes &c.

The best-known and much discussed 'City Road' verse must have already been in circulation by 9 April 1855, when J. R. Planché quoted it in his Easter extravaganza at the Theatre Royal, 'The New Haymarket Spring Meeting'. The genii of various London theatres were introduced, amongst them that of the Grecian Saloon attached to the Eagle Tavern (proprietor, B. O. Conquest). An eagle appeared on stage and sang:

> I'm the Bird of Conquest—made
>   First by Romans famous,
> Though 'Grecian' my Saloon was named,
>   By some ignoramus.
> 'Up and down the City Road,
>   In and out the Eagle,
> That's the way my money *comes*,
>   Pop goes the weasel!'

The significance of 'weasel', if any, has been a favourite subject for speculation. It has been suggested that a 'weasel' is a tailor's flat-iron, a hatter's tool, a piece of silver plate, or a 'weasel and stoat' (rhyming slang for coat) which must be 'popped' or pawned because of visits to the Eagle; that it is a mishearing of weevil or *vaisselle* (which leads to further obscurities); that it was James I's nickname ('because of his thin sharp features and red hair') and that, 'rice' and 'treacle' being slang terms for potassium nitrate and charcoal respectively, the rhyme refers to the Gunpowder Plot; that the phrase describes a sixpence expended, a cork being drawn out of a bottle, or the sinuous weasel-like movement of the dancer passing under the arms of his partners. But even when the dance was at the height of its popularity nobody seems to have known what the phrase meant, and W. R. Mandale, in his comic song 'Pop Goes the Weasel', says that after enquiring of everyone he met,

> I'm still as wise as e'er I was,
>   As full's an empty pea-shell,
> In as far as the true history goes
>   Of 'Pop goes the weasel'.

VIII

The Downfall of the Ring

ACROSS Europe ring games are played in which the *pièce de résistance* consists of flopping to the ground, 'a proceeding', remarked an observer in 1891, 'which seems to be a source of hilarious and side-splitting mirth'. In such games the subject of the song may be the getting into a barrel which falls apart, as in the Dutch game 'Jan Huygen in de ton'; or bread being put in an oven that is not hot enough, and the loaf collapsing, as in the French game 'Rondin, picotin'; or a potter placing a pot of water in an oven, and the whole oven collapsing, as in an Austrian version of 'Ringel, Ringel, Rosenkranz'; or a mother putting bread in an oven successfully, but then cutting herself, as in a Tuscan version of 'Giro, giro tondo'.

The players may make-believe they are to picnic on potatoes, and all sit down on the ground together, as in the Spanish game of 'La Rueda la Patata'. They may think of themselves as being apples and pears hanging on the trees, and when they are ripe they all fall down, as in Norway:

> Epler og paerer henger på traerne,
> Når de blir modne, så faller de ned.

They may pretend to be 'All the soldiers in the town', and, for some unexplained reason, 'all bop down', as in a game Alice Gomme reported from Norfolk at the end of the nineteenth century. Or they may go round and round and feel, when they all fall down, they are enacting the downfall of the world, as they commonly do in Italy:

> Giro, giro tondo,
> Casc' il mondo,
> Casc' la terra,
> E cosi giù per terra.

Such games, however, amongst which may be numbered the present-day 'Ring a Ring o' Roses', are simple amusements, the sport of little children, generally played under the direction of a parent or an older child. What is uncertain is whether all of them have always been nursery games, or whether some of them (including 'Ring a Ring o' Roses') were formerly more graceful games, which have come down in the world literally with a bump. In Argyllshire, at the turn of the century, little girls playing 'Round About the Punch Bowl' did not fall down at the end but made a low curtsy. In Surrey, about 1909, girls playing 'Our Boots Are Made of Leather' did not drop down at the end but curtsied 'till our frocks shall touch the ground'. Scots children, playing the wedding game 'Merry-ma-tansie', have long dropped to the ground at 'Twice about and then we fall', but they have done so to determine which of them is to be wedded. The players of the now popular game 'Orange Balls' do the same to decide who shall make known her loved one; and the evidence seems to show that at one time the point of playing both 'Ring a Ring o' Roses' and 'Ring Around the Rosie' was to determine who amongst the players was to be the next to reveal the object of her affection. Likewise in versions of 'Gira, gira rosa' in Italy, and 'J'ai un rosier' in France, the player in the middle has to kiss whom she likes best; while in a version of 'Giro, giro tondo', popular amongst Italian children, there is a link with 'Water, Water Wallflowers' as played in north Britain. After dancing round in a ring, and giving a bunch of violets to her who is liked best, the singers command that the littlest one must kneel, 's'inginocchi la più piccina', and this instruction may be compared with that in 'Water, Water Wallflowers' when the youngest one, or the littlest one, is told to turn her back to the others before the game recommences.

48

Ring a Ring o' Roses

Stepney, London E1, 1976

Ring a ring o' roses,
A pocket full of posies,
A-tishoo, a-tishoo,
We all fall down.

'Ring a Ring o' Roses', the nursery game in which players join hands in a circle, dance round while they sing, and aim not to be last to reach the ground when 'all fall down', is today almost a synonym for childhood: the first of the singing games an infant is likely to learn; the only one he or she plays with older members of the family; and the inevitable choice of illustrators when they wish to depict the supposed joyfulness of being young. The game is therefore scorned as soon as a child becomes independent and goes to school; although seven- and eight-year-olds, when asked about the ring games they know, tend to think first of 'Rin-ga, Rin-ga Roses' (so pronounced in the Midlands), and the game becomes good sport at the shallow end of the swimming pool on a chill day when the bathers are reluctant to get wet. However, in satisfaction of the adult requirement that anything seemingly innocent should have a hidden meaning of exceptional unpleasantness, the game has been tainted by a legend that the song is a relic of the Great Plague of 1665; that the ring of roses was the purpuric sore that betokened the plague, that the posies were the herbs carried as protection against infection, that sneezing ('a-tishoo, a-tishoo') was the final fatal symptom of the disease, and that 'all fall down' was precisely what happened. This story has obtained such circulation in recent years it can itself be said to be epidemic. Thus the mass-circulation *Radio Times*, 7 June 1973, gave it a double-page headline, to advertise a documentary programme on the plague-village of Eyam (although a 1909 guide book to Eyam does not mention the rhyme); lecturers at medical schools have repeated it as fact both in Britain and America (men of science are notoriously incautious when pronouncing on material in disciplines other than their own); and we ourselves have had to listen so often to this interpretation we are reluctant to go out of the house. Those infected with the belief seem unperturbed that no reference to 'Ring a Ring o' Roses' appears in Pepys's careful record of hearsay during the long months of the Plague; or that Defoe's brilliant evocation in *A Journal of the Plague Year* does not indicate that either sneezing or redness of spots was on men's minds at the time; or that two recent studies, Philip Ziegler's *The Black Death* (1969) and Professor J. F. D. Shrewsbury's *History of the Bubonic Plague in the British Isles* (1970), give no support to the theory, unless, that is, Thomas Vincent's observation in *God's Terrible Voice in the City*, 1666, is thought relevant, that roses were then neglected, since 'People dare not offer them to their noses, lest with their sweet savour that which is infectious should be attracted'.

The legend linking the plague with the game-song seems in fact to be comparatively new. It was not given by Alice Gomme in 1898, who would certainly have mentioned it had she known it; and has not been found in the work of any commentator before the Second World War, although—under the protection of *The Golden Bough*—the mythologists were not wanting in fancifulness (e.g., 'The falling down is a fragment of prostration that was practised when the shadows swept over the cornfield, and the corn spirit was passing by'). Probably the story grew out of the long-alleged connection between sneezing and the plague. A writer in *The Monthly Packet*, January 1875, commented: 'It is strange how many educated English people will persist in dating the national "God bless you!" from the time of the Great Plague; though we have clear proof to the contrary in *The Golden Legend*, which was printed by Caxton in 1483, which particularly mentions that the goodly practice of saying "God help you!" or "Chryste help!" endured at that time.'

The association of the plague with 'Ring a Ring o' Roses' looks even more improbable when the history of the game itself is examined. Alice Gomme's failure to devolve it from Stuart times is commendable, seeing that, when she was writing, the game had not been on record in England for more than twenty years, and versions continued to vary considerably. The following are the seven earliest reports known to us in Britain:

The children join hands and run round in a ring, and then sneeze and flop down at the words 'Atch chew!'

> A ring, a ring o' Roses
> A pocket full o' Posies—
> Atch chew! atch chew!
>
> *Bolton le Moors, Lancs., probably c.1880*

For 'pocket' there are variations: 'bottle', Bury, Lancs., and 'pottle', Reddish, Lancs., both *c.*1880 (Crofton MS, i, p. 166)

Ring-a-ring-a-roses,
A pocket full of posies;
Hush! hush! hush! hush!
We're all tumbled down.

Kate Greenaway's Mother Goose, 1881

A ring, a ring o' roses,
A pocket-full o' posies;
One for Jack and one for Jim
And one for little Moses!
A curchey in, and a curchey out,
And a curchey all together.

Edgmond, Shropshire, 1883. Children curtsy at the end

A ring, a ring o' roses,
A pocket-full o' posies;
One for Jack and one for Jim
And one for little Moses!
A-tisha! a-tisha! a-tisha!

'Common' in Shropshire, 1883. At end players stood still imitating sneezing

Ring a ring o' roses,
Pocketsful o' posies,
A maiden's fairy crown,
We all fall down.

London, 1891. 'The last line finds all the little maidens seated on the pavement with gleeful and delighted faces'

A ring a ring of roses,
A pocket full of posies,
Ashem, Ashem.
All fall down.

Sheffield, 1891. 'They fall either on their knees or flat on their faces . . . "Ashem" is said by some to express the noise made by sneezing'

Ring-a-ring o' rosies,
A bottleful o' posies,
Ashum! ashum! ashum! (ad lib.)

Leeds, 1896, 'At each "ashum" the players jump upwards and throw their heads forward in imitation of one sneezing, and so the singing and concomitant action of the last line (or word) continue till one or more fall down through sheer exhaustion'

In only four of these recordings is sneezing a feature; and in only two (the Yorkshire versions) is sneezing, or supposed sneezing, coupled with falling or kneeling down. That some-such entertainment was in existence in the middle of the nineteenth century may be adduced, perhaps, from *The Cricket on the Hearth* (1846), where Tilly Slowboy, the baby's nurse-maid, 'with a melodious cry of "Ketcher, Ketcher"—which sounded like some unknown words, adapted to a popular Sneeze—performed some cow-like gambols round that all unconscious Innocent'. But the game, if it was a game, and if performed to a nursery song, cannot have had the circulation it has today. Halliwell, whose ever-enlarged collections of nursery diversions appeared 1842–53, seems to have been as unaware of it as was his counterpart in Scotland, Robert Chambers. In America, however, Newell, writing in 1883, remarked that versions of a little round called 'Ring around the Rosie' were 'universally familiar', for instance:

> Ring around the rosie,
> Squat among the posies.

And,

> Ring around the roses,
> Pocket full of posies,
> One, two, three—squat!

And he added that the following had been known in New Bedford, Massachusetts, about 1790:

> Ring a ring a rosie,
> A bottle full of posie,
> All the girls in our town,
> Ring for little Josie.

This is not altogether unlike a version that was still well-known to children in Devon, Somerset, Herefordshire, and South Wales in the 1920s:

> Ring a ring of roses (or 'a rosie'),
> A pocket full of posies,
> One for you and one for me,
> And one for little Moses.
> Hush! Hush! Hush!

In America, it will be noticed, hushing or sneezing noises were virtually unknown: and the game sometimes had more to it than merely seeing who squatted last:

> Round the ring of roses,
> Pots full of posies,
> The one who stoops last
> Shall tell whom she loves best.

Newell reported that at the end of these words the children quickly stooped; and the last to get down had either to undergo a penalty or to take the place of a child in the centre who represented the 'rosie', i.e. *rosier* or rose-tree. The demand that the last down should tell whom she loved best (one little player is said to have answered 'God') continued in America into the present century, and was not unknown in Britain. At Grayrigg, near Kendal, 1903, the last down had to select a player from the ring, and the others then raised the embarrassing cry 'Shak', shak', feather bed! Wedding's coming on!' Games of this class were also widespread on the Continent. In Venice, a hundred years ago, when girls played 'Gira, gira, rosa', they danced round in a circle with one girl in the middle who skipped and curtsied as required by the song, and at the end kissed the one she liked best, who then took her place in the middle:

> Gira, gira, rosa,
>   Co la più bela in mezo;
> Gira un bel giardino,
>   Un altro pochetino;
> Un salterelo,
>   Un altro de più belo;
> Una riverenza,
>   Un'altra per penitenza;
> Un baso a chi ti vol.

> (Ring a ring a roses,
>   With the most beautiful in the
>   middle;
> Ring a pretty garden,
>   Another circle round,
> A little skip,
>   Another even better,
> A curtsy,
>   Another for penitence:
> A kiss for the one you like.)

And in Paris, about the same time, roses or a rose-tree were associated with this freedom—or compulsion—to choose and kiss whom the player liked best:

A la main droite j'ai un rosier
   Qui fleurira
   Au mois de mai,
   Au mois de mai,
   Qui fleurira.
Entrez, entrez, charmante rose;
Embrassez celle que vous voudrez,
   La rose
   Ou bien le rosier.

In Germany one of the most popular ring games amongst the young was, and still is, 'Ringel, Ringel, Reihe', in which, according to the song, three children sit up in an elder bush crying 'Musch, musch, musch! Sit you down!'—a game that was recorded in an antiquarian magazine as long ago as 1796:

Ringe, Ringe, Reihe!
Sind der Kinder dreie,
Sitzen auf dem Holderbusch,
Rufen alle: musch, musch, musch!
Setzt euch nieder!

The song a nine-year-old girl in South Shields gave Alice Gomme a century later is so similar it could almost be a direct translation:

Ring a ring a row-o,
See the children go-o,
Sit below the gooseberry bush;
Hark! they all cry Hush! hush! hush!
Sitty down, sit down.

In Switzerland, according to a version recorded in 1857, the children were not sitting in an elder bush but dancing round a rose tree:

Ringel, Ringeli, Reihe,
D'Chind göhnt i d'Maie.
Sie tanzet um die Rosestöck
Und machet alle Bode-Bodehöck.

(Ring-a, ring-a, row,
The bairns go into the greenwood.
They dance round the rose bush
And all squat down.)

Indeed roses or rosaries pervade such games. However common the saying 'There are as many roses as flowers', it can hardly be coincidence that in Languedoc, in the south of France, where the patois was such as to test a linguist, the children used to play 'The little branle of the Rose', bowing down and standing up straight at the end:

Lou brandet de Roso: (*Le petit branle de Rose*:
Tant de rosos coumo de flous   *Il y a autant de roses que de fleurs*
De touto meno de coulous,   *De toutes sortes de couleurs,*
   Cagassounet,   *Baisse-toi,*
   Levo-te dre!   *Lève-toi droit.*)

Likewise in Holland and Germany, where such games are common, the following lines (arguably medieval according to Gerrit Kalff) are sometimes sung to tunes very similar to the English 'Ring a Ring o' Roses':

Roze, roze, meie   (Rose, rose, May
Twintig in de stye   Twenty in the score
Dertig in de rozekrans   Thirty in the rose garland
Veertig in de mooie meisjesdans   Forty in the beautiful maidens' dance
Alle juffertjes nigen of knielen.   All the girls bow or kneel.)

Thus in 'Ring a Ring o' Roses' we have, or so it seems, a spray from the great Continental tradition of May games, that preserves the memory, however faintly, of the rose as the flower of Cupid, the wreath of roses with which Aphrodite crowned her hair, the chaplet of roses that a lover presented to his lady or with which, if she spurned him—and he followed Ovid's advice—he adorned her gatepost, the emblem that passed naturally into the social ceremony of the Middle Ages as in Chaucer's *The Romaunt of the Rose*, where the lover is instructed not only to 'harpe and giterne, daunce and play', but to

> Have hat of floures freshe as May,
> Chapelet of roses of Whitsonday.

Whether the English like to think of the rose as a symbol of pagan love or an insignia of the Virgin Mary, a race of rose-growers might surely have been expected to have taken more kindly to the idea that a ring o' roses was a rose wreath rather than a death-portending rash.

> Of a rose, a lovely rose,
> Of a rose is al myn song.

USA: New Bedford, Massachusetts, *c*.1790 (*Games of American Children*, pp. 127–8) | Washington DC, *c*.1885 (*American Anthropologist*, i, p. 253) | St Louis, *c*.1900; also 1944, 'Ring around a rosy, Pocket full of posy, Last one down is a nigger baby' (*JAFL*, lx, pp. 32 and 42) | Cincinnati, 1908 (ibid., xl, p. 25) | North Carolina, 1920s, five versions (*North Carolina Folklore*, pp. 150–1) | East Texas, 1938, 'Ring round the rosy, Bottle full of posy, Last one squats Will be old Josey' | Princeton, New Jersey, 1977, consensus opinion of mothers from various places: the game is now chiefly, as in Britain, an amusement for infants; it is called 'Ring around the Rosey', but the words are 'A ring a ring o' roses, A pocket full of posies, Ashes, Ashes, All fall down!' Tune similar to English.

Canada: Toronto, 1909, 'Ring around a rosy, Pocket full of posy, Who pops down first?' (*JAFL*, xxxi, p. 57); also Grey County, Ontario, 1918 (ibid., pp. 106–7) | Toronto, 1962 (Fowke, 1969, p. 11).

Britain: *Mother Goose*, Kate Greenaway, 1881, p. 52 | *Shropshire Folk-Lore*, C. S. Burne, 1883, pp. 511–12 | *Sheffield Glossary, Supplement*, S. O. Addy, 1891, p. 191 | London, 1891 (*Strand Magazine*, ii, p. 518) | *Traditional Games*, ii, 1898, pp. 108–11 | Ubiquitous in twentieth century.

Additional verses: Taunton, 1902; Milford Haven, 1947; Oban, 1974; and elsewhere (probably abetted by Alfred Moffat's *What the Children Sing*, 1915), 'The king has sent his daughter, To fetch a pail of water, A-tishoo, a-tishoo, We all bow down. The robin on the steeple Is singing to the people, A-tishoo, a-tishoo, We all kneel down. The merry bells are ringing, The boys and girls are singing, A-tishoo, a-tishoo, We all fall down. The cows are in the meadow Eating all the grass, A-tishoo, a-tishoo, Who's up last?' | Hayes, Middlesex, 1956, 'Take a pinch of snuff, And we all jump up' | Charing Cross Road, 1966, St John's Wood, 1973, and Dulwich, 1976, 'Picking up the daisies, Daisies, daisies, Picking up the daisies, We all jump up' | Manchester, Salford, and Scarborough, 1975, 'Fishes (*or* Ashes) in the water, Fishes (*or* Ashes) in the sea, We all jump up with a one, two, three' | Swanage, 1975, 'The cows are in the meadow Eating up the grass, Along came a fat bull And slipped upon his arse' | Oxford, 1976, 'Daddy's in the teapot, Mummy in the cup, Baby's in the saucer, We all jump up'.

Scotland: The song beginning 'Roon, roon, rosie', 'Ring a ring a rosie' or 'Ring a ring o' roses, A cappie, cappie shell, The dog's awa tae Hamilton Tae buy the wean a bell. . .', often referred to as the Scottish 'Ring o' Roses', but chiefly repeated during other amusements e.g. knee rides, is to be compared with 'Dingle dingle doosey' in *ODNR*, pp. 149–50.

Ireland: Dublin, 1976, 'Ring a ring a rosy A bucketful of posy, Ashah, ashah, We all fall down'.

Australia: Footscray, Victoria, *c*.1915, 'Ring a ring o' rosey, Pop down a posey, A-tishoo, a-tishoo, We all fall down'.

New Zealand: As Australia, 'played mainly by younger children' (Sutton-Smith, p. 12).

Germany: *Bragur*, iii, 1796, p. 245, as quote, with second verse, 'Es sitzt 'ne Frau im Gartenhaus Mit sieben kleinen Kinderlein. Was essens gern? Fischelein. Was trinkens gern? Rothen Wein. Setzt euch nieder!' (*Deutsches Kinderspiel*, F. M. Böhme, p. 439). Similar versions in *Des Knaben Wunderhorn*, L. Achim v. Arnim and C. Brentano, iii, 1808, pp. 88–9; *Kinder-Märchen*, Brüder Grimm, ii, 1819, p. 15; and *Das deutsche Kinderbuch*, Karl Simrock, 1848, p. 166 | *Salzburgische Volks-Lieder*, M. V. Süss, 1865, p. 22, 'Ringa, ringa, reia Dö Gans dö gehnt en Meia; Dö Vögel sand en Hollebusch, Schrei, mein Kinderl, husch, husch, husch!'

Austria: *Oberösterreichische Kinderspiele*, Otto Kampmüller, 1965, p. 70, 'Ringa, ringa, reiha, San ma unser dreier, Setz ma uns auf d'Hollerstaudn, D'Hollerstaudn bricht ab, Fall ma alle in Bach.'

Switzerland: *Alemannisches Kinderspiel aus der Schweiz*, L. E. Rochholz, 1857, p. 183, as quote | *Deutsches Kinderspiel*, F. M. Böhme, 1897, p. 439, 'Ringe, Ringe, Reihe! 's sind der Kinder zweie: Sie tanzed um e Rosebusch Und mached alle: husch, husch, husch!'

Netherlands: *Het Lied in de middeleeuwen*, G. Kalff, 1884, p. 526, as quote | Zwolle, *c*.1925, 'Roze, roze meije, Twintig in de reije, Dertig in de rozekrans, Veertig in de mooie meisjesdans, Van alle juffertjes kreije!' (at the end, all the 'fair maids' fell down and made a crowing noise).

France: *Chants populaires du Languedoc*, A. Montel and Louis Lambert, 1880, p. 577 | *Rimes et jeux de l'enfance*, E. Rolland, 1883, p. 71.

Italy: *Giuochi Popolari Veneziani*, Giuseppe Bernoni, 1874, p. 30.

49

Our Boots Are Made of Leather

adapted from Old Surrey Singing Games, *A. E. Gillington, 1909*

Our boots are made of leather,
Our stockings are made of silk,
Our pinafores of calico
As white as any milk.

Here we go around, around, around,
Until we touch the ground;
Here we go around, around, around,
Until we touch the ground.

On the last word the players stopped dancing in a circle and dropped to the ground; or, in some places, stopped and made a curtsy. Sometimes, while they sang the first verse they stood still, pointing in turn to their boots, stockings, and pinafores. Then, when they sang 'Here we go around', they sped round as fast as they could before 'jumping to the ground'. Sometimes the last player down had to go into the middle of the ring; and after the next round the last down had to join the first in the middle, and they continued until more children were crowded into the middle of the ring than there were players to dance round them. The game was a favourite at the turn of the century. Mrs Morel, in Lawrence's *Sons and Lovers*, could hear the children in the darkness of the street singing away:

My shoes are made of Spanish leather,
  My socks are made of silk;
I wear a ring on every finger,
  I wash myself in milk.

'They sounded so perfectly absorbed in the game as their voices came out of the night, that they had the feel of wild creatures singing.' It stirred her; and she understood how it was with them 'when they came in at eight o'clock, ruddy, with brilliant eyes, and quick, passionate speech'. The refrain 'Here we go around, around, around', stems, it seems, from the refrain of 'We Be Three Poore Mariners', printed in *Deuteromelia*, 1609:

Shall we go daunce the round, the round, the round,
  and shall we goe daunce the round?
And he that is a bully boy,
  come pledge me on the ground.

For further on this song see 'Jolly Sailors' (p. 197).

Merrie Games in Rhyme, E. M. Plunket, 1886, p. 48, 'Our boots are made of Spanish' | London, 1891, popular amongst small girls (*Strand Magazine*, ii, p. 518) | London, Barnes; Crockham Hill in Kent, and Liphook, Hampshire (*Traditional Games*, i, p. 205, and cf. ii, p. 436) | Tyneside, *c*.1895, similar to 1913, plus refrain 'Hi tiddly anca, yes, ianca, Hi tiddly anca, yes, i-o' | Soho, 1907, for skipping (*St Anne's Soho Monthly*, p. 180) | *Old Surrey Singing Games*, A. E. Gillington, 1909, p. 12 | Somerset, 1912 (*Children's Singing Games*, Cecil Sharp, v, p. 16) | *Sons and Lovers*, D. H. Lawrence, 1913. ch. iv, set in Nottinghamshire | *London Street Games*, 1916, p. 64 | Crewkerne and Ilminster, 1922 (Macmillan Collection) | *Street Games of North Shields Children*, M. and R. King, 1926, p. 9, 'My boots are made of Spanish leather', with refrain similar to *c*.1895 | Forfar, 1954, 'Our handkerchiefs are made of cotton As white as any milk' | Cf. *Mother Goose*, Kate Greenaway, 1881, p. 9, 'We're all jolly boys, and we're coming with a noise, Our stockings shall be made of the finest silk, And our tails shall touch the ground' | *Less Familiar Nursery Rhymes*, Robert Graves, 1927, p. 17, 'Our stockings shall be silk As white as the milk'.

50
The Leaves Are Green

Tune: 'Nuts in May'

The leaves are green, the nuts are brown,
They hang so high they won't come down;
Leave them alone till frosty weather,
Then they'll all come down together.

Sung while the children dance round in a ring, and fall down together at the end. Walter de la Mare included the lines in his anthology *Tom Tiddler's Ground*, 1932.

Berkshire, 1893 (*The Antiquary*, xxvii, pp. 254–5) | Somerset, 1922 (Macmillan Collection).

51

Round About the Punch Bowl

> Round about the punch bowl,
> One, two, three;
> If you want a bonnie lassie,
> Just take me.

This game, played in the manner of 'Ring o' Roses', seems to have been already vestigial when collected in Scotland and Northern Ireland in the nineteenth century. At Fochabers the children apparently jumped at the end, and if a player fell she had to leave the ring. In Belfast the players all crouched down at the finish, and in Argyllshire the girls made a low curtsy. In Swansea, in 1952, children were chanting:

> Round and round the mulberry bush,
> One, two, three;
> Jump little maiden
> And out goes she.

But the rhyme seems to have been used only for dipping, as was,

> Round and round the butter dish,
> One, two, three;
> If you want a pretty girl
> Just pick me,

which has been current in both Britain and America since the 1930s.

Belfast and Fochabers, Morayshire, 1898 (*Traditional Games*, ii, pp. 84–5) | *Games of Argyleshire*, 1901, p. 80.

52

Gallant, Gallant Ship

Joyous Book of Singing Games, *John Hornby, 1913*

Three times round goes the gallant, gallant ship,
   And three times round goes she;
And three times round goes the gallant, gallant ship,
   Till she sank to the bottom of the sea.

Pull her up, pull her up, cried the jolly sailor boy,
   Pull her up, pull her up, cried he;
Pull her up, pull her up, cried the jolly sailor boy,
   Till she comes to the top of the sea.

The verses are so neatly adapted to a ring game in which the players dance round, sink to the ground, and rise up again, that it is little wonder that children have felt the need for the game to be more elaborate. In Galloway (1898) the girl who was first down on the word 'sea' was led away, asked whom she loved best, and, when the ring re-formed, had to stand in the middle and hear the rest singing her sweetheart's name as they danced round. In Glasgow *c.*1912 the children in the ring jumped four times 'to a crouching position', and remained crouching while they sang the second verse, after which the last to rise had to pay a forfeit. At Helensburgh (1952) the players rose gradually while singing the second verse, and only reached 'full height' when the ship came 'to the top of the sea'. On Stornoway (1961), after sinking down, the players counted to twenty, and, according to a ten-year-old who described the game as her favourite, the last person to stand up went in the middle, 'and we all sing her name and her surname and then we tell her to take her place'. The source of the verses—which in Swansea are sung in the skipping rope—is apparently the ballad or sea chanty known as 'The Mermaid', 'The Seaman's Distress', or 'The Stormy Winds Do Blow'. This ballad tells of a ship's crew sighting a maiden on a rock, with comb and glass in her hand, and realizing one by one that they are doomed:

> Then up spoke the cabin-boy of our gallant ship,
>   And a brave little boy was he;
> I've a father and a mother in old Portsmouth town
>   And this night they will both weep for me.

The ballad was in print in the eighteenth century; and several versions were known early in the nineteenth century (a little boy from Glasgow sung one in 1826); but the genetic verse has not been found before 1840:

> Three times round went our gallant ship,
>   And three times round went she;
> Three times round went our gallant ship,
>   Then she sunk to the bottom of the sea.

The 'gallant, gallant ship' has received almost as much battering from the sound waves over the years as she once had from the sea, being found as 'aller-galler ship' (c.1890), 'gala-gala ship' (1901), 'galley galley ship' (1952), and 'golly golly ship' (1961).

Manchester, c.1890 | Aberdeen, Cullen, and Galloway, 1898 (*Traditional Games*, ii, pp. 143 and 422) | *Games of Argyleshire*, 1901, p. 53 | Keswick, 1901 (Gilchrist MSS, 231 Aiii, p. 100) | Stromness, 1909, in list (*Notes & Queries*, 10th ser., xi, p. 445) | Forfar, c.1910 | Glasgow, 1912 (*Kerr's Guild of Play*, p. 27) | Somerset, 1912 (*Children's Singing Games*, Cecil Sharp, v, p. 6) | Winsham and Lower Coombses, near Chard, 1922 (Macmillan Collection) | Helensburgh, 1952 | Stornoway and Stromness, 1961.

  Skipping: Swansea, 1952, 1957, and 1962, very popular, 'Three times Banbury overboard the ship, And three times Banbury over. . .'

53

Orange Balls

Liss, 1978

> Orange balls, orange balls, here we are again,
> The last one to sit down is out of the game.

'Orange Balls' seems to have acquired its present form and popularity only
about 1960. The girls dance around in a circle singing the words to a tune
similar to 'Jingle Bells'. At the end they flop down on the ground, the last
one down being firmly identified and ordered to leave the circle. She does
so (usually reluctantly), while the others have the ever-delightful task of
deciding, not without some giggling, who they will choose for her lover,
who may be a boy in the school, or a television star, or a pop singer.
Sometimes, not to be overheard, they rush to a corner, forming a tight
circle that looks, commented one observer, 'exactly like a rugger scrum',
pushing and shoving with their arms round each other's shoulders, as they
whisper their suggestions. Then—in one performance witnessed—they
called out 'All right', and a girl named Mandy (aged eight), who had been
last down, was encircled. They sang:

> Donny Osmond says he loves you,
> Donny Osmond says he loves you,
> Donny Osmond says he loves you,
> Is it true?

There was a flurry as they watched Mandy's reaction. She turned pink,
crossed her feet, and swivelled in embarrassment. They sang:

> Clap your hands if you love him,
> Clap your hands if you love him,
> Clap your hands if you love him,
> Is it true?

She said 'Yes' in a small voice, having forgotten to clap her hands, and the
circle continued:

> Stamp your feet if you hate him,
> Stamp your feet if you hate him,
> Stamp your feet if you hate him,
> Is it true?

She didn't stamp her feet, and one of the girls said 'You *hate* him!' 'I don't,'
she said, though they had deliberately chosen someone they knew she
disliked. They sang:

> Clap your hands if you'll marry him,
> Clap your hands if you'll marry him,
> Clap your hands if you'll marry him,
> Is it true?

She clapped her hands, and they sang:

> Hold your hands if you'll cuddle him,
> Hold your hands if you'll cuddle him,
> Hold your hands if you'll cuddle him,
> Is it true?

She held her hands as if she was cuddling someone, rocking gently from side to side while they sang. Then they started circling again, singing 'Orange balls, orange balls, here we are again', and a new round of the game had begun.

Children have been found singing similar words throughout the south and midlands, the words 'Orange balls' clearly being a rationalization by players without Irish connections, to whom 'Orange boys' means nothing. In Salford, however, they sing:

> Orange boys, orange boys, let the bells ring,
> Orange boys, orange boys, who's the only king?

And continue, when a boy's name has been picked for the girl who was last down:

> She loves him, she kisses him, she sits him on his (sic) knee,
> And she says, Dear *Colin Daily*, won't you marry me?
> She says tomorrow, and he says today,
> And all the little dicky birds go Hip, hip, hooray!
> If you love him clap your hands,
> If you hate him stamp your feet.

She does as she feels, and the game restarts.[1] Likewise in Bristol, in 1962, they sang as they danced round:

> Orange boys, orange boys, let the bells go ting-a-ling-a-ling,
> Orange boys, orange boys, God save the King!

And thereafter, when one girl had gone in the middle:

> *Howard Hunter* says he loves her,
> All the boys are crowding round her.
> Take her in the garden, sit her on your knee,
> Say, pretty darling, will you marry me?

---

[1] Usually they seem to stamp their feet. We asked one of them (age 8) after her ordeal, 'Was it a boy you knew?'
  'He's a boy in our class.'
  'I forget, did you hate him?'
  'Yes.'
  'Do you hate most of them?'
  'I hate every one of them.'

To this she replied either 'Yes' or 'No'. A similar song was collected by Anne Gilchrist, probably at Southport about 1920 (Gilchrist MSS 231 B iv):

> Orange boys, orange boys, let the bells ring,
> Orange boys, orange boys, God save the King.
> *Teddy Jones* says he loves her,
> All the boys are fighting for her,
> Let the boys say what they will
> But *Teddy Jones* loves her still . . .

And earlier, in *Shropshire Folk-Lore*, 1883, p. 508, Charlotte Burne reported the game being played at Berrington, near Shrewsbury:

> Oliver, Oliver, follow the King!
> Oliver, Oliver, last in the ring!

'They curtsy, or "douk down" all together,' Miss Burne explained, 'and the one who is last has to tell her sweetheart's name.'

> *Jim Burguin* wants a wife, and a wife he shall have,
> *Nelly* he kissed at the back-cellar door,
> *Nelly* made a pudding, she made it over sweet,
> She never stuck a knife in till he came home at night,
> So next Monday morning is our wedding-day,
> The bells shall ring, and the music shall play!

For a comment on these last lines see under 'All the Boys in Our Town' (p. 130) with which this game must be compared.

Britain: Shropshire, in 1880s, similar to *Shropshire Folk-Lore* (Crofton MS, i, p. 44) | Penrith, 1957, with 'Merry-ma-tansie' mechanism for disclosing sweetheart's name, 'Orange boys, orange boys, let the bells ring, Orange boys, orange boys, God save the King.' The ring 'think up a name like Billy Bunter' and sing to the returned victim 'B is his first name. . . Y.O.U.' and so on | Recordings after 1960 include Ashbourne, Derbyshire, 1977, 'Orange boys, orange boys, Here we are again—boom, boom' | Huddersfield, 1978, 'Orange bells'.

Ireland: Dublin, 1976, 'Orange bells, orange bells, Here we go again, The last one to tip the ground Has a boyfriend's name. *James* says he loves her, Early in the morning. Clap your hands if you love him, Early in the morning. Stamp your feet if you hate him . . . Roll your hands if you love him. . . Kneel up if you'll marry him. . . Stand up if you'll kiss him . . .'.

USA: Cf. Washington DC, 1886, 'Roly-boll, roly-boll, let your beau's name'. Girl in centre of ring gives a boy's name. Circle sings: 'Mr Blank is handsome, Mrs Dash is handsome as he; And they will get married, As they wish to be . . .' (*Lippincott's Magazine*, xxxviii, p. 325).

IX

Witch Dances

LINKING hands and dancing round in a circle with the back to the centre gives much the sensation of riding on a merry-go-round. The body is propelled outwards by the swing of the movement, yet kept on course by the constraint of the ring. The fun children have from this amusement is as nothing, however, compared with the enjoyment antiquarians obtain from it, who associate the sport with witches, one of whose sins when attending sabbats is alleged to have been dancing in rings back to back. Thus early in the seventeenth century the witch-hunter Pierre de Lancre, persecutor of Basque-speaking women in the old province of Guienne, alleged that those who danced with the devil always did so with their backs turned to the centre of the dance, 'which means that the girls are so accustomed to carry their hands backwards in this round dance, that they pull their whole body in that direction and give it a backward curve, having the arms half turned: so that most of them have a stomach commonly *grand, enflé & avancé*'. Although it occurred to him that the swollen bellies might be a result of the wretched diet of the district, and although those supposed to have taken the principal part usually denied it, saying the dance was impossible in the manner he described, de Lancre induced children to dance in this way, partly, he said, to show that it was possible, and partly—a revealing admission—'to deter them from such filth by making them realize how the smallest movement was filthy, vulgar and unbecoming to a virtuous girl' (*Tableau de l'Inconstance des mauvais Anges*, 1612, p. 207).

Dr Margaret Murray, (*The Witch-Cult in Western Europe*, 1921, p. 135) suggested that 'one form of the witches' dance' had survived among children in a Belgian ring game she had read about (probably ''k Heb een wit-zwart spiegelke gevonden'); and Dr K. M. Briggs permits a similar inference in *The Anatomy of Puck* (1959, p. 173): 'The back-to-back ring was used by both witches and fairies, and occurs in a few children's singing games, of apparently ritual origin. "Water Water Wallflowers" is the best known of these.' Evidence exists, however, to show what would anyway be expected, that such a dance-form was the amusement of ordinary people, and already in disrepute when the witch-hunters pressed their ludicrous charges. Sir Thomas More in his *Confutacyon of Tyndales answere*, 1532

WITCH DANCES

Right: Witches and devils dancing with their backs to the centre of the ring, in Nathaniel Crouch's accusatory *Kingdom of Darkness*, 1688. The musician, apparently non-denominational, takes the normal position in a tree.

Below: 'Wallflowers' (No. 56), the descendant of the alleged 'witches' dance', Workington, Cumberland, 1962.

(*Works*, p. 707/2), makes reference to 'A mainy of leud mocking knaues, which . . . would gette them into a roundell turnynge theym backe to backe'; and although 'leud' is not here to be taken to mean lecherous, it is apparent from the repeated expressions of disapproval made by the Church in the Middle Ages that such dancing by the common folk was looked upon as the remnant of pagan custom. The association of such dancing with the devil's disciples was merely a further way of bringing it into discredit. And the absurdity is compounded, today, when a children's game is thought to be descended, however remotely, from a practice of witches; since such an assumption necessitates, or so it would seem, belief in the reality of the transvective gatherings.

Games in which players turn their backs to the centre of the ring, one by one, are found on the Continent as well as in Britain. Madame Celnart observed in 1827 that children in the Bourbonnais commonly held hands in a circle while singing the refrain:

> J'ai des bourses à vendre.
> Quelle couleur ont-elles?
> Elles sont vertes et grises.
> Tourne le dos, ma mie.

When one of the dancers had turned her back, the circle continued going round and repeating the lines. Indeed versions of this 'ronde à se retourner' continue to be popular in France to this day. In Germany children have long played 'Ringel ringel Rosenkranz, Fuchsschwanz', one version ending—some would say significantly, although witches are a familiar feature in German games—'Alte Hex' dreh' dich um'. In Austria the game is 'Wine, wine, wette'; in Norway 'Vinne, vinne, nøstegarn' (Wind, wind the ball of yarn, As fine, as fine as spindle yarn, For *Kari* we will bow like this, For *Kari* we will curtsy like this, For *Kari* we will turn ourselves round); and in Denmark 'Vinde, vinde Nøglegarn'. In Holland they sing 'Ik heb een rond, rond spiegeltje gevonden' (I have found a round, round mirror, I have tied it round my neck, Turn round, turn round, *Marie* turn round once. *Marie* has turned round, She learned that from her mother); in Belgian Flanders they sing ' 'k Heb een wit-zwart spiegelke gevonden' and the youngest daughter is told to turn herself around. In Hungary, where children sing of a myrtle chain, 'Lánc, lainc eszter lánc', the game is played the same way, as also in Spain when children play 'San Pantaleón'; while in Italy and Sardinia children have apparently long played 'Ballate, ballate o vergini' or 'Balliam, balliamo o virgini', for further details of which see under 'Wallflowers' (p. 244).

Nevertheless it must be noted that none of these games has been found
before the nineteenth century (a singing game called 'Rum-riot', in
Dorothy Kilner's *The Village School*, *c.*1783, in which the children bow,
kiss, and curtsy in a ring, has the players with their backs to each other at
the commencement, but does not otherwise appear to be related); while
the turning-about of a player, after she has had some part in a game, can
also be a device to mark the player as having had his or her turn, or as
having failed in an allotted part, as was the practice, for instance, in the
girls' game of 'Allicomgreenzie'—a version of 'Drop Handkerchief'
—described by Mactaggart in his *Scottish Gallovidian Encyclopedia*, 1824.

54

Green Gravel

adapted from Shropshire Folk-Lore, *1883*

> Green gravel, green gravel, the grass is so green,
> The fairest young lady that ever was seen.
> We'll wash her in milk, and dress her in silk,
> And write down her name with a gold pen and ink.
> Oh *Mary*, oh *Mary*, your true love is dead,
> He sent you a letter to turn round your head.

In the usual game of 'Green Gravel' the players join hands in a ring, walk round as they sing, and when they have sung the words through, the player who has been named turns about, re-links her hands facing outwards, and remains that way while the song is repeated, and another child is named. Everyone who has heard the song seems to have found it unforgettable. Hardy appears to have been mesmerized by it, and fancied 'green gravel' was originally 'green grave, O'; William Barnes, Dorset's earlier poet, was another who recalled it in old age; and for years folklorists have been fascinated by the obsolescent floweriness of the phrases, the mysteriousness of the words 'green gravel, green gravel', and the turning of the head when death is announced. They have wondered whether 'green gravel' (alternatively 'green grover', 'green griver') could come from *green graff*, meaning green grave; or whether 'green' might be a mis-transmission of *greete*, for grit, linked with gravel and graves in the line of a Percy ballad, 'Make my grave of gravel and greete'; and whether it is relevant that, in eighteenth-century Scotland, when a corpse was newly laid out, the attendants retired from the death chamber to re-enter walking backwards.

The six lines above seem to constitute the basic text and they are certainly the lines that most often recur in recordings of the second half of the nineteenth century. Lengthier texts exist, but made lengthy by the addition of verses from other games. The earliest record of the game being played is in the Gorton district of Manchester, about 1835, where the children sang:

> Green gravel, green gravel, the grass is so green,
> The fairest young damsel that ever was seen,
> O *Mary*, O *Mary*, your true love is dead!
> He sent you a letter to turn round your head.
> O mother, O mother, do you think it is true?
> O yes, O yes, and what shall I do!
> I'll wash you in milk, and dress you in silk,
> An' write down your name with a gold pen and ink.

In 1875 a writer in *Notes & Queries* reported a version he had heard children singing at Thornes, near Wakefield, at the end of which the players, who had formed a circle with one in the middle, crouched down 'as if in profound respect':

> Around a green gravill the grass is so green,
> And all the fine ladies ashamed to be seen;
> They wash 'em in milk, an' dress 'em in silk.
> We'll all cou' down together.

And in 1877 Eleanor Boyle recorded a yet more mysterious verse:

> Green gravel, green gravel, The grass is so green,
> The fairest young maiden That ever was seen.
> Oh, Mary! Oh, Mary! Your true love is dead;
> He's sent you a green bough, To tie round your head.

> *(A New Child's-Play*, no. 2)

In the United States Newell reported (1883) that children were singing, somewhat similarly:

> Green gravel, green gravel, the grass is so green,
> And all the free masons are ashamed to be seen;
> O *Mary*, O *Mary*, your true love is dead,
> The king sends you a letter to turn back your head.

Here, when all the players were facing outwards, the game sometimes continued, the children being named a second time, and turning inwards when their name was called. The game finished when every child was facing inwards again. However, towards the end of the century, Alice Gomme reported that in the Forest of Dean, and similarly in Kiltubbrid, Co. Leitrim, when the children had sung:

> Round the green gravel the grass is so green,
> And all the fine ladies that ever were seen;
> Washed in milk and dressed in silk,
> The last that stoops down shall be married,

the last child to reach the ground had to tell who he or she was courting; and almost exactly this game was found being played at Forden, near Welshpool, in 1952. Here the children in the circle sang:

> On the green gravel the grass grows green,
> All the fine ladies are fit to be seen,
> Dressed in white and dressed in green,
> Last down is to be married.

The last down had then to name her sweetheart, the name being made public with the formula:

Benjie Evans says he loves her,
All the boys are waiting for her,
Benjie Evans still loves *Stella Whitaker*.

A similar game was being played in Bristol in the 1960s, but details about it were not readily forthcoming. One informant protested 'I think it is very soppy'. 'Green Gravel' is, in fact, now usually a skipping game.

The luxury that children continue to commemorate, that of washing in milk and dressing in silk (sometimes 'drying with silk'), was formerly common in ballad literature, for instance in the ballads 'Prince Heathen', 'Gil Brenton', and 'The Cruel Mother'. However, the washing in milk and dressing in silk of a *corpse* in Jamieson's version of 'Burd Ellen' is not of significance, being recounted in a stanza of which Jamieson himself was undoubtedly the original singer.

Britain: *Nursery Rhymes of England*, J. O. Halliwell, 1842, p. 148 | *Notes & Queries*, 4th ser., vii, 1871, pp. 415 and 523, Staffordshire and Gorton; 5th ser., iii, 1875, p. 482, Thornes | *Mother Goose*, Kate Greenaway, 1881, p. 47 | *Shropshire Folk-Lore*, 1883, p. 510 | *Merrie Games in Rhyme*, E. M. Plunket, 1886, p. 13 | *Folk-Lore Journal*, vii, 1889, pp. 214–15 (Dorset) | *Northumberland Words*, R. O. Heslop, 1892 | *English County Songs*, 1893, pp. 26–7, Lancashire and Derbyshire | *Traditional Games*, i, pp. 170–83; and ii, 426, 18 versions | Southport, 1898; Silverdale, 1900, etc. (Gilchrist MSS, 231 Aiii) | *Games of Argyleshire*, 1901, pp. 83–4 | Gosport, *c.*1910 (*Hampshire Field Club*, xiv, p. 407) | *Children's Singing Games*, Cecil Sharp, v, 1912, p. 18 | Somerset, 1922, four versions (Macmillan Collection) | Alderwasley, near Derby, *c.*1930 | Countesthorpe, Leicester, *c.*1946 | Forden, 1952 | Swansea, 1956 | Bristol and Lydeard St Lawrence, 1960 | Belfast, 1974, 'Green gravel, green gravel, your grass is so green, You're the fairest young damsel that ever was seen; We washed her, we dried her, we dressed her in silk, And we wrote down her name in a ball pen and ink. Oh *Kathleen*, oh *Kathleen*, your true love is dead, And we wrote you a letter to turn round your head' (David Hammond record, 'Green Peas and Barley O').

Ireland: County Down, 1947 (*Children's Games Throughout the Year*, Leslie Daiken, 1949, pp. 81 and 139).

USA: *Games of American Children*, 1883, p. 71 | Washington DC, 1888 (*American Anthropologist*, pp. 244–5) | Cincinnati, 1908, a marching game, moving forwards and backwards (*JAFL*, xl, p. 13) | *The Ozarks*, Vance Randolph, 1931, pp. 220–1 | Kentucky, *c.*1935 (Jean Ritchie, *Folkways Record* no. 754) | St Louis, 1944 (*JAFL*, lx, p. 42) | Maryland, 1944 (Howard MSS) | *North Carolina Folklore*, 1952, pp. 56–7, refers to 1920s and 1930s.

Canada: Toronto, 1893 (*JAFL*, viii, p. 254) | Elora, Ontario, *c.*1910 (Fowke, 1969, p. 25).

Australia: *The Bulletin*, Sydney, 19 March 1898, and Western Victoria, *c.*1900 (Turner, pp. 55 and 124).

New Zealand: Fordell, Wanganui, 1900 (Sutton-Smith, p. 17). Game said to have been known in every province.

55

Round Apples

Kerr's Guild of Play, *Glasgow, 1912*

Round apples, round apples,
By night and by day,
There stands a valley
In yonder haze.
There stands *Moira Rogers*
With a knife in her hand,
You dare not touch her
Or else she'll be hanged.

Her cheeks were like roses
But now they're like snow,
Poor *Moira*, poor *Moira*,
She's dying I know.
We'll wash her with milk
And dress her in silk,
And write down her name
With a gold pen and ink.

None of the recordings of this Scots ring game, with its sharp echoes of 'Green Gravel' (p. 239), has a long history, yet some of the texts are as compelling as traditional ballads, in the way they reach out to uncontrollable, foredoomed tragedy. This feeling is reinforced by the fact that the central texts do not vary in story, only in expression. 'There stands a valley in yonder haze' was, in Argyllshire, 'The stars are a valley down yonder by day'. 'You dare not touch her or else she'll be hanged' was, in New Galloway, 'There's no one dare touch her, or she'll go mad', a warning renewed in Kirkcaldy in 1952, 'You dare not touch her or else she'll go mad'. This consistency perhaps indicates that the original verses are not far to seek. Maclagan says one child stood in the middle of the ring grasping a chip of wood, or other implement, for a knife; and that the singer of the second verse, who stepped into the centre of the ring and wept, represented the mother.

Scotland: New Galloway, 1898 (*Traditional Games*, ii, p. 426) | *Games of Argyleshire*, 1901, pp. 85–6 | Edinburgh, *c.*1910, 'Pine apple, pine apple, By night and by day, I try to steal poor *Lizzie* away; But here comes her father, With a knife in his hand, Stand back! stand back! Or else you'll be stabbed'; tune similar to 'Queen Mary' (*Rymour Club*, i, p. 150) | Forfar, *c.*1910 | Glasgow, 1912, 'Growing apples, growing apples' (*Kerr's Guild of Play*, p. 23) | Kirkcaldy, 1952, 14-year-old girl.

56

Wallflowers (I)

Dudley, Worcs., 1969

> Wallflowers, wallflowers, growing up so high,
> We are all maidens, and we shall all die;
> Except for little *Julie*, she's the only one,
> Fie for shame! Fie for shame!
> Turn your back to the wall again.

'Wallflowers' is now the foremost game in which players turn their backs to the centre of the ring as their names are called, until the whole ring is, as it were, inside out. Descriptions of it in modern times are numerous ('The last time I play it was last week,' remarked one informant); but no account of it in England is known before it was found being played at Thornes, on the outskirts of Wakefield, in 1874. Here a circle of girls had one player in the middle while they sang:

> Willy, Willy Wallflower, growin' up so high;
> We are all maidens, we shall all die,
> Exceptin' *'Liz'beth Fawcitt*, she's the youngest daughter;
> She can hop, she can skip,
> She can turn the candlestick.
> Fie, fie; shame, shame;
> Turn your backs together again.

All the girls then turned round to face outwards, sang the verse a second time, turned inwards, and continued:

> *Eliz'beth Fawcitt*, your sweetheart is dead;
> He's sent you a letter to turn back your head.

Upon which all of them turned outwards, repeated the verse, and turned inwards again.

The opening phrase 'Wallflowers, wallflowers', or 'Willy, Willy Wall-flower', is sometimes rendered 'Wally, wally, wallflowers', or 'Waly, waly, wallflowers', which has led some commentators to think the song was originally a lamentation, in the manner of the eighteenth-century Scots song:

> O waly, waly, up the bank,
> And waly, waly, down the brae,
> And waly, waly yon burn-side,
> Where I and my love wont to gae.

However the game has been found with a variety of openings, as 'Walter, Walter, wallflower' (Milngavie, nr. Glasgow, *c.*1880), 'Mayflowers, mayflowers' (Cincinnati, 1908), 'Little Molly white-flower' (Hanbury, 1898), 'Lily, lily, white-flower' (Philadelphia, 1883, and Washington DC, 1886), 'Lily, lily, wallflowers' (Hampshire, 1909, and Somerset, 1922), 'Whitey, whitey, wallflowers' (Halifax, *c.*1900 and 1952), 'Walter, Walter, white flowers' (Cincinnati, 1908), and 'Walty, walty, wildflowers' (Work-ington, *c.*1910). Furthermore, in North Shields, *c.*1900, it was 'Water, water, wildflower'. In parts of Scotland, such as Edinburgh, Aberdeen, and Golspie, it has long been 'Water, water, wallflower'. In Arbroath, about 1845—according to the local poet John Christie—it was 'Water! water! wellflower'; and at Dyke in Morayshire, also in the nineteenth century, it was 'Water, water, well stones'. That the game was at one time associated with wells, and perhaps had some connection with well-worship, is indicated by the recollection of Robert Craig Maclagan. He wrote that in Perthshire, about 1850, the following verse 'was habitually sung when several girls reached the well to draw water at the same time. They formed a ring, and, after the first had drawn water, sang:

> Water, water, welsey, soaring up so high,
> We are all maidens, but we must all die,
> Especially *Annie Anderson*, she's the fairest flower,
> She shall dance, she shall sing, in a lady's bower.
> Turn your back to the well again.

'This the collector remembers quite well from childhood, and though it is in English, all the children who sang it spoke Gaelic habitually.'

However outside Scotland and the United States few texts contain reference either to wells or water; and the possibility must be considered that in the north the game-song became entwined with a well-dressing or 'well-flowering' song. More definite evidence exists to show that the girl who was first called, the beautiful one, the 'fairest flower', was generally the youngest one; and to this day the youngest player is likely to be called first. The lines,

> She can hop, she can skip,
> She can turn the candlestick,

which often recur in England, may be related to the rhyme,

> Jack be nimble, Jack be quick,
> Jack jump over the candle stick,

and to the ancient sport of candle-leaping (*ODNR*, pp. 226–7). On the other hand in Yorkshire 'Turning the candlestick' has been said to refer to the child who plays 'candlestick' on a seesaw, the one who stands mid-plank to help the ends rise and fall. These lines, too, are subject to variation. They have been found as 'She can hop and she can skip, and she can turn the mangle stick' (or 'mangle quick'), which is presumably a corruption of 'candle stick'; and as 'She can dance and she can sing, and she can turn the wedding ring', 'she can show the wedding ring', 'she can dance the wedding ring', and 'she can dance the Highland fling'. Likewise 'She can dance and she can sing, she can play the tambourine', 'she can play the wire', and—eight recordings, widely distributed—'She can hop and she can skip, and she can play the organ'. Yet more weird and, in Scotland, more common is 'She can dance, and she can fling, and she can turn the sofa', which may bear phonetic relationship to 'She can dance and she can sing, and she can lick the sugar' (Midlothian, *c.* 1905), and 'She can dance and she can sing, and she can ding a soldier' (Forfar, *c.* 1910). In fact several texts contain a hint, or more than a hint, of menace. Children at Golspie in 1953, like their grandparents in 1892, serenaded 'the youngest of us all' as their champion:

> She can dance and she can sing,
> She can knock us all down.

So did children in Milngavie, near Glasgow, *c.* 1880, in Workington before the First World War, and on the Isle of Arran, *c.* 1925. Alternatively the players may threaten the youngest one, as at Chardstock in Devon, *c.* 1922:

> Turn your back behind you, and say no more to me,
> For if you do I'll cut your throat, and tie you to a tree.

And at Cardington, near Bedford, in 1956:

> Turn your back you saucy cat, and say no more to me,
> Or if we do we'll set on you, and tie you to a tree.

Yet violence in this game seems out of place. The vocabulary of the verses accompanying the game on the Continent is a gentle one of garlands, curtsies, spinners, sweethearts, and angels. As an example the game 'Ballate, ballate o vergini', played by children in Rome in 1892, or 'La Ballata delle virgini', played by children in Sardinia in 1962, may be cited:

Balliam, balliamo o virgini,	(Let us dance, dance O virgins
Che gli angeli ci sono.	Who are angels all.
Balliam, balliamo o virgini	Let us dance, dance O virgins
Che gli angeli suoneram.	For whom the angels play music.
La (Anna) si girasse	Let (Anna) turn around
E l'angelo l'abbracciasse,	That the angel may embrace her,
Pieno di fior, pieno di fior,	Full of flowers, full of flowers,
Con l'angelo bello facciamo l'amor.	With the lovely angel let us make love.)

Britain: Thornes, Yorkshire, 1874 (*Notes & Queries*, 5th ser., iii, p. 481) | Milngavie, near Glasgow, *c.*1880 (Crofton MS, ii, p. 72) | Hersham, Surrey, 1882 (*Folk-Lore Record*, v, p. 84) | *Shropshire Folk-Lore*, 1883, p. 513 | *Arbroath: Past & Present*, J. M. McBain, 1887, pp. 347–8 | Symondsbury, Dorset, 1889, 'very popular' (*Folk-Lore*, vii, p. 215) | *Traditional Games*, ii, 1898, pp. 329–42, 35 versions including the above | Highfields and Southport, 1898 (Gilchrist MSS 231 Aiii) | *Games of Argyleshire*, R. C. Maclagan, 1901, pp. 84–6 | *Old Hampshire Singing Games*, A. E. Gillington, 1909, pp. 15–16 | *Children's Singing Games*, Cecil Sharp, v, 1912, p. 4 | *Joyous Book of Singing Games*, 1913, p. 32 | *100 Singing Games*, Kidson and Moffat, 1916, p. 42 | *London Street Games*, 1916, pp. 73–4 | *Lark Rise*, Flora Thompson, 1939, p. 165 | Opie MSS, over 80 further recordings | Versions from 48 places since 1950; also occasionally used for skipping.

USA: New York, 1883, 'Water, water, wild-flowers, growing up so high, We are all young ladies, And we are sure to die, Excepting *Susie Allen*, She is the finest flower. Fie, fie, fie for shame; Turn about and tell your beau's name' (*Games of American Children*, pp. 67–8 | Washington DC, 1886 (*Lippincott's Magazine*, xxxviii, pp. 326–7 | Cincinnati, 1908 (*JAFL*, xl, pp. 13–14).

X

Dramas

THESE games are descended from once-popular Europe-wide adult rituals and pastimes: fertility plays, social dance-and-song, and knock-about comedies. They have in common a theatricality which is enhanced by the power of tradition.

The two death-and-resurrection dramas, 'Old Roger' and 'Jenny Jones', seem linked to the European folk play and sword-dance, in which a Hero or Fool is slain and brought back to life by a comic doctor. Folk plays, which were still being acted in this century in Thrace, Thessaly, and Southern Macedonia, encompassed a human life-cycle of wooing, wedding, coition, birth, violent death, and resurrection. They were performed at seed-time, with invocations for a bumper harvest.[1] It is usually assumed that such plays have evolved from religious ceremonies of an entirely serious nature; yet the surviving texts are exuberantly nonsensical, and when the dead man is cured with 'a drop of Inkum Pinkum' and jumps to his feet again the effect is as zany as when Old Roger leaps up to give the old woman a knock, or Jenny Jones springs to life and chases the funeral party.

Two others, 'Daughter Ellen' and 'Three Sisters', are survivals of a hypnotic activity practised in the Middle Ages—dancing with a rocking step in a circle, while singing a ballad of many verses. Hjalmar Thuren described how epic singing-dances were still, in 1908, the favourite amusement of the Faroese during the week of Christmas and at midsummer (*Folk Songs in the Faroes*). Although the first written record is in a manuscript of 1669, the ballads sung are medieval, and tell of Tristram and Iseult, the hero Roland, and Olufa, daughter of the French King Pipin. Probably the oldest ballad used is that of Sigurd and Brynhild, whose story appears in the thirteenth-century *Vǫlsunga Saga*. The songs sometimes extend to a hundred verses, with many repetitions and long drawn-out descriptions, and this prolixity, Thuren says, 'is explained by the inclination of the Faroese to go on dancing as long as possible'. On these small volcanic islands between Iceland and the Shetlands, the *carole*, ubiquitous dance of the Middle Ages, has survived intact into the twentieth century (see also pp. 5–10).

[1] See *English Ritual Drama*, E. C. Cawte, Alex Helm, and N. Peacock, 1967, pp. 23–4, 30.

Professor Child (*Ballads*, ii, p. 346) says that children's games are 'the last stage of many old ballads', but although this should be true, and one believes it to be true, examples are hard to find. Child himself only supported his statement by mentioning a German game-version of the ballad 'Ritter Ulinger' (i, 33 n.) and including among the texts of 'The Maid Freed from the Gallows' a game-version from Forfarshire, *c.*1840 (the game-version of this ballad is usually known as 'Mary Brown' or 'Daughter Ellen' (p. 261)). Böhme has three game-versions of 'Ritter Ulinger' (pp. 545–7, nos. 349–51), one of 'Lord Randal' (p. 551, no. 359), and one of 'The Maid Freed from the Gallows' ('Schäferin und Edelmann', p. 549). Wolfgang Wittrock, 'Zur Tänzeballade in Schleswig-Holstein' (*Jahrbuch für Volksliedforschung*, xiv, 1969, pp. 53–61), added four more instances of ballads turned into singing games, 'Müller und Edelmann', 'Dienende Schwester', 'Königskinder', and 'Jäger und Graserin'. Games made from ballads, however, often take a different form from their progenitors, and sometimes tell a different story. In the ballad of 'Ritter Ulinger', for instance, the abducted lady, about to be added to Ulinger's row of murdered wives, is rescued by her brother; in the game-version (e.g. 'Mariechen sass auf einem Stein', Vienna, 1973) the brother inexplicably stabs her to death.

'Fair Rosie' can lay no claim to antiquity. It was made from the tale of 'The Sleeping Beauty' at the time when the aesthetic movement was drawing on all the resources of oral tradition in its zeal for beautifying the lives of children. Other translations of fairy tales into singing games were not so successful. 'The Glass Mountain' ('A princess stood on a hill of glass') found its way into the streets of Leeds during the 1920s, but has not survived. An incomplete game of 'Red Ridinghood' was discovered by Professor Pinon in East Flanders in 1938; and a fragment of a Bluebeard game in West Flanders,[1] but it seems that, on the whole, children prefer their fairy tales to remain in prose.

'Lazy Mary' and 'Milking Pails' are out-and-out comedies of ordinary life. Both deal with the relationship between adolescent girls and their mothers, an acid relationship that can be assuaged by laughter.

---

[1] *Fabula*, 2, 1958, pp. 32–3.

57
Old Roger

Mosspark, Glasgow, 1961

Old Roger is dead and laid in his grave,
Laid in his grave, laid in his grave,
They planted an apple tree over his head,
Hee! hi! over his head.

The apples grew ripe and ready to fall,
Ready to fall, ready to fall,
There came an old woman a-picking them all,
Hee! hi! a-picking them all.

Old Roger got up and he gave her a knock,
Gave her a knock, gave her a knock,
Which made the old woman go hippety hop,
Hee! hi! hippety hop.

The circle usually stand all the time and act as chorus, though sometimes, if they feel like it, they prance round. Old Roger lies flat on his back in the circle; in days gone by his body was covered by an apron (or several aprons) or a pocket handkerchief was spread over his face. When the third line is sung a child from the circle goes and stands beside Old Roger to represent an apple tree. Then another child hirples round about, pretending to pick up the fallen apples, and Old Roger chases and hits her. The old woman becomes Old Roger in the next performance.

'I think it was mean of him not to let the old woman have the apples,' said an eight-year-old girl (Alton, 1954). But the apple tree was evidently Old Roger himself, and one may be forgiven for kicking anyone who is stealing parts of one's body. The belief that the soul can pass into a plant or tree is old. In the ballad of 'Fair Margaret and Sweet William' the lovers are reunited after death: 'Out of her breast there sprung a rose, And out of his a brier', which 'grew in a true lovers' knot Which made all people admire'. In some versions of Cinderella (the Grimms' for instance) the lonely orphan is looked after by a tree which grows out of her mother's grave. And John Aubrey, in *The Remaines of Gentilisme*, 1686–7, comments on the naivety of village faith: 'M^ris Smyth's notion of men being metamorphosed into Trees, and Flowers is ingeniose; they planted a Tree, or a flower on the grave of their friend, and they thought the soule of the party deceased went into the tree or plant.' Two hundred years later, in neighbouring Dorset, belief in the green shade was still alive, and found expression in Hardy's poem 'Voices from Things Growing in a Churchyard'.

As with other of the more mysterious and primitive-seeming games, we have no recordings before the mid-nineteenth century. We can only feel that this dramatic comedy was a shout of laughter in the face of death, enacted by a whole community hand in hand and probably fortified by liquor. It may have been played at wakes. That it is old is to be deduced from the variety of wordings that existed by the second half of the nineteenth century, and from parallel games in Europe such as 'Dead Man Arise', in which the corpse lying in the circle leaps up and chases the mourners (see *Street and Playground*, pp. 106–8), though the Spanish 'Buena viejecita', a singing game in which the good old woman's husband dies and comes to life again, has no chasing at the end. Also, the phrase 'dead and laid in his grave' is antiquated, being used, for instance, by Dame Custance in Udall's *Ralph Roister Doister* (V, ii) *c.*1553, where she sighs 'Then would I were dead, and fair laid in my grave'.

Little can be concluded from the evidence about the original name of the deceased. He was 'Old John Rogers' in the 'childhood rhyme' from Rhode Island, USA, sent by 'a lady of over sixty' to the Revd T. Allen Moxon for his parish magazine, *St Anne's Soho Monthly Paper*, July, 1907:

> Old John Rogers is buried and dead,
> They planted an apple-tree over his head.
> Apples are ripe and ready to fall,
> There came an old woman and gathered them all.
> Old John Rogers gave her a whack
> Which made the old woman go whickety wack.
> She ran till she got to the top of the hill,
> And then she sat down, and made her will.

The name 'Old Roger' (or 'Poor Roger', or 'Sir Roger', or, less dignified, 'The lodger') far outnumbers other names in the seventy-odd recordings available; and 'Roger' was a popular Christian name during the Middle Ages. Usually, as in real life, the corpse is referred to as 'Old' or 'Poor' somebody; but in many places reality is put at a remove by the substitution of that other principal character at a funeral, Cock Robin. A name can be the most unstable element in traditional lore; it is seldom if ever part of a rhyme scheme; and people are notoriously 'bad at names'. Moreover the temptation must sometimes have arisen to slip a local character or a joke name into Old Roger's place (if, indeed, he was the original). Thus 'Poor Tommy' reigns beside 'Old Rodger' (a surname) in Edinburgh (*Golden City*, J. T. R. Ritchie, 1965) and has done since Edwardian days. 'Poor Johnnie' was dead in Sporle, Norfolk, *c.*1898 (*Traditional Games*, ii), and 'Poor Toby' in Belfast (ibid., and at St Mary's Primary School, Divis Street, *c.*1974, on David Hammond's record 'Green Peas and Barley O'); 'Poor Gracie' in North Shields before 1930 (*Street Games*, M. and R. King) and in an Aberdeen playground in 1952. The bogeyman Oliver Cromwell was named in Liverpool *c.*1890, in Suffolk ('learnt from a boy') *c.*1893 (*English County Songs*), and in Lancashire in 1956; and he acquired respectability in BBC Schools broadcasts in 1963. But Oliver Cromwell may only be a rationalization of 'Old Cromley', sent to Lucy Broadwood in 1907, which in turn was probably a mangling of 'Old Crummle', 'Old Grumble', or 'The Old Grumbler', beloved in the United States and Canada, which, to turn full circle, may be a corruption of 'Old Cromwell', since Newell (1883) reported 'In Cambridge, Mass., the name of the deceased was "Old Cromwell" '.

The refrains are equally various. They usually consist of a couple of exclamatory syllables (such as 'Heigh ho!', 'Hum, ha!', 'Hee haw!', 'E! I!' or 'I! O!') at the end of each verse or line, followed by the last three or four words in the line just sung. However, when Thomas Carrick played 'Cock Robin' at Brandlingill, near Cockermouth, *c.*1890, 'as a very little lad', a boy lay down on his back, his arms folded on his breast, while the rest circled round chanting:

> Cock Robin is dead and laid in his grave,
> Fiff-faff, laid in his grave

(*Journal of Lake District Society*, 1951, pp. 34–5). There can be near-extempore refrains, or no refrains at all; and neither refrains nor names fit any geographical pattern.

The words vary, so that the irate corpse can give the old woman a 'thump', 'kick' (common), 'tap', 'knock' (common), 'clout', or 'slap'. The tunes vary, so that each is different from the next. And it is possible that 'Old Roger' may have been a song which was later acted, rather than originally a dance-song, since the closing lines are often those sung at the end of folk songs:

> The bridle and saddle they lie on the shelf,
> If you want any more you must sing it yourself.

In short, the multifarious 'Old Roger' is a prime example of the lack of consideration shown to folklorists by the folk.

USA: Rhode Island, c.1850, as quote | New York streets, 1883, 'this unintelligible round', 'Old Grimes is dead and in his grave laid . . . O aye O! There grew up an apple-tree over his head—The apples were ripe and ready to fall—There came an old woman a-picking them up—Old Grimes got up and gave her a kick—And made her go hobbledy, hobbledy, hip—The bridles and saddles they hang on the shelf—And if you want any more you must sing it yourself' (*Games of American Children*, pp. 100–1) | Washington DC, 1886, 'Old Humpsy was dead . . . Heigho! heigho! heigho!' (*Lippincott's Magazine*, xxxvii, p. 244) | Cincinnati, 1908, 'Old Kramer . . . He, hi, ho!' (*JAFL*, xv, p. 20) | 'Old Grumley' and 'Old Crummle', c.1915, 'Old Grumble', c.1922 (*North Carolina Folklore*, pp. 46–8) | Raleigh, North Carolina, c.1920, 'Granddaddy is dead' (*JAFL*, xxxii, pp. 112–13).

Britain: Derbyshire, 1883, 'Cock Robin . . . Hum ha!' (*Folk-Lore*, i, p. 385) | Berkshire, 1893, 'Old Roger . . . Heigho!' (*Antiquary*, xxvii, no. 163, p. 255) | *Traditional Games*, ii, 1898, 11 versions, orally collected, including seven 'Rogers' and one 'Cock Robin' from Deptford with the refrain 'O my, flippity flop' | Stourport, 1899, 'Cock Robin . . . I.O., I.O., I.O.' (*Folk-Lore*, xxxv, pp. 268–9) | Calder Valley, c.1900, 'Old Johnny is dead . . . Ha, ha, lies in his grave' | Great Horksley, Essex, c.1912, 'Cock Robin' | Worksworth, Derbyshire, 1916, 'Sir Roger got up and he gave her a nudge, Hey! High!' (*Journal of EFDSS*, v, p. 295) | *London Street Games*, 1916, pp. 76–7, 'Old Roger (or Poor Robin) is dead and gone to his grave' | Somerset, 1922, 'A game which I find a large number of my young friends are very fond of playing is called "Old Roger is dead". Some of them call it "Poor Robin" or "Cock Robin", but it is all the same' (Macmillan Collection) | Beadnell, Northumberland, 1952, 'Poor Roger' | Berriew, Montgomery, 1952, 'Old Roger' | Forfar, 1956, 'Old Roger' | Penrith, 1957, 'Old Roger' | Glasgow, 1960, 'Old Roger' | Sutton, Surrey, 1961, 'Sir Roger' | Workington, 1965, '"Old Roger" or "Cock Robin" is played all over the town with no rival whatsoever' | Oban, 1974, 'Old Roger', taught in infant school.

Ireland: Dublin, 1975, 'Old Roger is dead' (*All In! All In!*, Eilís Brady, pp. 118–20).

Canada: Brantford, Ontario, c.1888, 'Old Grumble is dead and in his grave, H'm, ha, in his grave' (*Folk-Lore*, xxv, p. 387).

Cf. the game played in 'the pretty village of Eccleston, Cheshire, in 1852, "Old Dobbin is dead, Ay, ay; Dobbin is dead, He's laid in his bed, Ay, ay. There let him lie, Ay, ay; Keep watch for his eye, For if he gets up He'll eat us all UP" and away they scampered and Dobbin after them' (*Notes & Queries*, 10th ser., ii, pp. 348–9).

58

Jenny Jones

Games of American Children, *W. W. Newell, 1883*

In November 1891 Alice Gomme wrote to *Notes & Queries* asking for help with her collection of singing games, and the following month William Patterson replied from Belfast with a description of 'Jinny Jo', 'which now comes back to me after many years'. 'It was very pleasant,' he said, 'to see the graceful figures of the little children, many of them barefooted, advancing and retiring, their steps keeping time to the very simple pretty air to which they sang their rhymes. The performance lasted a long time . . . but in the long fine summer evenings it was repeated many times by many little parties of young performers.' The children, it seems, were willing to put themselves under the spell of this strange comedy of baulked love, of death and resurrection, and of preoccupation with the colour of burial clothes.

This is how Patterson remembered the game:

Jinny, who is a very small child, is concealed behind her parents. All the other children form the party of suitors. The suitors retire some little distance off, and then approach Jinny's 'house', singing:

> We've come to court Jinny Jo,
>   Jinny Jo, Jinny Jo,
> We've come to court Jinny Jo,
>   Is she within?

Something tragic has happened; but the father and mother wish to temporize so they sing in answer:

> Jinny Jo's washing clothes . . .
>   You can't see her to-day.

The visiting party, who are holding hands, retire slowly, walking backwards, while all sing:

Top: 'Jenny Jones' (No. 58), Nelson, Lancs, 1969. The dead Jenny is propped up in the doorway.
Bottom: 'Mary Malloga She Lifted her Leg' (see No. 113), Workington, Cumberland, 1962.

> So fare ye well ladies,
>   O ladies, O ladies,
> So fare ye well ladies
>   And gentlemen too.

The suitors return immediately, singing as before, and this is repeated a number
of times; each time they receive an excuse that Jinny is 'drying clothes', 'starching
clothes', 'ironing clothes', &c., till at last the parents are forced to announce the
sad fact that:

> Jinny Jo's lying dead . . .
> You can't see her to-day.

And then they add:

> So turn again ladies,
>   O ladies, O ladies,
> So turn again ladies
>   And gentlemen too.

But instead of going to their own homes again, the suitors remain and sing:

> What shall we dress her in?
>   Dress her in, dress her in?
> What shall we dress her in?
>   Shall it be red?

Then the unhappy parents answer:

> Red's for the soldiers . . .
> And that will not do.

Various other colours are suggested in song, but are found unsuitable: black,
because 'black's for the mourners'; green, because 'green's for the croppies';[1] and
so on, till at last white is named, and the parents sing:

> White's for the dead people,
>   The dead people, the dead people,
> White's for the dead people,
>   And that will just do.

Then the father and mother step aside, and Jinny is seen lying quite still; a hush
falls upon the little party; the funeral must be arranged; when suddenly Jinny
comes to life again, and springs up, when the play ends amid wild rejoicing.

'Jinny Jo' was 'Janet jo' when Chambers discovered the game in
Edinburgh in the 1820s. He listed it in the 1826 edition of *Popular Rhymes
of Scotland*, and by 1842 he was able to give the words:

Janet lies on her back behind the scenes. The father and mother stand up to
receive the visits of the lover, who comes forward singing:

---

[1] 'Croppies' were the Irish rebels of 1798, who showed their sympathy for the French
revolution by cutting their hair short.

> I'm come to court Janet jo,
> Janet jo, Janet jo,
> I'm come to court Janet jo—
> How's she the day?

Mother and Father:

> She's up the stair washin,
> Washin, washin,
> She's up the stair washin
> Ye canna see her the day.

The lover retires, and again advances with the same announcement of his object and purposes, to which he receives similar evasive answers from Janet's parents, who successively represent her as bleaching, drying, and ironing clothes. At last they say—

> Janet jo's dead and gane,
> Dead and gane, dead and gane,
> Janet jo's dead and gane,
> She'll never come hame!

She is then carried off to be buried, the lover and the rest weeping. She sometimes revives (to their great joy), and sometimes not, *ad libitum*—that is, as Janet herself chooses.

The antiquary James Napier sent his local version from Bothwell, Lanarkshire, to the *Folk-Lore Record*, 1881 (iv, pp. 173–4): 'I'm come to court Janet-jo . . . How is she the day?' 'She's butt the house washing' ('ironing', 'very sick', 'dead'). Each time the thwarted lover retired he sang 'Fare ye well ladies, Ladies, ladies, Fare ye well ladies, For I must away'.

'Janet jo' means 'Janet sweetheart' (*jo*, from French 'joie'). In England this was rationalized into 'Jenny Jones', and the romantic 'Fare ye well ladies' became, tartly, 'Very well, ladies'. The courting theme faded as children announced 'We've come to see Jenny Jones', giving the impression they wanted a little friend to come out to play. White, usually approved as the right colour for dead people to wear (a white shroud or white shift being the last clothing over many centuries), was sometimes accepted for another reason, that 'White is for the angels, And that will do' (e.g. Nairnshire, 1898). In some versions the story became so muddled that the questioners, instead of asking what colour they should dress the corpse in, asked what colour they themselves should wear to the funeral, and for that purpose black was of course chosen ('Black is for the mourners', Southampton, 1898). And the parents, who once protected their daughter from an unworthy suitor (or perhaps, with false replies, staved off the discovery that the girl was already dead), became the Mother alone, or, occasionally, the Servant.

The game was extremely popular in the late nineteenth century and up to the First World War. Lady Gomme said 'It is played very generally throughout the country', and she was sent so many similar versions that it was 'needless to print them in full'. The appeal of the game must have lain in the mesmeric to-ing and fro-ing of request and repulse, and the mock solemnity of the funeral, which burst into sudden excitement when 'Janet jo' or 'Jenny' came to life and chased the mourners. The other resurrection-drama 'Old Roger' (p. 250) possesses the same qualities of tension and release; and both games have the saving element of absurdity. In 'Jenny Jones' the reclusive daughter is usually upstairs doing her laundry, and dies, apparently, because 'She fell down the stair and broke her big toe' (Argyllshire, 1901) or 'She let the smoothing-iron fall on her toe' (Paisley, Ontario, 1909). Sometimes, when the girl has died, knocking noises are heard from the coffin, and the mother explains it is only 'a gig running past' or 'the boys playing at marbles' (Nairnshire, 1898). Whether these two games have died out because they were taught to children in the belief that they were dying out, is probable but difficult to prove. Even W. H. Patterson, harking back to his Belfast moppets, suggested that 'the children of the well-to-do . . . might find pleasure for themselves and give pleasure to their elders by learning and playing such a game'; and this was before Cecil Sharp's teaching crusade, and the Board of Education's recommendation that singing games should be taught in schools.

In the present day the game has been found only in Nelson, Lancs, first by Julian Pilling in 1957 and again by Father Damian Webb in 1969 when, at St Joseph's RC Junior School, it was called 'Janie Jones'. The 1957 version had, curiously, preserved many of the old features, but it had no chase at the end. Father, mother, and Mary Jones sat on a doorstep. The rest visited forward and back, singing to the tune of 'Nuts in May':

> We've come to see your Mary Jones,
>   Mary Jones, Mary Jones,
> We've come to see your Mary Jones,
>   How is she today?

The parents reply:

> Mary Jones is washing,
>   Washing, washing,
> Mary Jones is washing,
>   You cannot see her today.

Mary Jones is then said to be 'ironing', 'ill in bed', and 'dead'; and the

visitors ask 'What colour will she be buried in . . . Buried in today?' They
are told 'She'll be buried in red . . . Will that be all right?' and reply 'Red is
for danger . . . For danger today'. White will be all right, and there is no
further questioning and no chase.

'Jenny Jones' has fascinated poets as well as pedagogues. Thomas
Hardy was recalling the game (probably from his childhood c. 1850) when
he composed his 'late lyric' 'The Colour':

> 'What shall I bring you?
> Please will white do
> Best for your wearing
>   The long day through?'
> 'White is for weddings,
> Weddings, weddings,
> White is for weddings,
>   And that won't do.'

And at some time, long ago, a song-writer in America turned it into the
song 'Jennie Jenkins':

> Will you wear red, Jennie, my dear,
> Will you wear red, Jennie Jenkins?
>   Oh, I couldn't wear red,
>   It's the colour of my head.
> Then I'll buy you a rolly-dilly-dolly
> Sukey-dukey-double-rosy-binder,
>   To wear with your robe, Jennie Jenkins.

Jennie finally agrees to wear white, but will not marry her suitor ''Cause I
couldn't marry two'.

Scotland: *Popular Rhymes*, R. Chambers, 1842, p. 66 | *Traditional Games*, ii, 1898, pp. 433–5,
Strichen and Fochabers, 'Georgina'; Nairnshire, 'Georgina' and 'White is for the angels';
Rosehearty, 'We've come to see poor Janet' . . . 'She's fallen downstairs and broken her horn
toes' | *Games of Argyleshire*, 1901, pp. 123–4, 'We come to see Genesis' | Forfar, c. 1910, 'We've
come to speir for Janny-jo, And hoo's she the day?' She breaks her leg and dies, and the others
sing 'Bad luck for Janny-jo' | Glasgow, c. 1912, *Kerr's Guild of Play*, p. 28, 'Georgina'.
    England: Brampford Speke, Devon, 1864, 'Come to see Jinny Jan', as song, with chorus
'Morning ladies and gentlemen too' (Baring-Gould MSS, printed in *Folk Songs of the West
Country*, G. Hitchcock, 1974, pp. 66–7) | Halifax, c. 1870, 'I've come to see Jennie Jones . . . How
is she now?' Jennie is washing, then drying, ironing, ill, dead; mourner asks 'What shall I wear for
her?'; white is for babies, pink is for ladies, blue for sailors, yellow is forsaken, red for soldiers,
green for jealousy, brown for gentlemen; but black is for mourning and that will do; from the Revd
Crofton's children's nursemaid (MS notebook, p. 63) | Hanwell, Middlesex, 1878, 'We've come
to see Jenny Jones . . . Very well, ladies . . . What shall we lay her in? . . . White's what the dead
wear, And that will just do' (*Traditional Games*, i, pp. 264–7) | Bocking, Essex, 1881 (*Folk-Lore
Record*, iii, 2, pp. 171–2) | *Shropshire Folk-Lore*, 1883, p. 517 | *Traditional Games*, i, pp. 260–83,
Southampton; Colchester; Sporle, Norfolk; Northants.; Enborne, Berks.; Liphook, Hants;
Deptford | Haddington, Cambs., 1896, 'White is for weddings' . . . 'That won't suit', 'Black is for
mourning, That will suit' (*The Study of Man*, A. C. Haddon, 1898, pp. 412–14) | Edgehill,
Warwicks., c. 1900, 'Please may we see Jenny Jones, And how is she today?', 'Jenny Jones is

washing, And can't come out today' | *Old Hampshire Singing Games*, A. E. Gillington, 1909, pp. 6–7 | Somerset, 1912, 'We've come to see poor Jenny Jones . . . Fare ye well ladies and gentlemen too . . . White is what the angels wear, And that *will* do' (*Children's Singing Games*, Cecil Sharp, iii, p. 2) | *Joyous Book of Singing Games*, John Hornby, 1913, 'Jilly Jo' | *100 Singing Games*, F. Kidson, 1916, p. 2 | Bradford-on-Tone, Somerset, 'Miss Jennie O. Jones . . . Where shall we bury her, Behind the stable door? The rats and mice will eat her up, And that will never do. We'll bury her in the old churchyard, And that will just do' (Macmillan Collection) | Upton Magna, Shropshire, 'Poor Jenny Jones', enquirers ask 'When can we see her?' and are told 'One o'clock', 'Two o'clock', etc. | Nelson, Lancs, 1957 and 1969.

Wales: Aberdovey, *c.*1890, 'We've come to see poor Jenny, And how is she now?' Jenny was ironing, cooking, scrubbing, 'and the rest of the chores', then dying and dead | In Welsh, remembered from childhood. 'Jacko John Bach' is a little boy who cannot come out to play because he is sweeping the floor, eating breakfast, cleaning the shoes, and so on (Gomme papers, ff. 112–13, letter 21 May 1920).

Northern Ireland: near Belfast, ? *c.*1855 (*Notes & Queries*, 7th ser., xii, pp. 492–3).

Eire: *Merrie Games in Rhyme*, E. M. Plunket, 1886, pp. 24–5, 'I've come to court Jinny Jo' | Holywood, Co. Down, 1893, 'I came to see Jenny jo', with disappointed suitors singing 'Oh but I'm sorry I can't see her today'. Amongst colours for the laying-out clothes, black is rejected as 'for the sweeps' and orange as 'for the Orange-men'; white is the right colour 'for the corpse'. The singers end 'We have lost a soldier, soldier, soldier, We have lost a soldier, and the Queen has lost a man. We will bury him in the bed of glory, glory, glory, We will bury him in the bed of glory, and we'll never see him any more' (Clara M. Patterson, *Belfast Naturalists' Field Club*, iv, p. 50) | *Traditional Games*, i, 1894, p. 264, Lismore, Co. Waterford, 'Jenny jo'; p. 277, Annaverna, Co. Louth, 'How's poor Jenny jo . . . He's very ill . . . He's fallen downstairs and broken his neck'.

USA: *Games of American Children*, 1883, pp. 63–6, chosen from many versions, 'I've come to see Miss Jennia Jones, And how is she today?' She is upstairs washing, ironing, baking, scrubbing, sick, worse, dead. Blue is for sailors, 'So that will never do'; red is for firemen, pink is for babies, green is forsaken, black is for mourners, white is for dead people, and Miss Jones is buried under an apple tree. Her ghost suddenly arises and the ring run away shrieking. Also 1903, pp. 243–5 | Cincinatti, 1908, 'We come to see Miss Jennia Jones . . . He, hi, ho!' (*JAFL*, xl, pp. 11–12 | Chicago, 1956, 'I come to see Miss Jennie Jones, And how is she today?' She is washing, ironing, sick, dead (*Did you feed my cow?*, M. Taylor, p. 26).

Canada: Highgate and Paisley, Ontario, 1909, 'We've come to bury Miss Jenny Ann Jones, This bright and sunny morning'; 'Miss Dandy Doe' (*JAFL*, xxxi, pp. 50–1).

Australia: Brisbane, *c.*1875, 'Jennie Jones washing clothes, Washing clothes today . . . sick in bed . . . dead and gone . . . What shall we dress her in?' . . . not 'blue for sailor boys' or 'red for soldier boys' or 'green for Irishmen' but 'white for angels' (Howard MSS).

New Zealand: Rockville, Nelson, 1885, 'Jenny Jones', with 'White's for the dead people'; Wellington, 1890 (Sutton-Smith, p. 18).

Spain: cf. *Cancionero Infantil Español*, S. Córdova y Oña, 1947, p. 296, 'Los ladrones'. The robbers come to abduct Doña Ana, but her mother fends them off by saying 'She is gathering flowers' or she is having her stockings, or other garments, put on. At the end mother and daughter try to escape from the ring of robbers. Similar delaying tactics are employed in some German versions of 'Three Brethren out of Spain' (p. 92).

Russia: Nurse sat in middle of circle with Kostroma lying across her lap. The dialogue went: 'Knock, knock on the gate!' 'Who is there?' 'Kuz'ma Squintmouth.' 'Why have you come?' 'Is Kostroma at home?' 'No she's not, she has gone to town.' The players continued to ask for Kostroma and were told 'she has gone to Mass, just come home from Mass, having lunch, resting, ill, very ill, dead, being taken away for burial'. The girls carried Kostroma off with much lamentation, and fell on the ground in grief. Kostroma leapt to her feet and struck at them, saying 'Bake pancakes in remembrance of me' (pancakes were served at Russian wakes). When she had struck all of them they leapt up and ran away, chased by Kostroma (*Folk-Lore*, lxxxi, 1970, pp. 276–9).

59

Daughter Ellen

Here we— all stand— a - round— the ring,— And
now— we shut— poor Ma - ry in.

adapted from Merrie Games in Rhyme, *E. M. Plunket, 1886*

Oh rise, daughter Ellen, and stand on thy feet,
For to see thy dear mother lie dead in yon field.

Oh no, I'll not rise or stand on my feet,
To see my dear mother lie dead in yon field.

Oh rise, daughter Ellen, and stand on thy feet,
For to see thy dear father lie dead in yon field.

Oh no, I'll not rise or stand on my feet,
To see my dear father lie dead in yon field.

Oh rise, daughter Ellen, and stand on thy feet,
For to see thy dear sister lie dead in yon field.

Oh no, I'll not rise or stand on my feet,
To see my dear sister lie dead in yon field.

Oh rise, daughter Ellen, and stand on thy feet,
For to see thy dear brother lie dead in yon field.

Oh no, I'll not rise or stand on my feet,
To see my dear brother lie dead in yon field.

> Oh rise, daughter Ellen, and stand on thy feet,
> For to see thy dear true love lie dead in yon field.
>
> Oh yes I will rise, and stand on my feet,
> For to see my dear true love lie dead in yon field.

Played at a primary school in Clifton, Lancashire, *c.*1910. 'Daughter Ellen' got up and chose someone else to lie in the centre of the ring. (If children were worried about logic, they would wonder whether it is the dead mother speaking, or whether Ellen has a step-mother, or whether 'Daughter Ellen' is a title in itself, like 'Burd Ellen' in the ballad of that name.)

The game has grown from part of an old ballad, 'The Maid Freed from the Gallows' (Child 95), which was sung in Italy, Spain, Sweden, Finland, Germany, Estonia, and Russia, and probably other European countries as well. The story is of a maid (or, in Sicily, a wife) who is kidnapped by pirates and is to be sold into slavery unless she pays a ransom in gold. She applies to the members of her family one by one, and each says flatly that their possessions are more important to them than she is. Finally she turns to her lover, who sells his possessions and sets her free.

In the British version the maid is to be hung, not enslaved; and even in 1770, when the Revd Parsons sent Bishop Percy fifteen verses of the ballad, which he had collected from oral tradition, the story begins with the maid standing by the gallows and gives no explanation of her plight. The folk tale 'The Golden Ball' tells this part of the story, too, but also supplies a wondrous beginning, in which a gold-bedecked man gives the girl a golden ball and tells her she must not lose it on pain of death. Happy-go-lucky, she plays with it until it rolls itself, as balls will, far away under the bushes. Hope is fading when her lover finds the ball and brings it to her just in time.

In the best-preserved ballad of the cycle, the Sicilian one quoted by Professor Child, the wife's unkind relations die soon after she has been rescued, and she refuses to mourn them. 'And after three days the father died. "And let him die; I will dress all in red." And after three days the mother died. "And let her die: I will dress all in yellow." And after three days the brother died. "And let him die; I will dress all in green." And after three days the sister died. "And let her die; I will dress all in white. And if my dear husband dies, I will dress in black."' It is this part of the drama that was kept alive in the children's game; but not until one reads the complete ballad does one understand the reason for Daughter Ellen's apparent callousness.

Britain: Ninfield, Sussex, *c.*1830, 'Rise up, rise up, Betsy Brown, To see your father go through the town. I won't rise up upon my feet, To see my father go through the street . . . I will rise up upon my feet, To see my lover go through the street' (*Traditional Games*, i, p. 365) | *Popular Rhymes*, J. O. Halliwell, 1849, pp. 119–20, Essex, 'Here we all stand round the ring, And now we shut poor Mary in, Rise up, rise up, poor Mary Brown, And see your poor mother go through the town', then poor father, brother, sister, beggars. Halliwell complains 'One would have thought that this tiresome repetition had been continued quite long enough, but two other verses are sometimes added, introducing *gentlemen* and *ladies* with the same questions.' The game ends with Mary rising 'To see my sweetheart go through the street' and she 'rushes with impetuosity to break the ring' | Kirkcudbrightshire, 1880, 'Rise up, rise up, and stand on your feet, For to see your dear father lie dead on yon field' (*Notes & Queries*, 6th ser., ii, p. 248) | *Merrie Games in Rhyme*, E. M. Plunket, 1886, p. 41, similar to Halliwell | Barnes, *c.*1890, two versions collected by Alice Gomme in her home town, one similar to Halliwell, and the other beginning 'Rise daughter, rise daughter, off of your poor feet'; also Sussex, 'Rise daughter . . . from off your knees, To see your poor father lie down at yonder trees' (*Traditional Games*, i, pp. 364–5) | Keswick, 1901, similar to text (Gilchrist MSS 231 Aiii, p. 106) | Churchinford, Somerset, 1912, 'Rise, daughter, rise, and stand on your feet, To see your dear mother lie dead at your feet . . . Oh yes, I will rise and stand on my feet, To see my dear lover lie dead at my feet' (Macmillan Collection).

USA: New York, 1917, sung by children in the slums (*JAFL*, xxx, p. 119) | *American Play-Party Song*, B. A. Botkin, 1937, p. 62, ' "Hangman, Hangman, Slack Your Rope" . . . has lent itself to dramatization not only as a game but also as a play, especially among Negroes of the South'.

Sweden: *Svenska fornsånger*, A. I. Arwidsson, iii, 1842, pp. 233–7, 'Hvi ron J så, hvi ron J så, Fru Gundela?' 'Jag må välle ro, må välle ro, Med' gräset det gror, Om sommaren!' etc. ('Why are you rowing like that, Lady Gundela?' 'I must row, I must row, while the grass it does grow, In the summer.' 'Now I have heard, your father is dead, Lady Gundela!' 'Much do I care about my father, my mother still lives, O, God be praised!' and so on with mother, brother, and sister, till 'Now I have heard, your betrothed is dead'. Lady Gundela swoons. The ring then announce 'Now I have heard, your father still lives, Lady Gundela' and she answers 'Much do I care, my betrothed is dead, O God have mercy on me!' The story winds back on itself until her betrothed is said to be alive. 'Is it true, what you say to me, That my betrothed still lives, O, God be praised!' She leaps up and joins the dancers) | *Svenska Folklekar*, C. Tillhagen and N. Dencker, ii, 1950, pp. 310–12, 'Vi ron I så, fru Engela'.

60

Three Sisters

Once three sisters went a walk,
Once three sisters went a walk,
Once three sisters went a walk,
Down by the bonnie banks of Airdrie, O.

They met a robber on the way,
They met a robber on the way,
They met a robber on the way,
Down by the bonnie banks of Airdrie, O.

He took the first one by the hand,
He birled her round till she could not stand,
He birled her round till she could not stand,
Down by the bonnie banks of Airdrie, O.

Will you be a robber's wife,
Or will you die by my penknife?
Will you be a robber's wife?
Down by the bonnie banks of Airdrie, O.

I'll not be a robber's wife,
I'd rather die by your penknife,
I'll not be a robber's wife,
Down by the bonnie banks of Airdrie, O.

Then he took out his penknife,
Then he ended her sweet life,
Then he ended her sweet life,
Down by the bonnie banks of Airdrie, O.

The second sister is treated in the same way, then:

He took the third one by the hand,
He birled her round till she could not stand,
He birled her round till she could not stand,
Down by the bonny banks of Airdrie, O.

She replies as the other two sisters did, and adds:

I wish that my two brothers were here,
I wish that my two brothers were here,
I wish that my two brothers were here,
Down by the bonnie banks of Airdrie, O.

The robber asks:

> What are your two brothers like,
> What are your two brothers like,
> What are your two brothers like?
> Down by the bonnie banks of Airdrie, O.

> One's a minister, and the other's like you,
> One's a minister, and the other's like you,
> One's a minister, and the other's like you,
> Down by the bonnie banks of Airdrie, O.

> God, O God, what have I done!
> Killed my sisters all but one,
> Killed my sisters all but one,
> Down by the bonnie banks of Airdrie, O.

> Then he took out his penknife,
> Then he ended his sweet life,
> Then he ended his sweet life,
> Down by the bonnie banks of Airdrie, O.

This ballad, 'The Bonnie Banks o' Fordie', is, Professor Child says (I, 171), 'familiar to all branches of the Scandinavian race'. At the beginning of the Second World War Dr Katharine Briggs was taught a game-version by some children evacuated from the Gallowgate of Glasgow; the words and tune were as above. 'It was played as a rule grouped round one of the outside stairs. The chorus stood on the steps and four children acted it. The tune was clearly a folk tune, and apparently of some antiquity. It is interesting to see how "turned her round and made her stand" has become "turned her round till she could not stand". At this point the wicked brother spun the sister round and round under his hand till she fell to the ground.' Later, she found that the game had also been well known in Edinburgh in the 1930s, in a version that began 'There were three sisters went to gather flowers'. This is closer to the graceful verses collected in Edinburgh by David Herd in the early 1770s, the first of which ran:

> There wond three ladies in a bower,
>   Annet and Margret and Marjorie,
> And they have gone out to pu' a flower,
>   And the dew it lyes on the wood, gay ladie.

Scotland: Herd MS I, 38 | Isle of Bute, 1911 (*Rymour Club*, ii, p. 77) | *Notes & Queries*, cxci, 1946, p. 34.

61

Fair Rosie

Nottingham, 1977

Fair Rosie was a lovely girl,
A lovely girl, a lovely girl,
Fair Rosie was a lovely girl,
A lovely girl.

Her ancient castle was her home,
Was her home, was her home,
Her ancient castle was her home,
Was her home.

Fair Rosie sat in her high tower,
Her high tower, her high tower,
Fair Rosie sat in her high tower,
Her high tower.

A wicked fairy found her there,
Found her there, found her there,
A wicked fairy found her there,
Found her there.

Fair Rosie slept a hundred years,
A hundred years, a hundred years,
Fair Rosie slept a hundred years,
A hundred years.

A handsome prince came riding by,
Riding by, riding by,
A handsome prince came riding by,
Riding by.

Fair Rosie did not sleep no more,
Sleep no more, sleep no more,
Fair Rosie did not sleep no more,
Sleep no more.

All the guests made merry there,
Merry there, merry there,
All the guests made merry there,
Merry there.

(*girl, 7, Ipswich, 1953*)

The other form of the game is 'The princess was a lovely child':

The princess was a lovely child, lovely child, lovely child,
The princess was a lovely child, long long ago.

A wicked fairy cast a spell . . .

The princess slept a hundred years . . .

The palace trees grew tall and straight . . .

A handsome prince came galloping by . . .

He cut the trees down one by one . . .

They all had a happy time, a happy time, a happy time,
They all had a happy time, long long ago.

Nelson, Lancs, 1956

The princess preened herself, alone in the ring. The fairy stepped into the ring from outside, waved her hands and scowled. The princess fell asleep. The ring held their arms high, making a forest. The prince detached himself from the ring and galloped round the outside; then, using his hand as an axe, entered the ring and woke the princess. The singing had been slow and dreamlike; but now the ring joined up again and frolicked round faster and faster, ending up by falling head over heels on the grass verge. Asked whether the princess should not have been woken with a kiss, they said 'Nope, we just gives 'er a shove'.

The game, which tells the story of the Sleeping Beauty, is a direct translation of the German 'Dornröschen war ein schönes Kind'. It was imported during the years leading up to the First World War, when the Aesthetic Movement was fighting the ugliness of mass production, the supposed spiritual starvation of the masses, and the threat of war, with every means at its disposal: fairy tales, folk dances, and, especially, internationalism. In Caroline Crawford's *Folk Dances and Games*, New

York, 1908, the translation has a literary flavour ('The princess was so beautiful . . . O, little princess, have a care . . . have a care of a wicked fay'). In Curwen's *Folk Dances of Europe*, 1910, the game is 'The Sleeping Princess', and the princess is faithfully described as 'a lovely child'; in *Fifty Figures and Character Dances*, by E. T. Bell, 1923, it is 'Briar Rose'.

The Sleeping Beauty was an immediate and continuing success. A. S. Macmillan, when girls sent descriptions of 'Briar Rose-bud' from four places in Devonshire in 1922 for his weekly column in *Pulman's News*, enthused 'Isn't this a lovely game?' but said he felt sad there were no accounts from his own county of Somerset, a sadness that was soon alleviated. The West Country versions were particularly lively, perhaps because boys and girls were playing together; and the prince cutting his way through the thorn hedge was usually Prince Charles or Prince Charlie.

Many village schools still treasure copies of Curwen's *Folk Dances* and John Hornby's *Joyous Book of Singing Games*, 1913 (his 'Fair Rosie' is like our text, except that in verse 7 she 'now need sleep no more'). The game is played at innumerable school Christmas parties, but is unusual in also having a vigorous life in playgrounds and on housing estates on summer evenings. The tune—perhaps another reason for the game's popularity—is that of the old, widespread Germanic ring game 'Mariechen sass auf einem Stein', in which little Mary sits on a stone weeping because, for an unknown reason, she must die. Her brother—or some soldiers, or a wicked hunter—kills her, and she is resurrected. The game has its ultimate origin in the ballad of 'Ritter Ulinger'.

Germany: *Deutsches Kinderspiel*, F. M. Böhme, 1897, pp. 552–3, 'Dornröschen war ein schönes Kind' from *Spielbuch für Mädchen*, A. Netsch, 1895. No texts older than the 1890s, and Böhme says it was 'written for children to sing in playschools'.

USA: *Folk Dances*, C. Crawford, 1908, pp. 64–5 | Greenwich Village, New York, 1935, 'The princess slept for a hundred years . . . A long time ago. She lived in a castle . . . It was a very high one . . . The prince came to waken her . . . She promised him to marry . . . And then they lived so happily'; also New Jersey, 1939, 'Thorn Rosa was a lovely maid' (*JAFL*, lx, pp. 421–2).

Britain: Leeds, *c.*1912, 'The princess was a lovely child . . . Love-ly child. She lived in a fine town . . . A wicked fairy cast a spell . . . The Princess sleeps a hundred years . . . A great big hedge grew giant high . . . A gallant Prince came riding by . . . He cut the forest with his sword . . . Oh, little princess, lovely child, rise and wake . . . And everybody's happy now' | Bromley by Bow, *c.*1955, 'Sweet Rosebud was a pretty child . . . Long, long ago. A wicked witch cast a spell . . . She fell asleep a hundred years . . . A handsome prince came riding by . . . He took her hand and kissed her once . . . And now she is a happy bride' (*East London Papers*, ii, 2, p. 75) | West Kirby, 1959, 'Fair Rosebud was a lovely child . . . A lovely child. She lives up in a wayside town' . . . thereafter orthodox till 'Now they're married and settled down' | 1960s, various predictable recordings, except Workington, 1960, which possessed a particularly fine version: 'The princess lived in a big high tower . . . Long long ago. O princess you should have a care . . . There came a wicked fairy there . . . She cast a spell and pricked her thumbs . . . The princess slept for a hundred years . . . The palace trees grew all around . . . Till a handsome prince came riding by . . . He cut the trees down one by one . . . He kissed the princess on the hand . . . She woke up and became his bride ... The people all made merry then' | Edinburgh, 1975, for ball-bouncing, 'There was a little princess ... many years ago' | Stepney, 1976, 'Fair Rosie was a lovely child ... Love-ly child' | Nottingham, 1977, and Leeds, 1981, 'There was a princess long ago, Long long ago'.

Ireland: Belfast, 1974, 'Fair Rosa was a lovely child' (on David Hammond's record 'Green Peas and Barley O') | Dublin, 1976, 'There was a princess in a tower ... In a tower. Sweet roses grew up to her bower ... She pricked her finger on a thorn ... She fell asleep for twenty years ... A handsome prince came riding by ... He kissed her lips that were so sweet ... And then she opened her eyes ... And they were married in a year'.

Belgium: c.1958, Woluwé-Saint-Lambert, 'La bell' au bois, la bell' enfant, Bell' enfant, bell' enfant! La bell' au bois, la bell' enfant, Bell' enfant! ... Vivait dans un très haut château ... Une vieill' sorcièr' y entra ... Toucha la bell' et l'endormit ... La belle dormit cent hivers ... Un jeune prince y entra ... Toucha la belle et l'éveilla ... "Ma bell', il ne faut plus dormir!" ... Et tout le monde fut heureux' (*Fabula*, Berlin, 2, 1958, p. 31).

Ecuador: *Rique Ran*, M. L. Goodwin and E. L. Powell, 1951, pp. 20–1, 'Rosita era linda'.

62

Lazy Mary

Tune: 'Nuts in May'

Lazy Mary, will you get up, will you get up, will you get up,
Lazy Mary, will you get up, will you get up today?

No, Mother, I won't get up, I won't get up, I won't get up,
No, Mother, I won't get up, I won't get up today.

What will you give me if I get up? etc.

A slice of bread and a cup of tea, etc.

No, Mother, I won't get up, etc.

What will you give me if I get up? etc.

A hunk of bread and a slice of cheese, etc.

No, Mother, I won't get up, etc.

What will you give me if I get up? etc.

A hunk of fat and a roasted rat, etc.

No, Mother, I won't get up, etc.

What will you give me if I get up? etc.

A nice young man with rosy cheeks, etc.

Yes, Mother, I will get up, I will get up, I will get up,
Yes, Mother, I will get up, I will get up today.

Lazy Mary, you had to get up, you had to get up, you had to get up,
Lazy Mary, you had to get up, you had to get up today.

A ring with mother and daughter in the centre, the daughter with closed
eyes. The mother advances and retreats. Not surprisingly the game does
not appear in any of the collections aimed at children—its morality is
indefensible. More surprisingly it was not known to Alice Gomme. The
game had in fact already retreated to the west by the late nineteenth
century. Crofton found it jumbled up with other games, in Dukinfield,
Cheshire, *c.*1875. The daughter sat 'wi' pinny up to her face' in the ring,
and asked:

> What shall I have to my breakfast,
> If I get up today?
> Tea and toast to your breakfast
> If you get up today.
> No, Mother, no! I winna get up,
> I winna get up today.

It had become entangled with 'The Keys of Heaven' in Devon and
Somerset by the 1920s, but at that time was fully alive as an independent
game in the United States and in Dublin, where it was 'still very popular' in
1975.

A mirror-image song was collected by David Herd in Edinburgh before
1776, where it is a man who refuses to behave properly until he is promised
the pleasures of sex. In 'The Shepherds Wife Cries O'er the Lee' the
recalcitrant shepherd is offered increasingly tempting food for his supper,
but will not come home till his wife proposes 'A pair of white legs and a
good cogg-wame [bump-belly]' upon which he exclaims 'Ha, ha, how,
that's something that dow, I'll haste me hame again e'en, jo!'

USA: *Games of American Children*, 1883, p. 96, 'The round is familiar in New York streets' | St
Louis, 1895, as text (*JAFL*, lx, pp. 17–18) | Cincinnati, 1908 (*JAFL*, xl, pp. 18–19) | Chimney
Rock, *c.*1927 (*North Carolina Folklore*, p. 55).

Britain: Crofton MS, I, p. 130 | *Old Dorset Singing Games*, A. E. Gillington, 1913, no. 5, 'O
lazy Cake, will you get up?' | Devon, 1922, 'I'll give you a pram, with a shade up . . . I'll give you a
doll with rosy cheeks' (Macmillan Collection).

Ireland: Dublin, 1920s, 'Lazy Mary will you get up . . . And cook yer auld wan's breakfast' (*Out
Goes She*, Leslie Daiken, 1963, p. 27) | *All In! All In!*, Eilís Brady, 1975, pp. 121–3, 'Lazy Mary,
will you get up . . . On a cold and frosty morning'.

Germany: *Folk Dances of Germany*, E. Burchenal, N.Y. 1938, p. 106, 'Spinnerliedchen', in
which the mother cannot induce her daughter to spin until she is promised a husband.

France: *Chants Populaire du Languedoc*, ii, L. Lambert, 1906, pp. 100, and 243–4; the mother
offers the daughter 'une belle robe', 'une belle coiffe', and finally 'un joli jeune homme'.

Cf. 'Whistle, daughter, whistle', *ODNR*, pp. 143–4. The daughter cannot whistle, but when
offered a man she 'will do the best I can'. Why the mother wants her to whistle is not easy to
understand.

63

Milking Pails

Mary's gone a-milking,
    Mother, mother,
Mary's gone a-milking,
    Gentle sweet mother o' mine.

Take your pails and go after her,
    Daughter, daughter,
Take your pails and go after her,
    Gentle sweet daughter o' mine.

Buy me a pair of new milking pails,
    Mother, mother,
Buy me a pair of new milking pails,
    Gentle sweet mother o' mine.

Where's the money to come from,
    Daughter, daughter,
Where's the money to come from,
    Gentle sweet daughter o' mine?

Sell my father's feather bed,
    Mother, mother,
Sell my father's feather bed,
    Gentle sweet mother o' mine.

What's your father to sleep on,
    Daughter, daughter,
What's your father to sleep on,
    Gentle sweet daughter o' mine?

Put him in the truckle bed,
　Mother, mother,
Put him in the truckle bed,
　Gentle sweet mother o' mine.

What are the children to sleep on,
　Daughter, daughter,
What are the children to sleep on,
　Gentle sweet daughter o' mine?

Put them in the pig-sty,
　Mother, mother,
Put them in the pig-sty,
　Gentle sweet mother o' mine.

What are the pigs to lie in,
　Daughter, daughter,
What are the pigs to lie in,
　Gentle sweet daughter o' mine?

Put them in the washing-tubs,
　Mother, mother,
Put them in the washing-tubs,
　Gentle sweet mother o' mine.

What am I to wash in,
　Daughter, daughter,
What am I to wash in,
　Gentle sweet daughter o' mine?

Wash in the thimble,
　Mother, mother,
Wash in the thimble,
　Gentle sweet mother o' mine.

Thimble won't hold your father's shirt,
　Daughter, daughter,
Thimble won't hold your father's shirt,
　Gentle sweet daughter o' mine.

Wash in the river,
　Mother, mother,
Wash in the river,
　Gentle sweet mother o' mine.

Suppose the clothes should blow away,
   Daughter, daughter,
Suppose the clothes should blow away,
   Gentle sweet daughter o' mine?

Set a man to watch them,
   Mother, mother,
Set a man to watch them,
   Gentle sweet mother o' mine.

Suppose the man should go to sleep,
   Daughter, daughter,
Suppose the man should go to sleep,
   Gentle sweet daughter o' mine?

Take a boat and go after them,
   Mother, mother,
Take a boat and go after them,
   Gentle sweet mother o' mine.

Suppose the boat should be upset,
   Daughter, daughter,
Suppose the boat should be upset,
   Gentle sweet daughter o' mine?

Then that would be an end of you,
   Mother, mother,
Then that would be an end of you,
   Gentle sweet mother o' mine.

This is another game which has been overtaken by time. It belongs to the days when being a milkmaid was a desirable and joyous occupation, giving opportunities for romance (as in 'Where are you going to, my pretty maid?'). The text above, learned by Alice Gomme from a London nursemaid in 1876, is typical of the older wording. An elder sister has gone a-milking, and the younger needs new pails (not cans, as in later versions) so that she, too, may escape to the freedom of the fields. She wheedles her mother with soft words and patient answers till at last logic takes its course and the mother, finally outraged, chases and chastises her.

    The part of the would-be milkmaid is usually taken by a whole row of little girls, the mother standing in front on her own; but sometimes the mother is represented by a second line, or occasionally the game was a ring game and the mother stood within a filial circle. Mother and daughter sing alternate verses; and when the chase occurs, the girl who is caught becomes the mother.

When Joseph Ritson included the game in *Gammer Gurton's Garland*, 1810, the daughter was even more exasperated with her unco-operative mother:

> Betty's gone a milking, mother, mother;
> Betty's gone a milking, dainty fine mother of mine:
> Then you may go after, daughter, daughter;
> Then you may go after, dainty fine daughter of mine.
>
> Buy me a pair of milk pails, mother &c.
>
> Where's the money to come from, daughter? &c.
>
> Pawn my father's feather-bed, mother &c.
>
> Where's your father to lay? &c.
>
> Lay him in the maid's bed &c.
>
> Where is the maid to lay? &c.
>
> Lay her in the pig-stye &c.
>
> Where are the pigs to lay? &c.
>
> Lay them at the stair-foot &c.
>
> There they will be trod to death &c.
>
> Lay them by the water-side &c.
>
> There they will be drowned &c.
>
> Then take a rope and hang yourself &c.

Perhaps, in the south of England, this game has passed quite out of fashion. Only once have we heard it played, in the playground of the small village school at Herriard, Hampshire, in 1954, and then the request was 'Mummy, would you buy me a bicycle?' (followed by 'Where can I get the money from? Sell father's feather bed. Where will he sleep? In the boys' room. Where will the boys sleep? In the coal shed. Where will the coal go? In the copper. What shall I wash in? In the thimble. What shall I sew with? Sew with the poker. What shall I poke the fire with? Poke it with your finger. What if I burn it? Good job too!') But Father Damian Webb found it in Workington and Cockermouth, 1966, and in the same year Rowland Kellett collected it in Leeds.

Britain: *Gammer Gurton's Garland*, 1810 | *Popular Rhymes of Scotland*, R. Chambers, 1869, pp. 36–7, 'Buy me a milking pail, Mother, mother', 'Betsy's gone a-milking, Beautiful daughter', etc. | Dukinfield, Cheshire, *c.*1880, ending 'What mun we sew wi'? Sew wi' th' poker! What stir t'fire wi'? Stir wi' your finger! If it burns my finger? Serve thee reet!' (Crofton MS, i, p.

132) | *Shropshire Folk-Lore*, 1883, p. 515, 'Mother, please buy me a milking-can, A milking-can, a milking-can, Mother, please buy me a milking-can, With a humpty-dumpty-daisy' | *Merrie Games in Rhyme*, E. M. Plunket, 1886, pp. 34–5 | *Traditional Games*, i, 1894, pp. 376–88, 11 versions from oral tradition | Sowerby Bridge, Yorks., *c.*1900, 'Mother, will you buy me a milking can' ending like Dukinfield | *Old Surrey Singing Games*, A. E. Gillington, 1909, p. 13 | Dorset, *c.*1910, played at Sunday School treats, 'Mother buy me a wat'ring can' (Mass Observation) | Liverpool, *c.*1915, 'Mother, buy me a milking pail . . . One, two, three' | Great Glenham, Suffolk, *c.*1918, 'Mother go buy a milking can . . . E I O' | Oldham, *c.*1930, 'Mother will you buy me a milking can' ending 'Where will the baby sleep? Sleep in the dolly-tub; Where'll I do my washing? Wash in the fireplace; Where'll I keep the poker?' whereupon the crowd shout 'Stick it up—' and other rude suggestions, and they all run for it | Luthermuir, Kincardineshire, *c.*1940, taught by evacuees from Dundee, 'Buy me a pair of shoes, gentle mother, Gentle mother of mine' ending remarkably like the 1810 version | Workington and Cockermouth, 1966, 'Mother will you buy me a milking pail . . . On a cold and frosty morning' ending like Oldham, *c.*1930 | Leeds, 1966, 'Mother will you buy me a milking can . . . This cold and frosty morning' ending with the proposal that the pigs should sleep in a thimble.

USA: *Games of American Children*, 1883, pp. 166–7, 'Will you buy me a pair of milking-pails, Oh, mother! Oh, mother!' from 'a child lately arrived from England' | Brooklyn, NY, 1899, children move slowly in a circle, singing 'Mamma bought me a pincushion . . . One, two, three' when each claps hands and turns round. The song proceeds 'What did Mamma pay for it?' etc. (*JAFL*, xii, pp. 293–4) | Cincinnati, 1908, 'Mother, buy a milk can . . . A-Rance, a-Dance, a-Jig' (*JAFL*, xl, pp. 31–2) | Clarksburg, Virginia, 1918, 'Buy me a milking-pail, O mother'; long version much like text, including 'Get a man to watch' sequence (*JAFL*, xxxi, pp. 275–6).

Twentieth-century versions are usually sung to the tune of 'Nuts in May'.

XI

Contests

IT is significant that only two singing games can be called 'Contests'. The competitive element in most singing games is of a more subtle kind: the players compete for popularity, and success comes with being chosen as the one to be 'loved best'. But 'Nuts in May' and 'Romans and English' are games in the fullest sense of the word. There is a trial of strength, and doubt about the outcome. One side or the other can be said to have won. It can only be a coincidence, however, that these two games have aroused fiercer philological warfare than almost any others.

64

Nuts in May

Lilliput, Dorset, 1978

Here we come gathering nuts in May,
    Nuts in May, nuts in May,
Here we come gathering nuts in May,
    On a cold and frosty morning.

Who will you have for nuts in May,
    Nuts in May, nuts in May,
Who will you have for nuts in May,
    On a cold and frosty morning?

We will have *Susan Jones* for nuts in May,
    Nuts in May, nuts in May,
We will have *Susan Jones* for nuts in May,
    On a cold and frosty morning.

Who will you have to pull her away,
    Pull her away, pull her away,
Who will you have to pull her away,
    On a cold and frosty morning?

We'll have *Janet Evans* to pull her away,
    Pull her away, pull her away,
We'll have *Janet Evans* to pull her away,
    On a cold and frosty morning.

'One of my favourite games,' said a girl in Welshpool, 1963, 'is called "Here We Come Gathering Nuts in May". It's a light and gay game where you have quite a number of girls, then split up into two groups. This is how you play it:

The one group of girls start off by skipping towards the other group which are a distance away and sing "Here we come gathering". When we have skipped back to where we started the other group start skipping towards us singing "Who will you have?" Then skipping towards them we decide who we will have from their group and sing "We will have Susan Jones" or whoever we decided. Then we choose one of our group to pull her away, and sing that bit. The captains of each group walk up to the middle of the distance between the groups and they put their left foot in front and right one behind. The two people picked, pull, but are not allowed to go over the two left feet. The person who drags the opponent over the feet and quite clear of the feet is the winner and the loser joins the winner's side. Then it is the other side's turn and it carries on till there are none left in one of the groups.'

She might have added that it is a cunning game. Since the choosing side name both contestants, and must not send the same puller-away twice, they have to ensure that the one fetching is slightly stronger than the one being fetched.

The words now seem standardized, though even in the present day they occasionally vary (e.g. Bishop Auckland, 1961, 'On a cold winter's morning'; West Ham, 1960, 'Here we go gathering nuts and may . . . E.I.O. Who do you want for your girl friend? . . . E.I.O.') But among the twenty-two versions sent to Alice Gomme in the early 1890s (*Traditional Games*, i, pp. 424–33) the dancers came gathering 'nuts in May' or 'nuts and may' indiscriminately, or came 'gathering nuts away'; and the time of day when they went out gathering could be 'On a summer's morning', 'At five o'clock (or six o'clock) in the morning', 'On a bright summer's morning', or 'So early in the morning', as well as 'On a cold and frosty morning'. Early rising was essential for Maytime expeditions into the woods to pick hawthorn blossom; and it seems likely that 'Nuts in May' is a May game, the phrase 'nuts in May' being a corruption of 'knots of May' (the little clusters of may bloom), or perhaps of Chaucer's 'knoppes', buds. A version of the game from Charleston, Virginia, given by Newell (1883) strengthens its Maytime imagery:

> Here we come gathering nuts of May,
> Here we come gathering nuts of May,
> Here we come gathering nuts of May,
> On a May morning early.

The conception of 'marriage by capture' (that is, the kidnapping of a girl from a neighbouring tribe) fascinated the late Victorian folklorists, especially Sir Laurence Gomme, who included many supposed survivals in his *Folk-Lore Relics of Early Village Life*, 1883. His wife Alice Gomme saw a survival of the custom in the game of 'Nuts in May'. It is true that the naming of a victim from the opposing side, the sending over of a raider (in Shropshire, 1883, the single raider was 'assisted by those behind'), and the forceful 'fetching away' to the home camp, seem to fit a picture of abduction. However, while there is little evidence for real marriage-by-capture, there is much evidence for mock marriage-by-capture. Playful scenes in which the bridegroom and his friends chase after the bride and bring her back, a willing captive, are performed all over the world, and continued in Britain into the present century. In Wales, says Westermarck (*History of Human Marriage*, II, p. 261), 'On the morning of the wedding day the groom with his friends demanded the bride. Her friends gave a positive refusal, upon which a mock scuffle ensued. The bride, mounted behind her nearest kinsman, is carried off and is pursued by the groom and his friends with loud shouts. When they have fatigued themselves and their horses, he is suffered to overtake his bride, and leads her away in triumph.' At Hungarian weddings the bridegroom and his party 'attempt to kidnap, or for fun actually kidnap, the bride; they besiege her house, all kinds of obstacles are placed before the wedding procession, even shots are fired' (Károly Viski, *Hungarian Peasant Customs*, 1932, p. 112). In 1980 television viewers saw the same kind of ritualized 'marriage by capture' in the western Himalayas (the programme was entitled 'The Last Place on Earth'); but as the bridegroom happened to be a young man of no fortune, and the bride was rich (and enamoured), the usual procedure was reversed and the man was the one to be captured and brought home. Westermarck has shown that such ceremonies are enjoyed in the remotest parts of the world: in the valleys of the Amazon, amongst the Araucanians of Colombia, and the Kikuyu of Kenya. Among the Lolos in the interior of China a full-scale fight takes place, the women of the bride's village defending her with sticks and stones against the bridegroom and his men. The bride is, in every case, obliged by tradition to cry and show reluctance, which may be feigned but allows her to express feelings of modesty, and sorrow at leaving her family.

The European May games seem to have depicted the different stages in the process of getting married: the informal choosing of a sweetheart, the official match-making procedure (see chapter III, Match-Making), the wedding itself (see chapter V, Wedding Rings). It is not inconceivable that 'Nuts in May' imitated the mock capture of the bride which preceded the wedding.

Unfortunately there are no early recordings of 'Nuts in May'. The earliest is a nursery version in Mrs Valentine's *Home Book of Pleasure and Instruction*, 1867, in which one side are called 'Dew-seekers' and the other, 'Roses'. The dew-seekers each provide themselves with a leaf and sing 'Here we come gathering May-dew'. The roses reply 'Our pretty cups are full of dew', bow their heads, and wait to be touched with a leaf. Thus it is impossible to know how old the game may be, though its movements (except the tug of war) are those of the old German stepping dance. We know that the tune it shares with its arboreal companion 'The Mulberry Bush' (earliest mention 1821) existed before 1760, when it accompanied the song of 'Nancy Dawson' in the *Universal Magazine*; it had already appeared as a dance tune called 'Piss upon the Grass', in the third book of *Caledonian Country Dances*, printed for J. Walsh, *c.*1740, no. 36 (in the Mitchell Library, Glasgow).

Perhaps after all the game may be no more than a celebration of the earth's flowering, a spiritual descendant of a Greek children's game played about 600 BC whose words would not seem out of place sung by modern children as they advanced and retreated:

> Where are my roses, where are my violets,
> And where is my fine parsley?
>
> Here are your roses, here are your violets,
> And here is your fine parsley.

Britain: Reddish, Lancs., *c.*1880, 'Here we come gathering nuts and May . . . On a fine and frosty morning'; also Giggleswick and Stackhouse, Yorkshire, with variations 'Upon a summer's morning' and 'Nuts *in* May' (Crofton MS, i, p. 64) | Bocking, Essex, 1880, 'Nuts in May . . . On a cold and frosty morning. Where do you gather your nuts in May? On Galloway hill we gather our nuts', etc. (*Folk-Lore Record*, iii, p. 170) | *Shropshire Folk-Lore*, 1883, p. 516 | *Merrie Games in Rhyme*, E. M. Plunket, 1886, pp. 42–3, 'Here we go gathering nuts in May . . . On a cold and frosty morning . . . Who will you gather for nuts and May?' | Argyllshire, 1906 (*Folk-Lore*, xvii, p.

221) | *London Street Games*, 1916, pp. 88–9 | As text: Somerset, 1922 (Macmillan Collection), and frequently thereafter, played at parties and by children on their own.

Ireland: Trentagh, Co. Donegal, *c.*1958, as text, but 'the loser is out'.

USA: *Games of American Children*, p. 89 | Holland, Michigan, as text (*JAFL*, xxvii, p. 99) | Chimney Rock, *c.*1927, 'Here we come, gathering nuts in May . . . So early in the morning' (*North Carolina Folklore*, p. 110).

Canada: Toronto, 1888, played by little children on Dominion Day, as text (*JAFL*, viii, p. 253) | Toronto and Ottawa, 1909, said to be 'common' (*JAFL*, xxxi, pp. 47–8).

Australia: well known, e.g. Mallee country, Victoria, *c.*1906; and Melbourne, 1954, similar to text but ending with a tug of war between sides.

New Zealand: 'the great picnic game of all periods' (Sutton-Smith, pp. 24–5).

Israel: Jerusalem, 1965, 'We Go Out to Fight with You', contenders chosen by their own side (*Determinants of Children's Game Styles*, R. Eifermann, 1970, p. 66).

65

Romans and English

Buck - le on your sword and a - way we go . . .

Workington, Cumberland, 1962

Have you any bread and wine,
    For we are the Romans,
Have you any bread and wine,
    For we are the Roman soldiers?

Yes, we have some bread and wine,
  For we are the English,
Yes, we have some bread and wine,
  For we are the English soldiers.

Will you give us some of it,
  For we are the Romans,
Will you give us some of it,
  For we are the Roman soldiers?

No, we'll give you none of it,
  For we are the English,
No, we'll give you none of it,
  For we are the English soldiers.

Then we'll tell our King of you,
  For we are the Romans,
Then we'll tell our King of you,
  For we are the Roman soldiers.

What care I for King or you,
  For we are the English,
What care I for King or you,
  For we are the English soldiers.

Are you ready for a fight,
  For we are the Romans,
Are you ready for a fight,
  For we are the Roman soldiers?

Yes, we're ready for a fight,
  For we are the English,
Yes, we're ready for a fight,
  For we are the English soldiers.

A dramatic dialogue between two lines of girls who advance and retreat as they sing alternate verses, 'Romans and English' ends with the only ritualized fight in the repertoire of singing games. In the Workington, 1962, version above, the combatants fight hopping on one foot, trying to push each other off balance. Anyone who puts the other foot down is out. When the fight is over, everybody forms a ring and dances round singing, to the tune of 'Nuts in May':

> Buckle on your sword and away we go,
>   Away we go, away we go,
> Buckle on your sword and away we go,
>   On a cold and frosty morning.

To judge from the large number of recordings available from the past hundred years this must have been one of the greatest of the singing games. But it has dwindled from the long slanging-matches of the late nineteenth century, in which each side might sing twelve or more verses, to a perfunctory exchange such as was popular in St John's Wood, London, in 1973, where the children said plainly 'We prefer the fighting to the singing'. One side sang,

> Are you ready for a fight,
>   We are the English,
> Are you ready for a fight,
>   We are the English soldiers?

to which the others replied that they were German soldiers, and ready. The first side then sang, rather as in 'Nuts in May', that they would 'have so-and-so for a fight', and chose a champion, and when the others had also chosen a champion the two had a tug of war across a line.

The older recordings tell a story of spell-binding irrationality. In a version from Perth, *c.*1898, for instance, unidentified scroungers ask for bread and wine; they are offered some; the wine is not enough; the purveyors of the wine lose patience, and refuse ('A bottle of wine ye *shall not* have'); the scroungers turn nasty and say they will send for the magistrates, the policemen, the redcoat men; the other side retort 'What care we?' to every threat, and then ask, puzzled, 'What kind of men are ye at all?' The scroungers (or marauders) turn out to be Prince Charlie's men; the owners of the wine, King George's. They agree to have a battle:

> Yes, we're for a battle of it,
>   A battle of it, a battle of it,
> Yes, we're for a battle of it,
>   My Theerie and my Thorie.

Refrains such as the above are usually found in Scottish and North Country versions, and may indicate the older form of the game-song. By the time Newell found the game in Plymouth, Massachusetts, 1883, and Babcock reported it from Washington DC (*Lippincott's Magazine*, xxxvii, 1886), the refrain had become corrupted to 'My fairy and my fory . . . Within the golden story' and 'Miss Oorie and Miss Aurie'. English refrains are scarcer, though the haunting 'E I-over' (or 'He I over', or 'E I V over') has been heard in various places in England.

The common English form of the game is that given in the text. Occasionally the song begins with the rational statement 'We are coming to take your land, We are the rovers' (Ellesmere, Shropshire, c.1875; Southport, 1898); and occasionally it lapses into nursery comedy—'We will fetch our big bull-dogs . . . our big tom-cats . . . our big strong axe . . . our big sharp swords' (Dean Street Orphanage, Southport, 1898).

In the years leading up to the First World War, when the children were ready for a fight they shouted 'Present! Shoot! Bang! Fire!' (first noticed at Bath, and Maxey, Northants, *Traditional Games*, ii, 1898); and they enacted the progress of the fight with gruesome exactitude (e.g. at Taunton, c.1906):

> Now we've only got one leg, We are the Romans,
> Now we've only got one leg, We are the Roman soldiers.
>
> Now we've only got one arm . . .
>
> Now we've only got one eye . . .
>
> Now we all must drop down dead . . .

finishing, fairy-tale fashion,

> Now we're all made well again.

After the war A. S. Macmillan was sent 'new and up-to-date versions' of the game by some of his child correspondents in the West Country ('Will you have a glass of wine . . . For we are the German soldiers', 'We won't have your glass of wine . . . For we are the English soldiers', 'Will you have a piece of cake?', 'We won't have a piece of cake') and in one, when the English have refused the wine, the Germans say 'We will tell the Kaiser of you'.

Children's sense of history, however, is usually vague. One king seeming much like another, the opposing sides in Scottish, Irish, and American versions of the game have owed allegiance to King George and King William (New Pitsligo, c.1860; Plymouth, Mass., 1883; Kirkcudbright, 1898; Banffshire, c.1910), or Prince Charlie and King George (Perthshire, 1898), or King William and King James (*Games of Argyleshire*, 1901, pp. 205–6; *80 Singing Games*, F. Kidson, 1907, p. 13 n., 'many places in Ireland'). Kings William and James, if the earliest of the royal antagonists, may have figured in the 'up-to-date version' of the song when William III was fighting James II in Ireland in 1690; for there is no knowing how old the game may be, and other versions admit no kings at all, the fighting men being 'gallant soldiers', 'guardian soldiers', 'robbers' or 'rovers'.

The best-known version (because promulgated by Cecil Sharp) is that
of 'Romans and English' and it is this version which has attracted most
interpretations. Cecil Sharp himself, in whose Somerset collectings the
plaintiffs say they will tell the King and the Pope, believed it to represent a
case of excommunication. The general feeling now is that it is a struggle
between the Roman Catholic and Protestant churches, the 'bread and
wine' being highly significant. ('I was taught the game in a Kensington
kindergarten,' wrote a clergyman correspondent in 1959, 'and it was not
till about thirty years later that I realized its theological meaning. I think
they were guilty of outrageously bad taste.') But, quite apart from the fact
that Romans and English are not the earliest known contestants, bread and
wine were everyday fare (wine well into the nineteenth century) and are by
no means to be confined to the bread and wine of the sacrament.

The structure of the game is that of the old German stepping dance,
with two lines of dancers advancing and retreating, and, like 'Three
Brethren out of Spain' and 'A Duke a-Riding' (pp. 92, 76), 'Romans and
English' has retained the circling with which the stepping dance properly
ends. When the fight is over, the fighters join hands and dance round
singing, as in Workington, 1962, 'Buckle on your sword and away we go',
or, as in Somerset, c.1912, 'Then we'll join in a merry ring', or, as in
Hartley Witney, c.1898 (*Traditional Games*, ii, p. 347), 'Then let us join our
happy ring'. Other marks of antiquity are the lack of rhyme, and the
meaningless caudal refrain in the older versions.

Scotland and North Country: Arbroath, c.1837, 'King George's loyal men' and refrain 'Cam a
teerie, arrie ma torry' (*Arbroath: Past and Present*, J. M. McBain, 1887, pp. 342–3) | New Pitsligo,
c.1860, refrain 'My theerie and my thorie' (*Buchan Observer*, 16 April 1929) | *Traditional Games*,
ii, 1898, pp. 350–6, Perthshire, three versions; Northumberland; Kirkcudbright, two versions, in
the second 'robbers' fight 'gallant soldiers' | *Games of Argyleshire*, 1901, pp. 205–6; another
version, p. 225, has refrain 'My Three and my Thory . . . Within our golden sory [*sic*]' (cf.
Plymouth, Mass., 1883) and King George's men produce the trump card 'King William's dead
and in his grave, King George is alive and on his throne. Are ye ready for the battle?' | Lanark-
shire, c.1902, 'Shall we have one glass of wine? Matheery Aye Mathorie . . . Within my golden
story . . . Not one glass of wine you'll get' | Forfar, c.1910, 'We are all King James's men, We are
the Rovers, We are all King James's men, We are the gallant soldiers. We are all Queen Mary's
men . . . We shall have a battle then . . . At what hour does the battle begin? . . . Half past three the
battle begins'.
   England: Ellesmere, c.1875 (*Shropshire Folk-Lore*, 1883, p. 518) | Darrington, Wilts., c.1880,
'Give us bread and give us wine, We are the Romans . . . Roman soldiers,' 'We won't . . . We are
the English' | Heaton Norris, Cheshire, c.1889, 'Have you any bread and cheese? Hee, haw, the
rover! Will you give us cake and wine? Whether we're drunk or sober?' 'Take a pint and go your
way', and so on with a quart, a gallon, etc. | Wrecclesham, Surrey, 1892, Romans and English.
Magistrates, noble lords, Prince, and King, are sent for in vain | Southport, Lancs., 1898
(Gilchrist MSS, 231 Aiii, p. 33) | *Traditional Games*, ii, pp. 343–56, 10 versions | *Children's
Singing Games*, Cecil Sharp, iv, pp. 8–9 | Leeds, 1920s, 'Here we are on the battle field, Ee eye
over . . . We are the English soldiers.' English ask Russian soldiers for 'Half your wine and half
your bread', and when refused say they 'will set our dogs on you', then cats | Leicester, c.1930,
'Are you ready for a fight? Ee i over . . . For we're the Roman soldiers . . . English soldiers', ending

'Now we all lie down and die, Now we're all alive again' | Shrewsbury, 1952, 'Have you any bread and wine?' Roman and English soldiers | Alton, Hants, 1954, 'Will you have a pint of ale? ... Romans ... British soldiers', 'A pint of ale won't serve us all.' The British finally accept a barrel, but fight the Romans all the same in individual tugs of war | Claverley, Staffs, 1961, 'Can we 'ave a glass of wine, Glass of wine, glass of wine, Can we 'ave a glass of wine, We're the English soldiers?' 'No, we've got no glass of wine ... We're the Roman soldiers', 'Can we 'ave a sip?' 'No ...' ending with 'Shoot! Bang! Fire!', lost limbs, and 'Now we get down in our graves, Now we're up and alive again' | London SE17, 1981, like St John's Wood, 1973.

Ireland: Dublin, c. 1890, 'We are ready for to fight, We are the rovers; We are all brave Parnell's men, We are his gallant soldiers', sung by Catholic boys (*I Knock at the Door*, Sean O'Casey, 1939, p. 115) | Dublin, 1975, 'Will you have a glass of wine? ... We're the Irish soldiers,' 'No ... We're the Roman soldiers,' 'Will you have a slice of cake? ...' ending with 'Shoot! Bang! Fire!' and lost limbs.

USA: Plymouth, Mass., 1883 (*Games of American Children*, pp. 248–9) | St Louis, 1895 (*JAFL*, lx, pp. 25–6) | Cincinnati, 1908 (*JAFL*, xl, p. 40) | *North Carolina Folklore*, p. 43.

XII

Mimicry

IN the following games the players have the opportunity to depict with summary actions a succession of occupations or states of life. 'The juvenile lyrical drama, of the most ancient Thespian model, wherein the trades of mankind are successively simulated to the running burthen "On a cold and frosty morning",' observed Robert Louis Stevenson, 'gives a good instance of the artistic taste in children.'

Stevenson was quick to warn, however, that we should not delude ourselves the children were being creative in their pretences. The activities they mimic, or people they characterize, under the guidance of tradition, are painfully humdrum; yet if we find their subjects crude and their value-judgements depressing, we have only ourselves to blame. What we are seeing is ourselves through their eyes. Indeed the chief interest in these games may be thought to be the changes that have taken place in the subjects of the mimicry. A century ago the chores of the household, the sorrows of marriage (husbands were usually depicted as drunkards), and the workings of various industries, brewing, baking, tailoring, and farming, were the basis of their song. Today, although romance still fades with the marriage bed, the wash-tub and scrubbing brush are forgotten, and the gainful occupation most often portrayed seems to be that of stripper.

66

The Mulberry Bush

Tune: 'Nuts in May'

Here we go round the mulberry bush,
The mulberry bush, the mulberry bush;
Here we go round the mulberry bush,
On a cold and frosty morning.

This is the way we wash our clothes,
Wash our clothes, wash our clothes;
This is the way we wash our clothes,
  On a cold and frosty morning.

Here we go round the mulberry bush,
The mulberry bush, the mulberry bush;
Here we go round the mulberry bush,
  On a cold and frosty morning.

This is the way we iron our clothes,
Iron our clothes, iron our clothes;
This is the way we iron our clothes,
  On a cold and frosty morning.

Here we go round the mulberry bush,
The mulberry bush, the mulberry bush;
Here we go round the mulberry bush,
  On a cold and frosty morning.

This is the way we scrub the floors,
Scrub the floors, scrub the floors;
This is the way we scrub the floors,
  On a cold and frosty morning.

Here we go round the mulberry bush,
The mulberry bush, the mulberry bush;
Here we go round the mulberry bush,
  On a cold and frosty morning.

This renowned game, which Alice found herself taking part in when she tried to shake hands with Tweedledum and Tweedledee simultaneously, is carried out in the manner of a medieval *carole*, the circle of performers dancing round holding hands while they sing the refrain; and standing still, releasing hands, and imitating the action suggested, when they sing the narrative stanza.

The song's orderly exposition of domestic skills was a gift to educationalists wanting to instil the virtues of personal hygiene. In Glasgow Infant Schools, it was said in 1834, 'the utmost attention is paid to cleanliness. The Teachers regularly inspect the children every morning, while chaunting':

This is the way we wash our hands,
We wash our hands, we wash our hands,
This is the way we wash our hands,
To come to school in the morning.

> This is the way we wash our face, &c.
> To come to school in the morning.
>
> This is the way we comb our hair, &c.
> To come to school in the morning.
>
> This is the way we brush our clothes, &c.
> To come to school in the morning.
>
> This is the way we show our hands, &c.
> Whether they are clean or dirty.
>
> It is a shame to come to school, &c.
> With dirty hands or faces.
>
> Clean children like to come to school, &c.
> But not with dirty faces.
>
> (*Glasgow Infant School Magazine*, 2nd edn., p. 130)

Nevertheless it must be admitted the domestic activities normally featured were scarcely mind-stirring. For instance in Edinburgh in 1821, 'This is the way the ladies bake'. In Kilbarchan in 1842, 'She bakes the scones three times a day, three times a day, three times a day'. In England in 1849, 'This is the way we clean our rooms, clean our rooms, clean our rooms'. And commonly in the United States in the nineteenth century, as also in Canada and New Zealand, seven stanzas were sung describing the duties of the week:

> This is the way we wash our clothes,
> Wash our clothes, wash our clothes,
> This is the way we wash our clothes,
> So early Monday morning.
>
> This is the way we iron our clothes . . .
> So early Tuesday morning.
>
> This is the way we mend our clothes . . .
> So early Wednesday morning . . .

But why children should claim to dance round a *mulberry bush* (ordinarily a mulberry is a tree not a bush), and for how long they have been doing so, is obscure. Thomas Hardy (born Bockhampton, 1840) knew the game as 'All around the gooseberry bush'; T. S. Eliot (born St Louis, 1888) seems to have known it as 'Here we go round the prickly pear' ('This is the way the world ends Not with a bang but a whimper'); and in *Pleasant Evenings; or, Fireside Amusements*, published 1847, the refrain went:

> Nettles grow on an angry bush,
> An angry bush, an angry bush,
> Nettles grow on an angry bush,
> So early in the morning.

The connection, if any, between this verse and one of the 'bagatelles for juvenile amusement' published in the second volume of James Hook's *Christmas Box*, 1798, will probably now never be known:

> The gooseberry grows on an angry Tree,
> About ye Maids and about ye Maids.
> Others are merry as well as we,
> Then about ye merry Maids all.
>
> Some are sad and some are glad,
> Thorns flourish not on every Tree.
> Then about ye Maids, about ye Maids,
> About ye merry Maids all.

The tree or bush has also been recorded as a 'bramble bush' (1849), 'barberry bush' (Massachusetts, 1882; Missouri, c.1900), 'holly bush' (Nottinghamshire, 1894), and 'ivy bush' or 'ivory bush' (Norfolk, 1894); yet if the word of Mrs Valentine (born Laura Belinda Jewry, 1814) can be accepted, mulberry bushes were what children said they danced round when she was young, and long before, although her assertion that the round had been 'danced by little English children since the days when mulberry bushes were common in every village' need not be taken too literally. Only an adult nurtured in unimaginativeness could feel it necessary (as do the writers of the manuals) to have one child standing in the middle of the ring, to be made to look foolish with nothing to do but pretend to be a bush. Chesterton, of course, was *Manalive* enough to know that no centrepiece was required:

'And now,' cried Moon quite suddenly, stretching out a hand on each side, 'let's dance round that bush!'

'Why, what bush do you mean?' asked Rosamund, looking round with a sort of radiant rudeness.

'The bush that isn't there,' said Michael—'the Mulberry Bush.'

However the custom or fancy of dancing round particular trees, which has been depicted by artists from the fifteenth century onwards, is too deep-rooted in Western Europe to be ignored, as also its extension the maypole or 'summer tree', whose surmounting garland was sometimes known as 'the bush'. In Sir John Davies's *Poeme of Dancing*, 1596 (verse 64), the tutor is Love:

> He taught them rounds and winding Heyes to tread,
> And about trees to cast themselves in rings.

And such circling of trees is on record as having romantic significance. At Polwarth in Berwickshire, according to *The New Statistical Account of*

'HERE WE GO ROUND THE MULBERRY BUSH'?

Top left: Prehistoric people circling a tree; a pottery group found in Cyprus.

Top right: Peasants dancing round a living maypole, from the fifteenth-century *Heures de Charles d'Angoulême*.

Left: late seventeenth-century country folk dance round a tree, in whose branches the piper sits. *La Dance de Village*, G. Landry.

Scotland, ii, 1845, pp. 233–4, two thorn trees used to stand near each other in the midst of the village, and 'round these every newly married pair were expected to dance with all their friends; from hence arose the old song of "Polwarth on the Green" '. (The song is in *Orpheus Caledonius*, 1726.) A verse from Symondsbury in Dorset, recorded in *Folk-Lore*, vii, 1889, p. 211, may be apposite, although no confirmation of it has been found elsewhere:

> All round the mulberry bush,
>   Maidens all together,
> Give a kiss and take a kiss,
>   And curtsy all together.

For further ceremonial encirclement of trees see *Folk-Lore*, xxiii, 1912, bottom of p. 203. It must be remarked, however, that when children in the past played 'As we go round the mulberry bush' or 'Nettles grow in an angry bush' they used to turn round at the end of each verse, and might also clap hands or make a curtsy; and that this turning round also occurs in the Spanish version of the game, 'San Severín del Monte', as played in Montevideo.

'Here We Go Round the Mulberry Bush' undoubtedly owes much of its popularity to its tune, shared with 'Nuts in May', which became well known in the eighteenth century under the name 'Nancy Dawson'. It was published in *The Universal Magazine*, October 1760, p. 208. The same tune was used for 'Merry-ma-tansie' (p. 150) which in Scotland in the early days of the nineteenth century was sometimes played in precisely the same way, the girls, according to one of Jamieson's informants in 1825, dancing round in a circle, singing as they did so. 'In the progress of the play, they by the motion of their heads imitate the whole process of the laundry, in washing, starching, drying and ironing.' The tune 'Nettles Grow On an Angry Bush', given in 1847, was also recognizably 'Nancy Dawson'.

An ingenious joke-history for the 'Mulberry Bush' was going the rounds in 1978. The knights who were intent on killing Thomas à Becket first hung their swords on a mulberry tree, still, of course, extant. They scalped the Saint, singing 'This is the way we do our hair'. They washed their hands afterwards to get rid of the guilt, and said their prayers round the body.

Britain: *Blackwood's Edinburgh Magazine*, x, 1821, p. 37, mentioned as sung to the tune 'Nancy Dawson' | *Popular Rhymes of Scotland*, 1842, p. 65, two versions | *Pleasant Evenings; or, Fireside Amusements*, 1847, pp. 25–6, as quote, with tune | *Popular Rhymes*, J. O. Halliwell, 1849, pp. 126–7 and 130–1, three versions including 'Nettles grow in an angry bush, With my High, Ho, Ham! This is the way the lady goes, With my High, Ho, Ham!' | *Old Nurse's Book*, C. H. Bennett,

1858, p. 16 | *Nursery Carols*, 1862, p. 110, 'All around the mulberry bush, We dance around, we dance around' | *Home Book of Pleasure and Instruction*, R. Valentine, 1867, pp. 4–5 | Bury, Lancs, *c.*1875, and Reddish, *c.*1880, 'Nettles grow in an angry bush . . . To my one, two, three' (Crofton MS, i, p. 176) | Frequently recorded thereafter. Played today in infants' schools and by Brownies, but also when children are on their own, e.g. at Ashbourne, Derbyshire, 1977, where the sequence was 'This is how we get out of bed . . . clean our teeth . . . have our breakfast . . . get dressed . . . clean our shoes . . . put on our shoes . . . put on our coat . . . wave goodbye . . . get to school'. A 7-year-old said 'The more trouble you take getting ready for school, the more times you are allowed to go round the mulberry bush' | Cf. *London Street Games*, 1916, p. 65, 'We are washing linen, linen, We are washing linen clean. This way, tra la la, That way, tra la la, We are rinsing linen,' etc. (undoubtedly derived from the Swedish singing game 'Washing the Clothes', translated into English in Elizabeth Burchenal's *Folk Dances and Singing Games*, New York, 1909, pp. 10–11).

New Zealand: 'The most widespread of the pantomime games' (Sutton-Smith, p. 19).

USA: *The Exercise Song Book* (Boston), 1858, p. 15 (Fuld) | New York (?) and Massachusetts, 1883, 'As we go round the mulberry bush' (*Games of American Children*, pp. 86–7) | Washington DC, 1886 (*Lippincott's Magazine*, xxxviii, pp. 331–2) | St Louis, 1895 (*JAFL*, lx, p. 17) | *Games for the Playground*, J. H. Bancroft, 1909, pp. 283–5, 'one of the oldest of traditional games, and probably one of the most widely known' | Frequently thereafter | Cf. Cincinnati, 1908, 'This is the way we eat our breakfast, So early in the morning. John, John, I'll tell your daddy, So early in the morning' (*JAFL*, xl, pp. 16–17) | Louisiana, 1883, 'Do, do, pity my case, In some lady's garden; My clothes to wash when I get home, In some lady's garden.' Followed by 'my clothes to iron', etc. (*Games of American Children*, p. 87) | *North Carolina Folklore*, p. 86, from *c.*1927 | Popular song: 'Stop Beatin' 'Round the Mulberry Bush', Bickley Reichner, 1938.

Canada: Ontario, *c.*1900 and *c.*1910 (*JAFL*, xxxi, pp. 54 and 178–9) | Port Perry, 1940s (Fowke, 1969, p. 16).

Germany: Krombach, 1952, 'Zeigt mal eure Füsse, Zeigt mal eure Schuh, Und sehet den fleissigen Waschfrauen zu. Sie waschen, sie waschen den ganzen Tag.' ('Show your feet, Show your shoes, Look at the busy washerwomen. They wash, they wash the livelong day.') They subsequently hang out the clothes, iron, fold, rest, and dance the livelong day, singing the first three lines between each action).

Denmark: *Danmarks Sanglege*, S. Tvermose Thyregod, 1931, no. 102, pp. 258–60, 'Saa gaar vi rundt om en Enebaerbusk, Enebaerbusk, Enebaerbusk, Saa gaar vi rundt om en Enebaerbusk tidligt Mandag Morgen' (So we go round a juniper bush . . . Early Monday morning).

67

Days of the Week

Tune: 'Nuts in May'

Monday: I went to visit a friend one day,
            She only lived across the way;
            She said she couldn't go out to play,
            Because it was her washing day.

            This is the way she washed away,
            This is the way she washed away,
            This is the way she washed away,
            The day she couldn't go out to play.

Tuesday: I went to visit a friend one day,
She only lived across the way;
She said she couldn't go out to play,
Because it was her ironing day.

This is the way she ironed away,
This is the way she ironed away,
This is the way she ironed away,
The day she couldn't go out to play.

Wednesday: I went to visit a friend one day,
She only lived across the way,
She said she couldn't go out to play,
Because it was her mending day.

This is the way she stitched away,
This is the way she stitched away,
This is the way she stitched away,
The day she couldn't go out to play.

Thursday: I went to visit a friend one day,
She only lived across the way,
She said she couldn't go out to play,
Because it was her baking day.

This is the way she kneaded away,
This is the way she kneaded away,
This is the way she kneaded away,
The day she couldn't go out to play.

Friday: I went to visit a friend one day,
She only lived across the way,
She said she couldn't go out to play,
Because it was her cleaning day.

This is the way she scrubbed away,
This is the way she scrubbed away,
This is the way she scrubbed away,
The day she couldn't go out to play.

Saturday: I went to visit a friend one day,
She only lived across the way,
She said she could go out to play
Because it was her playing day.

This is the way we play away,
This is the way we play away,
This is the way we play away,
The day she could go out to play.

The children danced round in a circle, sometimes in couples, with one player in the middle as leader. When they sang 'This is the way she . . .' they stood still, and pretended to 'wash away', or 'iron away', or 'stitch away', or whatever was the activity of the day. The game is clearly related to 'The Mulberry Bush' (p. 286); but it is uncertain whether it is an offshoot, or whether it blossomed independently, cross-fertilizing 'The Mulberry Bush' to produce the nineteenth-century hybrid:

This is the way we wash our clothes,
   Wash our clothes, wash our clothes,
This is the way we wash our clothes,
   So early Monday morning.

West Country, 1922, as text (Macmillan Collection) | *North Carolina Folklore*, p. 86, probably referring to 1920s | *Dae Ye Min' Langsyne?* A. S. Fraser, 1975, p. 20, learnt years before in Airdrie from an elderly minister.

68

When I Was a Lady

Dumfries, 1960

When I was a lady, a lady, a lady,
When I was a lady, a lady was I.
'Twas this way and that way, and this way and that way,
When I was a lady, a lady was I.

When I was a gentleman, a gentleman, a gentleman,
When I was a gentleman, a gentleman was I.
'Twas this way and that way, and this way and that way,
When I was a gentleman, a gentleman was I.

When I was a baker, a baker, a baker,
When I was a baker, a baker was I.
'Twas this way and that way, and this way and that way,
When I was a baker, a baker was I.

When I was a teacher, a teacher, a teacher,
When I was a teacher, a teacher was I.
'Twas this way and that way, and this way and that way,
When I was a teacher, a teacher was I.

The players amble round in a circle singing, and each time they come to
' 'Twas this way and that way', they stop going round, face inwards and do
the action felt appropriate to the type of person named. They pretend to
powder their faces, to shave, to roll dough with a rolling pin, and, as a
twelve-year-old put it, to 'do the action of a teacher belting a pupil'. An
Aberdonian lady, recalling the fun they had playing this game at the
beginning of the century, says:

We all minced round in what we imagined was true ladylike fashion, holding up
our 'tails', as we saw our mothers doing with their long skirts on a wet day, and
singing:

> When I was a lady, a lady, a lady,
> When I was a lady, oh then, oh then, oh then,
> It was ee-o this way, this way, this way,
> It was ee-o this way, oh then, oh then, oh then.

Next came 'When I was a gentleman', and we smiled and doffed our hats to
imaginary ladies; 'When I had a baby', we rocked our babies to and fro in our arms;
and 'When I was a schoolmaster':

> It was ee-o scud the kids, scud the kids, scud the kids.

We suited the action to the words with great gusto.

A. S. Macmillan, in the 1920s, found a number of children playing the
game in the West Country. At Yarcombe in Devonshire they sang 'When I
was a schoolgirl 'twas this way I went', followed by 'When I was a
milkmaid', dressmaker, nurse, laundress, soldier, sailor, and dairymaid.
At Combses in south Somerset they professed to have been a teacher,
washerwoman, fish woman, soldier, sailor, butcher, baker, and beggar.

After they had sung 'When I was a butcher', they bowed to the player next to them and said:

'Any pork today, ma'am?'

'Any mutton today, ma'am?'

'Any beef today, ma'am?'

After they had sung 'When I was a baker', they bowed and asked:

'Any bread today, ma'am?'

'Any cakes today, ma'am?'

'Any flour today, ma'am?'

When they pretended to be fish women, they put their hands on their heads and cried out 'Bloaters' or 'Mackerel'. And Newell shows that the game was played little differently in America a century ago. In the streets of New York children sang:

> When I was a gentleman, and a gentleman was I,
> A this a way, and a this a way, and a this a way went I.

'The gentleman', Newell observed, 'places his hands in his waistcoat pockets, and promenades up and down; the lady gathers her skirts haughtily together; the fireman makes a sound in imitation of the horns which firemen formerly blew; the shoemaker and hairdresser are represented by appropriate motions, etc.'

Britain: *Merrie Games in Rhyme*, E. M. Plunket, 1886, p. 47 | Staffordshire, 1896, 'When I was a housemaid, a housemaid was I, An' o' thisnin', an' o' thatnin', an' o' thisnin' went I' (EDD 'Athisning') | *Traditional Games*, ii, 1898, pp. 362–74 passim, versions from Staffordshire 'When I wore my flounces', Wiltshire 'When I was a lady', and Berkshire 'Oh! when I was a soldier' | *Games of Argyleshire*, 1901, pp. 139–40 | Uist, 1905 (*Folk-Lore*, xvi, p. 343) | *Children's Singing Games*, Cecil Sharp, ii, 1909, pp. 10–11, 'O when I was a schoolgirl' | Aberdeen, c.1910 | Macmillan Collection, 1922 | Swansea, 1952 | Golspie, 1953 | Dumfries, 1960 | Cumnock, 1961, as text | *Cub Scout Songs*, B. J. Sims, 1972, p. 33, 'When I was a tailor' | *All In! All In!*, Eilís Brady, 1975, pp. 126–7, from Dublin, 'When I was a washerwoman'.

New Zealand: Dunedin, 1890s (Sutton-Smith, p. 19).

USA: New York, 1883, 'When I was a shoemaker'. 'Inquiry has shown us the song is old in America' (*Games of American Children*, p. 88) | Washington DC, 1888 (*American Anthropologist*, i, p. 264) | Buncombe County, c.1927 (*North Carolina Folklore*, p. 86).

Flanders: *Chant Populaires des Flamands de France*, C. E. Coussemaker, 1856, pp. 342–3, 'Langst een groen meuletje Kwam ik getreden' (I happened to pass by a little green mill, There we saw two gentlemen, Yes, gentlemen, Who were going our way, And they went thus, This was their manner). In succeeding verses they imitate farmers, nuns and monks.

France: *Chants du Languedoc*, L. Lambert, 1906, pp. 307–8, 'Sur le pont d'Avignon, Tout le monde y danse, y danse; Sur le pont d'Avignon, Tout le monde y danse en rond. Les messieurs font comm' ceci, Les messieurs font comm' cela, Les messieurs y passent.' The children make ladies, cripples, hunchbacks, shoemakers, etc., pass over the bridge of Avignon in succession, making comic gestures to imitate them. After each imitation, they circle round singing 'Sur le pont d'Avignon'.

Germany: *Deutsches Kinderspiel*, F. M. Böhme, 1897, p. 497, no. 241, 'Zwischen Köln und Paris, Wo die neue Mode ist, So, machen die Herren! . . . So machen die Damen . . . So machen die Schuster . . . So machen die Schneider . . . So machen die Frauen . . . So machen sie Alle!'

(Between Cologne and Paris, Where the new fashion is, Thus, go the gentlemen . . . the ladies . . . the cobblers . . . the tailors . . . the wives . . . Thus, go they all!).

Holland: *Kinderspel in Zuid-Nederland*, A. de Cock and I. Teirlinck, ii, 1903, pp. 183–4, 'Op den berg van Gilia' ('On the mountain of Gilia, There were so many gentlemen, And all the gentlemen went walking, Thus go the gentlemen.' Thereafter, on the mountain, are seen and imitated stampers, dancers, seamstresses, stoppers, priests, and nuns. The gentlemen swagger, the stampers stamp, the seamstresses—who are given two verses—sew and then put their thimbles in their mouths as stoppers, the priests kneel and the nuns make the sign of the cross).

Italy: *Giuochi Popolari Veneziani*, G. Bernoni, 1874, pp. 39–40, 'Abasso le Muneghete' (Get down, milkmaids). A variety of people go down on their knees in penitence, first milkmaids, then tailors, cooks, milliners, and so on | Anghiari, Tuscany, 1961, 'Maestro Ciliegia insegnava alle sue scuolare, Bambine mie care facciam cosà cosà. Le monachelle passano, Ros'e Rosella, Le monachelle passano, Ros'e Rosa' (Mr Cherry, you were teaching your pupils, including my dear ones, to go like this and like that. The nuns go by, Rose Rosella, The nuns go by, Rose Rosa). The children make the nuns go by, praying, and in succeeding verses aeroplanes go by with spread wings, washerwomen go by scrubbing on their knees, and trumpeters trumpet.

Sardinia (Sassari), 1965, from schoolchild: 'Sul campo di viole i campanari passano'; the bell-ringers are followed, on the field of violets, by carpenters, ladies, washerwomen, etc. (*Conte cantilene e filastrocche*, M. M. Lumbroso, p. 13).

Portugal: Lisbon, 1960, 'Bóia, bóia, binha, Faz assim assim assim, Ora agora lavadeira Faz assim assim assim' (Two little floating corks, Go like this, like this, like this, Look now at the washerwoman She goes like this, like this, like this). The children walk round imitating the various people mentioned: the dressmaker, the woman ironing, the student, the teacher.

Spain: *Cancionero Infantil Español*, S. Córdova y Oña, 1947, p. 291, 'San Selerín, de la buena buena vida, San Selerín, de la buena buena vi: así, así hacen las costureras; así, así. San Selerín, a la buena buena vi; así, así hacen las costureras; así, así, así me gusta a mí.' After the seamstresses, they imitate shoemakers, washerwomen, ironing-women, carpenters, clerks, bakers, smiths, little old men and little nuns.

Uruguay: *Rique Ran*, M. L. Goodwin and E. L. Powell, 1951, p. 11. In Uruguay, but not in Spain, they ask San Severín of the Mountain what trade he wishes them to learn: 'San Severín del Monte, San Severín cortés, dime tú que officio quieres aprender. Hacen así, así las lavanderas.' The circle of children kneel and pretend to wash clothes 'the way the laundress does it'. Thereafter they sew 'the way the seamstress does it', grind corn 'the way the miller does it', and so on.

The tune of the British game is said to be that of a Spanish dance, the Guaracha, as are that of 'Isabella' and 'Jack-a-needle' (*Journal of EFDSS*, 1946, p. 19).

69

Did You Ever See a Lassie?

Tune: 'O du lieber Augustin'

Did you ever see a lassie, a lassie, a lassie,
Did you ever see a lassie who acted like this?
This way and that way, this way and that way,
Did you ever see a lassie who acted like this.

This is the troop-leader and teacher-taught version of 'When I Was a Lady' (p. 294), an amusement that has not always met with adult approval.

As recommended at the beginning of the century 'Did You Ever See a Lassie?' was said to be 'the source of some very good exercise':

All of the players but one form a circle, clasping hands. They circle around, singing the first two lines of the verse. While they are doing this, the odd player stands in the center and illustrates some movement which he chooses for the others to imitate. During the last two lines of the verse the players stand in place, drop hands, and imitate the movements of the center player, which he continues in unison with them . . . The player may imitate any activity, such as mowing grass, raking hay, prancing like a horse, or turning a hand organ.

The game appeared in Marion Bromley Newton's *Graded Games and Rhythmic Exercises for Primary Schools*, published New York, 1908; in Jessie H. Bancroft's *Games for the Playground, Home, School, and Gymnasium*, New York, 1909; in the officially sponsored *Social Plays, Games, Marches, Old Folk Dances, and Rhythmic Movements for Use in Indian Schools*, printed in Washington DC, 1911; in Mrs Florence Kirk's *Rhythmic Games and Dances for Children*, produced in London in 1914; and in many another volume up to, and possibly after, Mary Chater's *A Baker's Dozen: Thirteen Singing Games for Brownies*, produced for the Girl Guides Association in 1947. It has however only rarely been found played by children on their own, though one group of seven-year-olds was enthusiastic about it, having added the embellishment that the leader twirled round after she had set the action, and the person pointed at when she stopped took her place. Fuld states that the tune 'O du lieber Augustin' was in print in 1788–9.

USA: Oklahoma, 1926–7, six recordings as a singing game (*American Play-Party Song*, B. A. Botkin, p. 28 n.) | St Louis, 1944, 'now a favorite kindergarten and elementary school game' (*JAFL*, lx, p. 34). The recollection of the game being played in the nineteenth century has not been confirmed.

Britain: Near-identical versions from four places since 1950.

70
The Peasant

Would you know how does the peasant,
Would you know how does the peasant,
Would you know how does the peasant
Sow his barley and wheat?

Look, 'tis so, so, does the peasant,
Look, 'tis so, so, does the peasant,
Look, 'tis so, so, does the peasant
Sow his barley and wheat.

Would you know how does the peasant,
Would you know how does the peasant,
Would you know how does the peasant
Reap his barley and wheat?

Look, 'tis so, so, does the peasant,
Look, 'tis so, so, does the peasant,
Look, 'tis so, so, does the peasant
Reap his barley and wheat.

Would you know how does the peasant,
Would you know how does the peasant,
Would you know how does the peasant
Thresh his barley and wheat?

Look, 'tis so, so, does the peasant,
Look, 'tis so, so, does the peasant,
Look, 'tis so, so, does the peasant
Thresh his barley and wheat.

Would you know how does the peasant,
Would you know how does the peasant,
Would you know how does the peasant
Sift his barley and wheat?

Look, 'tis so, so, does the peasant,
Look, 'tis so, so, does the peasant,
Look, 'tis so, so, does the peasant
Sift his barley and wheat.

Would you know how rests the peasant,
Would you know how rests the peasant,
Would you know how rests the peasant
When his labour is done?

Look, 'tis so, so, rests the peasant,
Look, 'tis so, so, rests the peasant,
Look, 'tis so, so, rests the peasant
When his labour is done.

Would you know how plays the peasant,
Would you know how plays the peasant,
Would you know how plays the peasant
When his labour is done?

Look, 'tis so, so, plays the peasant,
Look, 'tis so, so, plays the peasant,
Look, 'tis so, so, plays the peasant
When his labour is done.

This game was widely propagated in Britain in the second half of the nineteenth century. The children walked round in a circle holding hands while they sang the first verse; stopped, let go hands, and pretended to scatter seed from their pinafores or an imaginary basket while they sang the second verse; resumed going round while they sang the third verse; pretended to reap while they sang the fourth verse; and so continued, alternately walking round and miming the actions suggested, while they sang the rest of the verses. Sometimes they sang of a farmer instead of a peasant (the word *peasant* is unfamiliar to children except in 'Good King Wenceslas'); and during the last verse they either clapped hands or danced and jumped about. Alice Gomme felt the game was a survival of ancient ritual; and was much impressed by the information that in Lancashire as many as a hundred children might take part in it at once. 'The fact that this game was played by such a large number of young people together, points conclusively,' she wrote, 'to a time when it was a customary thing for all the people in one village to play this game as a kind of religious observance, to bring blessing on the work of the season, believing that by doing so, they caused the crops to grow better and produce grain in abundance.' In reality, as the words give warning, the game was an importation. It was brought to Britain by Johannes and Bertha Ronge, who printed it, with tune, as above, in their influential exposition of Froebel's system of infant training, *A Practical Guide to the English Kinder Garten*, 1855. The method of playing the game, which was said to have 'the tendency to awaken a love for usefulness and labour', was there minutely described, the text being as above with the addition of a refrain 'La, la, la, la, la, la', (which did not catch on) at the end of every second verse. The Ronges had adapted the song from the Continental game 'Der Bauer', which was popular at that time in their native land:

Wollt ihr wissen, wie der Bauer seinen Hafer aussät?
Seht so machts der Bauer, wenn er Hafer aussät.

Wollt ihr wissen, wie der Bauer seiner Hafer abmäht?
Seht so machts der Bauer, wenn er Hafer abmäht.

However the Ronges, as immigrant teachers in Tavistock Place, were wise enough not to be specific about the way the farmer or 'peasant' enjoyed himself when his toil was done.

Usually, in Germany, when he has sown his oats, and reaped them, he goes to a *Wirtshaus* for relaxation, and spends his hard-earned coppers on schnapps. The fun and point of the game comes, as with all good games, at the end, with the faithful imitation of the farmer's condition when he emerges from the inn:

Wollt ihr wissen, wie der Bauer aus dem Wirtshaus geht?
Seht so machts der Bauer, wenn aus dem Wirtshaus er geht.

Britain: *English Kinder Garten*, Joh. and Bertha Ronge, 1855 (1858, pp. 70–2) | *Home Book*, Mrs R. Valentine, 1867, p. 6, 'The Swiss Peasant' | *Merrie Games in Rhyme*, E. M. Plunket, 1886, p. 46 | *Traditional Games*, ii, 1898, pp. 399–401 | *Songs and Games for Little Ones*, E. R. Murray, 1902, p. 129 | *Folk-Lore*, xvi, 1905, p. 343, from Uist | *Joyous Book of Singing Games*, John Hornby, 1913, p. 3.

Germany: *Deutschen Volkslieder mit ihren Singweisen*, Ludwig Erk, ii, pt. 3, 1844, p. 17 | *Deutsches Kinderspiel*, F. M. Böhme, 1897, pp. 496–7, several versions.

Netherlands: *Kinderspel in Zuid-Nederland*, A. de Cock & I. Teirlinck, ii, 1903, pp. 189–94, 'Hoe zaait de boer zijn koreke, zijn koreke?'.

Hungary: *Hungarian Peasant Customs*, Károly Viski, 1937, pp. 155–6, adult mimic play current in Transylvania and Transdanubia, 'I'd like to know how Hungarians sow their oats . . . I'd like to know how Hungarians reap their oats . . .' ending, 'I'd like to know how the wife steals the oats . . . I'd like to know how the wife drinks its price'.

Cf. 'Oats and Beans and Barley Grow'.

71

Mary Was a Bad Girl

Tune: 'Nuts in May'

Mary was a bad girl, bad girl, a bad girl,
Mary was a bad girl, and this is what she said:
    I won't, I won't,
    I won't, I won't, I won't.

Mary was a good girl, good girl, a good girl,
Mary was a good girl, and this is what she said:
    I will, I will,
    I will, I will, I will.

Mary went to school, school, to school,
Mary went to school, and this is what she said:
   I write, I write,
   I write, I write, I write.

Mary left school, school, school,
Mary left school, and this is what she said:
   Hooray, hooray,
   Hooray, hooray, hooray.

Mary went a-courting, courting, a-courting,
Mary went a-courting, and this is what she said:
   A boy, a boy,
   A boy, a boy, a boy.

Mary got engaged, engaged, got engaged,
Mary got engaged, and this is what she said:
   A ring, a ring,
   A ring, a ring, a ring.

Mary got married, married, got married,
Mary got married, and this is what she said:
   A veil, a veil,
   A veil, a veil, a veil.

Mary had a baby, baby, a baby,
Mary had a baby, and this is what she said:
   Sh-ssh, sh-ssh,
   Sh-ssh, sh-ssh, sh-ssh.

Mary's baby died, died, died,
Mary's baby died, and this is what she said:
   A boo, a boo,
   A boo, hoo, hoo.

Mary's husband died, died, died,
Mary's husband died, and this is what she said:
   Hooray, hooray,
   Hooray, hooray, hooray.

Mary died herself, herself, herself,
Mary died herself, and this is what she said:
   A-down, a-down,
   A-down, a-down, a-down.

The players sing as they process round in a circle; and when they come to
the end of the first verse, shouting 'I won't, I won't', they turn their backs
and stamp their feet. In succeeding verses they nod their heads in
agreement, pretend to write, cheer when Mary leaves school, hug themselves when they go courting, and so on. They cheer again when Mary's
husband dies; and clearly this is traditional. In or before 1898 Alice
Gomme collected a version at Barnes beginning 'When I was a young girl'
in which the heroine also went to school; and thereafter became a teacher,
had a sweetheart, married, had a baby, lost her baby, took in washing, went
out scrubbing, and was beaten by her husband. The song ended:

> When my husband died, oh, died, oh, died,
> When my husband died, how happy was I.
> And this way and that way, and this way and that way,
>   And this way and that way, and this way went I.

'Each child walks round joyfully,' she observed, 'waving a handkerchief
and all calling out Hurrah! at the end.' Similarly at Crewkerne in the early
1920s when children came to the last verse and the husband died, A. S.
Macmillan reported, 'They laugh and shout "Hurrah!" and clap their
hands, which seems to me very sad and unbecoming'. Nonetheless they
were almost certainly maintaining the spirit of the original song. At
Belford, in the nineteenth century, as also at Golspie, the game was
recorded as beginning:

> When I was a lady, a lady, a lady,
> When I was a lady. Oh then, oh then, oh then!

One of Sam Cowell's songs, printed about 1857, began in much the same
manner:

> When I was a maid, O then! O then!
> When I was a maid, O then!
> As many bright stars as appear in the sky,
> So many lovers were caught by my eye;
> But I was a beauty then, O then!
> But I was a beauty then!

This song of a maid who married and quickly wished herself a widow
seems to have been modelled on an earlier piece. In fact the forebear of
Burl Ives's well-known 'When I was single, oh then, oh then' appears in
The Careless Bachelor's Garland, a northern songster, printed about 1775:

> When I was a Bachelor, O then, O then,
> I could smoke my pipe,
> And carouse all the night;
> The world it went rowling and bowling,
> And the world it went very well with me, O then.

In the succeeding verse, however, the hero ceased to be either a bachelor or without care:

> I marry'd a wife, O then, O then,
> I marry'd a wife, O then;
> I marry'd a wife, and she plagued my life,
> Oh! the world it went worser and worser,
> And the world it went very bad, &c.

Thereafter the wife was in labour, the wife and child died, the widower went to the graveside and, the song continued, 'the piper did play, and we danced all the way . . . the world it went very well'.

This devil-may-care attitude to life's responsibilities, characteristic of popular song in the eighteenth and nineteenth centuries, is also reflected today in the hand-clapping song 'When Susie Was a Baby' (p. 458) and the relationship of both games to 'When I Was a Lady' (p. 294) does not need emphasizing. The earliest record of children playing the present game is at Thornes, near Wakefield, in 1874, a recording (made by James Fowler, a Fellow of the Society of Antiquaries) notable for its good text and careful observation of the action of each verse:

> When I was a young gell, a young gell, a young gell,
> When I was a young gell, i' this a way went I.
> An' i' this a way, an' i' that a way,
> An' i' this a way went I.
>
> *(here each holds her dress coquettishly)*

> When I wanted a sweetheart, a sweetheart, a sweetheart,
> When I wanted a sweetheart, i' this a way went I.
> An' i' this a way, an' i' that a way,
> An' i' this a way went I.
>
> *(here each beckons with her finger)*

> When I went a-courting, a-courting, a-courting,
> When I went a-courting, i' this a way went I.
> An' i' this a way, an' i' that a way,
> An' i' this a way went I.
>
> *(here they take one another's arms)*

When I did get married, get married, get married,
When I did get married, i' this a way went I.
An' i' this a way, an' i' that a way,
An' i' this a way went I.

    (*here each holds her dress proudly*)

When I had a baby, a baby, a baby,
When I had a baby, i' this a way went I.
An' i' this a way, an' i' that a way,
An' i' this a way went I.

    (*here each folds and presses her apron to her bosom*)

When I went to church, to church, to church,
When I went to church, i' this a way went I.
An' i' this a way, an' i' that a way,
An' i' this a way went I.

    (*here 'we reckons to hold our frocks up' as if to kneel*)

My husband was a drunkard, a drunkard, a drunkard,
My husband was a drunkard, i' this a way went I.
An' i' this a way, an' i' that a way,
An' i' this a way went I.

    (*here they fist and beat one another*)

When I was a washerwoman, a washerwoman, a washerwoman,
When I was a washerwoman, i' this a way went I.
An' i' this a way, an' i' that a way,
An' i' this a way went I.

    (*here they make-believe to wash clothes with their. aprons*)

When I did peggy, did peggy, did peggy,
When I did peggy, i' this a way went I.
An' i' this a way, an' i' that a way,
An' i' this a way went I.

    (*here they revolve their bodies half round backwards and forwards to imitate
    'Peggying'*)

My baby fell sick, fell sick, fell sick,
My baby fell sick, an' i' this a way went I.
An' i' this a way, an' i' that a way,
An' i' this a way went I.

    (*here, holding up aprons to eyes, 'we reckons to cry'*)

My baby did die, did die, did die,
My baby did die, an' i' this a way went I.

An' i' this a way, an' i' that a way,
An i' this a way went I.

(*here 'we reckons to cry again'*)

My husband did die, did die, did die,
My husband did die, an' i' this a way went I.
An' i' this a way, an' i' that a way,
An' i' this a way went I.

(*here they shake their hands behind them as if to say, goodbye
and done for*)

Further, James Fowler makes clear the young girls playing this game were
not parading round in a circle when they sang but 'standing promis-
cuously'; and it seems likely that in Yorkshire in 1874 the game was not yet
the formal ring game it was to become (possibly under the influence of
'Here We Go Round the Mulberry Bush'), but in much the state of
development that 'When Susie Was a Baby' is today.

Britain: Thornes, Wakefield, 1874 (*Notes & Queries*, 5th ser., iii, p. 482) | *Nursery Rhymes and
Country Songs*, M. H. Mason, 1877, p. 42, version similar to Cowell's song | *Shropshire Folk-
Lore*, 1883, pp. 514–15, 'When I was a naughty girl' (pretends to tear clothes) ending 'Then my
age was a hundred and four, and a-this a-way went I' (hobbles along and finally falls down).
Another version starts 'First I was a school-maid, how happy was I', and ends 'And then my life
was ended, how sorry was I!' | Dorsetshire, 1889, 'When first we went to school' (*Folk-Lore
Journal*, vii, pp. 218–19) | Golspie, 1892, 'When I had a bustle, Oh! then, oh! then, oh! then . . .
When my bustle fell, Oh! then, oh! then, oh! then' (*Golspie*, E. W. B. Nicholson, 1897, pp. 164–
5) | Girton, Cambridgeshire, 1898 (*The Study of Man*, A. C. Haddon, pp. 339–40) | *Traditional
Games*, ii, 1898, pp. 363–74 | Exmouth, 1907 (*Notes & Queries*, 10th ser., viii, p. 206) | *Chil-
dren's Singing Games*, Cecil Sharp, set ii, 1909, pp. 12–13 | *Old Hampshire Singing Games*, A. E.
Gillington, 1909, pp. 20–1 | Edinburgh, *c.*1910, 'When my baby died . . . Guess where I rolled it
. . . Guess where I buried it . . . I buried it in the ashpan' (*Rymour Club*, i, pp. 81–2) | Wyld, near
Burnley, *c.*1910, 'My husband got drunk and this way went I'. Players fought their neighbours
| Somerset, 1922, 'Then I had a baby, 'Twas this way went I'. 'The little girls roll up their
pinafores and hold them in their arms to represent a baby' (Macmillan Collection) | Paisley and
Workington, 1961 | Bishop Auckland, 1961, and Birmingham, 1969, 'Sally is a naughty
girl' | Dudley, 1969, as text | Garforth, near Leeds, 1976 | Birmingham, 1977, Sally eats ice
cream (slurping noises in rhythm), watches telly ('Cor-cor-look at that!'), goes to her auntie
('Hello, hello, hello, hello, hello') etc.

Ireland: Dublin, 1970s, 'There was a girl in our school, And this is the way she went' (*All In! All
In!*, Eilís Brady, pp. 124–6).

USA: Cincinnati, 1908, 'As I was a baby, a baby was I' (*JAFL*, xl, p. 15).

Canada: Ontario, 1963, 'When I was a baby' (Fowke, 1969, p. 22).

72

I'm a Little Dutch Girl

Tune: 'Poor Jenny Is a-Weeping'; also sung to 'O du lieber Augustin'

Oh, I'm a little Dutch girl, a Dutch girl, a Dutch girl,
Oh, I'm a little Dutch girl, from over the sea.

Oh, I'm a little Dutch boy, a Dutch boy, a Dutch boy,
Oh, I'm a little Dutch boy, from over the sea.

Oh, go away I hate you, I hate you, I hate you,
Oh, go away I hate you, from over the sea.

Oh, why do you hate me, hate me, hate me,
Oh, why do you hate me, from over the sea?

Because you stole my necklace, my necklace, my necklace,
Because you stole my necklace, from over the sea.

Oh, here is your necklace, your necklace, your necklace,
Oh, here is your necklace, from over the sea.

Now we're getting married, married, married,
Now we're getting married, from over the sea.

Now we're having babies, babies, babies,
Now we're having babies, from over the sea.

Now we're getting older, older, older,
Now we're getting older, from over the sea.

Now we're in our coffins, coffins, coffins,
Now we're in our coffins, from over the sea.

Now we're up in heaven, heaven, heaven,
Now we're up in heaven, from over the sea.

Now we're little angels, angels, angels,
Now we're little angels, from over the sea.

The players form up in two lines facing each other. The 'Dutch girls' skip
towards their partners and retire, sometimes doing a Scottish dance step,
with one hand on hip and the other above their head. The 'Dutch boys' do
likewise in the second verse, perhaps having both hands on their hips.

When the girls sing 'Go away, I hate you', they turn their backs and stamp their feet. The 'boys' make their peace, pretending to hold out a necklace, or dropping on to one knee and imploring,

> Oh, please will you forgive me, forgive me, forgive me,
> Oh, please will you forgive me, from over the sea.

When they announce they are to be married they link elbows and dance round, or cross arms and twirl. Thereafter, as an eight-year-old cockney put it: 'We 'ave babies, and we fold our arms, we make out there's a baby in them, and we shake them. And then when we get older, we bend our knees down and down and down. And when we're up in 'eaven, we go up and up and up. And when we are angels we flap our arms like that.' When they are in their coffins, remarked another girl, they should lie on the ground, 'only we don't want to get our clothes dirty'. Instead they lean the coffins against a wall.

In recent years the song has become so lengthy its break-up seems imminent. In Stepney, for instance, the hating part of the game is grotesquely protracted:

> Why do you hate me, hate me, hate me,
> Why do you hate me, far across the sea.
>
> Cos you stole me necklace, me necklace, me necklace,
> Cos you stole me necklace, far across the sea.
>
> Here is your necklace . . .
>
> Go away I hate you . . .
>
> Why do you hate me . . .
>
> Cos you stole me ring . . .
>
> Here is your ring . . .
>
> Go away I hate you . . .
>
> Why do you hate me . . .
>
> Cos you stole me bracelet . . .
>
> Here is your bracelet . . .
>
> Now we're getting married . . .

The hating part of the game is, it must be reported, the part that most arouses the players, the enactment of domestic quarrels and reconciliations being a constant source of satisfaction to the young.

Britain: Aldgate and Sevenoaks, 1952 | Alton, 1954 | Swansea, 1956 | Thereafter versions from 20 places including the Channel Islands and Outer Hebrides. Extensions and improvisations sometimes have local currency, e.g. at St Peter Port, Guernsey, 'Now we've got a baby, from Holland we came', is followed by 'Now its growing bigger . . . Now it can ride a scooter . . . Now it can ride a pony . . .'

    Australia: Melbourne, 1968 (Turner, p. 59).

    Canada: Chatham, Ontario, *c.*1948, seven verses (Fowke, 1969, p. 40).

73
Green Peas and Barley

Dudley, Worcs., 1969

> Green peas and barley O,
>   Barley O, barley O,
> Green peas and barley O,
>   On a Sunday morning.
>
> This is the way the teacher stands,
>   Fold your arms and clap your hands,
> This is the way the Scotchies dance—
>   Whoops Maryanna!

The players tear around in a ring—usually—during the first verse, and then stop and imitate the teacher and the Scotchies—sometimes derisively—and then continue dancing round. But this is a popular lively little game which is still developing. In some places they have one player in the middle who calls in another player, who in the next round calls in another player, until there are seven players in the middle who dance round in a circle in the opposite direction; and in some places, particularly in the north (from Newcastle-under-Lyme to Newcastle-upon-Tyne) they sing an additional verse (usually part of the skipping rhyme 'I'm a Little Scotch Girl'):

> The king does this (*bows*)
> The queen does this (*curtsies*)
> The girls show their panties (*lift skirts*)
> And the boys blow a kiss (*kiss hands*).

England: Bearpark, Co. Durham, *c.*1925, 'Green peas and barley O . . . All on a Saturday morning. This is the way the teacher stands, This is the way she folds her hands, This is the way she clasps her hands, And this is the way she dances' | Like text, with third verse, Workington, 1962, 'The girls do the can-can, The boys do the twist'; Harrogate, 1965, and Coseley, Staffs, 1969, 'Green peas and barley oats' | Like text, 2 verses, Newcastle, Staffs, 1965, and Dudley, Worcs, 1969 | Stepney, 1976, 'One stick of barley, O . . . On a Monday morning, Two sticks . . .' up to seven, who make the central circle | Nottingham, 1977, 'One piece of polly ann . . . Saturday afternoon. This is the way the teacher goes, Fold your arms, clap your 'ands, Whoops, Mary Anna', and similar at Rocester, Staffs.

Scotland: Stornoway, Isle of Lewis, 1961, 2 verses, 'Green peas and barley O . . . Sugary cake and candy, This is the way the teacher stands, This is the way she claps her hands, This is the way she dances'. Similar at Paisley, 1961, and Greenock, 1975, 'This is the way the farmer stands'.

South Africa: Pretoria, 1972, 'This is the way the teacher stands, Fold your arms, clap your hands, This is the way the Scottish dance, Whoops! don't be cheeky'.

74

Ancient Auntie

Tralee, Co. Kerry, 1975

> I have an ancient auntie, her name is Monica,
> And when she goes out walking, I have to say 'Ha, ha'.
> She has a swinging hat, a hat swinging so,
> And when she goes out walking, her hat is swinging so.

The attributes of the ancient auntie accumulate until finally:

> I have an ancient auntie, her name is Monica,
> And when she goes out walking, I have to say 'Ha, ha'.
> She has swinging knees, knees swinging so,
> And when her knees are swinging, her knees are swinging so.

She has swinging hips, hips swinging so,
And when her hips are swinging, her hips are swinging so.
She has a swinging skirt, a skirt swinging so,
And when her skirt is swinging, her skirt is swinging so.
She has a swinging bag, a bag swinging so,
And when her bag is swinging, her bag is swinging so.
She has a swinging mouth, a mouth swinging so,
And when her mouth is swinging, her mouth is swinging so.
She has a swinging feather, a feather swinging so,
And when her feather's swinging, her feather's swinging so.
She has a swinging hat, a hat swinging so,
And when her hat is swinging, her hat is swinging so.
I have an ancient auntie, her name is Monica,
And when she goes out walking, I have to say 'Ha, ha!'

The girls stride briskly round, making fun of their ancient (but apparently absent) relative, who seems either to have St Vitus's dance, or to be pathetically caught up in the 'swinging' life-style of the 1960s. In the mid-1970s every girl in Great Britain might have been presumed to know the game, and minor variations abounded (e.g. in Liss, 1976, 'I had an auntie, an auntie Monica, And when she went out shopping They all said "Ooh la la!"'). The game's country of origin may have been Norway. It was recorded by Berit Østberg in Kristiansund in April 1973:

> Vi har ei gammel tante, som heter Monika,
> og når 'a går på torget, vi hermer etter 'a.
> For sånn svaier hatten, og hatten svaier sånn,
> og sånn svaier hatten, og hatten svaier sånn.
>
> (We have an ancient aunt, her name is Monika,
> And when she goes to market, we mimic after her.
> For she has a swinging hat, and a hat swinging so,
> And like this swings her hat,
> And her hat swings like this.)

Østberg gives a rather different version, from Trondheim, in her book *På livets landevei*, 1976, in which auntie goes into the centre of the ring to be mocked.

Curiously, the Girl Guide Movement seems to have adopted—or even originated—this faintly unpleasant pantomime; it appears in the *Girl Guide Jubilee Song Book*, published in Canada, and is played at Girl Guide and Brownie meetings. We include it as a contrast to the other games of mimicry, in which the singers make fun of themselves.

XIII

Bachelor Games

IF, in a game, one player is on his own, and his only means of acquiring a partner is to deprive someone else of his partner, the game is likely to have a certain edge to it however stylized the ritual, or good-natured the company. Yet the necessity for actions that in real life are considered intolerable seldom inhibits the enjoyment of a game, and it was only to be expected that games and dances in which predatory bachelors (of either sex) pair themselves with other people's partners would be found to be not only international but kept going by adults as well as by children. In the Southern Appalachian Mountains, for instance, Cecil Sharp found that the 'Running Set', which perhaps dates back to the sixteenth century, customarily ended with a dance known as 'Tucker', in which an extra man ran into the middle of the set and endeavoured to obtain a partner whenever the couples were briefly separated. In the Hebrides the traditional 'Pin Reel' or 'Bachelor's Reel' was on a similar plan, an equal number of men and women dancing round a single player who had no wish to remain single; and if the ladies were in the majority, it was a lady who rushed for a partner. In Berlin, in the first half of the nineteenth century, adults as well as children played 'Der Gänsedieb', in which the player in the middle, the goose-thief, was blindfolded and secured a partner by pointing (F. M. Böhme, *Deutsches Kinderspiel*, p. 465). Since the war, children in Berlin have had a similar sport under the name 'Fünfundzwanzig Bauernmädchen', an uneven number of children going round in a ring and pairing off at the end of their song (Reinhard Peesch, *Berliner Kinderspiel*, pp. 20–1). In Upper Saxony, in the 'Basket Dance', the odd-man-out, whether boy or girl (let us say girl), dances alone with a basket, and when the music suddenly stops she grabs a partner, and some other girl, who consequently is without a partner, has to take the basket. The others then circle round her, before the dancing recommences, wagging their fingers and singing:

Nun stehst du da, und has't kein Mann,	(Now you stand here and have no man,
Und ärgerst dich zu Tode.	And worry yourself to death.
Ein andermal, pass besser auf,	Another time be more alert,
Und mach' mit uns die Mode.	And do like we do.)

The players also jeer in the Oklahoma play-party game 'Pig in the Parlour'. Ordinarily, when a partnerless player is in the middle, the song commences:

> We kept a pig in the parlour,
> We kept a pig in the parlour,
> We kept a pig in the parlour,
> And that was Irish too.

But if at the end of the round the player has failed to secure a partner the others are likely to alter the ditty to his discomfort:

> The same old pig in the parlour,
> The same old pig in the parlour,
> The same old pig in the parlour,
> And that was Irish too.

(B. A. Botkin, pp. 290–3, and Edith Fowke, 1969, p. 28 and note; see also *North Carolina Folklore*, pp. 107–8). By such trials may many an American youth have learned imperviousness to ridicule as do the Swiss to this day with their 'Broom Dance', in which one dancer amongst the couples has a broom for a partner, which, happily, after circling the room surveying the other dancers, he may exchange for the girl of his choice (a glorified form of the Anglo-Saxon 'Excuse Me' dance), leaving her partner to dance with the broom, or to sweep the floor with it if he wishes, or, if he is wise, to exchange it for some other man's partner. At Antdorf, south of the Starnberger See in Germany, the lad who is left with a broom is less fortunate. On the first Sunday in May, every three years, the 'Mailaufen' is held. A group of girls carrying two brooms and a lantern between them are said to run across a meadow to a bench on which are seated a number of young men with their backs turned, three more than there are girls. The girls come up behind them, tip the bench over, and in the ensuing mêlée hope to seize the boy they like best, leaving three youths with the doubtful consolation of a broom or lantern for dancing partner (Richard Thonger, *Calendar of German Customs*, p. 45). The supposition that such practices, whether conducted in fun or earnest, are of long standing, is reasonable enough; yet Alice Gomme's straight-faced suggestion that the game 'Jolly Miller' (hereafter) is a memory of some custom such as that said to have been proposed by St Cowie at Campbeltown, that dissatisfied couples should be allowed to assemble at the church once a year, be blindfolded, and made to run round the church at full speed until the word 'Cabbay' was pronounced, when each man would lay hold of the first female he met and be her husband until the next performance of the custom, seems as helpful as suggesting that the Scots custom is also commemorated in the streets of London by the cry of 'Cabbie', when stranded pedestrians wish to engage a taxi-cab.

75
Jolly Miller

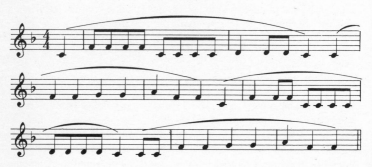

Cambo, Northumberland, 1978

> There was a jolly miller, and he lived by himself,
> By grinding corn he made his wealth;
> One hand in the hopper, the other in his bag,
> As the wheel went round he made his grab.

'Jolly Miller' was one of the most popular singing games at the end of the nineteenth century. In 1894 Alice Gomme possessed so many recordings and found the words so stereotyped that for once she felt it unnecessary to set out all, or even the majority of, her texts. Today the game has been taken over by teachers and is rarely played except under instruction —which is surprising, since the dance movements are ingenious and satisfying. The players process round in a circle in couples, arm-in-arm (perhaps this is now found embarrassing), and sing the song with one player, 'the miller', the odd-man-out, moving about within the circle. When the players come to the end of the song, the word *grab* is the signal for the inside player of each pair to dart forward and grasp, or attempt to grasp, the arm of the outer player of the couple in front, while 'the miller' tries to be first to reach one of the vacant arms. If he succeeds the player he displaces goes in the middle.

Since no recording or recollection of the game is known earlier than the 1870s it is tempting to think it is modern. On the other hand Addy speaks of 'Jolly Miller' being played in Sheffield by young men and women (which seems to indicate the game has a history); and in America the sport was in vogue for some forty or fifty years at play-parties. At these parties the game tended to be more formal and, seemingly, more fun. Often the last couplet contained a call to the players to change partners:

> One hand in the hopper and the other in the sack,
> Gents step forward and the ladies step back.

Alternatively the game was played with the boys and girls forming two concentric circles, girls in the inner circle, boys in the outer, and they sang as they moved in opposite directions, so that when the singing stopped each boy took the girl nearest to him, in the manner of 'Paul Jones', with the additional hazard that the miller, too, was after a partner, and one player would find himself on his own. Those who were paired off then paraded round singing a chorus of no obvious relevance, such as

> We're sailing east, we're sailing west,
> We're sailing over the ocean.

And this manner of playing the game may well be old.

In 1883 Newell printed a text from Cincinnati which was subsequently found to be well known elsewhere:

> Happy is the miller that lives in the mill;
> While the mill goes round, he works with a will;
> One hand in the hopper, and one in the bag,
> The mill goes around, and he cries out, Grab!

In *Wit and Mirth: or, Pills to Purge Melancholy*, 1699, p. 64, a song appears of rather doubtful humour, but with a first verse that is comparable:

> How Happy's the mortal,
>   That lives by his Mill,
> That depends on his own,
>   Not on Fortune's Wheel;
> By the slight of his hand,
>   And the strength of his back;
> How merrily, how merrily,
>   His Mill goes *Clack, clack, clack*.

A dance 'The Happy Miller' is printed in *The Second Part of the Dancing Master*, 1696, p. 22, but the directions for the dance are not those for the game, and the tune is not similar to that of the English game, nor to the American tunes for 'Happy is the Miller'. In fact the English game-tune is a version of 'Bobby Bingo' in augmentation, and has no resemblance to the

American 'Happy is the Miller' tunes; nor do the American tunes all have a close relationship to each other. Nevertheless the possibility must not be ignored that, as Newell felt, the song of 1699 is as likely, or more likely, to have been founded on a children's verse then current, as the present children's verse is to have descended from the seventeenth-century song.

Britain: Manchester, *c.*1875 (Gilchrist MSS 231 Aiii, p. 32) | *Cassell's Book of In-door Amusements*, 1881, p. 32 | Sussex, 1882, 'As the wheel went round he made his wealth' (*Folk-Lore Record*, v, p. 86) | *Shropshire Folk-Lore*, 1883, p. 512 | Derbyshire, 1883 (*Folk-Lore*, i, p. 385) | St Ives, Cornwall, 1884 (*Folk-Lore*, v, p. 57) | *Sheffield Glossary*, S. O. Addy, 1888, p. 120 | *Traditional Games*, i, 1894, pp. 289–93, and ii, 1898, pp. 436–7 | *Children's Singing Games*, Cecil Sharp, set ii, 1909, p. 6 | *Joyous Book of Singing Games*, John Hornby, 1913, p. 60 | *100 Singing Games*, Frank Kidson and Alfred Moffat, 1916, p. 115 | *London Street Games*, 1916, p. 73 | Macmillan Collection, *c.*1922, game sent by 'quite a lot of young people' | Claverley, near Bridgnorth, 1961.

USA: Muncie, Illinois, 'remembered from not long after the Civil War', 'Happy is the miller who lives by himself, As the wheels roll around, he is gaining his wealth. One hand in the hopper, and the other in the sack, As the wheel rolls around, the bags fall back' (*JAFL*, xxxii, pp. 490–1) | Boone County, Missouri, *c.*1880, 'Oh, the jolly old miller boy he lived by the mill' (*JAFL*, xxiv, p. 306) | Michigan, *c.*1915 (*JAFL*, xxxiii, pp. 101–2) | *Games of American Children*, 1883, pp. 102–3 | Oklahoma, 1920s (*American Play-Party Song*, B. A. Botkin, pp. 247–52, four versions and many references. The song apparently well-known at this time; but the historical note confuses unrelated songs about millers) | *North Carolina Folklore*, pp. 110–13.

Canada: Ontario, 1909, 'Old dusty miller, all alone by himself' (*JAFL*, xxxi, p. 54); and 1940s (Fowke, 1969, p. 28).

New Zealand: 'Played in all the provinces before 1900.' A similar game was 'Would you lend my mother a saucepan?' (Sutton-Smith, pp. 27–8).

Sweden: *Svenska fornsånger*, A. I. Arwidsson, iii, 1842, pp. 24–6, 'Vore jag kungens dotter, Visste jag hvad jag gjorde; Nu är jag ett torparbarn, Måste dra den tunga qvarn. Jag mal och jag mal, och jag mal, och jag mal, etc.' (If I were the king's daughter, I know what I'd do; Now I am a crofter's child, I must turn the heavy quern. I grind and I grind, and I grind, and I grind, etc.) Played on the principle of 'Musical Chairs'.

76

Joggle Along

'*The Baptist Game*', Games of American Children, *1883*

Come all ye young men, with your wicked ways,
Sow all your wild oats in your youthful days,
That we may live happy, that we may live happy,
That we may live happy when we grow old.
The day is far spent, the night's coming on,
Give us your arm and we'll joggle along . . .

Described in 1886 as 'a very favourite open air game' in Cornwall, and in
1913 as 'popular in Birmingham district', 'Joggle Along' was played in
exactly the same way as 'Jolly Miller' (p. 314). Boys and girls paired up,
sang as they walked arm-in-arm round a boy who had no partner, and
when they came to the words 'joggle along' each boy let go his partner and
tried to catch the arm of the girl in front of him before the boy in the middle
could take it. Whoever was then without a partner went in the middle for
the next round. The words have the coyness of a middle-aged folk song,
and it was doubtless easily displaced everywhere by the more nimble 'Jolly
Miller'.

Britain: Cornwall, 1886 and 1894 (*Folk-Lore*, v, p. 57, and *Traditional Games*, i, pp. 285–6,
Penzance) | Birmingham, 1913, the tune is 'curiously like the Dutch lullaby, "Slaap, kindje,
slaap"' (*Joyous Book of Singing Games*, John Hornby, p. 61).
    USA: Boone County, Missouri, 1870s or earlier, 'Come all ye young people that's wending
your way' (*JAFL*, xxiv, p. 314) | Albemarle County, Virginia, 1883, 'The Baptist Game' enjoyed
by 'pious people who will not dance'; New York 'a few years since'; and Massachusetts, similar but
'Come all ye old maids in your sinful ways' (*Games of American Children*, pp. 101–2) | South
Carolina, 1920s (*American Play-Party Song*, B. A. Botkin, pp. 170–1).

77

Fire on the Mountains

Kerr's Guild of Play, *Glasgow, 1912*

Fire on the mountains, run, boys, run!
You with the red coat, follow with the gun.
The drum shall beat and you shall run,
Fire on the mountains, run, boys, run.

An eight-year-old Devonian, giving these words in 1922, explained:

The children form two circles, one within the other, the outer circle having one more child in its number than the inner. The children in the inner circle sit on the ground and sing while those in the outer ring run round them one after the other. At a given signal the song suddenly ceases and each child in the outer circle tries to place himself immediately behind one of the seated children. The player who fails to do this has to pay a forfeit and change places with one of the children in the inner circle.

This forfeit could, it appears, be a source of embarrassment. An observer in 1912 reported:

In some parts of the country this game is played by boys alone, who arrange their caps in a large circle on the ground, with one cap less than there are players in the game. Then, having closely buttoned their clothes, the boys run round the outside of the circle singing the song, until the leader chooses to call "Stop", at which point everyone endeavours to kneel beside a cap, the odd-man-out being compelled to "lowse a button" of his jacket as a forfeit. As the game goes on, any player who has a garment completely unbuttoned must take it off, a penalty which results on occasion in the doffing of as many garments as the player is willing to discard.

The song itself has roots both in Britain and America. In a nursery book, *Mother Goose's Quarto*, published in Boston about 1825, appears the verse:

> Hogs in the garden, catch 'em Towser;
> Cows in the corn-field, run boys, run;
> Cats in the cream-pot, run girls, run girls;
> Fire on the mountains, run boys, run.

Adaptations of these lines feature in the American play-party game 'Jim Along Josie', whose actions confirm the relationship. In *Popular Rhymes of Scotland*, 1842, Robert Chambers gives—with what justification is uncertain—the following verse as a cry of juvenile bands 'when, at a particular season, they observe the conflagration of the heath, which takes place annually on many mountains in Scotland:

> Rabbit wi' the red neck, red neck, red neck,
>   Rabbit wi' the red neck, follow ye the drum:
> Fire on the mountains, the mountains, the mountains,
>   Fire on the mountains, run, boys, run.'

From time to time similar couplets have been adrift in the Scottish breeze, that seem to have had as little meaning to those who shouted them as to those who hear tell of them today, for instance:

> Sammy in the reid coat, Tammy wi' the drum,
> Fire on the mountains, run boys, run!

and,

> There's a rotten in the cotton and a crow in the bin,
> Fire on the mountains, rin boys, rin!

However the song—whatever its significance—is not essential to the action of the game; and throughout the twentieth century 'Fire on the Mountains' has also been played as a straightforward racing game (sometimes adult-organized in the gymnasium), and, indeed, Alice Gomme in 1898 knew only the plain game, unadorned by singing.

Britain: Auchterarder, Perthshire, 1898 (*Traditional Games*, ii, p. 421) | Glasgow, 1912, *Kerr's Guild of Play*, p. 13, with tune | West Country, 1922, descriptions from 22 children, both singing and plain versions (Macmillan Collection) | Plain versions: Knighton, 1953; Penrith, 1957; St Martin's, Guernsey, 1961; Welshpool, 1963; Accrington, 1964.

New Zealand: South Clutha, Southland, 1875, 'Fire on the mountains, lit by the sun' (Sutton-Smith, pp. 28–9).

USA: Missouri, *c.*1880, 'Cat's in the cream-jar, Run, girls, run! Fire in the mountains, Fun, boys, fun! Hey, Jim along, Jim along, Josie! Hey, Jim along, Jim along, Jo!' (*JAFL*, xxiv, p. 298) | *Games for the Playground*, J. H. Bancroft, 1909, pp. 86–7 | Bath, Michigan, *c.*1910 (*JAFL*, xxxiii, pp. 105–6) | *American Play-Party Song*, B. A. Botkin, 1937, pp. 214–15.

78

Skip to my Lou

Stepney, London E1, 1976

> Lou, lou, skip to me lou,
> Lou, lou, skip to me lou,
> Lou, lou, skip to me lou,
> Skip to me lou, my darling.
>
> Lost my partner, what shall I do?
> Lost my partner, what shall I do?
> Lost my partner, what shall I do?
> Skip to me lou, my darling.

> I've found anuvver one, just like you,
> I've found anuvver one, just like you,
> I've found anuvver one, just like you,
> Skip to me lou, my darling.

Thus, small cockneys tearing round in a circle at the foot of high-rise flats in Stepney, April 1976, whirling so fast that afterwards they collapsed on the grass among a litter of lemonade cans. In Nottingham, 1977, Jedburgh, 1972, and Louth, Lincolnshire, 1961, children confirmed that the way to play the game was to 'go quickly round, singing the song'; and in spite of more sophisticated wordings in, for instance, Brian J. Sims' *Cub Scout Songs*, 1972, and more sophisticated movements in teaching manuals such as Janet E. Tobitt's *Singing Games for Recreation*, ii, *c.*1938, this is usually the preferred *modus operandi* in Britain today. Only once was a more shapely dance discovered, by Father Damian Webb at Moss Park School between Glasgow and Paisley in 1961 ('Skip, skip, skip to m' loo . . . Skip to m' loo, my darling. Dance, to your partner, dance . . . Skip to m' loo, my darling. Slice the butter, choo, choo, choo . . . Skip to m' loo, my darling'), when the girls interrupted their circling to dance a *pas de basque* step opposite their neighbour.

However, the dance-game properly belongs to the Bachelor Games group. Botkin, in *The American Play-Party Song*, p. 75, says 'generally, in Oklahoma, a ring is formed with an extra boy in the center who tries to steal another boy's partner and swing her across to his place, while the boy left without a partner tries to steal another. In Indiana, the deserted boy may recover his partner if he succeeds in overtaking the couple before they get back to her former position after swinging round the circle'; and he gives lists of improvised or traditional verse-lines, a new one being needed each time a girl is stolen ('Pig's in the parlor, what'll I do?' 'Mice in the buttermilk, two by two,' 'Little red wagon painted blue')—a nice exercise in rhyming. Also, in Grace Cleveland Porter's *Negro Folk Singing Games*, 1914, 'the game is played exactly like the Jolly Miller'. 'Lou' is of course an old form of 'love'. Simpson, *The British Broadside Ballad*, says the tune of 'Skip to my Lou' bears 'strong traces' of the tune 'Dargason', first found in the sixteenth century.

XIV

Calls of Friendship

THESE games are examples of what must be the Ur ring game, which is of the utmost simplicity. One player in the middle of a ring calls someone to join her, and having danced with her relinquishes her place. All of them are performed at exhilarating speed except 'Poor Jenny' which, being a long saga and usually played by very young children, is sung slowly and mournfully. (There is, in any case, no dancing in 'Poor Jenny'.) Böhme points out that this kind of dance was known in the sixteenth century in the south of Germany, and quotes a dance-song from Wolfgang Schmeltzel's *Quodlibet*, 1544:

Jungfrau in dem rothen Rock,	(Girl in the red dress,
kommt her zu mir!	come here to me!
Es sein nit hübscher' Leute hie,	There's no one here more handsome
denn ich und ihr.	than I and thee.)

79
Queen Mary

> My name is Queen Mary, my age is sixteen,
> My father's a farmer on yonder green;
> He's plenty of money to dress me sae braw,
> But there's nae bonnie laddie will tak' me awa'.

> One morning I rose and I looked in the glass,
> I said to myself what a handsome young lass;
> My hands on my sides, and I gave a ha-ha,
> But there's nae bonnie laddie will tak' me awa'.

The circle sings the first verse with one player in the middle who chooses someone from the circle, and dances round with her while the rest sing the second verse. The first player then joins the circle, and the second player becomes the chooser in the next round. Most early reports are from Scotland and the north country, where the game was well-established by the turn of the century; but derivatives, or apparent derivatives, have been current in the south since Edwardian days. In 1907 girls in the streets of Soho sang as they skipped:

> My name is sweet *Dolly*, my age twenty-three,
> My father's a farmer over the Red Sea.
> Got plenty of money to dress me in silk,
> But no one to love me but *Amy*.

At Yarcombe, East Devon, in the early 1920s, when boys were still not ashamed to play ring games, the circle sang:

> Queen Mary, Queen Mary, my age is sixteen,
> So come pretty *Nancy* and marry me quick.

The girl chosen came forward, took hold of the boy's hand, and they both hopped round in the centre singing:

> Hop, hop, hop, to the butcher's shop,
>   I dare not stay any longer;
> If I did my mother would say,
>   I'd been playing with the boys over yonder.

In Herefordshire, Monmouthshire, and north Somerset, after the children had sung,

> Queen Mary, Queen Mary, my age is sixteen,
> My father's a farmer on yonder green,
> He's plenty of money to dress me in silk
> But nobody loves me but *Gertie*,

they continued with a scrap from 'Monday Night' (p. 339), but without making further contribution to the sense:

> Hey ho! *Gertie* oh,
> She shall have a baby oh,
> Wrap it up in calico,
> Send it off to Jericho.

And in a version of the game played in the Quantock Hills by Ruth Tongue in 1911, lines from 'Green Gravel' (p. 239), as also the tune, were assimilated:

> My name is Sweet Mary, my age is sixteen,
> My father's a farmer on yonder green;
> With plenty of money to wrap me up warm,
> And plenty of barley to put in his barn.
> O Mary, O Mary, your true love is dead,
> He sent you a letter to turn round your head.
> I loved him, I loved him, far more than my brother.
> Well if you can't have him you'll soon get another.

In Scotland, however, the text verses have generally prevailed; and even in England, for instance Harrogate, 1959, nine-year-olds were repeating lines with little more difference than would be expected from their Anglicization (e.g. 'a walk' for *awa'*):

> Queen Mary, Queen Mary, my age is sixteen,
> My father's a farmer on yonder green;
> He's plenty of money to clothe me in rich,
> Till along comes a laddie to take me a walk.
>
> I rose up one morning and looked in the glass,
> And I said to myself I'm a handsome young lass,
> With my hands on my hips and a ha, ha, ha, ha,
> Till along comes a laddie to take me a walk.

This transmission speaks well for the cadence of the lines, which evidently belong to the end of the eighteenth century. They occur in a homely composition said to have been written by a Thomas Scot of Falkirk in honour of, or rather at the expense of, the daughter of a local farmer named Russel or Russell. The verses, fifteen in number, as given in Maidment's *Scottish Ballads and Songs*, begin:

> My name it is Jean, and my age is fifteen;
> My father's a farmer, he lives on the plain,
> Of money he's plenty, which makes me so bra'
> Yet there's no bonny laddie will take me awa'.
>
> Each morning I rise, and make myself clean,
> With ruffles and ribbons, and everything fine,
> With the finest hair cushions, and French curls twa,
> Yet there's no bonny laddie will take me awa'.

And the tenth verse goes:

> It's ten times a-day I look in my glass,
> And I think in my heart that I am a fine lass;
> Then with a loud laughter I give a gaf-ha,
> Saying, Will no bonny laddie come take me awa'.

These verses were presumably printed on a slip sheet at the time, and may have entered oral tradition through adult singing. (Some of them, including the first and tenth verses, were heard sung by a fisherman in Newfoundland in 1929.) The tenth verse probably attracted children with its *gaf-ha*. Indeed Maclagan in *Argyleshire* (1901) particularly noted that while the game was being played, 'the ring at one time stops for a sort of laughing chorus'. The tune, according to Anne Gilchrist (*Journal of EFDSS*, v, pp. 222–3), is a variant of the melody 'Bonny Dundee', earlier known in Scotland as 'The Band at a Distance'. She adds that the resemblance the game-tune has to the hymn tune 'Hail, Queen of Heaven, the Ocean Star' is no coincidence. The musician Henri Hemy, who was responsible for the hymn tune, adapted it from the singing of little girls at play in the village of Stella, near Newcastle. This he published in his *Easy Music for Church Choirs*, 1851, and by so doing supplied the earliest notice of the game by more than forty years.

Scotland: Golspie, 1892, 'And I laughed a ha ha! For some bonnie laddie Will take me awa' ' (*Golspie*, E. W. B. Nicholson, pp. 132–4) | Eyemouth, Berwickshire, 1893 (*Antiquary*, xxx, p. 17) | Cullen, and elsewhere in north-east, 1898, played either in a ring or a row (*Traditional Games*, ii, pp. 10–14) | Loanhead and Lossiemouth, 1900 (*Journal of EFDSS*, v, p. 221) | Tarry Croys, near Keith, *c.*1900 | *Games of Argyleshire*, 1901, p. 85 | Lorn, 1905, 'Sweet Mary, sweet Mary, my age is sixteen, My father's a farmer in sweet Aberdeen' (*Folk-Lore*, xvi, p. 94) | Kirkcaldy, *c.*1905, when a boy was in the middle he sang 'An this bonnie laddie 'll tak' her awa' | Since 1950: Edinburgh, 1951 (*The Singing Street*, Norton Park School, p. 5) | Golspie, 1953.

England and Wales: Hexham, Northumberland, 1898 (*Traditional Games*, ii, pp. 102–3) | Belford, Northumberland, *c.*1900 (*County Folk-Lore*, iv, p. 118) | North Shields, *c.*1900, second verse 'Green peas and mutton pies' (*Street Games*, M. and R. King, p. 26) | *Old Surrey Singing Games*, A. E. Gillington, 1909, p. 5, 'My name is Sweet William' | *Children's Singing Games*, Cecil Sharp, v, 1912, pp. 8–11, two recordings 'Queen Mary' and 'Sweet Daisy' | *Joyous Book of Singing Games*, John Hornby, 1913, pp. 44–5, players stand in line | North and south of the Severn, 1920–5, eight recordings | Llanymynech, Salop, 1925 | Amlwch, Anglesey, 1952, 'Queen Silvia, Queen Silvia, your age is sixteen, Your father's a king and your mother's a queen, There's plenty of money to dress you in silk. Your hair is long and your skirt is short, And your shoes are of meadow silver, A red cross here and a red cross there, And a ring to go round your finger' | Harrogate, 1959 | Rhos, Denbighshire, *c.*1965.

Cf. skipping: *St Anne's Soho Monthly*, 1907, p. 180 | *London Street Games*, 1916, p. 72, apparently for skipping.

Ireland: Dublin, 1975, 'Dear Anne, Dear Anne, you're only sixteen' (*All In! All In!*, Eilís Brady, pp. 123–4). Game became popular in Dublin some five years before this.

Newfoundland: fisherman's song, *Ballads and Songs of Newfoundland*, E. B. Greenleaf and G. Mansfield, 1933, pp. 127–8.

80

Poor Jenny

Ilkley, 1975

Poor Jenny is a-weeping,
  A-weeping, a-weeping,
Poor Jenny is a-weeping,
  On a bright summer's day.

Why are you weeping,
  Weeping, weeping,
Why are you weeping,
  On a bright summer's day?

I'm weeping for a loved one,
  A loved one, a loved one,
I'm weeping for a loved one,
  On a bright summer's day.

Stand up and choose your loved one,
  Your loved one, your loved one,
Stand up and choose your loved one,
  On a bright summer's day.

Shake hands before you leave 'er,
  You leave 'er, you leave 'er,
Shake hands before you leave 'er,
  On a bright summer's day.

When infants play this game (text from Stepney, 1976) an engaging repertoire of emotions may be observed. Jenny, in the middle of the ring, supposedly abject while the other players skip round her, kneels or, according to temperament, sits stolidly, or delicately tucks her legs under her, or crouches, picking self-consciously at the asphalt. If too shy to sing alone when she is asked why she is weeping, the others respond for her; but if she does sing solo the sparkle on the faces of the little girls in the circle, leaning forward to catch her words, is delightful; as is the way Jenny, thereafter, enjoys her power, delays choosing her loved one, and struts round with a small smile on her face, pausing in front of someone as if to choose them, and then walking on again.

The game assumes a different character when played by nine- and ten-year-olds. As witnessed in Birmingham (1977) the girls joined hands in a circle, and sang in an exaggeratedly funereal style, with one girl in the middle who kept bringing her hands down over her nose, as if blowing it, in time with the singing:

> Sweet Jenny is a-weeping, a-weeping, a-weeping,
> Sweet Jenny is a-weeping,
> On a bright sunny day.

> Jenny wotcha-weeping-for, wotcha-weeping-for,
>   wotcha-weeping-for,
> Jenny wotcha-weeping-for,
> On a bright sunny day?

Jenny sang—as well as she could while blowing her nose:

> I'm weeping for my true love, my true love, my true
>   love,
> I'm weeping for my true love,
> On a bright sunny day.

The circle instructed her:

> Stand up and pick your true love, your true love,
>   your true love,
> Stand up and pick your true love,
> On a bright sunny day.

She then closed her eyes and fell into someone's arms—literally letting herself flop—upon which the rest sang:

> Sweet Jenny's got her true love, her true love, her
>   true love,
> Sweet Jenny's got her true love,
> On a bright sunny day.

> Jenny's getting married, getting married, getting married,
> Jenny's getting married,
> On a bright sunny day.

> Jenny has a baby, has a baby, has a baby,
> Jenny has a baby,
> On a bright sunny day.

Jenny was then released from the union:

> Jenny's husband di-ies, di-ies, di-ies,
> Jenny's husband di-ies,
> And she shouts out Hooray.

This was followed by a fresh source of grief:

> Her baby di-ied, di-ied, di-ied,
> Her baby di-ied,
> On a bright sunny day.

> And Jenny starts a-weeping, a-weeping, a-weeping,
> And Jenny starts a-weeping,
> On a bright sunny day.

> Then Jenny dies 'erself, 'erself, 'erself,
> Then Jenny dies 'erself,
> On a bright sunny day.

'Now we carry her away,' they explained, and the two biggest girls hooked their hands under the armpits of the rigid body and dragged Jenny away, her heels scraping on the asphalt, while the rest sang:

> We carry her a-way, a-way, a-way,
> We carry her a-way,
> On a bright sunny day.

They propped her against a bank ('She's supposed to be in a coffin'), and came back to join in the finale:

> Now Jenny is de-ead, de-ead, de-ead,
> Now Jenny is de-ead,
> On a bright sunny day.

'And now it's somebody else's turn,' they said matter-of-factly.

This continuation of the game, reminiscent of 'Mary Was a Bad Girl' (p. 301), is probably a recent innovation, yet it has precedents. In the nineteenth century after Jenny or 'Nellie' or 'Sally' or, quite often, 'Mary' had chosen her loved one, she might be told (in the manner of 'Isabella', p. 171):

> Pray, go to church love, go to church love, go to
>   church love,
> Pray, go to church love,
> On a fine summer's day.

> Pray, put the ring on, put the ring on, put the
>   ring on,
> Pray, put the ring on,
> On a fine summer's day.
>
> Pray, come back love, come back love, come
>   back love,
> Pray, come back love,
> On a fine summer's day.

And whether or not these formalities had been endured, the game often ended with one of the metrical blessings for newly-weds, such as the explicit verse chanted in Bean Street, Hull, in the 1890s, while Mary and her lover knelt in the middle of the ring:

> Now you're married we wish you joy,
> To every girl, a girl and a boy;
> One won't do, there must be two,
> So pray may you cuddle and kiss together.

Although 'Poor Jenny' or 'Poor Mary' had been one of the most consistently popular of singing games during the great period of folk song collection (in 1898 Alice Gomme knew nineteen versions, and today we have above a hundred), our knowledge of the game goes back no earlier than *c.*1880. It is thus not possible to determine whether Jenny was originally weeping for a particular sweetheart or for lack of any sweetheart; or whether, even, she was not weeping for a brother or a sister—seemingly lost at sea; or because her father was 'dead and gone'; or because she had no playmate. And mystery surrounds the game Edward Thomas saw played by five little girls 'on a green in front of their cottages', at the end of which Mary stood up and crossed hands with her true love, while the others sang:

> Your true love is a shepherd's cross, a shepherd's
>   cross, a shepherd's cross,
> Your true love is a shepherd's cross, by the bright
>   shining shore.

Britain up to First World War: Settle, Yorkshire, *c.*1880, 'Poor Mary sat a-weeping . . . On a bright, shining night, Get up and choose your lover'. They crossed hands while the circle sang 'Poor Mary has got a bonny cross' (Crofton MS, i, p. 102) | Dorset, *c.*1889, 'Pray, Sally what are you weeping for, On a bright shiny day? I'm weeping for a sweetheart' (*Folk-Lore*, vii, p. 209) | Dublin, *c.*1890, 'Poor Jennie is a-weeping on a bright summer day' (*I Knock at the Door*, Sean O'Casey, pp. 119–20) | South Devon, 1892, 'Poor Mary is a-weeping, On a fine summer's day', ending 'Her lover is a-sleeping . . . at the bottom of the sea' (*Notes & Queries*, 8th ser., i, p. 249) | Grundisburgh, 1893 (*County Folk-Lore: Suffolk*, E. C. Gurdon, p. 66) | Upton-on-Severn, Worcestershire, and Masham, Yorkshire, 1893 (*English County Songs*, p. 76) | Berkshire, 1893, ends 'Poor Mary's got a shepherd's cross'; Eyemouth, Berwickshire, 'Oh, what is Jeanie weeping for? I'm weeping for my own true love. Rise up and choose another love, All on this summer's day' (*Antiquary*, xxvii, p. 254, and xxx, p. 16) | Hull and Wrecclesham, Surrey, *c*.1895 | Colchester, 1896, 'Oh, Mary is a weeping, all by the seaside' | Earls Heaton, Yorkshire, 1898, 'Poor Mary, what are you weeping for? My father he is dead, sir', and, probably Scotland, 'Because my father's dead and gone' (*Traditional Games*, ii, pp. 46–62) | Highfields, Sussex, 1898 (Gilchrist MSS 231 Aiii, with five later recordings) | Midgley, near Halifax, *c*.1900, 'I'm weeping for my playmate' | Ardrishaig, Argyllshire, 1905 (*Folk-Lore*, xvi, pp. 93–4) | *Heart of England*, Edward Thomas, 1906, ch. xi | Soho, 1907, a version largely taken over by 'Pretty Little Girl of Mine' (p. 125) (*St Anne's Soho Monthly*, p. 182) | *Old Surrey Singing Games*, A. E. Gillington, 1909, pp. 7–8 | Wakefield, *c*.1910, 'Poor Sally sat a-weeping, down by the seashore, She's crying for her sister, down by the seashore' | Kent, 1912 (*Children's Singing Games*, Cecil Sharp, iii, pp. 18–20) | Glasgow, 1912 (*Kerr's Guild of Play*, p. 26) | *Joyous Book of Singing Games*, John Hornby, 1913, p. 53, 'Poor Ellen is a weeper'.

Very common thereafter. Since 1950 Jenny, or Mary, has often wept for a 'playmate' rather than a 'sweetheart', and has shaken hands rather than kissed. In Salford, 1975, she wept for 'my soldier'.

Australia: Western Victoria, *c*.1900, 'Nellie is a-weeping' (Turner, p. 60) | Mallee, Victoria, *c*.1906, 'Poor Mary is a-weeping', and Footscray, Victoria, *c*.1915, 'Poor Alice lies a-weeping' (Howard MSS).

New Zealand: Has been known in all provinces, e.g. in Canterbury, 1890, 'Poor Alice is a weeping'. Elsewhere 'Poor Sally', 'Poor Jenny' and 'Poor Mary' (Sutton-Smith, pp. 14–15).

Canada: Toronto, 1918, 'Poor Mary was a-weeping' (*JAFL*, xxxi, p. 132)

Cf. *Treasury of Jewish Folklore*, Nathan Ausubel, 1948 (1972, pp. 691–2), 'Vus-zhe, vils-tu, vus-zhe vils-tu? A shny-der far a mann?' ('What do you want, what do you want? A tailor for a husband?' She does not. She sits on a stone and weeps: all the girls are getting married. She is satisfied when offered a rabbi for a husband.)

It is extraordinary how partisan people can be, over whether the heroine should be 'poor Jenny' or 'poor Mary' (especially if they are determined that she is 'really' Joanna of Castile). All we can say is that, as far as records go, the score stands at 55 for 'Poor Mary' (23 pre-World War I), 33 for 'Poor Jenny' (five pre-World War I), and 13 for 'Poor Sally' (six pre-World War I), with a few poor Ellens, Nellies, and Sarahs. The tendency is for Londoners to sing about 'Jenny', while in the north and west of England, as also in Australia and Canada, 'Mary' is favoured. The game is not as popular in Scotland as it is in England.

81

Green Peas, Mutton Pies

Mother GOOSE's Melody. 67

WE'RE three brethren out of *Spain*,
Come to court your daughter *Jane*:
My daughter *Jane* she is too young,
She has no skill in a flattering tongue.
Be she the young, or be she the old,
'Tis for her gold she must be sold;
So far ye well my lady gay,
We must return another day.

Maxim. Riches serve a wise man,
and govern a fool.

E 2   *A Logical*

The little c Play.

THREAD the NEEDLE.

HERE Hand in Hand the Boys unite,
And form a very pleasing Sight;
Then thro' each other's Arms they fly,
As Thread does thro' the Needle's Eye.

RULE of LIFE.

Talk not too much; sit down content,
That your Discourse be pertinent.

FISHING.

SINGING GAMES IN EIGHTEENTH-CENTURY CHILDREN'S BOOKS

'Thread the Needle' in John Newbery's *A Little Pretty Pocket Book*,
1744 (1767).

'Three Brethren out of Spain' in *Mother Goose's Melody*, 1780
(edition of *c*.1795).

> Green peas, mutton pies,
> Tell me where my mother lies;
> I'll be there before she dies,
> So call me in my bosom.
> I love *Evelyn* over, over,
> I love *Evelyn* in the clover,
> I love her and she loves me,
> And that's the way we both agree.

This little ring game, in which a player in the middle calls another to join her, and swings her round as fast as may be while protesting her love, was in full throat at Dean Orphanage, Edinburgh, in 1955. It is a game that before the First World War was much indulged in by Scots girls, sometimes with an even less cheerful lyric, as in Glasgow about 1910, and in the Gorgie district of Edinburgh:

> Green peas, mutton pies,
> Tell me where my mother lies;
> I'll be there before she dies,
> And cuddle her in my bosom.
> My coffin shall be black,
> Six angels at my back;
> Two to sing, and two to pray,
> And two to carry my soul away.

And as in New Pitsligo, about 1875, and Aberdeen in the present century:

> Green peas, mutton pies,
> Tell me where my true love lies;
> I'll be there before she dies,
> Green peas, mutton pies.
> I'll hae on a fite goon,
> Festened at the back,
> Silk an' satin at my side
> An' ribbons in my hat.
> Weary, weary waitin' on her,
> I can wait no longer on her;
> Three times I've whistled on her,
> Lassie, are ye comin'?

It is a game with a hint of a pedigree. In his *Journal of a Tour to the Hebrides*, 26 September 1773, Boswell describes meeting the daughter of Alexander Macdonald of Kingsburgh, who had entertained Flora Macdonald and the Young Pretender in his house. He was a man, she said, who had but one song 'which he always sung when he was merry over a glass'; and Boswell noted it down from her dictation:

> Green sleeves and pudding pies,
> Tell me where my mistress lies,
> And I'll be with her before she rise,
> Fiddle and aw' together.
>
> May our affairs abroad succeed,
> And may our kind come home with speed,
> And all pretenders shake for dread,
> And let *his* health go round.
>
> To all our injured friends in need,
> This side and beyond the Tweed!—
> Let all pretenders shake for dread,
> And let *his* health go round.
>
> Green sleeves, etc.

The second and third verses had obviously been provided under the influence of the political situation; but a set of verses that with their Burnsian freeness are more likely to have kept the song alive had, as it happens, already been noted about 1776 by the Glasgow solicitor's clerk David Herd. Two stanzas are repeatable:

> Green sleeves and pudden-pyes,
> Come tell me where my true love lyes,
> And I'll be wi' her ere she rise:
> Fidle a' the gither!
>
> Green sleeves and yellow lace,
> Maids, maids, come, marry apace!
> The batchleors are in a pitiful case
> To fidle a' the gither.

That these lines, or ones similar, are rooted in the seventeenth century, sung to the ever-adaptable 'Green Sleeves' (the earliest known tune to have gone straight to the top of the pops on publication; and the only one to have stayed thereabouts for four hundred years), is shown in the seventh edition of *The Dancing Master*, 1686, where the tune is called 'Green-Sleeves and Pudding-Pies'; while in the seventeenth edition, 1721, it is called 'Green Sleeves and Yellow Lace'.

Ring game: New Pitsligo, *c*.1875 (*Buchan Observer*, 16 April 1929, p. 2) | Golspie, 1892, 'Green peas, mutton pies, Tell me where my Bella lies. I love Bella, she loves me, And that's the lass that I'll go wi'' (*Golspie*, E. W. B. Nicholson, pp. 157–8) | Eyemouth, Berwickshire, 1893 (*Antiquary*, xxx, p. 17) | Glasgow, *c*.1900 and *c*.1910 | *Games of Argyleshire*, R. C. Maclagan, 1901, p. 81 | Edinburgh, *c*.1910, two versions (*Rymour Club*, i, p. 150, and *Singing Street*, J. T. R. Ritchie, p. 13) | Aberdeen, *c*.1915 | *London Street Games*, 1916, p. 71 | Beccles, *c*.1920 (*Eastern Daily Press*, 6 March 1972) | Matching Green, Essex, 1954, 'Cold meat and mutton chops, Tell me when your money drops; I'll be there to pick it up, Roast beef and mutton chops' | Edinburgh, 1955, as text.

Skipping or dipping: Battersea, 1898, 'Cold meat, mutton chops, Tell me when your mother drops; I'll be ready to bury her, Cold meat, mutton chops. Pork meat, mutton pies, Tell me when your father dies; I'll be ready to bury him, Pork meat, mutton pies' | Southport, 1915 (*Journal of EFDSS*, vi, p. 89).

82

The Salmon Fishers

Cam' ye by the salmon fishers,
Cam' ye by the roperie,
Saw ye my dear sailor laddie
Sailing on the raging sea?

I cam' by the salmon fishers,
I cam' by the roperie,
I saw your dear sailor laddie,
Sailin' on the deep blue sea.

Sit ye doon my bonnie lassie,
Tak' yer bairnie on yer knee,
Drink a health to a jolly sailor,
He'll come back an' cherish thee.

Sailors they are bonnie laddies,
Ah but they are neat and clean;
They can kiss a bonnie lassie
In the dark an' no be seen.

In Aberdeen, in the middle of the nineteenth century, 'The Salmon Fishers' was a favourite song with the mill workers; and it is said to have been no uncommon sight to see two or three hundred mill girls coming up the Justice Port at night from the Bog Mill, singing this song, with a kind of cheer-leader in front of them. All recordings are from the north-east of Scotland, and versions were still known to older Aberdonians in 1959.

New Pitsligo, *c.*1880 (*Buchan Observer*, 16 April 1929, p. 2) | Rosehearty, Fochabers, and elsewhere, 1898, long versions with accretions (*Traditional Games*, ii, pp. 179–81) | Lossiemouth, *c.*1900 (Gilchrist MSS 231 Av) | Aberdeen, *c.*1915; and see *Aberdeen Press and Journal*, December 1959.

83

Knees Up Mary Muffet

Manchester, 1975

Knees up Mary Muffet,
Knees up Mary Brown,
Knees up Mary Macaroni,
Take your partner's hand, oh!

Swing 'er to the right,
Swing 'er to the left,
Swing 'er to the right again
And let 'er do the rest.

'We all stand in a ring and one girl skips round the outside. Then when we sing "Take your partner's hand" she comes in and chooses a friend. They hook arms, and they go round to the right, and to the left, and to the right again, and at the last line they change places. We clap our hands twice after *right*, *left*, and *rest*.' The girls at Wythenshawe said they had known this game 'for ages'; but it is doubtful whether their 'Knees up Mother Brown'-style words had long been a feature of the game, which seems to be a legacy of the square-dance era. At St Peter Port in 1961 children were singing:

She's the merry Murphy,
She's the merry Ann,
She's the merry Murphy,
Swing her by the hand.

And similar lines seem to have been popular in Dublin about 1970.

St Peter Port, Guernsey, 1961, second verse, 'Swing her to the right hand, Swing her to the left, Throw her in the middle And make her do the rest'. Player from the circle is 'thrown' into the middle of the ring to restart the game | Dublin, *c.*1970, 'Oosha Mary Murphy, Oosha Mary Anne' (*All In! All In!*, Eilís Brady, p. 123) | Wythenshawe, Manchester, 1975.

84

My Lad's a Terry

My lad's a terry,
My lad's a toff,
My lad's a terry toff.
He says he loves me,
I know it's true;
My lad's a terry toff—
Sez you!

This naive little love song is apparently only known in Scotland. The girl in the centre of the circle makes her declaration, and then, as in Aberdeen in 1952, 'points to any person in the group and twirls with them, then they are the one to sing the words'. In Forfar, 1954, where, they said, ' "My Lad's a Terry" is one of the most popular games', the chooser 'danced to one in the circle' and they swung before changing places. The words were:

My lad's a Terrie,
My lad's a toe,
My lad can wear a hat,
My lad can dance like that.
He says he loves me,
I know it's true,
My lad's a Terrie,
Too-oo-oo!

The song just possibly celebrates the inauguration of the Territorial Force in 1908, which caused much excitement at the time and was the source of a number of popular songs. The teasing 'Sez you!' at the end may be a later addition; it is not believed to have arrived in this country from the USA until about 1930.

XV

Up Against the Wall

THE amusements in this section with their rudimentary actions seem the impulse of a moment, scarcely to be dignified by the name of 'game'. The song-verses are inconsequential, and might be thought to be improvisations, forgotten tomorrow, were it not known that some have lasted for hundreds of years and all have proved tough survivors in oral tradition. One of them will suddenly turn up in a playground and be pronounced 'our favourite game' by girls who are as besotted by it as by the latest pop song; yet its first sighting may have been fifty years before, and in quite a different part of the country. The songs are in fact vintage pop songs, too good to be relinquished; and, because little girls instinctively move to music, it is natural to choose a partner from a row of friends lined up against a wall, to dance round with linked arms or do a 'twizzle' while they sing, and to let the chosen girl be chooser for the next turn. Even more than the strongly-established games, these back-alley pastimes are varied according to whim: 'If you haven't got a wall you can make a big circle instead,' they say.

85

Mrs Macaroni

Top: 'Here comes Mrs Macaroni' (No. 85), Leyland, Lancs, 1968.
Bottom: 'O princess you should have a care!' in 'Fair Rosie' (No. 61), Egremont, Cumberland, 1965.

Ilkley, 1975

> Here comes Mrs Macaroni
> Riding on a big fat pony,
> Looking for a house of glory—
> This is *Sarah*'s wedding.
> Om pom Susianna,
> Om pom Susianna,
> Om pom Susianna,
> Mrs Macaroni.

Everybody stands in a line (sometimes a circle) with one player in front of them who sings until she has to say whose wedding day it is. She chooses a friend, and they link right arms, so they are facing in opposite directions, and skip round singing 'Om pom Susianna'. After which 'the person who was on first goes with the group and the person who she picked starts to sing it all over again and we have different people on each time'. Modern as this game may sound, particularly when it is played in the skipping rope, it was well known in Scotland at the beginning of the century. It is conceivable, knowing the vagaries of oral tradition, that the game-song evolved from 'Come, my Lads', as taken down by Baring-Gould from the thatcher Edmund Fry of Lydford probably in 1889. The second verse goes:

> Solomon in all his glory,
>   Told us quite another story,
> In our cups to sing and glory,
>   When we're met together.
> Come let's live and we'll agree,
>   Always shun bad company,
> Why should we not merry be,
>   When we're met together.

Edinburgh, *c.*1900, 'Here comes Solomon in his glory Riding on a pretty pony; Standing by the house of glory, This is *somebody*'s wedding day' (*Rymour Club*, i, p. 75) | Huntly, Aberdeenshire, *c.*1900 | Lanarkshire, *c.*1902, 'Here comes Billy in his glory' | Kingarth, Bute, 1911 (*Rymour Club*, ii, p. 75) | Ipswich, 1953 and 1960 | Wolstanton, 1961 | Annitsford, Northumberland,

*c.*1967 | Leyland, 1967 | Covent Garden, 1974 | Ilkley, 1975 | Stepney, 1976. Versions
from 10 other places as a skipping rhyme. The tune is related to 'Bobby Shaftoe'. The folk song
'Come, My Lads' from Baring-Gould MSS, ed. G. Hitchcock as *Folk Songs of the West Country*,
1974.

86

Monday Night

Birmingham, 1975

Monday night up the lane,
Tuesday night back again,
Wednesday night a visitor,
Out comes—Nina,
Bonny bonny Nina.

Take 'er by the riverside,
Take 'er by the water,
Give 'er a kiss an' make 'er wish,
That's my daughter.

The Revd Stewart Headlam, who wrote the School Board Notes for *The
Church Reformer*, reported in June 1894, 'Benevolent West-end ladies who
have not yet recognized that their main duty towards the poor is to see that
all unauthorized people get off their backs, have once or twice lamented to
me that "poor" children do not know how to play. So being in a school in

the poorest part of Hoxton talking to the girls about temperance, I asked
them what games were then in season.' One of the games he was shown in
the playground after school was 'Monday Night, or, Pimlico'. 'It is
accompanied,' he said, 'With a kind of chaunt of a very fascinating kind.'

The chaunt had been found fascinating for more than three hundred
years, and although the words of the song have been deliberately or
accidentally changed over that time, it can still be recognized as the
Restoration love song 'The Scotch Wooing of Willy and Nanny',
published 1685–8 (Roxburghe Ballads, III), which had the chorus:

> It's Nanny, Nanny, Nanny O,
> The love I bear to Nanny O,
> All the world shall never know,
> The love I bear to Nanny O.

Many of the verses, for instance the seventh and the ninth, are also later
echoed in the singing game:

> Some pluck up the Finckel (fennel) seed,
> and some pull up the Tansie O,
> A bonny boy to pull off my boots,
> and to gang to bed to Nanny O.
>
> Some takes delight in cards and dice
> and other some in dancing O,
> But I take delight in a bonny lass,
> and her name is called Nanny O.

The poet Allan Ramsay wrote a more sophisticated version, full of
classical allusions, for inclusion in his *Poems*, 1721. No need to seek
courtesans and brothels, he said, while 'Nanny—O' is willing:

> While some for pleasure pawn their health,
> 'Twixt Laïs and the Bagnio,
> I'll save myself, and without stealth,
> Kiss and caress my Nanny—O.
> She bids more fair t'engage a Jove
> Than Leda did or Danae—O.
> Were I to paint the queen of love,
> None else should sit but Nanny—O . . .

Chorus.

> My bonny, bonny Nanny—O,
> My lovely charming Nanny—O.
> I care not though the world know
> How dearly I love Nanny—O.

The song was continuously popular throughout the century, appearing in the different editions of Ramsay's *Tea-Table Miscellany*, 1724, and William Thomson's *Orpheus Caledonius*, 1726, and in Johnson's *Musical Museum*, vol. I, 1787. Versions were collected from oral tradition, it was printed in pedlars' song-garlands, and, inevitably, Burns used the rhythm to make a song of his own, 'My Nanie, O' (Johnson's *Museum*, vi, 1803). It is hardly surprising that a song of such longevity should be pensioned off among schoolchildren.

At Thornes, near Wakefield, in the summer of 1874, James Fowler F.S.A. observed the following game, and in 1875 sent an account of it to *Notes & Queries*:

A number of girls range themselves against a wall, while one stands out and sings, stepping backwards and forwards to the time:

> Sunday night an' Nancy, oh!
> My delight an' fancy, oh!
> All the world that I should keep,
> If I had a Katey, oh!

Then she rushes to pick out one, taking her by the hand, and, standing face to face with her, the hands of the two being joined, sings:

> He, oh! my Katey, oh!
> My bonny, bonny Katey, oh!
> All the world that I should keep,
> If I had a Katey, oh!

In Golspie, 1892, Nicholson found the romantic verses:

> And my delight's in tansies;
> My delight's in pansies;
> My delight's in a red, red rose,
> The colour of my Maggie, oh!

> Heigh oh! my Maggie, oh!
> My very bonny Maggie, oh!
> All the world I would not give
> For a kiss from my Maggie, oh!

but in the south a more down-to-earth version had established itself. A correspondent wrote:

As children in Sussex, about 1895, we used to stand in a row on the seat under our covered shed. One child stood in front of us and we sang,

> Monday night, Band of Hope,
> Tuesday night, pull the rope,
> Wednesday night, put on your coat
> And come along with me,

while we held out our right hands for her to choose one of us. The girl she chose jumped down and the two girls swung round together, while the others sang,

> O! my Daisy O!
> Bonny bonny Daisy O!
> Of all the girls that I love,
> I love my Daisy O!

By at least 1939 the lines which fulfil the marriage function in 'Rosy Apple, Lemon and a Pear' had attached themselves to the game (as they have attached themselves to other games). In Swansea girls were singing:

> Monday night, Band of Hope,
> Tuesday night, pull the rope,
> Wednesday night a visitor,
> And out comes Nance,
> Oh bonny, bonny Nance.
> Take her to the river,
> Take her to the water,
> Give her a kiss and send her back,
> My fair daughter.

This is the present stage of the game's evolution; and although scarcely a trace remains of the original structure, yet the bouncing jollity of the 1680s song somehow survives.

Britain: Thornes, near Wakefield, 1874 (*Notes & Queries*, 5th ser., vol. iii, p. 482) | Golspie, 1892 (*Golspie*, E. W. B. Nicholson, p. 130) | Earls Heaton, Yorkshire, 'Sunday night and brandy, O! My life and saying so . . .' (*Traditional Games*, vol. ii, 1898, pp. 221–2) | *Games of Argyleshire*, R. C. Maclagan, 1901, p. 63, 'Sandy likes in tansie O, But my delight's in brandy O; Sandy likes in a red, red nose, Caller on my (Cuddie). Hey ho for Cuddie O, My bonny, bonny Cuddie O; All the world that I wad gie If I had my Cuddie O'; boys and girls played together | *Old Surrey Singing Games*, A. E. Gillington, 1909, p. 20, 'Monday night, Band of Hope! Tuesday night, Pull the rope! Thursday night, put on your cloak And come and meet your sweetheart!' (or, 'Friday night for Pimlico! Come along *Clara*, ho!') | *Joyous Book of Singing Games*, John Hornby, 1913, p. 33, 'Monday night; Tuesday night; Wednesday night; Thursday night; Friday night. Pick me, O! (Sally) was a lady Dressed in calico. Of all the girls that I like, I like (Sally), O!' This is reprinted in Mary Chater's *A Baker's Dozen: Singing Games for Brownies*, 1947 | *London Street Games*, p. 61 | Seaton, Devon, *c.*1922, 'Maudie lights and dancy-o, Tuesday night's a pleasure-o, Friday night's a holiday, Call upon my Nancy-o. N-O for Nancy-o, Bonnie, bonnie Nancy-o; Of all the world I love the best, I love my little Nancy-o' (Macmillan Collection) | *Street Games of North Shields Children*, M. and R. King, 2nd ser., 1930, p. 14, 'Brown bread and brandy-O, My mother said so: If I had a one to choose, I'd choose my bonny Joyce-y-O. J stands for Joyce-y-O, Bonny, bonny Joyce-y-O, If I had a one to choose I'd choose my bonny Joyce-y-O'; also 'Monday night, Tuesday night' version | Newcastle-on-Tyne, 1951, 'Monday night's the banjo, Tuesday night's the fiddle-O, Wednesday night's a visitor And in comes Mary-O' for skipping | West Newcastle, 1966–7, similar to *North Shields* (Pandrich, p. 6); also Manchester and Liverpool | Harborne, near Birmingham, 1970, 'Monday night, down the lane; Tuesday night, back again. Wednesday night a visitor, Out goes——. Take her by the riverside, Take her by the water. Give her a kiss and throw her in, My fair daughter.'

Ireland: *Irish Country Songs*, Herbert Hughes, vol. i, 1909, 'B for Barney, C for Cross, R for my love, Barney Ross! All the world will never, never know, The love I have for my Barney

O' | Dublin, *c.*1975, 'Monday night the gramophone, Tuesday night we're all alone, Wednesday night we call the roll, In comes (name) Oh! (name) My bonny, bonny (name) All the boys, and all the girls, They love (name)' for skipping (*All In! All In!* Eilís Brady, p. 82).

USA: *American Play-Party Song*, B. A. Botkin, 1937, p. 204, dancers march round singing 'Hay-O-my-Lucy-O, hay-o-my-Lucy-O, My darling, darling Lucy-O, I'd give this world and all I know To turn and swing my Lucy-O' then promenade singing 'Lucy-O, Lucy-O'.

87

Spanish Lady

Forfar, 1905

As I was walking down the street
A Spanish lady I did meet;
Patent slippers on her feet,
And the baby in her arms.
Tinkle, tinkle, tra la la, tra la la, tra la la,
Tinkle, tinkle, tra la la, and the baby in her arms.

This song about an exile in disgrace was probably at the height of its popularity in Edwardian days. Maclagan described girls in Lorne, Argyllshire, 'standing in a row with one walking up and down in front, singing,

As I went walking down the street
A German lady I did meet
With a pair of slippers on her feet
And a baby in her arms.'

The one in front then chose a partner and they marched up and down together singing 'Jingo-ring fal lal la'. Girls in Helensburgh in 1952 had inherited the song almost intact, except they sang of 'silver slippers' and their chorus was, picturesquely, 'Weary, weary, weary, tra la la . . . And a baby in her arms'. In England, as often happens, the words became corrupted. Norman Douglas found a surrealist Spanish lady wandering in the streets of London:

> As I was walking through the City,
> Half past eight o'clock at night,
> There I met a Spanish lady
> Washing out her clothes at night.
>
> First she rubbed them, then she scrubbed them,
> Then she hung them out to dry,
> Then she laid her hands upon them,
> Said: I wish my clothes were dry.

And in 1922 the Juvenile Editor of a West Country newspaper was sent 'a bouncing ball game' for his games column:

It must be a clever girl to do this. We must catch hold of the wall with one hand, and we do 'Alara' about six times; then they go round with one leg ever so fast till they can't keep it up any longer. This is how it begins:

> As I went down the lane,
> I saw a German lady,
> And she says,
> Oh, la, la, la, la, la, la, la.

Forfar, 1905, as text (*Lang Strang*, Jean C. Rodger, 1948, p. 28) | R. C. Maclagan, *Folk-Lore*, xvi, 1905, p. 94 | *London Street Games*, p. 28 | Macmillan Collection, 1922.

88

Keiller's Jam

> Keiller's jam, Keiller's jam,
> I love Keiller's jam.
> My mother said to me,
> 'What shall we have for tea?'
> So I looked upon the table,
> I saw butter, bread, and ham,
> But the thing that caught my eye
> Was a pot of Keiller's jam.

In 1962 the game of 'Keiller's Jam' arrived at Dalneigh Primary School, Inverness, brought by a newcomer from Falkirk. It was an immediate success.

We all stand in a circle with someone in the middle, and we sing these words to the tune of Jingle Bells. Then the person in the middle goes to someone in the circle and twirls her gently round. Then she does the same with the person opposite the person she's just been with. She keeps doing this till we have finished the song again. At the end you are meant to jump up and shout 'Whoopee!'

The game was by no means new. Ten years before, an Aberdeen girl had described it as 'an old favourite of mine, played with people standing in a row'; and in Swansea, in the 1950s, a longer version was current which showed that the children were aware the song had something to do with war:

> When I came home from Blighty
> My mother said to me,
> 'Oh Johnny, you've been fighting,
> What do you want for tea?'
> She laid upon the table
> Some fried eggs and some ham;
> The only thing was missing was
> A tin of Tommy Tittler's jam.
> Oh Tittler's jam! Oh Tittler's jam!
> I do love Tittler's jam!
> Apple, plum, apricot,
> All together in a pound pot.
> Every night as I lie dreaming, dreaming as I am,
> Hittler's Tittler's little moustache,
> With a tin of Tommy Tittler's jam.

Eric Partridge's 'authentic rendering' of the song (*Songs and Slang of the British Soldier: 1914–1918*, Brophy and Partridge, 3rd edn. 1931, p. 244) was, however, shorter and slightly different:

> Tickler's jam, Tickler's jam, how I long for Tickler's jam;
> Sent from England in ten-ton lots,
> Issued to Tommy in one-pound pots;
> Every evening when I'm asleep I'm dreaming that I am
> Forcing my way up the Dardanelles with Tommy Tickler's jam.

T. G. Tickler Ltd. had the army contract for jam during the First World War, and, unscathed by calumny, has gone on producing its excellent preserves ever since. In 1970 the firm was taken over by Robertson's, who wanted its 'Chunky' matured marmalade.

89

Sailor Laddie

Penrith, Cumberland, 1957

My sailor laddie's gone far away,
Red rosy cheeks and black curly hair;
He sent me a letter to say he's coming back,
And he left poor *Margaret* on the railway track.
Singing 'I love coffee, I love tea,
I love the boys and the boys love me.
I wish my mother would hold her tongue,
For she loved the boys when she was young'.

'You line up against the wall in a straight line, and one person walks up and down in front of the others singing the rhyme. When you get to "poor" you pick somebody. Then the two do a fast skitter-skatter, and then the person who was chosen carries on with the game,' says a ten-year-old girl from Penrith (1957).

Bearpark, near Durham, *c.* 1925, 'My sailor laddie, he's far, far away, With his red rosy cheeks and his black curly hair; He sends me a letter for when he's coming back, For he's my sailor laddie with his hair curled back' | County Durham, 1920s, sung by Em Elliott on the record *The Elliotts of Birtley*, 1962. 'I love coffee, I love tea' is a skipping rhyme.

90

The Butcher's Shop

Chesterton, near Newcastle-under-Lyme, c.1910

Hop, hop, hop to the butcher's shop,
I dare not stay any longer,
For if I do my mother will say
I've been playing with the boys down yonder.

Red stockings, blue garters,
Shoes tied up with silver,
A red, red rose upon my breast
And a gold ring on my finger.

D for Dorothy, pretty little Dorothy,
Of all the girls that I love best
I love Dorothy.

This is a good example of the way a game-song made from several
unrelated verses can not only fulfil its function but create a fascination in
the mind. The version above was written down by a ten-year-old girl in
Swansea in 1960. She explained:

To play this game you all stand in a long line with one person standing about four
feet away and this person hops up and down and sings the song. Then the person
who is singing picks a girl or boy from the other children and they dance round
singing the last part. This goes on till everybody has had a turn.

The first and second verses do not belong to each other, and the third is borrowed from 'Monday Night' (p. 339).

Nicholson collected a tripartite version beginning 'Green grass set a pass' in Golspie in 1892, and this, though somewhat obscure, seems to have been the standard Scottish version of the time, since the Revd Dr Gregor sent Lady Gomme a game with much the same wording which he had found in Tyrie:

> Green grass suits us,
> As my boots are lined with silver;
> E.I.O., E.I.O., my ain bonnie (a girl's Christian name).
> I kissed her once, I kissed her twice,
> I kissed her three times over.
> Hop, hop, the butcher's shop,
> I cannot stay any longer.
> If I stay my mother will say
> I played with the boys up yonder.

In fact these odd little verses have been fondly preserved and used on a variety of occasions and in a variety of renderings. They have been sung in children's May Day ceremonies (at Headington, for instance, in 1952) and at family gatherings. One distinct variation celebrates the one o'clock gun still fired from Edinburgh Castle (midday guns used to be fired as time-keepers in a number of northern cities):

> One o'clock, the gun goes off,
> I must stay no longer,
> If I did, Mama would say
> I'd been with the boys down yonder.

When the Revd Addison Crofton observed children playing a ring game in Milngavie, Glasgow, c. 1880 (to the tune, he noted, of 'Phairson swore a feud, Against the Clan McTavish'), they were singing yet another set of words:

> My boots are lined with gold,
> My stockings lined with silver;
> A red rose on my breast,
> And a gold ring on my finger.
>   Tar a ring, ding, ding!
>   Tar a ring, ding, dido!
>   Tar a ring, ding, ding,
>   I wish the war was over!
>
> My lover he came in,
> He drew his chair to the fire,
> He said, 'My love, sit down,
> For I wish the war was over!'

'Hop, Hop, Hop to the Butcher's Shop' enjoyed a revival when in the 1950s it occurred to a child somewhere, or to a lot of children in a lot of different places, that the rhyme ought to be accompanied by hopping. Since then every kind of hopping game has been found ornamented with the old verse: cockfighting (Enfield, 1951, and Bristol, 1964), hopping races (Ruthin, 1952), and the game described by a schoolgirl in Ayr in 1975:

Birds Eye Shop ['Birds Eye' is a brand of frozen foods]. Everybody stands in a row except one person. They all turn round and the person that is out hits one of them on the back then runs away. When the person that was hit shouts stop the running person must stop. Then the girl that was hit must hop round the girl that is standing, singing,

> Hop, hop, hop, to the Birds Eye shop
> And see how long it takes you,
> For when you get there your mother will say
> Don't play with the boys on the king's highway.

When she finishes singing the rhyme, if she is near enough the girl that is standing to touch her toes she is out but if she is not she just goes back to the line.

Britain: Berwick-on-Tweed, *c.*1870, 'One o'clock, the gun goes off' as quote | Milngavie, Glasgow, *c.*1880 (Crofton MS, ii, p. 40) | *Golspie*, 1897, p. 156 | *Traditional Games*, ii, p. 428 | Keswick, 1901, 2 verses, 'Pop, pop, pop, the barber's shop, I can't stay here no longer' (Gilchrist MSS 231 Aiii, p. 101) | Edinburgh, 1911, 3 verses beginning 'One o'clock' (*Rymour Club*, i, p. 149) | Glasgow, 1912, 3 verses beginning 'Green grow the rashes O, My boots are lined with silver' (*Kerr's Guild of Play*, p. 10) | Gloucestershire, 1912, 3 verses 'Off to the butcher's shop I'll go . . . Red stockings, blue garters, Shoes tied up with silver, Red rosettes upon my breast, And a gold ring on my finger' (*Children's Singing Games*, Cecil Sharp, iii, p. 16) | *London Street Games*, 1916, p. 93 | *Street Games of North Shields Children*, M. and R. King, 1926, p. 23, 'One o'clock' | London, Walworth, 1960, as Ayr, but 'hop to the baker's shop' | London, West Ham, 1960, as Ayr, but 'hop to the lollipop shop, As far as you can hasten. When you get back your mammy will say You've been playing with the boy down Hay Street' | Montrose, 1974, 'You've been with the boys at Trafalgar Square'.
   Ireland: Dublin, *c.*1975, 'Hop, hop . . . You were playing with the boys From the USA' (*All In, All In*, Eilís Brady, pp. 164–5).
   USA: Cincinnati, 1908, 'Skip, skop, to the barber's shop, To buy a stick of candy. One for you And one for me And one for Sister Annie' (*JAFL*, xl, 1927, p. 28).

91

The Bonny Bunch of Roses

> Up against the wall for the London Ball,
> The London Ball, the London Ball,
> Up against the wall for the London Ball,
> For the bonny bunch of roses.

Mother, mother, may I go,
  May I go, may I go?
Mother, mother, may I go
  To the bonny bunch of roses?

Yes, my darling, you may go,
  You may go, you may go,
Yes, my darling, you may go
  To the bonny bunch of roses.

She buckled up her skirt and away she went,
  Away she went, away she went,
She buckled up her skirt and away she went
  To the bonny bunch of roses.

She met her lover on the way,
  On the way, on the way,
She met her lover on the way,
  To the bonny bunch of roses.

He gave her a kiss and a one-two-three,
  A one-two-three, a one-two-three,
He gave her a kiss and a one-two-three,
  For the bonny bunch of roses.

She shook her head and said goodbye,
  Said goodbye, said goodbye,
She shook her head and said goodbye
  To the bonny bunch of roses.

James Ritchie filmed the children of Norton Park School, Edinburgh, playing this game for 'The Singing Street', in 1950, and said 'few singing games are played more'. It was a line-game, with the girl out in front taking the part of the daughter. She chose a lover from the line and swung with her; and they kissed while still swinging.

In other parts of Scotland the game seems to have died out—or at least there are no records of it having survived; and elsewhere in the 1950s it was only found as a fragmentary ring game in Swansea:

Stand on the wall for the London Ball,
Stand on the wall for the London Ball,
Stand on the wall for the London Ball,
And choose your prettiest maiden.

Please, Mother, may I go, may I go, may I go,
Please, Mother, may I go to see the London roses?

A verse from 'The Butcher's Shop' and a verse from 'Weary, Weary' were tacked on to make the performance long enough.

In the early years of the century, and as far back as records go, it had been a favourite romantic drama with little girls. Willa Muir knew it as a ring game when she was at a primary school on the north-east coast of Scotland in 1901:

> Father, Mother, may I go?
> May I go? May I go?
> Father, Mother, may I go,
> On a cold, cold frosty morning?

The daughter, instead of being 'Up against the wall for the London Ball' says 'Guess who I met in the London Row?', the answer of course being her 'lad', who gave her 'a kiss and a guinea gold ring'. In Forfar in 1880 the words had an equally old-fashioned sound:

> Father, mother, may I go, may I go, may I go,
> Father, mother, may I go to the bonnie banks o' roses?
>
> Yes, my darling, you may go, you may go, you may go,
> Yes, my darling, you may go to the bonnie banks o' roses.
>
> She buckled up her tails and away she went, away she went, away she went,
> She buckled up her tails and away she went to the bonnie banks o' roses.
>
> She met a lad wi' a tartan plaid, a tartan plaid, a tartan plaid,
> She met a lad wi' a tartan plaid at the bonnie banks o' roses.
>
> A tartan plaid is my delight, my delight, my delight,
> A tartan plaid is my delight at the bonnie banks o' roses.

To 'buckle up one's tails' was to buckle up one's skirt-tails for easy walking.

In some curious way the game appears to be connected with an old Scottish song, 'The Birks [Birches] of Abergeldie', the tune of which was included as a 'Scotch Ayre' in Playford's *Dancing Master*, 17th edition, 1721. David Herd printed two verses in the second edition of his *Scottish Songs*, 1776:

> Bonnie lassie, will ye go,
>   Will ye go, will ye go,
> Bonnie lassie, will ye go
>   To the birks o' Abergeldie?
> Ye shall get a gown of silk,
>   A gown of silk, a gown of silk,
> Ye shall get a gown of silk,
>   And coat of calimancoe.

> Na, kind Sir, I dare nae gang,
>   I dare nae gang, I dare nae gang,
> Na, kind Sir, I dare nae gang,
>   My minnie she'll be angry.
> Sair, sair wad she flyte,
>   Wad she flyte, wad she flyte,
> Sair, sair wad she flyte,
>   And sair wad she ban me.

These verses were given in Johnson's *Musical Museum*, 1788, along with Burns' more flowery song on the same pattern, and the tune:

As the song staggered to near-extinction in the form of a singing game the tune was gradually overcome, as is so often the case, either by 'Nuts in May' or 'London Bridge', or 'Sheriffmuir' (a 'London Bridge'-like tune), though the opening of the tune remembered by Willa Muir still shows some traces of it:

Forfar, 1880 (*Lang Strang*, Jean C. Rodger, 1948, p. 34) | Golspie, 1892, 'Clap your tails and away you go' (*Golspie*, E. W. B. Nicholson, 1897, pp. 129–30) | *Traditional Games*, ii, pp. 102–3, the children of Hexham Workhouse sang, to the tune of 'London Bridge', 'Father, mother, may I go . . . to buy a bunch of roses? Oh yes, you may go . . . Pick up her tail and away she goes' | N.E. Scotland, 1901 (*Living with Ballads*, Willa Muir, 1965, pp. 15–16) | Keswick, 1901, 'Mother, mother, may we go, For to gather roses', to 'London Bridge' (Gilchrist MSS 231 Aiii, p. 103) | Isle of Bute, 1911, 'Up against the wall for a London Ball . . . And a big, big bunch of roses' (*Rymour Club*, ii, pp. 75–6) | *Golden City*, James Ritchie, 1964, p. 157, text.

'The Birks of Abergeldie': *Ancient and Modern Scottish Songs*, David Herd, ii, 1776, pp. 221–2 | *Musical Museum*, John Johnson, ii, 1788, pp. 115–16 | *Scottish Ballads and Songs*, T. G. Stevenson, ed. J. Maidment, 1859, p. 59, a 10-verse song of a seduction, from an undateable broadside; clearly the same song as Herd's, though a different version.

92

Weary, Weary

Edinburgh, 1911 (Rymour Club, *i*)

> Weary, weary, waiting on you,
> I shall wait no longer now;
> Three times have I whistled on you—
> Lovie, are you coming now?

This plaintive 'come out to play' call (and presumably a lover's call before that) was still sung in Forfar *c.*1910; but otherwise it was only noted as a separate rhyme by Norman Douglas for *London Street Games*, 1916:

> Willie, Willie, I am waiting, I can't wait
>   no longer for you,
> Three times the whistle blows, are you
>   coming, yes or no?

However, children hate to waste a good verse, and 'Weary, Weary' was, about the turn of the century, grafted on to 'I'll Tell Mother' (p. 356) to make 'a common Row Game' (Edinburgh and Aberdeen) or was used for skipping (Edinburgh, *c.*1910). Also see the New Pitsligo version of 'Green Peas, Mutton Pies'.

93

Chinese Government

Inverness, 1962

> Chinese government, blackman's daughter,
> Tra la la it's a very fine day.
> Let the wind blow high,
> To reach the sky,
> And in comes *Karen* with a big black eye.

A game that is now only known in Scotland and Ireland. It can be played
'with the one in front of the row walking towards and away from them in
time to the tune', and then 'saying a person's name and they dance'
(Aberdeen, 1952); or 'the person chosen runs round the one standing out
until all the line are making a ring' (Edinburgh, 1955). But the song is the
chief attraction. When Madge and Robert King printed it in *Street Games
of North Shields Children*, 1926, they thought it 'may be derived from a
sailors' shanty':

> Chinee love a girl,
> White man's daughter.
> Tra la la,
> Tra la la,
> Velly big sea.
>
> Wind blew velly high—
> Think about a domini.
> Blew the little
> Girl away—
> Poor Chinee!

It is, however, more likely to have descended from one of the many songs current during the late nineteenth-century Chinese craze, such as G. W. Hunt's 'Poor Chinee', 1876. The chorus was:

> Me likey bow-wow, welly good Chow-Chow,
> Me likey lilly gal, she likey me,
> Me fetchey Hong-Kong, whitey man come along,
> Take a lilly gal from poor Chinee.

Britain: Glasgow, 1952, 'Chinese chinkiman' | Dundee, 1952, 'Chinese clever girls, black man's daughter, Tra la la the bonnie blue sea. Wind blows high, dashes through the sky, O cheefoo cheefoo Chinee' | Edinburgh, 1955, 'Chinese crackerman'.

Ireland: Dublin, *c.*1975, version similar to text (*All In! All In!*, Eilís Brady, p. 110).

USA: St Louis, *c.*1895, a hand-clapping game, 'I am a Chin, Chin, come from China, I like Amelikan girl, she lika me; I say a hunca, modacala, chunka, Say, O gal, the big Chinee!' (*JAFL*, lx, 1947, p. 28).

94

Jack-a-Needle

West Hartlepool, Co. Durham, 1926

> Jack-a-Needle, Jack-a-Needle,
> I'll sew with my needle,
> And when I get married how happy I'll be;
> I'll go to my garden and sit there all morning,
> And whistle to (Moira) to come and see me.

This, both words and tune, was sent to the *Rymour Club* in 1917 by a contributor in Perth. It was already old. The Revd Crofton had jotted down the following appealingly dilapidated version *c.*1880 from Polly Toft, his grandchildren's nursemaid, who came from Youlgrave, in Derbyshire:

> Jack Beetle, Jack Beetle,
> I live by my needle;
> And when I have money,
> Or apples are ripe,
> I go round my garden,
> And stay there while morning,
> And whistle my duty
> Till when I am gone!

'In this game,' he noted, 'the children place their arms a-kimbo, and keep jumping up and down . . . At the last line they turn round twice and begin again.'

Crofton MS, i, p. 16 | Forfar, 1890 (*Lang Strang*, Jean C. Rodger, 1948, p. 31) | Southport, *c.*1905, 'Jack Needle, Jack Needle, I work by my needle, And when I get married it's apples I buy. I go to my garden, And I stay there till morning, And I whisper my (Mary) for a gooseberry pie', followed by the dialogue 'Will you come?', 'No', 'Naughty maid, you won't come out' from 'Three Brethren out of Spain' (p. 92) (Gilchrist MSS 231 Bv, p. 2: also see 231 Bi, pp. 17 and 29) | *Rymour Club*, ii, p. 187 | West Hartlepool, 1926, 'Japaneedles'. The tune, like that of 'Isabella' and 'When I Was a Lady', is said to be that of a Spanish dance, the Guaracha (*Journal of EFDSS*, 1946, p. 19).

95
I'll Tell Mother

Aldershot, 1890

> I'll tell mother when I get home,
> The boys won't leave the girls alone;
> They pull their hair and break their comb—
> Oh, I'll tell Ma when I get home.

A ditty that was the rage in late Victorian days. The tune, above, is close to that of a music hall song 'I'm Ninety-five', which was adopted by the 95th Rifle Brigade; and later, like so many other verses with the same rhythm, it was sung to 'The King Pippen Polka', which is also the verse-tune of 'So Early in the Morning'.

Two of the earliest recordings are parodies. In *Ally Sloper's Christmas Number*, 1885, the boy Sloper (Ally's son) looks round the end of a fence at two girls sitting on the other side. The girls say: 'We'll tell our mothers when we get home, The Boys won't let the Girls alone.' The boy Sloper remarks: 'And what they'll say, if so you do, Is that the Girls don't want 'em to.' And in Wrecclesham, near Farnham, *c.* 1900, when the church bells pealed the little girls sang:

> I'll tell my mother when I get home,
> The boys won't let the girls alone;
> If it's true what I've been told,
> It's the girls won't let the boys alone.

A more orthodox version was, in Scotland, attached to 'Weary, Weary' (p. 353) and used for various games including the 'up against a wall' choosing game. In Edinburgh *c.* 1910, for instance, girls were skipping to:

> Weary, weary, waiting for you,
> I shall wait no longer for you,
> Three times whistle on you,
> Are you coming out?
>
> I'll tell Mamma when I get home,
> The boys won't leave the girls alone,
> Pull my hair and break my comb,
> That's the way they carry on.

It is an article of faith among folklorists that a once-popular rhyme will have survived somewhere. In the spring of 1969 children in Lower Gornal, Worcestershire, were heard skipping to this wail of woe:

> I'll tell Ma when I get home,
> The boys won't leave the girls alone;
> They pull my hair and break my bones,
> I'll tell Ma when I get home.

Britain: Combined version: Aberdeen, *c.* 1895 (*Traditional Games*, ii, pp. 360–1) | Edinburgh, *c.* 1900 (*Rymour Club*, i, pp. 74–5) | Edinburgh, *c.* 1910 (letter to *Sunday Companion*, Feb. 1971).

Single text verse: *London Street Games*, 1916, p. 55 | Belfast, *c.* 1945, 'So that's all right—till I go home' (*John o' London's Weekly*, 9 May 1952) | Anglesey, 1952, 'I'll tell my mother when I go home, The boys won't leave my hair alone. They pull my hair and break my comb, I'll tell my mother when I go home'.

USA: a fragment appears in an 'odd jumble' W. H. Babcock heard in Washington DC, 1886, 'I like coffee, and I like tea, I like boys, and the boys like me. I'll tell my mother when I get home, The boys won't let the girls alone. O sweet beans and barley grows'. . . . (*Lippincott's Magazine*, xxxviii, p. 328).

XVI

Static Circles

IF most players in a game are to be kept standing still most of the time, they need, by way of inducement, the anticipation that strenuous action is going to be suddenly thrust on them. This is the case in each of the well-known games whose framework is a static circle. It occurs in 'Cat and Mouse', where the circle of players are kept alert by the desire to let the mouse pass by but to deny passage to the cat; it occurs in the adult-sponsored game of 'Twos and Threes', in which the player being chased obtains sanctuary by placing himself in front of a static player and instantly puts at risk a third player; and it occurs, with more subtlety, in the game that has been known during three centuries as successively 'I Sent a Letter to My Love', 'Kiss in the Ring', and 'Drop Handkerchief' (see *Street and Playground*, pp. 114–15, 82–4, and 198–202).

The four singing games that follow, in which the majority of players have to keep fixed positions, anyway at the outset, nicely illustrate how one game may decline and another take its place due to intellectual upheavals occurring far beyond the perimeter of the playground; and they raise questions (for those of a questioning disposition) about the mutation of customs.

In the nineteenth century, it will be seen, the young were eager to play 'In and Out the Windows', a formal and repetitive ring game in which there were only two protagonists at a time, the other players merely forming a circle and singing, until it came to their turn to run in and out of the circle as pursuer and pursued. Today they play a game 'In and Out the Dusty Bluebells' that initially is similar, but which develops into a scrimmage. Meanwhile teachers perpetuate, at end of term parties, a sedate dance-song called 'Here Comes a Bluebird Through My Window', which remains a party game because it lacks the emotional mainspring to function on its own. However, the reason children now choose the rumbustious game in preference to the passive one is not, as might be supposed, because the young are not as quiet and well-behaved as they used to be; rather they seem to have been driven into playing rough-and-tumble games when unsupervised because it is no longer felt proper that children should be allowed to mature as early as they used to do. Apart from the adult-generated party game, any child who likes to play quietly is now likely to be viewed with distrust by those in authority, who comment that she is old-fashioned—a kindly description of one who is felt to be unnatural.

96

In and Out the Windows

Oban, 1974

In and out the windows,
In and out the windows,
In and out the windows,
As you have done before.

Stand and face your lover,
Stand and face your lover,
Stand and face your lover,
As you have done before.

Follow her to London,
Follow her to London,
Follow her to London,
As you have done before.

Shake hands before you leave her,
Shake hands before you leave her,
Shake hands before you leave her,
As you have done before.

All the players but one form a circle, link hands, stand still, hold their arms high to make arches, and sing the first verse, while the free player runs in and out under their arms. The player then selects a lover (or a 'partner'), chases her as she zig-zags in and out round the circle ('to London'), and shakes hands with her when she is caught; whereupon the pursued player goes into the middle, the first player joins the circle, and the singing restarts. This is the game that in the 1950s and 1960s was progressively replaced by 'Dusty Bluebells' (p. 366), a game which commences in exactly the same way, and which is now played as enthusiastically as 'In and Out the Windows' used to be. The reason for the changeover is obvious: children are now self-conscious of their gender, boys can no longer be persuaded to take part in the game, and without boys 'In and Out the Windows' has little to commend it. Its old attraction, lovingly recalled by Sean O'Casey in *I Knock at the Door*, was that the young were given playful opportunity to make known their feelings. The song might end not 'Shake hands before you leave her' but 'Kiss her before you leave her'. A display of affection was not merely permitted, but expected; and if the approach was rejected the rebuffed player could pass off his (or her) gesture of affection as merely a requirement of the game.

The earliest recordings of this game are American; and certainly it was in the States that the game was played with the greatest finesse. For instance, in the region of San Antonio in Gonzales County, West Texas, around 1880, grown-up 'boys' and 'girls' as well as children used to play 'Walking Round the Levy' (a 'levy' or 'levee' was the quay, or main gathering place in a town), which started much as in Britain, with one player strutting round the outside of the ring.

> We're walking round the levy,
> We're walking round the levy,
> We're walking round the levy,
> For we have won the day.
>
> Stand forth and face your lover,
> Stand forth and face your lover,
> Stand forth and face your lover,
> For we have won the day.

The player then knelt before his choice:

> I kneel because I love you,
> I kneel because I love you,
> I kneel because I love you,
> For we have won the day.

The chosen one made reply:

> I measure how much I love you,
> I measure how much I love you,
> I measure how much I love you,
> For we have won the day.

And while singing these lines the girl showed the dimension of her love by holding her hands apart as wide as she could spread them, or by holding them close together, sometimes teasing her suitor by starting with a small space and coyly edging her hands wider apart, or sometimes brazenly starting with her hands stretched wide and then, at the last moment, slapping them together. Whatever the reply the suitor would beg:

> One kiss before I leave you,
> One kiss before I leave you,
> One kiss before I leave you,
> For we have won the day.[1]

Despite this sophistication there is no reason to suppose the game originated in the New World. It was widespread in Britain before the turn of the century; and in some places, such as Wrecclesham, near Farnham, the play-song was considerably protracted, a sure sign of it being in favour.

> I went to the ball the other night,
> The ladies there were dressed in
>   white,
> Some were short and some were tall,
> And I asked God to bless them all.
>
> In and out the window,
> In and out the window,
> In and out the window,
> Just as you did before.
>
> Lady won't you marry,
> Lady won't you marry,
> Lady won't you marry,
> Before the break of day.
>
> In and out the window,
> In and out the window,
> In and out the window,
> Just as you did before.
>
> My ma won't let me marry,
> My ma won't let me marry,
> My ma won't let me marry,
> Until I'm twenty-four.

[1] Mrs D. L. Ames, recalling a version of this game at play-parties in Missouri around 1880, stated that in her experience this demand was never complied with. 'It may have been tempting to some of the players, but public sentiment was dead against kissing-games, and public sentiment was respected.' She does admit, however, that in the previous verse, when the love was being measured, 'the boy took the girl's hands in his own and extended his arms as far as possible to the sides, throwing the boy and girl close together' (*JAFL*, xxiv, 1911, p. 307).

In and out the window,
In and out the window,
In and out the window,
Just as you did before.

So follow her to London,
So follow her to London,
So follow her to London,
Before the break of day.

In and out the window,
In and out the window,
In and out the window,
Just as you did before.

The end-line 'Before the break of day', which also occurs in a Gomme version (1898) from Fraserburgh, appears to confirm that the tune is that of the sometime chorus of 'The Blue-tailed Fly':

So early in the morning,
So early in the morning,
So early in the morning,
Before the break of day.

That these lines were current in the early years of the nineteenth century is apparent from their inclusion in the *Narrative of Sojourner Truth*, the account of a female Negro slave, emancipated by New York State in 1828, who sometime in the 1840s, it seems, broke up a riot by singing a spiritual that included the lines.

The familiarity of the game in the early years of the twentieth century seems apparent from this song sung by the troops in the First World War:

Breaking out of barracks,
Breaking out of barracks,
Breaking out of barracks,
    As you have done before.

Parading all unbuttoned . . .

Take his name and number! . . .

Up before the C.O.! . . .

Fourteen days detention! . . .

Pack-drill, bread and water! . . .
(*Songs . . . of the British Soldier*, Brophy and Partridge, 1931 edn., p. 29)

USA: Gonzales County, West Texas. *c.*1880 | Missouri, *c.*1880 (*JAFL*, xxiv, pp. 306–7) | New York, 1883, 'Go round and round the valley, As we are all so gay' (*Games of American Children*,

p. 128) | Washington DC, 1888 (*American Anthropologist*, i, pp. 255–6) | St Louis, 1895 onwards, 'Go round and round the levee'. Reference is made to latter-day children no longer wanting to kneel and kiss, shaking hands instead (*JAFL*, lx, pp. 21–3; see also p. 38 and pp. 39–40) | Cincinnati, 1908, 'Go in and out the window' (*JAFL*, xl, p. 26) | Frequently recorded thereafter. See B. A. Botkin, *American Play-Party Song*, 1937, p. 29. Botkin himself collected 61 variants in Oklahoma alone.

Canada: Toronto, 1888, similar to New York, 1883 (*JAFL*, viii, p. 253. See also xxxi, p. 132) | Toronto, 1960 (Fowke, 1969, pp. 22–3).

Britain: West Grinstead, 1892, 'In and out the willows' (*Notes & Queries*, 8th ser., i, p. 249, tune given as 'Early in the morning' | Wrecclesham, 1892 | Devonport, 1893 | Hull, 1895 | *Traditional Games*, ii, pp. 122–31, 19 recordings including 'Out and in the villages', 'Go round and round the village', 'Walking round the village', and 'All round the village' | Several recordings from Sussex and the north country (Gilchrist MSS 231 A | *Games of Argyleshire*, 1901, p. 65, 'Round and round the valleys' | Very many recordings, with little variation in words, 1901 to 1920. During 1920s, some eccentricities, such as Somerset, 1922, 'Round and round the village . . . In and out the windows . . . Sit down upon the doorstep . . . Stand and face your lover . . . Carry her off to London . . . Bring her back to Devonshire . . .' (Macmillan Collection) | Bearpark, near Durham, c.1925, last verse 'Buy a penny ticket, As you have done before' | Southampton, 1940, also remembered by old people from 1890s, 'Walking round the village . . . Chase her off to London . . . Bring her to Southampton . . . Lock her up in prison' | Recordings from 15 places since 1950.

Ireland: Dublin, c.1890 (*I Knock at the Door*, Sean O'Casey, p. 120) | Belfast, 1898, 'Marching round the ladies' (*Traditional Games*, ii, p. 129) | Dublin, c.1965 (*All In! All In!* Eilís Brady, 1975, pp. 115–16).

Australia: Sydney, 1898, including verse 'Follow her to London' (Turner, p. 122) | Toowoomba, Queensland, c.1903; New Norfolk, Tasmania, c.1910; Footscray, Victoria, c.1915 (Howard MSS).

97

Bluebird

Poole, Dorset, 1930

Here comes a bluebird through the window,
Here comes a bluebird through the door,
Here comes a bluebird through the window,
   Hey diddle i dum day.

Take a little dance and hop in the corner,
Take a little dance and hop on the floor,
Take a little dance and hop in the corner,
   Hey diddle i dum day.

Probably of American origin, this game has never really caught on in Britain, and has small reason for doing so. The players form a circle, join hands holding them high, and stand still. One player runs in and out of the circle under the raised arms while the rest sing 'Here comes a bluebird'. She then chooses a partner, and dances with her outside the ring, while they sing 'Take a little dance and hop in the corner'. She then joins the ring; and it is the turn of the second player to thread her way round the circle, and to select a dancing partner. The game, which sometimes has lines attached to it from 'Dusty Bluebells' (p. 366), is now played chiefly by Brownies; and in 1962 a ten-year-old reported that in Inverness the song went 'There came a little Brownie through my window'. The particular charm of the game as played in Cincinnati about 1883 and in Somerset in the early 1920s was that each time the song was sung it used to be adapted to tell of 'a pink bird', 'a yellow bird', 'a grey bird', and so on according to the colour of the dress of the player going round the circle. This feature has now apparently been lost.

USA: Cincinnati, 1883 and 1908 (*Games of American Children*, pp. 118–19, and *JAFL*, xl, p. 24) | Michigan, 1914–15, as play-party game (*JAFL*, xxxiii, p. 94) | St Louis, 1944, 'Here comes a bluebird through my window, Oh, Johnny, I'm tired! Take a little partner, and pat him on the shoulder, Oh, Johnny, I'm tired' (*JAFL*, lx, p. 43, several references, 'versions known throughout the United States') | The American School in London, 1975, 'Blue bird, blue bird, fly through my window . . . And buy molasses candy'.

   Britain: *London Street Games*, 1916, p. 93, 'Here comes a little bird through the window . . . Take a little bird and hop in the corner' | Dorchester and Lyme Regis, 1922 (Macmillan Collection) | Poole, *c.*1930, as party game | Edinburgh, 1949 (BBC record no. 13869) | Harwich, 1948 | Welwyn, 1952, and Hucknall, 1960, 'Bluebird, bluebird, through the window . . . Pat a little girl upon the shoulder, One fine day' | Inverness, 1962 | Nottingham, 1977, played like 'Dusty Bluebells' | Subsequent versions adult transmitted.

   Australia: Taught in nursery schools.

   Scandinavia: Taught in Norwegian schools (very similar words); and has apparently taken root in Denmark.

98

Dusty Bluebells

East Tisted, Hants, 1964

Huish Episcopi, Somerset, 1978

In and out the dusty bluebells,
In and out the dusty bluebells,
In and out the dusty bluebells,
Who shall be my master?

Tippitty tappitty on your shoulder,
Tippitty tappitty on your shoulder,
Tippitty tappitty on your shoulder,
You shall be my master.

One of the most popular of song-games in the present day, and with good reason: it is humorous, cumulative, has a good tune, plenty of action, is seldom found in recreation manuals, and is little known to the older generation. One player is 'on' and the rest make a circle of arches by joining hands and holding them up. The player who is 'on' weaves her way through, while the rest sing 'In and out the dusty bluebells, Who shall be my master?' When they stop she stands behind one of the circle, and 'taps' the person on the shoulder as they sing 'Tippitty tappitty on your shoulder'. The player who has been tapped detaches herself from the circle, links on behind the first player, and together they set off ducking in and out under the arches while the first verse is repeated. A further girl is tapped on the shoulder, she links on behind, and the game continues, though with increasing difficulty as the line becomes longer and the arches fewer. 'I like this game,' confessed a nine-year-old, 'because in the end you get muddled up.' Indeed chaos may rule long before the end. The words the girls sing may be as coy as 'Pat a little friend upon her shoulder', but their actions belie their words. The shoulders are not patted but thumped; and when a girl links up she tends to hold on to her forerunner's skirt ('It's awful, they nearly pull your skirt off'); and if they join up by putting their hands on the shoulders of the girl in front of them, they will feel it necessary, each time they come to 'Tippitty tappitty on your shoulder', to thump the shoulders of the girl in front of them. The game, therefore, is not lacking in action.

'Dusty Bluebells' was unknown to Alice Gomme (1898) and seemingly unknown in the nineteenth century. 'Running in and out the bluebells', listed as a ring game in *London Street Games*, 1916, is presumably this game, though probably in an embryonic state. It is not in the Macmillan Collection, 1922.

Manchester and Portsmouth, *c.*1925 | Perth and Tipton, *c.*1935 | Swansea, 1939 | Abergavenny and Nailsworth, *c.*1940 | Garforth, near Leeds, 1940, 'In and out the shady bluebells' | Sidlesham, *c.*1945 | Wrexham, *c.*1945, 'In and out the Turkish bluebells' | Versions from 80 places since 1950, including 'In and out the dusky bluebells', 'In and out the rushing bluebells', 'In and out the bonny bluebells', 'In and out the Scottish bluebells', 'In and out the Scottish windows', 'In and out the bluebell windows', 'In and out the dusty daffodils', 'In and out the cottage windows', and 'In and out the dancing bluebells'.

The tune is related to that of 'O Belinda' (p. 215) and other American play-party games, e.g. 'The Paw-Paw Patch' and 'Boston'.

99

One Little Elephant

Manchester, 1975

One little elephant went out one day
Upon a spider's web to play;
He had such tremendous fun
He sent for another elephant to come.

Two little elephants went out one day
Upon a spider's web to play;
They had such tremendous fun
They sent for another elephant to come.

Three little elephants went out one day
Upon a spider's web to play;
They had such tremendous fun
They sent for another elephant to come . . .

A circle is formed, and one player tramps round the outside. She holds her
nose with one hand, and has her other hand hanging through the looped
arm. ('This is meant to be like an elephant.') When the first verse has been
sung she nudges whoever is nearest to her, and that player too, takes hold
of her nose, puts her other hand through the loop, and joins on to the first
person with her 'trunk'. This continues until as many verses have been
sung as there are players, and every player has joined on. So trivial an
amusement would scarcely be worth noticing were it not that the young of,
anyway, France, Belgium, Norway, Spain, Canada, and the United States,
are also familiar with it. In France children sing:

Un éléphant se balançait
Sur une toile d'araignée,
Il trouva ça si amusant,
Qu'il appela un autre éléphant.

Deux éléphants se balançaient
Sur une toile d'araignée,
Ils trouvèrent ça si amusant,
Qu'ils appelèrent un autre éléphant . . .

In Norway:

> Det kom en elefant spaserende
> en av edderkoppen synes han.
> Han synes dette var så iverig,
> at a *Sissel* måtte kom . . .

The kindergarten play manuals in which it appears do not state that this game is apparently founded on a round formerly danced by peasants in the south of France making mock of cuckolds. At Coux, in the department of Ardèche, two men used to link up and sing:

> Dous coucù se soun troubas, dins eno assemblado;
> O se trouvaron bé mai pèr eno autre annado.
>   Un coucù fai l'autre,
>   Un coucù meno l'autre,
>   Lou darriè vengù
>   Vai querre en autre coucù . . .

(Two cuckolds at an assembly, There will be many more next year. One cuckold pushes the other, One cuckold leads the other, The one who came last Goes to look for another cuckold).

Louis Lambert, in his *Chants et Chansons du Languedoc*, ii, 1906, pp. 343–5, recorded that 'La Ronde des Cocus' was especially for men, although little boys might be heard innocently singing it at carnival time. The first verse was danced by two people only, who held hands; a third joined them who had to go and look for a fourth, and so on until the lastcomer could not find anyone. There was no change in the verses, except that, of course, the number changed each time.

Britain: *Singing Games for Recreation*, iii, Janet E. Tobitt, *c.*1938, pp. 7–8, described as 'French' | Bath, 1940, as Girl Guide song | Swansea, 1951, two versions including 'One little elephant galloping Foot by foot on a piece of string' | Shrewsbury, 1951 | Glasgow and Wigan, 1960 | Lambourn and Leeds, 1973 | Manchester, 1975.
  USA: Camp Kiwanis, near Crete, Nebraska, *c.*1940, as camp stunt.
  Canada: Toronto, 1964 (Fowke, 1969, p. 42).
  France: Vichy, 1951 | *Les Comptines*, Jean Baucomont and others, 1961, p. 317, five references | *Chansons et Comptines*, W. J. Perry, 1968, p. 16.
  Spain: Madrid, *c.*1971.
  Norway: Trondheim, 1973 (*På livets landevei*, Berit Østberg, pp. 94–5).

XVII

Eccentric Circles

HERE are games whose structure is different from those in the main singing-game tradition in Britain. Many of them have two or three 'choosers' within the ring at once, a sharing of the central role which, though time-saving, has not historically suited the British character. In 'Push the Business On' the ring itself, with its neat mechanism for providing a new dancing partner at the end of each round, is the anomaly. It appears to be a circular jig, but 'jig' is a diffuse term applied to almost any dance that is brisk and vigorous. The two direct imports from abroad are played with two rings (side by side in the case of 'In a Fine Castle', and one within the other in the case of 'Hey Little Lassie'); while the foreign-seeming way in which 'The Muffin Man' is now danced may be accounted for by the probability that it was brought across the Channel by Dutch Scouts.

100

In a Fine Castle

Bedford, 1975

There are two rings of children, quite close to each other. The first ring skip around singing:

> In a fine castle,
> In a fine castle,
> In a fine castle,
> Have you seen my Cissy O?

The second ring skip round and sing:

> We are the prettiest,
> We are the prettiest,
> We are the prettiest,
> Have you seen my Cissy O?

The first ring skip and sing:

> We want one of you,
> We want one of you,
> We want one of you,
> Have you seen my Cissy O?

The second ring reply:

> Which one do you want,
> Which one do you want,
> Which one do you want,
> Have you seen my Cissy O?

The first ring:

> We want *Valerie*,
> We want *Valerie*,
> We want *Valerie*,
> Have you seen my Cissy O?

Valerie joins their ring, and the second ring ask for someone in exchange:

> We want one of you,
> We want one of you,
> We want one of you,
> Have you seen my Cissy O?

The first ring offer them somebody:

> We'll give you *Stephen*,
> We'll give you *Stephen*,
> We'll give you *Stephen*,
> Have you seen my Cissy O?

The second ring don't like Stephen:

> He's too ugly,
> He's too ugly,
> He's too ugly,
> Have you seen my Cissy O?

The first ring suggest somebody else:

> We'll give you *Melia*,
> We'll give you *Melia*,
> We'll give you *Melia*,
> Have you seen my Cissy O?

The second ring don't like Melia either:

> She's got a terrible voice,
> She's got a terrible voice,
> She's got a terrible voice,
> Have you seen my Cissy O?

The first ring offer Mandy, and Mandy has to be accepted:

> We'll give you *Mandy*,
> We'll give you *Mandy*,
> We'll give you *Mandy*,
> Have you seen my Cissy O?

> That will do,
> That will do,
> That will do,
> Have you seen my Cissy O?

As Mandy joins the other circle, the first circle skip round singing:

> Bye bye *Mandy*,
> Bye bye *Mandy*,
> Bye bye *Mandy*,
> Have you seen my Cissy O?

'We used to play that game a long time ago, about two years ago,' said the ten-year-old West Indian girl at Bedford, 1975. 'We used to play it in the playground and up the field, just amongst ourselves. The boys always play it with the girls.' 'Nobody ever does see Cissy,' she added, 'And I don't know who she is, unless she is somebody's sister. And I don't know where the game came from, it just arrived.'

At Wereham, Norfolk, in the same year, the game had much the same words as at Bedford, but was played in a less geometrically-satisfying way, with only one circle. As at Bedford, too, the boys thought it permissible to join in. A boy circled the circle and picked a girl he wanted to join him, singing, for instance, 'I want Mary'. The circle asked 'What will you give us?' and he thought of 'something Mary might want, like a pony'. If she refused a pony, the person outside had to think of something else, but the third time she had to go—'because that is the game'. If Mary agreed she nodded her head and went to the middle of the ring. The ring sang 'Goodbye Mary' and 'somebody gently pushed Mary to the person who chose her'. Then those two began circling the outside of the ring and singing the song, and the game continued until there was nobody left in the ring. Significantly, there is an American Air Force base fairly near Wereham, and about eight years before there had been a family of American children at Wereham primary school.

It seems that the game has been brought over from the USA; and that this is the second time it has been imported. It has long been a recreation on the Continent, especially in France and Italy, and was translated and taught in Britain during the wave of idealistic internationalism that preceded the First World War. Frank Kidson, for instance, included 'Ah! My Pretty House' ('a highly popular French Ronde freely translated') in *Eighty Singing Games*, 1907.

The French and Italian games present a *tableau vivant* of the Middle Ages. The two circles are rival castles; and each boasts that it is finer and stronger than the other (a late nineteenth-century dialogue from the Midi goes: 'We have a castle, La tan viro, viro, viro . . . Ours is finer . . . In ours there are squires . . . In ours there is a marshal . . . In ours there is a great court . . . In ours there is the flower of love'). The castle worsted in the bragging-match says it will destroy its rival, and sends a mason to seize one of the stones from the circle; and this goes on until the attacking castle is nearly twice its original size and the beseiged castle has only one or two stones left.

Britain: Bedford and Wereham, Norfolk, 1975.

France: *Chants et Rondes Enfantines*, T. M. Dumersan, 1846, 'Ah! mon beau château (1859, pp. 10–13) | *Chants du Cambresis*, A. Durieux and A. Bruyelles, 1864, pp. 278–9 | *Chants du Languedoc*, Louis Lambert, i, 1906, pp. 269–71.

Italy: Piedmont, 1858, 'Me castel l'è bel' (My castle is fine, Lantantirolirolena . . . Mine is still finer . . . We will seize it . . . We will guard it . . . We will burn it down . . . We will defend it . . . What are you searching for, all round my castle? . . . I have come to look for Madam Pülisera . . . You won't find her, she is dead under the earth . . . I shall find her all right . . . she is the most beautiful), *Germanische Mythen*, W. Mannhardt, 1858, p. 512 n. | Venice, 1874, 'El mio castel xè belo' (*Giuochi Popolari Veneziani*, G. Bernoni, pp. 33–4) | Naples, *c.*1930, 'O che bel castello, Marconticonticontello' (. . . And we will take away the stones . . . Which stone will you take? . . . We'll take the most beautiful) | Anghiari, Tuscany, 1961 | Capri, 1976.

Cf. Spain: Guadalajara, 1928, 'Yo tengo un castillo, Matarilerilerile' (I have a castle . . . Where are the keys? . . . At the bottom of the sea . . . Who will go to fetch them? . . . *Agatha* will do . . . What gift will you give her? . . . A garment of gold and silver . . . To whom will you marry her? . . . To the king's son . . . What job will you give her? . . . Embroiderer to the queen . . . There, take my daughter) | *Cancionero Infantil Español*, D. Sixto Córdova y Oña, 1947, p. 299. A girl's virginity was thought of as a fortress to which the keys might be obtained. In the Trifaldi story in *Don Quixote*, pt. 2, ch. 38, the waiting-woman laments that she did not guard her charge, the fourteen-year-old princess, against the charms of a knight of low degree: 'But all his graces and charms . . .

would have been ineffectual against the fortress of my child's virtue, if the shameless thief had not resorted to the expedient of winning me first. First the . . . vagabond set about gaining my goodwill and buying my consent to hand over to him, like a bad custodian, the keys of the fortress I was guarding.'

101

The Castle Gate

Bedford, 1975

Mandy's at the castle gate,
Mandy's at the castle gate,
Mandy's at the castle gate,
Open up the door and let her in.

She does a wiggle woggle, wiggle woggle, with her bum,
She does a wiggle woggle, wiggle woggle, with her bum,
She does a wiggle woggle, wiggle woggle, with her bum,
Turn around and choose the one you love.

This crisply syncopated dance-song seems to be an offshoot of 'In a Fine Castle', and has only been found in Bedford, 1975. Mandy was the girl who was outside the ring. She skipped round while the others sang the first verse, and they let her into the ring when they sang the last line. She wiggled her hips as they sang the second verse, then turned around and chose the one she loved. The one who was chosen went outside the circle and the game began again.

102

I Lost My Lad

Birmingham, 1977

I lost my lad in the cairnie,
The cairnie, the cairnie,
I lost my lad in the cairnie,
Y-O-U.

I met him in the shake-hand,
Shake-hand, shake-hand,
I met him in the shake-hand,
Y-O-U.

Red cheeks and roses,
Roses, roses,
Red cheeks and roses,
Y-O-U.

I met him in the dance-hall,
Dance-hall, dance-hall,
I met him in the dance-hall,
Y-O-U.

Oh, this is the one that I love,
I love, I love,
Oh, this is the one that I love,
Y-O-U.

At the beginning of the game the girls and boys make a circle and two people go outside the ring and one goes one way and the other goes the other way, and the people in the circle sing and clap. The two people go round the circle and then they come into the middle and shake hands and they sing 'I met him in the shake-hand'. After that they sing 'Red cheeks and roses', then they sing 'I met him in the dance-hall', then the girl and boy who were in the middle go to the ones they wish to be in the middle next and sing 'This is the one that I love' and those two people just go out and do the same thing again (*girl, 10, Govan, Glasgow, 1960*).

When this game was first tape-recorded in 1960 the word 'cairnie' was a mystery. Scottish dictionaries were consulted. Enquiries were made in Glasgow to find out if it had a local meaning. Eventually it was concluded that, since 'cairnie' was a heap or quantity of anything, the lad had been lost in a crowd. It was not until Willa Muir's *Living with Ballads* was published in 1965 that the story became clearer, and more carefree. About 1902, she said, in an elementary school playground in Montrose, 'rushing round in a kind of gallop we shouted rather than sang:

O, I've lost my lad an' I care-nae,
I've lost my lad an' I care-nae,
I've lost my lad an' I ca-are-nae,
A ramshy-damshy-doo!
O, we'll get anither canary,
We'll get anither canary,
We'll get anither cana-a-ry,
A ramshy-damshy-doo!'

'It was,' she remarked, 'a wholesome enough repudiation of romantic sentiment.'

Willa Muir and her friends were excited into circling by the force of a song: hers could scarcely be called a singing game. Yet in 1892 when Bodley's librarian E. W. B. Nicholson was gathering folklore from schoolchildren at Golspie, on the same Scottish coast, the game was being played in the same way as it is today. 'Jane Stuart tells me,' he wrote, '[that] two girls go out of the ring and then return to the middle of it, and dance, while the others walk round. They end by each taking another girl out, and the two girls so taken repeat the performance—the first two joining the ring in their stead'. The words had a lunatic gaiety:

> Hull many an auld man,
> An auld man, an auld man,
> Hull many an auld man,
> A dip, a dip a day.
>
> The auld man is jumping in the sky
> With his bonnie crucie wife,
> A dip, a dip a day.
>
> This is the one I choose, Oh!
> I choose, Oh! I choose, Oh!
> This is the one I choose,
> A dip, a dip a day.

But it may be that the song is the older form. After the shearing-supper was over, in Hardy's *Far from the Madding Crowd*, 1874, ch. xxiii, Jan Coggan (that 'crimson man with a spacious countenance') struck up:

> I've lost my love and I care not,
> I've lost my love and I care not,
> I shall soon have another
> That's better than t'other;
> I've lost my love, and I care not.

The game never seems to have had a tune of its own. Willa Muir sang it to 'Malbruk s'en va t'en guerre' ('For He's a Jolly Good Fellow') and so did girls in Moss Park, Glasgow, and Paisley, 1961. The Golspie girls' tune was on the pattern of 'There's Nae Luck About the House'. In Glasgow the tune is more like 'Weel May the Keel Row'; and in Birmingham it gravitates towards 'Nuts in May'.

Britain: *Golspie*, 1897, p. 185 | Argyllshire, 1905, a simple choosing game, 'Cherry cheeks and roses, cherry cheeks and roses, Cherry cheeks and roses, drumpy, drumpy, dry. Here's the one that I love best . . . drumpy, drumpy, dry' (*Folk-Lore*, xvi, p. 95) | Mosspark, Glasgow, 1961, 'Oh I lost my love in the kerney . . . A humpty, dumpty doo' | Paisley, 1961, 'I lost my lad in a tairney . . . Y-O-U' | Stirling, 1961, 'I lost my little kenny . . . Whatever shall I do?' | Welshpool, 1963, 'I lost my love in the curlie . . . Humpty diddle de dee' | Cumnock, 1965, 'Rosa love a canary . . . Y-O-U. This is the one that I love . . . Y-O-U' (*Those Dusty Bluebells*, p. 26) | Glasgow, 1970, 'I lost ma wee canary' | Glasgow, 1975, 'I lost my lod [lad] McCarney . . . a walla walla woe' ending 'Oh cowboys and Indians . . . a walla walla woe' | Birmingham, 1977, 'Rosy cheeks and cherries

... Y-O-U. I lost my friend Killarlie ... Y-O-U. They ended up in a dance hall ... Y-O-U. This is the one that I love ... Y-O-U.' 'Killarlie is a French boyfriend,' they said confidently.

103

Hey Little Lassie

Windermere, 1966

Hey, little lassie, will you have me?
I've leather gloves if you will have me.
I'm from the east and you're from the west,
I've wooden shoes but leather ones are best.
We'll dance together,
In any sort of weather,
Oh, we will dance together
And bow just so.

This is a Swedish game which is played at Brownies and occasionally in the playground. It appeared in Janet E. Tobitt's *Singing Games for Recreation*, book ii, no. 2, c.1938, with words almost as above, and directions for dancing in a double circle, boys inside and partners facing each other. The children were to clap their hands above their heads and jump where they stood; then hold out their hands as if showing their gloves. They shook their fingers at each other, stamped their wooden shoes on the ground, and put their leather shoes forward for admiration. During the singing of the last four lines they held each other's hands and slip-stepped counter-clockwise, pushed each other's hands back and forth, slip-stepped in the other direction, curtsied and bowed. In the next round the preliminary leap carried the dancers to the right, to face a new partner.

In Sweden the game is danced round Christmas trees, and round maypoles at Midsummer. The words (in a version from Gävle, 1970) are:

Hej, gosse lilla, vill du ha mig?	(Hey, my boy, will you have me?
Här är handskarna som du gar mig.	Here are the gloves you gave me.
Östbo är du och Västbo är jag,	You're from the East and I'm from the West,
Träsko har du och träsko har jag.	
Jänka bast du jänka vill,	You have wooden shoes and so do I.
Mig ska' du höra till.	Dance as well as you can,
Jänka bast du jänka vill,	You shall be mine,
Mej ska' du ha.	Dance as well as you can,
	You shall have me.)

Also see *Finlands Svenska Folkdiktning, 3, Sånglekar,* Otto Andersson, 1967, no. 223.

104

The Muffin Man

Cambo, Northumberland, 1978

> Do you know the muffin man,
>> The muffin man, the muffin man,
> Do you know the muffin man
>> Who lives in Drury Lane?

> Yes, I know the muffin man,
>> The muffin man, the muffin man,
> Yes, I know the muffin man
>> Who lives in Drury Lane.

This is the most eccentric of the eccentric ring games: it has changed its shape at least four times in the past hundred and sixty years. The first verse is found as a manuscript addition to Douce Adds 134(8) no. 3, *c.* 1820, in the Bodleian Library:

> Don't you know the Muffin-man
> And don't you know his name
> And don't you know the muffin-man
> That lives in Drury Lane?

Thus the game may have been in existence for many years when Frank Bellow described, in *The Art of Amusing*, 1866, an evening gathering in London where the guests had dropped in 'quite promiscuous':

An officer in the Guards, genus Swell, 'pwoposed' that we should play the Muffin man. As none of us had ever heard of this gentleman, or the muffin business, there was a general cry for light.

'Oh, it's vewy jolly, I asshua yaw. We all sit wound in a wing, yaw know, and one of us, yaw know, sings:–

> Do yaw know the muffin man,
> Do yaw know his name,
> Do yaw know the muffin man,
> That lives in Cwumpet Lane.

Then the next person answers:–

> Oh, yes, I know the muffin man,
> Oh, yes, I know the muffin man,
> Oh, yes, I know the muffin man,
> Who lives in Cwumpet Lane.

Then he turns to the next person, and when each person has sung his verse, yaw know, he then joins in the cawus, until it has gone all wound; then, yaw know, we all sing together:–

> We all know the muffin man,
> We all know his name;
> We all know the muffin man,
> Who lives in Cwumpet Lane.

The game is, yaw know, to keep a gwave face all the time. If yaw laugh yaw pay a forfeit.

'The ring,' said Bellow, was quickly constructed 'from individuals of every age from three up to seventy . . . but before he got half way through his verse we were all in convulsions of laughter . . . there was something so utterly idiotic and absurd in a large party of respectable, rational beings, congratulating themselves in song that they "knew the muffin man of Crumpet Lane".'

However, the social climate was changing, and children were being separated from their elders. In Mrs Mackarness's *Young Lady's Book*, 1876, the 'Muffin Man', though still played with question and answer round a seated ring, is in a section of 'Games for the Little Ones Indoors' and there is no mention of forfeits. And by the time Alice Gomme was sent the game, *c.* 1894, it was played in a standing circle, with a blindfolded child in the centre who had to touch or catch one of those in the ring and guess who they were (sometimes by asking questions and guessing by the person's voice).

The latest but probably not the last shape of the game is a dancing ring, in which, said a girl in Golspie, 1952, 'One boy or girl stands in the middle and begins by going to someone, dancing in front of them, and singing "Do you know the Muffin Man . . . who lives in Drury Lane?" and that person answers "Yes, I know the Muffin Man" and they join hands and dance round, but this time instead of singing "Yes, I know the Muffin Man" they sing "Two of us know the Muffin Man". Then the two separate and each dances to a new partner and it goes on until everyone is dancing round and singing that they "all know the Muffin Man".' This has been the way the 'Muffin Man' has been played from the 1920s onwards. Even so, in 1961, a boy in Offham, Kent, declared the game must be played like this: 'You all stand in a circle except One and that One skips round the circle and every time he picks up a Person and takes them with him.'

As rhyme only: *Shropshire Folk-Lore*, 1883, p. 571, 'Don't you know the Muffin-man, Don't you know his name, Don't you know the Muffin-man That lives in our lane? All around the Butter Cross, Up by St Giles's, Up and down the Gullet Shut, And call at Molly Miles's'.

Forfeits game: *The Young Lady's Book*, Mrs Henry Mackarness, 1876, pp. 278–80, first person chants 'to some sing-song tune' 'Do you know the muffin man . . . who lives in Drury Lane?' Next person replies 'Yes, I know etc.' 'Upon this they both exclaim "Then two of us know the muffin man etc."' and so on round the ring with more and more people knowing the muffin man | *Merrie Games in Rhyme*, E. M. Plunket, 1886, pp. 32–3.

Guessing game: *Traditional Games*, i, pp. 402–4 | *Eighty Singing Games*, Frank Kidson, 1907, 'O do you know the Muffin Man . . . who lives in Crumpet Lane' with, pedantically, the reply 'O yes we know . . . They call him Tom the Muffin Man . . . Of forty Crumpet Lane' | Chard, Somerset, 1922 (Macmillan Collection).

Dancing ring: Crewkerne, Somerset, 1922, 'That lives down Dorset Lane', with the chooser dancing with stretched legs, as in the Dutch game (Macmillan Collection) | Parkstone, Dorset, c.1930 | *A Brownies' Dozen*, Mary Chater, 1955, p. 18 | Scarborough, 1960 | Truro, 1961 | Welshpool, 1963, 'who lives down Cherry Lane, O' | Oban, 1974 | Cambo, Northumberland, 1978.

Well known in USA; and also in Holland, where the game is played much as in present-day Britain, but the chooser dances round with a kicking motion of his legs. The question 'Zeg, ken jij de mosselman . . . die woont in Schéveníngen?' (Say, do you know the musselman . . . who lives in Scheveningen?) is answered 'Ja, ik ken de mosselman . . .' and then, as the two dancers twirl round with crossed hands, 'Samen kennen wij de mosselman . . .' (Together we know the musselman).

Muffins were eaten throughout the eighteenth, nineteenth, and early twentieth centuries but conceded popularity to crumpets during the 1930s and were not widely obtainable again until about 1965. The earliest quotation for 'muffin man' in OED is 1810.

105

Push the Business On

Keswick, 1901, Gilchrist MSS 231 Aiii

I'll hire a horse and steal a gig,
And all the world shall have a jig,
And I'll do all that ever I can
To push the business on:
To push the business on,
To push the business on—
And I'll do all that ever I can
To push the business on.

The dancers hold hands in a ring, boy and girl alternately, and circle round. At 'To push the business on' the boys turn to the girl on their left and they clap hands three times. During the repetition the partners dance round together, and during the last two lines the girls are passed to the right of each boy, so that everyone has a new partner for the next turn.

Alison Uttley remembered this singing game vividly from the days when, as a child, she played it with grown men and girls on a farm in Cromford, Derbyshire, *c.*1897; and then the last line was 'To pass the music on' (*The Swans Fly Over*, 1959, p. 128).

The game was popular at Sunday School socials, was taken up by Frank Kidson, Cecil Sharp, and the other revivalists, and finally died out in the 1920s. Whether it has been put back into circulation by appearing in the Ladybird book of *Dancing Rhymes*, 1976, remains to be seen.

Askam-in-Furness, *c.*1890, 'To push the business on' | *Traditional Games*, ii, pp. 86–8 | National School, Keswick, 1901 | *Eighty Singing Games*, F. Kidson, p. 76 | *Children's Singing Games*, Cecil Sharp, ii, 1909, p. 18 | *Kerr's Guild of Play*, 1912, p. 17 | Great Glenham School, Suffolk, 1918, 'an Inspector taught the Infants "I'll buy a horse and steal a gig . . ." We did not care a lot for this game' | Somerset, 1922, three versions, including 'Barrow a horse, barrow a gig, And all the world shall have a rig, To pass the music on'.

106

Sailors Sailing on the Sea

Driffield, Yorks., 1975

Oh there were two sailors sailing on the sea,
If you want to choose a partner you've got to choose me.
Oh wishy washy, wishy washy, wishy washy woo,
If you want to choose a partner you've got to choose me.

You have two dancing in the middle and the rest go round. When it comes to 'You've got to choose a partner' they've each got to choose a partner. They put their hands on each other's shoulders and they dance with their legs out—like rag dolls—and then they go into the middle and cross hands and swing round. Then the first people go back into the ring and the new ones stay in the middle and it starts again (*girl, 10, Driffield, Yorkshire, 1975*).

This is a Scottish song far from its natural habitation and origins. In Scotland the words (too outlandish for English tongues) concern not sailors but unruly lassies:

Oh, we are three wee gallus[1] girls, sailing home from sea,
And if you pick the fairest one, the fairest one shall be—
Oh, rishy tishy petticoat, rishy tishy shawl,
Rishy tishy petticoat, the fairest one of all.

And in this Glasgow game one can just recognize the song Jeannie Robertson, the folk singer, remembered from her childhood *c.*1915:

We are three wee Glasgae molls,
We can let you see,
An' if you hate the one wee moll
Ye'll hate the heart of three.
Flashy dashy petticoats,
Flashy dashy shawls,
Twelve and a tanner's worth of boots,
And a'm a gallus moll.

The tune varies. In some places it is reminiscent of 'Pistol Packin' Momma', in some of 'The Laughing Policeman', and in some it is like the tune of 'Going to Kentucky' (p. 420).

Game: Moss Park, Glasgow, 1961 | West Walker, Newcastle upon Tyne, 1963, 'Oh sailor, sailor, sailing on the sea, If you want another one, why don't you come to me? Oh tishy tishy petticoat, oh tishy tishy tee, If you want another one, why don't you come to me?'; and eight other recordings in England and Scotland in the 1960s and 70s, including Glasgow, 1975, as quoted.
    Song: Jeannie Robertson, cassette 'What a Voice', side A, 7(5) | *Tradition*, i, 1966, p. 16, 'The Street Songs of Glasgow', 'As I went doon the Gallowgate, Ma hert began tae beat, Seein' a' the factory lassies, Comin' doon the street, Wi' their flashy, dashy petticoats, Their flashy dashy shawls, Five-an-a-tanner gutty [gutta percha] boots "Oh, we're big gallus molls!" ', with chorus 'Oh, ye're ma wee gallus bloke nae mair, etc.'.

---

[1] *Gallus*, spirited, plucky. The earlier meaning was 'fit for the gallows'.

107

There Was a Young Couple

Tune: 'Nuts in May'

There was a young couple a-skating away,
  Skating away, skating away,
There was a young couple a-skating away
  On a cold and frosty morning.

The ice was thin and they both fell in,
  Both fell in, both fell in,
The ice was thin and they both fell in,
  On a cold and frosty morning.

People form a ring, and the two people in the middle do the actions. Then they
pick two more people to go in the middle and the game continues as before (*girl,
10, Penrith, 1957*).

In January 1969 little girls in the playground of Old Street School,
Ludlow, were galloping round and singing, while two 'twizzled' in the
middle:

There came a cobbler skating along . . .
  On a cold and frosty morning.

The ice is in the orphan in . . .
  On a cold and frosty morning.

Then the ring stood still and clapped their hands while the middle two
went skipping in and out of them in opposite directions. They all sang:

You skip out and we'll skip in . . .
  On a cold and frosty morning.

The two people finished up in front of two members of the circle, who
went into the middle. 'We usually play it at home outside our houses,' they
said, 'In the summer.'

These are the only two instances found in Britain of a favourite
American play-party song, 'Three Old Maids'. As played in Cleveland
County, Oklahoma, in the 1920s, the song began:

Three old maids skating went,
  Skating went, skating went.
Three old maids skating went,
  So early in the morning,

the second verse being 'Ice was thin and they fell in', and the third 'Ask some one to help them out'. It was played with 'three ladies joining hands inside of a large circle of standers-by. While the outside circle of people sing, the three old maids skip around and around. During the last stanza they choose a partner . . . The chosen partners swing the three old maids, and then the three old bachelors remain in the center and the song is repeated . . . This play dance is repeated for hours at play-parties or square dances, each time the girls and boys choosing the one they liked best—so to speak, had a crush on' (B. A. Botkin, *American Play-Party Song*, 1937, p. 331). In a dance tradition which has turned even 'Twinkle, Twinkle, Little Star' into a 'swinging play' it is not surprising to find that the 'Three Old Maids' is based on the nursery rhyme 'Three children sliding on the ice' (which, in turn, derives from a burlesque ballad *The Lamentation of a Bad Market; or the Drowning of three Children in the Thames*, c. 1680: see *ODNR* no. 99).

USA: Missouri, c.1914, 'Three old bums went down to town' (*JAFL*, xxvii, p. 301) | Michigan, c.1914, 'Three little girls a-sliding went' (*JAFL*, xxxiii, p. 128).

108

Three Jolly Fishermen

Salford, 1970

There were three jolly fishermen,
There were three jolly fishermen,
There were three jolly fishermen,
And they'd just come home from sea.

> They cast their nets into the sea,
> They cast their nets into the sea,
> They cast their nets into the sea,
> The jolly jolly fishermen,
> A-men!

Opinions of this game have differed. Nine-year-old enthusiasts at Salford in 1970 said 'We usually have all the playground, all the *school* nearly, doing it. When they see us playing it they always join in.' On the other hand the folk-song collector Anne Gilchrist, who had played it 'in nursery days' in Manchester about 1880, commented 'It was not a particularly interesting game, and perhaps on that account not well known.'

This was the Salford way of playing:

We all get in a ring, and there's three people we pick, see. Then they join hands and then they skip around, and then we sing, and we skip the opposite way to the people in the middle, and when we say 'They cast their nets into the sea' we stand back as if we're casting the nets, and then we pull—you know, as if we're pulling the net in. And then the three persons in the middle, they pick another three out of the ring, and then they skip and sing 'There were *six* jolly fishermen' and then when they've finished the first three goes out, and then it starts again.

Anne Gilchrist's version, played with a little friend in Manchester, was much the same but ended 'And very fine fish caught we'. The friend's mother remembered a different ending from her own childhood, before 1850:

> We cast our nets into the sea,
> We cast our nets into the sea,
> We cast our nets into the sea,
> And silv'ry herring caught we.
> We sell them three for twopence,
> We sell them three for twopence,
> We sell them three for twopence,
> While the merry bells do ring;
> Come buy or you'll be too late,
> We sell them three for twopence,
> While the merry bells do ring.

It is strange that even in a shortened form such a vapid, and probably pedagogic, game should have survived; its survival seems, in any case, to be confined to Lancashire and Staffordshire, perhaps because it used to be much played at Sunday School parties there.

Gilchrist MSS 231 Aiii, p. 18 | *Traditional Games*, i, pp. 286–7, two versions, both from north Staffordshire | Whitmore, Staffs., *c*.1910 | Somerset, 1912, *Children's Singing Games*, Cecil Sharp, iv, p. 10 | Hanley, Staffs., *c*. 1915 | Somerset, 1922, 'a game our governess taught us at school' (Macmillan Collection) | Tunstall, Staffs., *c.*1930 | Sneyd Green, Staffs., 1965, 'There were three jolly fishermen . . . And they went out to sea. They cast their nets into the sea . . . And see what they have caught'.

109

Draw a Bucket of Water

Fringford, Oxon., 1950

> Draw a bucket of water
> For my lady's daughter,
> One in the tub, two in the tub,
> Three in the tub, four in the tub.
> Four little dollies in a rub-dub-dub,
> Four little dollies in a rub-dub-dub.

Four girls stand with hands clasped in couples, one pair of arms over the other pair of arms, so that they form a cross. They see-saw backwards and forwards as they sing the first two lines. As they sing 'One in the tub' one of the players is brought inside the circle by the joined hands of the people each side of her, which are lifted up over her head and around her waist (see illustration facing). The other 'dollies' are brought into the tub in the same manner, and they all jump up and down singing the last lines. The 'dollies' are not toys but the wooden appliances with arms and legs which were used to agitate dirty clothes in laundry tubs.

In the nineteenth century only one girl was entwined during the singing of the verse, which was repeated for each of the others; and the words were more romantic, as can be seen in a version from Halliwell's *Nursery Rhymes of England*, 1842:

'Draw a Bucket of Water' (No. 109), Workington, Cumberland, 1962. As they sing 'Wee laal sister creeps under the bush' the two players either side of her lift their arms over the 'laal sister's' head and round her waist, thus bringing her into the circle.

Draw a pail of water,
For my lady's daughter;
My father's a king, and my mother's a queen,
My two little sisters are dressed in green,
Stamping grass and parsley,
Marigold leaves and daisies.
One rush, two rush,
Pray thee, fine lady, come under my bush.

The action of this ingenious plaiting game is an old dance-figure called 'the basket', which occurs for instance in the dance 'Cottagers', and in the running set as observed by Cecil Sharp and Maud Karpeles in the Appalachian Mountains in 1917, when the figure was 'The Californian Show Basket' or 'Old Shuck Basket'. In American square dances it is usually 'Chicken in a Basket'.

Britain: *Nursery Rhymes of England*, J. O. Halliwell, 1842, p. 108, 'Sieve my lady's oatmeal, Grind my lady's flour, Put it in a chesnut, Let it stand an hour; One may rush, two may rush, Come, my girls, walk under the bush' | *Shropshire Folk-Lore*, 1883, p. 521 | Milngavie, c.1885, 'Draw a bucket of water, For a lady's daughter, One in a bush, Two in a bush, Let the fair lady come under'; then they jump about and sing 'A bunch of rags, A bottle of beer' till they fall down (Crofton MS, ii, p. 70) | *Traditional Games*, i, pp. 100–3, 12 versions from oral tradition | Newcastle upon Tyne, c.1910, 'Tansy and Pansy, Marigold, daisy, One on the bush, two on the bush, Let the young lady be under the bush', 'then we jumped round yelling "Chow, chow the baccy, chow"' | Yarcombe, Devon, 1922, 'Draw a bucket of water, For my lady's daughter; Milk her cows and serve her pigs, And drive her ducks to water. All the bells in Bethlehem, Will ring for my young lady; One a rush, two a rush, Pray, young lady, creep under a bush' (Macmillan Collection) | Bedford, 1945, 'Four little dolls in a tub, tub, tub . . . One goes in, two goes in, three goes in, four goes in. Four little dolls in a tub, tub, tub . . . One goes out, two goes out, etc.'; other 'dolly' versions from Sale, 1953, Leeds, 1966, and Macclesfield, 1980 | Ipswich, 1953, 'Draw a bucket of water, For my lady's daughter, One in a bush, Two in a bush, Pray, young lady, pop under', and similar from Crowcombe, 1956, Workington, 1962, and London w4, 1975.

USA: Somerville, Mass., c.1895, for jumping over a swaying rope, which was held higher and higher, 'Wash the lady's dishes, Hang them on the bushes, One on the bush, Two on the bush, Let the young lady jump over' (or 'step under') | Cincinnati, 1908, 'Draw buckets of water, Susie and her father, One bucket full, Two buckets full, Let the old lady under' (*JAFL*, xl, pp. 15–16).

Australia: Brisbane, c.1935, 'Draw a bucket of water, For a lady's daughter, One in a rush, two in a rush, This young lady get under the water', ends with jumping up and down and singing 'Shake up the pepper pot'; similar in Cairns, 1953, and Sydney, 1945.

Germany: *Deutsches Kinderspiel*, F. M. Böhme, 1897, pp. 544–5, 'Wo gehst du hin? An den Rhein. Was thust du da? Wasser schöpfen. Was gibst du mir? Einen gold'nen Ring. Schlüpfe durch!' (Where are you going? To the Rhine. What to do? To draw water. What will you give me? A golden ring. Slip through!). Then the players jump about shouting 'Herentanz, herentanz!'

Norway: Oslo, 1959 and 1974, 'Tak over skapet, (Berit) ut av skapet, Sullan dullan loppan dei, Dra din vei!' (Ceiling over the cupboard, (Berit) out of the cupboard, [nonsense], Go along with you!).

XVIII

Buffoonery

THESE games generate gaiety. With heady tunes, prankish gestures, fantastic words, and whirlygig motion, they can arouse such excitement that the players fall down laughing at the end as if they were drunk. When the 'Okey Kokey' is danced by young adults the hilarity may be caused partly by alcohol; but children's high spirits can bring them to a state of self-intoxication in which the only reality is the dizzy pleasure of the game, and they need this release from the real world as much as do their elders.

The only game to lack the proper verve is 'Punchinello', although the French pedagogue who wrote the original 'Polchinelle' undoubtedly thought he had given it the right touch of fancifulness.

110

Okey Kokey

Oxford, 1979

> You put your right arm in,
> You put your right arm out,
> In, out, in, out,
> Shake it all about;
> You do the Okey Kokey
> And you turn around,
> And that's what it's all about.
> Oh, Okey Kokey Kokey!
> Oh, Okey Kokey Kokey!
> Oh, Okey Kokey Kokey!
> Knees bend, arms stretch,
> Ra ra ra!

Thereafter they usually put their left arm in the circle, their right foot, left foot, head, and 'whole self'; but the parts of the body to be 'shaken all about' can include elbows, hips, ears, eyes, nose, and, as a nine-year-old in Langton Matravers said in 1977, 'your stummick and your bottom'. The dancers in the circle follow their own sung instructions, and wiggle their bodies when they sing 'You do the Okey Kokey'. They join hands for the chorus, then, raising their arms as they go, plunge three times into the middle ('Hurting ourselves like anything,' said one gleefully); and, after bending their knees and stretching their arms, they thrust their fists in the air cheering 'Ra, ra, ra'.

This must be the most gloriously boisterous, the noisiest, and probably the most popular ring game of the present day. The children get quite carried away by the performance and collapse in hysterical laughter, gasping 'That was good fun, that was'. They like it because 'it tires you out' and 'makes you puffed'. It is of course based on Jimmy Kennedy's action-song of 1941, which was, as Kennedy himself said, 'the big dance favourite' in Britain during the Second World War.

Curiously enough the Kennedy game does not seem to have entered the playground till the late 1950s. In the early fifties the words were still those in Frank Kidson and Alfred Moffat's *Eighty Singing Games*, 1907, from whence they were taught in infant schools:

> Here we go Lubin Loo,
> Here we go Lubin Light,
> Here we go Lubin Loo,
> All on a Saturday night.
> Put your right foot in,
> Put your right foot out,
> Shake it a little, a little,
> And turn yourself about.

In the late nineteenth century the verses were far from standardized, although 'Here we dance Lubin, Lubin' (or 'Looby looby') was the most common form. Mrs Henry Mackarness, for instance, in *The Young Lady's Book*, 1876, said the children must go round singing 'Looby looby looby, All on a Saturday night' but that they 'must take care when they put their heads in the middle of the circle, or they may come unpleasantly near their neighbours'; but the Revd Addison Crofton found a more joyful rendering in Reddish, Lancashire, *c.*1880:

> We come here to be merry,
>   Why should we be sad?
> We'll all join hands together
>   And dance like somebody mad!
> Then hey for laddie my gaddie,
>   And hey for laddie my gay,
> And hey for laddie my gaddie,
>   And hey for laddie my gay!
>
> Come put your right foot in,
> And put your right foot out;
> And give yourself a wriggle,
> And turn yourself about!

The version John Bell of Newcastle recorded *c.*1840 (in his interleaved copy of *Gammer Gurton's Garland*, p. 47) had the same convivial gaiety:

> Up with Ailie, Ailie,
>   Up with Ailie now,
> Up with Ailie, Ailie,
>   We're a' roaring fou.
> Turn your Right leg in,
>   Turn your left Leg out,
> Shake your Body a little,
>   And turn you round about.

And (as George Sturt reports in *William Smith, Potter and Farmer*, pp. 189–90) a Rector of Farnborough tried to gladden the hearts of his parishioners with the disreputable ditty *c.*1835. The Rector

seems to have looked upon his parish as a toy. He had once tried to revive a Maypole festival. Ann Smith . . . could tell of the rector's rather excited efforts to egg on the dancers with a rhyme:

> Turn your toes in, turn your toes out,
> Twist a little and turn a little,
> And shake yourself about!

In Scotland, however, where old words and customs linger, Robert

Chambers found a dance which has all the characteristics of the medieval *carole*, which was danced slowly in exactly the way he describes, with the refrain sung while the circle moves and the verse sung while it is standing still:

The party form a circle, taking hold of each other's hands. One sings, and the rest join, to the tune of *Lullibullero*, 'Fal de ral la, fal de ral la'; while doing so they move a little sideways, and back again, beating the time (which is slow) with their feet. As soon as the line is concluded, each claps his hands and wheels grotesquely round, singing at the same moment the second line of the verse, 'Hinkumbooby, round about'. Then they sing . . . throwing their right hand into the circle and the left out, 'Right hands in, and left hands out', still beating the time; then add as before, while wheeling round with a clap of the hands, 'Hinkumbooby round about'.

The movements continued with 'Left hands in, and right hands out', 'Right foot in, and left foot out', 'Left foot in and right foot out', 'Heads in and backs out', 'Backs in and heads out', 'A' feet in and nae feet out', 'Shake hands a', shake hands a''', and 'Good night a', good night a''', when the boys bowed and the girls curtsied (*Popular Rhymes of Scotland*, 1842, pp. 65–6).

One wonders whether Chambers' 'Hinkumbooby' is the same as the jollification in Brome's *Joviall Crew*, 1641: 'That were wont to see my Ghossips . . . daunce clutterdepouch, and Hannykin booby'. It would seem likely, for the dance was known at least as early as 1745, when it was used as the basis of a political song 'IN and OUT and TURN ABOUT: A New C——t Dance, To the TUNE of John Bob'd in, and John Bob'd Out: Or, Bob in Joan: Or, The Miller of Mansfield'. The song sheet is headed:

> One TOOL In, The Other TOOL Out,
> And so they DANCE LOOBY round about.

The first verse goes:

> Ye people at Home
>   Who H–n—r hate,
> How partial's your Doom,
>   How fickle the State!
> Dependent on Chance,
>   The Whole is a Doubt,
> Like this Courtier's Dance,
>   Call'd *Looby about*,
> Like this Courtier's Dance,
>   Call'd *Looby about*.

The eleventh verse gives an idea of how 'Looby Loo' was danced in the year of the Forty-five Rebellion:

Mhe Pl–m–s cut clean
  (B—h danc'd like a Clown)
John caper'd so high,
  He soon tumbl'd down,
With one Foot In,
  And the other Foot out,
But yet he hops
  Looby round about, &c.

Our belief that the game is far older than this earliest appearance in print is reinforced by the fact that it is well known in other parts of Europe. In France it is 'La Mistenlaire', and, as given by Madame Celnart in *Manuel Complet de Jeux de Societé*, 1830, is danced with a 'captain' in the centre of the ring, who demonstrates the movements which the dancers copy:

Savez-vous comment l'on danse
A la nouvelle façon? A la nouvelle façon?

Une main, deux mains,
Et voici comment l'on danse
A la nouvelle façon. A la nouvelle façon.

culminating in:

Il faut finir cette danse
A la nouvelle façon.
Une main, deux mains,
Un pied, deux pieds,
(*kiss to the right, kiss to the left*)
Et voici comment l'on danse
A la nouvelle façon.

(Do you know how they dance, In the new fashion? One hand, two hands, And this is how they dance, In the new fashion . . . This dance must be finished, In the new fashion. One hand, two hands, One foot, two feet (kiss to right and left), And this is how they dance, In the new fashion.)

In French Switzerland at the turn of the century (see *Schweizerisches Archiv für Volkskunde*, ii, 1898, p. 154) and probably still today, the boys made one circle and the girls another. The boys began:

Dites-nous, Mesdames,	(Tell us, ladies,
Que voulez-vous faire?	What would you like to do?
Voulez-vous jouer	Would you like to play
De la mistangaine,	Some thingamybob,
Le *pied* à terre, terre, terre, terre,	The *foot* to the ground . . .)
Ah! ah! ah!	
De la mistangaine?	

They stopped, let go hands, and all struck the ground with their feet. Then the girls sang:

Dites-nous, Messieurs,
Que voulez-vous faire?
Voulez-vous jouer
De la mistangaine,
Le *coude* à terre, terre, terre . . .

(Tell us, gentlemen,
What would you like to do?
Would you like to play
Some thingamybob,
The *elbow* to the ground . . .)

The boys began the round again and at the words *thumb, head, hand*, and *behind* the dancers struck the ground with these different parts of the body. Then the two circles combined, and everyone sang:

Dites-nous vraiment,
Que voulons-nous faire?
Voulons-nous jouer
De la mistangaine,
Les têtes à têtes, têtes, têtes, têtes,
Ah! ah! ah!
De la mistangaine?

(Tell us truly
What shall we do?
Shall we play
Some thingamybob;
Heads to heads, heads, heads, heads,
Ah! ah! ah!
Some thingamybob?)

In the Netherlands, where 'De Zevensprong' is as popular as the 'Hokey Cokey' is in Britain, they sing with actions:

Heb je wel gehoord van de zeven, de zeven,
Heb je wel gehoord van de zeven-sprong?
Ze zeggen dat ik niet dansen kan,
Ik kan dansen als een edelman.
Dat is een,
Dat is een, dat is twee, etc.

(Have you ever heard of the seven, the seven,
Have you ever heard of the seven springs?
They say that I cannot dance,
I can dance like a nobleman.
That is one,
That is one, that is two, etc.)

The actions are: one step forward, two steps forward, kneel with one knee, kneel with the other knee, one elbow on the ground, the other elbow on the ground, the head on the ground.

In Germany, as one might expect, the dance is also 'The Seven Springs'. Böhme prints, amongst many others, a version from H. Smidt's *Bremer Kinderreime*, 1836 (1859, p. 29):

Danz mi mal de seven Sprünge,
Danz mi mal de seven.
Meenst dat ick nich danzen kann?
Kann danzen as 'n Edelmann—
Spring hoog up! Spring hoog up!

(Dance me the seven leaps,
Dance me the seven.
Do you think I can't dance?
I can dance like a nobleman—
Leap up high! Leap up high!)

He says the dancer must perform the following movements: two with the feet, two with the knees, two with the elbows, and must finally hit his forehead on the ground. Another version printed by Böhme goes 'Kennt ihr nicht die sieben Sprünge?'. When the Germans were retreating up Italy during the Second World War the soldiers sang what seems to be a parody:

Kennst du den Avanti schritt?	(Do you know the forward step?
Ein Schritt vor und zehn zurueck.	One step forward and ten back.
Ja, ja, den kenn ich schon,	Yes, yes, I know it well,
Denn ich komm direkt von Rom.	For I come direct from Rome.)

The song goes on 'If you want to see a German You've got to go to the Brenner—Now they are at the Alps, Adolf can't hold them any longer —What are Adolf's new weapons? The young laddies and the old apes' (*Ballads of World War II*, Hamish Henderson, pp. 39–40).

England: *Popular Rhymes*, J. O. Halliwell, 1849, p. 129, 'Now we dance looby, looby, looby, Now we dance looby, looby, light. Shake your right hand a little And turn you round about'; the actions accumulate until, in the last verse, the dancers shake their right hands, left hands, right feet, left feet, and heads | Manchester, 1870s, 'Here we dance Lubin, Lubin, Here we dance Lubin light ... Every Saturday night', and Loanhead, 1900, 'Halla-by looby loo' (Gilchrist MSS 231 Aiii, p. 97) | *Merrie Games in Rhyme*, E. M. Plunket, 1886, pp. 16–17, 'Here we go Lubin, Lubin' | Cornwall, 1887, 'Friskee, friskee, I was and I was, A-drinking of small beer. Right arms in ...' (*Folk-Lore*, v, p. 49) | *Sheffield Glossary*, S. O. Addy, 1888, p. 320, 'Can you dance, looby looby (thrice) ... All on a Friday night? You put your right foot in, And then you take it out, And wag it, and wag it, and wag it, Then turn and turn about' | *Traditional Games*, i, 1894, pp. 352–61, nine recordings from oral tradition (eight from England and one from Belfast). Most begin 'Here we dance 'Lubin loo' or 'looby loo' and end on different nights (e.g. on 'Christmas night', Epworth, near Doncaster, and on 'New Year's night', Nottingham); some are eccentric (e.g. 'I love Antimacassar, Antimacassar loves me' from Dorset) | Midgley, near Halifax, *c.* 1900, 'Now we're marching as we go, And here we march for ever, March as high as in the west, And then we'd stop for ever. Put all your right arms out, Put all your right arms in, Shake 'em, shake 'em, shake 'em, Turn yourselves around' | Gloucestershire, 1912, 'Here we dance looby looby ... On a summer's night' (*Children's Singing Games*, Cecil Sharp, iv, p. 2) | *London Street Games*, 1916, pp. 74–5, 'Here we go Loobeloo' ending 'Put your noddle in, Put your whole self in' | *Street Games of North Shields Children*, M. and R. King, 1930, pp. 33–4, 'Ha-la-ga-loo-ga-loo, Ha-la-ga-loo-ga light ... Upon a Saturday night' | Recordings of 'Here we go looby loo' from various places as taught by teachers, e.g. Alton, 1954, 'Here we go loopy loo'; Wilmslow, 1960 'Here we come looby loo'; East Tisted, 1964, 'looby loo'. Since late 1950s, recordings of the 'Okey Kokey' (or 'Hokey Kokey', or 'Hokey Pokey') from 27 places: but one can count on finding the game in any playground in Britain.

Scotland: Golspie, 1891, brought from Edinburgh, 'Hilli ballu ballai, Hilli ballu ballight ... Upon a Saturday night. Put all your right feet out, Put all your left feet in, Turn them a little, a little, And turn yourselves about. Chu!' Then 'right and left hands', 'noses', 'neighbours'. At 'Chu!' the circle moves in the opposite direction (*Golspie*, pp. 176–8) | *Traditional Games*, ii, 1898, pp. 430–1, 'Hulla-balloo, ballee ... All on a winter's night' from Nairnshire | Forfar, 1910 and 1952, 'Hallabuloobaloo; also Dundee, *c.*1915 | Golspie, 1953, almost identical to Golspie, 1891.

USA: Boston (?), *c.*1820, 'Put your right elbow in, Put your right elbow out, Shake yourselves a little, And turn yourselves about', followed by left elbow, ears, and feet: 'the game was danced deliberately and decorously, as old fashion was, with slow rhythmical motion. Now it has been turned into a romp ... in Boston, "Ugly Mug"' (*Games of American Children*, p. 131) | Cincinnati,

1908, 'Let us dance, Luby, Luby, Let us dance, Luby light, Let us dance, Luby, Luby, All on a Monday (or whatever) night. Put the right hand out, Take it back again, Shake your hand a little bit, And turn about again' (*JAFL*, xl, pp. 25–6) | St Louis, 1944, 'Here we go Looby Loo, Here we go Looby Light, Here we go Looby Loo, All on a Saturday night, etc.' (*JAFL*, lx, p. 43).

Spain: *Jochs de la Infancia*, F. Maspons y Labrós, 1874, 'Jan petit', pp. 8–9.

A good song-and-dance is used over and over again. In the First World War the troops danced to their own version: 'Oh, here's to Ronnel McConnel, Oh, here's to a bottle of beer, Oh, here's to Ronnel McConnel, We're all good company here, So put your left leg out, etc' (*Tommy's Tunes*, F. T. Nettleingham, 1917, p. 90). In 1963 the night clubs of London were captivated by a new dance ('a mixture of Twist, Madison and Hully-Gully') set to Frankie Vaughan's currently popular 'Here we go loop-de-loop'.

A 'looby' is a clumsy, stupid fellow; and Lubin is a generic name for a country bumpkin.

I I I

Sally Go Round the Sun

Birmingham, 1977

> Sally go round the sun,
> Sally go round the moon,
> Sally go round the chimney pots
> On a Sunday afternoon.

Girls in Birmingham in 1977 said that 'Molly go round the moon' was one of their best games. 'Some say Molly, and some say Sally,' they said impatiently, 'It doesn't matter which.' With lightning speed they were numbered round by 'the boss of the game' and were set in motion by the song. Each time they said 'afternoon' a girl turned outwards, and 'when you've all been outwards you turn back inwards when you're singing it again'.

The Birmingham girls were entitled to play the game in the manner of 'Wallflowers' (p. 244) if they wanted; but usually the circle romp round to the right singing the verse, kick their legs high in the air at the end, shouting 'Oh!' or 'Whoops!', and then dance round in the opposite direction. The game has, however, been in a decline (probably ousted by the 'Okey Kokey') and is more likely to furnish romantic memories of childhood than to be found in a local playground.

H. E. Bates recalled, from his childhood in the Midlands during the First World War, '"Sally Go Round the Moon" . . . a game of singing and swinging under lamp-posts that I then thought rather cissy and that now carries for me a lovely memory of pinafores and pigtails bright under gaslight' (*Everybody's*, March 1954). In South Shields in the mid-1920s James Kirkup, at the age of two, was 'a little uneasy about the whole display—something rather wild about the words and the abandon of the dancing faintly shocked my infant primness; and on the final word, the girls lifted up their frocks at the back and shoved their bottoms out in a way which I found very distressing. The words went something like this:

> Halligal, eagle, eagle,
> Halligal, eagle, ee!
> Halligal, eagle, eagle,
> Upon a Sarrada' neet
> Whee!'

(*The Only Child*, pp. 99–100)

Twenty years before that, in Bean Street, Hull, the words had been:

> Alley galoo, galoo,
> Alley galoo, galoo,
> Alley galoo, alley galoo,
> I lost me father's shoe—Hi!

It seems from these northern verses that the song may have some connection with the Scottish form of 'Looby Loo' (Nicholson's 'Hilli ballu ballai' from *Golspie*, for instance, which ended 'Chu!' and the circle reversed direction), and it is significant that the tunes are the same. On the other hand Sally was already travelling in space when the Revd Addison Crofton interviewed Mary Martha Mason in Giggleswick *c.*1880. The verse she sang was:

> Sally go round the sun,
> Sally go round the moon,
> Sally go round the Rainbow
> On Sunday afternoon,

and she added 'This game goes on for a very long time' (Crofton MS, i, p. 96).

Britain: Deptford, London, 1898 (*Traditional Games*, ii, p. 149) | Whalley, *c.*1900, 'Sally go round the moon . . . the stars . . . On a Sunday afternoon, Ch!' (Gilchrist MSS, 231, Aiii, p. 71) | *Old Surrey Singing Games*, A. E. Gillington, 1909, p. 6, 'Sally go round the Sun; Sally go round the Moon; Sally go round the Chimney-Pots, On a Sunday afternoon. Whoop!'; and many similar recordings from oral tradition *c.*1910 to *c.*1937 | Chesterton, Staffordshire, *c.*1910, 'Sally go round the moon . . . the stars . . . the churchyard, Sunday afternoon—Hoop la!' | Somerset, 1912, 'Sally go round the moon . . . the stars . . . the chimney pots, Ev'ry afternoon, Bump!' (*Children's Singing Games*, Cecil Sharp, v, p. 12) | *London Street Games*, 1916, p. 52, 'Sally go round the moon, Sally, Sally go round the sun, Sally go round the ominlebus On a Sunday afternoon' | Since 1950: Amlwch and Swansea, 1952 | Welshpool, 1952, 'Sally go round the sun . . . the moon . . . the mulberry bush Every afternoon. Boo!' | Alton, 1954.

Ireland: Dublin, 1975, 'Sally go round the moon . . . the stars . . . the chimney pot, And an Oosha Mary Ann' (*All In! All In!* Eilís Brady, 1975, p. 12).

Australia: Footscray, Victoria, *c.*1915, as Gillington.

Canada: Toronto, 1909, 'Sally go round the sun . . . the moon . . . the chimney-top Every afternoon' (*JAFL*, xxxi, p. 55).

USA: Cincinnati, 1908, 'Mary go round the sun . . . the moon . . . the mulberry bush, On a Sunday afternoon' (or, 'With a yellow coon') (*JAFL*, xl, p. 27) | St Louis, 1944, 'Jolly go round the sun . . . the moon . . . a hickory stick, On Sunday afternoon' (*JAFL*, lx, p. 43).

112

Hey, Jock ma Cuddy!

Tune: 'Okey Kokey'

> Hey, Jock ma cuddy,
>   Ma cuddy's o'er the dyke,
> And if you touch ma cuddy,
>   Ma cuddy will give you a bite—
>   Hooch!

Another game, like 'Sally Go Round the Sun', which has the charm of perpetual motion. The children dance round, fling their legs in the air at 'Hooch!', and start off again in the opposite direction. It is perhaps more sung than played, nowadays; it lingers on in kindergartens, and is sometimes used for counting-out (e.g. Edinburgh, 1954). This rhyme about a snappish donkey had however already undergone one metamorphosis. In 1824 John Mactaggart included in his *Gallovidian Encyclopedia* an 'old riddle respecting the *nettle*:

> Heg Beg adist the dyke—and Heg Beg ayout the dyke—
> Gif ye touch Heg Beg—Heg Beg—will gar ye byke.'

All recordings are Scottish: Forfar, 1910 and 1952, 'Hey, Jock ma cuddy, Ma cuddy's on the dike, And if ye meddle ma cuddy, Ma cuddy'll gi'e ye a bite—hooch!' (*Lang Strang*, Jean C. Rodger, p. 34) | Isle of Bute, 1911, '. . . And if you touch my cuddy' (*Rymour Club*, ii, p. 74) | *County Folk-Lore: Fife*, J. E. Simpkins, 1914, p. 306, as riddle | Since 1950: Kirkcaldy, 1952 | Glenrothes, 1974, as a 'saying' | Oban, 1974, teacher-taught | Glasgow, 1975, 'And if you want ma cuddy, Ma cuddy will give you a kick'.

113

Ellen McGiggin

Ellen McGiggin was put to the jiggin'
   For lifting her leg so high, oh;
All of a sudden a big black pudden
   Came flying through the sky, oh!

A saw the kilties comin',
   A saw them gaun awa',
A saw the kilties comin',
   Comin' through the Broomielaw.

Another set of verses adopted for singing in the ring, and sometimes, too, adapted for other purposes. The second verse is part of the old song calculated, by those who sang it at a safe distance, to rouse the fighting spirit of the 42nds. The Broomielaw is on the north side of Glasgow harbour.

Glasgow, 1954 | Bishop Auckland, 1961, for two-baller, 'All of a sudden a big black pudden Came flying through the air; It missed my ma and hit my pa, And knocked him off the chair' | Workington, 1962, 'Mary Malloga she lifted her leg, She lifted her leg so high, yow! All of a sudden a great surprise Came floating through the air-O. Yaw-saw magamazoni, Yaw-saw magamazoni, Yaw-saw magamazoni, Early in the morning'. All kick their legs in the air at 'yow!'; then the one in the centre chooses her successor by dancing 'a kind of pas-de-basque step' in front of her.

114

This Way Hen-er-y

Liss, 1978

A nine-year-old girl brought this game to Liss from Denmead, near Portsmouth, in 1974. 'We all get in pairs like this, in a long line,' she said. She took her partner's hands in hers and pushed them backwards and forwards with a boxing action, while they sang:

> This way, Hen-er-y,
> That way, Hen-er-y,
> This way, Hen-er-y,
> All day long.

'And everybody is doing the same,' she said, 'and then I walk off, anywhere I like, doing some action. Say I might be putting my hands up beside my head, one after the other—like Morecambe and Wise do on the television. You can do any kind of action, just what you like. Some people clap their knees, or skip. Anyway, I walk off as far as I like, and I sing:

> Strakmus, Lizzie,
> Strakmus, Lizzie,
> Strakmus, Lizzie,
> All day long.'

('Strakmus?' we said. 'Have we got it right? What does it mean?' 'It doesn't mean anything,' she said impatiently, 'but it doesn't matter.') She went on 'Then the other person follows you, doing just what you are doing, and she sings:

> Here comes this one,
> Just like the other one,
> Here comes this one,
> All day long.'

In Lilliput, 1978, two lines of girls clapped while singing:

> Here comes Sally down the alley,
> Here comes Sally down the alley,
> Here comes Sally down the alley,
> On the North Carolina.

'Sally' skipped through the alley, and round and through again until the song stopped, when she chose as the next 'Sally' one of the pair of girls she was standing between, and took her place.

In 1969 girls in Bristol were overcome by a dancing craze which had the words:

> Here we go shoo sha, shoo sha, shoo sha,
> Here we go shoo sha, all night long.
>
> I walk down the alley and what do I see?
> I see a big fat man from Tennessee:
> To the front, to the back,
> To the s-s-side.
> I got a pain in me leg,
> I got a pain in me back,
> And I do the camel walk.

(The 'camel walk' was bent double, with legs kicking out to the side.)

And in Stepney, 1976, lines of little girls were wiggling their hips to another variation on the theme:

> Pick up the telephone, what do you hear?
> An iddy biddy man from Kanassee:
> Going boom shawawa, boom shawawa,
> Boom shawawa, all day long.
> Going boom shawawa, boom shawawa,
> Boom shawawa, all day long.

The next telephone call is from 'a big fat lady from Kanassee' when, they said, 'you comb your hands round the front of your body, making it very fat'; and the next is from 'an iddy biddy baby' when 'you put your knees together, point your fingers down and wiggle your way down to baby size'.

At first sight, these sets of words seem to be hopelessly muddled immigrants from the USA, and scarcely related to each other. On closer inspection, it can be seen that they are based on lines which were embedded in the equally higgledy-piggledy clapping chants of the mid-nineteenth century, to which modern lines have adhered:

Where have you been all day long?
Up the alley, courting Sally,
Picking up cinders, breaking winders,
All—day—long.

See p. 442.

See p. 442.

Britain: Bristol, 1969 | St John's Wood, London, 1973, 'This way, Valerie, That way, Valerie, This way, Valerie, All day long. Here comes Valerie, Here comes the other one, Here comes Valerie, All day long' | Liss, 1975 | Stepney, 1976 | Lilliput, Dorset, 1978 | Walworth, London, 1981, 'Step back, Charlie'.

USA: Negro children, Chicago, 1956, 'Strut, Miss Susie! Strut, Miss Susie! Here comes another one, Just like the other one. Strut, Miss Susie! All day long!' (*Did you feed my cow?*, M. Taylor, p. 51) | New York, 1960, probably played like Boston, 1974, 'This is the way we will-a-be, will-a-be, will-a-be, This is the way we will-a-be, all night long. Stepping back Sally . . . all night long. Stepping down the alley . . . all night long' (*New York Times*, 3 July 1960, p. 12) | Boston, 1974, 'Here we go willowbee, willowbee, willowbee, Here we go willowbee, all that long. Step back Sally, Sally, Sally, A walkin' through the alley, all that long. I peeked around the corner, And what did I see? A big fat man from-a Tennessee. I raised my dress above my knee, To show that man from-a Tennessee. My mother called the doctor and the doctor said, Oo ah I got a pain in my side. Row row row row, Shake sha-ma-ma, shake sha-ma-ma shake!' Partners hold hands with one hand and one foot forward, the other back, jumping to the opposite position on every other beat. 'Step back Sally': alternate jumping backward and clapping. 'A walkin' through the alley': walk towards each other, pass, then face each other. Other actions as appropriate, ending with twirling an imaginary lariat (*Circle Round the Zero*, M. Kenney, p. 66).

115

Flee Fly Flo

Salford, 1970

This is a typical gibberish campfire song, sung by Scouts and Guides in this country and at summer camps in the USA. During the 1970s the incantation gripped the imagination of junior school children, who inevitably muddled it into unorthodox playground variations. A Salford ten-year-old explained (November, 1970):

There's this game called Flee Fly Flo. It's the strangest game I ever played. There's one person in the middle, and whatever she says, the others in the circle repeat. She sits down cross-legged, with the others sitting round her, and begins by saying 'Flee fly'.

> 'Flee fly,' they repeat.
>
> 'Flee fly flo,' she says.
>
> 'Flee fly flo.'
>
> 'Vesta.'
>
> 'Vesta.'

She sings,
> 'Esta mella fella mella,
> Oo-ah a fella mella.'

They copy,
> 'Esta mella fella mella,
> Oo-ah a fella mella.'

She sings, 'Oh no no, no no nonesta', and they sing it after her. Then they all sing together,

> 'Bobo be ditten datta,
> Bobo be ditten datta,
> Bobo be ditten datta,
> Ssh!'

The one in the middle keeps crossing and uncrossing her hands, and taps on her knees in time to the rhythm. And then she picks another person, and that person goes in the middle, and they do it again.

In a Birmingham junior school in 1977 the leader's chant was,

> Flee.
> Flee fly.
> Flee fly flo.
> Comberlye comberlye comberlye vista.
> Hey, no no, no no the vista.
> Essa menie sella menie,
> You are the one-a menie,

and all shouted at the end,

> Flee, fly, flee fly flo,
> Flee fly flo flum—
> Boom boom!

The Irish girl who had been taking the lead said 'My sister learned it me. She's fourteen. She learned it from the others at her school. They made it up.'

   The song was recorded at Kristiansund, Norway, in 1973, but the recorder did not attempt a translation because, she said, 'In Norwegian the words have little sense.'

USA: *Circle Round the Zero*, Maureen Kenney, 1974, p. 51, 'Flee, Flee fly, Flee fly flow, Vishka. Cooma lotee cooma lotee cooma lotee vishka. Oh no, oh no no vishka. Eska meenie, sola meenie, Oo ah, oo ah na meenie, Ee skiddle-ee oaten doaten, Oo ah oo ah na an choo!' Learnt at summer camp.
   Cf. the calling-and-answering song sung by girls in the yard of Peabody Buildings, London wc2, 1974: 'Chargerlo-o-sa. Go way te ta-ar-bo. Simulassie boomberlassie. When u love a laker, Go way te ta-ar-bo. Simulassie boomberlassie.'

116

Wee Melodie Man

Kerr's Guild of Play, *Glasgow*, *1912*

> I'm the wee melodie man,
> The rumpty tumpty toddy man,
> I always do the best I can
> To follow the wee melodie man.
>
> *Kerr's Guild of Play*, 1912

This is the most rational of the verses which were used for a game of musical follow-the-leader, and it is still cherished in the far north and Scotland (but as a rhyme for juggling two balls against a wall). The children sat in a circle with the Melodie Man in the centre, all of them playing an imaginary musical instrument. At any time the Melodie Man might choose to imitate any of the instruments being played in the circle round him, and the player had immediately to change to the instrument just relinquished by the Melodie Man. If he did not do so, he was punished with a forfeit and took the Melodie Man's place in the centre.

Anne Gilchrist played the game as a small child in Manchester in the 1870s, with the words,

> Oh my little Hielandman,
> My rantin', tearin' Hielan'man,
> I'll do all that ever I can
> To please my little Hielan'man.

The Hielandman began by 'clapping his hands or bringing the palms near together in dumb show' and this, Miss Gilchrist believed, was a vestigial imitation of playing the bagpipes. The Highland variety of the game was also known at Clifton, on the outskirts of Manchester, *c.* 1910:

> John Healyman, John Healyman,
> Is a ranting roving Irish.
> I'll do all that ever I can
> To please my little John Healyman.

And in a Lincolnshire childhood of perhaps the 1920s:

> I am a gay bolony man,
> A ramping tearing Highlandman;
> And I'll do all that ever I can
> To follow the gay bolony man.

But in Dublin, 1939 and 1975, it was 'I'm the wee Polony man' and no Highlandman remained.

Alice Gomme's collectors sent her garbled versions from Earls Heaton, Yorks., and Redhill, Surrey ('Follow my gable 'oary man . . . I'll do all that ever I can To follow my gable 'oary man'; 'Holy Gabriel, holy man, Rantum roarum reeden man . . .'), and it is these versions, apparently laden with religious meaning, which have been made into mythical stories by fakelorists. ('Follow my Gable,' said Christine Chandler in *A Year Book of Folklore*, 1959, 'must have had its origin in the processions once held on Lady Day . . . The word "oary" is thought to be a corruption of holy.') It is these versions, too, which have been subjected to philological examination. Anne Gilchrist wrote to Alice Gomme that she considered 'gable oary man' to be a corruption of 'gaberlunzie man', 'gaberlunzie' being Scottish for 'beggar'. Frank Kidson, further confusing the issue, probably invented a game for his *100 Singing Games*, 1916, called 'The Scotch Beggar', which began:

> I am a Gaberlunzie man,
> A puir auld Gaberlunzie man,
> And I will do whatever I can
> To carry the Gaberlunzie on.

His game has no connection with music. The beggarman 'must not ask for anything that does not contain the letter S, under penalty of a forfeit, and the goodwives must not offer him, under a like penalty, anything that has an S in the name'.

The words, in fact, have been so inconsistent that one wonders whether they ever had an identity at all. It may be that in this country a popular Continental game, having no English words, was played to whatever verse came handy; and that one of the available verses was the chorus of the Jacobite song 'The White Cockade':

> O he's a rantin' rovin' blade,
> O he's a brisk and bonnie lad,
> Betide what may, my heart is glad,
> To see my lad wi' his white cockade.

The game itself, under the name 'Adam had Seven Sons', has long been popular in Germanic countries. Fischart knew it, and quoted the first line in *Gargantua*, 1590. 'It was originally a social game,' says Böhme. 'The company went round in a circle, singing. One stood in the middle who, at the end of the song, took up a position or made some motion that all the others must copy. Whoever did not do it well had to pay a forfeit and take the place in the middle.' He gives several versions, including the following slightly disreputable one from Thüringen:

Adam hatte sieben Söhn, sieben Söhn hat Adam.
Sie assen nicht, sie tranken nicht,
Sie waren alle lüderlich
Und machtens alle so wie ich.

(Adam had seven sons, seven sons had Adam.
They did not eat, they did not drink,
All of them were profligate,
And all did as I do.)

Britain: Gilchrist MSS 231 Aii, p. 24 | *Traditional Games*, i, pp. 129–30 | Argyllshire, 1905, 'I'm the wee melody man' (*Folk-Lore*, xvi, p. 344) | *Joyous Book of Singing Games*, John Hornby, 1913, p. 13, 'I'm the Gabel Huntsiman' | Cumberland, *c.*1930, 'I'm the Tinkle-airy man' (a 'tinkle-airy' is a street piano) | *The Countryman*, Autumn 1969, p. 187 | Many northern and Scottish recordings, 1950s–70s, usually for 2-balls and usually on this pattern, 'I'm a wee mulody man, A rufty tufty toady man, I'll always do the best I can To follow the wee mulody man' (or, 'follow the gipsy caravan').

Ireland: Dublin, 1939, 'I'm the wee Polony man, The ratterin' tatterin' Tory man . . .', all players copy the leader (*Irish Wake Amusements*, S. Ó'Súilleabháin, 1967, p. 104) | Dublin, 1975 (*All In! All In!*, Eilís Brady, pp. 127–8).

Germany: *Deutsches Kinderlied*, F. M. Böhme, 1897, pp. 494–6: often the imitating part of the game has the words 'Mit dem Fingerchen tip, tip, tip, Mit dem Köpfchen nick, nick, nick, Mit den Füsschen trab, trab, trab, Mit den Händchen klapp, klapp, klapp', which were borrowed by Humperdinck for Gretel's song in the opera 'Hänsel und Gretel', 1893 | Krombach, 1952.

Holland: *Kinderspel in Zuid-Nederland*, A. de Cock and I. Teirlinck, ii, 1903, pp. 181–2, 'Adam had een zevenzoon'.

Belgium: *Vlaamsche Kinderspelen uit West-Brussel*, Aimé de Cort, 1929, pp. 144–5, 'Adam had zeven zonen, Zeven zonen had Adam, Zij aten niet, ze dronken niet, Maar deden allen zóó!'.

Denmark: *Børneses Musik, Sange, etc.*, Serine and Sophus Hagen, 1879, 'Adam havde syv Sønner, Syv Sønner havde Adam. Alle gjorde hoad han bad, Alle vare lige glad, Se alli paa mig, gjør ligesom jeg som saa!' (Adam had seven sons, Seven sons had Adam. All his sons would gaily do, Everything he told them to. Now imitate me, Whatever you see, Do so!) | *Danmarks Sanglege*, S. Tvermose Thyregod, 1931, pp. 283–7.

France: *Every Girl's Book*, Louisa Lawford, 1860, pp. 21–2, 'La Follette', the will-o'-the wisp plays a harp or guitar, the circle imitate trades | *200 Jeux d'Enfants*, *c.*1892, p. 236, 'Les Musiciens'.

Egypt: Lower Egypt, 1927, 'All the players choose a particular occupation, e.g. cobbler, tailor, blacksmith, musician, etc., and all begin to play their parts, at the same time watching the chief. He will suddenly change his occupation and imitate that of someone else. At once the player whose occupation that is must imitate what the chief was doing previously' (*Folk-Lore*, xxxviii, pp. 379–80).

'The White Cockade', from *Songs of Scotland*, R. Chambers, 1862, also contains the verse 'I'll sell my rock, I'll sell my reel', which Gomme gives as a game-verse, on its own, for 'Follow my Gable'. 'I'll sell my rock [distaff]' is attached to various songs in which a girl proposes to follow her soldier lover, e.g. 'Johnny has gone for a soldier'.

117

Bobby Bingo

Dundee, 1975

> There was a farmer had a dog,
> His name was Bobby Bingo;
> B-I-N-G-O, B-I-N-G-O, B-I-N-G-O,
> His name was Bobby Bingo.

You make a ring with one person in the middle and you all go round singing. When you get to B-I-N-G-O the person in the middle points for each letter, and the person she lands on with 'O' goes in the middle. You all got a fair chance, see—depending which one she starts on (*girl, 8, Salford, 1970*).

'Bobby Bingo' is an example of how, when a popular song is no longer popular with adults, children can be found singing it in makeshift games. The comic song 'Little Bingo' was sung by Mr Swords at the Theatre Royal, Haymarket, *c.*1780:

> The Farmer's Dog leapt o'er the Stile,
> His name it was little Bingo,
> The Farmer's Dog leapt o'er the Stile,
> His name it was little Bingo;
> B with an I—I with an N
> N with a G—G with an O
> His name was little Bingo,
> B, I, N, G, O,
> And his name was little Bingo.
>
> The farmer lov'd a Cup of good Ale,
> He call'd it rare good Stingo, etc.
>
> And is not this a sweet little Song,
> I think it is—by Jingo, etc.

The song remained in favour and was still being sung (for instance at harvest suppers) at the end of the nineteenth century. During Wake Week at Little Hucklow, Derbyshire, *c.*1850, men and women danced in a ring from house to house, singing 'There was a man, he had a dog, And Bingo was his name O', and 'they would dance in the houses if they could get in' (*Notes & Queries*, 9th ser., xii, p. 474). But at least by 1849, when E. F. Rimbault included it in his *Nursery Rhymes*, it was thought of as suitable for children.

By the end of the century it had been turned into a game, played in a variety of ways and with a variety of wordings, but always hinging on the spelling of the dog's name. In Shropshire in the 1870s the girls sang:

> A farmer's dog lay on the floor,
> And Bingo was his name, O!
> B, i, n, g, o, B, i, n, g, o!
> And Bingo was his name, O!

'The girl in the middle then cries, B! and signals to another, who says, I! the next to her N, the third G, the fourth "O! his name was Bobby Bingo!" Whoever makes a mistake, takes the place of the girl in the middle.' A second verse was then sung, 'The farmer likes a glass of beer, I think he calls it Stingo!', and the word Stingo was spelt round in the same manner (*Shropshire Folk-Lore*, pp. 513–14). When played like this, as was usual, the game generates a certain excitement, since no one knows who, in the circle, will have to start the spelling. But in Metheringham in the early 1890s the girl in the centre was blindfolded; when the song was over she pointed at the circling players and whoever was opposite her when she said 'Stop!' was next in the centre. In some places (e.g. Liphook, 1894, and Lilliput, 1978) the game was more like a dance, with the girls clapping the letters, and, in Liphook, turning round at the end. And in the present day the pleasure of the game must lie entirely in rhythmic motion, since the action is usually either shut-eyes-and-point or a kind of counting-out.

Britain: London street children, 1891, 'There was a farmer had a boy, And his name was Bobby Bingo' (*Strand Magazine*, ii, p. 517) | *Traditional Games*, i, 1894, pp. 29–31, seven versions including Monton, Lancs, 'The miller's mill-dog lay at the mill-door', three verses; Liphook and Wakefield, 'There was a jolly farmer, And he had a jolly son'; Eckington, Derbyshire, 'The shepherd's dog lay on the hearth'; Enbourne, Berks., 'Pinto went to sleep one night'; Metheringham, mentioned | Upper Calder Valley, Yorks., *c.*1900, 'The farmer's dog lay on the ground' | Glasgow, 1912, 'The farmer's dog's at our back door' (*Kerr's Guild of Play*, p. 19) | Somerset, 1922, 'There was a farmer had a dog' (Macmillan Collection) | 1950s–1970s, similar to text, but also Blackburn, 1952, 'B-I-N-G-O, And Bingo was his name, O. Wrap him up in calico, Send him to Americo . . .' | Aberdeen, 1952, 'The farmer's dog is in the yard . . . And Jumbo is its name' | Glasgow, 1960, 'There was a man who had a dog, His name was Bobby Bingo, He dressed him up in sailor's clothes, And sent him to America, B-I-N-G-O . . .'.

   USA: Michigan, 1914, play-party version, 'There was a farmer had a dog, Bingo was his name, sir, B-i-n-g-o . . . Right hand to your partner, Left hand to your neighbour . . .' (*JAFL*, xxxiii, pp. 93–4).

   Canada: Toronto, 1907, 'There was a farmer owned a dog', with the one in the middle counting round (*JAFL*, xxxi, p. 130).

   'Bingo' was a cant word for brandy, and was also a name for a dog (whether or not because of the song), e.g. in Scott's *Guy Mannering*, ch. xxiv, where the Colonel's terrier is so named. Nowadays 'Bingo' is likely to mean the game of chance once known as 'Housie-Housie' or 'Lotto', and holiday-makers at Butlin's camps are summoned to a gambling session with the song of 'Bobby Bingo' played over the loud-speakers.

118

Punchinello

St John's Wood, London NW8, *1973*

What shall we do, Punchinello, little fellow?
What shall we do, Punchinello, little dear?

We'll do the same, Punchinello, little fellow,
We'll do the same, Punchinello, little dear.

Punchinello is the person in the middle of the ring. When the question has been asked Punchinello does something, such as hopping, jumping, or clapping, and everybody does the same. After that everybody sits down and the last one to sit down is the next Punchinello (*girl, 10, Aberdeen, 1952*).

A game-rhyme with the word 'little' in it is immediately suspect. It is probably purpose-written for children and is not part of oral tradition. 'Punchinello' is a case in point. Even in the original French (*Rounds for Singing and Dancing*, Augener Ltd., *c.*1910) it seems to have been created for kindergarten use:

> Pan qu'est-c'qu'est là?
> C'est Polichinel' mam'selle,
> Pan qu'est-c'qu'est là,
> C'est Polichinel' que v' là.
>
> Il est mal fait
> Et craint de vous déplaire.
> Mais il espère
> Vous chanter son couplet.
>
> Toujours joyeux,
> Il aime fort la danse.
> Il se balance
> D'un petit air gracieux.

(Ah! who is here? Punchinello, little fellow. Ah! who is here? Punchinel', my little dear. Though he be plain, Yet he hopes to please you. Would it displease you To see him once again? Lively and gay, He loves to keep you cheery. Should you be weary, Then come and see him play.)

The instructions for playing were: 'The children walk slowly, keeping time with their feet and at the same time moving their arms in imitation of the gestures of Punchinello.'

When children began playing the game spontaneously is not known. In *A Baker's Dozen: Singing Games for Brownies*, 1947, Mary Chater noted that it 'seems to have caught on in Britain and has become more popular than most such importations'. Certainly it was being played in a great number of places in the 1950s, 60s, and 70s, whether at Brownies or in playtime, and both words and method of playing varied from place to place.

Britain: Birmingham, 1952, and Penrith, 1957, 'Who comes here, Punchinello' etc. | Arncliffe, Yorks, 1952, 'What can he do, Punchinello' etc., 'the one in the middle chooses the person he thinks has done it best' | 1960s, versions from Edinburgh, Glasgow, Inverness ('Punch-in-Ella'), Dumfries, Swansea, etc. | St John's Wood, London, 1973, with choosing verse, '[Catherine] does it best, Punchinello little fellow, [Catherine] does it best, Punchinello little man'.

USA: *Nursery Friends from France*, Miller (Chicago), 1925.

New Zealand: Sutton-Smith, p. 30, 'Punchinello, introduced into schools by physical education specialists [during the 1940s] has become widespread'.

Canada: from childhood in Toronto, Fowke, 1969, p. 14.

XIX

Impersonations and Dance Routines

IT seems natural to little girls to act a part and put actions to a song. Certain songs in which a character is described have been made into miniature dramas, and are acted by each girl in turn in the centre of the simplest stage known to man—a circle of dancers who are also the chorus. Some of the songs are of known authorship; most, even if modern, are traditional. The acting games given here are all established favourites. If a game has been noticed only once, it may have been a transient enthusiasm and we have not included it. In Belfast in 1950, for instance, girls were seen circling while acting out the anonymous comedy song 'Mrs O'Grady' (also known as 'Mistress Shady' and 'Mrs Brady'):

> Mrs O'Grady, she was a lady,
> She had a daughter whom I adore.
> Each day I'd court her,
> I mean the daughter,
> Every Monday, Tuesday, Wednesday,
> Thursday, Friday, Saturday, Sunday
> Afternoon at half past four.
> She's tall and fair, and her hair
> Is a delicate shade of *ginger*.

But we have not heard of its being used as a game in the thirty-odd years since then.

Pop songs are sung in the playground either with the actions believed to have been performed by the pop groups singing them on television, or, more often, with actions fitted to them by the children. 'Come and see our new game,' they say, 'We've just made it up.' However, these games usually only last as long as the pop song. Sandie Shaw's 'Puppet on a String', which won the Eurovision Song Contest in 1967, was faithfully copied by rows of little girls in playtime, but died away when, eventually, the song died. 'Save Your Kisses for Me', sung by the Brotherhood of Man in 1976, also seemed a candidate for survival. The cynical 'Just One More Dance', sung by Esther and Abi Ofarim, was turned into a mime dance, at the height of its popularity in 1968, which lasted well into the 1970s (at least in Leyland, Lancs., and thereabouts), though whether it is still played anywhere we do not know. The song-dances in this section are the exception to the rule. They have taken root in oral tradition, and often both words and movements have grown over the years. Two older dances are also included. 'Wind the Bobbin' is both an impersonation and a dance, being a dance imitating the actions of cobblers. 'Shoo Fly' is an American square dance which has been taken to British children's hearts chiefly, it seems, for the strangeness of the words and the often-mentioned virtue, in a game, that 'it tires you out'. Other old dances are in chapter VII, 'Longways for as Many as Will'.

119

Diana Dors

Liss, 1975

> My—name—is
> Diana Dors
> And I'm a movie star,
> I've got a cute cute face
> And a monkey guitar.
> I've got the lips (kiss, kiss)
> I've got the hips, boom boom,
> I've got the le-egs, sexy le-egs,
> Turn around, movie star, boom boom boom,
> Turn around, movie star, boom boom boom.
> Firecrack, firecrack, boom de boom boom,
> Firecrack, firecrack, boom de boom boom.
> Boys got the muscles,
> Teacher's got the brains,
> We've got the sexy legs
> And we've won the game—Hey!

One imagines that 'Diana Dors', and similar solo performances such as 'I'm Shirley Temple' (p. 417), must be of American origin, yet our only evidence (apart from the word 'movie' star) is the declaration by occasional American newcomers to Liss school that 'of course' they know the game.

J. A. Pandrich was the first to locate the game in this country. Children in Newcastle, 1966, told him 'You get in a big ring, somebody goes round; at the end somebody else is in and it goes on and on.' The star in the centre was the pop singer Matt Monro, who was made to sing, rather curiously:

> I'm Matt Monro, I'm a famous star,
> I've got a coo-coo figure, and a driving car.
> I've got two big hips, so what do you say,
> Come up, pretty baby, and dance today.

Other children at the same school were singing about 'Marlon Rose', and it seems possible that the original heroine was Marilyn Monroe.

Sometimes the last lines, when the action hots up, are used as a separate game. At Farnham in 1972, for instance, no star was mentioned; the game started 'Crackerjack, crackerjack, boom boom boom', sung twice while the children in the circle bumped their hips into each other, and ended with the pantomime 'The boys have got the muscles' ('everyone flexes their biceps'), 'The teacher's got the pay' ('stretch out hands'), 'The girls have got the sexy legs' ('lift skirt showing off leg'), 'Hurrah, hurrah, hurrah!' ('jump up and down').

In Salford, 1975, the first part of the game was thought quite sufficient. The girls stood in a line, with an audience of boys watching every movement. The girls sang, with appropriate actions, 'Diana Dors, she is a star' (here they drew a star in the air), 'She's got a cute, cute face and a musky guitar. She's got those lips, She's got those hips, She's got those legs, those beauty legs. One, two, three, four, five, six, seven, eight, nine, ten—Sorry, boys, down again!' As they counted they crept their skirts up their legs with two fingers. The boys went 'Oooh' as the skirts went up, and 'Aah' as they fell again. '*What* sort of guitar was it?' we asked, and the leader of the girls answered 'A musky guitar. It's a kind of colour, a very dark brownish colour—like rusty, you know.'

Newcastle, 1966, Pandrich thesis | Liss, 1974 (both parts of game, as text) | Salford, 1975, as quote | Belfast, *c.*1974, David Hammond record 'Green Peas and Barley O', similar to Newcastle, but 'Diana Dors' | Greenock, 1975, '(girl's name) she's a movie star, She's got the fabulous figure that nobody has, She's got the hips, the lips, the legs of a star, And she walks like a movie star, oh yeh!' | Birmingham, 1977 | Garforth, 1978.

'Firecrack' part only: Farnham, 1972, as quote | Coram Fields, London, 1974 | Birmingham, 1976, ending 'The Queen does the curtsy, The King does the bow, The girls go (blow kisses) And the boys go "Wow"' from the skipping rhyme 'I'm a Little Scots Girl' | London, 1979, *New Statesman*, 21 Dec., 'Pat a cake, pat a cake, boom zi ay, Pat a cake, pat a cake, boom zi aah. Boys've got the muscles, Teachers got the brains, Girls have got the sexy legs, One, two, three, four, Come on boys if you want to see more, Five, six, seven, eight, Sorry, boys, you're far too late'.

120

I'm Shirley Temple

Dulwich, London SE19, 1976

I'm Shirley Temple, the girl with curly hair,
I've got two dimples, and wear me skirts up there;
I'm not able to do the Betty Grable,
I'm Shirley Temple, the girl with curly hair.

I've got a leg like nobody's business,
I've got a figure like Marilyn Monroe;
I've got hair like Ginger Rogers,
And a face like I don't know.

Oh Salome, Salome,
You should see Salome,
Hands up there, skirts up there,
You should see Salome.

Swing it, swing it,
You should see her swing it,
Hands up there, skirts up there,
You should see her swing it.

This game emerged fully fledged, as far as we are aware, at the beginning of the 1960s in Scotland, and gradually spread. By the mid-70s every little girl in Britain seemed to know it. The actions are predictable:

You all get in a giant ring—anybody can join in. There's somebody stands in the middle who is Shirley Temple, and the rest dance round singing. When they sing 'two dimples' if you are Shirley Temple you push two fingers into your cheeks, and when they sing about the skirts you pull your skirt up a little, rather short. Then you choose someone in the ring, and stand in front of them, and put your hands on your hips and wiggle your bottom from side to side. Then you hold her hand or you link arms and you swing round in the middle singing 'Oh Salome, Salome' and when it says so you put your hand in the air and hitch your skirt up.

(girl, 11, Liss, 1970)

The fact that the names are meaningless to the players is evident from the variations. Instead of being unable 'to do the Betty Grable' they are liable to say they cannot do the 'Bessy Grable', 'Betsy Cable', 'Betsy cradle', 'sexy cradle' (common), 'hipsy cradle' or 'gipsy cradle' (they rock their arms maternally). In Scotland, by 1975, Marilyn Monroe had been replaced by Matt Munro; they had pimples rather than dimples on their cheeks, and a face 'like an elephant's toe'. Salome, whose history was unknown to them (is the New Testament now bowdlerized?), was rendered 'Selomi', 'Salone', 'Salolie', 'Saraly', 'Salami', 'Supreena', and 'Sabrina';[1] while in Stepney children were found singing:

[1] Sabrina was a bosomy beauty who became the nation's pin-up girl briefly c.1960.

> Slowly, slowly,
> You've got to do it slowly.

Everyone, however, was aware that the game was a bit naughty. Outside the circle the boys take up vantage points, clambering on to windowsills or hanging on drainpipes like monkeys. 'It's because when we lift our skirts up the boys can see our knickers,' explained a nine-year-old.

The Salome verse (which is also used for skipping) came into being when Maud Allan, clad in little more than pearls, was scandalizing London with her dance 'The Vision of Salome', first performed at the Palace Theatre on 17 March 1908. The adult version, still fondly remembered, goes: 'Salome, Salome, you should see Salome, Standing there with her arse all bare, Waiting for someone to slip it there' (or, 'with her tits all bare, Standing by the lions in Trafalgar Square').

Paisley, 1961 | Dunoon and Edinburgh, 1962 | Newcastle upon Tyne and Birtley, Co. Durham, 1966 | Penshaw, Co. Durham, 1967 | Canterbury and Farnham, Surrey, 1968 | Liss, and Abergele, 1969 | Nelson, Salford, Birmingham, Street, and Dublin, 1970 | Versions from 29 places since 1970.

121

Macnamara's Band

My name is Macnamara, I'm the leader of the band,
My wife is Betty Grable, she's the fairest in the land.
Oh, she can dance, she can sing, she can show a leg—
The only thing that she can't do is make my ham and eggs.
Tra-la-la-la boom boom
Tra-la-la-la boom,
The only thing she can't do is make my ham and eggs.

'Macnamara's Band', written by John J. Stamford (copyright J. H. Larway, 1914) has been a song too good for children to abandon, and is particularly cherished in Scotland. The original words were:

My name is Macnamara, I'm the Leader of the Band,
And though we're small in number we're the best in all the land.
Oh! I am the Conductor, and we often have to play
With all the best musicianers you hear about today.

By the 1950s Betty Grable had been brought in to strengthen the cast, and the song became a playlet performed in a circle, as well as being used for skipping. Sometimes the children in the circle clap the rhythm while the child in the centre sings the words, acting the parts of conductor and film star before choosing another child to take the stage.

Text from Paisley, 1975. Other recordings from Glasgow and Ipswich, 1960, and from Edinburgh, 1962. Also, for skipping, from Kirkcaldy, 1952, and Dundee, 1954.

122

Going to Kentucky

Lymington, Hants, 1976

Top: 'Going to Kentucky' (No. 122), Leyland, Lancs., 1968. The circle sing 'Rumble to the bottom, Rumble to the top', while the small onlookers imitate.

Bottom: 'Sunny Side Up' (No. 127), Egremont, Cumberland, 1965.

> We're going to Kentucky,
> We're going to the fair,
> To see the señorita
> With flowers in her hair.
> Oh shimmy, shimmy, shimmy,
> Shimmy if you dare,
> Round and round and round she goes
> And where she stops nobody knows.

The señorita in the middle of the ring (at Adderbury, Oxfordshire, 1970) looked animated but a little shamefaced, as if she suspected the character she was playing, being foreign, was not quite nice. 'When you say "flowers in her hair" you sort of draw circles round your ear, so I think it must be a ball of flowers. Then you wiggle your hips for "shimmy, shimmy", and at the end you twizzle round with your eyes shut, and point, and whoever you point to, she goes in the middle next.'

The game swept the country with the speed of a pop song in the mid-1960s, and exploded into a multiplicity of wordings, such as this, collected in Islington in 1969:

> I was going to the tatty,
> I was going to the fair,
> When I met a Cinderella
> With flowers in her hair.
> Oh, twisty, twisty, twisty,
> Twisty all around,
> Twisty, twisty, twisty,
> Twisty all around.
> Oh rumble to the bottom,
> Rumble to the top,
> Turn around, turn around,
> Till you may not stop.

The children did their best with the unfamiliar 'Kentucky', rendering it 'going to the shankey', 'honky tonky', 'tacky', 'Toky-okee', 'hockey hockey', 'ratty tatty', 'Turkey', 'Yogi' ('I'm on my way to Yogi, To Yogi Yogi Bear', Perth, 1975), and sometimes, rebelliously, 'We're going to Chicago'. There is now a strong lobby for the comprehensible 'I'm going to the country' (e.g. Montrose and Glasgow, late 1970s, and Birmingham, 1980). On the other hand, 'Kentucky' has survived intact in a number of places, and a twelve-year-old from Harrow (town, not school) wrote to the *New Statesman* in January 1980 to say 'The words I know for this song are:

> I went to see Kentucky,
> To see a summer fair,
> I saw a señorita
> With flowers in her hair.'

So odd have the words become that they seem full of allusions which beg to be interpreted. Who was this 'señorita with a rosebud in her hair' who, in the Salford version, 1970, was 'hired by an Irish man'? Even we, in a moment of enthusiasm, felt sure that the original song must have been written to celebrate a World Fair, but the resources of the Bodleian Library's Harding Collection produced nothing closer than the waltz written at the time of the World's Exposition at St Louis in 1904:

> Meet me in St Louis, Louis,
> Meet me at the fair . . .

However, the game is not entirely modern, since it embodies the 'shimmy' in some versions, a foxtrot popular after the First World War and in the early 1920s.

USA: The American School in London, 1975, 'I'm going to Kentucky, I'm going to the fair, I met a senorita with a buckle in her hair. Shake it, shake it, shake it, Shake it if you can, If you cannot shake it, Do the best you can'.

  Canada: Toronto, 1969, 'We're going to Chicago (or Kentucky), We're going to the fair, To see a senorita with a ribbon in her hair, Oh, shake it, baby, shake it, shake it if you can, Shake it like a milkshake, and drink it like a man' (Fowke, 1969, p. 26).

  South Africa: Pietermaritzberg, 1975, 'As I went to Hoky, to Hoky Toky Fair, I met a senorita with curlers in her hair. Oh shaky, shaky, shaky, do the best you can, Oh twisty, twisty, twisty, and if you cannot twisty, Do the best you can'.

123

I've Got a Daughter

Driffield, Yorks., 1975

> I've got a daughter, lives in the ocean,
> I'd do anything to keep her alive—Whoo!
> She's got a pair of hips, just like two battleships,
> That's where my money all go-o-oes.
> Toesie toesie, kneesie kneesie, elbow elbow, clap clap!
> Toesie toesie, kneesie kneesie, elbow elbow, clap clap!

'When we were in the second year, the fourth-years started playing "I've Got a Daughter" on the field, and we picked it up,' said ten-year-olds at Driffield, 1975. They were in several minds about the last word of the first line. 'Some say "Majorca" and some say "autumn" and some say "ocean", but Majorca's the most sensible really,' said one. The action is as varied as the words. In some places the game is played with one player running round outside the ring and pushing her successor into the arena; in some, with a player skipping round inside the ring and choosing her successor. Sometimes the circle hold their arms up and shut their eyes while the single player runs in and out, and when her time is up she pushes another player into the centre. Sometimes the one chosen is tossed, as if in a blanket, before having her turn. Occasionally the game is played by two lines of girls facing each other.

   This cheerfully insulting song derives from the much-parodied American popular song 'My Girl's a "Corker", or The Race Track Girl', 1895, words by William Jerome and music by John Queen, of which the chorus ran:

> My girl's a 'corker'!
> She's a New Yorker;
> She plays the races,
> She gets the 'dough'!

> She loves me dearly,
> And so sincerely!
> Tell me how you found that out?
> She told me so!

Popular in the 1960s and 70s, with much variation in words: e.g. Govan, Glasgow, 1960, 'My girl's a corker, She's a New Yorker, I'd give almost anything To keep her in style. She's got a pair of hips Just like two battleships, That's where all my money goes. Oompah, oompah, oompah-pah, Oompah-pah, oompah-pah, Oompah, oompah, ommpah-pah, That's where all my money goes'; Leyland, 1968, 'My girl's a Quaker'; Edinburgh, 1975, 'I know a foreign girl, She comes from Yorkshire'; Scarborough, 1975, 'My girl's a conker, She's a New Yorker, I'd do most anything to keep her away—Hey!'; Greenock, 1975, 'My girl's a bonny girl, She's got victorious'.

Parodies of the song were popular with students, and, in bawdy versions, with service men, long before it was used as a singing game: see *A Book for Singing Occasions*, compiled by the Welsh Regional Council for the NUS, 1949; *Song Fest* (USA), D. and B. Best, 1948; and *Bawdy Ballads*, E. Cray, 1970.

124

She Wears Red Feathers

Birmingham, 1977

> She wears red feathers and a hooley hooley skirt,
> She wears red feathers and a hooley hooley skirt,
> She lives on fresh coconuts and fish from the sea,
> With a rose in her hair, and a gleam in her eye,
> And love in her heart for me.

In the backstreets of Britain in the early 1960s, circles of little girls could be heard singing this song while admiring a performer in the centre who, flapping her hands daintily to right and left, and swinging her hips, gave her interpretation of a hula-hula dance. 'You have to have about thirteen people to make it fun,' said a ten-year-old girl in Norwich in 1961. 'You put your hands up for coconuts, and down for fish. You put your hand in your hair for to show the rose, and point to your eye to show it gleams, and then you put your hands out and say "Eee". And then it's somebody else's turn.'

The origin of even the most modern-sounding singing game can rarely be discovered to enable one to see the changes wrought by oral tradition. 'She Wears Red Feathers' was written and composed by Bob Merrill in 1952 (copyright Oxford Music Corporation, New York), but as the chorus possesses all the qualifications for a successful children's dance-song, and as the song has been heard frequently on the radio and published in song albums, changes over the past thirty years have been few.

In some places (e.g. Towyn, Denbighshire, 1969, and Liss, 1970) children sang 'I'm a little Indian' and held up their fingers for Red Indian feather head-dresses; and this belief has been backed up by introductory verses such as,

> Me big chief, alla walla big chief,
> Ain't got a girl, ain't got a girl,

from Merseyside *c.*1975. But a certain geographical confusion is also noticeable in the story line of the original song, where a lovelorn London bank clerk follows his hula-hula sweetheart home not to Hawaii but (for the sake of the rhyme) to Mandalay.

125

Down in the Jungle

Dundee, 1975

Down in the jungle
Where nobody goes,
Lives a big fat mamma
Who washes her clothes;
With a rub a dub here,
And a rub a dub there,
That's how she washes her clothes.
Dye, dye, duby, duby, duby,
Dye, dye, duby, dup dup,
Dye, dye, duby, duby, duby—
That's how she washes her clothes.

This is a game which I used to play when I was smaller. It consisted of about six or more people making a circle, two of them would stand in the middle back to back and do the actions. The two people who stand in the centre do the actions while the other people sing it. When it comes to a rubadub here they rub one of their sides with their hand and then a rubadub there they rub their other side. Then when it comes to the dye dye bit the two people in the centre go and face somebody and the two in the centre and the two in the outside start rubbing their sides while the others say it. The name of the game is 'Down in the Jungle'. I hope it is understandable for you (*girl, 12, Aberdeen, 1960*).

The boogie-woogie rhythm, the big fat mamma herself, and the fact that all the earliest recordings are Scottish, would seem to indicate that the game was an American importation; but it was being played before the American Air Force families arrived in Holy Loch and brought their games with them. However, similar alien activities in deserted places were the subject of song in Scotland by at least the early 1950s, when students at Glasgow University were singing in the pubs:

Down in the valley where nobody goes,
There once lived a maiden without any clothes;
Along came a cowboy as tough as a brick,
Down came his trousers and out came his prick.

And this itself was probably an outcrop of the well-known American folk ballad whose chorus is,

> Down in the valley, the valley so low,
> Hang your head over, hear the wind blow.

The usual flow is in this case reversed; the new game first appeared in Scotland and worked its way southward. In 1960 we had recordings from Aberdeen and Dumfries; and in 1961 from Cumnock ('A big fat mamma stood washing her clothes . . . Tiddly ay tie, a do-be-do-be-do'). Thereafter recordings were from the north of England as well as Scotland, e.g. Newcastle, 1966 (Pandrich thesis); Leeds, 1973; Oban, 1974; Paisley, Dundee ('Diddly um, pum, rubadub Susie'), Manchester and Belfast, 1975; and by the mid-1970s the song was sufficiently familiar to need enlivening with lines from other songs, 'Diana Dors' for instance.

126

O Alla Tinka

> O alla tinka, to do the Rumba,
> O alla tinka, do the
> Rumba umba umba umba Ay!
>
> I paula-tay paula-tuska,
> Paula-tay, paula-toe;
> I paula-tay paula-tuska,
> Paula-tay, paula toe.
>
> O alla tinka, to do the Rumba,
> O alla tinka, do the
> Rumba umba umba umba Ay!

This song is included to show the persistence of scraps of rhythmic utterance, and the esteem in which they are held, as if they were magic incantations. The song has only been noticed at Norton Park School, Edinburgh, first as a skipping rhyme, when it was recorded for the BBC Record Library (No. 13869), and then as a rumba ring, with a girl wiggling her hips in the centre, in the printed version *The Singing Street*, 1951. The mumbo-jumbo of the second verse was, however, being chanted at the evening sing-songs of the Holiday Fellowship before the First World War, in a part-song which went like this:

> Hi politi politaska, polita, polito.
> Hi politi politaska, polita, polito.

O Nicodemuss—O Sara numper,
O Nicodemuss, Sara—numper, umper,
    umper, umper . . .

One half of the singers continued to sing 'umper, umper' while the others
sang the first two lines again, and it is not impossible that the 'umper
umpering' turned into the 'rumba umba umba' of the Edinburgh rumba
song. The part-song also bequeathed its rhythms to a clapping song, see
'Em pom pee' (p. 464).

127

Sunny Side Up

Alton, Hants, 1972

Keep the sunny side up, up,
And the other side too, too,
See the soldiers marching along,
See the sailors singing a song,
So keep the sunny side up, up,
And the other side too, too.
Turn round and touch your toes,
Just like the Eskimoes;
Turn round and touch your knees,
Just like the Japanese,
Turn round and touch your chin,
Just like an Indian—
Whoooo. How!

(girls, 9, Wareham, Dorset, 1975)

From the moment the film 'The Best Things in Life Are Free' was
released in 1929, little girls recognized that one of its hit songs, 'Sunny
Side Up', might have been specially written for them. Imitating the snappy

Hollywood chorus-line of the time, they put their arms round each other's shoulders, kicked their legs in the air, and sang the words they had heard the adults singing:

> Keep your sunny side up, up!
> Hide the side that gets blue.
> If you've eleven sons in a row
> Football teams make money, you know!
> Keep your funny side up, up!
> Let your laughter come through, do!
> Stand upon your legs, be like two fried eggs,
> Keep your sunny side up![1]

During the next decades the words became more pictorial. In Bristol, 1961 (when the boys joined in, as they will when a craze is big enough), the version used seemed to belong to the Second World War. Boys and girls marched in pairs, hands crossed behind their backs, and, after doing the routine high kicks, they acted the part of American soldiers:

> Keep your sunny side up, up,
> And the other one too, too.
> See the GIs marching along,
> See Sabrina singing a song.
> Keep your sunny side up, up,
> And the other one too, too.
> Bend down and clap-a-knees,
> Look like a Japanese.
> Keep the sunny side,
> Keep the sunny side,
> Keep the sunny side up.

But in Petersfield the same year, the words were distinctly different:

> Keep the sunny side up, up,
> Though the ocean is blue,.blue,
> See the soldiers marching along,
> Hear the sailors singing a song.
> Keep the sunny side up, up,
> Though the ocean is blue, blue.
> Bend down and touch your knees,
> Be like a Japanese,
> But keep the sunny side up.

In Workington in 1965 it was Cliff Richard who was singing the song, and the gymnastic Japanese had been joined by an Eskimo and an Indian.

---

[1] Copyright De Sylva, Brown & Henderson, Inc., New York.

Once a framework has been established daring additions and variations can be made: Leeds, 1966, 'See Sabrina waggle her bum'; Alton, 1972, 'See the boys shout "I love you"'; Liss, 1974, 'See the babies down on their knees, And the ladies doing strip-tease'. Children in a Scarborough park in 1975 were singing 'See the soldiers in red, white and blue, See Larry Grayson say "How do you do?"', but, after explaining that Larry Grayson 'is the one that says "Shut that door!" on television', they said 'We don't always put him in—we put in whoever we feel like'. In some places they finish the game with a cheerful shout of 'Olé!', or drop down on one knee, throw their arms wide, and exclaim 'Cha cha cha!'.

Since 1960, recordings from 22 places in Britain. The game seems to be growing in popularity and consequently in length. Throughout the 1970s there seemed to be no school playground where the girls would not immediately volunteer a performance.

128

Tennessee Wig-Walk

Aylesbury, 1978

I'm a bold-headed chicken, with a hole in me head,
I ain't been happy since I don't know when;
Oh she walks with a wiggle, and a woggle and a walk,
Doin' the Tennisis—Wig Walk.

Toes together and knees apart,
Bend your back and you'll make a start,

> Clap your hands, one, two, three,
> You've never seen a monkey go just like me.
> Oh she walks with a wiggle, and a woggle and a walk,
> Doin' the Tennisis—Wig Walk.
>
> You're the King and I'm the Queen,
> You're the one that stole my ring,
> Oh she walks with a wiggle, and a woggle and a walk,
> Doin' the Tennisis—Wig Walk.

Ten-year-old girls in Driffield, Yorkshire, 1975, gave directions for playing:

You stand in two long lines, and you each have a partner opposite you. When you sing the first line you jump towards each other with both feet and you put both hands on each other's head. Then you jump back again while you're saying 'I ain't been happy since I don't know when'. Then you put your hands on your hips and change places with your partner, walking with a wiggle and ending up shaking your bottom from side to side when you say 'Wig Walk'. Then you put your toes together and your knees apart, like it says; then you bend backwards and stay like that clapping your hands and singing 'You've never seen a monkey go just like me'. The next bit is the same as before. Then you point to your partner and say 'You're the King' and point to yourself and say 'I'm the Queen'. Then point to them and sing 'You're the one' and point to your finger and sing 'Who stole my ring'. Then you wiggle and change places with your partner again. No, 'Tennisis' doesn't mean anything, it's just a funny word.

'The Tennessee Wig-Walk', words by Norman Gimbel and music by Larry Coleman, 1953, was, like 'Underneath the Spreading Chestnut Tree' of 1939, an action-dance in which adults could allow themselves to be childish, and thus was immediately taken up by children. At first there was a spate of parodies:

> I'm a bow-legged chicken,
> I'm a cockney sparrow,
> I went to London on a four-wheeled barrow.
> Had some radishes for my tea—
> Felt a bit peculiar—
> Burp! Pardon me.

By the late 1960s the comedy song-and-dance itself had invaded the playgrounds. During the 1970s it was the rage, and exhibited the usual characteristics of a craze by developing stranger and stranger words and actions, and acquiring extra verses of unknown origin. In Dublin, 1970, children sang:

> I'm a one-legged chicken and an ugly duck,
> I ain't got married so I don't know what.
> With a walk and a wiggle, and a wiggle and a walk,
> Do what the hen says, wig walk.

In Poole, 1975, small viragos on a housing estate sang with unstoppable energy:

> I'm a bow-legged chicken, and a woggeny head,
> I haven't been so happy since I don't know when.
> I walk with a wiggle and a woggle and a squawk,
> Doin' the Tennessies Wig Wog.
> Won't you come, my darling, along with me;
> We're all in together, side by side,
> I walk with a wiggle and a woggle and a squawk,
> Doin' the Tennessies Wig Wog.
> Rockaberry, rockaberry, rockaberry rock, hey!
> Rockaberry, rockaberry, rockaberry rock.
> Indians come from Tennessee,
> Cowboys come from the USA.
> They wear red ribbons and they shout 'Hooray!'
> So rockaberry, rockaberry, rockaberry rock.

This was followed, without pause for breath, by 'The Queen does the curtsy, The King does the bow, The boys go "Hup!" And the girls go "Wow!"' from the skipping rhyme 'I'm a Little Scots Girl'.

Britain: Salford, 1975, learnt at 'a real dancing school', with movements according to the music sheet, with Lady and Gent circling each other | Notting Hill, 1975 | Lymington, 1976 | Aylesbury, 1978, 'Doin' the Tennessee—ping pang pong' | Garforth, 1978, like text, but accretions from 'Sunny Side Up' and ending 'Walking round a lamp-post singing a song So she walks, etc. Put your feet together and your legs apart, Flap your wings and get ready to start, So she walks,' etc. | Warwick, 1980, 'I'm a bone-headed chicken, I'm an ugly hen, I haven't been so happy since I don't know when; And I walk with a wiggle and a woggle and a swing, Doing the Texan, dog walk', followed by the King and Queen verse, then 'Indians come from Indians' land, Cowboys come from USA, Ladies come from Abbaville, Rockababy, rockababy, rock rock. I'm swinging on a straw, I'm swinging on a string, Boomeracker, boomeracker, boom boom boom. The boys got the muscles, Teachers got the brains, Girls have got the sexy legs And we won the game' | Walworth, London, 1981, 'I'm a stuffed-up chicken and a back-boned hen, My mother goes to Heaven but I don't know when'.

Published version, copyright Village Music Co., New York, 1953, 'I'm a bow-legged chicken, I'm a knock-kneed hen, Never been so happy since I don't know when. I walk with a wiggle and a giggle and a squawk, Doin' the Tennessee Wig-Walk.'

129

Drunken Sailor

Birmingham, 1977

What shall we do with a drunken sailor,
What shall we do with a drunken sailor,
What shall we do with a drunken sailor,
Ear-lie in the morning?

Oo-ray and up she rises,
Oo-ray and up she rises,
Oo-ray and up she rises,
Ear-lie in the morning.

Children have restored the 'Drunken Sailor' to its original use. James Fuld (*World-Famous Music*, 1971) says it is first known as a dance tune, 1824–5, titled 'Columbus'. Stan Hugill (*Spin* magazine, ix, 4, 1973) says it was printed, with its music, as a sea shanty in F. A. Olmsted's *Incidents of a Whaling Voyage*, 1841. Girls in a Birmingham playground in 1977 said 'You are all in a circle. You just join your hands and go round and at "Early in the morning" you sort of go down as if you were weary or drunk. Then you stand and haul the rope till your hands are high in the air. We sing it any time we like—outside our houses, or out in the playground—or you can sing it on a ship if you like.'

North Kensington, 1960, danced in two lines, 'with a bit of hornpipe attached, but the best part is when they kick their legs in the air for "Up she rises"' | Glasgow, 1961, danced in circle with bowing to partners for 'Yea, yea, up she rises'.

130

Dinah

Dundee, 1975

Someone's in the kitchen with Dinah,
Someone's in the kitchen I know, I know,
Someone's in the kitchen with Dinah,
Strummin' on the old banjo.

Fee, fi, tiddley i oh,
Fee, fi, tiddley i oh,
Fee, fi, tiddley i oh,
Strummin' on the old banjo.

'Someone's in the House with Dinah' was sung by Ethiopian minstrels in the 1840s and 1850s, but with a different tune from that known today.

James J. Fuld, in *The Book of World-Famous Music*, says no early printing of
the present-day tune has been found, and, as Sigmund Spaeth pointed out
to him, it is basically an embellishment of 'Goodnight Ladies'. The
playground tune is slightly different again.

Girls were dancing to the song in Swansea, 1962, and in Lilliput,
Dorset, 1978. In Dundee, 1975, it had been adapted so that the dancers
could tease each other about their boyfriends:

> *Elaine*'s in the kitchen wi' *Andy*,
> *Elaine*'s in the kitchen we know, we know,
> *Elaine*'s in the kitchen wi' *Andy*,
> Kissin' when the lights are low.

131

When Grandmama Met Grandpapa

Birmingham, 1975

When grandmama met grandpapa, they danced the minuet,
The minuet was too slow, so they danced the rock and roll:
Heel toe, heel toe, give me that kick,
Heel toe, heel toe, give me that kick,
Heel toe, heel toe, give me that kick,
That's the way to do it!

Hands up, stick 'em out, drop down dead,
Hands up, stick 'em out, drop down dead,
Hands up, stick 'em out, drop down dead,
That's the way to do it!

This game was suddenly popular about 1975, and was still popular in 1980. It is more fun than the words might suggest. Anybody can join in if they have a partner. It starts with a careful representation of a minuet, and then explodes into whatever improvisations may occur to the dancers. In Dundee, 1975, for instance, two of the additional verses went 'Cha cha cha and a boo boo boom . . . That's the way to do it' and,

> Shake those shoulders, birl around,
> Shake those shoulders, touch the ground,
> Shake those shoulders, birl around,
> That's the way to do it!

In at least two places, Birmingham and Walworth, London SE17, 'minuet' has become 'miluet' and 'milulet'. The tune is reminiscent of 'Away in a Manger'.

132

Shoo Fly

Garforth, Yorks., 1978

> Shoo fly, don't bother me,
> Shoo fly, don't bother me,
> Shoo fly, don't bother me,
> I belong to somebody.

> I feel, I feel, I feel
> Like a morning star;
> I feel, I feel, I feel
> Like a morning star.

We get a partner and join in a ring. Then we run to the middle and back again singing 'Shoo fly, don't bother me, I belong to somebody'. Then we go round our partner singing 'I feel, I feel, I feel like a morning star', and then we go round the other way singing the same thing (*girl, 9, Wolstanton*).

This game, based on the minstrel song by Billy Reeves and Frank Campbell, said to have been popular in the American Civil War though the copyright date is 1869, enjoyed energetic approval in the 1960s, apparently following the singing of 'Shoo Fly' by Burl Ives. However the game seems to be founded on more than the casual adoption of familiar words. It was reported being played in a similar manner in places that are widely separated; it was current in Oklahoma in the 1920s at play-parties; and a calendrical sport or ritual that took place in Wales during the First World War seems to have been plagued by the same fly. An informant recalls that on May Day at Rhos in Denbighshire the children used to black their faces and go from door to door asking for pennies. While they were waiting for the door to be opened they formed themselves into a circle and sang a verse which can have done their cause little service:

> Shoo fly, shoo fly, to follow me.
> We went to the baker's shop
> To buy a penny bun;
> He asked us for the money
> And away we run—
> Shoo fly, shoo fly.

Forfar, *c.*1955 | Wigan, 1960 | Wilmslow and Wolstanton, 1961 | Hindon, Wiltshire, 1965 | Garforth, Yorkshire, 1978. Cf. *American Play-Party Song*, B. A. Botkin, 1937, pp. 304–8.

133
Wind the Bobbin

Manchester, 1975

> Wind the bobbin up,
> Wind the bobbin up,
> Pull, pull,
> Tug, tug, tug.

Players wind their fists round each other, first one way, then the other. At 'Pull, pull' they thrust their fists away from each other, and at 'Tug, tug, tug' pull their elbows back. Although now a playground game it seems originally to have been a nursery game, in fact one young informant said she had known it so long she could not remember where she had learnt it: 'I think me aunt and me Mum taught it me.'

Yorkshire County Magazine, Pt 3, 1891, pp. 80–1, 'Winnd a bobbin, winnd a bobbin, Bum, bum, bum' (ad infinitum) | *Folk-Dances and Singing Games*, Elizabeth Burchenal, 1909, pp. 8–9, 'Shoemakers' Dance' (Danish). No words. Winding fists, pulling elbows, and tapping fists, followed by polka which 'should be danced lightly on the toes with much spring and life'. | Bristol, 1960 | Manchester, 1975.

Cf. *Singing Games for Recreation*, Janet E. Tobitt, iii, *c.* 1938, p. 2, 'The Shoemaker. Wind, wind, wind the thread and pull and pull and tap, tap, tap,'; and in USA, *Social Plays, Games, Marches* (Washington DC), 1911, p. 34.

XX

Clapping

THE earliest rhythmic hand-clapping game in Europe was probably 'Pat-a-cake, Pat-a-cake, Baker's Man', first recorded in 1698, in which a nurse claps a baby's hands gently together before moving them through the other actions of pricking and marking the cake and throwing it into the oven; and modern hand-clapping is still referred to as 'patty-cake' in the USA. Later, but it is not known when, it became the custom for two children to clap their hands against each other's to the forceful rhythm of 'Pease Porridge Hot, Pease Porridge Cold', a song which first appeared in *The Newest Christmas Box*, *c.*1797.

Hand-clapping (called 'hand-work' in Salford, 1970, 'hand-games' in Glasgow, 1975, and 'hot hands' in Dublin, 1975) is a social game for two: 'It's friendly', 'It's clever', 'It passes the time', 'You can't think about anything else while you're doing it', 'It's better than sitting around talking.' Boys sometimes clap hands fiercely in pairs, to keep warm, or 'to drive the other chap back', and this they call 'Hand Drive'. Girls clap hands to rhymes, which time the hand-beats, and their aim is to go on as long as possible without making a mistake. This kind of clapping has been going on for more than a hundred and fifty years. It was recommended by Madame Celnart, in her *Manuel Complet des Jeux de Société*, 1827, as a nice game for two children, 'especially when one gets the knack of doing it very quickly'. It could be played standing or sitting, and 'the two, with fingers very straight, well in front of each other, and with hands flat, clap their hands as if they were applauding; then they open their hands, and apply them both to those of their neighbour: straight afterwards they clap them again as if to say *bravo*, then the left hand of one must be clapped against the right hand of the other; again they clap hands, and the right hand must be clapped against the left hand in its turn' (the sequence is the same as in the English 'pat-a-cake'). A variation, Madame Celnart added, could be made, after crossing the hands, by giving oneself a clap on the right side, clapping both hands with partner, clapping oneself on the left side, and so on. And 'when one is used to this game and can perform it without interruption, one can sing the following verse as an accompaniment:

Dans sa cabane, jeune et saint ermite
  Vivait de noix et de pain bis;
Jamais poulet n'entra dans sa marmite,
Ni poulette dans son taudis.
  Un certain soir il en vient une.
Notre saint fit si bien, qu'il l'attrapa.
    La bonne fortune,
    Lui dit-il, ma brune,
Jamais mondain ne te croquera.
	(In his hut, the young and saintly
	    hermit
	Lived on nuts and brown bread;
	There was never a chicken in his
	    saucepan
	Nor chick in his hovel.
	  A certain evening one came by.
	Our holy man did so well that he caught
	    her.
	    You are lucky, my brunette,
	    He said to her,
	A worldly man will never snap you up.)

When the Revd Addison Crofton was a curate in Walmersley, Lancashire, *c.*1875, he watched children 'clap their hands together, alternately their own and their partner's hands, and sing:

> My mother *said* (clap)
>   That I never *should* (clap)
> Play with the gipsies (clap)
>   In the wood (clap)
> Because she said (clap)
>   That if I did (clap)
> She'd smack my bottom (clap)
>   With a saucepan lid! (clap)

The fashion for hand-clapping seems to have reached a peak during the late nineteenth century and up to the First World War. Various verses were strung together and clapped in a long sequence, as happens when hand-clapping is the rage. The following were the most popular at that time, and might be used in any order:

> Old Mrs Brown went up to town
> Riding on a pony,
> When she came back, she took off her hat
> And gave it to Miss Malony.

> *Suffolk, 1850s. One of the many polka verses, it often began the clapping sequence. Golspie, E. W. B. Nicholson, 1897, 'when she came back, With a Dolly Varden hat, They called her Miss Meroo-oo-nie'. Belford, Northumberland (County Folk-Lore, iv, 1904) 'Susan Brown went to town, With her breeches hanging down'. The rhyme has survived to the present day in both polite and impolite versions and for a variety of uses.*

John, John, where have you been,
All this live-long day?
Down the alley, courting Sally,
Picking up cinders, breaking windows,
Feeding monkeys, riding donkeys,
Chasing bull-dogs,
All this live-long day.

Ballarat, Australia, learnt from mother born c.1850 (Turner MS). Usually only four lines, e.g. 'Where have you been, all this day? Up the alley, courting Sally, Picking up cinders, breaking winders, Sally courting me', Wrecclesham, Surrey, 1892. It was still known in the 1930s.

My mother said that I never should
Play with the gipsies in the wood.
If I did she would say
'Naughty girl to disobey,
   Disobey, disobey,
   Naughty girl to disobey'.
The woods are dark, the grass is green,
Here comes Sally with a tambourine,
   A tambourine, a tambourine,
   Here comes Sally with a tambourine.

Cradley Heath, Worcs., c.1900. Sung to 'The King Pippen Polka'. Correspondents to Notes & Queries (1931–4) remembered it from the 1860s and 1870s, and it was still used for clapping in the 1950s.

'I have a bonnet trimmed with blue.'
'Why don't you wear it?' 'So I do.'
'When do you wear it?' 'When I can—
When I go out with my young man.
My young man's away at sea,
When he comes back he'll marry me;
Buy me a biscuit, buy me a tart,
What do you think of my sweetheart?'

Orpington, 1906. Sung to 'King Pippen Polka', and known from c.1850 to the 1930s.

San-tee-ti, san-tee-ti,
San-tee doodle-um, doodle-um di.
There was a farmer, so full of greed,
Planted his meadow full of seed.
When the seed began to grow,
Like a meadow full of snow.

When the snow began to melt,
Like a ship without a belt.
When the ship began to sail,
Like a bird without a tail.
When the bird began to fly,
Like a diamond in the sky.
When the sky began to roar,
Like a lion at your door.
When the door began to crack,
Like a stick upon my back.
When my back began to smart,
Like a penknife in my heart.
When my heart began to bleed,
'Twas death and death and death indeed.

Ipswich, c.1897. Usually, 'There was a man, a man indeed'. Versions, with or without the introductory sounds, Golspie, E. W. B. Nicholson, 1897; Games of Argyleshire, R. C. Maclagan, 1901; Kerr's Guild of Play, c.1910; and from a number of correspondents. Also see ODNR, no. 322

America was in the grip of a clapping craze at this time, too. Mr Babcock observed children in the streets of Washington 'clapping the palms together, and alternating with this movement a similar clapping against the knees or face' while they chanted 'Pease porridge hot' and 'Missy Massy gone away, Won't come back till Saturday' (*American Anthropologist*, i, 1888, p. 275). Leah Yoffie also began clapping-sequences with 'Pease porridge hot' in a St Louis playground in the 1890s (*JAFL*, lx, pp. 27–8). But from America, during the years between the wars and into the 1950s, there is no more news of hand-clapping; nor is there mention of it in the Frank C. Brown Collection of the 1920s, nor in Dr Dorothy Howard's massive collectings of the 1930s–50s, nor in Carl Wither's collectings of the late 1930s to 1945.

During those years, in this country, the art of hand-clapping did not exactly die out; but it came a poor third to ball-bouncing and skipping amongst the games of agility. It was not till the wave of sparkling and spirited chants came over from America that it could be said to enjoy a revival.

The clapping actions, being subject to the laws of folklore, have of course changed over the years. The actions of the 1890s were described thus by Nicholson (*Golspie*, pp. 187–8), using the rhyme of 'Mis-sis Brown went to town' as his model:

Two girls stand facing each other, each with her hands raised and linked in the hands of the girl opposite. They then begin to sing the verse . . . At the syllable *Mis* the players bring their hands smartly on the leg above the knee. At the syllable -*sis* they clap them in front of their chests. At *Brown* they link them as at first . . . and so on.

A recollection of clapping games in North Shields (*Street Games*, M. and R. King) confirms that this was the fashionable method of the time, though there the routine was interspersed with 'clapping hands separately and with each other'.

At the beginning of the revival the clapping method was not much different. 'I am a pretty little Dutch girl, as pretty as pretty can be' was, for instance, clapped thus at Wilmslow, 1960: hands crossed on chest, clap thighs, clap own hands together, clap right hands, clap own hands, clap left hands, clap own hands, and so on, ending with clapping partner's hands three times on 'be, be, be'. The usual modern method, however, is horizontal rather than upright. Two girls stand in front of each other and clap each other's palms with hands held horizontally, right palm upwards and left palm downwards. On the second count they clap each other's palms forwards, both hands held vertically, and on the third count they clap their own hands together. These three movements follow each other in a gentle, slithery flow, with a pause on the fourth beat to allow for a special action or simply a rest. (The pattern of clapping rhythms always seems to have been 'One, two, three—rest', since the days of 'Pease Porridge Hot' and 'My Mother Said'.)

Innovations creep in all the time. The girls may do the basic actions in a different order; or they put their hands together as if praying and strike them against their partner's similarly held hands during a slow lead-in to the rhyme, thereafter keeping their hands in the same general position but clapping right hands together above the neighboured left hands, then left hands together below the neighboured right hands; or they simply open and clench their hands alternately, right hand open and left hand clenched, then right hand clenched and left hand open, synchronizing the movements so that one player's open hand is placed against the other player's fist, and vice versa. It is Junior- and Middle-School children, however, who use the 'horizontal' method and its variations. The seven-year-olds clap slowly and ponderously with the old upright 'pat-a-cake' actions.

The whole process can be complicated, and made more hospitable, by the clapping being performed in a circle, a girl's right hand clapping against her neighbour's left, her left hand against her neighbour's right. This dextrous performance is nothing new. Leah Yoffie was clapping 'Pease Porridge Hot' in a circle in a St Louis playground in 1895. But girls in Liss playground find circular clapping a strain: 'It's really easier with two, cos there's not so much hassle,' said a nine-year-old, 'I get it all mixed up when it's in a circle—your hands go sideways, you see, not straight.'

Girls clapping a long game like 'Miss Mary Mack' or 'A Sailor Went to Sea' have no time to think whether the words they are chanting are sense or nonsense. They are concentrating all their energies on saying them in the right order and remembering the actions that go with them. 'It's very difficult,' they say: and it is. They are being driven by the need to keep in time with their partner. They are being driven by the momentum of the game itself, and the compulsion to reach the end. When the game is over, it is over and something else is happening. Children are no more reflective than other people. If they are asked what they think of the words, or what they think a particular word means, they will—most of them—say the first thing that comes into their heads.

The prime requisite of a successful clapping song is that it should have a pleasing rhythm. Wit and euphony seem to be secondary considerations. When clapping is in fashion the girls experiment with any song that floats their way. Over the years they have clapped to pop songs like 'Hello Dolly', 'The Nickelodeon', 'The Merry-go-Round Broke Down', Harry Lauder's 'Roamin' in the Gloamin' ', and Tommy Steele's 'Little White Bull'; to community songs like 'Polly Wolly Doodle', and 'Under the Lilacs She Played Her Guitar'; to Guide and Brownie songs like 'Ging Gang Gooly What Shang' and 'Kookaburra Sits in the Old Gum Tree'; to ball-bouncing jingles like 'Mickey Mouse is Dead' and 'Over the Garden Wall'; and to naughty rhymes like 'My Friend Billy Had a Ten-foot Willy'. In 1979, when a disreputable rhyme about the characters in the television serial *Dallas* was in circulation, seven-year-olds patted it into domesticity in the playground:

> I'm only a poor little Ewing,
> JR's always picking on me.
> Sue Ellen's a drunk,
> The baby's a punk,
> And Bobby lives under the sea.

But such songs do not satisfy for long, and the girls go back to the steady favourites which, though not custom-made, have been adapted for the job. The last words of lines, or of alternate lines, are repeated ('be, be, be'), and clapped with forward-facing hands, which makes an effective sound-pattern and an interval for the clappers. Snappy endings are added, which can be used whenever felt to be appropriate, and which seem to express the triumph of finishing the game: 'Boom, boom!' they exclaim, like Basil

Brush; or 'Boom, boom, boom, Esso Blue!', or 'Hoo!' or 'Too!' or 'Fish face!' or 'Boing!' or 'Olé!'. One of the most popular endings is 'Sex-y!', when they flick their skirts up ('Really, we should kick our legs up, to show we're sexy,' said a Brighton eight-year-old, 'But they would get in the way'). Another ending, 'Um tiddley um dum, sex-y!' is patterned on the old, cheerful coda 'Hi tiddley i ti, brown bread!',[1] a musical phrase first suggested in print (says James J. Fuld, *World-Famous Music*, p. 495) in Fischler's 'Hot Scotch Rag', 1911.

Many of the games, if they do not have their own tune, are clapped to the same monotonous drone as 'I Am a Pretty Little Dutch Girl' (p. 450); though often the girls do not even pretend to sing: 'It's all right if they're just *said*,' they declare. In fact everything about hand-clapping is emphatic. It is the most zestful, speedy, and energetic of the singing games, and, in the modern phrase, one of the chief growth areas.

There can be no country, now, where hand-clapping games are not played. The following are samples of rhymes used in different parts of the world:

France: *Chants du Cambresis*, A. Durieux & A. Bruyelles, 1864, pp. 308–9, 'Dans sa cabane était un saint ermite', clapping knees, right hands, left hands | *Rimes et Jeux de l'Enfance*, E. Rolland, 1883, pp. 132–3, 'Mon père m'a donné des rubans' and 'Jean, Jean, Jean, Ta femme est-elle belle?' | Bon–Encontre, 1978, 'La Rosalie, ti-ti, pom-pom, Elle est malade . . . Du mal d'amour', the cure being to eat salad three times a day (*Le Folklore de Bon Encontre*, R. Brinton, unpublished dissertation).

Spain: *Cancionero Infantil Español*, S. Córdova y Oña, 1947, p. 247, 'Celedín, Celedín, Celedón, hizo una casa nueva, Celedín, Celedín, Celedón, con ventana y balcón; Cantan y bailan las truchas en el río, Cantan y bailan y nunca tienen frío' (Celedin, Celedin, Celedon, made himself a house . . . with window and balcony. The trout sing and dance in the river, They sing and dance and are never cold).

Norway: 'The most popular "klappesang" is "Praerien lá". The girls still use the old method of clapping for one song, "Min far han er barber, fallera", but otherwise use the new horizontal way' (correspondent, 1974).

Canada: one of the most popular is 'Take me out to the hospital, Take me up to my room; Needles and needles and I don't care, For I'm in love with Doctor Kildare' (*Macleans*, 6 July 1963, p. 43, from Toronto).

USA: 'Eeny, meeny, gypsaleeny, Oh, oh, animal-eeny, Achapacha, libavacha, I love you' (*New York Herald Tribune*, 2 August 1964).

India: Ramapura, Uttar Pradesh, 1975, translation, 'Betel, flower, leaf, Rose colour is not fast!' and 'Fire is in the dish, I am your sister-in-law', 'with great mirth at the end'.

China: a correspondent who reports, 1975, that in Peking (and probably all over China) children play clapping games, saw one 'played almost word for word as "My mother said, that I never should"'.

Korea: *Swing High: Korean Folk Recreation*, Chunga Elaine Cho, 1954, p. 23, gives 'among the clapping games so universal among girls in the orient', 'High there in the deep blue sky, Down the Milky Way, Rides a ship without a sail, With no oars, they say. White the ship, its only crew Is a rabbit white, Westward they're floating onward, Quietly through the night'.

---

[1] Often extended to 'Hi tiddley i ti, brown bread, Look at your father's—bald head!', or 'Rum tiddley batchcakes, brown bread, I struck a sausage—down dead!'. The phrase has also been recorded as 'How is your father? Blind drunk!', 'Tripe and bananas, fried fish!', and, in the army, 'Guard to the guard-room, dis-miss!'. In America it is 'Shave and a hair cut, Bay rum!'.

134

My Mummy Told Me

South Baddesley, Hants, 1983
(also text)

> My Mummy told me,
> If I was goody,
> That she would buy me
> A rubber dolly.
> My Auntie told her
> I kissed a soldier—
> Now she won't buy me
> A rubber dolly.

This all-purpose ditty may well be based on a music-hall song of the 1890s, though no likely candidate has been found. It has the same coy pseudo-childishness as Vesta Victoria's 'Daddy wouldn't buy me a bow-wow', and rubber dollies were in fashion at the time. About 1910 the song was being used for skipping:

> My mother told me,
> She would buy me,
>   A rubber dolly;
> But someone told her
> I kissed a soldier,
> And so she will not buy me
>   One at all.

Farringdon, Hants

and thereafter was employed for other ludic purposes including hand-clapping (e.g. Sidcup, 1945, 'My mother told me, That she would buy me, A rubber dolly, If I was good. But if you tell her, I kissed a feller, She will not buy me, A rubber dolly'). Later the clapping game, already very popular, may have been given a boost by Shirley Ellis's pop version, 'The Clapping Song', 1965.

Twins at Bamber Bridge, Lancs., 1984, play 'Who stole the cookies from the cookie jar?'. This is, nowadays, sometimes clapped by only two players. When it first arrived in this country about 1972 it was clapped in a circle, and became one of the most popular clapping games, the words diversifying as 'Who stole the cookies from the cookie shop?' or 'cookery shop', or 'Who stole the apples from the old man's tree?'. A ten-year-old girl from Lymington here describes the earlier version (1976):

> Everyone stands in a circle and has a number, and everyone claps their own hands and their next door neighbour's, alternately, and everyone chants:
>
> 'Who stole the cookies from the cookery shop?
> Number One stole the cookies from the cookery shop.'
>
> Number One says: 'Who, me?' and they all answer: 'Yes you.'
> Number One: 'Couldn't have been.'
> All: 'Then who stole the cookies from the cookery shop?'
> Number One: 'Number Two stole the cookies from the cookery shop.'
> Number Two: 'Who, me?'

and so it goes on till the last number, and she can't accuse anybody, so they all chase her.

The game—one of several on the same pattern—had been known in America since at least 1952 (New York City, Folkways Record FP 703) and the accusation of theft was not made in orderly fashion round the circle but was flung at random at any of the other players. It is in fact simply the old and international game of 'The Priest of the Parish', furnished with new words and a clapping accompaniment. In the *Spectator* 7 Jan. 1712, it was called 'the merry game of "The Parson has lost his Cloak" '; in *The Gentleman's Magazine*, Feb. 1738, 'The Parson hath lost his Fuddling Cap'; and in Captain Marryat's *The King's Own*, 1840, 'The game of the goose'.

The actions are usually: *first line*, own hands together, right hands, own hands together, left hands; *second line*, own hands together, cross arms and touch own shoulders, slap thighs; and so on. Sometimes an ending has been added to each line, to accommodate the cross-arms-and-slap-thighs movement (e.g. 'criss cross', Liverpool, 1960; 'tiddly-winks', Workington, 1962; and, frequently, 'full stop', Goring-by-Sea, 1969, and Langton Matravers, 1975). The rhyme is occasionally followed by 'Three, six, nine, the goose drank wine', see below.

Britain: In some places it has been felt that an extra line would improve the song, e.g. Swansea, 1952, 'My mother told me, That she would buy me, A rubber dolly, To play with Molly. But if I told her, I kissed a soldier, She would not buy me, A rubber dolly'.

Ireland: Belfast, 1974, 'My Mammy told me' (David Hammond's record 'Green Peas and Barley O').

Australia: Melbourne, 1967, 'My mother told me, criss cross'.

USA: Carmel, California, 1983, 'My Mammy told me . . . Now don't you tell her, I've got a feller, Or she won't buy me, A rubber dolly'.

135

Three, Six, Nine

Notting Hill Gate, London W11, 1983

Three, six, nine, the goose drank wine,
The monkey chewed tobacco on the street car line.
The line broke, the monkey got choked,
And they all went to heaven in a little row boat.

This is shouted rather than chanted, and is clapped with special vigour, the girls nearly pushing each other over in the process. In Langton Matravers, 1975, they clapped their own hands together, in praying position, then right hands against partner's, twice, then left hands against partner's, twice. They clutched their throats at 'choked', and at 'clap, clap, full stop' (the local ending) they clapped straight forward with their partner, twice, crossed arms on chests and clapped their thighs.

The clapping rhyme was known in Britain in the late 1950s, and in America as a 'narrative' rhyme in the 1930s, when it began 'Once upon a time':

> Once upon a time, the goose drank wine,
> The monkey chewed tobacco on the street car line;
> The street car broke, they all began to choke,
> They all went to heaven but the poor billy goat.

It is, of course, simply a version of the old nonsensical beginning to fairy tales, such as appears in *The History of Four Kings*, *c.*1750: 'Once upon a time when geese were swine, and birds built nests in old men's beards . . .'.

USA: Gloucester, Mass., 1937 (Howard MSS) | Boston, 1974, 'Three, six, nine, The goofs drank wine . . .' (*Circle Round the Zero*, M. Kenney, p. 23).

Britain: Warwick, 1957, as text but 'They went together' | Birmingham, 1966, ordinary version, and parody 'Three, six, nine, his spunk met mine, I wagged him off on the railway line. His johnny broke and his cock got soaked, And they all went to heaven in a little johnny boat—Clap hands, clap hands' | Bristol, 1969, and Birkenhead and Langton Matravers, 1975, 'Monkey chews tobacco in the street Caroline' | Other recordings as text.

Ireland: Belfast, 1974 (David Hammond's record, 'Green Peas and Barley O').

The rhyme was part of Shirley Ellis's hit 'The Clapping Song', 1965.

136

I Am a Pretty Little Dutch Girl

Ashbourne, Derbyshire, 1977

I am a pretty little Dutch girl,
As pretty as can be, be, be,
And all the boys in the baseball team
Go crazy over me, me, me.

My boy friend's name is Fatty,
He comes from Senoratti,
With turned-up toes and a pimple on his nose,
And this is how the story goes:

My mother sent me to the shop,
And told me not to stay, stay, stay,
I met my boy friend on the way
And stayed till Christmas Day, Day, Day.

First he gave me peaches,
Then he gave me pears,
Then he gave me 25 cents
To kiss him on the stairs, stairs, stairs.
I gave him back his peaches,
I gave him back his pears,
I gave him back his 25 cents
And kicked him down the stairs, stairs, stairs.

One day when I was walking,
I saw my true love talking,
To a pretty little girl
With a strawberry curl,
And this is what he said:
I will T-A-K-E take you
To the P-A-R-K park,
I will K-I-S-S kiss you
In the D-A-R-K dark;
I will L-O-V-E love you
All the T-I-M-E time,
And the wedding bells will chime.

This light-hearted love story would be recognized as American even if the earliest recording did not come from New York. It appears to have arrived in Britain in 1959, when it was first noted, and it spread through the country like wildfire. A girl from Twickenham taught it to the children of her new school in Wilmslow. A girl from London SE8 taught it to the children in her new school in Worcester. A girl brought it back to her

school in Spennymoor from the children's ward of Durham County
Hospital, where 'everybody was playing it'. It was too exciting a game to
keep to oneself. But oral tradition, under pressure, could not preserve the
unfamiliar words, which diversified charmingly. The boy friend Fatty,
originally from Cincinnati, is now said to come from 'Sixolatti',
'Switzerlatti', 'Madagassi', or 'an Irish Naafi'; or his identity is now 'Tony
from the land of Polony', or 'Shallow from Portomallow', or 'Martin from
the Isle of Tartan', or 'Sailor from Venezuela' (it seems that rhyming a
boy's name with a home town is part of the game); or he has 'a red, red nose
and cherries on his toes', or 'a pickle on his nose and ten black toes', or
'bubble gum feet that smell so sweet'.

   The text given here is an assemblage of all the possible component parts
of the story, which stem from different places. Children most often
combine the first, second, and fifth parts, or the first, third, and fourth. In
the very many versions collected almost every combination has been
found, except all five parts in one version.

   Sometimes, instead of proposing to the little girl with the strawberry
curl, the boy friend rejects her less than gallantly:

> I love you dearly,
> But I love someone else sincerely,
> So jump in the river
> And swallow a snake,
> And come out with the belly-ache.

Bristol, 1962

This part of the song was once separate, and the rejection was of a boy by a
girl (see Chicago quote).

USA: New York, *c.*1940, 'I'm a pretty little Dutch girl, As pretty as can be, And all the boys around
the block, Are crazy over me. My boy friend's name is Michael, He rides a motorcycle, With a
pimple on his nose, And ten flat toes, And that's the way my story goes' (*Ready or Not*, Carl
Withers, 1947, p. 100) | Chicago, 1956, two separate rhymes, 'I am a pretty little Dutch girl, As
pretty as pretty can be; And all the boys on the baseball team, Are crazy over me'. 'One day when I
was walking, I saw my boy friend talking, To a pretty little girl With a big fat curl, And this is what
she said: "I love you very dearly, But I love another sincerely; So go climb a tree, And don't bother
me, And we will both live happily"' (*Did you feed my cow?* M. Taylor, pp. 51 and 55) | Bucks
County, 1974, 'I am a pretty little Dutch girl . . . And all the boys around my way, Go nutty over
me. My girl friend's name is Patty, She comes from Cincinnati, With a pickle on her nose And
forty-eight toes, And that's the way my story goes' (*Pennsylvania Jumpster*, for 'pat-a-cake').
   Australia: Melbourne, 1956, 'Oh, I'm a pretty little Dutch girl, As pretty as can be, pom pom,
And all the boys around the place, Are crazy over me. My boy friend's name is Fatty, He comes
from Cissinatti, With a pimple on his nose, And two auburn toes . . .' (Turner MS).
   Britain: 37 versions, from 1959 onwards, including Harrogate, 1959, 'I am a pretty little Dutch
girl . . . And all the boys in my block, Are crazy over me. My boy friend is a caddy, Comes
from Sissinady . . .' | Hendon, 1961, '. . . My boy friend's name is Fatty, He comes from
Cincinnati . . .'.

137

Under the Bram Bush

Under the bram bush,
Under the sea, boom, boom, boom,
True love for you, my darling,
True love for me.
When we get mar-ried,
We'll have a fa-mi-ly,
A boy for you, a girl for me,
Um tiddley um dum, sex-y!

Stepney, 1976

This is the kind of love song that appeals to little girls: it also has a nice crisp rhythm. The clapping is horizontal; the partners point at each other when they sing 'A boy for you' and at themselves when they sing 'A girl for me'. The words have a ninety-year-old history.

In 1895 Harry Harndin's comic song 'A Cannibal King' was published (music by Harriet Harndin), and in 1902 Cole and Johnson's 'Under the Bamboo Tree'. Both were catchy, and survived (with a third element, 'If you'll be M-I-N-E') as a composite student song known as 'The Cannibal King Medley'. This student song was adopted as a clapping game, and was sung thus in Liverpool, 1960:

A cannibal king with a big nose-ring fell in love with a dusky maid,
And every night in the pale moonlight across the lake he sailed.
He hugged and kissed his pretty little miss in the shade of a bamboo tree,
And every night in the pale moonlight he sang like this to me:

A rum pee pee, a rum pee pee, a rum tilly iddy aye aye,
A rum pee pee, a rum pee pee, a rum tilly iddy aye aye.
We'll build a bungalow big enough for two,
Big enough for two, my honey, big enough for two.
And when we are married happy we will be,
Under the bamboo, under the bamboo tree.

If you'll be M I N E mine,
I'll be T H I N E thine;
And I'll L O V E love you all the T I M E time.
You're the B E S T best of all the R E S T rest,
And I'll L O V E love you all the T I M E time.
Pack 'em up, stack 'em up any old time—
Ashes in the ash pan,
Bum bum!

Whereas 'A Cannibal King' and 'If you'll be M I N E' had a brief innings as ball-bouncing rhymes and clapping songs, the middle part, 'We'll build a bungalow big enough for two', became probably the most-played of the clapping games. In Dick and Beth Best's *Song Fest* (USA, 1948) it even had the 'boom, boom, boom' ending much favoured by bram-bush performers. From the 1960s till about 1975 the verse could begin 'Under the bamboo', 'Under the brambles', 'Under the brown bushes', 'Under the branches', or 'Under the shade of the blackberry tree', but recently it seems to have settled down to 'bramble bushes', or 'bram bush' (which is better for clapping). And because the rhyme and rhythm fit, girls sometimes lead from the first line of 'bram bush' into the skipping rhyme 'Down by the ocean, down by the sea' and sing:

Under the bram bushes, under the sea,
Johnny broke a bottle and blamed it onto me;
I told my mamma, I told my papa—
Johnny got a smacking on his oompa, cha cha cha!

Pimlico, 1976

Australia and USA: Australian and American children have a different amalgam. They sing (e.g. Sydney, 1973): 'Under the bram bush, Under the sea—boom boom boom, True love for ever, True love for me. And when we're married, We'll raise a fam'ly, Of little children All in a row, row—Row your boat, Gently down the stream, Kick your teacher overboard And see how loud she screams—Aah!'. 'Row, Row Your Boat' was possibly a minstrel song, and was copyrighted 4 October, 1852, by Firth, Pond & Co., New York (see James J. Fuld, *Book of World-Famous Music*, 1971).

Norway: in Norway the words are nonsense, except where the two languages coincide, but the rhyme is very popular: 'Ande liane, Ande masji, bom bom bom, Ande masji, mai darling, Ande masji, mai darling, Klapp for mi, Klapp for ju, Ande liane—si si' (Oslo, 1975).

138

I Had the Scarlet Fever

Tune: 'I Am a Pretty Little Dutch Girl'

I had the scarlet fever,
I had it very bad,
They wrapped me up in a blanket
And threw me in a cab.
The cab was very shaky,
I nearly tumbled out,
But when I got to the hospital
You should have heard me shout:
Oh Mummy, Daddy, take me home,
From the convalescent home,
I've been here a week or two,
And now I want to be with you.

Here comes Dr Glannister,
Sliding down the banister;
Half way down he ripped his pants,
Doing the hula hula dance.

North Grecian Junior School, Salford, 1975

At another school in Salford the rhyme ended:

Here comes the doctor, Doctor Brown,
Asking questions all around,
'Are you ill, or are you not?'
'Yes I am, you silly clot!'

'The way you clap it,' they said, was 'You just clap "together, right, together, left, and together twice at the end".'

The days are long past when children were taken in a black fever van to the isolation hospital, and consequently the song now often begins 'I had a magic fever' (London SE21, 1970), or 'I had the tonsillitis' (Swanage, 1975), or, commonly, 'I had the German measles' (Birmingham, 1966, 1975, and 1977; Birkenhead, 1975; Redditch, 1977). Little is known of its early history, though a *Sunday Mirror* reader (summer 1969) remembered singing, as a child-patient in the Lord Mayor Treloar Hospital, Alton, *c.*1920:

> Mother, mother, take me home
> From this convalescent home,
> I've been here a week or two,
> Now I want to be with you.
> Goodbye all the nurses,
> Goodbye Sister too,
> Goodbye all the doctors,
> And Convalescent Home.

It seems likely that this is the 'girls' song' mentioned by Norman Douglas in *London Street Games*, 1916: 'Mother, mother, fetch me home'.

Nelson, Lancs., 1960, 'I had the scarlet fever . . . They wrapped me in a blanket, And put me in a van . . . Along comes the doctor, Doctor Cline, Asking questions all the time. "Do you feel bad or do you feel worse? If you feel worse, I'll send for the nurse." Along comes the nurse with a red-hot poultice, Puts it on your face and takes no notice. All the children shout "It's hot!" The nurse shouts "Of course it's not". Goodbye all the doctors, Goodbye all the nurses, Goodbye all the sisters, And jolly good luck to you—salt fish!' | Wilmslow, 1960 and 1964, similar to Nelson, but the scarlet fever 'wasn't very bad' | Birmingham, 1966, ends 'Here comes Nursie down the stair, Doing up her brassière'.

139

Have You Ever Ever Ever?

Market Weighton, Yorks., 1975

> Have you ever ever ever in your long-legged life
> Seen a long-legged sailor with a long-legged wife?
>
> No, I've never never never in my long-legged life
> Seen a long-legged sailor with a long-legged wife.
>
> Have you ever ever ever in your knock-kneed life
> Seen a knock-kneed sailor with a knock-kneed wife?

No, I've never never never in my knock-kneed life
Seen a knock-kneed sailor with a knock-kneed wife.

Have you ever ever ever in your bow-legged life
Seen a bow-legged sailor with a bow-legged wife?

No, I've never never never in my bow-legged life
Seen a bow-legged sailor with a bow-legged wife.

'Every time you start a new bit you put your hands on your knees and then clap your own hands together—that's for "Have you" and "No, I've", because they are slow. Then you go quicker and clap against the other person's right hand and your own hands again and the other person's left hand and your own again, and when you say "long-legged life" you separate your arms out sideways. And when you come to "knock-kneed" and "bow-legged" you imitate those as well' (Birkenhead, 1975). In Scarborough, 1965, they also managed to swing their right legs across, when clapping right hands with each other, and left legs when clapping left hands.

The ancestors of the rhyme are American. Carl Withers printed this amusement in *A Rocket in my Pocket*, 1948:

> Did you eever, iver, over,
> In your leef, life, loaf,
> See the deevel, divel, dovel,
> Kiss his weef, wife, woaf?
>
> No, I neever, niver, nover,
> In my leef, life, loaf,
> Saw the deevel, divel, dovel,
> Kiss his weef, wife, woaf.

In Michigan, *c.*1918, a plainer and somewhat scurrilous question was asked: 'Did you ever, ever, ever, In your life, life, life, See a nigger, nigger, nigger, Kiss his wife, wife, wife?' (*JAFL*, xxxi, p. 531, for counting-out).

Britain: Only the descriptions of the sailor and his compatible wife can be varied, and for this reason, perhaps, the game is not particularly popular. Only found in 17 places between 1961 and the present day. The most vivacious performance was recorded by Father Damian Webb in Edinburgh, 1961, where the sailor and his wife were successively long-legged, short-legged, bald-headed, cheeky, nosey, and teenage. Otherwise, the wording has been conventional, except for 'pigeon-toed sailor' in Birmingham, 1966, and 'tea-pot sailor' in Nelson, 1972.

Australia: Melbourne, 1967, as text, the sequence of adjectives being 'long-legged', 'short-legged', 'elbow', 'knee-cap', 'ankle', and 'nosey', and ending 'Yes, I've many many times in my nosey life, Seen a nosey sailor with a nosey wife'.

Canada: Shawnigan Lake, BC, 1964, 'Did you ever ever ever in your long-legged life, See a long-legged sailor with a short-legged wife?'. Then 'a bow-legged sailor with a flat-footed wife', and 'a knock-kneed sailor with a pigeon-toed wife'.

140

When Susie Was a Baby

Bedford, 1975

When Susie was a baby, a baby Susie was,
She went a goo, goo,—a goo, goo, goo.

When Susie was an infant, an infant Susie was,
She went a A, B,—a A, B, C.

When Susie was a junior, a junior Susie was,
She went a 'Miss, Miss, I can't do this'.

When Susie was a teenager, a teenager Susie was,
She went a kiss, kiss,—a kiss, kiss, kiss.

When Susie was a mother, a mother Susie was,
She went a smack, smack,—a smack, smack, smack.

When Susie was a grandmother, a grandmother Susie was,
She went 'Me back, me back—me back, me back, me back'.

When Susie was a-dying, a-dying Susie was,
She went 'Aah, aah,—aah, aah, aah'.

When Susie was a skeleton, a skeleton Susie was,
She went a creak, creak—a creak, creak, creak.

When Susie was a nothing, a nothing Susie was,
She went——(*Silence, except for giggles*)

Hand-clapping game that has emerged from 'When I Was a Lady' (p. 294). Two players—rarely more—do the usual routine of a horizontal clap, an upright clap, and a clap of their own hands, interrupting the clapping to demonstrate how Susie went. The game was taken up enthusiastically in the late 1960s, and additional stages and descriptions of Susie's career came into circulation. By the mid-1970s the game seemed to be known throughout England, little girls of eight or nine being enchanted by the audacity of the words, which were taken up in one place after another with little variation. Thus, two girls we came upon in a village on the Berkshire Downs:

> When Susie was a baby, a baby Susie was,
> And she went ooh aah, ooh aah aah.
>> (*They each popped a thumb in and out of their mouths in time to 'ooh, aah, ooh aah aah'*)

> When Susie was a toddler, a toddler Susie was,
> And she went
>> (*They toddled to the rhythm*)

> When Susie was a schoolgirl, a schoolgirl Susie was,
> And she went 'Please Miss, I can't do this!'
>> (*They each held up a hand and waved strenuously*)

> When Susie was a teenager, a teenager Susie was,
> And she went 'Ooh, aah, take off my bra'.
>> (*Signs of itching and discomfort*)

> When Susie was a-pregnant, a-pregnant Susie was,
> And she went 'Ooh, aah, ooh aah aah'.
>> (*Each clutched a very imminent infant*)

> When Susie was a-married, a-married Susie was,
> And she went 'La la la—la la la la'.
>> (*They swayed to the opening bars of the Wedding March*)

> When Susie was a granny, a granny Susie was,
> And she went
>> (*They peered through spectacles made of their forefingers and thumbs*)

> When Susie was a-dying, a-dying Susie was,
> And she went 'Ooh—aah, ooh aah aah'.
>> (*They staggered about dying*)

> When Susie was an angel, an angel Susie was,
> And she went 'Oooh, aaah, ooh aah aah'.
>> (*They flapped their arms*)

> When Susie was a devil, a devil Susie was,
> And she went 'Ooh, aah, ooh aah aah'.
>> (*They placed fingers on their heads for horns, and moved them up and down*)

> When Susie was a nothing—Stop!
>> (*They stopped clapping, and stood still, dangling their arms*)

In Covent Garden, London, a group of girls chanted verses that were only slightly different:

When Susie was a baby, a baby Susie was,
And she went 'Mama, mama, mama'.

When Susie was a nuisance, a nuisance Susie was,
And she went 'Nah, nah, nah nah nah'.

When Susie was a junior, a junior Susie was,
And she went 'Miss, Miss, I can't do this'.

When Susie was a teenager, a teenager Susie was,
And she went 'Um, ah, I lost my bra. I left my knickers in my boy friend's car'.

When Susie was a stripper, a stripper Susie was,
And she went 'Ooh, ah, off with me bra, down with me knickers—chi la!'

When Susie was a mother, a mother Susie was,
And she went
    (*They rocked a baby*)

When Susie was a granny, a granny Susie was,
And she went tap, tap, and a tap tap tap.
    (*They pretended to walk with a stick*)

When Susie was a skeleton, a skeleton Susie was,
And she went rattle, rattle, rattle rattle rattle.

When Susie was a devil, a devil Susie was,
And she went 'Nah, nah, nah nah nah'.
    (*They put up finger-horns*)

When Susie was an angel, an angel Susie was,
And she went
    (*Sighing noises*)

When Susie was a cloud, a cloud Susie was,
And she went 'Ooh, ooh,—ooh ooh ooh'.
    (*Ethereal noises*)

At Alton in Hampshire, although the structure of the song was the old one of 'When I Was a Lady', and familiarity with city night-life minimal, they were equally knowledgeable about Susie becoming a stripper:

> When Susie was a baby, a baby, a baby,
> When Susie was a baby, she went like this:
>   'Ooh, gee, go, gah'.

When Susie was a schoolgirl, a schoolgirl, a schoolgirl,
When Susie was a schoolgirl, she went like this:
    'Oh Miss, I can't do this'.

When Susie was a teenager, a teenager, a teenager,
When Susie was a teenager, she went like this:
    'Ooh, ah, I lost my bra,
    I left it in the vicar's car.'

When Susie was a mummy, a mummy, a mummy,
When Susie was a mummy, she went like this:
    'Down with me knickers, cha, cha, cha'.

When Susie was a stripper, a stripper, a stripper,
When Susie was a stripper, she went like this:
    'Ooh, ah, I lost my bra,
    I don't know where me knickers are.'

When Susie was a granny, a granny, a granny,
When Susie was a granny, she went like this:
    'Ooh, ooh'.
    (*Hobbling about*)

When Susie was a skeleton, a skeleton, a skeleton,
When Susie was a skeleton, she went like this:
    'Oooooh!'.
    (*Eerie moan*)

These performances may be compared with the singing of 'When I Was a
Young Gell' exactly a hundred years earlier (pp. 304–6). As with other
games it was noticeable the children had difficulty in remembering the
words unless they were performing at the same time.

Britain: Aldershot and Liss, 1966 onwards | Ilford, 1969, 'When Molly was a baby, she went this
way and that way, And this way and that way' | Cheam, Chichester, Street, and Salford,
1970 | Versions from 22 places thereafter including Four Marks, 1971, 'When Susie was a
schoolgirl, a schoolgirl Susie was, She went "Mummy, Mummy, the boys don't like
me"' | Dudley, 1973, 'When Twiggy was a baby, a baby Twiggy was, And she went "Ha, ha, ha,
ha, ha, ha, Agro"' | Ilkley, 1975, 'When Susie was a teenager . . . I've left my knickers in the
Osmonds' car', and 'When Susie was a grandma, She went a knit, knit, "I've lost my
stitch"' | Notting Hill Gate, 1983, 'Miss, Miss, I want to go to the piss, But I don't know where
the toilet is'.

    South Africa: Johannesburg, 1969, 'When Susie was a granny, She acted just like this: "Ek het
'n Steek vergeet"'.

    Israel: Jerusalem, 1960s, 'Oh when I was a baby, a baby, a baby . . . in nursery school, etc. . . . in
the army . . . a young lady . . . went out with my boyfriend . . . was pregnant, etc. . . .' ending 'And
when I was in the grave' (players call 'Help!') (*Children's Game Styles*, Rivka Eifermann, 1970, pp.
27–9).

    USA: Boston, *c.* 1973, 'When I was a baby, baby, baby' (*Circle Round the Zero*, Maureen Kenney,
p. 35).

141

O Susie Anna

Tune: 'Fair Rosie'

I saw my boy friend walking down the street,
  Walking down the street, walking down the street,
I saw my boy friend walking down the street,
  O Susie Anna!

And in his arms he had a box . . .

And in that box there was a dress . . .

And in that dress there was a pocket . . .

And in that pocket there was a note . . .

And on that note there was four words . . .

And those four words were 'Will you marry me?' . . .

And her reply was 'Yes I will' . . .

And they got married the very next day . . .

And she had four to five chil-dren,
  Four to five chil-dren, four to five chil-dren,
And she had four to five chil-dren,
  O Susie Anna!

'O Susie Anna' is built on the same mnemonic pattern as the medieval Corpus Christi carol and the folk song 'The Tree on the Hill'; each verse takes its theme from the end of the previous verse. It was first noticed in Liss and Aldershot in 1966, and although not one of the foremost clapping chants is still firmly in the repertoire. When the girls sing 'O Susie Anna' they put their index fingers to their foreheads, then to their waists, and then do a little bob on 'Anna', bending and straightening their knees.

Northern versions take a tragic turn: the pocket contains a rose, on which is a bee, on which is some poisoned honey, which Susie Anna eats with fatal results ('It's dead sad, that bit,' remarked a ten-year-old Mancunian).

142

Em Pom Pee

Liss, 1965

Em pom pee para me
Para moscas,
Em pompee, para me.
Acca dairy, so fairy,
Acca dairy—
Poof poof!

A clapping chant that became epidemic in the mid-1960s, but was a cause of wonder more to adults than to children. 'My niece's daughters clap to this rigmarole all day long,' said a Liss woman in the summer of 1965, 'even the two-year-old tries to join in. They say they learnt it at school, and they say it's French—but it's complete nonsense.' By 1970 there were two recognized versions at Liss school. The second, which had arrived from Aldershot, went:

Em pom pee diddy vee diddy voskus,
Em pom pee, diddy vee;
Diddy voskus, diddy voskus, diddy voskus—
Poof poof!

As children moved from school to school and, eager to pass on the latest game, fudged new syllables in place of those they could not remember, a multitude of variations came into existence: among them, 'Em pom pee polanee polaneski' (Leyland, 1968); 'Oushka oushka vi, davvy davvy, Oushaka vi, follow me, Acadeema, so far me, Acadeema, poof poof!' (Cheltenham, 1969); 'In pom pee pomerlee pomerlastus, Sen pom pee, pomerlee, Eccatamus, so famous, Eccatamus, poof poof!' (Portsmouth, 1969); 'In bom bee ally ally ally aster' (Salford, 1975); 'Um van vee valeree valeruski' (Prenton, Merseyside, c. 1975); 'Pom pom pee palla lee pa lee ex ki' (Longdon-upon-Tern, 1976); 'Om pom pee choorelay choora laska' (Dublin, 1976); 'Om pom pay pollo-ay polloneski' (Nottingham, 1977).

In the same way, perhaps, the method of clapping has varied. The earliest method noted (at Liss) involved hands, chest, and head. At Cheltenham in 1969 two children clapped against each other with alternately clenched and open palms; for the third and fourth phrases they crossed their arms one at a time against their shoulders, and they finished by clapping with the old upright 'pat-a-cake' actions. At Salford in 1975 some players clapped with the now orthodox 'horizontal' movements; others alternately opened and closed their hands against their partner's; and others again held their hands together as if praying and struck them against their partner's sideways, from one side and then the other, and when they came to 'Poof poof!' one player clenched her fists while the other patted them with forward-held palms.

The children are usually convinced the words are foreign, and the usual choice is French; but at Huddersfield a little girl 'learnt it from a Polish friend, and as I didn't understand the words I thought they must be Polish'. Gibberish songs are truly international, and partly for that reason are often sung round Scout and Guide camp fires and at other fraternal gatherings. Guests at Holiday Fellowship Centres just before the First World War used to sing:

> Hi politi politaska, polita, polito,
> Hi politi politaska, polita, polito.
> O Nicodemus—O Sara numper,
> O Nicodemusss, Sara—numper,
>   umper, umper, umper . . .

Half the singers went on singing 'umper, umper', while the rest sang the first two lines again. Both joined in lines three and four, and those who had been singing 'umper, umper' then sang the first two lines and vice versa (see pp. 428–9).

Children, too, have been using this *lingua franca* to make friends abroad. In Capri in 1976 one of the favourite clapping rhymes went, to the same tune and horizontal actions as in England:

> Em pom pi poloni polonaste,
> Em pom pi.
> Accademi sofare,
> Accademi—pom pof!

143

I Went to a Chinese Restaurant

Liss, 1974

I went to a Chinese restaurant,
To buy a loaf of bread, bread, bread,
They wrapped it up in a five pound note
And this is what they said, said, said:
    My—name—is—
    Alli alli,
    Chickerlye chickerlye,
    Om pom poodle,
    Walla walla whiskers,
    Chinese chopsticks,
    Indian chief says 'How!'

A steady favourite at Liss for at least ten years. By 1980 the last line had become 'Indian chief—corn beef, How!' The clapping is horizontal, but for the statement 'My—name—is' the hands are held together as if praying and swashed against the partner's hands on each word.

As with other nonsense rhymes, the words vary considerably from place to place. 'Indian chief' becomes 'Indian cheese' and then 'Cheese paste'; or, instead of saying 'How!' he warbles 'Ooo, ooo, scoobi doobi doo'; or he pluralizes into 'Cowboys and Indians', who go 'Whoo–oo–oo' and flap their skirts up and down. In some places the rhyme begins, prosaically, 'I went into a baker's shop'; in others, the restaurateur emphasizes his foreignness by declaring he is a 'Chinese-Japanese-Indian chief'; often, the rhyme consists only of the recitation of the long name.

The possibility of being addressed by a Chinaman seems to have had a perennial fascination for children. Before the clapping craze absorbed the rhyme in the late 1960s it was used for counting-out, and the venue was not a restaurant but a Chinese laundry. The laundryman wrapped the loaf in a tablecloth and rattled off the currently popular form of 'Chinese counting': 'Air I dominacka, Chicka bocka, lollipoppa, Om pom push'. Before this, in the 1920s, the 'Alli alli, chickerlye chickerlye' rigmarole was enjoying a heyday. A reader of the *Times* Business Diary (28 October 1971) sent in a little 'hymn to tea' he remembered from his childhood in the East End of London:

> Hi chi chicker chi
> Chicker chi, chicker chi,
> Ooni pooni, om pom pini,
> Alamana cushay,
> Chinese tea,

which prompted a flood of similar recollections. And the humdrum ball-bounce formula, 'When I was one I ate a bun', was sometimes enlivened with a Chinese adventure:

> When I was one I ate a bun,
> I used to go to sea;
> I jumped on board of a Chinaman's ship
> And the captain said to me:
> Ari-ari chikari-chari,
> Roly-poly inkumpanyin,
> Waly-waly whiskers Chinese chunks.

Street Games of North Shields Children,
M. and R. King, 1930

It is tempting to think that heydays occur every forty years, for in the late 1880s the Revd Walter Gregor found boys in Fraserburgh counting-out with the following string of sounds:

> Ra, ra,
> Chuckeree, chuckeree,
> Ony, pony,
> Ningy, ningy, na.

Addy, caddy, westce,
Anty, poo,
Chutipan, chutipan,
China, chu.

Britain: a great variety of recordings from 30 places, e.g. St John's Wood, London, 1969, 'I went to a Chinese restaurant once . . . Suey, ah ha ha, Ching chang, walla walla wing bang, Suey, ah ha ha, Ching chang, walla walla, wing bamboo' | Wordsley, Staffs., 1969, 'My name is Lili, Chickily i chickily, Hom pom poodle, Deputie and doodle, Wolla wolla whiskers, China's chopsticks, Indian chief, How!' | Edinburgh, 1975, 'My name is Ella Bella, Cinderella, Chinese chopsticks, Indian feather, Woo woo woo woo, How!' | Wool, Dorset, 1975, 'I went to a Chinese restaurant . . . Willie, Willie Whiskers, Chinese chopsticks, One, two, three' | Virginia Water, 1983, 'I went to a Chinese restaurant . . . My name is—Elvis Presley, Girls are sexy, Sitting on the back seat, Drinking Pepsi, Boys go (kiss, kiss), Girls go "Whoo!" '.

New Zealand: Christchurch, 1970, 'My name is Ay wy, ay wy, Chickapi chickapi, Pom pom poodle, Wally wally whiskers, Charlie Chopsticks, Indian chief'.

144

A Sailor Went to Sea

Wool, Dorset, 1975

A sailor went to sea, sea, sea,
To see what he could see, see, see,
But all that he could see, see, see,
Was the bottom of the deep blue sea, sea, sea.

A sailor went to chop, chop, chop . . .

A sailor went to knee, knee, knee . . .

A sailor went to toe, toe, toe . . .

There can scarcely be a school playground in Britain where this is not known, from Littlehampton on the Sussex coast to Benbecula in the Outer Hebrides. The clapping nowadays is horizontal. The girls touch their eye, or more often salute, when they say 'sea, sea, sea'. They chop their hands into the angles of their elbows, and slap the other parts of their bodies. About 1970, the sailor began going to China (or Hawaii, or Africa) and making appropriate motions ('When you say "Chi-i-na" you bow with your hands together, like a Chinaman': girl, 10, Manchester, 1975). They perform at manic speed, and the aim is not to make a mistake; or it could be that they hope to make mistakes, for a girl in Market Weighton in 1975 pronounced the game 'A good one because you can't do it properly, you're forgettin' to do the actions all the time and you get a good laugh.'

This joke originated, or was perpetuated, in the Fred Astaire and Ginger Rogers song 'We joined the Navy to see the world, But what did we see? We saw the sea' (*Follow the Fleet*, 1936). In the 1950s the rhyme was used for ball-bouncing:

> A sailor went to sea,
> To see what he could see,
> But the only thing that he could see
> Was the deep blue sea.

('At every "sea" or "see" we have to put the ball under our leg': girl, 13, Aberdeen, 1952.)

By the 1960s it had been converted into a clapping game by the repetition of 'sea' and 'see', and each time the verse was chanted a different part of the body was slapped. Thus, the cheeks were patted at 'sea, sea, sea' and 'see, see, see' the first time round; next, the hands were crossed on the chest; next, the knees were slapped; and, with the fourth recitation, cheeks, chest and knees were touched.

By 1969, at least, the present standard form had evolved, in which parts of the body are named and the movements are summed up in the last verse in a memory-testing résumé (for instance, Birmingham, 1975, 'A sailor went to sea, chop, China, Russia, knee, tangalang talang, toe').

USA: New York, *c.*1940, for ball-bouncing, 'A sailor went to sea, sea, sea, To see what he could see, see, see, And all that he could see, see, see, Was the bottom of the deep blue sea, sea, sea' (*Ready or Not*, Carl Withers, 1947, p. 94) | Boston, 1972, 'A sailor went to sea, sea, sea . . . chop . . . knee . . . toe'; tune and actions as in this country.

Britain: Worcester Park, Surrey, 1969, 'A sailor went to sea, sea, sea . . . chop, chop, chop . . . knee, knee, knee' | Stockport, 1971, 'A sailor went to sea, sea, sea . . . chest . . . waist . . . knee . . . foot'.

Ireland: Belfast, 1974, similar (David Hammond's record, 'Green Peas and Barley O') | Dublin, 1976, 'A sailor went to sea, sea, sea . . . chop . . . knee . . . toes'.

145

Miss Mary Mack

Miss Mary Mack, Mack, Mack,
She's dressed in black, black, black,
With silver buttons, buttons, buttons,
All down her back, back, back.
She asked her mother, mother, mother,
For fifty cents, cents, cents,
To watch the elephant, elephant, elephant,
Jump over the fence, fence, fence.
He jumped so high, high, high,
He reached the sky, sky, sky,
And never came back, back, back,
Till the end of July, ly, ly.

Huish Episcopi, 1978

These words, as clapped today by girls all over the country, are a combination of an old English rhyme and an oldish American one. In the 1844 edition of Halliwell's *Nursery Rhymes of England* is a 'marching song':

Darby and Joan were dress'd in black,
Sword and buckle behind their back;
Foot for foot, and knee for knee,
Turn about Darby's company.

Professor Kittredge heard this sung by white children in Boston *c.*1865, as:

Mary Mack is dressed in black,
Silver buttons all down her back,
Walking on the railroad track

(*American Negro Folk-Songs*, N. I. White, 1928, p. 288); and Miss Jackson, in the 1870s, saw children skipping along in pairs, with crossed hands, singing:

> Betsy Blue came all in black,
> Silver buttons down her back.
> Every button cost a crown,
> Every lady turn around.
> Alligoshi, alligoshee,
> Turn the bridle over my knee.

(Shropshire Folk-Lore, p. 523)

'At the end of the last line,' she said, 'they turn themselves about without loosing hands'—in other words, they were performing the entrancing exercise of Alligoshee, which is possibly descended from the skipping movement in the old French 'allemande' dance.

The episode of the elephant's spectacular leap over the fence is purely American; usually he comes back to earth for the Fourth of July. The rhyme was 'heard at commencement speeches' in Auburn, Alabama, *c.*1915 (*American Negro Folk-Songs*, N. I. White, 1928, p. 249); it also appears in *Negro Folk Rhymes*, T. W. Talley, 1922, and *JAFL*, xxxi, 1918, p. 62, from Ontario.

USA: St Louis, 1895, for clapping, 'May Mac, dressed in black, Three gold buttons down her back' followed by 'I love coffee, I love tea, I love the boys and the boys love me', 'I asked my mother for fifty cents' and 'One flew East, one flew West, One flew over the cuckoo's nest' (*JAFL*, lx, p. 27) | Hollywood and San Francisco, 1973, 'Oh Mary Mack, Mack, Mack, All dressed in black, black, black, With silver buttons, buttons, buttons, All down her back, back, back, She asked her mother, mother, mother, For fifteen cents, cents, cents, To see the elephant, elephant, elephant, Jump over the fence, fence, fence, He jumped so high, high, high, He reached the sky, sky, sky, He never came back, back, back, Till the Fourth of July, ly, ly'.

Australia: Townsville, 1935, 'Mary Mack, Mack, Mack, dressed in black, black, black, Silver buttons, buttons, buttons, down her back, back, back. She likes coffee, she likes tea, She likes sitting on a black fellow's knee'. The same from Melbourne, *c.*1935, and 1957 (Turner MS).

Britain: Salford, 1970, 'To see the kanga, kanga, kanga, Jump over the fence . . . He never came back . . . Till the Fourth of July' | London NW8. and Leeds, 1973, 'never came back . . . till next July, ly, ly' | Birmingham, 1977, 'To watch the ants . . . Fall off the fence'.

146

Popeye the Sailor Man

Leeds, 1973

I'm Popeye the sailor man, full stop,
I live in a caravan, full stop.
I open the door and fall through the floor,
I'm Popeye the sailor man, full stop,
Comma comma, dash dash, full stop.

Leeds, 1973

I'm Popeye the sailor man, full stop,
I live in a caravan, full stop.
And when I go swimmin'
I kiss all the women,
I'm Popeye the sailor man, full stop, full stop,
Comma comma, dash dash, full stop.

Bedford, 1975

In the early 1970s the less vulgar versions of 'Popeye the Sailor Man' were converted into hand-clapping songs by the addition of spoken punctuation (a convention taken from 'My Mummy Told Me' (p. 447)). The clapping is horizontal but, typically, 'When it comes to "full stop" you cross your hands and hit your shoulders. And when it comes to "comma comma" you close your hands and stick your thumbs behind your right shoulder and left shoulder. And when it says "dash dash" you push your knees forward alternately'.

The songs sung by the small cockneys of Peabody Buildings, Wild Street, WC2, 1974, were, however, more daring than most:

I'm Popeye the sailor man, full stop,
I live in a caravan, full stop.
I slept with Queen Mary,
Cor blimey, she's 'airy!
I'm Popeye the sailor man, full stop,
    full stop,
Comma comma, full stop.

I'm Popeye the sailor man, full stop,
I live in a caravan, full stop.
I slept with me granny
And tickled 'er fanny,
I'm Popeye the sailor man, full stop,
    full stop,
Comma comma, full stop.

Recordings in the 1980s show that the punctuation endings are going out of favour, and the song is now often ornamented only by the ending 'Too too!' or 'Poo poo!', an echo of the tugboat whistle in the original cartoon song written by Sammy Lerner in 1932.

147
The Johnsons Had a Baby

Tune: 'I Am a Pretty Little Dutch Girl'

The Johnsons had a baby,
They called him Tiny Tim, Tim, Tim,
They put him in a bath tub
To see if he could swim, swim, swim.
He drank a bowl of water,
And ate a bar of soap, soap, soap,
He tried to eat the bath tub,
But it wouldn't fit down his throat, throat, throat.
Mummy, Mummy, I feel ill,
Call the doctor down the hill.
In came the doctor, in came the nurse,
In came the lady with the alligator purse.
'Doctor, doctor, will I die?'
'Yes, my son, but do not cry,
Close your eyes and count to ten.'
'One, two, three, four, five, six, seven, eight, nine, ten.'
Out went the doctor, out went the nurse,
Out went the lady with the alligator purse.

Langrish, near Petersfield, 1974

This saga is constructed, like a caddis-worm case, from odds and ends stuck together, and is chanted to the same tune as 'I Am a Pretty Little Dutch Girl'. The first eight lines can be recognized as part of a bawdy song about a whore called Lulu, who had a baby which 'was an awful shock, She couldn't call it Lulu 'cos, The bastard had a cock'. In the 1920s Lulu and her baby featured in one of the joke verses popular at the time, in which the rude words are never actually said; it was sung to the 'Soldiers' Chorus' from Gounod's *Faust*:

> Lulu had a baby, she called it Sunny Jim,
> She took it to the bathroom to see if it could swim.
> It swam to the bottom, it swam to the top,
> Lulu got excited and grabbed it by the—
> Cocktails, ginger ale, two and six a glass . . .

The rhyme was next employed for ball-bouncing. In Kirkcaldy, 1952, it was 'Rena had a baby, she called it Tiny Tim, She took him to the bathroom to learn him how to swim. It sunk to the bottom, it floated to the top, Rena got exhausted and grab it by the cocktail'; while children in Harrogate, 1959, knew the full story, complete with the voracious baby who tried to eat the bath tub and the medical team accompanied by the mysterious lady with the alligator purse. This medical episode has been a game-rhyme in the USA for many years; it was, for instance, a jump-rope rhyme in West Medford, Mass., in the 1920s:

> In goes the doctor, in goes the nurse,
> In goes the lady with the big black purse;
> Out goes the doctor, out goes the nurse,
> Out goes the lady in the big black hearse.

The couplet 'Mother, mother, I feel ill, Call the doctor down the hill' is an old ingredient of macabre child-medleys. It must have been in circulation when the source of the sequential couplet was enquired for in *Notes & Queries*, 1864 (3rd ser., vi, p. 514): 'Doctor, doctor, I shall die!' 'Yes, pretty maid, and so shall I.'

USA: earliest recording, Westchester County, New York, 1938, 'I had a little brother, His name was Tiny Tim, I put him in the bath tub, To teach him how to swim. He drank up all the water, He ate up all the soap, He died last night with a bubble in his throat' (Howard MSS, no use given).

Britain: for ball-bouncing, many versions late 1950s–70s, the chief being 'I had a little monkey, his name was Joey Brown, I took him to the wash tub to see if he would drown. He drank all the water, he ate all the soap, He died last night with a bubble in his throat' (Aberdeen, 1960).

For clapping, all versions with medical episode; North London, 1972, 'Miss Lucy had a baby, she called it Tiny Tim . . . Miss Lucy called the doctor, Miss Lucy called the nurse, Miss Lucy called the lady with the alligator purse. "Operation," said the doctor, "Operation," said the nurse, "Operation," said the lady with the alligator purse' | Edinburgh, 1975, 'Miss Jenny had a baby, she called it Tiny Tim' | Poulner, Hants, 1975, 'Susie had a baby . . . Tiny Tim' | Lilliput, Dorset, 1978, 'I had a baby brother, his name was Tiny Tim'.

'Miss Lucy' may have arrived from another baby-minding verse, 'Miss Lucy had a baby, And she laid him on the straw, And every time the baby cry, She slap the baby's jaw' (Howard MSS, East Orange, New Jersey, c.1935).

148

See, See, My Playmate

See, see, my playmate,
Come out and play with me,
Under the apple tree,
And bring your dollies three.
Slide down the drainpipe
Into the cellar door,
And we'll be merry friends
For ever more, more, more.

Ilkley, 1980

When you sing 'See, see' you hook your little fingers in each other's and shake them up and down twice, and then you clap your own hands together, and right hands against each other, and hands together, then left hands, then two claps of your own hands together for a pause after 'playmate'; then backs of hands against other person's backs, then fronts of hands, own hands together, right hands, own hands, left hands, then two claps of own hands after 'me', then backs, and fronts, and all that all over again, and it goes on the same all through, except three frontways claps for 'more, more, more' (*girl, 9, Virginia Water, 1983*).

The words of this clapping game have not drifted very far from its source, the popular song 'Playmates', words and music by Saxie Dowell, 1940:

Play-mate—come out and play with me,
And bring your dollies three,
Climb up my apple tree,
Look down my rain pipe,
Slide down my kitchen door,
And we'll be jolly friends
For ever more.

I'm sorry, play-mate, I cannot play with you,
My dollies have the flu,
Boo hoo hoo hoo hoo hoo.
Ain't got no rain pipe,
Ain't got no kitchen door,
But we'll be jolly friends for ever more. Oh![1]

The 1940 song was, in its turn, based on H. W. Petrie's tale of a childish quarrel 'I Don't Want to Play in Your Yard', 1894, which, however, had a quite different tune. The chorus went: 'I don't want to play in your yard, I don't like you any more; You'll be sorry when you see me, Sliding down our cellar door. You can't holler down our rain barrel, You can't climb our apple tree, I don't want to play in your yard, If you won't be good to me'.

Britain: the game was very popular in the mid 1970s, and we have no recording before Leeds, 1973, 'Oh little playmate, come out and play with me'. The words are by no means standardized, and vary from 'See, see, my baby, My baby's got the flu, Since 1972. Slide down the drainpipe, Slide down the banisters, And we'll be jolly friends, For ever more, more—droopy drawers!' (London W4, 1975) to 'See, see, my baby, I cannot play with you, Because I've got the flu, Chicken pox and measles too. Flush down the lavatory, Into the drainpipe, And that's the way they go—go—go' (Liss, 1979; the 9-year-old performers said defensively 'We didn't make it up—it's going round the school'). Often the invitation is to 'Slide down my rainbow' (e.g. Pimlico, 1976).

Australia: Townsville, 1978, 'Say, say, my playmate, Come out and play with me, And bring your dollies sweet, Right up the apple tree, Slide down my rainbow, Into my sailing boat, And we'll be jolly friends For ever more, more, more', with the reply 'Sorry, sorry, my playmate, I cannot play with you, My dolly's got the flu, I think I've got it too, Boo hoo hoo hoo hoo hoo . . .'

USA: *Circle Round the Zero*, M. Kenney, 1974, p. 39, 'O Jolly Playmate' | The American School in London, 1975, 'Say, say, my playmate, Come out and play with me, And bring your dollies three, Climb up my apple tree; Slide down my rainbow, Into my cellar door, And we'll be jolly friends, For ever more, more, more more more', played for at least the previous two years.

[1] Copyright Santly-Joy-Select Inc., New York. Campbell, Connelly & Co., London.

149

My Mother Is a Baker

Tune: 'When Susie Was a Baby'

My mother is a baker, a baker, a baker,
My mother is a baker, she bakes like this—
    Yummy, yummy.

My father is a butcher, a butcher, a butcher,
My father is a butcher, he smells like this—
    Yummy, yummy,
    Pooey, pooey.

My sister is a modeller, a modeller, a modeller,
My sister is a modeller, she went like this—
    Yummy, yummy,
    Pooey, pooey,
    Mrs Susie.

My brother is a cowboy, a cowboy, a cowboy,
My brother is a cowboy, he goes like this—
    Yummy, yummy,
    Pooey, pooey,
    Mrs Susie,
    Hands up, drop yer guns, turn around, touch the ground.

My grandpa is a flasher, a flasher, a flasher,
My grandpa is a flasher, he went like this—
    Yummy, yummy,
    Pooey, pooey,
    Mrs Susie,
    Hands up, drop yer guns, turn around, touch the ground,
    Flash, flash, flash.

My grannie is a hairdresser, a hairdresser, a hairdresser,
My grannie is a hairdresser, she went like this—
    Yummy, yummy,
    Pooey, pooey,
    Mrs Susie,
    Hands up, drop yer guns, turn around, touch the ground,
    Flash, flash,
    Comb, comb.

Sung in the modern manner with two performers standing opposite each other clapping hands, first clapping their partner's hands horizontally, then their partner's hands vertically, then their own hands together. Then they illustrate the verse, followed by the actions of the preceding verses, so that each verse becomes more difficult than the last. When their mother bakes, 'Yummy, yummy', they rub their tummies; when their father smells, 'Pooey, pooey', they hold their noses; when their sister models, 'Mrs Susie', they take up an elegant stance with one hand on hip and the other curving above their head; when their brother is a cowboy they raise their hands, turn around, and touch the ground; when their grandpa is a flasher they confuse flashing with flushing and pull an imaginary lavatory chain; and when their granny is a hairdresser they comb their hair. The headmaster who came upon us recording this song was dismayed. 'I don't know where they learn these things!' he said, and enjoined us not to associate it with his school. The song is Transatlantic, and was first heard in England at the beginning of 1975; it was widespread, it seems, by 1976.

Canada: Toronto, 1962, for skipping: 'My father is a garbage man—Pheew! My mother is a baker . . . My sister is a hairdresser . . . My brother is a cowboy . . . My baby is a cry-baby, Pheew! Yum yum! Curl curl! Bang bang! Waaaa!' (Fowke, 1969, p. 57).

  USA: Harlem, 1970, for hand-clapping, 'My mother is a baker', father a garbage man, sister a beautician, brother a cowboy, auntie a telephone director, grandfather a tickler, grandmother a wicked old witch. 'Yummy yum, pee yew, la de da de do, roll 'em up, stick 'em up, take 'em out, hello, tickle tickle, Boo!' (*New York*, 10 August 1970, pp. 25–6) | Boston, *c.*1970, 'My mother works at the bakery' (*Circle Round the Zero*, Maureen Kenney, p. 30).

Twelve Less Popular Clapping Songs

THE following are the less popular and more ephemeral clapping songs:

I'm not going to school any more, more,
  more,
There's a great fat teacher by the door,
  door, door,
  She pulls me by the hair,
  And sits me in a chair,
I'm not going to school any more, more,
  more.

> Street, Somerset, 1971. An old-established American rhyme, 'I won't go to Macy's any more, more, more, There's a big fat policeman at the door, door, door ...' (Macy's is the famous store in New York). First noted in this country as a ball-bounce rhyme in Leeds, 1966, 'Don't go to Grannie's any more, There's a great fat copper on the door, He'll grab you by the collar, And make you pay a dollar, So don't go to Grannie's any more'

I want to get married, I do, mama,
I want to get married, I do, ha ha,
I want to get married, but don't you tell
  pa,
'Cos pa wouldn't like it at all, mama.

I want six children, I do, mama . . .

I've got married, I have, mama . . .

I've got six children, I have, mama . . .

> Leeds, 1973. A well-known Transatlantic folk song sometimes sung by children, for instance by Leah Yoffie in a St Louis playground c.1895 (JAFL, lx, p. 33); also see Ozark Folksongs, ii, V. Randolph and F. C. Shoemaker, 1949, pp. 98–100

My mother gave me a necklace,
My father gave me a dime,

My sister gave me a lover-boy
Who kissed me all the time.

My mother took my necklace,
My father took my dime,
My sister took my lover-boy
And gave me Frankenstein.

He made me dust the windows,
He made me scrub the floor,
He made me sew his smelly socks,
So I kicked him out the door.

> Salford, 1975. Derived from the skipping rhyme 'Nine o'clock is striking', especially the early American versions, e.g. Poughkeepsie, NY, 1926, 'Twelve o'clock striking. Mother, may I go out? All the boys are waiting, For to take me out. One will give me an apple, One will give me a pear, One will give me fifty cents, To kiss behind the stair. I'd rather wash the dishes, I'd rather scrub the floor, I don't want an apple, I don't want a pear, I don't want fifty cents, To kiss behind the stair (JAFL, xxxix, pp. 84–5). 'Necklace' is an approximation to 'nickel'

We are the barbie girls,
We wear our hair in curls,
We wear our dungarees
To hide our dirty knees.

We wear our father's shirt,
We wear our brother's tie,
And when we want a guy
We simply wink the eye.

> Glasgow, 1975. In Tralee, Co. Kerry, the same year, it was 'We are the mercy girls ... And when it comes to boys, We treat them as toys' (Saydisc record, Children's Singing Games, 1983)

My father was born in Germany,
My mother was born in Italy,
My sister was born in the USA,
And my baby followed me, me, me.

My father likes to smoke his pipe,
My mother likes to read her book,
My sister likes to show her legs,
And my baby follows me, me, me.

My father died in Germany,
My mother died in Italy,
My sister died in the USA,
And my baby followed me, me, me.

> *Bedford, 1975. First noted at Swansea, 1962, 'My father works in the bakery, My mother works in the Grand B., My sister works in the boogie-woogie shop, And they do it all for me, me, me. My father likes to ring a bell, My mother likes to yell, yell, yell, My sister likes to smoke, smoke, smoke, And they do it all for me, me, me'. Melbourne, 1967, '. . . My sister comes from a go-go show'. Tune: 'I Am a Pretty Little Dutch Girl' (p. 450)*

When Jimmy got drunk on a bottle o' gin,
'E called for the doctor and the doctor come in.
Now let's get the rhythm of the head, ding dong,
We've got the rhythm of the head, ding dong.
Now let's get the rhythm of the feet (stamp, stamp),
We've got the rhythm of the feet (stamp, stamp),
Now let's get the rhythm of the hands (clap, clap),
We've got the rhythm of the hands (clap, clap),
Now let's get the rhythm of the hot dog (pant like a hot dog),
We've got the rhythm of the hot dog (pant like a hot dog).
Now put it all together and see what we've got,
Ding dong, (stamp, stamp), (clap, clap), (pant like a hot dog),

Hot dog, hot dog, yeah, yeah, yeah! (shouted)

> *Stepney, 1976. It more often begins 'Doctor Knickerbocker, Number Nine, He sure got drunk on a bottle of wine', which is how it is known in the country of its origin, the USA. It can also be played as a ring game, with two girls doing the actions in the middle*

Dinah, Dinah, show us your leg,
Show us your leg, show us your leg,
Dinah, Dinah, show us your leg,
Beyond, above the knee.

Rich girls they wear brassies,
Poor girls they wear rags,
But Dinah don't wear anything,
She lets her bosoms sag.

Rich girls they use frillies,
Poor girls they use hankies,
But Dinah don't wear anything
Because her bum's too hard.

> *Street, Somerset, 1976. The adult version, in e.g. Rugby Songs, ed. Harry Morgan, at least makes more sense*

Georgie Best, Superstar,
How many knickers have you wore so far?
Ninety-four, maybe more,
Ten in the gutter and the rest on the floor.

> *Birmingham, 1976. Georgie Best verses, sung to the theme song from 'Jesus Christ Superstar', were at the height of their popularity in 1972 (the best known was 'Georgie Best, Superstar, Walks like a woman and wears a bra'). When the craze was over they lingered for a while as clapping verses*

My father went to war, war, war,
In nineteen-seventy-four, four, four,
He brought me back a gun, gun, gun,
And shot me in the tum, tum, tum.

> *Ashbourne, Derbyshire, 1977. Girls poke each other in the tummy when saying 'tum, tum, tum'*

Milly Molly Mandy,
Sweet as sugar candy,
I'm in love with you.

Milly Molly Mandy,
Sweet as sugar candy,
Your pretty little eyes are blue.

Milly Molly Mandy,
Sweet as sugar candy,
I'm—in—love—with—you.

Garforth, Yorks., 1978. 'Every time it says "you", you have to point at the other person.' The first Milly-Molly-Mandy Stories, by Joyce Lankester Brisley, were published in 1928

All the girls in France
Do the hula-hula dance,
And the dance they do
Is enough to make a shoe,
And the shoe they make
Is enough to make a pill,
And the pill they eat
Is enough to pluck a chicken,

And the chicken they pluck
Is enough to make a duck—
Boom, boom, boom, Esso Blue!

Thurso, Caithness, 1975. In Ormskirk, 1978, it began 'The girls in Spain, Wash their knickers in champagne'. At the American School in London, 1975, they were singing 'All the girls in France, Do the hootchy kootchy dance, And the way they shake, Is enough to kill a snake, When the snake is dead, They put roses in their head, When the roses die, They put diamonds in their eye—Hoo!'

I know a little Dutch girl
Called 'Hi Susie Anna'.
All the boys at the football match
Go 'Hi Susie Anna!'
'How is your father?' 'All right—
Died in the fish shop—last night.'
'What was he eating?' 'Raw fish.'
'How did he die?' 'Like this—' (one girl
falls into the other girl's arms)

South Baddesley, Hants, 1983. An amalgam of 'I Am a Pretty Little Dutch Girl' (p. 450), whose tune it uses, 'O Susie Anna' (p. 462), and a quadruple 'Hi tiddley i ti' ending

Select Bibliography

BOOKS additional to those in the list of Abbreviations (p. xxi). (Published in London unless otherwise stated.)

American Anthropologist, Washington, i, 1888, W. H. Babcock, 'Games of Washington Children', pp. 243–84.

Andersson, Otto, ed., *Finlands Svenska Folkdiktning*, v, 3, Sanglekar, 1967.

Arnold, Dr Samuel. *Juvenile Amusements*, nursery rhyme music sheets, 1796–98?

Arwidsson, A. I. *Svenska Fornsånger. En Samling af Kämpavisor, Folk-Visor, Lekar och Dansar, samt Barn- och Vall-Sånger*, 3 vols., Stockholm, 1834–42.

Babcock, W. H. see *American Anthropologist* and *Lippincott's Magazine*.

Bernoni, G. *Giuochi Popolari Veneziani*, Venice, 1874.

Botkin, B. A. *American Play-Party Song*, Nebraska, 1937.

Brady, Eilís. *All In! All In!*, Dublin, 1975.

Braga, Theophilo. *O Povo Portuguez*, 2 vols., Lisbon, 1885.

Cassell's Book of In-door Amusements, 1881.

Celnart, Madame. *Manuel Complet des Jeux de Société*, Paris, 1827, 1830, 1846.

Chabreul, Madame de. *Jeux et Exercises des Jeunes Filles*, Paris, 1856.

Chappell, W. *The Ballad Literature and Popular Music of the Olden Time*, 2 vols., 1855–9.

Chater, Mary. *Baker's Dozen: Singing Games for Brownies*, Girl Guides Association, 1947.

Child, F. J. *The English and Scottish Popular Ballads*, 5 vols., Boston, 1882–98, (reprint, Folklore Press, New York, 1957).

Child, L. M. *The Little Girl's Own Book*, Boston, 1831; the first issue of the very popular *Girl's Own Book*. The London '4th' edition was printed 1832, from the American 2nd edn.

Cock, A. de, and Teirlinck, I. *Kinderspel & Kinderlust in Zuid-Nederland*, 8 vols., Ghent, 1902–8.

Córdova y Oña, S. *Cancionero Infantil Español*, Santander, 1847.

Cort, Aimé de. *Vlaamsche Kinderspelen uit West-Brussel*, Brussels, 1929.

County Folk-Lore: Suffolk, vol. I, no. 2, E. C. Gurdon, 1893.

County Folk-Lore: Northumberland, vol. IV, no. 6, collected M. C. Balfour, edited N. W. Thomas, 1904.

Coussemaker, E. de. *Chants Populaires des Flamands de France . . . avec les mélodies*, Ghent, 1856.

Daiken, Leslie. *Children's Games throughout the Year*, 1949.

Durieux, A., and Bruyelle, A. *Chants et Chansons Populaires de Cambresis*, 2 vols., Cambrai, 1864–8.

East London Papers, vol., II, no. 2, Ocotober 1959, 'An Introduction to East London Folklore', A. W. Smith, pp. 63–78.

Fraser, A. S. *Dae Ye Min' Langsyne?*, 1975.

Gammer Gurton's Garland: or, The Nursery Parnassus, 1784; enlarged *c.*1799, 1810.

Gennep, A. Van. *Folklore du Dauphiné, Isère*, 2 vols., Paris, 1932–3.

Gillington, A. E. *Old Hampshire Singing Games*, 1909.

—— *Old Isle of Wight Singing Games*, 1909.

—— *Old Surrey Singing Games*, 1909.

—— *Old Dorset Singing Games*, 1913.

Goodwin, M. L. and Powell, E. L. *Rique Ran: games and songs of South American children*, Delaware, Ohio, 1951.

Haddon, A. C. *The Study of Man*, 1898.

Hagen, Serine & Sophus, *Børneses Musik, Sange, Lege, og Dandse fra en Børnekreds, samlede af En Moder*, Copenhagen, 1879.

Halliwell, J. O. *The Nursery Rhymes of England*, 1842, 1843, 1844, 1846, 1853, *c.*1860.

—— *Popular Rhymes and Nursery Tales*, 1849, *c.*1860.

Hammond, David, *Green Peas and Barley O: children's street songs and rhymes from Belfast* (St Mary's Primary School, Belfast) L.B.J. Recordings Ltd., Belfast, 1974.

Herd MS. David Herd, *Scots Songs and Ballads*, 2 MS vols., completed 1776 and partially printed the same year (British Library MS Adds. 22311–2).

Hornby, John. *The Joyous Book of Singing Games*, Leeds, [1913].

Kampmüller, Otto. *Oberösterreichische Kinderspiele*, Linz, 1965.

Kerr's Guild of Play, containing 49 Singing Games with pianoforte accompaniments, Glasgow, [1912].

Kidson, Frank, and Moffat, Alfred. *Eighty Singing Games*, 1907.

—— *100 Singing Games*, 1916.

King, M. and R. *Street Games of North Shields Children*, privately printed at Tynemouth by Robert King, 1926; 2nd series, 1930.

Lambert, L. *Chants et Chansons Populaires du Languedoc*, Paris, 1906.

Leslie, E. *American Girl's Book: or, Occupation for Play Hours*, Boston, 1831. Many subsequent editions, including London, 1835. Pirated editions are titled *The Little Girl's Own Book*.

Lippincott's Magazine, Philadelphia, xxxvii and xxxviii, 1886, W. H. Babcock, 'Song-Games and Myth-Dramas at Washington', 'Carols and Child-Lore of the Capital', pp. 239–57, pp. 320–42.

Lirica Infantil Mexicana, *Artes de Mexico*, no. 162, Año XX, 1973. Whole number devoted to children's lore.

Lumbroso, M. M. *Giochi descritti e illustrati dai bambini delle varie regioni d'italia*, Rome, 1967.

McBain, J. M. *Arbroath: Past and Present*, Arbroath, 1887.

McIntosh, D. S. *Folk Songs and Singing Games of the Illinois Ozarks*, New York, 1957.

MacTaggart, John. *The Scottish Gallovidian Encyclopedia*, 1824.

Maidment, James. *Scottish Ballads and Songs*, Edinburgh, 1859: from material assembled by T. G. Stevenson.

Marín, F. R. *Varios Juegos Infantiles del Siglo XVI*, Madrid, 1932.

Maspons y Labrós, F. *Jochs de la Infancia*, Barcelona, 1874.

Montel, A. and Lambert, L. *Chants populaires du Languedoc*, Paris, 1880.
Mother Goose's Melody: or, Sonnets for the Cradle, 1780; ? assembled by Oliver Goldsmith; published by John Newbery possibly *c*.1765.
Østberg, Berit. *På livets landevei: sangleker fra Trondheim*, Oslo, 1976.
Ó Súilleabháin, Seán. *Irish Wake Amusements*, Cork, 1967.
Peesch, Reinhard. *Das Berliner Kinderspiel der Gegenwart*, Berlin, 1957.
Pennsylvania Jumpster. Booklet compiled for Pennsylvania Library Association, 1974.
Pitrè, G. *Giuochi fanciulleschi Siciliani*, Palermo, 1883.
Plunket, E. M. *Merrie Games in Rhyme*, 1886.
Rimbault, E. F. *Nursery Rhymes with the tunes to which they are still sung*, 1846.
Ritchie, J. T. R. *The Singing Street*, Edinburgh, 1964.
—— *Golden City*, Edinburgh, 1965.
Rochholz, E. L. *Alemannisches Kinderlied und Kinderspiel aus der Schweiz*, Leipzig, 1857.
Rodger, Jean C. *Lang Strang: Being a Mixter-Maxter of Old Rhymes, Games, etc.*, Forfar, 1948.
Rolland, E. *Rimes et Jeux de l'Enfance*, Paris, 1883.
Rutherford, Frank. *All the Way to Pennywell: Children's Rhymes of the North East* (University of Durham Institute of Education), 1971.
Rymour Club, Miscellanea of the, Edinburgh, 1906–28.
Sachs, Curt. *World History of the Dance*, trans. from German, New York, 1937.
St Anne's Soho Monthly Paper, June, July, and August 1907; series of articles 'Games of Soho' by the rector, Revd T. Allen Moxon.
Sharp, Cecil. *Children's Singing Games*, five sets, 1909 (2), 1912 (3).
Simpson, Claude M. *The British Broadside Ballad and Its Music*, New Brunswick, USA, 1966.
Simrock, K. *Das deutsche Kinderbuch*, Frankfurt a. M., 1848.
Støylen, Bernt. *Norske Barnerim og Leikar*, Oslo, 1899.
Ström, F. *Visor, ramsor och andra folkrim*, Stockholm, 1941.
The Singing Street, N. McIsaac, Edinburgh, 1951. The verses of the games of Norton Park School, Edinburgh, shown in the documentary film of the same title. A detailed commentary on the film and games by N. McIsaac appears in *Folk-Lore*, lxiii, 1952.
Thuren, Hjalmar. *Folk Songs in the Faroes*, F.F. Publications, Northern Series, 2, 1908.
Thyregod, S. Tvermose. *Danmarks Sanglege*, Copenhagen, 1931.
Tillhagen, C. and Dencker, N. *Svenska folklekar och danser*, 2 vols., Stockholm, 1949–50.
Tobitt, Janet E. *Singing Games for Recreation*, four booklets, *c*.1938.
Tommy Thumb's Pretty Song Book, vol. II, *c*.1744. (Volume I is not extant.)
Uyldert, Mellie. *De Verborgen Schat in het Kinderspel*, Amsterdam, [1962].
Valentine, Mrs. *Home Book of Pleasure and Instruction*, 1867.

General Index

Index of Songs, Games, and Dances